*Camille Arnaud Jules Marie, Prince de Polignac. From
a painting in Confederate Memorial Hall in New Orleans,
by courtesy of the United Daughters of the Confederacy,
Stonewall Jackson Chapter, New Orleans, La.*

FOREIGNERS
in the
CONFEDERACY

ELLA LONN
Professor of History, Goucher College

CHAPEL HILL
THE UNIVERSITY OF NORTH CAROLINA PRESS
1940

To My Sister

E. V. L.

Whose Aid in Its Preparation
Has Been Invaluable
This Book Is Dedicated

PREFACE

RECOGNITION of the part played by the foreign-born in the brief span of life of the Confederate States of America has been long delayed. The rôle played by the knights-errant and the soldiers of fortune has found its way into some southern publications, but the rôle played by the large number of foreigners who fought in the ranks of the Confederate army has hitherto been hidden away in the Confederate descriptive and muster rolls. The present work is an effort to fill that gap.

The investigation has presented many difficulties—some of them insuperable—owing, in the first place, to the absence of thousands of company rolls, which were destroyed or lost in the confusion and destruction of war; and, in the second place, to the failure of authorities to record the data which were requisite for this study—the native land of the recruit. However, sufficient data have survived so that it is possible to present a fair picture, as a cross section of the entire Confederate army is presented. A goodly number of descriptive rolls have survived for each of the states which joined the Confederacy. That errors and serious omissions will appear is inevitable. This is to be deplored but accepted as unavoidable in a study of this sort conducted so long after the war and after so many of the characters concerned have disappeared from the stage.

There remains the grateful task of making acknowledgment to the many persons to whom I am indebted. To the men and women in charge of the various archives where material is located I wish to express gratitude for the uniform courtesy and helpfulness with which materials were made available: to Mr. Peter Brannon, of the Alabama Archives; Miss Ruth Blair, formerly of the Georgia Archives; Professor A. R. Newsome for help at the North Carolina Historical Commission; Mr. Winfred Beck, of the Confederate Archives, War Department (now retired); and Miss Harriet Smither, of the Texas Archives. To the latter and to Mr. Peter Brannon I am especially grateful for thoughtfulness and kindness in sending me data which came to light in their own work after my visit to their respective archives. To Mrs. P. M. Howell I owe thanks for the use of the rolls preserved at Memorial Hall of the United Daughters of the Confederacy in New Orleans.

I am deeply indebted to the following librarians: Mr. Robert Usher, of Howard Memorial Library in New Orleans; Miss Harris, of the Mobile City Library; Miss Ella May Thornton, of the Georgia State Library; Miss Alice S. Wyman, librarian at the University of Alabama; and Mr. Harry Clemons, of the library of the University of Virginia. Members of the staff of Peabody Library and Enoch Pratt Library in Baltimore, of the University of Texas Library, and of the Library of Congress have been unfailing in courtesy and sympathetic coöperation. To Mr. William Baehr, librarian of Augustana College, I make acknowledgment for copying some excerpts.

Mr. August Dietz kindly afforded me opportunity to consult his file of the *Richmonder Anzeiger,* the only file, it is believed, extant. Likewise Mr. Albert Orth, of Charleston, graciously placed before me some materials in his possession. Permission was granted me by Miss Elizabeth Cutting to use some materials from a letter in her possession which helped to clear up the rôle played by Professor Schele de Ver, of the University of Virginia, in the Confederate drama. To Mr. A. L. Crabb, of George Peabody College for Teachers, I owe the use of a rare pamphlet on the Nashville Female Academy. The Reverend Anthony J. Bleicher, S. J., furnished me with some data concerning several Catholic chaplains which I should not otherwise have secured.

To Mrs. S. V. Pfeuffer, of New Braunfels, Texas, and to Mr. Alex Brinkman, of Comfort, Texas, I extend thanks for the use of materials in their private libraries. For data contributed orally by Mr. David Pipes, a survivor of the Washington Artillery of New Orleans; by Mr. Allison Owen, also of New Orleans; by Mrs. Crockett Riley (now deceased), of Fredericksburg, Texas; by Dr. J. P. Bibb, of Montgomery, Alabama; by Mrs. Jack Ross, of Mobile; and by Miss Marian Reed, of Fredericksburg, Virginia, I make acknowledgment. To Mrs. Henry Lewis, of Fredericksburg, Texas, and to Mrs. H. F. Mengden, of New Braunfels, Texas, I am indebted for aid in providing contacts and for making it possible for me to complete my work in those two cities in a limited space of time.

The painstaking care shown by Mrs. Catherine Anderson of the University of North Carolina Press in preparing the manuscript for the press has my grateful acknowledgment.

Finally, Professor Anna Irene Miller, of the department of English at Goucher College, who has read the entire manuscript, has my gratitude for helpful suggestions.

ELLA LONN

Goucher College
May, 1939

CONTENTS

ILLUSTRATIONS

FOREIGNERS IN THE CONFEDERACY

I

NUMBERS AND DISTRIBUTION OF FOREIGNERS IN THE CONFEDERACY IN 1860

PROBABLY NO impression has been more deeply cherished by the population living south of Mason and Dixon's line and none more widely accepted by those who dwell north of that line than that which affirms that in the veins of the southerners flowed the purest Anglo-Saxon blood in the New World and that their soil was the freest from the tread of foreign races. If confronted with the historical record, the layman would doubtless admit that some Germans had filtered into the valley of Virginia from Pennsylvania in the eighteenth century; that some French Huguenots and Scotch Highlanders had made their way into the mountain region of South Carolina; and that some Italians had been encouraged in colonial days to enter Georgia in order to promote the silk culture. Few Confederate veterans entertained any doubt that the Civil War resulted as it did because the meager ranks of the Confederates, consisting of native-born sons, were overwhelmed by hordes of European-born Federal soldiers and European mercenaries. The facts may prove surprising.

To present an adequate picture of the various racial strains in the Confederate States, it is desirable to sketch in bold lines the different geographical divisions of the South as they appeared to travelers during the late fifties. The bare figures of population statistics as presented in the census of 1860 are quite inadequate to convey the picture, even with careful interpretation. It colors the entire slavery question to grasp firmly the fact that in the eleven states of the Confederacy there was a total of somewhat over three hundred thousand slaveowners, and that in this total were included a number of unnaturalized foreigners.[1]

Virginia, the mother state, although on the seaboard and, therefore, presumably offering the easiest access to foreigners who cared to

[1] De Bow in an open letter to R. N. Gourdin of Charleston, S. C., published in January, 1861, claimed 347,255 as the correct number of slaveholders in the entire South.—"The Non-Slaveholders of the South," in *De Bow's Review*, XXX (O. S.), 67. The census of 1861, *Agriculture*, 247, gives 384,884, but that includes Delaware and the territories. De Bow's figures are modified so as to include only the states which seceded.

enter the South, does not in 1860 present a picture of large numbers
of unassimilated aliens. While there were numbers of foreigners and
foreign sections in her cities, as will appear later, most of what Virginia would have termed her foreign population were descendants of
the Pennsylvania Germans who had settled in the valley of the
Shenandoah in the eighteenth century, where they now constituted a
majority of the population. These Americanized Germans, or "old
Germans," as they were often termed, became the core of the Stonewall Brigade and produced some of the leaders of the Confederate
forces—Armistead and Kemper, to name but two—but they are outside the scope of this story.[2] Among the 1,047,411 whites of Virginia's population, only a relatively few thousand, compared with the
many thousands of German descent, had been born in Germany. Still
these amounted to over 10,500.[3]

Economic considerations had led the Germans to cast their eyes
in the direction of Virginia in the early decades of the nineteenth cen-
tury. Several wholesale houses of Bremen sent their representatives
to Richmond with a consequent increase in the export of tobacco to
Germany. As many as six or eight German vessels were, before the
middle of the century, to be seen at one time in Richmond's harbor.
It was in the fourth decade that the German element, particularly in
Richmond and in several country towns, received large additions of
German immigration, representing nearly all the German states. A
Mr. Nolting, who was a Richmond merchant, imported by sailing
vessel from Bremen to Rocketts[4] a large number of German laborers
and artisans to be employed in building the James River or Kanawha
Canal.[5] Numerous German Jews settled in various county seats of
the state and established stores. They had become sufficiently numerous in Richmond to establish a synagogue by 1840 and a commercial
college, Handelsschule, by 1859-60. The capital city became, rather
naturally, the nucleus of German life in Virginia. Here occurred the
celebration of national events in the history of the Fatherland; as

[2] Dr. H. Ruffner, who served for years as president of Washington College, was descended
from this old German stock. It is worthy of passing comment that in 1847 he and Franz
Lieber at the South Carolina College lifted their voices against slavery.—Wilhelm Kaufmann,
Die Deutschen im amerikanischen Bürgerkriege, 141.

[3] Hermann Schuricht, History of the German Element in Virginia, II, 50. The census of
1860 gives 10,512.—Statistics of the Population of the United States, liii.

[4] Rocketts seems to have been the name given to the lower neighborhood of Richmond, the
portion known as Fulton. The Nolting referred to may have been A. W. Nolting, uncle of
the man referred to on p. 330.   [5] Schuricht, op. cit., II, 29.

early as 1840 a *Volksfest* in memory of Gutenberg was held. And there came into existence German organizations such as the *Sänger-bund*, *Krankenverein*, *Schiller-Loge*, *Turnverein*, and *Theaterverein*. German farmers, among whom were many gardeners,[6] settled in middle Virginia and the tidewater belt during the period from 1840 to 1860. Prosperous German settlements were founded at New Hessen and Helvetia in western Virginia, where German Hungarians and Poles built up the village of Hungary.[7] Also just before and during the Civil War, English, Scotch, and Welsh had come in to labor in the coal mines.[8]

In 1860 Richmond had 37,910 inhabitants, of whom 4,956 were foreigners, representing 13.07 per cent of the whole, or about 23 per cent of the white population. Moreover this city had before the war drawn large numbers of mechanics and munition workers, though in that class there was a lower percentage of aliens than in other large cities of the South. Samuel Phillips Day has left a graphic description of German Richmond as it was at the opening of the war. "A large proportion of the inhabitants are Germans, who either keep lager-beer saloons, or clothing-stores. They occupy the lower part of the city, support their own private theatres, 'Volks-Garten'—a favorite resort on Sundays—two newspapers, and a few churches. The German population is not liked in Virginia; they seldom associate, and never assimilate, with the regular citizens, and are generally dirty and untidy in their habits. In some parts of Richmond more German than other names appear over the doors; and to judge from the conversation heard on the streets, one might be at a loss to ascertain whether German or English was the language of the country."[9]

Norfolk County, with its large Gosport Navy Yard, sustained a population of 12,000, of whom 7,000 were located at the southern

[6] *Ibid.*, 57.　　　　　　　　　　　　　　　　[7] *Ibid.*

[8] Mrs. Logan writes as follows: "I had every opportunity of observing them, [the Negroes] as my father owned the Clover Hill coal mines, where he employed a large number of colored people in addition to men of other nationalities, English, Scotch, and Welsh."—*My Confederate Girlhood; the Memoirs of Kate Virginia Cox Logan*, 27.

[9] *Down South; or an Englishman's Experiences at the Seat of the American War*, I, 139, published in 1862. Similar, though sharper in its criticism, was the comment recorded by Frederick Law Olmsted on his visit in 1855: "There is a considerable population of foreign origin, generally of the least valuable class; very dirty German Jews, especially, abound, and their characteristic shops, (with their characteristic smells, quite as bad as in Cologne), are thickly set in the narrowest and meanest streets, which seem to be otherwise inhabited mainly by negroes."—*A Journey in the Seaboard Slave States*, I, 55. Hereafter cited as *Seaboard Slave States*. For Norfolk County see census of 1860, *Population Statistics*, 521.

extremity of Portsmouth around this important naval station. Among the 1,500 foreign inhabitants of the county were many mechanics and laborers, Germans and Irishmen. Alexandria, Petersburg, and Lynchburg all had a considerable foreign element.

A group of Scotch Highlanders in the vicinity of Fayetteville, North Carolina, merit mention, if not for their numerical importance, for their intrinsic interest. These people, who, it is well known, commenced to emigrate to the Carolinas in colonial days, continued to migrate directly to Wilmington. Olmsted, who traveled widely through the South during the decade before the war, found people in that state who spoke Gaelic and occasionally a small settlement in which that language was the common tongue. There were even one or two churches in the state where services were performed in Gaelic. Most of the Scottish Gaels were very poor upon arrival, but their natural thrift, unless offset by intemperance, as was too often the case, usually brought them to the status of owner of a few acres of piney woods, a cabin, and a family or two of Negroes, to be divided as a patrimony among their children.[10]

South Carolina received her new foreigners largely between 1840 and 1860. Franz Melchers, editor of a German paper in Charleston, has left on record the statement that when he arrived in 1846 there were scarcely fifty German families, but that in the following fifteen years a large number of young people, chiefly from North Germany, wandered in and engaged in petty shopkeeping.[11] Irish as well as Germans were found in large numbers in Charleston, living in the northern part of the city, but Charleston, despite the importance of 1,944 Germans and 3,263 Irish, had a foreign element of only 15.5 per cent in its relatively large population of 40,578. That figure rises to 30 per cent as soon as one compares the alien to the native white element. That indefatigable war correspondent of the London *Times*, Sir William Howard Russell, informs us that the Emerald Isle had contributed largely to the population of Charleston. "In the principal street there is a large and fine red sandstone building with the usual Greek-Yankee composite portico, over which is emblazoned the crownless harp and the shamrock wreath proper to a Saint Patrick's Hall, and several Roman Catholic churches also attest the Hibernian

[10] *Seaboard Slave States*, 396-397.
[11] Cited by Anton Eickhoff, *In der neuen Heimath*, 214.

presence."[12] A few years earlier Olmsted had noted in a Charleston paper the statement that the most prosperous community in the state was one composed exclusively of Germans in the hill country of the western section, the settlement poetically named Walhalla.[13]

Although the foreign-born population in Alabama in 1850 was negligible, only 7,638, the number had grown to 12,352 by the next census, more than twice the percentage of increase of the native white population of that state. Most of the foreign population was to be found in the towns and cities, though here and there one might have noted a German or an Irishman settled on the land. One notable instance is that of Thomas Friel, a thrifty, hard-working Irishman who had settled in the Jones Valley, later to become famous through its metropolis, Birmingham, and accumulated sufficient means to build a modest home.[14] The town of Selma acquired, through the visit to Germany of the merchant prince, Colonel Philip J. Weaver, sometime before 1852, about 300 immigrants, artisans and mechanics chiefly, who added materially to the industrial life of that community. McMorris' diary records on January 26, 1851, the arrival in Wetumpka of 270 Irish passengers by the steamboat *Arkansas*. Despite great loss by smallpox and cholera, a number of Irish were added to the population.[15]

In Montgomery, a thriving town of 8,800 people, although there were only 578 foreigners all told, the foreign element was sufficiently conspicuous so that travelers noted that it constituted a considerable proportion of the business and artisan class. To the small white population it contributed about 6.5 per cent of the entire population. Commerce Street led then, as now, to the modest railroad station. Just across the tracks passengers descended the bank to board the palatial vessels which plied the Alabama River to Mobile. Up the

[12] *My Diary North and South*, 121 (ed. of 1863).

[13] This observation, Olmsted states, was apropos of the foundation among them of an educational institution of a high order and it appeared that they had considerable manufacturing in successful operation and were succeeding so well in farming and in other industries as to have capital to spare to aid a railroad enterprise.—*Op. cit.*, II, 148-149. This was the community founded by Wagener through the German Settlement Society, in Pickens District, an area of nearly 18,000 acres. It remained exclusively German until shattered by the war.— Wm. Yeaton Wagener, "John Andreas Wagener," Chap. IV.

[14] The war swept away his competence, but the discovery of the finest coal under his fields soon replaced manifold what the war had deprived him of.—Mary Duffee, "Sketches of Jones Valley," No. 10, 2-3, a manuscript in the Alabama Military Archives. The sketches appeared in the *Birmingham Weekly Iron Age* in 1886.

[15] Minnie Clare Boyd, *Alabama in the Fifties*, 19; John Hardy, *Selma; Her Industries and Her Men*, 41; McMorris, "Diary," a manuscript in private possession.

river lay the race track, soon to become the camping ground of soldiers as company after company was mustered into the Confederate
service.

Certain families, representative of various racial strains, held a
well-recognized position: among the Germans the families of Römer,
Crusius, Fabel, Englehardt, and Schüssler. Several German Jewish
families were to send sons to the war. Among the business houses
which lined the main streets a visitor would have noted the modest
provision houses of several foreigners and the cobbler shop of Bohlae,
Fritz-in-the-Hole, as the naughty boys called him. Two Englishmen
were respected as good gardeners. An English half-wit named Johnson sold papers and proved during the war as eager to wipe out the
Yankees as the fiercest native fire-eater. Other races were represented
in smaller numbers: the French by Louis Cardinal, to name but one
illustration, who conducted a confectionary store at 32 Market Street;
the Belgians by a lacemaker who plied her craft on Wilkinson Street;
the Italians by Joseph Pizzala who conducted a restaurant on Perry
Street; the Dutch by J. R. Ilko who boasted of the superiority of his
watch repairing; and the Cubans by J. A. Díaz who offered imported
Havana cigars at 38 Market Street. Not the least interesting of the
aliens was the Polish city engineer, Ferdinand Okelomski, curiously
stared at by the boys because of a disfiguring scar on his face, but
whose ability as cartographer is attested by a map which is still to be
seen in the Montgomery Museum of Fine Arts.[16]

It was, however, the Gulf port of Mobile which presented a cosmopolitan air. "I looked out on the quay of Mobile," wrote Russell
when he reached this point on the morning of May 11, 1861, "fringed
by tall warehouses with shops at the basement; with names French,
German, Irish, Swiss, Italian, Scotch, Spanish, English, and Jewish;
and I thought what manner of city is this? For there was no sign of
life in the streets with all these great buildings, from most of which
the Confederate flag was flying." Straightway he answered himself:
"Then the market in the evening! A throng of mulattoes, quadroons,
Mestizos, in striking and pretty costumes, gabbling in Spanish, Italian, and French, a *lingua franca*. The most foreign looking city in the
states, a very turbulent, noisy, parti-colored 'Marseilles!' "[17] At this

[16] See Olmsted, *op. cit.*, II, 191. For details the writer is indebted to Dr. J. P. Bibb and the
file of the Montgomery *Daily Post*, February-April, 1861.
[17] "Recollections of the Civil War," *North American Review*, CLXVI, 492.

point Olmsted in 1855 had noted English merchants who wished themselves recognized as members of Mobile society. Many of these merchants owned slaves, while all probably employed them.[18]

In truth Mobile had a strikingly large proportion of the foreign element in her population. In a city of a little more than twenty-nine thousand, almost a fourth were foreigners, a ratio only equaled among the really large centers by New Orleans. While the French influence dominated to such a degree that many Negroes in Mobile spoke French, the Gulf city was truly cosmopolitan. An advertisement in the city directory of 1861 by the druggist, A. Castened, is illuminating: "English, French, Spanish, and Italian spoken by the attendants of this Establishment." Miss Walker's Ladies Book Exchange and Variety Store at 102 Dauphin Street announced that French, German, Spanish, and Italian books, papers, and magazines were to be had there. And J. Louis Launoy proclaimed a Restaurant Français at Rue Conti, 11. It is difficult to find an important nationality not represented in the business houses. Gustavus Adler managed a drugstore; Patrick Pepper, a County Clare man from Ireland, had a drygoods store at the Golden Sheep on Dauphin Street; Louis Bacho sold beer; John Lozo parceled out cigars; Augustini and Company and the more renowned S. Festorazzi and Company were confectioners;[19] Baarcke and Kienecke made men's clothing; Jules l'Etondal was a watchmaker who was to leave his watches for the front; A. P. Horta was a commission merchant for wines and cigars; and John Leversayne was a machinist at the Phoenix Foundry. Here are represented the Fatherland, Erin, Italy, Spain, and France. Dauphin and Royal were then, as now, the main retail streets; Water and Commerce were the haunts of the wholesale merchants.

The wealthier of the foreign-born and the better placed among them, such as the foreign consuls, sought residences on Monroe and Summerville streets and on the Shell Road, away from the heart of

[18] He thought that slavery seemed to be of more value to them in the amusement it afforded them than in any other way. So-and-so advertises a "valuable drayman, and a good blacksmith and horse-shoers for sale at reasonable terms"; "an acclimated double-entry book-keeper, kind in harness, is what I want," said one; "those Virginia patriarchs haven't any enterprise, or they'd send on a stock of such goods every spring, to be kept on through the fever so they could warrant them."—*Op. cit.*, II, 212.

[19] Lest it may be thought the Italians had a monopoly of confectionery, it should be added that the Frenchman, Pascal Larrouil, came to Mobile from Toulouse early in the thirties and enjoyed the reputation of being the best pastry maker in the southland. He was reported to have made the bread and pastry for La Tourette's Café in Paris. He lived through the war.

the business section, but many of them lived on business streets and above places of business on Dauphin, Conti, and Conception streets. The humble tended to be crowded on Jackson, Michael, and lower Royal streets in the southern part toward the bay. It is of interest that Adelina Patti and her sister Carlotta made their home at this time near Government and Repar streets.[20] A wharf builder, Captain Robert Gregg, well enough esteemed when the war came to head a Scotch company, lived on the corner of Government and Lafayette streets.

Among the chief cities of the South, Savannah and Memphis offer the greatest surprises. The presence of 3,100 Irishmen swelled the percentage of foreigners to 20.86 in Savannah, and in Memphis 4,100 Irish and 1,400 Germans brought it to 30.66. Always, it must be remembered, the proportion rises if the ratio is taken to the native white residents instead of to the total population. In these two cases it would mount to about 33 per cent and nearly 42 per cent respectively.

Despite Russell's designation of Mobile as the most foreign-looking city in the states—he had not yet visited New Orleans—the palm in that respect must undoubtedly be awarded to New Orleans. The metropolis of the cotton kingdom with its population of 168,675 was by far the most cosmopolitan in the South. In addition to the French and Spanish Creoles, who were not foreigners in the strict sense of the word, there were many Irish, Scotch, and Germans. Indeed the census corroborates the ante-bellum visitors' impression of representatives of all nations jostling each other, for one finds listed, in addition to the chief nationalities, immigrants from Denmark, Italy, Mexico, Portugal, Poland, Sweden, and Switzerland. From the West Indies alone more than 1,000 persons had entered. The greater portion of the mechanic and artisan class were natives of the northern states or Europeans; with the clerks of the various nationalities they constituted a considerable proportion of the population. The laboring classes were composed largely of Irish and Germans, most of whom after the requisite period of residence went through the form of naturalization in order to secure the coveted ballot.[21]

[20] These facts concerning the places of business and residences of foreign-born in Mobile have been compiled from the city directory of 1861 and the census statistics data of 1860 preserved in the bureau of the census. For details of the business section of the city, etc., the writer is indebted to Miss Harris, librarian of the city library.

[21] William Watson, *Life in the Confederate Army*, 22; Frederick Law Olmsted, *The Cotton Kingdom*, I, 296.

The Irish were present in almost overwhelming numbers. Of the 64,621 foreigners in 1860, 24,398 were Irish. This city had a special attraction for that race because of its predominant Catholic population, and also because of its being the logical port of entry for the adventurer whose goal was the frontier lands of the Southwest or even of the Northwest. Once landed on the wharves of the Crescent City, many Irish stayed. Likewise many young Germans direct from Bremen settled in the city so that the Germans constituted a large mass, 19,752 strong. France rose to third place with 10,564, as is not surprising in a community originally French. England, including Scotland and British America, dropped to fourth place with only 4,343 representatives. Three taverns symbolized to Olmsted the chief races: one, bearing the sign "The Pig and Whistle," indicated the recent English; a cabaret, the Universal Republic, with a red flag, the French; and the *Gasthaus zum Rhein Platz*, the Teutonic contribution to the strength of our nation. A policeman with a rich Irish brogue added the ever pervasive Hibernian touch.[22] In all about 40 per cent of the population represented foreign elements and two thirds of the businessmen of the city were probably of foreign birth.[23]

If the reader could transport himself to the New Orleans of early 1861, he could stroll in sections where he would feel at home. The Vieux Carré, covering pretty much what it does today, stretched from Canal Street to the Esplanade, and from Rampart to the Levee. For one seated in Jackson Square facing the cathedral it would not be difficult to imagine the beat of drum and bugle call up on Canal Street as the Washington Artillery went marching by for drill. Perhaps little French Creole children would be running through the Square and swinging themselves from limb to limb of the old trees where today Italian children would be more likely to disport themselves. But if he crossed Canal Street from the French quarter, he would behold a city of far smaller dimensions, required to house a population of only 168,000 as compared with nearly 460,000 in 1930. He would recognize the famous St. Charles Hotel, reputed the finest

[22] Edward F. Roberts, *Ireland in America*, 143; Eickhoff, *op. cit.*, 318; Kaufmann, *op. cit.*, 139. Indeed so numerous were the Germans by 1847 that a German company was founded in New Orleans to protect immigrants and to help needy countrymen. The war interrupted its activity as no immigrants came through the port and its membership declined by one half.—Eickhoff, *op. cit.*, 318. Olmsted makes the comment about the taverns in his *Seaboard Slave States*, II, 232.

[23] *American Annual Cyclopaedia*, 1862, 646.

hostelry in the entire South, on the same site as the present hotel; he might perhaps have to turn to the City Hotel on Camp Street as second choice, if he arrived at a time when the city was crowded, and he would note the number of banks, for the city had never been so prosperous. Lafayette Square, inclosed by an iron railing, would not look natural, though he would recognize the First Presbyterian Church facing it and feel that he had best take advantage of the opportunity to hear the noted divine, Dr. Palmer, the next Sunday. He would probably smile at the mule-drawn street cars, but he would feel at home marching out on the broad strip of ground on Canal Street known as "neutral ground."[24] As elsewhere, the distinguished foreigners had built for themselves ample, elegant structures in the style that came into vogue during the forties and fifties. The Del Valle residence is a splendid example at 613 Royal Street, for the Italians and French cling to the Creole quarter. The visitor would probably also note the superb façade and doorways of the mansion of Felix Grima at 820 St. Philip Street. He would notice the handsome, costly White House on South Rampart Street near Tulane, only recently erected by Charles Kock, a German commission merchant, and shudder if he could have foreseen that it was to be taken over by the United States militia in the impending war.

The visitor would find the famous Frenchman, Pierre Soulé, destined to greater fame as a minister of the Confederacy, residing on Rampart Street, and his distinguished fellow countryman, Pierre Rost, on Victory at the corner of Mandeville. The First German Lutheran Church was located modestly at the corner of Port and Cross streets, almost rubbing shoulders with the place of worship of the German Methodists between Port and Enghien streets, while not a great distance away the Irish Cathedral faced Cross between Marigney and Mandeville streets. But to find the stately home of the distinguished German lawyer, Christian Roselius,[25] the visitor would have to wander out to the suburb of Greenville.

[24] The writer secured these details about the old city from D. W. Pipes, a veteran of the war, who was a frequent visitor to the city with his father just before the war.

Canal Street derives its name from a waterway intended to unite the Mississippi River with Lake Pontchartrain. By about 1838 it had been partially filled in, giving place to a neutral ground or embankment extending from the river front to Claiborne Street.—John S. Kendall, *History of New Orleans*, II, 676.

[25] Roselius was born in 1803, came to New Orleans at the age of sixteen a redemptioner, was first a printer, learning French by setting French type. He then studied law in the office of A. Davezac, acquiring a passion for French civil law. He gradually rose to prominence,

But the more humble aliens, whether French, Irish, or German, were likely to be living on Carondolet, Royal, and Magazine streets. Irish steamboat men lived in lodgings on Delord Street near Magazine. In the squalid slums of the city near Old Levee and the Basin were packed large numbers of Irish and Germans, where race prejudices not too infrequently flamed out into bloody riots, especially at election time.

Foreigners were, however, by no means confined to the chief city of Louisiana. Until shortly before the war many people of German descent lived on a tract of land above the city along the Mississippi River, which was called the German Coast. Although the story of this Teutonic settlement goes back to the days of Law and his Louisiana Bubble and the settlement is therefore not foreign in the sense in which that word is used in this book, some few native Germans in the last decade before the war found their way to this section.[26] An interesting German colony in Louisiana was that established in Claiborne Parish, on the road from Minden to Frankville. Close to the parish line lay Germantown, preserving in its name the hint of its origin. Farther inland was an even more significant settlement. Count de Leon with his able wife led a company of forty-five persons down the Mississippi and up the Red River to found a communistic religious community six miles from Natchitoches in 1833. Upon the death of the count from an epidemic shortly after their arrival, the widow moved the remaining colonists to good land twelve miles southwest of Homer on the military road from Natchitoches to Fort Towson (now Fort Smith), Arkansas. It seems fairly well estab-

becoming attorney general in 1841. Shortly afterwards his legal reputation had become so great that he was offered a partnership by Daniel Webster, but Roselius preferred to remain in New Orleans. For years he was dean of the law faculty at the University of Louisiana and for over twenty years a professor there of civil law.—Henry Rightor, *Standard History of New Orleans*, 400-401.

[26] John Law realized that he needed good farmers for his concession in Louisiana. Accordingly he sent propaganda pamphlets, filled with wild promises, printed in German, into Germany. As a result more than 10,000 Germans set sail for Louisiana during the years 1718-24. Though many of the German ships were so badly provisioned that hundreds never lived to reach America, other shiploads made their way up the river to Arkansas, where they founded a colony on Law's concession. Soon dissatisfied, they built rafts and floated down the rivers to New Orleans, arriving just as the bubble burst. Here some settled in the city proper; others took up their residence on the river bank near the city—the German Coast, which was the bank of the Mississippi, beginning at a distance perhaps 25 miles above New Orleans, extending about 20 miles on each bank of the stream up the Mississippi. By industry they won their way through hardships to prosperity.—Lyle Saxon, *Fabulous New Orleans*, 95-98; Louis Houck, *A History of Missouri, from the Earliest Explorations and Settlements until the Admission into the Union*, II, 187; Walter H. Ryle, *Missouri, Union or Secession*, 8-9.

lished that Count de Leon was an exile because of participation in an uprising against the Austrian government of one of the small Italian duchies, probably Parma or Modena, and was saved through the influence of the Masons and a prominent Prussian prince. This community existed and throve throughout the war period, failing financially only in 1870 because of excessive generosity to the war-impoverished planters.[27]

In the Hope Villa country not far from Baton Rouge there was a trading point which went by the suggestive name of Dutch Settlement. The inhabitants of Washington, a humble scattering village on a narrow bayou in the midst of a large planting and grazing district near Opelousas, were chiefly Germans. When a session of the court brought in the residents from the surrounding country, there proved to be also large numbers of Frenchmen with the leading and richest men, English. Irishmen in this section were, apparently, conspicuous by their absence.[28] Near Natchitoches there was located a considerable number of Italians, chiefly mechanics, some of them refugees from the revolution of 1848, who proved valuable citizens. There were a sufficient number of Spaniards in that neighborhood so that a politician boasted of having overreached his opponent in an election by getting out the "Spanish vote." The Spaniards and Indian half-breeds seem to have served in this section as cattle herders of the considerable herds of poor cattle.[29] In St. James Parish were established a group of French citizens, computed at 257 in the census of 1860. Toward

[27] The community prospered on agriculture and merchandising so that it did a business worth $100,000 in 1870. Its religious views were based on the imminent return of the Messiah, when a new kingdom should arise. Until after that event couples were forbidden to marry, so that some couples had delayed their nuptials for over fifteen years. One of the number, William Stakowsky, a scholar in German and English literature, was still living near the site of the colony in 1891. The best account of the colony is given in John H. Deiler, *Eine vergessene deutsche Colonie.* A brief account occurs in D. W. Harris and B. M. Hulse, *The History of Claiborne Parish, Louisiana,* 89-93.

[28] Howell Carter, *A Cavalryman's Reminiscences of the Civil War,* 113; Olmsted, *Seaboard Slave States,* 298, 301-302. Olmsted notes the presence on the jury of a Spaniard who understood very little French and scarcely any English. He also mentions a disagreeable group of German peddlers at his inn who spoke, even to each other, a bastard English, decorating it with a profusion of cant and profane and obscene phrases. They carried knives in their bosoms and were constantly offering familiar observations to Olmsted. One of them denounced the others with great contempt as Jews who pretended to be infidels.—*Ibid.,* II, 298.

[29] *Ibid.,* II, 282, 286. He met one Italian refugee from Trieste who spoke German, French, Russian, and English besides his native Italian. As indicative of the mixture of nationalities near Opelousas, Old Man Corse might be introduced. He was an Italian-French emigrant who for forty years had been christened "Old Man Corse" from his birthplace, the island of Corsica. He had learned some French but no English. His wife could speak some "American" as she properly termed the tongue she heard about her.—Olmsted, *A Journey Through Texas,* 395-396.

the northwestern part of the state in and near the little town of Many, Sabine Parish, were a handful of Belgians.[30]

All in all, the population of Louisiana outside the Crescent City presented a considerable variety of nationalities but the foreign elements do not roll up huge figures. The census statistics show the presence in the state, exclusive of New Orleans, of approximately 5,000 Germans, 1,000 English, 4,000 Irish, and almost 5,000 French.

In some ways the foreign population of Texas was to prove the most significant alien element in the Confederacy. For one thing, as will be detailed later, it was the only state in which the foreign population ventured to offer opposition to the Confederate forces. Furthermore the foreign element, instead of being concentrated in cities as in South Carolina, Virginia, Alabama, and Louisiana, was dotted over the Texan hills and plains in agrarian colonies or villages. All the settlements were of comparatively recent development and date from almost the same period. Finally, the foreigners constituted a far larger percentage of the entire population of this sparsely settled state than of any other state, barring Louisiana alone. In all Texas there were in 1860 only 421,294 white people, at least three fourths of whom were recent immigrants into the state and nearly 10 per cent of whom had been born under an alien flag. And, finally, the strongest single national strain was preponderantly the German strain.

The Peters' Colony, an English venture, was one of the first in the field. Under an act of the Texas legislature of February, 1841, to encourage settlement of the wilderness, a contract was executed the following August by President Sam Houston for the creation of the Peters' Colony Company. This enterprise drew attention to the open wilderness and led to the beginning of its settlement. The colony covered a large district lying on the south side of the Red River and extending south 100 miles to include a large part of Ellis and all of Dallas County except a strip about three to eight miles wide on the east side and extending west about 164 miles. The natural advantages of this virgin country, widely advertised by the company, and inducements of grants of 640 acres of land to each family drew an excellent population. Agents passed throughout England in the year 1847

[30] See John G. Belisle, *History of Sabine Parish*, 218, 317, etc., for biographical statements of a half dozen of these Belgians. All were in humble stations in life.

luring the people to Texas to enable Peters to fill his stipulated quota of settlers for the colony. Though a majority of the families were drawn from Devonshire, several came from Ireland and Scotland.[31]

Even earlier in point of time were a group of German colonies. As early as 1823, when Texas was still a part of Mexico, Baron von Bastrop founded the earliest of the German colonies on the Colorado River. Settlers were mostly Oldenburgers. By the early thirties many German families had located between the Brazos and Colorado rivers. These settlers fought for Texas in her revolt against Mexico.

Texan independence brought an increase of immigration. In the early forties Henri Castro, a Frenchman of Portuguese origin, received a contract from the Republic for a grant of 28,000,000 acres of land west of San Antonio and founded Castroville in 1845 in what is now Medina County, on the right bank of the beautiful limpid Medina River. The village contained a colony of Swiss and Alsatians who spoke French or a mixture of French and German. The enterprise seems to have been under the special patronage of the Roman Catholic Church as every colonist was a communicant of that church, and the first concern of the infant village was the founding of the church edifices. By 1858 the colony numbered possibly 800 souls.[32]

Beyond Castroville, at a distance of about twenty-five miles, there were two small villages, also established by Castro, settled mostly by Rhinelanders; one, Quihi, upon the Quihi Creek, a branch of the Seco; the other, Dhanis, upon the Seco itself, resembling one of the meanest of the European peasant hamlets.[33]

About this time the *Mainzer Adelsverein*, composed of a number of minor princes and nobles, made its appearance. Its purpose was to preserve the national German traits and to encourage the concentra-

[31] For a circumstantial account of the first families of this settlement, see George Jackson, *Sixty Years in Texas*, 1, 75-76, 85, 156-157. See also pp. 65 ff. for a list of the first families to settle in the area. Jackson came out with a family of eight, four sons and four daughters, and settled in Dallas County.—*Ibid.*, 2. This section was also known as Hedgecox's Colony.

[32] The cornerstone of the church was laid by Bishop Odin of Galveston with imposing ceremonies ten days after the arrival of the colonists. The one stone house erected in the village was for M. Castro, but up to 1861 it had never been occupied. Each colonist received a town lot and a farm of 320 acres of fertile soil. Castro himself was to receive an amount of acreage two and one-half times the amount taken by the colonists. Within a fortnight a common garden had been plotted, civil officers had been chosen by ballot, and the colony was fully inaugurated.—Olmsted, *A Journey Through Texas*, 276-277, 278. See also Martin Maris, *Souvenirs d'Amérique. Relations d'un Voyage au Texas et en Haiti*, 20-21, 89-90; Albert B. Faust, *The German Element in the United States*, I, 490-498. Maris hunted for some days with some French emigrants recently arrived from Strasbourg.—*Op. cit.*, 109.

[33] Olmsted, *A Journey Through Texas*, 278-281.

tion of German emigration in one area. Prince Carl of Solms-Braunfels, official representative of the society, arrived in Texas in July, 1844, and in March, 1845, after some vicissitudes, settled the first colony of about 200 Germans on the Guadalupe River in Comal County. Here they erected New Braunfels as their county seat. Another colony was planted some ninety miles away in the higher mountainous country at Fredericksburg.[34] The society brought over to that neighborhood between 1842 and 1846 several thousand Hessians and Nassauers and planted the villages of Comfort, Boerne, and several others. Some 2,000 persons perished in the desert which interposed as a desperate obstacle between the coast and the German settlements.

The valley through which the marvelously beautiful Guadalupe River flows would readily remind a German of Thuringia in the Fatherland and was named Sisterdale for the Sister Creek, formed by two parallel-running brooks. In this lovely valley Ottomar von Behr from Kötlin settled in 1850; here came the Degeners, one of whom rose to the dignity of serving in the national congress for his adopted state, and Fritz Tegener, whom we shall meet in the Nueces Massacre.

The state received its strongest German influx during the forties and fifties from the revolutionary movements which swept Europe during those decades. By 1860 Texas was one of the most German states of the entire American Union. It is no exaggeration to say that one fifth of the white population of Texas were then of German blood; of this number twenty thousand had been born in Germany. The number of residents born in Germany was twice as large as the domiciled Irish, English, French, and Spanish taken together. The German portion of the state lay in the southwest between the Colorado and San Antonio rivers with the valley of the Guadalupe in the vicinity of the Comal Mountains forming the middle. The region is rich in water, and the many valleys are extraordinarily fertile, a blossoming garden in the midst of wide-spreading prairies and desert.[35]

[34] For a fuller account of these settlements of the Mainzer Verein see John J. Linn, *Reminiscences of Fifty Years in Texas*, 348; Faust, *op. cit.*, I, 490-498; Olmsted, *A Journey Through Texas*, 172-177; Thomas North, *Five Years in Texas*, 189; and the very complete, scholarly work by R. L. Biesele, *The History of the German Settlements in Texas, 1831-1861*.

[35] An enumeration of the German villages will give some conception of the extent of the German settlements: Neu Ulm, High Hill, Berlin, Catspring, Millheim, Content, Felsburg,

These Texan Germans held themselves apart in four purely German counties and founded three German cities in that section; namely, Fredericksburg, New Braunfels, and Boerne. To these towns, as market centers, came the country folk who surrounded the villages. The entire region may properly be denominated a small Germany. The children spoke only German in the home until outside contacts forced them to learn English;[36] even some of the few Negroes of the section spoke German. There were to be found only German churches,[37] and as early as 1860 there was a well-conducted and influential German press.[38] Among the fugitive revolutionists were many comfortably situated, even rich, Germans, who acquired large landholdings and created extensive plantations. But wealth counted for less in the creation of this Germany than the love of liberty, industry, and virtue. The Latin colony in the Sisterdale, so called because many of the settlers had received the classical training of the German gymnasia, was chiefly the spiritual center of Little Germany in Texas. Many cultured Germans belonged to the circle: Julius Dresel, a fugitive from Wiesbaden; Professor Ernst Kapp, a distinguished geographer of Westphalia; and Dr. W. I. Runge of Mecklenburg.[39] Dr. Ferdinand Lindheimer, who had found a botanist's paradise in the Guadalupe Valley and to whom we owe the

Sisterdale, Kerrville, Ufnau, Concrete, Meyersville, and Hochheim. LaGrange, Columbus, and several other places were largely peopled by Germans.—Kaufmann, *op. cit.*, 144.

[36] Even now German is the medium of communication for large numbers of the population in this section, though it is often corrupted by English perversions. The first words the writer heard in Fredericksburg as she reached the main street were in German. German influence even in matters of diet was observable in the serving of a compote of prunes at dinner to the group of men in the restaurants drinking beer. She met several people who could not speak English, though they had been born here. One of the leading citizens declared with pride that Fredericksburg was "the most German place south of the Mason and Dixon line." The interesting octagonal structure in this place serving as a museum is a replica of the old church. Several of the old houses antedating the war are still extant, as the John Peter Tatsch home and the old Klingelhoefer house. No visitor could fail to observe the great width of the main streets in Fredericksburg, San Antonio, Seguin, and New Braunfels—even the side streets are far from narrow—which are indications of German forethought, for they must have streets wide enough to permit the turning of the four-team oxcarts. The writer is indebted to Mrs. Henry Lewis for a visit to the old houses and for other kindnesses.

[37] Many of the settlers, true forty-eighters, especially among the cultured classes, were freethinkers, and were quite indifferent to the erection of churches. Their influence is reflected even today.

[38] Among the papers printed in German were the *Neu Braunfelser Zeitung*, *Galveston Union*, *Der Texas Demokrat* (Houston), and *Texas Staats Zeitung* (San Antonio).

[39] The hotel register of the inn on the public square of New Braunfels, the Markt Platz of earlier days, which shows the list of distinguished visitors, is preserved in the New Braunfels Museum. The hotel still faces the square, is still serving its original purpose, and well rewards a visit to see its thick walls, its quaint staircase, and the old wine cellar, quite separate from the rest of the basement. These visitors usually made their way to the Latin colony.

best data on Texas flora,[40] Dr. Adolf Douai, editor of a German newspaper in San Antonio, and other "forty-eighters" often visited in Sisterdale. The rude Texas backwoodsmen, shrinking as pioneers from no hard work or privations, clung to the memory of a Fatherland deeply beloved but sacrificed for liberty. They often gathered for lectures and classical music. Every home possessed a library of scientific and inspirational works. The youth grew up in the speech and views of their elders, but because of the breadth of view of these men instruction in the flourishing schools was bilingual. There were no illiterates here as in the rest of Texas, for in the German hamlets there were free schools for elementary education, a more advanced free school for the higher grades, and a private classical school.[41] There existed as in Richmond several organizations for social improvement—an agricultural society, a mechanics institute, a harmonic society, a society for political debates, and a *Turnverein*. A horticultural club expended twelve thousand dollars in one year to introduce new trees and plants.[42]

Another area of German settlement of perhaps two hundred families was to be found in 1860 on the Brazos River near San Filipe. Almost all the settlers owned only small farms or were farm laborers. When they first arrived, they were very poor and hired themselves out at such wages as they could get. But they prospered, all cultivating cotton, so that Olmsted, on the occasion of his visit, found many of them enlarging and decorating their homes. He saw no Negroes among them.[43]

In the extreme southern part of Texas is the peninsula of Matagorda, a narrow strip of land one to two miles wide and seventy-five miles long, bordered by the Gulf of Mexico on the south and Mata-

[40] Lindheimer was not only a famous botanist; he edited the *Neu Braunfelser Zeitung* and earned for it recognition as a very well conducted newspaper. We shall have occasion to refer to him again in connection with the discussion of the attitude of the aliens toward secession. The building in which he wrote so many editorials still stands on the main street of New Braunfels and still houses this paper.

The Guadalupe is the most rarely beautiful stream the writer has ever seen. Lined on both sides in the lower courses with elephant's-ears, the river changes when one reaches the head springs. The bottom of the stream is covered with vegetation so that one sees through the crystal-clear water bands of pale green, deep green, and red vegetation, alternating with bands of gray stone. The play of the sunlight on the water makes a scene of loveliness unsurpassed for pure natural beauty.

[41] Lovingly the New Braunfelsers of the second and third generation are cherishing and preserving by tree surgery the oak under which Hermann Seele gathered the children and conducted his first school in August, 1845.

[42] Kaufmann, *op. cit.*, 146, 147, 148.   [43] *A Journey Through Texas*, 358, 359.

gorda Bay on the north. It connects with the mainland at Caney and comes to a focus at Decros Point or Schura Pass, now Cavallo Pass. About midway between the two lay the Dutch Settlement, consisting of half a dozen houses.[44]

Certain Texan cities, notably San Antonio, Dallas, Galveston, Houston, and Austin, felt the influence of the German stream of immigration, securing large additions after 1848. A large number of unfortunate immigrants who arrived with exhausted purses remained in Houston as laborers, or acquired a little patch of ground or a cabin in the vicinity. The greater part of the small tradesmen and mechanics of this city were German.[45] About half of Victoria, consisting of a population of one thousand, were Germans. Several tracts of land on the outskirts were divided into plots for them, which they eagerly bought with their savings or first earnings, but which they were unable to sell without the loss of their improvements. Before the war Victoria was a small, poor town, standing on the great flat coast prairie near the edge of the river bottom. The situation of the Germans there was pitiable compared with that of their more prosperous countrymen in the upper country.[46]

On the very eve of the war Germans were arriving in large numbers. The *Neu Braunfelser Zeitung* reported on December 2, 1859, that the steamboat *Matagorda* had just brought via Berwick Bay the largest number of genuine settlers which had arrived within a year in any ship. The ship was packed with passengers, it added. On January 4, 1861, it recorded the ship *Juno* as arriving in December and bearing several families bound for New Braunfels and Fredericksburg, a number of Bohemians, and several men of distinction, as a certain Dr. Steffens F. of Hildesheim and an architect of Oranienburg.[47] By this time Germans were spread in important numbers from Calhoun County on the coast to Gillespie and Bastrop counties on the north along the upper Colorado, the Llano, Pedernales, Guadalupe, and San Antonio rivers.[48]

[44] Charles A. Siringo, *A Texas Cow Boy*, 13.
[45] Olmsted, *A Journey through Texas*, 362.   [46] *Ibid.*, 240-241.
[47] No further information could be found concerning these two men.
[48] The subjoined table shows the widespread distribution and the proportion of Germans through the Texas counties as only statistics can:

TEXAS

County	Per Cent	County	Per Cent
De Witte	32	Galveston	30
Harris	31	Calhoun	27

Colonies of other nationalities existed in Texas. A group of Irishmen had founded Religion not far from Goliad in the early days of settlement. Though it had not increased very rapidly, still the inhabitants there were comfortable. They owned no slaves, not from conscientious scruples but from caution for their property, as Negroes could escape too easily across the Rio Grande.[49] Another well-known Irish settlement existed at San Patricio Hibernia, then called San Patricio.[50] A sort of religious colony of Silesian Poles had been established near San Antonio in 1855-56 by Father Leopold Moczygemba, a Franciscan monk who had been sent to Texas by the general of his order and who had been enraptured by the new country. Several hundred arrived in February, 1855, coming from Polish villages in the vicinity of his birthplace, 700 more in the autumn, and some 500 additional in 1856. Unfortunately the site in Karnes County chosen by their spiritual father proved so unhealthy as to induce a desertion of about one half of the survivors, who founded a new settlement in the upper eastern corner of Medina County.[51] A group of French agrarians, about 1,000 strong, who had settled on the Trinity River near Dallas in 1855, dispersed after one disastrous season. A few remained on the domain of the association, a few followed their leader, Victor Considérant, to the Sabinal River as a communist group, but the great bulk scattered over the state.[52]

County	Per Cent	County	Per Cent
Victoria	27	Austin	20
Fayette	24	Bastrop	18
Colorado	24	Matagorda	9
Washington	21	Lavaca	6

WEST TEXAS

County	Per Cent	County	Per Cent
Comal	85	Medina	36
Kendall	81	Guadalupe	22
Gillespie	75	Bexar	20
Kerr	55	Llano	10
Mason	46	Travis	8

See Biesele, *The History of the German Settlements in Texas*, 62, 164, and maps on 61, 163. It should be noted that he includes in the text the first generation born in America.—*Ibid.*, 159.

[49] Olmsted tells of seeing an Irishman at work in this vicinity making a novel fence of squares of turf piled into a wall.—*A Journey Through Texas*, 266.

[50] Mrs. Susan Francis Miller, *Sixty Years in the Nueces Valley (1870-1930)*, 5.

[51] Olmsted, *A Journey Through Texas*, 270; Miecislaus Hainan, *The Poles in the Early History of Texas*, 38; *Catholic Encyclopedia*, XII, 205; Rev. Edward Dworaczyk, *The First Polish Colonies of America in Texas*, 1-7.

[52] Olmsted, *A Journey Through Texas*, 285. A few German-Swiss became members of this communist colony in 1855.—Moritz Tiling, *History of the German Element in Texas*, 132.

As was to be expected in a state bordering on Mexico, represent-atives of the adjacent nation were to be found in considerable num-bers. Spanish-speaking citizens, obtained in 1845 by annexation alone, reached nearly 20,000, large numbers of whom, of course, were still alive in 1860. In the neighborhood of San Antonio there were a large number of Mexican ranches. Some Mexicans were large landholders and stock raisers; a few even owned slaves. But the great bulk made docile and patient laborers, working indiscriminately alongside slaves as cattle herders.[53] As the border was approached, the Mexican influ-ence became more marked. Eagle Pass on the Rio Grande, 160 miles west of San Antonio, was chiefly inhabited by Mexicans, and the ma-jority of the inhabitants of Brownsville were of the same race.[54] Zapata County was thoroughly Mexican and rural. During the fifties the Americans and foreigners who came to Starr County were single and married the daughters of leading Mexican families so that Rio Grande became a cosmopolitan little place. The Spanish-speaking population of the state was strong enough to support several Spanish papers. The *Ranchero*, established at Corpus Christi in 1852 and removed just before the war to Brownsville, was published during the war years at Matamoros across the river; and *El Bejareño*, started by General Debray and A. A. Lewis in 1855, was abruptly terminated when General de Bray joined the army at the outbreak of war.[55]

Scattered references to other nationalities and strange racial mix-tures occur. A Texas cowboy states that his father came from Italy and his mother from Ireland. The French traveler Maris tells of a hotel in Bexar kept by an Italian immigrant who spoke almost all languages and who also had the prescience to divine the contents of all purses and fix his prices accordingly.[56] G. W. Kendall, editor of the New Orleans *Picayune*, owned a sheep ranch a few miles north of New Braunfels under the charge of an imported Scotch shepherd. A colony of 240 Bohemians settled at Alleyton, Colorado County, and another 100 passed through Columbus on their way to Fayette

[53] Olmsted, *A Journey Through Texas*, 271-272, 427.
[54] R. H. Williams, *With the Border Ruffians*, 279, 315. As the census of 1860 did not distinguish between persons of Anglo-American and Mexican stock, exact numbers cannot be determined.
[55] Dudley G. Wooten, *A Comprehensive History of Texas, 1615-1897*, II, 391-392.
[56] Siringo, *op. cit.*, 14; Maris, *op. cit.*, 86. Maris prudently adds, "Il est donc prudent de convenir avec lui du prix en arrivant."

County at the very close of 1860. A few scattered Hungarians and Swedes were to be encountered, also.[57]

The Norwegian settlements in Texas, three in number in 1860, have won a fame out of all proportion to the number of actual settlers, owing largely to the letters and writings of certain pioneers, which received wide circulation and attention during the two decades just before the war. Despite this wide advertisement the settlements remained relatively small, as the Norwegians in general preferred to settle in the north central and western states.

Two of the settlements center about Johan Reiersen, a prominent journalist and editor of Kristiansand, Norway, who advocated emigration from Norway for economic opportunity. After an exploratory visit, sweeping from Texas to Wisconsin and Illinois, in the course of which he met Governor Houston, who promptly manifested interest in his plans for a colony, he led a small party of Norwegians as an advance guard to northeastern Texas in 1845, where he planted a colony in Henderson County. The romantic name of his first village, Normandy, later suffered change to the more prosaic Brownsboro. The next year a second group of about fifty augmented the earlier emigrants. Early in 1848 illness in the colony and discouragement led Reiersen to move to a point southwest of Dallas known as Four Mile Prairie, where on the border line between Kaufman and Van Zandt counties he located the village of Prairieville as a nucleus. Soon the settlers from Brownsboro followed him to the new location, including the justly famous J. M. C. Wärenskjold and his cultivated wife, Elise, both of whom wrote incessantly in praise of the new home. In 1850 the second Norwegian settlement was further strengthened by the addition of fourteen families from the homeland.

Bosque County, southwest of Dallas, became the site of the third Norwegian colony. A certain Cleng Peerson, an incessant traveler who had arrived in America in 1821, visited Texas in 1849, exploring the Eros, Brazos, and Trinity rivers. Convinced that this new state

[57] Olmsted, A Journey Through Texas, 183. The arrival of the Bohemians is noted by the Neu Braunfelser Zeitung, December 28, 1860. The most interesting Hungarian encountered was the exile, Ladislaus Ujházy, a nobleman who had removed to a point near San Antonio from Iowa after the death of his wife. With his children he cultivated his own land. He did not take part in the Civil War as he was appointed consul at Ancona by President Lincoln in 1861.—Eugene Piványi, Hungarians in the American Civil War, 8. For the Swedes see Carl Rosenquist, "The Swedes in Texas"; August Anderson, Hyphenated or The Life Story of S. M. Swenson; Erik Norelius, De Svenska Luterska Församlingarnas och Svenskarnes historia i Amerika, 37; and Ernest Severin, Svenskarne i Texas i Ord Och Bild, I, 151.

offered greater advantages than the northwest, he returned to the Fox
River colony in Illinois and induced some of his fellow countrymen
to set out for Texas with him. Among them was Ole Canuteson, who
had arrived in America with his parents in 1850. As a ten-year-old
lad in Norway he had first caught the American fever from hearing
Peerson, on one of his visits home, tell stories about the "promised
land." When he met Peerson, just back from Texas, in La Salle,
Illinois, he was ready for the venture. They arrived at an opportune
moment, for two years later the Texas legislature voted to bestow
land on actual settlers. Canuteson found vacant land near the Bosque
River and there, a few miles northwest of Waco in a rich, lovely spot,
he founded in 1853 what was to become the chief Norwegian settlement in Texas, centering around the village of Clifton. The rest of
the group followed him from Dallas County in 1854.

In the early part of 1853, 150 new immigrants arrived at Galveston with several hundred more expected on the next steamer from
New Orleans. On the eve of the Civil War the oldest settlement at
Brownsboro had about 145 souls; at Four Mile Prairie there were 63
Norwegians; and in Bosque County, 75. Mrs. Wärenskjold estimated
350 in the three settlements, including farmers near the villages, a
figure which approximates closely the official count of the census of
1860, which was 321.[58]

The conglomerate character of many of the Texas cities and towns
may prove surprising. The population of San Antonio, for instance,
fell into three approximately even divisions: 4,000 Mexicans, 3,500
Americans, and 3,000 Germans. Founded by the Spaniards in 1650,
the city had sunk to a miserable Spanish nest when the first Germans
arrived in 1843. By 1860 it was the largest city in Texas, a veritable
work of art wrought by the Germans.[59] However, upon the right
bank of the San Antonio River there was still a sort of suburb composed of poor cabins occupied chiefly by the Mexicans who passed

[58] For fuller details about the Norwegian settlements see Carlton C. Qualey, *Norwegian
Settlement in the United States*, 198-205; T. C. Blegen, *Norwegian Migration to America,
1825-60*, 177-182; Olaf M. Norlie, *History of the Norwegian People in America*, 175-176;
Rasmus Björn Anderson, *The First Chapter of Norwegian Immigration (1821-1840)*, 370-395.
Elise Wärenskjold, who lived until 1895, has left an account of the early settlement which
appeared in *Billad Magazine*, copies of which are to be found in Decorah, Iowa. The San
Saba Colonization Company, a Texas project, was definitely interested in promoting Scandi-
navian immigration. Its leaders prepared to bring to Texas 1,000 families of German, Dutch,
Swiss, Norwegian, Danish, and Swedish immigrants. See R. L. Biesele, "The San Saba
Colonization Company," *Southwestern Historical Quarterly*, XXXIII, 175.
[59] Kaufmann, *op. cit.*, 146.

over to the city by a wooden bridge. Olmsted found the composite character of the town portrayed through its architecture: "For five minutes the houses were evidently German, of fresh, square-cut blocks of creamy-white limestone, mostly of a single story and humble proportions, but neat and thoroughly roofed and finished. Some were furnished with the luxuries of little bow-windows, balconies or galleries.

"From these we enter the square of the Alamo. This is all Mexican. Windowless cabins of stakes, plastered with mud and roofed with river-grass or 'tula,' or low windowless, but better thatched, houses of adobes (gray, unburnt bricks), with groups of brown idlers lounging at their doors. . . . From the bridge we enter Commerce Street, the narrow principal thoroughfare, and here are American houses, and the triple nationalities break out into the most amusing display, till we reach the main plaza. The sauntering Mexicans prevail on the pavements, but the bearded Germans and the sallow Yankees furnish their proportion. The signs are German by all odds, and perhaps the houses. . . . The American houses stand back, with galleries and jalousies and a garden picket-fence against the walk. . . . The Mexican buildings are stronger there than those we saw before, but still of all sorts, and now put to all sorts of new uses."[60]

Galveston likewise offered its claims to cosmopolitanism. Maris, who visited it in 1857 when its population was seven thousand, declared that in no other place had he encountered a population more heterogeneous. All the nations of Europe had sent their contingents. Embarking on the boat which he took from Galveston to Port Lavaca, he encountered a crowd of immigrants recently arrived from Europe on their way to the colony at Castroville in the interior of Texas. Stated in concrete terms, according to Maris, about one half of the population of Texas only was American, the other half emigrants from Ireland, France, Italy, Spain, and Germany, the last-named contributing at least one third of the foreign contingent. His impressions were not of course entirely correct.[61]

Of the states which were to contribute soldiers to the Confederacy

---

[60] *A Journey Through Texas*, 149-150. It is impossible, of course, to recognize Olmsted's city in the huge modern city of San Antonio. Even the huts of the Mexicans in the outskirts, miserable as they are, are wooden shacks, not adobe or thatched huts.

[61] *Op. cit.*, 14. Maris felt that Galveston owed its prosperity solely to its advantageous position at the entrance to the bay. See also *De Bow's Review*, III, Ser. 1, 348.

only three others require particular mention. Germans and Irish were found in Arkansas. In 1836, 60 families had migrated from Rheinhessen to settle under their pastor, the Reverend Mr. Klingelhöffer, and were the advance guard for over 1,000 of their countrymen who settled near Little Rock. This home state of General Patrick Cleburne of the Confederate army rallied many Irish followers to his standard.[62] The number of Germans scattered in Missouri was far from negligible. Except in St. Louis, where 50 per cent were congregated, they were not segregated in any one section, but were scattered rather broadly over the state. Those outside of the metropolis of the state were engaged in farming and soon were assimilated by the native white stock, thus losing their identity as a foreign group. In contrast to their brethren of the cotton states, they avoided the "Black Belt" of Missouri, the slaveholding counties.[63] Of Irish in that state there were 43,464 and of Germans no less than 88,487.

There were several small colonies of Swiss in Eastern Tennessee who had come over in 1845 after a period of failure of crops and general depression in their mountainous country. After an interval of negotiations between the Tennessee Colonization Company and the canton authorities, who wished, on the one hand, to protect their countrymen against exploitation, and, on the other, to protect the infant colony against a potential band of paupers or criminals, a group settled in Grundy County on the Cumberland Plateau, naming their settlement Grütli to give the new location a home flavor. An agricultural union, consisting of twenty members, gave advice to the farmers and helped in the purchase of tools. A coöperative society established a shop where the colonists could secure necessities at cost. With subsistence farming was combined the practice of the wood carving they had learned in Switzerland and for which they found a market in adjacent watering places. Four similar Swiss colonies were planted at Warburg in Morgan County, at Winchester in Franklin County, at Newbern in Dyer County, and at South Pittsburg in Marion County.[64]

The foreigners resident in the South represented naturally every

[62] Faust, op. cit., I, 439; census of 1860. There were only 3,600 foreigners in all Arkansas.
[63] Walter H. Ryle, Missouri, Union or Secession, 7-8, 18-21.
[64] Adelrich Steinach, Geschichte und Leben der Schweizer Kolonien in den Vereinigten Staaten von Nord-Amerika, 163, 170; Grace Stone, "Tennessee: Social and Economic Laboratory," Sewanee Review, XLVI, 39-43.

class and rank of society from nobleman to ditchdigger, from Hungarian exile to humble Irish nationalist,[65] from German geologist to Mexican herder, from college professor to cobbler, from leading member of the bar to pack peddler. There were, as has been indicated, a number of British slaveholders owning plantations of greater and less size, men of wealth, culture, and refinement. There were educated editors of foreign papers.[66] Occasionally the foreign-born citizen rose to real prominence at the bar and in public life. Many such will be brought forward in a later chapter. Suffice it here to note as illustrative of a minor group Robert B. Lindsay, a well-educated Scotchman who practiced law at Tuscumbia, Alabama, until he was sent to Montgomery to sit in the lower house of assembly in 1857; Michael Ryan, who fled Ireland to escape the priesthood and settled at Alexandria, Louisiana, to become a leading figure at the local bar; another son of the Emerald Isle, Jere Boyle, who played an important rôle in the grading for new railroad lines in the Cahaba Valley in north central Alabama; Dr. Anthony Michael Dignowity, who built up a good practice in medicine in San Antonio;[67] and S. M. Swenson who ran away from a disagreeable apprenticeship in Sweden to Galveston in 1838, married romantically the widow of the wealthy planter for whom he had served as overseer, became highly respected as an able planter, and finally won the friendship of Sam Houston.[68] It is striking that many of these foreigners who showed talent and ability married into prominent southern families.[69]

Here and there one encounters a British clergyman, such as the Reverend T. O. Summers, who for many years edited the official

[65] Sir William Russell tells of encountering at Jackson, Mississippi, a namesake who had been involved in the Irish national movement of 1848 and who "had left the country for his own good." He possessed influence and dollars, "which he would never have attained in Dublin."—"Recollections of the Civil War," *North American Review*, CLXVI, 499. He tells of another Irishman who had come over from the north of Ireland to New Orleans as a cabin boy and by 1857 had possession of 44,000 acres of land.—*Ibid.*, 498.

[66] The reader will readily recall J. A. Wagener of Charleston and K. D. A. Douai of San Antonio already mentioned.

[67] Lindsay was returned to the state senate in 1865, after the war. See William Garrett, *Reminiscences of Public Men in Alabama for Thirty Years*, 732; G. P. Whittington, "Rapides Parish, Louisiana,—a History," *The Louisiana Historical Quarterly*, XVII (July, 1934), 548. For information concerning Dr. Dignowity, an interesting Czech to whom reference is again made below, in Chap. IV, see Estelle Hudson, *Czech Pioneers of the Southwest*, 45-49.

[68] The romantic story of this fascinating Swede is told in Anderson, *Hyphenated*. He tried to bring colonists from his native land to Texas but actually succeeded in bringing over only a few families before the war.

[69] Duffee, *op. cit.*, 6-7. The marriage of Swenson is noted in the text; Lindsay married the daughter of Anthony Winston; Boyle married Helen Lee of a prominent family of that section of Alabama.

organ of the Southern Methodist Church and was the author of many
tracts and books on Methodism.[70] Many political French exiles, indeed exiles of all nations, had located in New Orleans during the last
decade before the war and were earning incomes as teachers, as petty
dealers, or as manufacturers of tobacco. There were numbers of foreign merchants everywhere in the towns and cities, among whom
German Jews were conspicuous. Many of the so-called "Latin
farmers" of Texas came from the higher classes and even the nobility
of Germany.[71] Aliens did some of the manufacturing. The Germans
of New Braunfels had given the manufacture of cloth more attention
than it had received elsewhere in Texas. The alien element, among
whom English, Scotch, and Germans should be especially mentioned,
furnished mechanics and skilled laborers out of all proportion to their
numbers.[72] The Germans, with exceptions, furnished the artisans
(Handwerker) and small dealers, and had bestowed on them the
sobriquet of Speckschneider (tailors of bacon). In some places,
Charleston for instance, Germans controlled almost exclusively the
drugstores, and thus enjoyed the title of doctor. The educated Germans had a good reputation among Americans, while the small
dealers were often in collision with the law by selling spirits to the
Negroes or by purchasing stolen articles from them at a low price.
These so-called "Dutch" formed a separate class, not recognized by
their own fellow countrymen or by other nationalities, and despised
because of their transactions with the Negroes. Here and there the
exiled Gaul was preserving under difficulties the traditions of a Paris
café.

Surprisingly enough, one might have found Irish waiters in some
of the best hotels of the South in ante-bellum days. Their presence
at the American in Richmond and at the Battle House in Mobile,
both run by northern men, is explicable. In some cases their employment was inspired by motives of economy, as the price of slave hire

[70] David R. Barbee, An Excursion in Southern History, 44-45.

[71] Ernest H. Hohenwart, Land und Leute in den Vereinigten Staaten, 69.

[72] Linn, op. cit., 348. Olmsted felt that there was not another town in the slave states in
which the proportion to the whole population of mechanics or of persons employed in the
exercise of their own discretion was one quarter as large as in New Braunfels unless one in
which the Germans were the predominating race.—A Journey Through Texas, 178. In 1855
Olmsted felt that the population of the skilled labor class was rapidly increasing and cited
the fact that previous to an election in 1855 foreigners had been naturalized in five
days.—Seaboard Slave States, II, 148, 238. The occupations of the men who enlisted in the
Confederate States army offers corroboration of the facts stated here.

was so high as to be prohibitive. Southerners did not like them as they often did not understand their brogue, a fact which irritated the Irish, and the planter class, moreover, did not know how to address servants of their own color. Hence they preferred hotels with Negro servants. Often where the Irish were used in the dining room, colored servants were used as chambermaids.[73]

The Germans, Scotch, and Irish, the latter especially because of their poverty on arrival, supplied the labor of the cities and did the heavy work on the docks and wharves. This fact explains their presence in the urban sections. The free white had to a surprising degree usurped from the Negro the field of labor in New Orleans. The majority of the carterers, hackney coach men, porters, railroad hands, public waiters, and common laborers appeared to a close observer like Olmsted to be white. He found this to be the case more often there than in any other town in the South, despite a torrid and dangerous climate, and explained it by the extensive commercial interests of that port and by the constant movement of immigrants through the city. That flow provided a sufficient number of free laborers to sustain by competition and association with each other the habits of free-labor communities. It was well known that there existed a great antipathy among the draymen and rivermen of New Orleans —almost to a man, foreigners—to the participation of slaves in this branch of industry.[74]

In the towns the Mexicans seemed to have no other business than that of carting goods. They carried on almost the entire transportation of the southwestern country with oxen or two-wheeled carts. Some had small shops to supply the needs of their fellow countrymen, and some lived upon the produce of farms and cattle ranches owned in the neighborhood. Out on the ranches they served almost exclusively as menials, the men as "hands," the occasional Mexican woman as a domestic.[75]

Foreign labor was employed in turpentine making near Fayetteville, North Carolina. Opinion differed as to the comparative merits of free white and slave labor, but a very interesting comparison made by the owner of a glue factory concerning the merits of Irishmen and

[73] Olmsted, *The Cotton Kingdom*, I, 51; Joseph H. Ingraham, *The Sunny South*, 504.
[74] Olmsted, *The Cotton Kingdom*, I, 299; *idem, Seaboard Slave States*, II, 238.
[75] *Idem, A Journey Through Texas*, 160.

Germans is recorded by Olmsted. The Irishmen worked well for a time but became in a fortnight too self-confident and officious. On the other hand Germans, who had been tried in time of stress, proved excellent hands, steady, plodding, reliable, ready to work without boasting or grumbling for less wages than Irishmen. The Welsh and English helped supply the labor of the coal mines in Virginia but were occasionally dissatisfied with conditions, even though better wages were paid for this labor than in the North.[76]

The crews of the river boats, or the rivermen as they were often called, were during the decade preceding the war partly Irishmen with an occasional English fireman, and partly slaves, hired out by their owners at the same wages paid the Irishmen, about thirty to forty dollars a month.

One fact which will strike the modern reader as extraordinary is that the labor of digging ditches and trenches, of clearing the waste lands, of hewing down the forests on the plantations, and of repairing the levees was generally done by the Irish laborers, who traveled about under contractors or were engaged by resident foremen of gangs. The high price demanded for this work was lamented but consolation was found in the reflection that it was much better to use the Irish, who cost nothing to the planter if they died, "than to use up good field hands in such severe employment." Many Irishmen were buried in the Louisiana swamps, leaving their earnings to the grogshop and to the contractor, and the results of their labor to the planter.[77]

A singular illustration of the way in which the Negroes were shielded from dangerous posts is revealed in a description of the loading of a boat with cotton. Negro hands were sent to the top of the bank to roll the bales to the top of the gangway, down which they slid with fearful velocity. Irishmen were at the foot of the gangway to move them into place. The callous reason given for this division of labor was that "the niggers are worth too much to be risked here; if the Paddies are knocked overboard, or get their backs broke, nobody loses anything."[78]

Only Irish or Germans would consent to work with the slaves.

[76] Idem, Seaboard Slave States, I, 412-413. His factory was located in Baltimore. One young Englishman had been warned away from the coal mine because of fraternizing with the Negroes.
[77] Russell, My Diary North and South, 104; H. G. Bunn, Reminiscences of the Civil War, bound with Charles E. Nash (ed.), Biographical Sketches of Gen. Pat Cleburne and Gen. T. C. Hindman, 191.   [78] Olmsted, The Cotton Kingdom, I, 276.

No American who recognized the racial prejudice among his fellow workers would let himself be seen working with a Negro. Still more degrading was it to serve under a Negro. To a native white "it was a most revolting sight" to see an Irishman waiting on a Negro mason, and yet it was one which could be seen any day on Canal Street in New Orleans. It led even the Negro to scorn the Irishmen, as the following story indicates: A Negro, seeing another slave carrying mortar, called out with a loud laugh, "Hallo! you is turned Irishman is 'ou?" And yet there is much evidence to indicate that white workers were rapidly displacing the slaves in all sorts of work.[79]

There is some evidence of seasonal migratory labor from Canada to the South on the eve of the rebellion. The *Mobile Daily Advertiser and Register* reports that "the number of young men who have left Quebec during the last few weeks, for Southern States . . . is positively astonishing, and surpasses by far the number of those who were in the habit of seeking their fortunes in the South during the winter of former years. The figure will scarcely fall short of six hundred. They nearly all belong to the working classes connected with shipping, and were bound for Savannah, New Orleans, Mobile, Pensacola, and other Southern ports."[80]

Statistics are seldom thrilling but in a study of this sort there is scarcely any escape from them. There were in the eleven states of the Confederacy nearly 5,500,000 white people, of whom nearly 250,000 had been born abroad, or roughly between 4 and 5 per cent. De Bow's general statement, indicative of southern opinion, is true: "Non slaveholders are not subjected to that competition with foreign pauper labor which has degraded the free labor of the North. From whatever cause it has happened, whether from climate, the nature of our products, or of our labor, the South has been enabled to maintain a more homogeneous population, and show a less admixture of races, than the North."[81] It is perfectly well known that the vast mass of

[79] *Ibid.*, 297. A master asked his slave which of the "boys" to send, as he must furnish some "niggers" to work on the fortifications during the war. "Well, massa," replied the old servant, "I doesn't know about dat. War's comin' on, and dey might be killed. Ought to get Irishmen to do dat work anyhow. I reckon you'd better not send any ob de boys—tell you what, massa, nigger property's mighty onsartin dese times!"—Albert D. Richardson, *The Secret Service, the field, the dungeon, and the escape,* 147.   [80] November 23, 1860.

[81] Open letter by J. D. B. De Bow to R. N. Gourdin in *De Bow's Review,* XXX, 72-73. The table as given by De Bow is as follows:

RATIO OF FOREIGN TO NATIVE POPULATION

Eastern States ....12.65 to every 100 natives
Middle States ....19.84 "   "   "   "

the immigrants turned north because they were a peasant and laboring class and unskilled white labor was not wanted in the South. Thirty per cent of all male immigrants were farmers, according to immigration authorities, and turned naturally to the public lands of the West, and 42 per cent, laborers, who just as naturally sought the best market for their brawn, the rapidly growing cities of the North. But it is difficult to see how De Bow arrived at his figures. His table, published in January, 1861, gives only 1.86 foreigners in the southern states to every 100 native-born and 5.34 to every 100 natives in the southwestern states as compared with 12.65 in the northeastern states and 19.84 in the north middle states. The census figures of 1860, which were, of course, not yet compiled at the time, show, according to a careful calculation by the writer, an average of 2.83 per cent foreign population to the entire population throughout the South. The further assertion that the foreigners "that are among us are of a select class, and, from education and example, approximate very nearly to the native standard" must have been written by De Bow with one eye cocked to the few British slaveholders and the other closed to the stevedores and draymen of New Orleans.

It is again true that 86.6 per cent of the foreign-born population of the United States inhabited the free states and that but 13.4 per cent were to be found in the slave states but, in a foreign population the size of that in the United States, the 13.5 per cent must still constitute a very appreciable and important number. It is also true that the four states with the smallest percentage of foreign-born were all southern states—North Carolina with only .33 per cent, Arkansas with only .86 per cent, Mississippi with only 1.08 per cent, and Georgia with only 1.10 per cent. Only two states rise relatively high—Texas with 7.19 per cent and Louisiana with 11.44 per cent. Florida, although its absolute number was 3,309, only a handful more than North Carolina's 3,298, rises much higher in proportion because of the paucity of the entire population in her swamps and everglades— 2.36 per cent. In all the southern states the Irish element outranked all others except in Texas where the Germans topped the list. The

---

Southern States .... 1.86 to every 100 natives
Southwestern States .... 5.34 "   "   "   "
Northwestern States .... 12.75 "   "   "   "

Germans ranked second in the South as a whole, while th[e]
came third.[82]

The Irish rolled up in 1860 a total of 84,763 in the Sout[h]
British, exclusive of the Irish but including other British A.......ans,
amounted to 53,304.[83] The total number of Germans within the
same limits amounted to the far from negligible figure of 73,579. Of
these Teutons 20,000 were scattered over eight states, while the
remaining 53,000 dwelt in Texas, Louisiana, and Virginia.[84] The
census of 1860 shows 20,555 Germans located in Texas. In Comal,
Gillespie, and Kendall counties 75 to 85 per cent of the population
were German; in Kerr, Marion, and Bexar (except the city of San
Antonio) counties about one third to one half were Teutons; in
Medina, Guadalupe, and Llano counties the German element ranged
from one tenth to over one third; while in Travis County it sank to
only 8 per cent. On the Lower Brazos, Colorado, and Guadalupe
rivers the Germans comprised in many counties one fifth to one third
of the population. Olmsted's estimate of the number of Mexicans
ranged from 1,000 in Uvalde, Goliad, and Nueces counties to over
8,000 in El Paso County including Presidio with a floating Mexican
population of several thousand. In all there were 12,443 Mexicans
in the state according to census figures for 1860.[85]

The actual figures of the foreign population in Virginia yield
details of interest. As the oldest state she had a white population of

[82] Census of 1860, *Population Statistics*, XXXI. The table follows:

DISTRIBUTION   IMMIGRANTS
Percentage of entire population in each state
Percentage English—Irish—German 1860 by states

	ENGLISH	IRISH	GERMAN	TOTAL FOREIGN
Alabama	.12	.59	.27	1.28
Arkansas	.09	.30	.26	.86
Florida	.23	.60	.34	2.36
Georgia	.11	.62	.23	1.10
Louisiana	.56	3.98	3.48	11.44
Mississippi	.11	.49	.25	1.08
Missouri	.85	3.68	7.50	13.59 (high)
N. Carolina	.07	.09	.08	.33
S. Carolina	.11	.70	.38	1.42
Tennessee	.18	1.12	.35	1.91
Texas	.28	.58	3.40	7.19
Virginia	.26	1.03	.66	2.19

[83] *Ibid.*, XXIX, compiled by the writer from the census statistics.

[84] Kaufmann gives 70,000 as the total.—*Op. cit.*, 139. The writer's compilation is from the census.

[85] For the Mexicans by counties see Olmsted, *A Journey Through Texas*, 165; for the Germans, Biesele, *History of the German Settlements in Texas*, 62, 164.

1,047,299, among whom there were 35,058 foreigners. The distribution among the nationalities was: 5,490 English and Scotch, 10,512 Germans, 16,501 Irish, while French and minor nationalities constituted only 517. The Irish therefore ranked first in point of numbers, the Germans second with almost one third of the foreign population. One fourth of the entire number had embraced American citizenship.[86]

[86] Schuricht, *op. cit.*, II, 58, bases these figures on a statement by General Gaspard Tochman in an article, "Der Staat Virginien," in the *Virginische Zeitung*, No. 17, January 25, 1868. Tochman had been appointed agent for European immigration by the Virginia government in 1867, and had had good opportunity for observation. The figures tally very closely with those given in the census. The article is found also in English as a pamphlet, *Virginia: A Brief Memoir for the information of Europeans desirous of emigrating to the New World* (see p. 12). The entire table for the chief cities appears as an appendix. Likewise the statistics for New Orleans are held sufficiently interesting to reprint. See Appendix I.

II

ATTITUDE AND MOTIVES OF FOREIGN CONFEDERATES

"OUR SERVICE offers but little inducement to the soldiers of fortune, but a great deal to the men of principle," said President Davis to a visitor at Charleston.

An Austrian officer visiting the fields and cities of the South in 1863-64 elaborated this thought as follows for his British readers: "The few who have entered the Confederate service have, almost without exception, distinguished themselves highly." He offers as evidence of disinterested motives: "The Southern Confederacy being very difficult of access, the foreigners who have taken service here have all been impelled to do so by their sympathy with the cause, which is in truth a noble one."[1]

In any discussion of the attitude of the foreigners living or sojourning in the South—especially of the Germans on the Atlantic seaboard—a distinction must be made between their attitude toward slavery and toward secession. It is probably safe to say that only one group of Germans were in sympathy with slavery—the Jewish slave traders. Captain Melchers and General Wagener, both of South Carolina, and Hermann Schuricht of Virginia, to name only a few representative leaders, had been lifelong opponents of slavery; indeed they had been long regarded by their fellows as abolitionists.

The position taken by Schuricht in negotiating a business deal for his newspaper is sufficiently indicative of his position. He had come to Richmond in 1859 and with Henry Schott, a native of Marburg, Hesse, had started the *Virginische Zeitung* and a comic Sunday paper, *Die Wespe*. In January, 1861, they were consolidated with the Richmond *Enquirer*. Under the name of the *Daily Richmond Enquirer* the consolidated sheet appeared with some columns of its outer pages printed in German until the opening of the state convention. The editor of the English section was O. Jennings Wise, whose interest in

[1] Quoted by Fitzgerald Ross writing anonymously.—*A Visit to the Cities and Camps of the Confederate States,* 219. This also appeared as an article in *Blackwood's Edinburgh Magazine* (XCVII, 184). Ross was the son of English parents, but in the service of Austria.

the German element of the population is to be explained by the fact that he had studied jurisprudence at Göttingen University. Schuricht consented to continue as editor of the German portion but stipulated that he should not be obliged to write in favor of slavery and that all contributions by English editors to the German portion of the paper should be signed.[2]

Yet though opposed to slavery, the Germans in Virginia, if one may judge by the comment of the *Richmonder Anzeiger* in its issue of October 31, 1860, were also bitterly opposed to any recognition of the Negro. "The negroes therefore rule in fact in Ohio; they will soon rule in every northern state, if the people express their approval of the honoring of negroes by Lincoln and Hamlin." This same paper on November 1 expressed the view that the free blacks of the North were in a hundred times more lamentable condition than the slaves.

Whatever might have been Editor Franz Melcher's personal views, the editorials of the *Deutsche Zeitung* of Charleston, South Carolina, during the months just before the outbreak of war seemed to accept slavery as a recognized institution of the South. It would have taken a hardy soul indeed to lift his voice against the principle of slavery in this stronghold of slavocracy. An editorial in the issue of January 29, 1861, entitled "Compromiss oder Bürgerkrieg" intimates that the abolition of slavery, combined with civil war, would bring upon the South the horrors of Santo Domingo. The attitude of the Charleston *Turnverein* in breaking from the national *Turner Alliance* upon the latter's condemnation of slavery was probably dictated partly, at least, by caution.[3]

Light is thrown on what Americans thought was the attitude of the Germans in Louisiana. A speaker in New Orleans was reported to have said, "Our large German population is hostile to it [slavery]. About all these Dutchmen would be not only Unionists, but Black Republicans, if they dared."[4]

The reaction of the Germans to the slavery issue is easy to understand. Those settled in Texas, especially in the rural sections, were

[2] Schuricht is himself authority for the statement as to his attitude toward slavery.— *History of the German Element in Virginia*, II, 40-41. The German columns in the paper were discontinued on February 25, 1861, after only four weeks.

[3] The Charleston *Turnverein* changed its name to *Independent Turnverein*. See jubilee edition of *Deutsche Zeitung*, November 22, 1913.

[4] Richardson, *The Secret Service*, 92.

decisive foes of slavery before they ever set foot on American soil. What they saw of it among their American neighbors in the rest of Texas turned them into abolitionists of the extreme type of Garrison or Brooks so that slavery among them was practically unknown. The German paper, the San Antonio *Staats Zeitung,* under Dr. Douai fought for abolition in Texas from 1853 to 1859; the *State Times* in Austin in return urged its readers to drown him, but his German compatriots of San Antonio gathered to defend him with arms. Despite this show of opposition, native feeling became so inflamed that Douai had to flee north toward the close of the fifties. His paper died honorably as a Union sheet after the outbreak of the war. The Germans, taking advantage of a musical festival in San Antonio in May, 1854, even held a political mass meeting at which as part of their platform they adopted a resolution declaring slavery an evil, and its removal absolutely necessary; nevertheless they held it a problem of the individual state in which the Federal government should not interfere. The announcement of this platform brought on a storm of protest from the American press of the state and from conservative Germans and even the threat of lynch law. In general it may be said that the bulk of the Germans felt that it was impolitic to antagonize the American settlers and to interfere in their affairs. The more prudent, feeling themselves in a suspected position, carefully avoided all open expression. In Galveston and Houston the Germans were chiefly in the cotton business and, wholly under the sway of the slavocracy, viewed the question in an entirely different way from their countrymen of the interior.[5]

Sharply distinguished also from the remainder of the German population in respect to their position on slavery stood the German Jews. It cannot be disputed that Jews were interested in the slave trade. The largest auction house for the sale of slaves in Richmond was owned and conducted by a Jew. As is well known, the trader in Negroes was regarded with contempt by the planter, despite the fact that the latter viewed slaves and hence the slave trade as a necessity. Therefore the general prejudice against the Jews was not mitigated by the fact that several of them had amassed fortunes by the sale of human flesh. It was, accordingly, natural that the Jews should be

[5] Kaufmann, *Die Deutschen im amerikanischen Bürgerkriege,* 145-146, 568; Olmsted, *A Journey through Texas,* 432-440. Olmsted says that there were probably not thirty German slaveowners in west Texas and had not himself met one.—*Ibid.,* 432 and n.

foremost among all the foreign element in advocacy of secession. However the alacrity and cheerfulness with which they entered military service for the Confederacy should be held as evidence of the sincerity of their devotion to the southern cause and was favorably noted by the Confederates.[6]

The British, despite the fact that slavery had perished in the British colonies three decades before the Civil War in America, were frequently defenders of the "peculiar institution" which they found established in the South. Sir William Russell's emphatic statement of the position he found assumed by his fellow countrymen in 1861 may well be quoted: "Among the most determined opponents of the North, and the most vehement friends of what are called her 'domestic institutions,' are the British residents, English, Irish, and Scotch, who have settled here for trading purposes, and who are frequently slave-holders. These men have no state rights to uphold, but they are convinced of the excellence of things as they are, or find it their interest to be so."[7]

Corroborative evidence as to the position of the resident Britisher comes from many sources. A naturalized Irishman spoke very warmly for southern rights and slavery according to the *Charleston Mercury* of November 17, 1860. Approval came also from the foreign-born Irishwomen. Olmsted tells of encountering in Texas an Irishwoman who declared that on arrival she had been an avowed abolitionist, but that she had soon changed her views. Now she had "just as lief whip a nigger as not." She used to think the "niggers hard used, but now she knew they weren't a bit more than they deserved to be."[8]

Through the pages of the Swedish newspaper *Hemlandet* the reader catches a glimpse of the attitude of a few Swedes resident in Texas. Svante Palm, who had settled near Austin in 1844 through the efforts of his nephew, S. M. Swenson, whom we have already encountered, protested to the editor of this nationality paper that he could not indorse all the sentiments voiced in his editorials. "We agree on Know-nothingism, but on slavery we hold an entirely different opinion. We live in a slave state and are in daily contact with masters and slaves. We find the slaves better treated than the work-

---

[6] Schuricht, *op. cit.*, II, 93.
[7] *Pictures of Southern Life, political and military*, 34.
[8] *A Journey through Texas*, 249.

ing classes in Sweden. Some of us Swedes own slaves and all want to own them as soon as we can. Our countrymen in the northern states write that they are treated worse than slaves. The abolitionists in the north are fanatics. We citizens of a slave state are good, 'renhåriga' [upright] democrats and believe in state rights." His letter in turn produced a chorus of protests from his fellow Swedish Americans. Many letters came to the desk of the editor of the *Hemlandet* expressing surprise that a Swede should defend slavery. From Texas came a letter to assure the reader that not all of Palm's fellow Swedes shared his attitude. The writer did not know a single Swede around Austin who had purchased a slave although many were financially able to do so. He admitted that wages were poor in Sweden, but saw no comparison between the condition of the laboring classes in Sweden and that of slaves in the South. It is true that Palm's nephew, S. M. Swenson, now a wealthy planter, owned slaves, but he clearly entertained doubts on the subject, and treated his slaves exceedingly well.[9]

The position of the Norwegians in Texas on the slavery question seems to have been divided. Mrs. Elise Wärenskjold, writing on July 9, 1851, expressed horror of slavery, but asserted that the slaveholders of American birth treated their slaves kindly; she felt that the slaves were often better off than laborers in Norway, but she still felt that there could be no compensation for loss of freedom. However K. H. Hajland, who visited the Norwegian settlements in 1860 and 1861, reported that the Norwegians owned slaves and felt themselves made if they owned one. Ole Canuteson of the Bosque County settlement seemed to assent to such a statement, for he declared in a later issue of the *Skandinaven*, a Norwegian American paper, that possession of slaves was in keeping with the society in which they had taken up residence. Knowing the inherent love of freedom of the Scandinavian, it is probably a safe assertion to say that in their hearts the Norwegians did not approve of slavery. Certainly it is significant

[9] Palm's letter appeared in the *Hemlandet*, August 28, 1855. For the criticisms of his stand see issues of October 20, November 10, 1855. At the close of the war a Swedish resident of Texas dropped into the office of the *Hemlandet* and told the editor that Palm had learned a lesson and was then a strong Union man.—*Ibid.*, June 21, 1865. See also George M. Stephenson, "Some Footnotes to the History of Swedish Immigration from about 1861 to 1865," *Year Book of the Swedish Historical Society of America*, 1921-22, 46. The writer believes from her study that there is no doubt about Palm's views with regard to secession, whatever he may have thought with regard to slavery. It is likely that his post as Swedish consul, accredited to the Federal government of the United States for some years prior to the war, may have predisposed him in favor of the Union.

that during the war Elise Wärenskjold's husband was assassinated for sympathy with the North and opposition to slavery.[10]

The attitude of the most humbly placed foreigners, irrespective of nationality, helps to explain their willingness to take up arms for the Confederate cause. We must turn to Olmsted again for the most clear-cut statement which the author has found of the position of this class in regard to slavery. "No native can exceed, in idolatry to Slavery, the mass of the ignorant foreign-born laborers. Their hatred of the negro is proportionate to the equality of their intellect and character to his; and their regard for Slavery, to their disinclination to compete with him in a fair field."[11]

Exceptions to the general attitude of the Britisher there were also, of course, ranging from those best designated as indifferent to those actively hostile to slavery. William Watson, a Scotch merchant and engineer resident in Louisiana in 1861, declared himself "not a votary of slavery. I had no interest in it, or connection with it, but was rather opposed to it," and he thought a "very large number in the South were opposed to it, although on quite different principles from the New England political Abolitionists." An Englishman by the name of Gardiner, residing near Wilmington, North Carolina, planting on shares, was arrested in February, 1861, as "a dangerous man" because he was regarded as unfavorable to slavery. His little property and improvements were ruthlessly seized and he was turned out of the state penniless. Out of consideration for his wife and children his case was "compromised" by his being hastily put on a boat and sent to New York. It was a foregone conclusion that the Vigilance Committee would seize and commit to prison a compositor for the *True Witness*, an Irishman in New Orleans, because he boldly avowed before the mayor his abolition sentiments at such a tense moment as December, 1860.[12]

Whatever his personal convictions might have been on the moral aspects of slavery and states' rights, General de Polignac was clear-

---

[10] Mrs. Wärenskjold's letter, published in two Norwegian papers, was reprinted in *Morgonbladet*, June 17, 18, 1852. See Blegen, *Norwegian Migration to America*, 186-187. For Hajland and Canuteson see Qualey, *Norwegian Settlement in the United States*, 207. The data appeared in *Skandinaven* in the issues of April 18, June 16, 1867, referring to the earlier date.   [11] *Seaboard Slave States*, II, 150.

[12] Watson, *Life in the Confederate Army*, 395. For the Englishman see John S. C. Abbott, *History of the Civil War in America*, I, 72; for the Irishman see *Mobile Daily Advertiser and Register*, December 1, 1860. He had been driven from Natchez ten years earlier for abolitionism, and had been notified to leave New Orleans fifteen days before his arrest.—*Ibid.*

sighted as to the slavery question. "Indeed," he wrote long after the war, "many of them [Confederates] knew too well that the institution of slavery proved the greatest bar to every hope of foreign assistance, and that the establishment of a new slaveholding community with the aid of a foreign power was an absolute impossibility."[13]

The views of General Patrick Cleburne, Irish-born and devoted to the South, are so interesting that they merit exposition. He had never owned a slave but had been so intimately connected with slaveowners that he had learned to recognize the great attachment which often existed between master and slave. Though the fact that he had no capital invested in slaves may explain the detachment with which he worked out a solution for the desperate situation of the Confederacy in 1864, credit is due him for the boldness and wisdom with which he advocated it: the enlistment of the young and able-bodied Negroes, with the promise that all who should be honorably discharged at the close of the war would have their freedom. His arguments were cogent. Considering slavery really at an end in the spring of 1864, he pointed out the only means left to the South to recruit her exhausted armies. He felt that the South could not risk putting arms in the hands of the slaves until the relation to them had first been entirely changed, not by military law, but by the action of the states. He felt that as soon as this change had been effected, the North could not keep its soldiers in the field and European recognition would be assured. He urged that that step, taken at this time of crisis, would mold the relations for all time between the races with the result that the South could retain the Negroes as laborers at less cost than as slaves. He insisted that it was the duty of the southern people to waive considerations of property and prejudice of caste in order to bring to their aid these powerful auxiliaries. He read a paper embodying these views to his fellow officers, some of whom approved it, but General Johnston declined to forward it to headquarters on the ground that the question was political, rather than military. General Walker thought it so incendiary that he asked for a copy to send to President Davis. Cleburne rejoiced at this opportunity to bring the matter before the authorities, although he anticipated a possible court-

[13] J. C. de Polignac, "Polignac's Mission," *Southern Historical Society Papers*, XXXII, 370.

martial and cashiering. After some weeks the paper was returned by Davis endorsed, "While recognizing the patriotic motives of its distinguished author, I deem it inexpedient, at this time to give publicity to this paper, and request that it be suppressed." Cleburne's proposition did not meet with the favor of either the government or the people, for he was in advance of his time. Before Cleburne's death, he had the satisfaction of knowing that a bill embodying most of his proposition was advocated, passed, and signed—but too late.[14] It is possible that if this paper had never been written Cleburne instead of Hood might have succeeded Johnston at Atlanta and the current of history been changed—temporarily.

When one approaches the foreign attitude towards states' rights and secession, one finds more of a cleavage in opinion within the different nationality groups than existed on the subject of slavery. Where there was little or no real difference of opinion among Germans toward slavery, one finds sharp differences toward the right of disruption of the Union. Schuricht claims that not one German Virginian—of American or German birth—was favorable to secession at the beginning. But this writer is forced to agree with Kaufmann in challenging that assertion.[15] This statement is hardly true of the old Germans, American-born descendants of old German stock, but is probably true of the small circle of recently arrived Germans. The descendants of Germans who had settled in the South very young and had long been associated with all the local interests of their fellow citizens tended to become Democrats in politics and felt that the question of slavery was a matter for the state and not for the general government. The more recent immigrants, whether in Virginia or Texas, many of whom came from Germany at a time when the nationalistic feeling was strong in that land and who as naturalized citizens had taken an oath of allegiance to the United States, felt a strong sense of obligation to the flag which had welcomed them when they fled persecution. Gustav Schleicher of Texas and the Germans in the valley of Virginia are illustrative of the first group; Degener

[14] It is interesting that General Hood believed that, if Cleburne's suggestion had been adopted, this additional strength would have given the South its independence.—John Bell Hood, *Advance and Retreat*, 296. See also Bunn, *Reminiscences of the Civil War*, in Nash, *Biographical Sketches*, 191-192; W. J. Hardee, "Biographical Sketch of Major-General Patrick R. Cleburne," *Southern Historical Society Papers*, XXXI, 157; Letter from Colonel A. S. Colyar to Colonel A. S. Marks, January 30, 1864, in *Annals of the Army of Tennessee and Early Western History*, 51.

[15] Schuricht, *op. cit.*, II, 66; Kaufmann, *op. cit.*, 141.

and the Germans in Texas, especially in the Upper Colorado Valley, in San Antonio, and in the Guadalupe Valley, of the second group. Schuricht declares that all recent comers who joined the ranks of the Confederates did it with a "bleeding heart" and under pressure of compelling circumstances. It is probably true that of those born in Germany few drew their swords voluntarily for the Confederacy. They would almost unanimously have preferred to remain neutral had pressure not been brought to bear upon them.[16] It is certain moreover that all the German citizens in Virginia heartily indorsed the resolution of the legislature to call a peace congress in the hope of avoiding civil war. Even in New Orleans, where the Germans were very numerous and concentrated, and where they were surrounded by states' rights proponents, there were only individual secessionists to be found. This indisposition toward the war among the German element was well known to rebel leaders. The Germans of the first group tended to feel that their constitutional rights had been invaded and, in any case, shared the general southern expectation that there would be no war. They awaited some compromise to avert war.[17]

As sentiment was crystalizing, the German citizens of Richmond held a well-attended mass meeting at Steinlein's Monticello Hall in April, 1861, to consider steps to assure peace. Wiegand, an avowed Unionist, occupied the chair, and Captain O. J. Wise, son of the former governor, addressed the meeting in German as one of the chief speakers. But no course of action to promote the maintenance of peace could be voted, as the majority held it the duty of every adopted citizen to submit to the will of the majority, particularly that of the native-born citizens, and to sacrifice his life and property, if necessary, for the defense of his adopted state.

The Germans felt it wrong that the North, after selling its slaves to the South, should attempt to force the slaveholders to free their slaves without compensation. Furthermore on the question of commercial independence many of the Germans shared the free-trade principles of their Anglo-Saxon southern neighbors. They resented the high tariff, firmly believing that northern manufacturers under its protection extorted tribute from every inhabitant of the South on

[16] Faust, *The German Element in the United States*, I, 565.
[17] Kaufmann, *op. cit.*, 139-140. "Doch wir wollen hoffen," said the *Richmonder Anzeiger*, "dieses Unglück einer Trennung unserer Union werde sich nie ereignen."—November 1, 1860.

almost every article he purchased, and demanded that that wrong should be corrected. Like other residents of the South, they could not escape the fear, aroused by the John Brown raid, of possible Negro insurrections. It must not be forgotten that, while opposed to slavery, they, like Lee, preferred seeing it abolished in a lawful, peaceable manner.[18] They were, naturally, not impervious to the passionate appeals poured out upon them by the Confederate orators and by the press. "The time has come when every man in the South capable of bearing arms must become a soldier, must prepare to strike for her defence. She calls upon all her sons to rally to her rescue. It is not enough that we send our armies to the fields to battle against the foe. Those who stay at home must organize, must drill, must arm themselves as best they can to resist the enemy. None who has an arm to strike should withhold it from the public defence."[19]

Where the Germans took up arms voluntarily, they did so for the perpetuation of liberty, as they saw it through the eyes of Confederate constitutionalism, not for the striking of the chains from the limbs of the Negro, but for the casting off of political and economic shackles from the limbs of the whites. The Germans were in large majority, certainly in Arkansas and Louisiana, Democrats, disciplined and tutored in the dogma of states' rights as taught by the Jacksonian catechism.[20] The degree to which this German element had identified itself with the sentiment of South Carolina may perhaps best be epitomized by an incident which occurred in front of the Charleston *Deutsche Zeitung*. The Palmetto Jäger, which had gathered for drill on Citadel Square, marched with closed ranks to the office of this paper in the lower part of the city, halted and saluted, and cheered the black, red, and yellow flag with the palmetto and star which fluttered in front of the office.[21]

There was some lukewarmness and hypocrisy among the German foreigners even in the older sections. Conrad, a German member of the Charleston Zouaves, though wholly in sympathy with the Confederacy, was not eager to shed his blood and, while his American companions chafed at the delay, found satisfaction in the fact that the

---

[18] Schuricht, *op. cit.*, II, 60, 68-70.

[19] Memphis *Avalanche*, November 18, 1861, copies of which are not extant. Reprinted in a pamphlet, *Her Great Men* (see p. 79).   [20] Nash, *op. cit.*, 95, 96.

[21] See issue of November 15, 1860, where the Jägers are referred to as the "Deutsche Compagnie." See also issue of November 20, 1860.

company was not to be sent at once to the front. He remarked of his friend Laitenberger, who had followed his example in joining the Cadets, that he, like himself, did not wish "to carry his hat to market."[22] Colonel Heros von Borcke bore testimony to a less pleasant phase of German feeling. At a hotel in Frederick, Maryland, he observed that the proprietor and many of the guests were German, and after the fashion of the homeland sat drinking beer and enveloped in clouds of tobacco. "I am quite sure that most of them were very decided Yankee sympathizers, but as a grey uniform was right among them, and many others not far off, they talked the hottest secession, and nearly floored me with their questions."[23] Occasionally when capture rendered avowal of their principles safe, they rejoiced in declaring themselves Union men.[24]

The pressure to which the foreigner was subject may perhaps be best illustrated by the complete about-face of the *Tägliche Deutsche Zeitung* of New Orleans. Throughout the entire presidential campaign of 1860 an ardent Douglas and Union sheet, by early December it instituted a complete reversal of policy. "The Europeans who by many years residence here are familiar with the institutions of the South, and acknowledge them as their own, know that the South not only can exist without the North, but indeed can prosper even better without it, by the creation and powerful support of its own factories, and by direct business connections with Europe." The editor no longer saw a dark future looming before a southern confederation if southern states defended their guaranteed states' rights by separating from the Union, but insisted on the need of unity and close watchfulness of the "enemy." "Nur Einigkeit macht stark." One after another the conservative organs found themselves—German papers among them—forced to abandon their principles of coöperation and

---

[22] "Die Charleston Zouave Cadets, nicht minder begeistert für eine Züchtigung der Yankees, fanden noch keine Befriedigung ihrer Sehnsucht, und setzten einstweilen ihre friedlichen Übungen fort, sodass für mich keine Gefahr darin lag, Mitglied derselben zu bleiben . . . Zum Todschiessenlassen hatte ich gerade keine Lust, wenn ich auch mit warmem Interesse an der Sache des Südens hing."—*Schatten und Lichtblicke aus dem amerikanischen Leben während des Secessions-Krieges*, 43.

[23] *Memoirs of the Confederate War for Independence*, I, 190.

[24] Joel Cook in describing a group of Confederate prisoners who had been captured near Richmond says, "The majority seemed rather glad to have been captured. One German, from the manner of his walk and the grin on his face, was evidently going North to search for the heart he could not find in the Southern country. 'There goes a good Union man,' cried a bystander. 'Yes, me a Union man,' answered the German, amid the cheers of the surrounding crowd."— *The Siege of Richmond*, 141.

to give heed to the all-powerful voice of the people. Directly they were printing secession arguments and sentiments as strongly as the strongest of the avowedly secession sheets. By August the New Orleans *Zeitung* was declaring that a part of the North saw that the war was not one of defense, but indeed of conquest and subjugation, and that northern enthusiasm had soon fallen from its high exaltation and could not find the objectives for the defense of which the men had armed themselves. It was calling Lincoln the "personification of despotism."[25]

The record of the *Richmonder Anzeiger*, noticeably cautious, is similar. Its editor, B. Hassel, substituted foreign news for editorials from the election in early November until November 30. On that date he spoke out on the political crisis which he called "long anticipated" and declared that Lincoln's election "on a platform which openly mocks southern rights guaranteed by the constitution must lead to a decision of the pending crisis." He later pointed to various fugitive slave laws of the northern states as proof that it was the North which had produced the crisis by its disregard of the Federal laws. He asserted that if the northern states would repeal those obnoxious laws, the conservative element of the South would seize the hand of friendship thus extended and would regard a secessionist as a high traitor to the common fatherland.[26]

On November 26 the paper quoted a number of northern German papers with the comment that they scarcely comprehended the danger at hand. By December 11 it recognized the situation as very grave, for a veritable avalanche was in motion, precipitated by the fanatics of the North. It felt that annulment of the fugitive slave laws and the removal of the slave question from politics would be the only steps which could prevent the other states from following South Carolina's example. The editor mourned openly over the disappearance of the "first star of the flag" and over the destruction of "the first pillar of this great and beautiful Republic, which was the Mecca of all the oppressed. . . . May the heart of the friend of the Country bleed over the destruction of the union, for now every com-

[25] Issue of December 7, 1860. For strong expression of loyalty to the Confederacy see the issues of August 1, 2, 28, and October 20, 1861.

[26] The fugitive slave laws of twelve northern states were printed in the issues of November 30 and December 1 under the heading, "The Political Crisis."

promise, every concession of the north will be too late."[27] On January 8 he dared to print an excerpt from the *Virginische Zeitung* asking whether the Charleston Germans, who were dedicating themselves so jealously to the "narrower Fatherland," had pondered the seriousness of breaking their oath of naturalization.[28] However the strong appeal which appeared on January 29 on the eve of the election of delegates to the peace convention in Washington, called by Virginia, was not from the pen of the editor, but was carefully labeled "Eingesandt." As sentiment for the Confederacy finally crystalized in Virginia, the editorials became more cautious or disappeared entirely from the sheet.

Meanwhile the Germans of Charleston, if the *Deutsche Zeitung* of that city may be regarded as their mouthpiece, were not yet entirely weaned away from the Union to which they had pledged allegiance and which Editor Melchers wrote, "lay close to their hearts." In an editorial of November 13, 1860, which bore the heading, "Die Deutschen Charlestons und die Secession," he reminded his readers that the Germans had fought nullification in 1832; that again in 1852, although they had reached the point of readiness for a southern confederation, they were against immediate withdrawal from the Union. The German feared not only for his own freedom but also for that of his fellows in Europe who still languished under the yoke of tyranny; he feared lest "the new world, which God had vouchsafed men as the altar of their eternal rights, will no longer be a homeland for the oppressed. For this reason the German loves the Union." But after this exposition of old loyalty, he declared a new one: "But when, as now, the constitution, which holds this Union together, is boldly violated by one section of the land; when the North openly declares war on the South and its institutions, then the German strives for the rights of his adopted country; then he is true to the section, which he voluntarily chose as his home; then he stands by those who assured him protection from tyrants, and who were friends, brothers and neighbors to him."

[27] December 21, 1860. It should be stated that before the election the editor had declared that his opposition to the Republican party was based on the conviction that he was fighting for the preservation of the Union.

[28] If the naturalized foreigner assumed any position except a purely passive one, "so bringt er sich in dieselbe Stellung, wie ein Soldat, der seinen Fahneid bricht, und der mit Recht strenger bestraft wird, als ein Bürger, der nur einer bei ihm vorausgesetzten Staatsbürgerpflicht untreu wird." For the first time on January 28 it spoke of the folly and selfishness of southern demagogues as causing, with the fanaticism of the North, the crisis.

The statement which appeared in the *Anzeiger* on December 17, 1860, is very revealing as to early German sentiment on secession. It declared that at that period, among the almost three hundred German papers in the United States, there were only three which upheld secession: the *Deutsche Zeitung* of New Orleans, the *Deutsche Zeitung* of Charleston, and the *Anzeiger des Südens* of Memphis.[29]

In the far west among the Germans in Texas opinion was more definitely formed on the question of secession, and expression more determined. One factor in determining opinion on the Texas frontier may have been the frequent enrollment before the war of settlers on the ranches as partisan rangers under the flag of the United States. It may have seemed, therefore, more natural for these men, when the call to arms came, to range themselves under that banner. Certain newspapers in this section boldly and fearlessly fought secession, such as the Galveston *Union* and the San Antonio *Zeitung*, the former sheet not hesitating to pour out its scorn on the heads of the secessionists. "If we are correctly informed," says the *Union*, "we must truly regret, that such measures by the majority were held necessary. A beautiful republic in which one must suppress a difference of opinion as to the ways and means to reach the same goal! To make the measure full, there is only lacking a mandate of the dominating party that no one shall vote for an anti-secessionist."[30] Still on December 18 it is cherishing a "feeble" hope that the Union may be preserved in an "honorable way for the South," but, if that be impossible, it hopes that Texas will turn her back on a southern union. On January 10 it prays that those who speak so lightly of the Union be made to realize whither the political passions are leading them. "Or is it so agreeable a consolation that with one's own ruin the ruin of one's rival is imminent?"

The San Antonio *Texas Staats Zeitung*, after Dr. Douai's flight, was in the hands of another abolitionist, Dr. Hertzberg, who through

[29] The writer has been unable to locate any copies of the Memphis paper. It is also naturally to be regretted that no copies of the *Virginische Zeitung* seem to be extant, as it wielded a wider influence than the *Anzeiger*. We caught one reflection of its opinion in the excerpt printed in the *Richmonder Anzeiger* on January 8. See above, p. 45.

[30] See the Galveston *Union*, December 11, 1860, where the editor says, "Wenn man uns recht berichtet hat, so müssen wir aufrichtig bedauern dass solche Massregeln von der Majorität nöthig erachtet wurden. Eine schöne Republik, in welcher man eine Meinungsverschiedenheit über die Mittel und Wege, um zu demselben Ziel zu gelangen, unterdrücken muss. Um das Maas voll zu machen, fehlt nun noch ein Mandat der dominierenden Partei dass Niemand für einen Anti-Secessionisten stimmen soll." See also the issue of December 13.

December, 1860, fought against a state convention as illegal and against a southern confederation, and apparently had to leave the country late in January, 1861. The paper appeared for the last time on January 19 as a quarto sheet with the announcement that its further publication was for the present discontinued due to inability to secure paper.[31]

Almost alone among the German sheets in Texas, the *Neu Braunfelser Zeitung* manifested secessionist sentiment during the critical months of December, 1860, and January, 1861. The views of its editor, Lindheimer, can best be set forth in his own words: "It is the Unionists who rob us of the last hope of a preservation of the Union. The greater part of the Union people in the South will surely be impelled to a conservative behaviour only by a true dependence on our glorious Union. . . . I, for my part, do not wish to go with the secessionists because they constitute, according to my judgment, the majority, but because the separation of the South from the North is now the only way to preserve the Union from race war, from amalgamation, and the decline of its civilization." His real conviction was undoubtedly that it was useless to oppose the irresistible trend of the times and that the Germans would be placed in an unfavorable position with their American neighbors if they attempted to swim against the stream.[32] As time moved on Lindheimer grew more fixed in his views and became involved in a bitter quarrel with Flake, editor of the Galveston *Union,* in which each gave the other the lie. Lind-

[31] On December 15, 1860, it expressed the opinion that a southern confederacy would for years have no time even to think of Texas and strongly doubted if it would be able to protect the Texan frontiers even as well as Uncle Sam had. On December 22 it was inclined, with the Union Club in Austin, to recommend refusal to participate in the election for the state convention. "Wir gestehen dass ein solches Verhalten· unserm Gesetzlichkeitsgefühle und der Logik entsprechend sein würde." In the issue of January 4, 1861, it emphasized the revolutionary character of the convention, a view in which the Galveston *Union* concurred.

For evidence that Hertzberg left Texas, see letter of Dr. F. Bracht to Governor Clark, under date of May 2, 1861, expressing a desire to secure possession of the San Antonio *Zeitung* in order to wrest it from the "freesoil league there." "You know that the editor of that paper was a noted Abolitionist, Dr. Hertzberg, who has left the country since about two months."—Governor's Letters, March-May, 1861, Governor Edward Clark, Archives, Texas State Library.

[32] December 21, 1860. In no place did Lindheimer reveal more clearly his real views than in a comment on the *Deutsche Zeitung* of New Orleans which, a zealous Douglas and Union sheet during the entire presidential campaign, after the election used phrases such as only the strongest secessionists could. "Wir sind weit davon entfernt, die Deutsche Zeitung desshalb zu tadeln, dass sie der unwiderstehlichen Wendung der Dinge Rechnung trägt und nicht den unnützen Versuch macht, gegen den Strom zu schwimmen." Since this sudden change in a widely read paper was a yardstick of public opinion in Louisiana and in the South, he made some excerpts for his readers. See issue of December 7, 1860. See also his editorial of January 4, 1861.

heimer pointed out that his opponent's views were those of the Black Republicans and prophesied the failure of Flake's predictions, especially his political jeremiads on the unhappy condition of Texas in the event of separation from the Union.[33] So strong was the feeling that Lindheimer felt that only justice had been done Flake when the printing press of the *Union* was demolished on January 6, an event which was precipitated by a particularly bitter article against South Carolina, which Lindheimer felt put the Germans of that section in an entirely false light.[34] This did not, however, prove fatal, for by January 10 another issue of the *Union* was off the press—new or restored.

So aroused and disturbed were the Germans that views of their leaders were published in the nationality papers: those of F. Bading, a jurist; of Frederick Ernst, one of the early settlers in Fayette County; of Jacob Wälder, member of the Texas legislature, written to the editor of the San Antonio *Zeitung*; and of H. Wickeland, who deplored the lack of unity in Comal County. Probably the conservative, cautious German sentiment could best be summed up in the phraseology of one of these correspondents: "But how would it be with us foreigners in such a possible and probable case, if we as a small minority were to set ourselves against the movement and show ourselves hostile to our fellow-citizens of the South. Of later good feeling and friendly understanding there could be no further thought."[35]

By early December the movement for mass meetings to marshal public opinion for secession was under way. Comal County, led by Lindheimer, George Pfeuffer, and others, both Germans and Americans, was in the field early with a call for a mass meeting of all citizens at the courthouse, "regardless of old parties," on Sunday afternoon, December 9. Though Lindheimer called the meeting to order, Dr. Felix Bracht, an ardent Confederate, although a German,

---

[33] See *ibid.*, issues of February 1, 8, 1861. Note especially the feeling manifested in the following: "Hierauf antwortet uns der Jüngling der Galveston Union mit, 'Bah'! Wie verschieden von dieser jungenmässigen Keckheit des Galveston Union-Jünglings ist dagegen die Ansicht eines Richters" (R. T. Wheeler).—*Ibid.*, December 28, 1860.

[34] "Ich bin kein Freund von solchen Handlungen, aber dem Flake ist recht geschehen. Jemand, der sich so gemeinschädlich, wie er gegen das deutsche Element, macht in einem Platze, wo keine Gegenpublikationen gemacht werden können,—mag sich merken—Lieber ein Glied abzuschlagen, als dass der ganze Körper zur Hölle geht und die Opposition der Deutschen Hölle uns eine wahre Hölle bereitet."—*Ibid.*, January 18, 1861.

[35] *Ibid.*, December 14, 21, 1860, January 4, 1861. The *Neu Braunfelser Zeitung* published articles which accorded with its editor's views.

was made chairman and a committee of eleven promptly named to draw up resolutions. In spite of the presence of Lindheimer and other Germans on the committee, the resolutions did not move smoothly and swiftly to acceptance, according to plan. Hermann Seele, the famous teacher who had opened the first school in New Braunfels under an oak tree and who was serving as secretary of the meeting, lifted his voice in dissent from the general attitude. Lincoln's election had been legal, and "we are rebels if we act against him before he has taken an unconstitutional step." There was nothing to fear from Lincoln, he added, since there was a Democratic majority in house, senate, and on the supreme court. It was his opinion that citizens must await the action of the legislature and that they should send to the convention, if one were called, thoughtful men, not demagogues or fire-eaters eager to throw the state into war. Dr. Ferdinand Römer, a geologist and naturalist of note, in similar strain remarked that the selection of Lincoln was no ground for secession, and that one should not allow himself to be led by hotheads. Dr. Bracht warned that they should not be deceived by the cry of union. "We wish also the Union, but with our full rights."

There was some objection to the resolutions, which were passed only after a very heated discussion and after the elimination of the second resolution which called for arrangement for an election of delegates to a convention. As passed, they called upon the governor to summon the legislature in special session to consider convoking a convention. The meeting adjourned after Seele demanded and secured three cheers for the Union!

Seele knew what he was about in gaining excision of the second resolution, for this embodied the heart and soul of the meeting. As Lindheimer complained in describing the meeting: "Even if the legislature were summoned at once, it could not assemble until January and then it would be too late to call a convention, as that body could convene only simultaneously or after Lincoln's inauguration," and then a result more favorable to the view of the anti-secessionists would be secured.[36]

[36] See *ibid.*, December 7, for the call; December 14, for the account of the meeting. The "Whereas" part of the resolutions ran in the usual tenor; namely, that since the southern institutions were injured by the election of Lincoln, Texans thought themselves justified in fighting for their rights and states' rights until guarantees were given, and claimed the right

Herr Seele stood his ground later when General Waul came to New Braunfels on December 21. After the public meeting in the courthouse, followed by fireworks in the Market Place and presentation of a Texas flag, a choral society serenaded General Waul in his room at the Hotel Schmitz. Here an exchange of views between General Waul and Seele occurred. The substance of the latter's speech was that the southerners should exhaust all constitutional means before resorting to extremes—the disruption of the Union.[37]

The current of the times was too strong for Seele to dam, and so an election for delegates to the convention was duly held in New Braunfels, as elsewhere; again the results were not exactly according to plan. The two out-and-out secessionists, Dr. Bracht and Gustav Dreiss, were defeated and two more conservative men were elected. Lindheimer's fellow Germans respected their editor, were proud of him as a botanist, and never held against him in postwar days his sympathy with secession, but outside of Comal County they refused to let him do their thinking for them.

Meanwhile mass meetings were being held elsewhere in the other German counties. On January 1, 1861, the men of Gillespie County were brought together at Fredericksburg. Franz van Stucken was made chairman, the purpose of the meeting was set forth and translated into German, and resolutions were adopted unanimously which approved a convention of the slave states as soon as possible; but the resolutions also approved the action of the governor in calling the legislature. While those present at the meeting supported the right of secession, they regarded it as a final resort, likely to lead to civil war; hardships within the Union should be adjusted, if they could, consistently with honor and safety. They expressed the belief that a realization of the unity of the slave states would cause the North to concede to them their rights within the Union. Again independence of opinion in German Texas! The claim of present-day Fredericks-

---

to take back, peacefully or by force, all the power and rights which they had delegated to the Federal government. Lindheimer declared that Seele had aroused such a storm as hitherto had been seen in no meeting of their peaceful population. Even then he felt it wise to print, "Auch wir sind für die Union, aber wir scheuen eine Abstimmung des Volkes von Texas nicht." The more loyal sheet in neighboring Seguin, the *Mercury*, remarked, "Comal hätte sich nicht diese Blösse geben sollen und wir hoffen, dass ein Umschlag in der öffentlichen Meinung stattfinden wird."—December 14, 1860 (copied in the *Neu Braunfelser Zeitung*, December 21 and quoted in German, as this issue of the *Mercury* is not extant).

[37] The occurrence is described at length in the *Neu Braunfelser Zeitung*, December 28, 1860. This paper appeared throughout the entire war, though in reduced size, of course.

burg citizens that sentiment there was solidly anti-secession is probably true.[38]

The Germans of Houston held a great mass meeting on Sunday, January 8, declared to be the largest party meeting which had ever been held there. Americans shared the program with Germans, and resolutions declared for immediate secession of the individual states. In Fayette County, Unionist sentiment was strong. The county papers throughout the closing months of 1860 record enthusiastic Union meetings and the German settlers were an important element in creating this sentiment and in determining the vote, though it is clear that the Americans voted with them.[39]

When it came to the referendum vote on the question of secession which Texas allowed her citizens on February 23, 1861, it must be recalled that 13,841 negative votes were counted, most of them cast by German citizens. In Austin, Comal, and Colorado counties alone among the German counties, so far as the author has been able to secure figures, did the vote for secession carry. In all the other German sections secession was defeated. In the narrow margin of twenty votes by which it was defeated in Fayette County the 250 German votes were an important factor. In the city of Seguin we get some hint of German sentiment in the election of members of the secession convention: 164 votes were cast for states' rights candidates as against thirty-three for Union candidates; in Guadalupe County as a whole the only opposition was in the German settlement of Schumannsville where all the votes, sixty-eight in number, were cast for the Union. As the results became public, great ill will began to be manifest on the part of the native-born population against the German counties and towns.[40] Nevertheless to offset this indifference or hostility to

[38] The meeting is described and the resolution published in *ibid.*, January 18, 1861. The claim of Union loyalty was made by Editor Kett, present editor of the Fredericksburg *Standard*.

[39] The *Tri-Weekly Telegraph* (Houston), January 8, 1861, states that the Germans were to meet in Perkins Hall that evening. One is therefore forced to regard as incorrect the date given for the meeting, January 7, in the *Neu Braunfelser Zeitung*, January 18, 1861. One cannot fail to note the continental use of Sunday for big gatherings. The *True Issue* (La Grange, Fayette County, Texas), of October 4, 1860, printed a bold slogan as its motto: "Our Country, Our State, The South, The Union."

[40] The following table is compiled from the reports of the returns from the referendum in the *Neu Braunfelser Zeitung*, March 8, 1861, and in the Galveston *Die Union*, issues of February 26, 28, March 5, 7, 9, 1861:

	FOR SECESSION	AGAINST SECESSION
Austin County	majority of 600	
Cat Spring-Millheim	8	99

the war, a good many of the official appointments for the defense works at Baton Rouge were given to such Germans as "were known to exercise considerable influence over their fellow-countrymen."[41]

With the actual outbreak of war the opposition perforce faded away, some few Germans becoming converted to the southern point of view. The vast bulk concealed their real sentiments. Some few refused to part with their Union convictions and suffered in consequence, as we shall see, severe persecution. The press either became zealous Confederate sheets, like the *Tägliche Deutsche Zeitung*, until the capture of New Orleans by the Federals made expression of its actual views safe, or, for both spiritual and material reasons, was forced, like *Der Texas Demokrat* of Houston, to become a colorless sheet of one or two pages, confining itself to the barest record of war news.[42]

	FOR SECESSION	AGAINST SECESSION
Industry ....majority of	81 (*Union*, Feb. 28)	
New Ulm	36	30
Shelby	16	51
Bastrop County		majority of 26
Colorado County ....large majority		
Columbus		90
Frelsburg	22 (*Union*, Feb. 25)	154 (*Union*, Feb. 25)
Comal County	239	89
Fayette County	580	626
La Grange	10 (*Union*, Mar. 7)	390 (*Union*, Mar. 7)
Roundtop	50 (*Union*, Feb. 28)	115 (*Union*, Feb. 28)
Gillespie County	17	400
Kendall County		
Boerne	6	85
Comfort	15	42
Travis County		majority of 75-150 (*Union*, Feb. 26)
City of San Antonio..............	538	662

For Cat Spring see Adalbert Regenbrecht, "The German Settlers of Millheim before the Civil War," *Southwestern Historical Quarterly*, XX, 30. Some hint of the trend is revealed in the votes for delegates to the convention.—*Neu Braunfelser Zeitung*, January 11, 1861.

	FOR STATES' RIGHTS CANDIDATES	FOR UNION CANDIDATES
Seguin	164	33
Shumansville	0	68

[41] Watson, *op. cit.*, 89.

[42] A comparison of the earlier issue of the New Orleans *Deutsche Zeitung* of November 10, 1861, with that of June 5, 1864, and of the *Louisiana Staatszeitung* with a later issue of October 16, 1864, is rewarding. On the earlier date the former is rejoicing over the victory at Columbus and minimizing the defeat at Port Royal. "Doch seien wir zufrieden mit dem Ruhm, der unsere Waffen aufs neue umstrahlt, und begnügen wir uns mit dem Sieg, den unsere Tapferen abermals errungen haben." On June 2, 1864, it refers to General Edward Johnson as "Der Rebellen-General," and on June 5 it reflects the northern attitude toward England. "Darum hatte es [England] nichts Eiligeres zu thun, als, so viel an ihm lag, den stattgefundenen Bruch unheilbar zu machen und indem es mit unzeitiger Hast die 'kriegführenden Rechte' des Südens anerkannte, nährte es in unehrlicher Absicht den Glauben in demselben, dass es später zu seinen Gunsten thatsächlich einschreiten würde." Note also the comment of the latter on October 16, 1864: "Die Lüge war die Mutter dieses unglücklichen

So far as the views of the French-born residents in the Confederacy found expression, they were probably reflected in the New Orleans *L'Abeille*. This newspaper reflected more properly the opinion of the French Creole population toward secession. Immediately after the results of the balloting showed Lincoln's election it urged the South to wait. "We are for the Union so long as it is possible to preserve it. We are willing to go with Louisiana, but every good citizen is bound to use his best efforts to make Louisiana go right." By December 18 it had been swept to the view that the South "is compelled to defend herself" against the North, "which regards our institutions with jaundiced eyes, envies our prosperity and progress, and endeavors to arrest both by annihilating the system of domestic servitude under which we have attained these blessings." By the end of January it was exulting in secession: "The state has seceded; Louisiana has recovered her sovereignty. The allegiance of her citizens is now due to her alone."[43] The American-born French were fighting for their freedom from oppression and French-born residents were helping her. "Liberté" in the sense of 1789 was again ringing in the ears of the American Gaul.

The Irishmen on the southern side were frequently actuated by a burning zeal for southern independence. Cleburne, as a naturalized citizen, had taken a solemn oath of allegiance to the United States and had sworn to protect her flag and support her constitution. He conscientiously took up arms against that flag, because he believed he was fighting for the old flag of thirteen stars and stripes and for the old constitution as framed by the founders. He often expressed the hope that he would not survive the loss of independence by the South.[44] Irish and English slaveholders held that they were entering the war to secure redress for the wrongs inflicted by the North, to prevent themselves from being robbed of their property, and to save themselves from being murdered by their freed slaves. Probably no

Bürgerkrieges, welche sich mit dem Mantel der Tugend und Gerechtigkeit schmückte, und in dieser Form Millionen gute Herzen bethörte."

Der Texas Demokrat had the hardest kind of a struggle for physical existence. On February 17, 1863, No. 15 appeared printed on both sides of very thin paper; on March 20, 1863, it was printed as No. 20 on both sides of one brown sheet of paper; on March 27 it issued No. 23 printed on one side of paper of almost the thinness of tissue paper. Scattered copies, by no means a full file, are preserved in the Archives Division of the Texas State Library. If it had dared, it could hardly have wasted space to print personal views.

[43] See issues of November 8, 14, December 31, 1860, and of January 27, 1861.
[44] Nash, *op. cit.*, 14.

fairer statement of the position of the average Irishman can be made
than that by John Francis Maguire who talked with many of them
shortly after the war. "Southern Irishmen believed, perhaps more
strongly than their countrymen in the North, that neither the circumstances of the country nor the character, capacity nor training of the
negro was suited to sudden emancipation; but they at the same time
expressed themselves as having always been in favor of gradual and
prudent abolition—the final extinction of that which they felt to be
a cause of grave social injury and national weakness, and likewise a
fruitful source of political trouble, possibly ultimate convulsion. But
these Southern Irishmen took their stand on the fundamental principle of State Sovereignty, as guaranteed by the Constitution, and
denied that Congress had any right whatever to interfere with the
institutions of individual States."[45] The humbler Irish echoed the
arguments which had been dinned into their ears in the hustings. A
certain big redheaded Irishman called "Colonel" Mulligan, possibly
in derision, was on one occasion early in the war drinking confusion
to the foe in some pillaged whiskey. "Ye coom like thaves in the
dark!" cried the melodramatic Celt. "Is this the way to make warr
on a civilized people? But ye'll niver, no niver escape!"[46]

As the threat of war grew more menacing, meetings were held
with audiences drummed up from every available source. "Irish
laborers, proud of their citizenship, fond of politics, easily led, and
always ready to take part in any political agitation, were now in great
demand, and were coaxed to attend the meetings and give their decisions on the great question of the day"[47]—favorable of course to
secession. Like all ardent youths, they feared that the war would be
over before they could get to Virginia, and took pleasure in bestowing
such epithets upon the foe as "dirty, nigger-loving Yanks."

The Irish were overwhelmingly Democratic in politics, but probably for reasons which had nothing to do with the Negro issue. In
fact evidence that as a race they held no positive convictions for or
against slavery or secession is found in the fact that, governed by the

---

[45] *The Irish in America*, 634.
[46] See the story of the long argument between an Irish officer of the New Orleans Tigers
and a Union chaplain told in James J. Marks, *The Peninsular Campaign in Virginia or
Incidents and Scenes on the Battlefields and in Richmond*, 338-350. This Irishman and his
father had accumulated considerable property, mostly in slaves.
[47] Victor M. Rose, *Ross's Texas Brigade*, 89; Maguire, *op. cit.*, Appendix, 634-635; Watson, *op. cit.*, 71.

places of their residence, they enlisted with equal readiness in both armies.[48] But once in the fight, they gave themselves with their usual warm ardor to the cause they were espousing. Neither Confederate nor Federal Irishmen could understand the position of the other. The northern zealot was shocked at a southern Irishman fighting against the land of liberty; the southern Celt failed to see how an Irishman who wished for the freedom of his native isle could fight against a people striving to secure their independence. They seemed perfectly able to level their guns against their fellow countrymen if they were arrayed on the "wrong" side. "Faix," remarked one son of Erin, when a southern officer asked him if he had killed many of his own race, "they must all take it as it comes." In the opinion of this officer southern Irishmen made excellent "Rebs" and had no scruples of any kind in killing as many of their northern brethren as they possibly could.[49] Perhaps a fair statement of the attitude of the Irish as a race is the old cliché, "the Irishman loves a fight."

And now one comes to the motives actuating the individual foreigner in placing life and limb at the disposal of the new republic. Here and there one finds an Englishman who seems to have viewed the war as did the best class of native southerners. One Englishman, still a British citizen after some years' residence in the South, who enlisted from Mississippi, called it a "holy war," and stated that his motive in bearing arms for the South was simply "that inherent love of liberty which animates every English heart. With all to lose and naught to gain in opposing the tyranny of Federal rule, and with no legal or political tie to North or South," he could not, in manhood, stand by and do nothing.[50] He was thoroughly imbued with the prejudices of the planter class when he could write, "Never did

[48] The writer finds it difficult to accept the following statement: "Southern Irishmen have told me that they shed tears of bitter anguish when, in vindication of what they held to be the outraged independence of their state, which to them was the immediate home of their adoption, they first fired on the flag of that glorious country which had been an asylum to millions of people."—Maguire, *op. cit.*, 546. Likewise the writer must contradict the statement of Edward F. Roberts, *Ireland in America*, 142, that the Irish in the Confederate ranks were almost entirely recruited from the descendants of the colonial Irish who had pushed South from Pennsylvania. She has found too many hundreds and thousands whose birthplace was recorded on the descriptive rolls as Ireland.

[49] Edward A. Pollard, *Southern History of the War. Second Year of the War*, 333. Hereafter cited as *Second Year of the War*.

[50] This youth who wrote anonymously seems to have been resident in America for some years, having gone to college here.—*Battle-fields of the South*, I, 178. He enlisted in a Mississippi company from Yazoo under General Evans and became a lieutenant of artillery on the field staff.—*Ibid.*, I, xiii; II, 64.

Louisianians use the bayonet with greater good will, for they had met for the first time 'real' Yankees [Vermont], who had done more lying and boasting than those of any state in the North—always excepting the arch-hypocrites and Negro-worshippers of Massachusetts."[51]

Very similar was the motive of the twenty-one-year-old lad, Frank Dawson, who made his way to America on Captain Pegram's ship. He declared after a lapse of twenty years that he had had no expectation of any gain for himself. "I had a sincere sympathy with the Southern people in their struggle for independence, and felt that it would be a pleasant thing to help them to secure their freedom. . . . I expected no reward and wanted none. . . ."[52] But Dawson left out of the reckoning the love of adventure which was undoubtedly thrilling his heart. This same motive of devotion to the cause, even when phrased in the extravagance of a toast, had undoubtedly some validity. Several English officers, arriving at Wilmington on board the *Stag*, were present at an entertainment to celebrate their safe journey. One voiced their motive: "We come, not as mercenary adventurers, to enlist under the banner of the Confederacy, but, like true knights errant, to join as honorable volunteers the standard of the bravest lance in Christendom, that of the noble, peerless Lee."[53]

This motive was undoubtedly a factor in bringing Prince Polignac, Von Borcke, and that host whom we call soldiers of fortune to the standard of the Confederacy, but, mingled with it in proportions which we shall not attempt to evaluate, was sheer love of adventure, that impulse that sends such lovers of a fight wherever fighting is to be had. Motives were, as always, mixed and not always easy to define. Occasionally ulterior motives of patriotism to another land entered into the complex. Here probably would be classified the offers, discussed later, of various Poles who were seeking friends for the Polish cause.

There was also the instinctive sense of the duty of joining one's fellows, of responding to the call upon one's own group. A striking illustration is that of a Prussian Jew who had for several years been a member of the Russell Volunteers while living in Montgomery, Alabama. Though he had moved to Tennessee for business reasons,

[51] *Ibid.*, I, 253.
[52] *Reminiscences of Confederate Service*, 3.
[53] James Sprunt, *Tales and Traditions of the Lower Cape Fear*, 179-180.

he came rushing back as soon as his old company was called to arms. A young Nova Scotian, only a short time in the country, when urged by a cousin to go home as he could not be expected to have the same feeling toward the foe as did the native-born southerners, insisted that this was not true, but that his highest ambition was "to have a shot at them."[54]

A Scotchman engaged in business at Baton Rouge, Louisiana, frankly acknowledges the motive which led him to enlist on the southern side. Put tersely, it was because he could not stay out of the army with decency. "I never was a very strong sympathizer with the South. I was much opposed to the secession movement, and would have done anything I could to have prevented it. But when the North declared war, I was in a position that I could not well withdraw from, and I served my time in the Confederate army, and that has given me a sort of veneration for the South, though I would now wish as far as possible to remain neutral. . . ." He even goes so far as to declare that, although he responded to the call for volunteers to secure the surrender of the arsenal at Baton Rouge, he would "much rather have been called upon to act with the United States troops to suppress the secession movement and maintain the Union," a feeling which he attributed to many others in the group. It is certainly strangely illuminating to have him state that on a reconnoitering expedition he hailed for the first time "with joy sincere the Confederate flag."[55]

Sometimes voluntary enlistments came from men so out of sympathy with the cause that their presence in the Confederate States army can only be explained by the phrase "drifting along with the tide." The words and acts of a certain Hungarian, Estvàn by name, can only thus be interpreted. "It was now thirteen years that I had been away from my native home," he explains, "and now, drawn into the whirlpool of events, I found myself, almost against my will, serving in the ranks of a foreign army, and fighting for a cause, with which neither my head nor my heart could thoroughly sympathize." Even more sharply did he state his reaction to the fall of

---

[54] Montgomery *Daily Post*, May 1, 1861; Kate Cumming, *A Journal of Hospital Life in the Confederate Army of Tennessee*, 70, 37; George A. Lawrence, *Border and Bastille*, v.

[55] William Watson, *Adventures of a Blockade Runner*, 131; *idem, Life in the Confederate Army*, 78, 301. In another place he declares his lack of sympathy with the cause and his opinion that the war had at first been brought about by corrupt and unfair means.—*Ibid.*, 121.

Sumter, "The church bells began to peal, and the cheers and shouts, and the bombastic boasting and speechifying of men in a condition of mind more like that of lunatics than reasonable beings, produced a most disagreeable impression upon me."[56] So distasteful did his position become that he left the service and even the Confederacy after his period of service had elapsed and repaired to England where he wrote his *War Pictures*, which he dedicated to General McClellan![57]

Similar motives actuated the Germans in entering the Confederate ranks. They had found a friendly reception and felt a moral obligation to rise to the defense of their new home. Business interests held many of them in the Confederacy until they were caught by the conscription net. Their entire material possessions, won by many years of labor, were in jeopardy. No one anticipated, when natives talked of a three weeks' war, a four-year war to the knife. The small fifty-dollar bounty offered under the act of December 11, 1861, could at no time be regarded as any real inducement, as the huge one-thousand-dollar bounty of the North undoubtedly was to many a poverty-stricken foreigner and to the unprincipled bounty jumpers who planned to reap the profits of enlistment without discharging any of the obligations. The isolation of those who were Unionists at heart, such as the Germans in Texas, left them defenseless against the persuasion, moral and physical, of their neighbors.[58]

Watson analyzes his motives in volunteering for the army and, since human motives are seldom unmixed and since these factors probably entered in varying degree into many of the voluntary enlistments of foreigners, it may be worth while to recapitulate them briefly:

1. Policy from the business point of view.—The firm of which he was a junior member, both the senior members of which were married and had families, had been kindly received and well patronized by a community which had unanimously and, as he supposed justifiably, declared itself for the cause. Enlistments from other firms composed of foreigners would make his firm appear singularly selfish and perhaps arouse suspicion against it if it did not send at least one man to the service. He, as the unmarried member, was indicated.

[56] *War Pictures from the South*, I, 304, 55.
[57] Of course his severe criticisms of the Confederates awakened their animosity so that he was accused of having deserted. The edition of 1864 is dedicated to the soldiers of both armies.
[58] Eickhoff, *In der neuen Heimath*, 214; Kaufmann, *op. cit.*, 139-140.

2. Sympathy.—He shared with a large body of loyal, law-abiding, even Union-loving people, in the disgust and contempt felt for the Federal government for its failure to afford loyal southerners aid and support at the proper time.

3. Honor.—He had been an active member of the Baton Rouge volunteer company of riflemen. Resignation in the hour of danger could scarcely stamp him as other than a coward in the eyes of Louisianians or fellow Scotchmen, or reflect credit on Scotland, his native country.

4. Love of adventure.—He acknowledged a little of that feeling. It is probably safe to assume a grain of that element present in the heart of most volunteers, foreign as well as native.[59]

Foreign-born citizens of prominence scattered here and there showed great independence of judgment and fearlessness. Christian Roselius, the German redemptioner who had risen high in the profession of the law in New Orleans, refused to sign the secession ordinance though a member of the secession convention of Louisiana; Dr. Anthony Michael Dignowity, a Czech, was so opposed to secession that he threatened to leave San Antonio if it occurred and found himself obliged to flee to Washington to escape hanging on the plaza; S. M. Swenson, a Swede, whose natural opposition to secession was doubtless strengthened by his friendship with General Houston, in the latter part of 1863 departed for Mexico, ostensibly for relief from rheumatism at Monterey Springs, but in reality to escape persecution for his Unionist views.[60]

Only from Tennessee and Arkansas was flight to the northern states easily available for Union loyalists. Not a few made good use of their opportunities at the beginning of the war. A number of Germans, estimated at over a thousand, made their way from Texas to Federal regiments in Missouri, leaving their properties and family behind them. This group furnished at least two officers of high rank

[59] For the interesting full exposition of his motives see *Life in the Confederate Army*, 122-123. The explanation of the motives of foreigners offered by a Union soldier is interesting if not very sound: "The American joined the service because he wanted to serve his country and put down the rebellion. So did the Irishman, whose earnestness was such that no man could question his loyalty. Englishmen were full of conceits, did not care much about the war, were willing to fight on that side which paid best, and as the Americans didn't know much about war, were sure always to want to give us a great deal of instruction as to how they did it in their country."—Francis C. Adams, *The Story of a Trooper*, 81.

[60] Hudson, *Czech Pioneers of the Southwest*, 45-49; Anderson, *Hyphenated*, 210-214. Swenson did not find it advisable to return until June, 1865, after the close of the war.

to the Union cause, General Küffner and Admiral Fahrenholt. Typical of one type of Unionist was Hermann Bokum, who arrived in America from Germany in his twenty-first year. After spending twenty-eight years in the North, a sojourn which naturally imbued him with loyalty for the institutions and historical traditions of that section, he moved to East Tennessee. When secession brought chaos to that region, his attachment to the Union was such that he felt obliged to forsake home and family to become a chaplain in the Union army.[61] Escape, far from easy at the opening of the hostilities, became later practically impossible for those who found themselves out of sympathy with the Confederate cause.[62]

With the passage of the conscription law in May, 1862, came a marked change in the attitude of the foreigners toward enlistment. The law seemed to many of them oppressive and even despotic. Hundreds who had resided in the South only a few months when the war came volunteered and served cheerfully during one year of war. To put such men on a perfect equality with those born on the soil who had rendered as yet no military service seemed like sheer absolutism—the sort of thing which they thought they had left behind in Europe. The act produced much murmuring, with the result that many, rather than serve for an indefinite period as the price of citizenship, abandoned both their plans for citizenship and the cause, seeking protection from the consuls of their several countries.[63]

If the issues of the war brought conflict and division within the families of native Americans, they brought them also to the families of the foreign-born. It was well known that General Cleburne had a brother in the Federal army as well as one in the Confederate army. He seldom mentioned the former, and never without classifying him with the mass of the Irish who had espoused the northern cause, of whom he always spoke in terms of strong indignation. The famous political scientist, Francis Lieber, had two sons in the Federal army, while one son volunteered for the Confederate service and died of wounds received in battle. The same division appeared in humbler families. The Jackson family, for instance, pioneer settlers in Texas, gave three sons to the Confederate ranks, and one, who lived during

[61] Kaufmann, op. cit., 139; Hermann Bokum, Wanderings North and South, 3.
[62] See below, Chap. XIV, for the story of the attempt of a group of Germans to cut their way through Texas to join the Union army via Mexico.
[63] Battle-fields of the South, I, 313.

the war in Kansas and Colorado, to the Federal ranks. The Brinkman family of Comfort, Texas, revealed the same division, although under compulsion. Alex Brinkman was drafted into the Confederate army; Charles, his brother, crossed the border to Matamoros and then made his way to New Orleans to join the First United States Cavalry—and ultimately, be it added, to die at Belleville, Austin County, October 12, 1864. Alex and Charles corresponded during the war in brotherly fashion. The brothers Inglis, Englishmen, show of what metal many of the foreign officers were made. Captain John L. Inglis was sent by a Confederate superior to silence a battery of Federal artillery. He hurled his gallant Florida men against the belching cannons so furiously that he captured them—commander and all. The Federal captain stood by his battery as long as he had men to work it and surrendered to his own brother. Two Irish brothers named Gwynn afford still another striking illustration. Hugh became a major in the Twenty-third Tennessee. His elder brother James served as a major general in the United States army. Finally the case of Dr. William J. Häcker may well close the several illustrations. His family, prominent in Westphalia, came to America when he wrote from London that he would not return to Germany, and settled in Louisville, Kentucky, where he married. His family were ardent abolitionists, but so strongly were his sympathies enlisted for the South, his chosen home, that he arranged with a brother-in-law to adjust his business so that he could enlist in the Confederate army.[64]

[64] Hardee, "Biographical Sketch of Major-General Patrick R. Cleburne," *Southern Historical Society Papers*, XXXI, 162; Joseph G. Rosengarten, *The German Soldier in the Wars of the United States*, 63, 169; *Confederate Veteran*, XXV, 517; Jackson, *Sixty Years in Texas*, 190 ff.; manuscript letters between the Brinkman brothers now in the possession of Alex Brinkman, a nephew.

Lieber had been professor of history and economics at South Carolina College (now the University of South Carolina) from 1835 to 1857, a fact which explains the sympathy of one of his sons with the Confederate cause. He himself became adviser to the United States government on military and international law.

For Hugh and James Gwynn see *Confederate Veteran*, XXXIV, 27.

III

IN THE EMPLOY OF THE CIVIL GOVERNMENT

ALTHOUGH a fact well known to the student of Confederate history, it may be a surprise to the lay reader to be confronted with the statement that no less than three members of Jefferson Davis' cabinet were born outside the limits of the Confederate States of America. The above statement is not to be interpreted of course as saying that they were aliens, for they would hardly have been invited to help direct the destinies of the infant republic if they had not been citizens by adoption, if not by birth. These three men were Judah P. Benjamin, who held several portfolios and was longest identified with the department of state, Christopher Memminger, secretary of the treasury, and S. R. Mallory, secretary of the navy. In no true sense, however, could the last-named be considered a foreigner, for he was born on the island of Trinidad while his father, a civil engineer and a United States citizen, was located there temporarily.

Judah P. Benjamin started his service for the infant republic as attorney general, was soon made secretary of war, and was finally transferred by President Davis to the department of state, thus having held no less than three separate portfolios in a cabinet of only six members. Descended from a Portuguese Jewish family, he was the son of Philip and Rebecca (de Mendes) Benjamin, who had gone out from London to the West Indies about 1808. The second child, Judah Philip, was born in 1811 on St. Thomas Island or St. Croix— the exact place is not certain—and was consequently a British subject. After the removal of the family to Charleston where Mrs. Benjamin had relatives, his father in 1826 took out naturalization papers and thus automatically conferred American citizenship on his children. The fact of his birth under the English flag proved later a great asset to the younger Benjamin for, when he fled to England after the fall of the Confederacy and turned to the practice of law, the British law swept aside forty-seven years of American citizenship as non-existent. "Once a Briton, always a Briton" proved to him a convenient technicality whereby he established British citizenship without formalities.[1]

[1] Pierce Butler, *Judah P. Benjamin*, 382-383; *Southern Historical Society Papers*, XXV, 379. The matter of Benjamin's birth as a British subject is often regarded as largely an

His education and experience up to the outbreak of the war were wholly American, as he had studied at Yale,[2] entering at the ripe age of fourteen years, and had practiced law in New Orleans, where he quickly forged his way to the front. His knowledge of law is sufficiently attested by the fact that he had been offered and had declined a place on the United States supreme bench before secession. His eloquence and ability won him a foremost place in the southern wing of the Democratic party of the senate during his years of service there from 1852-61. His farewell address, delivered on February 4, 1861, on the occasion of the withdrawal from the senate of the two Louisiana senators, John Slidell and himself, was one of the strongest expositions of states' rights ever formulated.[3]

Under the provisional government of the Confederacy[4] he was appointed attorney general, for which post he was highly qualified, serving in this capacity only until September, 1861, when he was made secretary of war. For this latter post he had had no training, but he brought to its problems his habits of a business man, acquired on his plantation in Louisiana,[5] and introduced some order into the office. It has been pointed out that he was given no real authority, and accordingly success could hardly be expected. Under constant criticism, he was censured by the Confederate congress in February, 1862, as he was blamed for the loss of Forts Henry and Donelson, and especially for the disaster at Roanoke Island.[6] Wisely however, for Benjamin was by all odds the ablest adviser in the official group,

---

accident. His parents were on their way from England to New Orleans. Arriving at the mouth of the Mississippi River, they found it blocked by a British man-of-war, so that the vessel put in at St. Croix. But see Butler, *op. cit.*, 23-24.

[2] He left Yale after three years, before taking the degree, for lack of funds.—H. T. Ezekiel, "Judah P. Benjamin," *Southern Historical Society Papers*, XXV, 298. His family relationships may have contributed to his understanding of international affairs. His wife, the brilliant Natalie St. Martin, moved to Paris, finding life too dull at his plantation, *Belle Chasse*, near New Orleans. He maintained his devotion to her and their only child through life, spending his last years with them in Paris after his retirement.—*Confederate Veteran*, XXXIX, 252.

[3] It is a significant fact that he is the first Jew ever to have been admitted to the United States senate. On one occasion, it is reported, a derogatory allusion was made to his race; he hurled the insult back and left the chamber until an apology was offered.

[4] It is interesting that a sharp personal controversy between Benjamin and Jefferson Davis in 1858, when both were serving as United States senators, seemed likely to cause a duel, but a conflict was averted when the latter apologized on the floor of the senate for the harsh language he had used.—Butler, *op. cit.*, 177-178.

[5] Benjamin's experiments with sugar cane on his plantation gained him prestige. But heavy floods at the very time he was obliged to meet a note for a large sum for a friend brought the loss of his plantation.—*Confederate Veteran*, XXXIX, 254.

[6] *Ibid.*, 253.

President Davis retained him in his cabinet, and advanced him to the portfolio of state while congress was still debating his removal from the war department. For a brief period Benjamin held the secretary-ship of both war and state. Since he filled the latter post until the close of the Confederate government, it is with this position that he is most completely identified.[7]

Benjamin cannot of course be regarded as a success as secretary of war, even when all due allowances are made for his magnanimous willingness to shoulder for the government the popular odium. He undoubtedly showed skill in organizing and guiding the routine work of the department, but he as undoubtedly manifested no talent for the far more difficult and important work of planning or directing actual campaigns. It is no part of a layman's task to criticize his work in the war department on technical grounds, but it is obvious to the veriest tyro that he had no victory of any importance to his credit, while for one, at least, of the two great disasters, one in the west and one in the east, which occurred during his incumbency in office, he must receive partial blame. The defeat at Roanoke Island must be ascribed, not to failure to support General Wise, for he could not send ammunition he did not have, but to grave error of judgment, for he should have warned General Wise and thus have saved the latter's command.[8]

Quite different is his record as secretary of state. Always busy, always cheerful, always courteous, unruffled and clearheaded, he was a tower of strength in this department. Eckenrode's estimate of him is probably just. As secretary of state he was at home, "for no man in the South had better diplomatic talents or wider knowledge of Euro-pean affairs." Eckenrode hazards the opinion that "if he had been sent to Europe with plenty of money and unlimited powers to make treaties, he might have secured the success of the Confederacy."[9] As it was, he became the trusted counselor in whom President Davis con-fided most, and directed with great skill the efforts of the Confederate agents sent abroad to secure European recognition. It was even said that he actually wrote the president's messages when other duties occupied the time of the chief executive.[10]

[7] James F. Rhodes, *History of the United States from the Compromise of 1850*, III, 603
[8] See Butler, *op. cit.*, 252-258.
[9] Hamilton J. Eckenrode, *Jefferson Davis, President of the South*, 137.
[10] *Ibid.*, 253, 254.

With his analytical mind he saw, according to Professor William Dodd, at the very beginning of the war that slavery was the stumbling block in the way of recognition by foreign governments. He determined to propose emancipation, his plan being to offer freedom to the Negro on the condition that he enlist in the army. Such a policy was so foreign to all southern reasoning on the most vital issue before the Confederacy that it took courage to propose it. It was a tribute to Benjamin's powers of persuasion that he finally won President Davis to his point of view and gained consideration of the plan by congress. But action came too late to be effective, and very few Negroes were put into service.[11] Davis came to lean ever more heavily on Benjamin, who remained faithful to the end, sharing his president's plight and looking to his own escape only when all was lost.[12]

Christopher Gustavus Memminger, the son of an army officer killed in battle, was a German, born in Württemberg, January 9, 1803, who had been brought to Charleston by his mother as an infant. Left an orphan at the age of four, he was fortunate enough to be adopted from the Charleston orphanage by Americans of wealth and refinement. He was given a college education and training in law under the personal direction of his foster father, later Governor Thomas Bennett, and was thus started on his distinguished career. He was naturally so fully Americanized that there was nothing German about him. His presence in the cabinet is undoubtedly to be explained as an effort to bring in conservative opinion. He had been a leader of the Union party during the nullification controversy of 1832 and the avowed opponent of Calhoun's views.[13] Yet he appeared at the convention at Montgomery as a mild secessionist, drafted the constitution of the new state, and was sent to urge Virginia to coöperate with her sister states. He served as treasurer through most of the period of the Confederacy, initiating at once a

---

[11] He was, of course, a pro-slavery man. His advocacy of the legal claims of slavery brought from Senator Wade of Ohio the remark that Benjamin was "a Hebrew with Egyptian principles."—*History of the Jews of Louisiana*, 23; Wm. Dodd, *Jefferson Davis*, 343-345.

[12] For the full story of his escape see Butler, *Judah P. Benjamin*, 363-366. In England he was made queen's counsel in 1872 and became so famous as to appear only before the House of Lords and the Privy Council. A farewell banquet was given in his honor at his retirement in 1883 in Inner Temple Hall, a truly unique honor. See *Confederate Veteran*, XXXIX, 252. See also A. J. Hanna, *Flight into Oblivion*, Chap. 10.

[13] To make the cause ridiculous, he wrote *The Book of Nullification*, a parody in biblical language satirizing the doctrines and leaders of nullification. He had, of course, the courage to hold the unpopular side.

series of efforts for the financial relief of the government.[14] Upon his shoulders fell the onerous burden of financing at home and abroad a nation which was without resources in the treasury and without even credit. Unfortunately he was neither an able financier nor a leader who could bend other men to his will. Congress lost confidence in him and passed legislation opposed in the most vital points to his judgment and contrary to his strongly urged recommendations. He negotiated a European loan on cotton, devised the tax in kind, and became the author of a plan to issue notes to be taken up with bonds, a scheme later followed by Secretary Chase in the northern states. But in view of the attitude of congress it became impossible for him to promote a financial program, and so he was driven to submit his resignation. Two claims have been made, both of which throw responsibility for the failure of the Confederacy at Memminger's door. General J. E. Johnston after the war held that the government should have shipped to Europe during the first year of the war 4,000,000 or 5,000,000 bales of cotton, which could have furnished a basis of credit sufficient for the needs of the government. Memminger answered Johnston's charges by endeavoring to prove that such a policy was impossible. He estimated that a fleet of 4,000 ships, each capable of transporting 1,000 bales, would have been necessary to carry over such an amount of cotton, and pointed out that a fleet of such size was not to be obtained. Further, he held that the cotton could have been procured only by seizure, purchase, or donation, none of which methods would have appealed to the government as feasible at that early period of the war. A citizenry convinced that the blockade could not last a year would not have tolerated them. The scheme could probably have been carried out only on a small scale.

The other criticism probably has more validity. It is well known that the French banking house of Erlanger urged at the outset of negotiations in 1863 a larger loan than the proposed $15,000,000; namely, $25,000,000. The Confederate agents could not, of course, extend the loan without authority from Richmond; even Émile Erlanger, through his agents during their visit to the Confederacy, was unable to persuade the secretary of the treasury to do so.[15] Some

[14] *Confederate Veteran*, XXXV, 17; Kaufmann, *Die Deutschen im amerikanischen Bürgerkriege*, 569; Clement A. Evans, *Confederate Military History*, I, 603-604; *The South in the Building of the Nation*, XII, 186-187.

[15] When it was seen that the blockade and war were to be a long-drawn-out affair, a loan was negotiated with the banking house of Erlanger and Company in Paris with cotton

loyal Confederates later insisted that a huge loan at that time could have been made and would have saved the Confederacy. Predictions of results based on hypotheses are always incapable of proof, but this was probably a blunder of major importance and must be attributed to Memminger. His selection for the important treasury post is probably to be deplored, but not on the basis of nativity.[16] Reared in the traditions of South Carolina, he had probably been little influenced by the strain of German blood, though there were some ardent southerners who criticized the selection of other than "native-born" sons for high posts in the government. "Mr. Memminger," declared one critic, "had not by inheritance of birth the southern instinct. His early and constant sympathy with the Washington government was normal. The Confederate government never developed a financial policy. No country ever had a better or safer foundation for one, but Mr. Memminger never understood the conditions about him."[17]

The Confederacy drew rather heavily on the foreigners for her diplomatic service. France furnished one diplomat to the Confederacy[18] in the person of Pierre Adolph Rost, a jurist born in the *departement* of Lot-et-Garonne, France, about 1797. He received his education at the Lycée Napoleon and at the École Polytechnique and served as a soldier in the defense of Paris in 1814 in the corps of cadets of the latter institution when Napoleon's régime came to an

as security. The cotton was to be delivered at certain ports within six months after the close of the war—or before the end of the war if possible. Erlanger took the 7 per cent bonds at 77 per cent. Memminger seems to have contemplated an extension of the amount in case the houses of congress would consent to amend the loan act so as to relieve all doubt as to his authority to do so; in January, 1863, he recommended to the speaker of the lower house amendment of the act so as to use the bonds provided for increasing Confederate specie credit in Europe. For the story of the Erlanger loan, which has been so sharply and justly criticized, see James Callahan, *Diplomatic History of the Southern Confederacy*, 60-61, 62. For the visit of the agents, see below, pp. 366-367.

[16] See Samuel B. Thompson, *Confederate Purchasing Operations Abroad*, 5, 53-55, 72-73; John C. Schwab, *The Confederate States of America, 1861-1865*, 30-31.

[17] For fuller accounts of Memminger see *Confederate Veteran*, XXXV, 16-17; Evans, *op. cit.*, I, 614; *The South in the Building of the Nation*, XII, 186-187; John W. DuBose, *General Joseph Wheeler and the Army of Tennessee*, 33; *Dictionary of American Biography*, XII, 527-528; and, especially, Henry D. Capers, *Life and Times of C. G. Memminger*.

[18] Some accounts state that Pierre Soulé, another citizen of the Confederacy who had been born in France, was sent on a special mission to Spain, but the writer can find no authoritative evidence of such a mission. Nothing is to be found in the official records. The story of Soulé's service on the staff of General Beauregard and promotion to a brigadier-generalship as recognition of service in the defense of Charleston belongs to a later chapter (V). For references to his prison experiences, see *The War of the Rebellion: A Compilation of the Official Records of the Union and Confederate Armies*, Ser. 2, III, 612, 615, 675; IV, 23, 35, 41, 49, 55, 744, 934, 936; V, 952. Hereafter cited as *O. W. R.*

end. After Waterloo he found the government of the Restoration so uncongenial that he preferred to emigrate to America. Arriving at Natchez, Mississippi, without money or friends in 1816, he turned to teaching for a livelihood. His intelligence and pleasing appearance won him many friends and an opportunity for him to study law in the office of Joseph E. Davis, brother of the future president of the Confederate States. After completing his preparation for the law, he located at Natchitoches for a time but about 1830 removed to New Orleans; here he married a Louisiana Creole[19] and brought upon himself the responsibility of managing a large plantation in St. Charles Parish. Upon his return from a visit to Europe in 1838 he was appointed to the supreme court of his state, a post which he held with distinction for two terms. When the southern states created a new nation, Rost was made one of the regular commissioners to Europe and was wisely selected for the post in Spain where he remained only until May, 1862. He was to seek recognition for the Confederacy on the ground of the close community of the Spanish and southern social systems and of the proximity of the Confederacy to Cuba. In March, 1862, Minister Calderón Collantes informed Rost to his disappointment that Spain would take no initiative in recognition. His resignation on May 28 was based on the plea of health but was probably influenced by his conviction of the hopelessness of the mission. The paucity of results in his mission is hardly to be charged against him.[20]

It seems necessary to discuss in connection with the persons sent abroad on diplomatic service the mission ascribed to Maximilian Schele de Ver in order to refute the claims made in his behalf. Two German writers record him as having been sent by the Confederate government toward the close of the war to the German States in order to gain their good will toward the new republic, but add that he achieved nothing as Germany remained throughout the war the faithful friend of the Union.[21] Certainly Professor Schele, who had been filling the chair of modern languages at the University of Virginia

[19] Louise Destrehan.
[20] Benson J. Lossing, *Pictorial History of the Civil War in the United States of America*, I, 260. For his report on his interview with Collantes see James D. Richardson, *Compilations of Messages and Papers of the Confederacy including Diplomatic Correspondence, 1861-5*, II, 202-206. Hereafter cited as *Messages and Papers*. For his resignation see *ibid.*, 326. See also *The South in the Building of the Nation*, XII, 360-361.
[21] The two Germans who make this claim are Kaufmann, *op. cit.*, 570-571, and Schuricht, *History of the German Element in Virginia*, II, 44.

since 1844, would have been a most suitable choice for such a mission. Although Swedish by birth, he had adopted the allegiance of his Prussian father, and would have brought to the post a background of service as officer in the Prussian Landwehr and experience as a jurist. This impression that he was sent to Germany probably arose from the fact that he was approached by Secretary Benjamin in the spring of 1863 concerning a mission to France. On April 27, 1863, the faculty of the university expressed its favorable opinion as to the "propriety of granting Professor Schele leave to proceed to Europe upon a mission at the instance of the Secretary of State of the Confederate States." His going was, however, delayed in order that he might "complete his course of instruction before his departure," but the mission was never carried out.[22]

In addition to the regularly accredited commissioners to the European courts, such as Mason, Slidell, and Rost, several men were sent on special missions. Among them we find some of the most distinguished foreigners associated with the Confederacy, several of whom had already served her honorably on the field of battle.

The first such special agent whom the writer has been able to find is Henry Hotze, a Swiss by birth but a naturalized citizen, who had come to America as a child. He was taken from the ranks of the Third Alabama Regiment and sent to Europe by Walker, who was then secretary of war, on a mission of which relatively little is known. His experience as secretary of legation in Belgium in 1858-59 was probably a factor in his choice.[23] Shortly after his return to America the Confederate state department commissioned him as "Commercial agent" in London. He arrived in England about the same time as J. M. Mason, at the close of January, 1862, and at once set about his

[22] The note of leave granted to Schele by the faculty at the request of the rector is recorded in the minutes of the faculty for the date cited in the text. Benjamin's reason for approaching Schele is probably to be found in a letter of February 7, 1863, from Benjamin to Slidell to which is appended a memorandum by a "professor of the University of Virginia, detailing an hour's interview with Napoleon III at Biarritz three years earlier." The emperor had plied the professor for all sorts of information about Louisiana, Texas, the disposition of the French residents, the tendencies of the German colonists, and the feeling on the Mexican border. Obviously, he was contemplating the Mexican adventure. See John Bigelow, *Retrospections of an Active Life,* I, 601-602, for a portion of the memorandum appended to Benjamin's letter to Slidell. The evidence seems to point to Schele's being the professor in question.

[23] See Donaldson Jordan and Edwin J. Pratt, *Europe and the American Civil War,* 166; *Mobile Daily Advertiser and Register,* May 11, 1887, for an account of his life; J. F. Jameson (ed.), "The London Expenditures of the Confederate Secret Service," *American Historical Review,* XXXV, 812.

work. He seems to have been a regularly appointed propagandist for the secession cause, if one may judge from the instructions issued him on November 14, 1861. "You will be diligent and earnest in your efforts to impress upon the public mind abroad the ability of the Confederate States to maintain their independence, and to this end you will publish whatever information you possess calculated to convey a just idea of their ample resources and vast military strength and to raise their character and Government in general estimation."[24]

Hotze's first method of procedure was to try to secure the insertion in the large metropolitan newspapers of editorials which he hoped would be helpful to the southern cause. In this plan he was fortunate and successful. He did not have large funds at his command, but editorials and leading articles were scarcely for sale. More adroit means had to be devised. He was favored by fortune for the papers were naturally eager for authoritative news from the blockaded Confederacy; in addition many of the journalists were so friendly to the Confederate cause that they did not cavil at publishing southern arguments as if they were their own. Hotze's method in placing these articles was to offer them to professional writers of "leaders" and then to allow them to claim the fee paid by the paper.[25]

As one means to his end Hotze founded a Confederate weekly newspaper in London, the *Index*, which first appeared early in May, 1862, and which he brought up to a circulation of 2,250. It partially paid its way in 1864 by netting over £2,000, but it cost £4,700. He also issued miscellaneous publications as they seemed advisable, aiming not at the general public but rather at those who molded public opinion. He secured for the organ the services of James Spence[26] and of another Englishman to serve him as assistant editor, but he himself did the major portion of the work. He used this medium also to secure the alliance of professional journalists. He reported to Secretary Benjamin on March 14, 1863, that he had given partial employment to seven writers of the daily London press, four of whom were colleagues of one editorial corps, as he made concentration of effort one of his main objectives. He thus secured the services

[24] James D. Richardson, *op. cit.*, II, 115.   [25] Jordan and Pratt, *op. cit.*, 167.
[26] Spence was a young business man of Liverpool who had been engaged in a number of commercial enterprises with American companies, and who had been hard hit by the panic of 1857. He threw himself with ardor into the work but, when some captured correspondence showing that he was a paid southern agent was published, his usefulness was destroyed.—*Ibid.*, 172. For cost of *Index* see Jameson, *op. cit.*, 822.

of Percy Greg, one of the ablest "leader" writers of London, who was also one of the strongest supporters of the South in the *Saturday Review* and other political and literary periodicals.[27]

As advertisements were few and indeed a secondary consideration, the *Index* was costing about forty pounds a week. The absence of direct communication with the Confederacy gave this paper a certain authority and caused it to be widely quoted in England. Its carefully edited material may have contributed somewhat toward beclouding the issue in the British Isles. Evidence of its being regarded as authoritative is the fact that the editor of the *Annual Register* applied to Hotze for data and documents for the issue of 1862.

A scrutiny of his list of expenses reveals very interesting phases of his activity. He had busts made of President Davis and photographs of General Jackson; he contributed to the library fund of the Anthropological Society and succeeded in getting himself on the council of that organization;[28] he inserted in the *Autographic Mirror* facsimiles of papers found on Colonel Ulrich Dahlgren which purported to enjoin his men to kill Davis and his cabinet;[29] and he placarded every available space in the streets of London with representations of the Confederate flag linked with the British national ensign, a little device which cost the Confederate treasury the sum of £107 12 *s.* 6 *d.* He secured promises from the London *Herald* and the *Standard* to print at least every other day from June 6 to July 1, 1863, leading articles in support of a motion sponsored by John Arthur Roebuck, a member of parliament, requesting the government to confer with other European powers regarding recognition of the Confederacy.[30] He had a German translation made of James Spence's *The American Union*, assailing federal government of all types and especially the American Constitution. It ran through four London editions between November, 1861, and March, 1862.[31] Undoubtedly his best piece of

[27] Jordan and Pratt, *op. cit.*, 167-168. To the end Greg was a defender of the South. See the obituary in the *Manchester Guardian*, December 30, 1889.

[28] The curious fact should be recorded here of Hotze's connection with the formation of the Anthropological Society which seceded from the Ethnological Society in 1863. The president, James Hunt, in a paper to the British Association for the Advancement of Science, delivered that year, declared that the Negro was more like an ape than a European and that slavery was his proper place.—Jordan and Pratt, *op. cit.*, 168-169. Hotze spent £15 for busts of Davis and £20 for photographs of Jackson. See his expense account published from his Letter and Cash Book, *American Historical Review*, XXXV, 818.

[29] Evidence as to the non-genuineness of the Dahlgren Papers is printed in *Battles and Leaders of the Civil War* (Robert U. Johnson and Clarence C. Buel, eds.), IV, 96.

[30] Jordan and Pratt, *op. cit.*, 184.

[31] See entry in his expense account.—Jameson, *op. cit.*, 814.

propaganda, and probably the cleverest stroke in this field during the war, was gaining the consent of a Presbyterian publishing house to lend itself to southern propaganda. In the summer of 1863 the clergy of the Confederate States, assembled in Richmond, had issued an *Address to Christians* throughout the world, which had appeared as a pamphlet in England, setting forth the claims of the Confederacy to Christian sympathy in the old familiar arguments. Hotze actually succeeded in having it stitched up under the same cover with the current number of every respectable religious publication in Great Britain as well as with the *Quarterly Review* and the *Edinburgh Review*. It was thus thrust upon the attention of 250,000 subscribers. Yet Hotze might well have moderated his satisfaction with this stroke, for anti-slavery proponents were shocked at the church leaders lending themselves to slavery propaganda and brought out counter blasts. Nearly 1,000 Scottish clergymen signed an indignant reply.[32] Hotze's plan, as has been seen, was to work on individual writers rather than on the newspapers with which they were connected, and for that purpose he had elaborated a system of correspondence to and from England and France and between Europe and the northern states of America.[33] In all he furnished some twenty papers in England, on the Continent, and in the North with regular newspaper correspondence. He also acted as a despatch agent, for nearly every mail from Bermuda and Nassau brought him heavy packages of mail to be distributed.[34] He made several trips to Paris after the recall of Edwin de Leon[35] in 1864, and was certainly still at his post in January, 1865. By gaining the ear of M. Havas of the Havas Bullier Telegraphic Company, he secured a virtual monopoly of the French press on American news. He thus attained a success even beyond his expectations.

[32] Jordan and Pratt, *op. cit.*, 169-170. The cost of this item was only $770.10 in American currency.

[33] Jameson, *op. cit.*, 823, letter to Benjamin.

[34] *Ibid.*, 813, letter of December 31, 1864.

[35] Edwin de Leon was another agent, appointed in 1862 as confidential agent of the state department and supplied with a secret service fund to be used for the special service of insertions in the journals of Great Britain and the continental countries of such articles as would enlighten public opinion in regard to the Confederacy.—James D. Richardson, *op. cit.*, II, 224, 233. He dealt especially with the French press, whereas Hotze until 1864 worked chiefly with the British press. After De Leon's withdrawal from Europe, Hotze is seen making arrangements with a M. Felix Aucaigne to secure insertions of his own writings or of the *Index* in the Paris papers.—*Official Record of the Union and Confederate Navies of the War of the Rebellion*, Ser. 2, III, 1026-1027. Hereafter cited as *N. R.* Hotze even had a certain Manetta working for the cause in Turin, Italy.

Hotze's expenses, paid from the secret service fund, had mounted by the end of 1864 to £5,905 16s. 2d. He spent for entertainment, wine, and gifts, $557.82, exclusive of some boxes of choice Havana cigars and other personal gifts. The degree of his success he himself estimated on December 31, 1864, in the following terms: "But it is pleasant for me to believe that if in the French press where before an occasional favorable mention had to be begged as a great favor, we have now the almost undivided ear of three-fourths of the newspaper reading public, and if in the English press no European question, not even that of the Dano-German war which touched English sympathies so nearly and threatened English interests so seriously . . . has ever been so generally and so thoroughly understood. . . . I have been one among the many moral and intellectual agencies which jointly contributed to the result." He refused to acknowledge discouragement, even though he admitted "grievous disappointment" at the failure of those agencies to affect the action of the government since the "good opinion of the world is a precious thing to every nation, whether old or young," and since he was convinced that "if we have gained no political victory in Europe we have sustained no moral defeat."[36]

It is probably true that Hotze was the best informed and shrewdest of the southerners in England but, as with all the missions abroad, little genuine success can be justly claimed despite the money and energy expended. The men with whom he established contacts were already southern sympathizers, and his handling of the slavery question, though skillfully done, merely strengthened the pre-existing anti-Union sentiment, and, directed at the clergy, proved a boomerang. It can hardly be urged that he increased the pressure for recognition. In France he awakened interest and perhaps aroused sympathy—but no governmental action.

The next special foreign-born agents in point of time of whom we find record were sent back to Ireland to undermine, as far as possible, the military enlistments which it was felt the Federal government was securing in disguised form from abroad, especially from Ireland, and to show the people the true nature of the war. Several of the Confederate commissioners who were greatly exercised by what they

[36] Letter of Hotze to Benjamin, accompanying his expense account.—Jameson, op. cit., 823.

thought was evidence of such enlistments duly reported the fact to the home government and protested to the governments to which they were accredited.[37] "Of course," reads a communication dated June 8, 1863, from Commissioner Mason to Robert Dowling, a Confederate commercial agent located at Cork,[38] "these enlistments are made by the Federal agencies under false pretences, such, it is said, as pretended engagements for laborers on railroads in the United States or as farm hands. You will best know in what manner most successfully to conduct these inquiries, with a view to get at the facts, however they may be disguised. . . ."[39]

It is true that at the outbreak of the war sympathy in Ireland tended to favor the North, probably owing to the fact that the majority of her emigrants had settled in that section; it is true that the early war years saw thousands of Irishmen leave for America; and it is also true that Federal agents had visited Ireland, the most distinguished being Archbishop Hughes, who had spoken in Dublin on the American situation. However to attribute all the migration to America to the stimulation of Federal agents is to overlook more obvious reasons, such as poor crops in Ireland in those years, the withdrawal of large tracts of land from cultivation for pasturage, the termination of remittances from prosperous sons in the United States, and the cotton embargo affecting labor for Irishmen in British factories. Federalists scarcely needed to send their agents to encourage the Irish youth to leave home.

So serious, however, did the Richmond government regard the matter that it decided that it could not depend upon the diligence of the regular commissioners but must send "two or three Irishmen, long residents of our country, to act as far as they can in arresting

[37] Letters on this subject are to be found from L. Q. C. Lamar, dated March 20, 1863, *N. R.*, Ser. 2, III, 718; from J. C. MacFarland to Benjamin, June 6, 1863, *ibid.*, 792. For a protest to M. Rogier, minister of foreign affairs in Belgium, as early as October 13, 1862, see *ibid.*, 1158. Similar letters regarding the securing of labor recruits in Germany were sent a year later by A. Dudley Mann to Benjamin from Brussels, July 7, 1864.— *Ibid.*, 1165.

[38] Dowling was an Irishman who served the Confederacy, but the writer is convinced that he was resident in his own land and not sent over from the Confederate States. At least she has found no evidence to substantiate the latter view, though Leo Francis Stock in his article, "Catholic Participation in the Diplomacy of the Southern Confederacy," *Catholic Historical Review*, XVI, 1-18, assumes that he was sent or found evidence which he fails to disclose. The first allusion the writer has found in the records is a letter from Mason under date of May 14, 1863, addressed to Dowling at Dublin, transmitting from Benjamin a commission as commercial agent.—*N. R.*, Ser. 2, II, 422. It does not appear why the commission was not handed Dowling before departure, if he were sent over from America.   [39] *N. R.*, Ser. 2, II, 436.

these unlawful acts of the enemy by communicating directly with the people."[40]

So far as appears, only three agents were sent to Ireland: Lieutenant James L. Capston, the Reverend Father John Bannon, and Captain Lalor.[41] Capston was a cavalry officer, detailed by the war department for special service under the department of state. He arrived in London on September 2, 1863, reported to Hotze for instructions, and then left the same evening for Ireland. Benjamin's instructions to this missionary, dated July 3, 1863, indicate more clearly than anything else the purpose of the mission:

"The duty which is proposed to entrust to you is that of a private and confidential agent of this Government for the purpose of proceeding to Ireland and there using all legitimate means to enlighten the population as to the true nature and character of the contest now waged on this continent, with the view of defeating the attempts made by the agents of the United States to obtain in Ireland recruits for their armies."

Regarding the procedure Benjamin says, "The means to be used by you can scarcely be suggested from this side, but they are to be confined to such as are strictly legitimate, honorable, and proper. We rely on truth and justice alone. Throw yourself as much as possible into the close communication with the people where the agents of our enemies are at work. Inform them by every means you can devise, of the true purposes of those who seek to induce them to emigrate. Explain to them the nature of the warfare which is carried on here. Picture to them the fate of their unhappy countrymen who have already fallen victims to the arts of the Federals. Relate to them the story of Meagher's Brigade, its formation and its fate. Explain to them that they will be called on to meet Irishmen in battle, and thus imbrue their hands in the blood of their own friends, and perhaps kinsmen, in a quarrel which does not concern them, and in which all the feelings of a common humanity should induce them to refuse

[40] *Ibid.*, III, 836.

[41] The third agent, a Captain Lalor, was dispatched, but whether he was, like Capston and Father Bannon, a native-born Irishman, it is impossible to ascertain. The records show that he sailed from Wilmington sometime after February 29, 1864, perhaps on the *Caledonia*, and that he reported to Hotze some days before April 16, the same year, delivering his letter of introduction, and that he thereupon proceeded to Ireland. The records yield no further data. See Holcomb's letter to Benjamin, February 29, 1864, and Hotze's report of April 16 to the secretary.—*N. R.*, Ser. 2, III, 1044, 1088.

taking part against us." Note the subtle argument used. "Contrast the policy of the Federal and Confederate States in former times in their treatment of foreigners, in order to satisfy Irishmen where true sympathy in their favor was found in periods of trial. At the North the Know-Nothing party, based on hatred to foreigners and especially to Catholics, was triumphant in its career. In the South it was crushed, Virginia taking the lead in trampling it under foot. In this war such has been the hatred of the New England Puritans to Irishmen and Catholics, that in several instances the chapels and places of worship of the Irish Catholics have been burnt or shamefully desecrated by the regiments of volunteers from New England." He gave Capston great freedom of means—the use of the press, mixing among the people, and spreading the facts among persons of influence, but warned against any violation of the law.

"The laws of England must be strictly respected and obeyed by you. While prudence dictates that you should not reveal your agency nor the purposes for which you go abroad, it is not desired nor expected that you use any dishonest disguise or false pretenses. Your mission is, although secret, honorable; and the means employed must be such as this Government may fearlessly avow and openly justify, if your conduct should ever be called into question. On this point there must be no room whatever for doubt or cavil."[42]

He was provided with a letter to the Confederate agent Hotze, through whom he was to report monthly. His pay was to be that of a first lieutenant of cavalry, about one hundred dollars a month. Passage to and from Europe, and small expenses, such as printing, were to be paid, "if allowed by the above-mentioned agent," Hotze presumably. Hotze reported Capston's arrival in London on September 5, 1863.[43]

In Dublin he called on several editors and influential citizens, and published several letters pointing out the dangers to emigrants as they landed in New York. Proceeding to Limerick, Galway, and

---

[42] As proof of the truth of his statements Benjamin cites the New York *Freeman's Journal*, where the details concerning the actions of New England soldiers are cited as coming from Federal officers. For the entire letter of instructions see *N. R.*, Ser. 2, III, 828-829. It is also printed in "Capston's Special Mission," *Southern Historical Society Papers*, XXIV, 202-204. One comment would make it appear that Lieutenant Capston himself proposed the mission, for Benjamin's instructions begin, "You have in accordance with your proposal made to the department, been detailed by the Secretary of War for special service under my orders."—*Ibid.*, 202.

[43] *Ibid.*, 204; *N. R.*, Ser. 2, III, 829, 895.

Cork, he found the Catholic clergy eager to do anything they could to hold their diminishing flocks. He circulated a poster, bearing in large type catch phrases: "Overthrown! The Blessed Host Scattered on the Ground! Benediction Veil Made a Horse Cover of! All the Sacred Vessels Carried Off! The Priest Imprisoned and Afterwards Exposed on an Island to Alligators and Snakes!" Such outrages, according to the poster, had been committed on Catholics by Massachusetts soldiers in the South. Let Irishmen remember, he cautioned, the Know-Nothing party, that child of Orangemen who had earlier entered convents and insulted nuns at their devotions. Let Irishmen recall the fate of Meagher's brigade at Fredericksburg, and the comment of a New York paper that the North could afford to lose a few thousand of the scum of the Irish. Allusions to his work and correspondence with Hotze indicate Capston's presence in Ireland as agent until May, 1864. His return to his military duties in America is indicated in a letter of April 22, 1864, from Benjamin to Hotze, unless the latter thought that his "continuance abroad will be of advantage." Nothing appearing to the contrary, it is reasonable to infer that he returned to America about this time.[44]

At about the time of Capston's arrival in England, September 4, 1863, almost identical instructions were issued to Father Bannon, who had left Ireland ten years before to labor in St. Louis. He was relieved by the war department from his duties as chaplain to Missouri troops under General Price and placed at the disposal of the department of state. He was a priest of large physique, a brilliant speaker of impressive personality.[45]

His instructions gave him discretion to associate with him any Catholic prelate from the North who shared his view of the Confederate cause, as well as to go to Rome to get such sanction from the pope as might strengthen his hands, but he evidently held both actions unnecessary, for he proceeded alone straightway to Ireland. At Dublin we find him by October 31 established at the Angel Hotel, the

[44] Benjamin writes: "I apprehend that Lieutenant Capston can scarcely be of much further service and you can intimate to him that the Department considers it now time that he should return to his duties here, unless you think that his continuance abroad will be of advantage." Since he disappears from the *Naval Records*, it is logical to assume that Hotze did not detain him.—*Ibid.*, 1098.

[45] For his instructions see *ibid.*, 893-895. He was allowed $100 a month for his salary, his passage to and from Europe was paid, and Hotze was to allow him a small sum for expenses such as printing, travel, etc. He was handed $1,212.50 in gold at his departure to cover his expenses to Europe; any surplus was to be delivered to Hotze.

chief resort of country priests visiting the city, and of middle-class farmers frequenting the neighboring market of Smithfield. Like Capston, he resorted to the press as his best instrument. He assisted the Irish revolutionist, John Martin, who was pro-southern in his sympathies, in the preparation of a series of articles for the *Nation*. He had 2,000 copies of a handbill printed, 1,000 of which he sent to Queenstown and 500 to Galway to be distributed to prospective emigrants and to be posted in the boarding houses usually occupied by them just prior to their departure. Under the *nom de plume* of Sacerdos, he prepared circulars, letters, and statements almost without end, reprinted contributions to the New York *Freeman's Journal*, lectured, and preached throughout the southern part of Ireland. Early in 1864 he put out a six-column broadside to the "Catholic Clergy and People of Ireland." Three thousand copies were sent to parish priests for widespread distribution. In this broadside were printed the letter of October 18, 1862, of Pope Pius IX to Archbishop Hughes of New York, urging every effort to secure peace in America, President Davis' letter of appreciation to the pope, and the pontiff's much discussed reply.[46] Father Bannon in his address interpreted the papal reply as favoring the South. He pointed out that the Yankees were descendants of Cromwell and his party, who had persecuted the Quakers, and, in the guise of the Know-Nothing party, the Catholics. On the other hand, the southern gentlemen were the natural allies of foreigners and of Catholics and should receive credit for crushing the Know-Nothing movement. He repeated Capston's cries of the defiling of chalices, ciboria, and sacred vestments. No Catholic, he was sure, would persist in countenancing actions condemned by the pope; as a Catholic priest he only desired to see the wishes of the Holy Father realized. These appeals were well tuned to Irish temperament.

Father Bannon followed the broadside with a plea to the "Young Men of Ireland," recalling the Irish revolutionary movement and its leaders, most of whom had expressed sympathy for the South. He warned them that, since immigrants had to sign a document pledging

[46] The letter expressive of appreciation for the papal effort was dated September 22, 1863, sent over by President Davis, and delivered personally by A. Dudley Mann, commissioner at Brussels, to the pope. The reply of the pope, which was worded ambiguously, was dated December 3, 1863. For the text of all three documents see *American Annual Cyclopaedia*, 1863, 819-820.

themselves not to work for any other than the parties furnishing the passage money, they would be virtually forced into military service. He next cited church theologians to discredit mercenary service in the army.

Thousands of his circulars were distributed and explained by the parish priests to the people, and he himself was widely sought for sermons and lectures. He issued a statement, trying to show that the pope had recognized the Confederacy, and one more broadside, carrying a letter by Earl Russell which had appeared in the Irish *Times*, suggesting discontinuance of passports for the United States to any but persons properly authenticated. A final letter to the "Catholic Clergy and People of Ireland" closed with an appeal to avoid the United States until after the war. Therewith he left in the hands of the local clergy further efforts to frustate northern agents.[47]

Father Bannon's labors seemed to bear fruit. Several bishops and a large number of parish priests declared themselves converts to his views; an apostolic delegate came out for the southern cause. In his final dispatch of May 28, 1864, he declared, "My mission has been accomplished." It was viewed at the time by Confederate authorities as a success, for Davis endorsed one of the Father's reports with the comment, "Course of the agent is very satisfactory," and thought his articles worthy of publication in the South. The clergy of Ireland sent to the Vatican a protest against the Federal government's using up the Irish "like dogs." Father Bannon claimed that the exodus from Ireland was stopped. But in any just evaluation it must be stated that the statistics, while showing a decline in 1864, do not show any real check! A decline in emigration from 117,000 in 1863 to 114,000 in 1864 could scarcely be regarded as a telling triumph.[48]

It was, however, Father Bannon who first proposed to Secretary Benjamin the possible advantages to the Confederate States of enlist-

[47] For details about his life and work see Stock, *op. cit.*, 7, 9-14.

[48] Benjamin wrote to Hotze on April 22, 1864: "I am much gratified with the zeal, discretion, and ability displayed by the Rev. Mr. Bannon in the service undertaken by him, and desire you should continue to provide him with the necessary means for continuing his labors as long as he remains satisfied that his efforts are useful to our cause." As he could not reach Father Bannon, he asked that the substance of his comment be communicated by Hotze, and added that the former had attracted the favorable notice of the president.—*N. R.*, Ser. 2, III, 1098, 1099. The figures in the text are from a statement by Sir Robert Peel, secretary for Ireland. The report of the United States commissioner for immigration gives the following number of immigrants from Ireland: 1863, 55,916; 1864, 63,523; 1865, 29,772.

ing the sympathies of the pope and thus through direct influence affecting the attitude of the Catholic countries.[49]

It was natural that, when President Davis was casting about for an emissary to send to the pope, he should select the outstanding Catholic cleric in the South, whom the church had itself honored. It is a matter of circumstance that he was born in 1817 rather than in 1819, for in the latter event he would not have entered this story. However the Right Reverend Patrick Niesen Lynch was born at Clones, Ireland, March 10, 1817, and was brought by his parents when he was only two years old to Cheraw, South Carolina. The fact that he had been a distinguished student at the College of Propaganda at Rome and therefore had some acquaintance with the Roman ecclesiastics probably counted in his favor. A doctor of divinity, a bishop, an ardent advocate of the cause of the Confederacy from the outbreak of war, he was obviously a proper choice to plead with the pope and to present a letter from President Davis, expressive of the desire of the Confederacy for peace. It was by no means held against him that he had intervened in behalf of Federal prisoners sent south from the battlefields of the war.

Bishop Lynch's appointment as special commissioner to the States of the Church, dated April 4, 1864, vested him with power to agree and "negotiate concerning all matters and subjects interesting to both Governments" and to conclude a treaty.[50] The bishop visited Ireland, was there joined by Father Bannon, who accompanied his suite as chaplain, reached Paris before June 11, made a favorable impression on Slidell as "admirably fitted for the duties assigned to him," had two interviews with the French minister of foreign affairs, and was accorded an audience by the emperor, on which occasion he was careful to wear his full episcopal robes.[51] In Rome he was graciously accorded several audiences by the pope, but only in his ecclesiastical relation, never as a representative of the Confederate States. His mission therefore cannot be regarded as other than a failure. He was caught abroad by the cessation of hostilities and used his kindness to Federal prisoners as a plea for permission to return. He returned to find his government overthrown and the church property

[49] *Ibid.;* Stock, *op. cit.,* 15.
[50] *N. R.,* Ser. 2, III, 172-173.
[51] *Ibid.,* 1148, 1162.

of his diocese destroyed. Obviously the mission, if it were to bring to an end the enlistment of Irish and German Catholics in the northern armies through intervention of the pope, should have been dispatched much earlier.[52]

Agents were sent also to several points in Mexico: J. T. Pickett as special agent at the beginning of the war to sound out the Mexican government on an alliance, and at a late period, January, 1864, General William Preston as envoy extraordinary and minister plenipotentiary, accredited to Emperor Maximilian. But particular diplomatic and commercial agents were sent for specific purposes, some of them foreigners. The most important of these minor officials was certainly John A. Quintero. The state of revolution in the northern provinces of Mexico at the opening of the American war undoubtedly prompted the sending of a special mission to the state of New Leon, though the pretext offered for such action was the distance of New Leon from Mexico City and the lack of speedy and constant communication with the central government.[53] H. W. Leach, a citizen of Texas, had proposed to his fellow Texans, Judge Reagan and Senator Wigfall, as early as May 11, 1861, the desirability of sending an agent with secret powers to assure the church party and Governor Vidaurri of Confederate friendship and mutuality of interest in order to prevent a collision on the Rio Grande. At first he suggested Father Anstead, a priest of Galveston, but later proposed J. A. Quintero, born in Havana, but then in charge of the land office in Austin. He, it was felt, had the necessary qualifications—clearheadedness, prudence, and a perfect command of Spanish, his mother tongue. As a Cuban he stood outside of Mexican politics and was free from any personal prejudices in local politics. A rather extraordinary proposition had been made by the Bishop of Monterey to Bishop Odin of Galveston to annex Texas to the Sierre Madre region.[54]

By May 22 Quintero had received his credentials from the Confederate government as commissioner to Governor Vidaurri of the province of New Leon, and departed from Galveston for Brazos

[52] Stock, *op. cit.*, 17-18.

[53] See letter of Secretary of State Toombs to General Vidaurri, governor of the Province of New Leon.—*N. R.*, Ser. 2, III, 101.

[54] Governor's Letters, March-May, 1861, Governor Edward Clark, Archives, Texas State Library. Bishop Odin became archbishop at New Orleans in February, 1861.

Santiago, armed with instructions and a draft for three hundred dollars as salary for six weeks, the time in which he was expected to accomplish his task. He also carried letters from the head of the clergy to influential priests in Mexico. He was to assure Governor Vidaurri of the friendly disposition of the Confederacy toward Mexico and of its desire for peace. His government would use every effort to insure the preservation of peace on the border by insisting on the observance of international law, and expected equal vigilance on the part of General Vidaurri to prevent outrages on the persons and property of Texas citizens; if the governor failed to stop the raids, the Confederacy would feel compelled to punish the invaders.[55]

After reporting at Richmond the success of his mission, Quintero was immediately asked to return as confidential agent to northeast Mexico with residence at Monterey, as his earlier mission had won the entire approval of the state department. It is interesting that this appointment was made in response to the expressed wish of the governor of New Leon. This second mission being of a secret and confidential nature, he was to declare his official character only to Governor Vidaurri and such other persons as he might deem prudent. It was manifestly to the interest of both people that intimate social and commercial relations should exist between the Confederates and the people of northern Mexico, but President Davis felt it "imprudent and impolitic" in the interest of both parties to "take any steps at present in regard to the proposition made by Governor Vidaurri . . . in reference to the future political relations of the Confederate States with the northern Provinces of Mexico." Quintero was instructed to send information concerning that country, to report especially on the prospects of getting powder, lead, saltpeter, and other munitions of war through Matamoros, and to purchase lead and powder in the amount specified. If Mexico had, as was reported, given the United States permission to transport troops and munitions across her territory, he was to induce the governor to throw his influence against it.[56] On November 4, 1861, Quintero reported that Vidaurri would oppose the passage of United States troops through New Leon but, as the war

[55] Quintero to Governor Clark, June 3, 1861; *ibid.*, June-December, 1861; *N. R.*, Ser. 2, III, 101, 217. Vidaurri's reply to the secretary of state, dated July 1, 1861, is found in Governor's Letters, Governor Edward Clark, Archives, Texas State Library.

[56] His instructions are dated September 3, 1861. See *N. R.*, Ser. 2, III, 253-255. For letters by Quintero to Lubbock, March 24, 28, 1862, see Governor's Letters, Lubbock Papers, Archives, Texas State Library; Pickett Papers, Quintero to State Department, August 19, 1861.

dragged on, the Mexican proved to be not wholly faithful to the Confederacy.[57]

In addition to Quintero, who was regarded as general agent of the state department on the Rio Grande frontier in Mexico, Richard Fitzpatrick was appointed commercial agent at Matamoros on November 15, 1862. Bernard Avegno of New Orleans received an appointment to the same post at Vera Cruz on December 18, 1862; and later, May 30, 1864, Émile la Sere of Louisiana received credentials to perform the same functions at Vera Cruz.[58] All three of these commercial agents were foreign-born. Fitzpatrick who was functioning at Matamoros as late as March 9, 1864, reported on activities in that vicinity, but felt that there was nothing for him to do there. Avegno departed for Vera Cruz with five hundred dollars advance salary via Nassau, and reached Havana in June or July, 1863. After months of silence which Benjamin generously ascribed to broken communications, quiet inquiries revealed that the agent had decided to resign and go to Europe. After several broken promises to Slidell he, together with some bonds, vanishes from the records. Nothing appears in the official records concerning La Sere other than the bare record of his appointment.[59]

It was about the middle period of the war that a Canadian of Irish parentage was sent at the request of General E. Kirby Smith to Mexico. Thomas J. Devine was born in Halifax, Nova Scotia, prepared for college in Tallahassee, studied law at Transylvania University in Kentucky, and located finally in San Antonio. With a brilliant record as district judge, he was immediately after the establishment of the Confederacy appointed Confederate judge for a Texas district. His Mexican mission only added to his reputation, for he adjusted amicably for the Confederacy the issues which threatened discord with her closest neighbor. In a sharp dispute with the house of P. Milmo of Monterey over the embargoing of some Confederate cotton for a debt, General Magruder had forbidden any cotton to pass into Mexico; in retaliation Vidaurri closed the port and would not allow any goods to pass into Texas. Judge Thomas J. Devine and

---

[57] For Vidaurri's bad faith in supporting the house of P. Milmo and Company, in seizing some cases containing funds for San Antonio and Shreveport, in December, 1863, see *O. W. R.*, Ser. 1, LIII, 942-943. See also 932, 941, 947.

[58] *N. R.*, Ser. 2, III, 136, 138-139, 175.

[59] For Fitzpatrick see *O. W. R.*, Ser. 1, XXXIV, Pt. 2, 1032; for Avegno, *N. R.*, Ser. 2, III, 904, 912, 1012-1013, 1107-1108; *O. W. R.*, Ser. 4, II, 257-258.

Colonel T. F. McKinney were sent as commissioners to Monterey about February, 1864, to settle the dispute. It is not strange that at the close of the war a judge who had served as a delegate to the secession convention of the state, who had served on the Committee of Public Safety, and who had officially represented the Confederacy on a special mission should have been indicted by the Union authorities for treason; accordingly, Judge Devine was confined at Fort Jackson for several months. For such fidelity Texas rewarded her adopted son by placing him on the supreme bench after his release from prison.[60]

A Swiss, Captain Henry Wirz, whose military service, especially as the unfortunate superintendent of the prison camp at Andersonville, will be discussed later, also played a rôle as a special agent. In the summer of 1863 he was deputed by Davis, at the instigation of General Winder, who befriended him on several occasions, to serve as bearer of secret dispatches to the Confederate commissioners, Mason and Slidell, in England and France and to certain financial agents in Europe. He discharged his mission successfully and returned in January, 1864, shortly to be put in charge of the military prison at Andersonville.[61]

There appears at least one more foreign-born citizen who played a minor rôle as emissary for the Confederacy. A. Supervièle, a Frenchman by birth, as his name suggests, but for the sixteen years preceding the war a resident of Texas, was sent to Mexico and Paris as the special representative of General H. P. Bee with the approval of Bee's superior commander, General E. Kirby Smith. His first mission to Mexico was an attempt to induce the French officers to seize Matamoros in order to insure the presence of a friendly, reliable power in control of that all-important point. His mission covered the period from his arrival at Havana, February 28, 1863, to about the last of June, when he was arrested by a Mexican officer as a spy. He was promptly released by the governor and succeeded in establishing friendly contacts with practically all the French leaders in Mexico, but he failed to bring about the desired military action at Matamoros.[62]

[60] Sid Johnson, *Texans Who Wore the Gray*, 105; *O. W. R.*, Ser. 1, XXXIV, Pt. 2, 318, 536. McKinney appears not to have been a foreigner.
[61] Ambrose S. Spencer, *A Narrative of Andersonville*, 56. See below, Chap. VIII, for his service at Andersonville.
[62] *O. W. R.*, Ser. 1, XXVI, Pt. 2, 140-151, gives Supervièle's report on his first mission.

The second mission, upon which he was dispatched very shortly after his return from Mexico, was a personal effort of General Bee, who was disturbed by the seizure of two British vessels loaded with arms for the Confederacy by a French frigate at the mouth of the Rio Grande, one in July, and the *Love Bird* in September, 1863. The special objective of Supervièle's efforts was to be the recovery of the arms originally on board the *Love Bird*. General Smith intrusted to the agent a communication to be delivered to Slidell, whose services were to be enlisted to the desired end. Supervièle was instructed to proceed to Vera Cruz to present to the French admiral the facts; he was to allow General Smith's letter to Slidell to be read by the admiral and by a French general, if there were an officer in Mexico able to control the movements of the army. The whole transaction was to be kept a profound secret. If he became satisfied from the conversation with the admiral that there existed no officer with power to carry out the views of General Smith, he was to proceed at once to Paris without the delay of going to Mexico City. But if he encountered a reliable man to whom he dared entrust the letter to Slidell, he might himself return to the Confederate States. General Smith's letter was delivered by Supervièle to the admiral about December 20, 1863. The London *Times* shortly afterwards carried a notice of the arrival in Paris of a M. Supervièle, who had sailed from Vera Cruz in a French steamer, as a special envoy to secure recognition for the Confederacy. Therewith he vanishes from the war and from the records.[63]

Military routine was broken for another foreign-born agent, Colonel James S. Reily, when he was dispatched by a superior military officer on what was largely a military mission. He was sent across the Mexican border from Texas into the states of Chihuahua and Sonora early in January, 1863, by General Sibley who charged him with the duty of establishing friendly relations with those two states, a general commission probably to cloak the more precise one of securing coöperation against the Indians and making arrangements for the storage of Confederate provisions in Mexico. Colonel Reily optimistically interpreted the results of his brief mission as "the first official recognition by a foreign government of the Confederate States of America"—a slight exaggeration, to say the least.[64]

[63] *Ibid.*, 188, 202, 234, 273, 308; *Daily Richmond Examiner*, January 12, 1864.
[64] *O. W. R.*, Ser. 1, IV, 167-174, gives the data on the entire mission.

On the very eve of the collapse of the Confederacy, two military men who had left their native lands to offer their swords to the Confederacy were sent back across the sea to serve in the diplomatic field. Each was a figure of the greatest interest.

Heros von Borcke, after two years of valiant service on Stuart's staff, had been so severely wounded that he was unable to return to active duty. As the winter of 1864-65 approached, a proposal which had already been placed before him several times, but which he had as often rejected because of hope of returning to the field, was renewed. Urged by Generals Hampton and Lee and by President Davis, and recognizing the unlikelihood of an active winter campaign for him, he consented to go on a government mission to England. Receiving a further mark of appreciation for his valuable services, Major von Borcke departed as Colonel von Borcke. Long and tedious delays on the journey ensued; he was four days reaching Wilmington, ran the blockade as the heavy guns opened the bombardment of Fort Fisher, and reached England in February, 1865, only after a circuitous route by way of the West Indies. He arrived at the Court of St. James too late to do more for the cause which was "just and noble" in his eyes than write a few articles for the press. But he personally was thereby spared the pain of witnessing the collapse of that for which he had spilled his blood.[65]

Much more ambitious and important was a second mission projected at about the same time, that of Prince Polignac, whom we shall meet shortly as a major general in the military ranks. Early in 1865 at the earnest request of Governor Allen of Louisiana, the Trans-Mississippi military authorities resolved to send him to Emperor Napoleon III. He had himself inspired the venture, for at the close of the campaign of 1864 he felt that he might awaken sympathy for the southern cause by carrying information abroad and capitalizing the curiosity which the presence of an active participant must arouse. Accordingly he suggested to General Smith the advisability of a six month's leave of absence for the purpose, which the latter had power to grant without consent of the secretary of war or of the president. The prince was relying on his personal acquaintance with an intimate friend of the emperor, the Duke de Morny, who, though known for

---

[65] See Von Borcke's own story of his effort as special envoy in *Memoirs of the Confederate War*, II, 317.

his lack of enthusiasm, was credited with shrewdness, freedom from prejudice, and readiness to receive information about the southern cause.[66] While the leaders of the Confederacy who were consulted entertained no sanguine hopes of French help as a result of the visit, it was felt worth while to grant the leave of absence. To give more dignity to his presence abroad the prince asked that his chief of staff, Major T. C. Moncure, be allowed to accompany him. Governor Allen also availed himself of the opportunity to send a letter directly to the emperor by his aide-de-camp, Colonel Ernest Miltenberger. The governor wrote as the official head of the state of Louisiana, a political division which might presumably on historical grounds lay special claims to French sympathy. On March 16, 1865, Colonel E. Miltenberger, Major Moncure, and Prince Polignac left Shreveport on what was definitely a special government mission, though only the first-named was invested with an official character, and that from the state of Louisiana, not from the Confederacy. As the party set out, traversing the entire breadth of Texas, deputations of citizens welcomed them at every stage and made Prince Polignac the guest of the state. Stagecoach travel was necessarily slow to the Mexican border; at Matamoros they were delayed awaiting the steamer to convey them to Havana, where they were again delayed before they could embark on a steamer for Cadiz. On the very last day of the journey into Paris, the prince learned from a newspaper of the death of the Duke de Morny and knew that his efforts could produce no practical results.

However a former friend who hastened to greet him, a member of the emperor's staff, secured an interview for him without difficulty. The interview with the emperor was quite informal and in the ensuing conversation the head of the French state manifested much interest in the progress of the war, making many remarks on the operations in the field, but he did not touch upon the political side. As he took his departure Prince Polignac asked permission to introduce an aide-de-camp of the governor of Louisiana, the bearer of a letter to the emperor.[67] Though the latter hesitated, he granted the

[66] For Polignac's own story of the mission see "Polignac's Mission," *Southern Historical Society Papers*, XXXII, 365-371.

[67] The *Washington Post* on March 16, 1901, stated that a paper was prepared to be sent to Napoleon, ceding Louisiana to France in return for armed intervention. The story circulated long as "The Lost Chapter," but there is no evidence for it. In 1895 it was categorically denied by J. Reagan, George Davis, and Attorney General Colonel L. Q. Washington. See the latter's "Confederate States State Department," *Southern Historical*

request and Colonel Miltenberger delivered Governor Allen's letter the next day in a purely formal interview of only a few minutes.

The close of the war in America ended all thought of Polignac's return to the South and, as he was *persona non grata* to Louis Napoleon, he retired to his estate in Austria, and took no part in the Franco-Prussian War.[68]

Of civil servants in minor posts in the Confederate government and in the employ of the various states there were probably many, but in the main the records were not concerned with minor folk in civil life and usually did not record the places of birth. One person in a more important minor post has not escaped the fine-toothed comb. William M. Browne, assistant secretary of state, was an Englishman of fine education who had come to the United States and became naturalized before 1861. He had been editing a paper in Washington, but at the outbreak of war he went South and became an aide-de-camp to President Davis with the rank of colonel of cavalry. He served with fidelity and gained the appreciation of Davis. His remarkably attractive personal appearance and his wide information on public affairs proved invaluable. His military record will be given later.[69]

A German, Gustav A. Schwarzmann, who was in the general post office at Washington at the outbreak of war, went to Richmond, as his sympathies were with the South, where he was at once appointed to the post-office department. The Ole Canuteson who had founded a Norwegian colony in Texas and who had served as postmaster at Norman Hill since its establishment was retained in that capacity by the Confederate government throughout the war.[70]

It is possible to discover a few Irish-born serving the government in a civil capacity, usually after they had been disabled in military service. Captain Blayney Townley Walshe, Andrew R. Blakely, and James Bratton fall in this class. The former, who had been in

Society Papers, XXIX, 344-346. Finally Prince Polignac silenced all doubts by his denial. —*Op. cit.*, 367.

[68] James C. Nisbet, *Four Years on the Firing Line*, 47.

[69] Evans, *op. cit.*, I, 628-629. For the account of his military record see below, Chap. V. After the war he engaged in agriculture in Georgia, and was later elected professor of history and political economy at the University of Georgia where he served until his death in 1884.

[70] See Schuricht, *History of the German Element in Virginia*, II, 84, for Schwarzmann. For Canuteson see Anderson, *The First Chapter of Norwegian Immigration*, 388.

New Orleans only since 1853, after a period of service in the Washington Artillery was severely wounded at Gaines's Mill. He was then made chief of the passport office in Richmond and in that important post directed the efforts of a lieutenant and twenty-six clerks. When able to dispense with his crutches, he returned to military service as major provost marshal of three parishes in Louisiana.[71] The next-named, Blakely, about to enter the University of Dublin at fifteen years of age, ran away to sea to escape studying for the church. He was in the field also with the Washington Artillery until incapacitated at Second Manassas, when he was detailed as a clerk to the treasury department. Nothing is known of Bratton except that he came from Shropshire, went to work for Texas in 1861, and was transferred to the Confederate service, serving till the close of the war.[72] Finally one notes some German Jews among the secret police which was organized by General Winder, provost marshal of Virginia, to put down the disorders rampant in Richmond.[73]

A very interesting group of civil servants working for the Confederate government were some lithographers. The largest lithographic establishment in Virginia was conducted by Hoyer and Ludwig, a German firm which during the period of the war printed Confederate notes and bonds. In the second year of the war a group of Scotchmen skilled in this work were secured to print paper money for the Confederate government. With a valuable cargo of military stores, ammunition, and a large quantity of lithographic material for the treasury department, twenty-six lithographers ran the blockade on the *R. E. Lee.* Although this craft ran aground on a flat of mud in Wilmington Harbor, the men were safely landed in one of her two quarter boats on December 29, 1862. The Scotchmen found abundant employment in Richmond, as the paper mills ran busily throughout the war turning out treasury notes; but it might be remarked that the style of their work was far from faultless, as is sufficiently attested by the fact that counterfeit notes printed in the North and extensively circulated through the South could be easily detected by the superior execution of their engraving.[74]

[71] *Confederate Veteran,* VI, 576.
[72] *Ibid.,* X, 178; Mamie Yeary (ed.), *Reminiscences of the Boys in Gray,* 79.
[73] Estvàn, *War Pictures,* I, 184-185.
[74] Schuricht, *op. cit.,* II, 49, and n.; Francis B. C. Bradlee, *Blockade Running during the Civil War,* 73, 74.

It is possible to identify a few foreigners in the civil service of the states. The secretary of Governor Lubbock throughout his term of office, for instance, was James Paul, a Texan citizen of English birth living at Castroville. Because of physical infirmities he was incapacitated for military service.[75]

Dr. Eugene Woldemar Hilgard, state geologist of Mississippi, had been born in Zweibrücken, Bavaria, on January 5, 1833. Although he was brought to America three years later and received his preliminary education in the schools of Belleville, Illinois, it was in Germany that he took his training for the doctorate, receiving the degree at Heidelberg in 1853. From 1855 through the entire period of the war and until 1873 he was state geologist and professor of chemistry at the University of Mississippi. One comes across frequent references to his work for the state, especially in connection with salt, which was a serious problem to all the states of the Confederacy. As a slight example of his work it might be stated that he visited a number of reputed salt springs of the state when directed by Governor Pettus to report on the salt resources of Mississippi, only to confirm his previous conviction that the state possessed no natural brines of sufficient strength to justify exploitation. However he prepared and disseminated a circular, giving general directions for making salt at the salt licks and suggested submission of specimens of salt for his analysis.[76]

Scattered here and there through the southern states were civilians of distinction who rendered services which were unique and which sometimes had a semiofficial relation to the state or central government. A striking example of this type was M. J. Raymond Thomassy, a French geologist who had made four or five tours of inspection of the Mississippi Delta on the eve of the war. He had in 1860 produced his *Géologie pratique de la Louisiane,* published by American subscribers in New Orleans and also in Paris, the first geological survey of Louisiana. His unique service is identified more fully than

[75] Francis R. Lubbock, *Six Decades in Texas or Memoirs,* 336. Hereafter cited as *Memoirs.*

[76] In 1873 he left the South to accept a professorship of geology and natural history at the University of Michigan. He left this institution in 1875 to become a professor of agriculture at the University of California. He died on January 8, 1916.—*South in the Building of the Nation,* XI, 491. See also Ella Lonn, *Salt as a Factor in the Confederacy,* 48, 79; and Hilgard, "Memoranda Concerning the Geological Survey," *Mississippi Senate Journal,* called Session, 1862, Appendix, 89-90, 94.

Hilgard's with what may perhaps appear as a rather unique subject to be connected with the Civil War—salt.

He had devised a way to improve production of salt by solar evaporation, the method which had been used in Italy since 1848, and which had resulted in the manufacture of salt from the weak brine of the Adriatic at a cost of one and one-half cents a bushel. His deep interest in the southern states, and more especially in salt, in view of the tremendous demand for it in that part of the country and the dependence on outside sources for its supply, led him after the outbreak of war to press his views about solar production first upon one state legislature and then upon another, upon prominent editors, and upon government leaders at Richmond. His path can be traced from Charleston through Montgomery to the Lake Bistineau region in northern Louisiana, down to the newly discovered salt mine near New Iberia on the Gulf coast, then to the Alabama salt wells in the southern part of that state, and finally to Richmond. He ultimately convinced the secretary of war of the value of his views, but he himself was removed from the scene by death in 1863. To understand the importance of the work of Thomassy in striving to aid the population in securing a supply of cheap salt from the sea which washed the shores of so many of their states, it is necessary to understand the frightful dearth of this necessity and the almost incredible size of the demand for it—6,000,000 bushels a year or 300,000,000 pounds, an amount computed on a reduced war basis rather than the 50 pounds per capita basis which was peacetime consumption. If Thomassy had lived, it is possible that he would have solved this problem for the Confederacy as he had been directed by the war department to go to Europe to secure workers skilled in the manufacture of salt by his process of solar evaporation.[77]

[77] Lonn, *op. cit.*, 72-77.

IV

CONFEDERATE MILITARY COMPANIES COMPOSED
OF FOREIGN-BORN

THE NEWSPAPERS during the early months of the war were crowded with advertisements concerning the formation of new companies of volunteers. Conspicuous among these were companies to be drawn from various nationality groups. Men of foreign birth or descent seemed drawn to a company composed of men of similar background. Such special organizations seemed to hold a particular attraction for Irishmen; the green flag seemed to exert a magnetic control over the brawny sons of the Emerald Isle. Their fondness for their own companies is explicable: the Irishman fights better shoulder to shoulder with Irishmen as comrades, and always yearns to reflect honor on "Ould Ireland." The strongest inducement in winning Irish recruits was the reputation of the company.

To appreciate the importance of the company in the Confederate army, it is necessary to point out that the position of military schools and military companies in the ante-bellum South was rather remarkable. Many southerners attended such schools and joined such companies although they had no thought of the army as a career. Admission to an exclusive company, like the Washington Artillery of New Orleans, was regarded in much the same light as admission to an equally exclusive club today, and the weekly military drill not as a burden, but as a pleasure and a recreation. These companies were semiofficial in that the state provided the arms, though the members had to bear the expense of most of the uniform. Their dues, however, assured them a clubroom with some gymnastic equipment, an opportunity to play chess, and pleasant companionship. The example of the native Americans soon begot military companies of Irishmen, Germans, or of mixed nationalities, the existence of which bred a spirit of friendly rivalry between the companies in their drills and parades, which were held especially on the Fourth of July. Occasionally a man who had not been born in the South was invited to join one of the elite companies.[1] One of the most noted of the nationality companies in the South was the German Fusiliers of Charleston, which traced a long and honorable history back to 1775.[2] For some conception of the prominence of these companies in the life of the South let us turn to Olmsted's description of Charleston in 1853. "The frequent drumming which is heard, the State military school, the cannon in position on the parade-ground, the citadel, the guard-house, with its martial ceremonies, the frequent parades of militia (the ranks mainly filled by foreign-born citizens), and, especially, the numerous armed police, which is under military discipline, might lead one to imagine that the town was in a state of siege or revolution."[3]

Even in distant Texas the exigencies of frontier life had produced militia groups. The French traveler Maris describes a company of light cavalry, well armed and uniformed and excellently drilled, organized by Prince Carl of Solms-Braunfels at the expense of the Mainzer society to convoy teams from Port Lavaca to New Braunfels. There was also at the outbreak of the Civil War a very strong company of militia at San Antonio composed of Germans who refused, as we shall see, to take the oath to the Confederacy and were disbanded, most of the members fleeing north. After the election of 1860 German *Turnvereine* became sometimes virtually such militia companies, for they added bayonet practice to their other exercises, and drilled secretly.[4]

[1] Oddly enough the best account of these companies which the writer has encountered is given by a German who was honored by an invitation to join the newly organized Charleston Zouaves, a company composed chiefly of Charlestonians whose parents were Germans, but also of some genuine Germans. Even in that group which spoke "more or less German," Conrad and a certain Laitenberger, who had been born in Stuttgart, gravitated together naturally as brothers-in-arms (Waffenbrüder). See Conrad, *Schatten und Lichtblicke*, 25-26, 33. Louis Sherfesse, who came from Germany as a babe, affords an instance of a foreign-born being asked to join the Washington Artillery of Charleston. He became the color-bearer.—*Confederate Veteran*, XII, 232. Another instance of a foreigner in an elite group was Andrew R. Blakely, a well-born Irishman, who became a member of the New Orleans Washington Artillery.—*Ibid.*, X, 178. Occasionally such companies died out, as did the Union Guard, a company composed exclusively of Irish-American citizens at Norfolk, Virginia, which disbanded about a year before the war.— John W. H. Porter, *A Record of Events in Norfolk County, Virginia, from April 19, 1861, to May 10, 1862*, 17. In the case of the Zouaves, South Carolina provided the musket, a knapsack of white leather, a sash, and side arms. Members provided the rest of the uniform, which was decidedly expensive.

[2] Grimball, "Glowing Tribute to the German Fusiliers," *Stories of the Confederacy*, 273. The object of the German companies was not entirely military, for they also wished to preserve German traditions and characteristics.   [3] *Seaboard Slave States*, II, 31.

[4] The uniform of the German company in Texas as described by Maris sounds practical as well as interesting with its gray blouse, long boots, broad-brimmed hat and wild

Interesting as it is to know that there were solid companies of Germans enlisted from several states of the Confederacy, a French legion, a Polish legion, companies of Italians, Spaniards, and Mexicans, a European brigade, entire regiments of Irish, it would be even more interesting if the suggestion contained in the Confederate law of February 16, 1864, encouraging the states to secure from each captain an historical record of his company, had been acted upon by all the states, if the efforts of the states had been fully complied with, and if all those precious historic rolls had been preserved.[5] For a few states, among them North Carolina and Mississippi, the record is gratifyingly complete; for a few, such as Louisiana and Texas, sufficient rolls can be found to reward well the search; but for others a diligent search has yielded such meagre results that one is forced to conclude that the suggestion was not complied with or that the records have been destroyed. It is perhaps logical to suppose that these records perished with the general destruction in Virginia, South Carolina, Tennessee, and Georgia. Unfortunately for the purposes of this study, at the time of enlistment officers were usually indifferent to the birthplace of the recruit; all alike made good cannon fodder. Hence muster rolls record such data only rarely.[6] But enough has been preserved so that, although this chapter cannot pretend to completeness,

---

turkey feathers. "Ils ont une espèce d'uniforme, qui consiste en longues bottes, pantalon gris, blouse grise et chapeau de feutre blanc à larges bords surmonté par quelques plumes de dinde sauvage. Leurs armes sont un long sabre de cavalerie, une paire de pistolets d'arcon et une carabine de fabrique allemande portant l'inscription suivante: Für die Auswanderer in Texas." He said that they drilled "avec une précision et un aplomb admirable."—*Souvenirs d'Amérique*, 90.

For the San Antonio company see Kaufmann, *Die Deutschen im amerikanischen Bürgerkriege*, 154, n. 2. An instance of a *Turnverein* turned into militia may be found in Missouri.—Edward C. Smith, *The Borderland in the Civil War*, 121-122. This company joined the Union army.

[5] This statute was passed February 16, 1864, and directed the secretary of war to grant passports and transportation to any state officers upon application of the governor, if the former were engaged in perfecting the records of its troops; he was also to be granted the right to purchase supplies from the commissary stores on the same terms as regular army officers of similar rank. The central government thus recognized and helped an activity which thus far had been initiated in Alabama alone.

As early as November 5, 1862, Alabama passed a law to preserve the names of all who had died in the war from that state. December 7, 1863, the law was amplified and the office of superintendent of records was created to execute the act. W. H. Fowler was accordingly appointed. By the end of April, 1864, Virginia had a "Recorder," Joseph Jackson, and South Carolina an "agent for the record of names," B. Johnson. Not until shortly before January, 1865, did Louisiana move to create a "Superintendent of Army Records," M. Favrot. North Carolina had also taken steps to preserve her records.

[6] The author found a very few instances where on the informal muster rolls of Texas the place of birth was recorded.

proof can be adduced of the existence of solid companies of foreign-born soldiers and a fair picture of their place in the Confederacy can be presented.[7]

In the beginning the reader must be cautioned to be on his guard against too great reliance upon specious-sounding company names, for the soldier of the Civil War period was fond of seizing on pompous and suggestive titles. Lafayette Guards were many, but by no means composed entirely of Frenchmen; the Pulaski Rifles at Mobile, which might at first seem a Polish company, awakens suspicion when one finds its members bearing perfectly good Anglo-Saxon names with not one Polish-sounding name among them; Emerald Guards did not always designate a group of men who had been born in Ireland.

As must be expected, Alabama with her large number of foreigners in Mobile, and Louisiana with her cosmopolitan population rank high in the number of foreign companies. Texas, although she did produce Mexican and German companies, did not produce them, for reasons which will appear later, in just proportion to the large percentage of foreigners in the state.

Before proceeding to Mobile one notes almost with surprise several companies from Montgomery, a small place then in the heart of Alabama, in which only about five hundred residents might properly be called foreign. The Irish Volunteers existed before the actual outbreak of war; the Alabama Rebels, a group of firemen in the city, composed in part of foreign-born, were organized in May, 1863, and offered their services to the governor for state defense under his proclamation of December 22, 1862. The total roll showed seventy-four names, for seventeen of whom foreign nativity is recorded. Equally

---

[7] The roll was variously named in different states. For instance, in Mississippi it was called Historic Roll, in Alabama and Louisiana, Record. In Texas, where some officers seem to have made some effort to secure data as best they could without official blanks, ruling off and pasting together great sheets of heavy coarse paper, it was occasionally headed Descriptive List and Muster Roll. For North Carolina the record is preserved in the archives at Washington; the author is still in doubt, however, as to whether the data were compiled at the behest of Richmond or had been made of the state's own wisdom at the first enlistment, for the rolls are called Original Muster and Descriptive Roll. Occasionally the Descriptive List and Account of Pay furnish desired data. Some lists of recruits record the place of birth.

The rolls are preserved in different places. In the Confederate Archives in Washington are found a few original records and many copies. In the state archives of Alabama, Mississippi, and Texas are preserved many rolls. In Louisiana a large number are preserved in Memorial Hall by the United Daughters of the Confederacy, though some 165 rolls have never been recovered since they were loaned to Mr. Booth for his compilation of the soldiers of that state.

interesting were the Montgomery Foreign Guards, a home guard company consisting of thirty-five officers and men, representing more nationalities than one would think Montgomery could boast. Most of the officers were British, although the third lieutenant and second sergeant were German and the orderly sergeant, French. The five corporals were all of different nationalities as if to divide honors with a fine view to avoid dissension: Swedish, Prussian, German, Canadian, and British. In the thin ranks a Spaniard rubbed elbows with an Austrian, a Pole with a Scotchman, and a German with a Briton. An effort of the German citizens to form a company of Montgomery Fusiliers failed, as they could not muster up the requisite number for a company. Hence many of them joined the Metropolitan Guards.[8]

Numerous were the Mobile companies composed of foreign-born citizens and residents. One of the first to leave Alabama for Virginia was Company I, Eighth Alabama Regiment, more picturesquely known as the Emerald Guards. In a company roster of 109 men, 104 show the place of birth as Ireland, with fourteen added later hailing from England, Scotland, Germany, and Sweden. Most of the officers had been born in Ireland. Under the leadership of Captain P. Loughry its members had responded promptly to the call of their adopted country. In those opening days of the war, costumes were colorful and picturesque. The men were dressed in dark green and carried a beautiful banner with a Confederate flag on one side, in the center of which was the full-length figure of Washington; on the other side, a harp, encircled with a wreath of shamrocks and the words, "Erin-go-Bragh." Below that was the Irish war cry, "Faugh-a-ballagh!"—Gaelic for "Clear the Way." As this group had been members of a fire company, it was escorted to the station by all the fire companies of Mobile and by a band.[9] The Scotch Guards, organized in 1861 or 1862, mustered in as Company I, Second Alabama, under Captain Garvin Watson, boasted eighty or ninety members, most of them of Scottish birth. The company rendered good service

---

[8] See a call for a meeting of the Irish Volunteers in the Montgomery *Daily Post*, February 20, 1861. For the list of the Alabama Rebels (Firemen) and the Montgomery Foreign Guards, see Beat Rolls, Muster and Descriptive Rolls, Alabama Military Records Division. One roll for the Rebels shows 84 names. The exact number in a company varied, of course, as men were lost by death. For the effort at a Germany company see Montgomery *Daily Post*, April 26, 1861; Montgomery *Daily Advertiser*, April 17, 1861. Its captain, Stephen Schüssler, was the son of a German, so that it is likely that some of its members were of German descent born in Alabama.

[9] Record, Alabama Military Archives; Cumming, *A Journal of Hospital Life*, 37.

at Fort Morgan where they were stationed for the year of their enlistment. At the expiration of that term the members entered various other organizations.[10]

In the Twelfth Alabama Infantry were to be found many foreign-born soldiers. Company A, the Gardes Lafayette, under Captain Heuilly and Lieutenants Jules l'Etondal, Eugene Olivia, and J. B. Concha, were a mixed group, largely French. Company C, the Mobile Independent Rifles, was made up almost wholly of men of German birth, many of whom had not renounced their foreign allegiance, as no less than sixteen secured discharge in 1862 on the ground of foreign citizenship, and twenty deserted, which argues an indifference to the cause more likely in aliens than citizens. Its officers were almost all Germans.

In the Twenty-first Alabama Infantry a group of mixed foreigners, with many Frenchmen, had enrolled under Captain Charles de Vaux as Company H under the name, the French Guards. A second company of French Guards distinguished themselves as the Mobile French Guards. They seem to have been composed in part of the reserves of the Gardes LaFayette and were duly recorded by the captain, Augustus Poitevin, before a justice of the peace on June 27, 1861. The roll still exudes a foreign flavor as the reader notes one Mathieu Franceschi as "Porte Drapeau," Pierre Augustini as "Trésorier," and scans the list of forty-eight men entered as "soldat." There was also a third company of French Guards, organized late in the war, which included some representatives of other nationalities. Also in this regiment was to be found the company of mixed French, Italians, and Spaniards led by the Italian confectioner, Sylvester Festorazzi, bearing the title of Southern State Guards, but enrolled as Company K, Twenty-first Alabama. The Emmett Guards, otherwise known as Company B, Twenty-fourth Alabama, officered by Captain Bernard O'Connell and Lieutenants William J. O'Brien,

[10] In a letter to Thomas M. Owen, John McArthur, writing June 24, 1909, says that the company broke up over the issue of home defense or field service and that members joined other companies. But the writer is inclined to think that Mr. McArthur had, after a half century, become confused, as Miss Cumming, writing at the time, speaks often of the Scotch Guards, of which her brother was a member.—*Op. cit.*, 197. It is probable that there was a Scotch company organized early in the war which broke up at once over the question of being taken to the front, when many thought that they had been organized for home defense only, as McArthur says, especially since he speaks of Robert Gregg as captain, whereas we know that the captain of the Scotch Guards usually referred to was Garvin G. Watson.

James Martin, and R. T. B. Porham, was composed largely of Irish-born citizens enlisted on October 15, 1861, for one year. There only remain to be enumerated the two companies of German Fusiliers, led by Captains John P. Emerich and Jacob Wittman; the Mobile Dragoons, largely an Irish Company; and Stuart's Horse Artillery. The last-named was probably the most famous single company in the Confederate army. Emphatic statements may be found that only one detachment of Pelham's original battery had any foreign flavor and that was made up of a group of French Creoles from Talladega County, Pelham's own home section, and so was called the "French Detachment." It seems impossible, however, to deny the testimony of Von Borcke who knew many of the men personally and who would salute them in English, French, or German when he galloped up to the batteries during a fight or passed them on the march. He states definitely that it was made up of Englishmen, Germans, Spaniards, Frenchmen, and Americans.[11] Probably the greater part of the French element was contributed by Alabama Creoles, but there was also undoubtedly an admixture of foreign adventurers.

For the war various groups of Citizens Guards were mustered into service for local defense or special service under the state act of August 20, 1861, to do duty only in defense of the city of Mobile and only in case of a threatened attack. It was expressly stipulated that they were not liable for service outside of the county (of Mo-

[11] No Record for Company A, 12th Alabama, is to be found in the Alabama Archives, but the names of the members have been printed several times, along with the names of the other foreign companies, in the Mobile newspapers. See the *Mobile News Item* for April 26, 1910, for all the foreign companies. A roll for the Southern Guards is to be found in the Alabama Archives. For Company C, see Record, Alabama Military Archives; Robert E. Park, *Sketch of the Twelfth Alabama Infantry*, 10, 11; *Southern Historical Society Papers*, I, 370 ff. There is a muster roll of the company, a most interesting paper, in the Alabama Archives, presented by Major Proskauer to the survivors of the Mobile Independent Rifles after the war.

The French Guards are particularly confusing as three almost entirely different lists of privates are found, with different officers. The explanation is probably that they were organized at separate periods of the war. The third is clearly of a late period—October 11, 1864. See Muster Rolls, Alabama Military Archives; also the *Mobile News Item*, April 26, 1910; Richmond *Whig*, May 27, 1863.

H. B. McClellan makes the "correction" regarding Stuart's artillery and declares the only foundation to have been that one detachment of the battery consisted largely of Frenchmen, by which he meant, doubtless, Creoles.—*The Life and Campaigns of Major-General J. E. B. Stuart*, 179. Von Borcke's emphatic statement is found in *Memoirs*, II, 13-14, n.

William C. Oates, *War between the Union and the Confederacy and its Lost Opportunities*, 735, says that Company K, Fifteenth Alabama was an Irish company, but the Record shows only eleven born in Ireland in the company of 113. The rest may have been Irish-Americans.

bile), but in case of necessity might be assigned to duty in the fortifications around the city. Until called out for service they were not liable to the rules of war, the orders of military authorities, or the army regulations, and they were not to be called into actual service until the enemy advanced on the city. Here we find the British Guards, Company A, known as British Consular Guards, who had offered their services to the mayor just before May 21, 1863, for duty not inconsistent with their neutrality; Company B in which were enlisted eighty-two British subjects; Company F, first Mobile Volunteers, also British; Company E, Captain John F. Leaven's company of Citizens Guards, consisting of sixty-four aliens of various allegiances; Company K, Captain Eugene Brook's company of mixed Frenchmen, Italians, and Spaniards; and Captain Gueringer's company, drafted from Beat Number 1, officially Company A, Ninety-fifth Alabama Militia, many of whose members show foreign citizenship papers, and all of whom were recruited from or around Mobile. The different companies of the regiment of First Mobile Volunteers under Colonel A. W. Lampkin were called out at various times for guard and police duty in and around the city after November 22, 1863.[12] The purpose of the foreigners in tendering their services may have been to evade conscription. In the Coast Guards, which was organized just after Lincoln's inauguration and served on the Gulf coast for several months until relieved by the cavalry and sent to Fort Gaines to finish a year of service, were to be found many foreign-born; a few aliens were enrolled in the Mobile County Reserves, which was organized as a battalion in the fall of 1864, when all residents able to bear a gun had been organized into companies for home protection; some served in the City Troop of Augustus Brook's cavalry and many in the Fire Battalion. The Home Guards are recorded as armed with pikes. Mention is also made of a group called the Spanish Guards. It is highly probable that the great majority, at least, of this company of eighty-one men from this Gulf port city were Spanish with possibly some sons of Spanish fathers.[13]

[12] See Muster Rolls, Company A, British Guards, Confederate Records, War Department, Companies E, F, and K.

[13] See rolls of Coast Guards; Mobile Company, Butt's Citizen Battalion, Mobile County Reserves; Muster and Descriptive List of Mobile County Reserves; Ninety-fourth Regiment Alabama Militia, Alabama Military Archives. Details of the Coast Guard were secured from a letter in the Alabama Archives by John B. Rabby, a relative of Captain Jacob M. Rabby, to Thomas Owen, dated Sept. 30, 1910. The evidence of the Spanish company seems

So numerous, so picturesque were the Louisiana troops which consisted of foreign-born that wherever they appeared they imparted a dramatic flavor. The Creole troops, descendants of French and Spanish fathers who had come to Louisiana generations before the war, in their diverse uniforms, with their Gallic appearance and temperament, speaking and drilling in French, seemed as foreign as a regiment of Germans on the northern side. That the Hibernian Guards were fond of donning green uniforms has been noted in the description of a Mobile company; several groups of Zouaves were conspicuous with their fantastic dress of baggy red trousers, blue jackets adorned with fanciful embroidery, white gaiters, and Turkish red fez; other groups of native-born troops wore gray and light blue or later a rusty brown. One can readily picture the scene which brought from Russell's facile pen the following account of the camp outside New Orleans: "It is scarcely possible to imagine a more heterogeneous-looking body of men; the variety of uniform, of clothing and of accoutrements were as great as if a specimen squad had been taken from the battalions of the Grand Army of 1812. The general effect of the men and of their habiliments is decidedly French, and there is even a small company of Zouaves. . . ."[14]

The Polish Brigade, the fantastic conception of a Polish revolutionary, never fully materializing and misnamed in addition, had best be first discussed. Major Tochman, who had seen European service in the Polish revolt of 1830, received authorization about May, 1861, to raise two regiments to be called the Polish Brigade, though it was obvious that that element of the population could only be represented in it.[15] The two regiments, when completed by late August, were

conclusive. Every name on the roll sounds Spanish except that of the second sergeant, one G. Smith. The officers were commissioned November 19, to date from November 6.—Descriptive Roll, Spanish Guards, Butt's Mobile County Reserves, Alabama Archives. Furthermore a letter turned up in the Confederate Archives, War Department, which reveals a member of the company stating that he had to get someone to write for him as he knew no English.

[14] *The Civil War in America*, 30. The Gardes d'Orleans, composed of the elite of the Creole population of New Orleans, wore a uniform of blue which resembled that of the Federals so that at times, since that color was not "in the odor of sanctity with Confederate sharpshooters," the men were ordered to turn them wrong side out, thus reminding the spectator of a masquerade ball.—Napier Bartlett, paper on "The Orleans Guard Battalion and Battery" in *Military Record of Louisiana*, 20.

[15] The comment of the New Orleans *Bee* reflects the desire of the southerners to see all nationalities of its population rally to the new flag. "This will be the first of the two Regiments that the gallant Major G. Tochman, of European military celebrity, has

composed of men of all nationalities: the Irish were largely represented; there were French, Germans, and some Americans; and many of them were steamboat hands. It was a labor of great difficulty to bend the spirits of a thousand passionate men, speaking different languages, accustomed to different usages, with no previous taste of discipline, to the discipline of a camp. The first regiment left Camp Pulaski for Richmond as the Fourteenth Louisiana just before August 26, 1861, with its full complement of officers, among whom Colonel Sulakowski was by all odds the most spectacular. He was the very incarnation of military discipline—cruel, despotic, and absolutely merciless. Nothing less could have cowed the wildest and most reckless body of men in the southern army—not barring the Zouaves or Tigers. One experience shows what manner of men they were. At a junction point on one of their trips—Grand Junction, Tennessee, to be exact—they were once detained; the men, tired and ill-tempered from being crowded in the cars, were marched into camp and orders were given to close all grocery and coffeehouses to prevent them from getting liquor. Execution of such an order proved, as often, impossible and liquor flowed freely. When one man was bayoneted in the course of efforts to procure order, the men became infuriated and disarmed the guards. When the officers ran into the hotel and barred the windows on the inside, the mob tried to set the hotel afire. On this terrible scene appeared Colonel Sulakowski, a commanding figure, six feet tall, his stern face livid and eyes flashing with fury. So awe-inspiring was his appearance that the men thought best to obey orders, though not until several shots had been fired, several men killed, and many wounded.[16]

Far more famous throughout the South were the Louisiana Zouaves—a name given to at least three distinct regiments adopting this outlandish dress: the Louisiana Zouaves, commanded successively by the brothers De Coppens; the Avegno Zouaves, more properly the Governor's Guards; and Bob Wheat's battalion, Zouaves by vir-

---

been authorized to raise and form into a body to be called the Polish Brigade which will represent in the ranks of the army of the South a very considerable element of our adopted citizens, who are anxious to fight side by side with Southerners born in the cause of honor and right."—June 3, 1861. See also issue of August 26, when it expressed the hope that Tochman's forces would be brigaded "with-out regard to a title so incorrect and absurd."

[16] See the account of this affair in Bartlett, "Louisiana Troops in the West," *Military Record of Louisiana*, 43-47.

tue of their dress, but more familiarly and distinctively known as "The Tigers."

The Louisiana Zouaves was a regiment composed of seasoned men, Frenchmen and Italians for the most part, and Creoles, many of whom had fought before Sevastopol in the Crimea, in Algiers, and in the Italian wars. Major Gustave de Coppens, a graduate of the Marine School of France, organized the body about the last of January, 1861, drilling them secretly for two months until he was ready to go to Montgomery to offer their services to President Davis. They were recruited from the most lawless and desperate material in New Orleans. It is said that the colonel, with the approval of the mayor, established booths in the different jails, giving criminals the choice of enlisting or serving out their terms. They were a strange mixture of desperate men of many nationalities, guilty of many types of crimes, inspired by no patriotism, but lured by the dream of exercising their chief occupation—freebooting. Their striking costume of red and blue, on which dust and grease were allowed to accumulate, their bronzed complexions, the countenance often terrifying with disfiguring scars which marked former desperate fights, and the catlike, elastic step acquired in the drill served to set their heterogeneous company apart from other soldiers.

They were the first troops to leave Louisiana in response to Beauregard's pressing calls for help after the fall of Fort Donelson, and their departure on February 25, 1862, was rendered dramatic by the address of Dr. Choppin, surgeon general, which closed with the clarion refrain of the "Marseillaise," sending a quiver through every heart, and with the ringing call, "Creoles of Louisiana, on to the work."[17] We can imagine the troops rolling away in their trains, making the woods ring with their wild yells and the roaring chorus of the song of the "Zou-Zou." The illusion of these being foreign troops in very truth was intensified in camp by the reveille of the

[17] The New Orleans *Daily True Delta*, March 24, 1861, tells the story of the secret drilling, the absence of street parades, and of how their commander urged them to say as little as possible about the organization. See also Sallie A. B. Putnam, *Richmond during the War; four years of personal observation*, 36, for a description of their appearance; and *American Annual Cyclopaedia*, 1862, 553, for the story of Choppin's address.

William H. Russell, who had, of course, seen the original Zouaves, thought they looked very like their prototypes, except that they were not so well developed at the back of the head, the heels, and the ankles, and did not wear the turban on the fez. Russell felt himself on several occasions back in the Crimea.—*The Civil War in America*, 83, 109.

Zouaves, the French rolls and clangors, and the drill calls in the French language.

The men were a great problem to their officers and to the unfortunate civilians into whose neighborhood they were injected. As De Leon happily phrases it, "They had the vaguest ideas of *meum* and *teum*," and resorted promptly to a bowie knife or brass buckle to settle little differences in an argument. In cases of insubordination the officers resorted as promptly to a revolver stock or a bullet. Wild are the escapades told of them! The privates once ran away with the train on the way to Montgomery, uncoupling the officers' car. They went through the drinking places in that city, burst into groceries and private homes, and threatened citizens. Serious trouble was only averted by the arrival of their officers.[18] Naturally citizens dreaded their arrival as they dreaded a scourge. "Whenever a Zouave was seen, something was sure to be missed," declared Mrs. Putnam of their arrival in Richmond. The poultry and garden stock around the city were favorite objects of depredation with these thievish soldiers. "It was common with them to walk into saloons and restaurants, order what they wished to eat and drink, and then direct the dismayed proprietor to charge their bill to the government." Always finding means to effect their escape from their barracks at night, "they roamed about the city like a pack of untamed wild-cats, and so clever were they in eluding the vigilance of the police, that few or none of them were brought to justice for the larcenies they committed."[19] It proved necessary to give them a separate encampment where strife became the usual order of the day until they were sent to the peninsula where many fell in battle or deserted. Finally the motley gang was dispersed.

The Avegno Zouaves, six companies of the governor's guards, to form later with four other companies the Thirteenth Louisiana, were an identical battalion in language, usage, and outer appearance with De Coppen's crew, except that they were a more cosmopolitan group and were a set of wild young fellows rather than low vagabonds. There were in the camp at Mandeville, where they were gathered,

[18] Thomas Cooper de Leon, *Four Years in Rebel Capitals: An Inside View of Life in the Southern Confederacy, from Birth to Death,* 71-72; n. 73-74 for the whole story of the theft of the train.

[19] *Op. cit.,* 36. Estvàn tells the same story of thieving.—*War Pictures,* I, 288-290. For evidence that they were chiefly French see Record, U. D. C. Memorial Hall in New Orleans.

Frenchmen, Spaniards, Mexicans, Italians, Germans, Chinese, Irishmen, and indeed persons from every clime. Just after enlistment they were likely to wear, in addition to the Zouave uniform, a black eye, a bandaged head, or a broken nose. Their impudence in remarks concerning new officers was proverbial and was one of their ways of testing the mettle of their superiors.[20] A most amusing story, which illustrates the polyglot character of the group, relates how an Irishman complained of an order just issued by General Twiggs to substitute English for the French language, which had been the language of the drill ground. Said he, "Leftnant, I don't know what oi'll do. You want us to drill in English, and the divil a word I know but French"—an astonishing but true statement so far as military terms were concerned.[21]

The first impression produced by the Avegnos upon General Tracy, who was the unfortunate officer in charge of Camp Moore, the rendezvous where the raw state troops were disciplined and drilled for transference to the Confederate service, was clearly unfavorable. He had just dispatched the Tenth Louisiana, and the appearance of the Thirteenth wrested from him the groan, "Heavens above! When I sent the tenth away I thought I would never see its like again, but these fellows are chips from the same block."[22]

The reader would not wish to lose the picture of the scene at the Jackson railroad station in New Orleans as this regiment was passing through the city on its way from Camp Moore to Camp Chalmette, as described by one of the officers. Nine tenths of the men of the Thirteenth came from the Crescent City so that there were few but had parents, sisters, brothers, wives, children, or at least scores of friends, at the station to greet them that Sunday morning as the train stopped. "Nor was that the worst, for it seemed that every wife, mother or sister in the mob expected her soldier boy to accompany her home for the day. 'Oh, Captain, for the love of God, let Patrick

---

[20] John McGrath relates that on his arrival at Camp Mandeville he heard one fellow remark in a rich brogue, "Oh, Mike, look at that new leftenant! Don't he think he is purty wid the new chicken guts [narrow gold lace, insignia of rank] on his arms. Look at his strut." This brought forth from the victim a blessing in strong language and, incidentally, a respect on the part of the rascal so that he saved McGrath's life later.—"In a Louisiana Regiment," *Southern Historical Society Papers*, XXXI, 104. McGrath is positive that there were bad men among them, but that the good predominated.—*Ibid.*, 106. Two of the companies added to the Zouaves to form the Thirteenth Louisiana were Irish companies.

[21] *Ibid.*   [22] *Ibid.*, 109-110.

go home with me. I have a good dinner cooked for him, and he'll be in camp tonight. Oh, do, Captain, maybe I'll niver see my boy again,' importuned an old Irish mother. 'Impossible, madam, strict orders to keep the men in ranks,' was the reply. 'Mon Dieu, Lieutenant! let my lil' Garçon, Jules, go my 'ouse. His petite sis-ter seek. Come back queek,' said another. 'Impossible, madam.' But Patrick slipped, and Mike followed; Jules dodged through passing crowds, and Pierre also. Of course, in such a crowd of admiring patriots, with the hearts overflowing with patriotism, whiskey was slipped to the boys going off to fight the battles of the country, and the liquor soon began to tell, so that by the time the march began many of the soldiers were decidedly groggy."[23]

One last episode in the career of the Thirteenth Louisiana and we shall turn from them. When they were sent up the Mississippi to Columbus, Kentucky, many of the Union soldiers who streamed down to the river to see the newcomers land had never seen a Zouave before. They took the baggy trousers for petticoats. One loud-voiced Hoosier shouted: "Jeems, come over here and see the Loosyane wimmen soldiers. All o' you'uns come." The remarks of the disgusted Zouaves were unprintable.[24]

The notorious Tigers acquired their name when three detached companies were thrown together into a battalion just before the first battle of Manassas, the strongest of the three giving character and name to all. Recruited on the levee and in the alleys of New Orleans by Major Bob Wheat, an American soldier of fortune who had served in the Crimean War, it was composed of the very lowest of the thugs who infested that city. They were largely Irish and dressed, like the two preceding groups, in the Zouave uniform. They were appropriately named, for tigers they were in human form. "I was actually afraid of them," admits one survivor of the war days, "afraid I would meet them somewhere and that they would do me like they did Tom Lane of my company; knock me down and stamp me half to death."[25] His fear was justified, for two of the number had to be court-martialed and shot for insubordination. They suffered from the usual Irish thirst for whiskey. Being mostly city or river men, they knew

[23] This delightful story is drawn by McGrath and printed in *ibid.*, 113.
[24] *Ibid.*, 120.
[25] W. A. McClendon, *Recollections of War Times by an Old Veteran*, 37.

the ropes and could get it from Richmond. They robbed the dead and, like most Irish, dearly loved a fight—from picking a quarrel with another company to a real battle.[26] When their commander was killed in the Seven Days' Battles around Richmond, the command passed to one White. Ultimately they were assigned to General Richard Taylor who made good use of his Tigers.[27]

All the Zouave companies were noted for hard, reckless fighting. The first group, the Louisiana Zouaves, fatalistic as Arabs, fought as naturally as they breathed and died with seeming carelessness. McGrath declared of his Avegno Zouaves that "none were braver, none more loyal to the cause, and none more easily handled in fight."[28] Along with questionable morals, all accord to the Tigers desperate courage, well suited to the shock of battle but unfitted to the steady pull of a campaign. That very bravery led to the destruction of their organization at Cold Harbor on June 27, 1862. Their method of fighting is described as follows by an Englishman: "Now, the battalion would keep up a lively fire from the woods, creep through the brush, make a sudden charge, upset a cannon or two, and retire. Again, they would maintain a death-like silence until the foe was not more than fifty paces off; then delivering a withering volley, they would dash forward with unearthly yells, and as they drew their knives and rushed to close quarters, the Yankees screamed with horror."[29]

Unlike many other groups of foreigners, the Louisiana Zouaves and the Zouaves of the Thirteenth Louisiana were not commanded by men of the same background as the privates. It is true that there were foreigners among the officers, but as a whole they were of a class entirely above the privates—gentlemen in every sense of the word— by birth and prestige, by education and travel. With a few exceptions they were French Creoles, gay, bright, dashing young soldiers, ready to lay down their lives for Louisiana as their forefathers had in earlier wars.

From the Irishmen in the Tigers one makes an easy transition to

---

[26] Nisbet tells how they came to the camp of the Twenty-first Georgia on the charge that the latter had stolen their whiskey. Although mollified by a drink all around from Captain Nisbet, they departed declaring belligerently, "We are much obliged, sor, but Wheat's Battalion kin clean up the whole dam . . . Twenty-first Georgia any time."—*Four Years on the Firing Line,* 55-56. [27] *Confederate Veteran,* XXXI, 213.
[28] McGrath, *op. cit.,* 106. [29] *Battle-fields of the South,* I, 65.

the Louisiana Irish Regiment and to the Irish Brigade, one of the many commands ordered away from New Orleans with nearly all the fighting forces on February 15, 1862, to defend the city against the impending Federal attack. The latter was organized in New Orleans in May, 1861, camped on the Metarie racecourse some eight days, and then started for Camp Moore, the first company to arrive at that noted place. It contributed much to the construction of that camp, through which every succeeding company passed and in which almost every Louisiana regiment was organized.[30]

As the threat of Federal attack became imminent, efforts to rally Irishmen to the defense were redoubled. "Irishmen desiring to enlist in the service of their adopted country have now an opportunity of doing so in accordance with their wishes—Company A, of the Irish Brigade, Captain Joseph Hanlon commanding, being authorized by the Confederate States government to increase its numbers to 125 men. The government bounty of fifty dollars, and other advantages, will be given. . . . Captain Hanlon especially solicits the attention of his own countrymen to the above call. The Southern Confederacy expects now that every man will do his duty." So read a card in the New Orleans *Commercial Bulletin* of February 24, 1862. This brigade was attached to the Sixth Louisiana commanded by Colonel I. G. Seymour, and was composed of stout, hardy sons of Erin recruited from New Orleans, turbulent in camp and requiring a strong hand, but ready to follow their officers to the death. The official record would seem to indicate but two companies in the Irish Brigade, A and B, which became respectively Company I and Company F of the Sixth Louisiana. It would appear that Captain Hanlon obtained at first only a first lieutenant's commission—for Company I was commanded by Captain S. L. James of Tennessee, a descendant of an Irish father—but he rose, it will be seen, to be lieutenant colonel in the Sixth Louisiana. Every other officer, however, of Company A and all the officers of Company B were Irish-born. While the great bulk of the privates also hailed from Ireland, the zeal for completing the requisite number for a company led enrolling officers to accept a few others. In Company A there were nine others, including four

[30] Henry Rightor, *Standard History of New Orleans, Louisiana*, 155. For the officers of the regiment and the captain of each company see the New Orleans *Bee*, February 17, 1862.

Germans and one Swede; in Company B there were eight non-Irish, though Pat Sweeney of New York and John Tolen from Canada doubtless derived their names from real sons "of the old sod." However John Johnson and George Copeland of England, John Morrison of Scotland, and William St. Clair Smith of Canada were doubtless accepted under the pressure of getting the company to the forts.[31]

The Irish Brigade must have felt at home in the Sixth, for Irishmen were present in the regiment in preponderant numbers. In Company B, 110 in a group of 140 privates were Irish-born; in Company H, 32 of the 90 privates; in Company K, 54 of the 87 privates. In all the companies other foreign nationalities were represented so that the companies in this regiment were usually overwhelmingly foreign. Company B, for instance, had only two native-born members; Company H had rather less than one-third natives; Company K had 72 foreign-born in a total of 109 privates; Company E, however, had just half foreign-born members. Company G, Pemberton's Rangers, presents features of unusual interest. Germans here constituted the predominant strain, as 69 in a company of 89 privates were born in the German states and all but two were born abroad. All the lower noncommissioned officers, sergeants and corporals, were German-born, but the names of the commissioned officers sound American, though nativity is not recorded. Even in this highly mixed company, for members hailed from France, Alsace, Switzerland, England, Pennsylvania, Michigan, Vermont, and Malta, 12 Irishmen were of the number. This company offers corroboration of the statement elsewhere made that distrust of the Germans led to their being thrown among other nationalities. The high number of deserters from this group, 30 privates, among whom Germans numbered 27, and 4 low-ranking officers, surely justified the distrust. Four recruits from the

---

[31] The words legion, battalion, and brigade, when applied to foreign groups, are used loosely. Although Joseph Hanlon was denied the captaincy at this time, he was rewarded by promotion to captain on June 6, 1862.—Record, U. D. C. Memorial Hall, New Orleans. It should be added that the names of the three American-born members of Company A— Dunnivan, Gleason, and Flynn—leave little doubt of their ancestry. The roll of Company B is complete when it is noted that the two men of Louisiana and the one of New York had Irish names.

The need for prompt enlistment is indicated in the following excerpt from the *Daily True Delta* of April 28, 1861: "The roll for Company B, Irish Brigade, will be opened at the Olive Branch Coffee-house, corner of Erato and Tchoupitoulas Streets, tomorrow, Monday, the twenty-ninth instant, at ten o'clock."

island of Malta form a particularly interesting element here.[32] The Sixth Louisiana may assuredly be put down as a foreign regiment.

The brigade was sent to Virginia, went through the memorable campaign in the Shenandoah Valley under Jackson, followed Lee in the Army of Northern Virginia through the Pennsylvania campaign of 1863, and Jubal Early in the Valley campaign from Richmond to Washington. Company A was reduced from 90 to 1 officer and 3 men by March, 1865; Company B from over 100 men to 2. Irishmen were fighters.

The Louisiana Irish Regiment commanded by Colonel P. B. O'Brien seems to have been a distinct organization, a militia body, composed of about eight companies, blessed with the usual suggestive names: Shamrock Guards, O'Brien Light Infantry, Laughlin Light Guards, each officered by Irishmen. The author is forced to the conclusion that it was an ephemeral organization produced by the threat of the attack on New Orleans, for the only record of it which the search has turned up is in the *Bee* of New Orleans for February 17, 1862. The officers do not appear in any of the official records. One wonders that there were enough Irishmen left in this city to form eight companies.

On the Tenth Louisiana under Colonel Waggaman should be bestowed the title of the Cosmopolitan Regiment. While Ireland figured largely in five of the companies, many other nations and bits of the globe were represented—Germany, England, Scotland, Canada, Norway, Austria, Hungary, Russia, Malta, Spain, Mexico, Italy, Cuba, Turkey, Poland, and France. In the most cosmopolitan company in the regiment, Company I, the roll of the various countries is so interesting that it may be permissible to print it. Note that Ireland is quite eclipsed and that no less than fifteen countries are represented.[33]

---

[32] This data is all gathered from the sheets of the Record. The Record in the Confederate Archives, War Department, Washington, does not agree perfectly with the Record in the U. D. C. Memorial Hall at New Orleans. They were probably compiled at slightly different times.

[33] Record, U. D. C. Memorial Hall in New Orleans. The proportion of Irish in the companies should be noted:

Company A, 66 in a total of 88 privates

Company B, Nativity blank or indecipherable. The two names that were decipherable indicated Irish origin

Company C, 74 Irish in a total of 81 privates

Company D, 43 Irish in a total of 71 privates

Austria	5		Louisiana	6
Corsica	1		Martinique	1
England	1		Portugal	4
France	7		Scotland	1
Germany	8		Sicily	1
Greece	5		Spain	2
Ireland	2		Switzerland	1
Italy	26			

The Irish companies from Donaldsonville must have their place in the roll call of Louisiana companies. Russell states at the time of his visit in 1861 that this city had furnished two companies of Irishmen and that a third was in process of formation, though the author cannot determine whether it was finally organized.[34]

The ambitious project of a Garibaldi Legion to be composed exclusively of Italians must have fallen far short of realization, as only one company seems to have completed its organization. As was usual in those early days of glowing hopes, the uniform was a matter of prime importance. If the Italians ever did parade in the uniform prescribed for this legion, they must have presented a striking appearance. It was to be much like that worn by Garibaldi's soldiers: a high-peaked black felt hat, boasting a moderate-sized brim turned up on the left side, with a small bunch of green, black, and white feathers; around the crown a green silk cord terminating behind in a tassel, with a gilt button in front; a round jacket of red woolen cloth; bottle-green pantaloons, cut wide and reaching below the knee, held in place by gaiters or leggings of the same material buttoned on the outside; and a black belt and cartridge box to complete the costume. The sponsors of this legion were unable to complete the two companies in time to turn out for the parade on February 22, as had been hoped, and were not able to get the fine equipment ready, but the first company did complete its organization on the twenty-first of that month by the election of a full complement of Italian-born officers. So far as the author has been able to learn, this remained the only company.[35]

Company G, 7 Irish in a total of 78 privates. Almost as mixed a group as Company I, 55 born elsewhere than in the United States
 Company I, as above
[34] Russell, *Pictures of Southern Life*, 109.
[35] The uniform was described in the *Bee*, January 28, 1861. See also the issue of Feb-

The Twentieth Louisiana Regiment stands in history as a German regiment, though it was far from filled with Teutons. Augustus Reichard, whose personal record is presented in another chapter, raised a battalion of his fellow countrymen. But the general distrust of the loyalty of the Germans precluded the Twentieth from becoming a pure German regiment. To Reichard's six German companies were added four Irish companies to complete the regiment. The New Orleans Jägers were a company which figures in the pages of the history of this war. Joseph Rosengarten in his *The German Soldier in the Wars of the United States* gives a list of eleven German companies of militia in Louisiana in existence in 1861, some of which antedated the war and were similar to the Charleston Zouaves. The Steuben Guards entered the war as Company A in the Twentieth Louisiana Regiment and it is logical to assume that most of the other five companies were drawn from the old militia companies.[36] Leon von Zincken raised a regiment, composed largely of Germans from New Orleans but with a large admixture of French and Irish, which was assigned to General Helm's division. The Florence Guards under Captain Brummenstadt was one of the few German companies raised in the state of Louisiana outside of New Orleans.[37]

In many of the Louisiana companies there were so many Irish that they must have colored the entire company; in others, nationalities were mixed, but the companies were composed largely of foreign-born so that they really constitute foreign companies, whether so designated or not. In the first class would fall certain companies of the First Louisiana: the Emmett Guards, Company D, in which

---

ruary 28, 1861. The future of a Scotch company, to be composed of natives or descendants of Scotland, to be called the Scotch Rifle Guards, enrolled for the defense of the city, is left in doubt.—The *Bee*, April 16, 1861.

[36] Rosengarten's list is as follows:

New Orleans Jägers	Captain Peters
Sharpshooters	Captain Chistern
Fusiliers	Captain Sievers
Lafayette Guards	Captain König
Jefferson Guards	Captain Wollrath
Turner Guards	Captain Bahnecke
Steuben Guards	Captain Burger
Reichard Rifles	Captain Reitmeyer
Louisiana Volunteers	Captain Ruhl
Black Jägers	Captain Robenhorst
Florence Guards	Captain Brummenstadt

Joseph Rosengarten, *The German Soldier in the Wars of the United States*, 188. The Record, U. D. C. Memorial Hall shows that the Steuben Guards became Company A in the Twentieth Louisiana Regiment. [37] Rosengarten, *op. cit.*, 188.

the Irish numbered almost two thirds; and the Montgomery Guards, Company E, with the Irish numbering 101 in 130, or three fourths.[38] Company C, Fifth Louisiana, the Sarsfield Rangers, officers and privates, and Company F, the Irish Volunteer Company in the Seventh Louisiana were almost solidly Irish-born. In the Eighth Louisiana, foreign-born comprised about two thirds of companies B and D, each a very cosmopolitan group; and Company E of the Ninth Louisiana presented an almost solid company of men who had been born abroad, almost four fifths of them in Ireland. Six of the companies of the Fourteenth Louisiana had from one half to over three fourths of their personnel foreigners or adopted citizens with the Irish in the ascendency except in Company I, the Tiger Bayou Rifles, where the Germans won out slightly over the Irish, and in Company C where the Germans equalled them. A slightly higher percentage holds true for two companies of the Fifteenth Louisiana: Company B, the Jefferson Cadets, and Company D, the St. Ceran Rifles, neither of which gives any hint of its foreign complexion in its name. In Company G in the Fifth Louisiana, the Louisiana Swamp Rangers, three fourths of the total number of privates had been born abroad, one third of the whole in Germany.[39]

From outside the metropolis we have a few records of interesting mixed companies. The Shreveport Rebels had eighty in the company, according to one writer, with not more than five American-born. While the record for this company is not forthcoming, the names of its officers suggest the probable country of their origin: Hunsicker, Scheffner, Hyans.[40]

Last but far from least in this procession from Louisiana come the French Legion and the European Brigade. The legion, consisting of five companies, was formed in April, 1861, of French citizens living in New Orleans, exclusively for the defense of the city. It came into existence only with much friction and heartburning over the selection

[38] George H. Hepworth comments on the heterogeneous character of the First Louisiana, noting twenty-seven nationalities in it.—*The Whip, Hoe, and Sword; in the Gulf Department in '63*, 111.

[39] The facts stated above may all be substantiated from the sheets of the Record in the U. D. C. Memorial Hall in New Orleans. The Record for Company E, First Louisiana, is a very interesting sheet, ruled by hand, and bearing a long history of the company at the end—five pages long! Even the Twenty-sixth Louisiana, which was composed largely of Creoles, had some Irish and a few Germans in the regiment.—Winchester H. Hall, *The Story of the Twenty-sixth Louisiana Infantry in the Service of the Confederacy*, 27.

[40] Maude Hearn O'Pry, *Chronicles of Shreveport*, 169.

of officers, the degree of power to be surrendered to the executive council (Conseil d'Administration), and the annexation of two minor groups, a company of Belgians and a company of Swiss citizens. The intrusion of some naturalized citizens, evidently in the effort to avoid regular service, caused some trouble. In September the plan of organization envisaged two battalions of six and five companies, a corps of musicians, a drum major, a number of drummers, and a corps of sappers. Two companies of sharpshooters (Tirailleurs français), retaining a few special rights and a slight difference of uniform, were admitted to the legion.[41] It did not however attain its ambitious dimensions. Thus it added to the streets of New Orleans one more gay uniform, for the French Legion donned that of the French army —red pantaloons and horizon-blue coat. The charm of the unusual appealed as always to the small boy, so that the tradition of the French colors passed into boyhood slang in this southern city and lived long after the war. The cry, "The Red Legs are coming," became a boy's warning to run. This body offered its services to the state and became a part of the First Brigade of Volunteer State Troops, although it should be noted that two of the companies, when confronted with the necessity of entering active service on February 24, 1862, withdrew from the legion under the plea of forming a wholly French Brigade.[42]

In the entire history of the military companies of the Confederacy, nothing is more picturesque than the European Brigade. The threatened movement by the Federal forces to take Forts St. Philip and Jackson early in 1862 drew away from New Orleans so many men that it caused great concern for the safety of the city. By February 21 the formation of the famous European Brigade resulted, largely from unnaturalized Europeans resident in the city, for the preservation of

[41] The story of the organization and friction is found betrayed in the pages of a pamphlet preserved at the Howard Memorial Library recording the minutes of the body.— *Légion française* (Conseil d'Administration), 10, 14. The meetings of the Conseil and of the organization through September and October were obviously stormy ones, as one can discern even through the concise language of the minutes. See also Rightor, *op. cit.*, 153. The body was functioning by November 23, 1861, for there exists a morning report for that date.—Confederate Archives, War Department. For difficulties over the entry of naturalized citizens see the *Bee*, December 5, 1861.

[42] The author owes the bits of detail concerning the costume to General Owens of New Orleans. For the withdrawal of part of the Legion, see the *Bee*, February 24, 1862. It is conspicuous that the brigadier general himself, Paul Juge of the European Brigade, a naturalized citizen, should have applied to the French government to be restored to his former citizenship at the very time that he was holding the command of this legion.— Statement of General Butler to Secretary Seward, October, 1862, in *O. W. R.*, Ser. 3, II, 722.

order and for the defense of the city, and was composed of four regiments of infantry, to which was attached one independent company of infantry and one troop of cavalry. To form the brigade went the regiment of the French Guard under Colonel Paul Juge, Jr., the battalion of six companies of Hansa Guards, the battalion of Italian Guards under Major Della Valle, and Captain Shannon's company of British Guards—this entire regiment under Colonel C. T. Buddecke; the regiment of the French Brigade; and the regiment of the Spanish Legion, Cazadores españoles, under Commandant P. Avendano. The independent company was that of French Veterans under Captain Fournier, and the troop of cavalry bore the name of Orleans Guides. There even exists in the Confederate Archives a roll for an Austrian company under Captain Cognavich. The European Brigade numbered about 4,500 distributed as follows: 2,500 Frenchmen; 800 Spaniards; 500 Italians; 400 Germans, Dutch, and Scandinavians; and 500 Swiss, Belgians, English, Slavonians, and others. Organization was completed by the election of Colonel Paul Juge as brigadier general.[43] Before the excitement had died down three European brigades in all had been formed, one exclusively of Frenchmen, the other two of Spanish, Italian, German, Dutch, Scandinavian, Belgian, and English citizens. The three brigadier generals to command these brigades, whom the *Picayune* tenderly called the "Three Guardsmen of the Crescent City," were selected from among the French residents. Altogether their numbers amounted to around 10,000 men.[44] The first brigade may not properly be regarded as wholly foreign as about 2,000 of the 3,000 members were Creoles, and are therefore not counted in the calculation of 10,000.

The foreign brigades rendered excellent service during the anxious period preceding and during the actual capture of the city by the Federals, from the time when the alarm was sounded—twelve strokes of one of the church bells four times repeated—to the taking over of

[43] The clearest statement of the organization of the brigade, completed on February 21, was found in the *Bee*, February 24, 1862, but see also *New Orleans Commercial Bulletin*, February 25, 1862. The Italian Guards had been formed prior to November 21, 1861, for the *Bee* of that date carries the note that it had been out for drill the preceding evening with full ranks and a field band under Major Della Valle. In the Confederate Archives, United States War Department, may be found the list of members of the Cazadores españoles, consisting of 10 companies and also Company A of Lake Borgne. It is recorded as Fifth Regiment of the European Brigade, giving names and residences. Some records were kept in Spanish. There were eighty-four members in the Lake Borgne company.

[44] See the *Picayune*, March 3, 1862. Twelve thousand foreigners in the brigades is probably an exaggeration unless the Creoles are counted.

the city by General Butler. As there were only 2,800 Confederate troops left in the city, the mayor called on the European brigades and placed the city in their charge to repress thugs and lawless elements. When the frenzied cry arose to burn the city rather than allow it to fall into the hands of the Federals, these brigades repressed the tumult and prevented the destruction of the town. At the request of the mayor and the solicitation of a number of citizens,[45] General Juge, although it had been his intention to retire as soon as the United States authorities took possession, kept the men, weary from four days of ceaseless vigilance, under arms until order was completely restored and fear was no longer entertained for the safety of life and property. The brigades were disbanded on the evening of May 2, their mission, a severe and disagreeable duty, accomplished. The violations of public order were few and slight according to the mayor, thanks to the European brigades.[46]

The British Guard, a group of only fifty or sixty Englishmen, on returning to their armory after the disbanding of the foreign brigades, took action which brought them into sharp conflict with General Butler. In a formal meeting they voted to donate their arms, accoutrements, and uniforms to General Beauregard at Corinth. General Butler, upon learning of this action a few days later, curtly gave those of the company still in the city the choice of accompanying their uniforms within twenty-four hours or of confinement in Fort Jackson, though he modified the order to the extent that members not present at the offending meeting, and thus not violating the law of neutrality, might appear before him with their arms and uniforms. As none could produce his arms or uniform, every member fled from the city except the captain and one other, who were promptly confined in Fort Jackson. When the British consul, George Coppell, protested that the action had been taken with no thought of wrongdoing and enlarged upon the inconvenience of Butler's order, the general replied with the exactness of a lawyer. These people, he declared, "thought

[45] General Juge consented to keep the brigades under arms if the arrangement with General Butler could be concluded. He felt further that Butler was responsible for the preservation of order.—Marion Southwood, *Beauty and Booty*, 21-22, 49. See also the tribute to the brigades given in the New Orleans *Daily Crescent*, May 3, 1862. Mrs. Southwood dedicated her book to the European Brigade.

[46] See also the statement of the value of their services by Mayor J. T. Monroe to the council on April 30, 1862, quoted in Southwood, *op. cit.*, 34. See the *New Orleans Commercial Bulletin* of May 3, 1862, for the address of General Juge, Jr., on the disbandment of the foreign brigades.

it of consequence that Beauregard should have sixty more uniforms and rifles. I think it of the same consequence that he should have sixty more of these faithless men who may fill them if they choose. I intend this order to be strictly enforced." Butler also held it against them that the company had received some form of authorization from the governor of Louisiana, and that a number of them had declared their intention of becoming citizens of the Confederate States. Consul Coppell finally secured for them from the prudent secretary of state, Seward, a recommendation for mercy. They were consequently released after only a few weeks' detention.[47]

In one other Louisiana parish there was a sufficiently large population of French subjects to produce a company of aliens, styling themselves the French Company of St. James, who tendered their services to the governor for active service in the parish of St. James, and pledged themselves to obey the commands of the governor and their superior officers in any active service within the limits of the parish.[48]

In considering foreign companies from Virginia, the student must be constantly on his guard, for writers are likely to claim anyone with a German strain in his ancestry as German. In this study the sturdy yeomen of the Shenandoah Valley who mostly filled the ranks of the Stonewall Brigade must be excluded. Schuricht counts as "entirely" German two Virginia companies in the regular forces and two companies in the Home Guards.[49] But we shall find more. In Richmond several companies were formed. The old German Rifle Company, which had been organized on March 1, 1850, was attached to the First Infantry Regiment as Company K. Another company composed of recent comers, the Marion Rifles, was mustered into service on May 1, 1861, and ordered to the peninsula on the twenty-fourth of that month. Colonel Rains recruited an artillery regiment composed in part of Germans from Richmond.[50] The First Virginia Regiment

[47] James Parton, *General Butler in New Orleans*, 95-96. See also John S. C. Abbott, *The History of the Civil War in America*, II, 296-297. Butler had not included the European Legion in his general order to all rebellious subjects to surrender with their arms, equipment, and munitions of war, as they were not in arms against the United States, but invited them to coöperate with the United States in order to protect life and property.—Southwood, *op. cit.*, 44.

[48] Muster Roll of the French Company of St. James Parish, Louisiana, Confederate Archives, War Department.

[49] Schuricht, *History of the German Element in Virginia*, II, 72-80.

[50] Nisbet, *Four Years on the Firing Line*, 61-62; Schuricht, *op. cit.*, II, 72, 74.

was, except for the German Rifle Company, composed of Irishmen, and was termed accordingly the Irish Battalion. It was attached to Jackson's division from December, 1861, to about December, 1862, when it was made provost guard for the Army of Northern Virginia. While Irishmen usually gave a good account of themselves, as we shall see, this battalion yielded to a panic in an engagement near Orange Courthouse about mid-August, 1862, and broke disgracefully, to the humiliation of the officers.[51] Two of the companies of the Seventeenth Virginia, G and I, formed after the beginning of hostilities, were composed of Irish citizens from Alexandria. Company H of the Eleventh Virginia was a Lynchburg company and had among its recruits many Irishmen.[52] The Nineteenth Virginia Reserved Forces were chiefly composed of foreigners, Germans, Frenchmen, and Italians, recruited for home defense from among the artisans in the government workshops. It would appear that the Italian laborers were organized as a company under Captain Alfred Pico. Very soon these forces were also ordered to the field about Richmond, although the members enjoyed the privilege of following their occupation if not on duty and of drawing rations from the government magazine for their families at government prices, no mean privilege toward the close of the war.[53] No muster roll can be found of another German company, an infirmary or sanitary company, recruited by a Captain John A. Herbig, formerly a lieutenant in the Bavarian army, but the word of a German officer recorded at the time should be accepted as evidence of its existence. The Confederacy, like the Union, had its aliens who found themselves in the front ranks after only a few months in this country.[54]

[51] The Irish Battalion with the Twenty-first, Forty-second, and Forty-eighth Virginia regiments was formed into the second brigade of Jackson's division.—John Hampden Chamberlayne, *Ham Chamberlayne—Virginian: Letters and Papers of an Artillery Officer in the War for Southern Independence, 1861-65*, 90. Day states that several of the commanders of the First Virginia were men of business who had accumulated fortunes in Richmond.—*Down South*, I, 125-126.

[52] George Wise, *History of the Seventeenth Virginia Infantry C.S.A.*, 18; Alexander Hunter, *Johnny Reb and Billy Yank*, 19; William H. Morgan, *Personal Reminiscences of the War of 1861-65*, 39.

[53] Schuricht, *op. cit.*, II, 100-101. Toward the close of the year 1863 Schuricht was obliged to resign as lieutenant of Company D, Fourteenth Virginia Cavalry, on account of his health, but, at the request of Governor Smith, he organized a German company for home defense, which became Company M, Nineteenth Virginia.—*Ibid.*, 78. Company H was the second German company in the Home Guards, which served in the field and guarded the prisons until April 3, 1865. For an episode in Pico's company, see *Daily Richmond Examiner*, February 10, 1864.

[54] Schuricht, *op. cit.*, II, 79; Henry N. Blake, *Three Years in the Army of the Potomac*, 124.

Richmond, as well as New Orleans and Mobile, had its Foreign Legion, composed almost exclusively of British subjects. By August, 1863, the newspapers at the capital were reporting it as thoroughly organized under a Captain Buxton, and drilling three evenings a week at the old market hall.[55]

Even from North Carolina, which boasts of its almost purely Anglo-Saxon population, hail several companies which were constituted of sons from other climes. But one has only to recall that Wilmington had a goodly proportion of foreign-born to understand the raising by Captain Cornehlson from its German citizens of the German Volunteers, a group which became afterwards Company A, Eighteenth North Carolina. Every officer and every enlisted man, 102 in all, except 30, had been born in Germany. Even of these 30, one came from France, one from Denmark, and from Bladen County 26, bearing names which indicate German parentage. On that basis it is perhaps just to call it a German company. This company was early in the field, for it was transferred to the Confederate States service on August 29, 1861.[56] At Wilmington also Edward D. Hall organized in the spring of the first year of the war a company made up chiefly of Irishmen. Stationed first at Fort Caswell, it was later sent to Weldon and attached to the Second North Carolina; after being sent to various points in Virginia, it was returned to North Carolina early in 1862 to be stationed at the fortification on the Cape Fear River.[57] Company H, Fortieth North Carolina, organized at Bald Head, at the mouth of the Cape Fear River in December, 1863, was composed principally of Irishmen.[58] Company D, Seventh North Carolina, the last which needs to be chronicled for the Old North State, was a mixed group of men gathered from Ireland, England, Germany, and Scotland to fight to erect a new state among the nations of the world. Most of the men gave their residence as Charlotte, though some came from Savannah and some from Charleston, but enlistment at Camp Mason caused the company to be recorded as

[55] *Daily Richmond Examiner*, August 5, 1863.
[56] The two other members of the company to be accounted for came from South Carolina and Philadelphia.—Original Muster and Descriptive Roll, Confederate Archives, War Department.
[57] See "Confederate Heroes," James Sprunt's *Chronicles of the Cape Fear River*, 264; Original Muster and Descriptive Roll.
[58] Sprunt, "Confederate Heroes," *Chronicles of the Cape Fear River*, 321. The Original Muster Roll is missing in the Washington Archives.

from Mecklenburg County. Over half of the company was foreign-born. Sprunt speaks of the "Scotch Boys," as if North Carolina could boast a company of that nationality.[59]

It was inevitable that a city, with as large groups of Germans and Irish as Charleston had, should send forth companies comprised in whole or in large part of men born in the German states or in Ireland. The German citizens of Charleston, many of them distinguished leaders of the German population of the United States, and long resident in the state of their adoption, determined to raise and equip a company of young men to represent them in the Confederate army. The leading spirit in the undertaking was Colonel John A. Wagener, whom we shall encounter again as a distinguished officer of the South Carolina Militia. He was enthusiastically supported by his brother and several of his young fellow officers, as well as by the German citizens in general. Officers were selected and authorization secured to recruit a company of infantry, members to be enlisted for five years. The company was christened the German Volunteers. Most generously and patriotically did the Germans of Charleston uniform and equip the company, with the exception of the arms, provided of course by the government. The personnel of the company was drawn partly from the members of the ante-bellum militia companies alluded to early in this chapter, and partly from men who had never been previously connected with a military organization, "but there was not a man in the company who owed allegiance to the Confederate States," according to Captain W. F. Bachman, "every man being a foreigner and unnaturalized." They came from the superior ranks of the German citizens, merchants, lawyers, teachers, clerks, and artisans. They were mustered into service as an infantry company, but were subsequently transferred to the light artillery so that they live in history as Bachman's battery.[60] In those early days of the war, when it was felt that their homes were assailed, the Germans volunteered freely, providing for the Fourth Brigade of the South Carolina Militia the German Riflemen (Schützen) under Captain J.

[59] Original Muster and Descriptive Roll, Confederate Archives, War Department: Sprunt, "Confederate Heroes," *Chronicles of the Cape Fear River*, 303.
[60] Simmons, "Sketch of Bachman's Battery," in Brooks (ed.), *Stories of the Confederacy*, 278; Rosengarten, *op. cit.*, 184-185. Bachman made this striking statement about the nativity of his men in a letter to Captain James Lowndes, dated February 16, 1864.— Bachman's File, Confederate Archives, War Department.

Small; the Palmetto-Schützen under Captain A. Melchers; the Marion Rifles, which had been a volunteer corps of the fire department, under Captain C. B. Sigwald; the German Fusiliers under Captain Schroder, Company C in the Charleston Battalion; and the German Hussars under Captain Theodore Cordes, a cavalry company known as Troop G, Third South Carolina Cavalry. But it was in the artillery that South Carolina Germans won their greatest glory. They provided men for three companies: Light Battery B, Hampton Legion (originally the German Volunteers); Light Battery A, under Captain F. W. Wagener, and Light Battery B under Captain F. Melchers.[61] At the very start the artillery organization was under the command of Major John A. Wagener.

Charleston also furnished Irish companies which did much good service to the cause. The garrison at Fort Sumter consisted of the Charleston Battalion, which was largely Irish, two companies of artillery, and the Old Irish Volunteers, an organization dating back more than seventy years, which was intrusted with the defense of the east wall of the rampart. Though the militia organization was old, there were many members of it who were recent comers. The Meagher Guards[62] changed its name promptly after the fall of Sumter to the Emerald Light Infantry, which was disbanded sometime before January, 1863.[63] As in other states of the Confederacy, aliens volunteered for service on the understanding that they would render service only in the city, though this claim of exemption by aliens was not

[61] Kaufmann, *Die Deutschen im amerikanischen Bürgerkriege*, 567-568; Rosengarten, *op. cit.*, 185-187. The companies A and B were sometimes alluded to as the German Flying Artillery. The German Fusiliers are included, though the writer knows that this group may have been composed of descendants from early German settlers. This organization dates back to the revolution. Company K, Fourteenth South Carolina Volunteers, is omitted as this company was recruited from the Germans long settled in the Dutch Settlement in Edgefield County. This group owned few slaves, did their own work, had little time for education, as the school term ran only from January to planting season, and were but slightly amalgamated with the rest of the population.—John A. Chapman, *History of Edgefield County from the Earliest Settlements to 1897*, 483.

[62] Thomas Francis Meagher, condemned to death for treason for his share in the Irish revolt, was instead banished to Tasmania and escaped to America in 1852. In 1861 at the outbreak of war he organized and led a company of Zouaves, the famous Sixty-ninth of New York. Of course a Confederate company did not wish to adopt the name of an officer fighting on the other side.

[63] Maguire, *The Irish in America*, 567. The Irish Volunteers, which ultimately became two companies, was the first company to volunteer "for the War" and was honored by being ordered to Virginia in July, 1861, where they were soon attached to Gregg's First Regiment of South Carolina Volunteers. Evidence concerning the Emerald Light Infantry appears in the obituary of Patrick Walsh, a member.—*Confederate Veteran*, VII, 177.

allowed by Beauregard. A Captain Moroso headed a company of aliens on this understanding.[64]

From Georgia seem to have come eight companies which may properly be designated as foreign. There was first a German artillery company, the German Volunteers, commanded by Captain John H. Steigen, which constituted one of the companies of the First Volunteer Regiment of Georgia. This company was engaged in the defense of Fort Pulaski. Among the besiegers was the Forty-sixth New York. On quiet evenings the northern soldiers were accustomed to sing German songs on the neighboring island of Tybee. They were answered by the Georgia Germans in the fort with the same melodies. The commander in the fort interpreted the songs as a signal and promptly forbade the singing. This is not the only instance of the foreign soldiers of the two armies joining in singing the songs of their own country. Estvàn tells the following story of a scene in the Kanawha Valley in West Virginia: "And when the firing was over, as night came on, nothing was to be heard but the roaring of the waters, intermingled now and then with snatches of song from some of the German soldiers on either side, which produced a touching effect at such an hour. Ofttimes one of our Germans could be seen leaning on his rifle, listening to the sounds of his mother tongue as they were wafted over from the enemy's camp. At times, one of the sentinels would shout across—'From what part do you come, countryman?' 'I am a Bavarian. From whence art thou?' 'Halt! Who's there?' The dialogue is interrupted by bullets whistling by in all directions." A second unit, an infantry company, came from Atlanta where there was a contingent of Germans. Some of them formed a company which they styled the Steuben Rifles, but the similarity of its name to that of the Stephen Rifles resulted in confusion so that the group chose a new designation, the Steuben Jägers. It elected for its captain Maurice L. Lichtenstadt. A second company of infantry was Company K, German Volunteers from Savannah under the command of Captain C. Werner.[65]

[64] Captain Moroso of Company D, First Charleston Guards, protested against his company's being detailed for service on the steamboats in the harbor as contrary to their agreement and their obligations to their own governments, as the service was outside the city limits.—Milledge L. Bonham, *British Consuls in the Confederacy*, "Columbia University Studies," XLIII, 129-130. For his protest to the chief of staff, see Pickens-Bonham Papers.

[65] Rosengarten, *op. cit.*, 189. The story of the singing was told Kaufmann by a member of the battalion.—*Op. cit.*, 140, n. For the Steuben Rifles see Lucian L. Knight,

The Irish units were at least five: the Irish Volunteers, a company from Augusta, which marched up with other volunteer units upon the command of Governor Brown, after the secession ordinance, to demand the surrender of the Augusta arsenal; two companies calling themselves the Irish Jasper Greens, companies A and B from Savannah; and Frazier's battery composed largely of Irishmen also from Savannah—gallant fellows, but wild and reckless, to be tamed only by a strong hand like that of their Methodist preacher captain, the Reverend Morgan Calloway, a rare combination of Praise-God-Barebones and Sir Philip Sidney. Then there were the Jackson Guards, Company B in the Nineteenth Georgia Infantry, all of whom were Irish, according to the testimony of their captain, John W. Keely.[66]

If the descriptive rolls for Florida could be located, there is no doubt that many companies would be found constituted fully or partly of foreigners. The writer examined few muster rolls without Irish, Italian, or Spanish names. When the nearness of Florida to Cuba is taken into consideration, the names Lopez, Pacetti, Padgetti, Papano, Sanchez, Ursina, and Zimavis, which appear on the muster rolls, take on added significance, especially when one finds the captain of such a company bearing the name Fernandez.

There came south with General Sterling Price's army from Missouri a fine, fully equipped battery of Irishmen. There was also a company in his legion composed entirely of Irish, which had bestowed upon itself the appellation of the Shamrock Guards, numbering more than eighty men and officered by Irishmen. The captain and first lieutenant had been railroad contractors and had good control of these men as a result of this previous business relationship; but the other two lieutenants and the noncommissioned officers, younger, less experienced, and with no former tradition of obedience on which to

History of Fulton County, Georgia, 87. For the scene in the Kanawha Valley see Estvàn, War Pictures, I, 226-227.

[66] For the Irish Volunteers see Charles C. Jones, Historical Sketch of the Chatham Artillery during the Confederate Struggle for Independence, 83-84, and Walter A. Clark, Under the Stars and Bars; or Memoirs of four years service with the Oglethorpes of Augusta, Georgia, 9; for Frazier's battery, Robert Stiles, Four Years under Marse Robert, 229-231.

Stiles declares he never saw any man give himself such a send-off as the Reverend Mr. Calloway did with his battery. A soldier made a lewd comment about a woman. Instantly the clergyman soldier delivered a blow with his sword on the scalp of the offender. When a move was made to go to the aid of his victim, he cried, "Stand fast in ranks! Eyes front." They stood as if carved in stone.—Ibid. For the Jackson Guards, Nineteenth Georgia, see Atlanta Constitution, Sunday Magazine, March 15, 1931, 8.

rely, found themselves frequently in difficulty with the turbulent Shamrocks.[67] In General Bevier's Missouri command there were two Irish regiments, but these probably had some American-born Irishmen in their ranks.

Tennessee presented a surprising array of foreign companies, owing, undoubtedly, to the presence of the river towns, Memphis and Nashville, where there was much opportunity for heavy labor. Captain St. Clair Morgan raised a company of Irish in Nashville; of the mutual devotion of these men and their leader more will appear later. Colonel Frazer recruited in Memphis a company of sturdy, fighting Irishmen which became Company I in the Twenty-first Tennessee, and after the consolidation of that regiment and the Second Tennessee bore the letter B in the consolidated Fifth Confederate Regiment of Infantry. This regiment was composed almost entirely of Irishmen and was suitably assigned to their great Irish compatriot, General Cleburne, and sent after his death to General Smith.[68] Naturally recruiting did not stop with a company; soon one company became a regiment of about seven hundred and fifty Irish Catholics, the Second Tennessee, which resembled in character the fine Sixty-ninth New York. The Tenth Tennessee was also an Irish regiment, a fact heralded to the world by the names adopted by some of its companies —Company H, for instance, which called itself Sons of Erin.[69]

The Germans in Tennessee were no whit behind the Irish in organizing and offering a company to the governor, for by April 27, 1861, the New Orleans *Daily True Delta* reports such a company completed in Nashville. Again we see the existing militia companies enlisting for active service. The old Washington Rifles in Memphis was a local company composed entirely of foreign-born citizens, a part of the old One Hundred and Fifty-fourth Tennessee Militia. In June, 1861, it enrolled for the war and became Company I of the Fifteenth Tennessee.[70]

[67] For one occasion when the Shamrocks got out of hand, see Basil W. Duke, *Reminiscences*, 60. The battery of Missouri Irishmen is mentioned in the *Confederate Veteran*, XXVII, 180.

[68] Julia E. Morgan, *How It Was; four years among the Rebels*, 51. See the *Confederate Veteran*, XXIX, 269, for Captain St. Clair Morgan; for Frazer's company see *ibid.*, V, 505. It was of this regiment that Benjamin la Bree wrote, "composed of as rascally a set of men as ever went unhung."—*Camp Fires of the Confederacy*, 71.

[69] W. G. Stevenson, *Thirteen Months in the Rebel Army*, 41, 68; the *Confederate Veteran*, XXIX, 269; New Orleans *Daily True Delta*, April 30, 1861.

[70] James H. Mathes, *The Old Guard in Gray*, 102.

The most surprising group to find mustering a company, unless one is aware of its presence in the state, is the French with a Garde française in Memphis. A card appeared in the *Memphis Appeal* on January 9, 1862, requesting the members to meet at the home of a M. François Filleul to consider measures concerning the company. The author is unable to determine whether it ever enlisted for the war.[71]

As might be expected, despite their disaffection for the Confederacy, the largest number of foreign groups sent by Texas to the field were Germans. Many of them were of course conscripted, while many of those who did enlist did it under the compulsion of vigilance committees or neighborhood threats, sometimes with the hope of reaching the Union army by way of desertion or capture. It is true that the members of the German militia company of San Antonio refused to take the oath and deemed it wise to flee north. However it is also true that when the call for volunteers was raised in Texas, the *Turnverein* of Houston, one of the best-drilled companies in the state, raised from its members the first volunteer company in that city with E. B. H. Schneider as captain. It was stationed at old South Battery on Galveston Island and was the first to be put under fire on Texas soil.

In 1862 when Waul's Texas Legion was being formed, the great majority of the remaining "Turners" from Houston joined it and became officers in the companies commanded by Otto Nathusius, Robert Voigt, and H. Wickeland, which were almost solid German companies.[72] To the number of forty strong, Germans entered Company F of the Second Texas. There were in the Twenty-fifth Texas many Germans who allowed themselves to be captured by General Osterhaus at Arkansas Post.

There was a German company of Mounted Volunteers in General Tom Green's regiment, technically Company E, Fifth Texas, which

---

[71] The writer found this copied in a pamphlet on *Memphis: Her Great Men*, 77 (author unknown). The card was signed by A. Beer, K. Duruy, E. Filleul, C. Rowland, A. Vioyas.

[72] Moritz Tiling, *History of the German Element in Texas*, 166-167. All in Nathusius' company had been born in Germany except three Swiss, and three born in the states; all in Voigt's company except three Russians, one Dutchman from Holland, and five Texans, who bear such German-sounding names that one naturally concludes that they are of the first generation born in Texas. All of Wickeland's company hailed from Germany with the exception of a few Bohemians (nine) and one Swiss. See Muster Rolls, Archives Division, Texas State Library. Here is one of the rare exceptions where the muster rolls show place of nativity.

had charge of the wagon supply train of Sibley's brigade in its invasion of New Mexico. This supply train had little opportunity to engage in actual combat, but was the one essential in military movements. These Germans shared with the brigade the service of the entire war period. Comal County, of which New Braunfels was the chief city, furnished three companies in addition to Buchel's regiment, one of which was Company E, Fifth Texas, just described, one in Waul's regiment, and one an infantry company which fought in Louisiana. Fredericksburg in Gillespie County sent forth three companies; Fayette County at least one, called the Long Prairie German Company, which may logically be assumed to have been largely German; Colorado County, one company of a hundred Germans; and La Grange County, a mixed company. Galveston provided several companies: the Island City Schützen under a Captain Müller, the Galveston Rangers under Captain Behrmann, and, most important of all, the German Bürgerwehr, apparently a home defense group of two hundred and fifteen men under Captain Theodore Oswald and Major Bruch. Captain Franz van Stucken organized Company E, First Texas Cavalry, in Fredericksburg, enlisting the men for three years or the war, the great majority being Germans. It was fondly hoped that they would be kept near home for defense against the Indians and thus escape service against the Union.[73] Several companies of Germans served in Terry's Texas Rangers, classified officially as Eighth Texas Cavalry: Captain Louis Ströbel's Company F, rather a wild lot who fought among themselves; and many Germans in Company B. Colonel Buchel's regiment of cavalry was organized, as just stated, in the settlement of New Braunfels. As sentiment had been divided there, it is possible that General Taylor's evaluation of Buchel's men is true: "The men had a distinct idea that they were fighting for their adopted country, and their conduct in battle was in marked contrast to that of the Germans whom I had encountered in

[73] Kaufmann, op. cit., 571. One of the companies from Comal County was under Captain G. Hofmann and fought in Sibley's brigade in New Mexico, one under Captain Podawill in Waul's regiment, and an infantry company under Captain J. Boses in Louisiana.—Gilbert G. Benjamin, The Germans in Texas, 110. The three from Fredericksburg were led by Captains E. Krauskopf, Wm. Warmant, and Henry Döring of Cherry Spring— the testimony of Mrs. Crockett Riley of that place. I did not find the muster rolls. The statement concerning a German company from Fayette County is from the roll though place of birth is not given. Every name on the roll is German-sounding, and the names are significant from this partly German county. A photostat of Van Stucken's muster roll is on view in the Fredericksburg Museum.

the Federal army in Virginia."[74] But the record of Company B, Eighth Texas Infantry, also raised in New Braunfels, of which the great majority were Germans—all but twenty-five, and all but fourteen foreign-born—must be placed in sharp contrast with General Taylor's statement. Twenty-seven Germans deserted besides four of other nationalities; no less than twenty-five had been conscripted. Their hearts were not in the cause.[75] In addition the writer came across the muster roll of a troop of local defense in Precinct No. 3, Mason County, enrolled December 9, 1863, bearing only twenty-six names, but every man had been born in Germany. This may be indicative of many home guard groups for which the rolls are missing.[76]

In 1861 the young men of the Irish settlement at San Patricio, Texas, were anxious to enlist and were tormented, like many others, by the fear that the war might be over before they could reach Virginia. They enlisted in Terry's Texas Rangers. The little group of forty-two men, officially known as Company F, First Texas Heavy Artillery, but popularly known as Davis Guards, who covered themselves with immortal glory at Sabine Pass were mostly Texas Irishmen.[77]

A state which had taken thousands of Mexicans into its citizenry some twenty-five years earlier could legitimately expect to recruit some companies of that nationality. The company of which F. J. Parker was captain, Company C of Buchel's Third Texas Cavalry, was a solid Mexican company, except for three men who had been born in Brownsville of parents who were obviously Mexican, and honored eight of the Mexicans with office. At a later period of the war Buchel had three companies of Mexican citizens on the Rio Grande enrolled for four months' service. Another company comes to view, Company C of Terry's Texas Rangers, in which all the officers except a sergeant and a corporal, and all the privates except four had been born in Mexico. By all odds the most surprising aggregation of Confederate soldiers was the regiment headed by Colonel

---

[74] Richard Taylor, *Destruction and Reconstruction*, 158. For the statement on Ströbel's company, see the *True Issue*, La Grange, Texas, issue of October 4, 1861.

[75] A copy of the descriptive roll of this company is found in the Confederate Archives, War Department, taken in 1903 from the original owned by Mr. Lichtenstein of Corpus Christi, Texas.

[76] Muster Roll, Archives, Texas State Library.

[77] For the first group see Miller, *Sixty Years in the Nueces Valley*, 5. For the value of the achievement of the Davis Guard, see below, Chap. XVI.

Santos Benavides which was almost exclusively Mexican. The companies of Captains Refugio Benavides and Christoval Benavides, probably relatives of Colonel Benavides and serving under him, were solidly Mexican, according to the statement of General Bee, and had apparently been recruited at Laredo near the border. Although the place of nativity is not given on the muster roll of the Jeff Davis Home Guards in Precinct No. 2, Refugio County, it is logical to conclude that it was composed almost exclusively of Mexicans. That Captain Rafalo Aldrate was a Mexican is established from other sources; all the officers, except one sergeant, and all the forty-six privates, except four, bear Mexican names. Most of the native whites had already been drained off to the army so that there were few males left except the unnaturalized or transient Mexicans. One scarcely expects that a muster roll can be amusing, but the reader will probably smile over the one in the Texas State Archives which begins, "Who desire to enter into the Cervice of the State of Texas for 6 months from time mustered for Cervice." The name of Clemente Bustilla heads the list of twelve officers and then come Mexican names for eighty-one privates, ranging from eighteen to forty-nine years in age. There is entered after each name a full description of the recruit, even to the state of his whiskers, designated as "scattered," "thick," "thin," or "none." Bustilla testifies at the end, "I certify foregoing of my co. of infantry or Cavalry determine, tendered this day for the middle division of the State of San Antonio. March 5/61." The writer scarcely expects to be challenged for putting down this company as Mexican, though she cannot prove it.

General Bee also had a plan for a sort of home guard of Mexican citizens, which he called a police force. He requested the commanding general to sanction the organization of two companies of Mexicans living on the Rio Grande River to serve during the war. They were to enforce police patrol and to enable him to send back three companies of cavalry stationed at Ringgold Barracks. Whether he secured the approval of his superior officer and actually created the home guard of Mexican citizens does not appear.

One encounters small commands filled with Mexicans, such as the rancher Williams speaks of, small groups of perhaps thirty men, drafted from various companies and sent on scouting duty. He also speaks of a Mexican company under a Captain Pattina. At the time of General Banks's plan to capture Brownsville that city was in such a turmoil that a home guard was felt necessary to assure order. With the help of the Americans and some Mexicans from Matamoros, a Mexican refugee in Brownsville by the name of General José Maria Cobos carried out the plan of organizing a company for local defense.[78]

It is with real surprise that the researcher discovers that there were enough Poles in the vicinity of the Texan village of Panna Maria to muster a Polish company, commanded by Captain Joseph Kyrisk, which assembled with three other companies on the Cibolo River. The Polanders were regarded by the drillmaster, an old regular from the United States army, as the best-drilled of the battalion, a fact which he attributed to their military discipline in the old country and to their habit of obeying orders.

There were, naturally, mixed companies here as elsewhere, which were foreign, although not made up of men of one nationality. The Third Texas Regiment, Buchel's command, a mixed group if ever there was one, was, Williams tells us, a fine body though made up of American, Irish, Dutch, and Mexican companies.[79] Captain Buquor's company and Captain Marmion's artillery company in Buchel's command were composed partly of Mexicans but chiefly of Europeans. Company A, Captain E. G. Bolling's Company, of the Waul Legion, was such a cosmopolitan group, with Germans in the ascendancy, but with Irish, French, Swiss, Italians, Scotch, Mexicans, and Swedes represented by one or more members. Captain Redewood's Company, Rio Grande Regiment, was another, except that here the Irish outnumbered other nationalities. Captain James Morgan's company in

[78] Several muster rolls in the Division of Archives, Texas State Library, show the place of nativity. The author handled several other rolls there and in Washington, which recorded what were undoubtedly Mexican companies, but did not show the place of birth. See R. H. Williams, *With the Border Ruffians*, 289-290, 343. For the story of the Brownsville Home Guard, the author is indebted to the master's thesis by Jovita Gonzales, "Social Life in Cameron, Star and Zapata Counties." Cobos later crossed into Mexico with the men he had enlisted at Brownsville to aid Maximilian and was killed by Cortina.

For the companies in Buchel's command see letter of Buchel to Major S. B. Davis, Dec. 5, 1861, *O. W. R.*, Ser. 1, IV, 152; for 1863, *ibid.*, XV, 1057; for General Bee's statement on Benavides' command, *ibid.*, XXXIV, Pt. 1,648. The data for Company C, Eighth Texas, Terry's Rangers, were found in a Descriptive List and Account of Pay, Confederate Archives, War Department. The Texas legislature provided for a regiment of Mexican lancers, but the scheme never materialized.—Lubbock's *Memoirs*, 380.

[79] Williams, *op. cit.*, 282-283; for the Polish company see Edward Dworaczyk, *The First Polish Colonies of America in Texas*, 26-27.

the Coast Defense was still another, where the heterogeneity extended to the officers.[80]

Finally the Confederacy secured another group of foreign soldiers by what might be termed immigration, enlisted from among the United States prisoners of war. There were two such foreign battalions—Tucker's regiment and Brooke's Foreign Battalion—both inelegantly referred to as Galvanized Yankees. Sometime toward the latter part of 1864 the Richmond authorities conceived the idea of enlisting in the Confederate ranks foreigners among the Federal prisoners, assuming that their convictions were little engaged. It is difficult to state authoritatively where the idea originated but it is suitable in this study to record the fact that credit for the idea has been given by some to Conrad Nutzel, who had come from Germany to the South in 1853 and had cast in his fortunes with the Fifteenth Tennessee. After the battle of Corinth he was mentioned for "gallant and meritorious service" and was assigned to the staff of Colonel Ben Hill, provost marshal at that time at Dalton, Georgia. It is claimed that he conceived the idea of converting to the southern cause six hundred Yankee prisoners, all of whom were Germans and unable to speak English.[81] Already on September 24, 1864, a commission was issued to Major Garnett Andrews to establish such a battalion of infantry from the prisoners at Millen, Andersonville, and other points in Georgia. Irish and French were to be preferred, few, if any, Germans accepted, and natives of the United States entirely eschewed. Enlistment was to be for a three-year term, and the battalion to be assigned for service elsewhere than in the armies of Tennessee and Northern Virginia. The problem of the method of selection of officers which was troubling General Lee was settled by stipulating expressly their appointment by the president.[82]

---

[80] See the Muster Rolls, Archives, Texas State Library; Kaufmann, *op. cit.*, 568. For the companies in Buchel's command, see *O. W. R.*, Ser. 1, IV, 153.

[81] J. N. Rainey, secretary of the Confederate Historical Association of Memphis, gives Nutzel credit.—*Confederate Veteran*, XIII, 87. It would appear that after the fall of Atlanta he was ordered to recruit from the prisons and got a regiment of 600. He made up a company of 100, nearly all Germans, who spoke no English.—Mathes, *op. cit.*, 172.

[82] On November 14, 1864, General Lee wrote Seddon on this subject and quoted General J. G. Martin, who had been on duty at Salisbury, as believing that 2,000-3,000 foreign prisoners of war could be recruited there. It is clear that he was commenting on a proposition already made and was trying to influence the war department not to allow the companies to elect their own officers, but to have them appointed by the president.— *O. W. R.*, Ser. 4, III, 822-823.

For the order to Major Andrews see Letters and Telegrams Sent, A and C. Co., Chap.

The First Foreign Battalion of ten companies was organized at Richmond on October 16, under Julius Tucker as lieutenant colonel, whence the name, Tucker's regiment. On November 10 authority was extended to include prisoners confined in any military prison. Somewhat later a second battalion was enrolled, known from its commander as Brooke's Foreign Battalion. It is quite explicable why Irish were preferred, in view of their well-known fighting qualities, and equally intelligible why Germans, in view of the problem they presented in Texas, were not desired, but it is difficult to see why so large a number of northern Americans were allowed to enlist under the pretense of being Englishmen. The result, a mutiny in Brooke's Foreign Battalion which might have been foretold, made its appearance at the siege of Savannah. For several miles around the city crossways had been constructed over the flooded fields for travel and trade between the country and city. After the Federal attempt to enter Savannah over these crossways had been repulsed by the Confederate artillery, the Federals entered into a conspiracy with some of the "galvanized" troops in the Confederate camp, led by the orderly sergeants of the seven companies of the Irish battalion. A general mutiny was to be executed late that night, on December 17, 1864. The guns were to be spiked, the officers to be bucked and gagged and carried off, the pickets to be forced and carried over to the foe. But the plot was betrayed in some way to the Confederate officers, who suddenly surrounded the Irish camp, disarmed the men, tried the ringleaders by drumhead court-martial and executed them, and put the other men of the battalion under guard during the rest of the siege.[83]

More successful were Nutzel's efforts at gaining adherents to the southern arms. Commanded by Colonel J. G. O'Neal, his detachment was sent to Mobile and ordered to follow Hood's army into

I, Vol. XLIII, August 29-December 31, 1864, p. 66, Confederate Archives, War Department. See Solon Hyde, *A Captive of War*, 268-270, for the story of the futile effort of Colonel O'Neal, who commanded an Irish brigade in the Confederate army, to win recruits for his brigade from a group of Irish prisoners in a hospital. He got one recruit, an American, who used it as a forlorn hope to reach his regiment.

[83] The details vary slightly in the several accounts of this affair. Chester C. Jones says that after a sergeant and fifteen men had successfully made their escape, two other privates of the same command were captured in the attempt to desert to the foe.—*The Siege of Savannah*, 137-138. Robert D. Chapman says that some local soldiers in the Irish camp, true to the cause, reported their designs in full.—*A Georgia Soldier in the Civil War, 1861-1865*, 190.

Tennessee. At Egypt Station, Nutzel's company of Germans was thrown out on picket duty and made a gallant stand behind a railroad embankment for several hours against Grierson's scouting force until forced into a small stockade where they finally surrendered after their ammunition was exhausted. They were ultimately sent to Johnson's Island as prisoners of war.[84]

[84] Mathes, *op. cit.*, 172-173. It should be noted that the Confederacy was not alone in recruiting from the foe. Davis, a lawyer in Texas, who was a strong Unionist, had had to leave when secession occurred, and went North. He was given a commission as colonel to raise a regiment for Federal service out of the disaffected elements in Southwest Texas and from the deserters and renegades who had crossed into Mexico.—Williams, *op. cit.*, 292. The Union also recruited from among its prisoners of war.—Lonn, *Desertion during the Civil War*, 97 ff.

V

FOREIGN-BORN CITIZENS AS OFFICERS*

The resident foreigner, as the foreign-born citizen, was inclined to complain that the Confederate authorities were unwilling to recognize military ability and bravery with suitable rank, if that ability and courage were found in a person who had not been born under the American flag. Exactly the same complaint was brought against the Federal authorities by the foreign-born serving in the Union army. Both Richmond and Washington were regarded as wishing to reserve commissioned offices, especially those of high rank, for the native-born.

Occasionally that prejudice against the foreigner was combined with other prejudices. One of the most conspicuous illustrations on record was the determination of Colonel Pickens to prevent the promotion of Captain Adolph Proskauer, a German Jew of Alabama. Proskauer had had an excellent education under the strict Prussian discipline, presented a handsome appearance, and was possibly the best-dressed man in the regiment. He applied for the position of major when a vacancy occurred in his regiment. Colonel Pickens preferred a certain Captain John McNeely for the post, although Proskauer was senior captain. To further his personal wishes, the colonel secured an examining court to which, it was rumored in camp, he had expressed the hope of an examination sufficiently rigid to fail the candidate. Unusual interest was manifested by the officers in the camp. After an all-day examination, one of the examiners reported to Colonel Pickens that the committee had done all they could to defeat Captain Proskauer, but that in a most searching examination on all phases of drill—squad, company, regimental, brigade, drill, and drill by echelon—the candidate had answered promptly and accurately every question. The examining officer added, "He knows

---

* The determination of the exact rank of the various officers and of their status as naturalized citizens or aliens has been one of the most baffling parts of the work connected with this study. In general the official status recorded in the war department has been accepted, except where there is indisputable evidence to the contrary. Where an alien is not officially recorded, rank has been assigned according to the best evidence available.

more about tactics than any of the Examining Committee, and we were forced to recommend his promotion."[1]

Accompanying prejudice was occasionally distrust, as in the case of Colonel Augustus Reichard of New Orleans. At the outbreak of war he put through the union of the German militia companies into a regiment, cherishing, it is said, the hope of ultimately attaining the rank of general. The authorities, however, distrusted the Germans on account of the occurrences in Missouri and their well-known attitude toward slavery. It is true that Reichard was suffered to become colonel of the Twentieth Louisiana when the German battalion was united with four Irish companies into a regiment, but he never achieved higher rank.[2]

A mere handful of officers who had attained the status of citizenship by naturalization reached the higher ranking positions. There was only one honored as major general; a very few attained the rank of brigadier general; there was a corporal's guard of colonels and majors. Naturally there was a much larger number of captains, and still more lieutenants. When it came to sergeants and corporals, noncommissioned officers needed for the disagreeable tasks of whipping the raw recruits into shape and of attending to the police duties of camp, foreign-born were numerous. It is relatively seldom that one finds any one but an American-born serving as officer in a wholly American company, though there are a very few exceptions in favor of a Scotchman or an Englishman. Company B, Eighteenth North Carolina, the Bladen Light Infantry, affords such an illustration, as Robert Tait, its captain, hailed from Scotland, and Company H, Fifty-second North Carolina, had a Swedish-born captain, Eric Erson by name. Usually foreign-born officers were put in charge of a full company of their fellow countrymen, though there are numerous instances of foreign companies having native officers over them, the commanders of regiments usually being Americans.[3] Occasionally the

---

[1] Park, *Sketch of the Twelfth Alabama Infantry*, 10.

[2] Kaufmann, *Die Deutschen im amerikanischen Bürgerkriege*, 569-570.

[3] As evidence of the accuracy of the above generalizations the following statistics may be adduced:

The Tenth Alabama had no foreign-born officers in any of its companies.

The Thirteenth Alabama had no foreign-born officers in any of its companies.

The Fourteenth Alabama had no foreign-born officers on the field and staff. There is no record of nativity for the companies.

The Fifteenth Alabama had a fourth corporal in Company H.

The Nineteenth Alabama had no foreign-born officers.

brief statement added by an old veteran to his record for some compilation of Confederate data indicated recognition of the existence of such prejudices against the foreign-born. Robert McNab, a Scotchman, reports, "I had three calls for promotion, but being of foreign birth, was refused."[4] Repeatedly occurs the terse phrase, "Never promoted."[5]

Probably it should be placed to the credit of the Confederacy, as evidence of willingness to reward merit, that one of her small group of six major generals was a naturalized citizen. Patrick Ronayne Cleburne was an Irishman by the accident of birth, but a Confederate soldier by choice. He was born in Cork County, Ireland, but had come to America in 1853 and was practicing law at Helena, Arkansas, at the outbreak of the war. Organizing a company,[6] the Yell Rifles, of which he naturally became captain, he found himself part of the First, afterwards the Fifteenth, Arkansas Regiment, of which he was at once elected colonel. Serving in Missouri under General Hardee, he accompanied that general to Bowling Green, Kentucky, where he was soon assigned to the command of a brigade, receiving his commission as brigadier general on March 4, 1862. At Shiloh he won great distinction and during the reorganization of the army at Tupelo brought his brigade to a very high state of efficiency, as he possessed the great gift of ability to enforce discipline without forfeiting the esteem of his troops.[7] At the battle of Richmond, by his handling of a division he aided materially, as will be shown later, in the splendid victory over General Nelson and proved that his abilities were not overrated. This was followed a few weeks later at Perryville by his usual success, despite a painful wound from the battle at Richmond.

Company K, Seventh Louisiana, the Livingston Rifles, had no foreign-born officers.

Many North Carolina companies could be cited.—Record, Alabama Military Archives; Record, U. D. C. Memorial Hall, New Orleans; Muster and Descriptive Rolls of North Carolina, Confederate Archives, War Department.

[4] Yeary, *Reminiscences of the Boys in Gray*, 504.

[5] *Ibid.*, 44, 73, 116, 121, 218, 327, 560, 666.

[6] There is some confusion as to this first company. Several authorities state that Cleburne "raised" a company; others that he enlisted as a private and was elected captain of the company, when its captain, Ed. Cawly, was injured. This may have been the company of several hundred men who in February, 1861, moved on Little Rock and captured the arsenal there. In any case Cleburne was active in the organization of this company or of another in April. See Nash, *Biographical Sketches of Gen. Pat Cleburne and Gen. T. C. Hindman*, 109. See also G. W. Gordon, "General P. R. Cleburne," *Southern Historical Society Papers*, XVIII, 261-271; *Confederate Veteran*, XIX, 212; Irving A. Buck, *Cleburne and His Command*, 25.

[7] Highly amusing stories are told of him as drill master. See below.

Major General Patrick Ronayne Cleburne. From an oil painting in the possession of the Arkansas History Commission, Little Rock, Ark., by courtesy of Mr. Dallas Herndon

This triumph led to his commission as major general on December 12, 1862, at the remarkably young age of thirty-six. It should be recalled that Cleburne's experience had much to do with this meteoric rise. He had had a fine home background, for he came of a good family, had received a sound education, and had enlisted in the Forty-first Regiment of Infantry in the British army in his humiliation at failure to pass the examinations at Trinity College, Dublin, where he was being educated for the medical profession. He thus brought to the Confederate army the knowledge of military tactics acquired by three years of service and had, furthermore, through his cutting himself off from his family, learned to depend upon himself.[8]

His brilliant record through the remainder of his service is well known and can be summarized in a few words. A few weeks after his promotion to a major-generalship he was conspicuous in the brilliant charge at Murfreesboro which routed the right wing of the Union army; at Chickamauga he and the men he had trained carried a position which had been assailed by others without success; at Missionary Ridge on November 30, 1863, he defeated Sherman at the tunnel, capturing hundreds of prisoners; at Ringgold Gap he guarded the rear of the army as Bragg retreated, saving the artillery and wagon train. In the carnage at Franklin on November 30, 1864, this Irish Confederate gave his last order, falling within twenty paces of the Federal army. The death of the Stonewall Jackson of the West, an apposite expression often applied to Cleburne, cast a deep gloom over the entire Confederacy. Eight million people mourned his loss and felt there was none to take his place.[9]

In some respects Cleburne was the typical Irishman and brought to his army Irish characteristics. He had accent enough to betray his nativity. This accent, perceptible in ordinary conversation, grew in times of excitement into a strongly marked brogue. He used to refer to Ireland as the "old country," always in the loving accents of a son

[8] It is regarded as no part of the task of this study to supply full details of the lives of the persons who move through its pages, as this is not a biographical encyclopedia. Such facts, however, as are illuminating to the understanding of appointments will be briefly included. Cleburne was a descendant of Richard Clyborne of Westmoreland and his mother was of the lineage of Maurice Ronayne. His father was a physician of much eminence.—Gordon, *op. cit.*, 262.

[9] In addition to the references above on Cleburne, the reader is referred to Hardee, "Biographical Sketch of Major-General Patrick R. Cleburne," *Southern Historical Society Papers*, XXXI, 151; Evans, *Confederate Military History*, X, 396-398; *The South in the Building of the Nation*, XI, 213-214; *Confederate Veteran*, XVII, 475, XXXVI, 174; David Y. Thomas, *Arkansas in War and Reconstruction*, 341-347; and Buck, *op. cit.*

referring to his mother. He had a strain of Irish wit, rather grim, owing no doubt to the stern influences which had molded his life. He was also the consummate Irish orator on occasion. His address to the southern soldiers before the battle of Tupelo was a great speech, declared by one hearer the most stirring patriotic speech he had ever heard. He explained the purpose of the rear move, the necessity of the forced march, stating the consequences of both success and failure. He drew a picture of Ireland in its humbled condition, declaring that the South would be in a worse state if the Confederacy failed, provided the spirit of hate and revenge lived on in the North. As a finale, he turned his face upwards, and with all the fervor of his Celtic emotions exclaimed, "If this cause which is so dear to my heart is doomed to fail, I pray heaven may let me fall with it, while my face is turned to the enemy and my arm battling for that which I know to be right."[10] Stories of his warmheartedness and impulsiveness are many.[11] In this very impulsiveness, which prompted his impetuous charges, lay the key to many of his successes. In one respect he was not a typical Irishman, for he had been baptized and educated in the Episcopal faith.

The most distinguished of the brigadiers who had begun life abroad was possibly General Xavier Blanchard Debray. With qualifications which could not be denied, embracing excellent military training and cultural advantages, it is not strange that he attained this high rank. Born in France about 1818 of a fairly prominent family, he was graduated with honors from the noted military school, St. Cyr. A brief period of diplomatic service for the Second Empire was abruptly terminated in 1852, when the converted Republican felt com-

---

[10] John L. McKinnon in *History of Walton County, Fla.*, 300, tells the story of this speech. One of his officers gives the following account of his accent: "His accent would at any time have betrayed his nativity, but when giving emphatic orders on the field, the harsh rolling of his R's was sometimes startling. Not one of his soldiers but can recall the peculiar intonation given to his command, 'Fore-ward Mar-r-r-ch!' the first word being syllabled with remarkable distinctness, while the latter was given with the broadest brogue imaginable. Nor can we forget his truly Irish rendering of (bar-r-rel) of the word 'barrel' when lecturing his class of officers on the rifle, its parts, uses, etc."—"A Sketch of Major-General P. R. Cleburne," *The Land We Love*, II, 460.

[11] The story of his dying in his stocking-feet because a few minutes before he fell he had drawn off his own boots for one of his Irish boys from Little Rock who was tramping barefooted over the frozen furrows of the cornfield has been denied.—Irvin S. Cobb, "The Lost Irish Tribes in the South," *Tennessee Historical Magazine*, Ser. 2, I, 122. See Duke, *Reminiscences*, 69, for his warm-heartedness and devotion to his friends. In Kentucky, when he found that his teamster's rear guard had, under pretense of illness, fallen behind to steal eggs and chickens, Cleburne paid for them out of his own pocket.—Thomas, *op. cit.*, 342-343.

pelled to resign from the imperial service. He came to the United States and located in Texas, first in San Antonio and then in Austin. His standing in his adopted city was clearly indicated in the mayoralty contest in 1859 when he was defeated by only one vote. At the outbreak of the war he raised a regiment of cavalry in Bexar and the adjoining counties and served throughout the war in Louisiana, Arkansas, and Texas, rising to the second highest rank in the army accorded a foreign-born officer.[12]

Two leaders among the Germans achieved distinguished position —John A. Wagener of Charleston and Robert Bechem of Texas. The former, though born in Bremen, had been identified with the South Carolina capital for some years before the war. Opposed to secession, indeed a Unionist at heart, he still felt that he could not avoid military service. He began his Confederate military career as a major of an artillery company, made up chiefly of Germans and descendants of Germans. He attained his rank and title of brigadier general as commander of the state troops within the city of Charleston, in which his two sons, the younger only fifteen years old, fought under him. It speaks well for the spirit of these last defenders of the "cradle of the Confederacy" that half of the garrison was killed or wounded before it surrendered to General Schimmelfennig. One is struck anew with the cleavage within the ranks of the foreign-born citizens when one notes that a German furled over Fort Sumter the Stars and Bars even as it was a German who again raised the Stars and Stripes. Wagener's best work was the defenses of Fort Walker, which he built in November, 1861.[13]

A second German likewise attained his brigadiership in state

[12] In San Antonio he had, as noted earlier, published a paper in Spanish for several years before the war. For twenty years after the war he served as translator of Spanish in the general land office. He did not die until 1895.—Austin *Evening News*, January 7, 1895. During the war he brought a regiment, impeded by a long wagon train, from a point 80 miles beyond Houston, 250 miles in less than 14 days.—Xavier B. Debray, "A Sketch of Debray's Twenty-Sixth Regiment of Texas Cavalry," *Southern Historical Society Papers*, XIII, 157.

[13] Kaufmann, *op. cit.*, 571-572. Wagener had had a military career before the war. In 1835, two years after his arrival from Germany, he became a member of the German Fusiliers. As his qualities of leadership were recognized, he rose rapidly in rank until in 1847 he became captain of the German Artillery, founded by a younger brother, but nursed by John until by 1859 it was large enough to be divided into two companies. Governor William H. Gist made him major of the First Artillery Regiment of South Carolina. It is worthy of note that another brother, Frederick Wilhelm Wagener, who had arrived from the homeland in 1848, rose to the rank of captain.—Wagener, "John Andreas Wagener," Chap. V. See also H. A. Rattermann, *General Johann Andreas Wagener, Eine biographische Skizze*, 20-21.

military service and not as rank accorded in the regular Confederate army. It is interesting to notice that when Robert Bechem of New Braunfels was first asked whether he would consider the headship of the Thirty-first Texas State Troops and formally urged to stand for election, he declined to do so, merely stating that he could not accept the post. Later he evidently thought better of his refusal, for he appears in the official records, both state and national, as brigadier general of that same body of troops.[14]

A Scotchman, Peter Alexander Selkirk McGlashan, rose all the way from private to brigadier general. His family emigrated from Edinburgh in 1848 when he was seventeen years old and settled in Savannah, Georgia. The war found him residing in Thomasville, Georgia; by August, 1861, he had volunteered in the Twenty-ninth Georgia and was serving on the coast. In March of the next year he was transferred to Company E of the newly organized Fiftieth Georgia and elected first lieutenant. This regiment was soon ordered from the Georgia coast to Virginia, which it reached in time to participate in the closing scenes of the Seven Days' Battles. He fought through the war in the Army of Northern Virginia until his capture on April 5, 1865. To his commission as brigadier general attaches a melancholy interest as the last commission signed by the president before the evacuation of Richmond. To McGlashan it probably brought scant comfort, for he was a prisoner at the time on Johnson's Island, from which point he was released only late in August after the close of the war.[15] To his family, for his father was a veteran of Waterloo, and to his buccaneering experience with Walker in Nicaragua he may have owed some part of his promotions.

Collett Leventhorpe was one of those rare Englishmen who could bring themselves to renounce their British citizenship. If he had not become an adopted son of North Carolina and a citizen of the United States, it is doubtful if even his commission and valuable experience in the British army would have made him a brigadier. Descended from a knightly family of Yorkshire—and that probably was no disadvantage in the southern states—he had been made an ensign at the age of seventeen in the Fourteenth Regiment of Foot by William IV.

[14] Bechem's letter of refusal is found in the valuable Pfeuffer collection of Texicana. He merely replies that he cannot accept the post.

[15] Evans, *Confederate Military History*, VI, 460-461; Louisville *Evening Post*, May 30, 1900.

After three years' service in Ireland, several more in the West Indies, and a year in Canada, he disposed of his captain's commission in 1842 and settled ultimately in North Carolina. He entered the war from his adopted state as colonel of the Thirty-fourth Regiment in November, 1861, and brought his regiment to so fine a state of discipline that by December he was given command of a brigade. In those early days of the war the Confederacy could not afford to neglect availing herself of the services of trained officers. A brilliant victory at White Hall in January, 1863, forwarded his interests, but capture on the retreat from Gettysburg lodged him in prison for nine months so that he was promoted to the rank of brigadier only in February of the closing year of the war. He served then with General Joseph Johnston until the surrender. The official record indicates that he took the unusual step of declining the appointment, but he is entitled to the rank of general by virtue of the fact that immediately after his exchange as a prisoner of war he had accepted from Governor Vance a commission as brigadier general of the North Carolina State Troops.[16]

To one other ex-subject of Her Majesty Queen Victoria went a commission as brigadier general—to William M. Browne, who was editing a newspaper in Washington early in 1861. When the Confederate States were organized, he went South, although he had taken out naturalization papers; and for his espousal of the cause he was appointed an aide-de-camp on the staff of President Davis with rank as colonel of cavalry. He served with such fidelity that Davis, as a mark of appreciation, made him a brigadier in December, 1864, and allowed him to serve at the siege of Savannah. His services after his promotion were not especially noteworthy. Although the senate refused to confirm his appointment, he was paroled as brigadier general.[17]

A small group of Irishmen fought their way up to this high rank. Patrick T. Moore, a Galway man, was commissioned a colonel of the First Virginia and assigned to Longstreet's brigade. He saw hard service on that general's staff during the battles before Richmond, though his brigadiership was not forthcoming until 1864. Generals James Hagan and Walter P. Lane were in a peculiar sense foreigners

---

[16] Evans, *op. cit.*, IV, 326-328; *Southern Historical Society Papers*, XVII, 61; *The Papers of Randolph Abbott Shotwell*, I, 273. Hereafter cited as *Shotwell Papers*. His commission was dated February 3 and refused March 6, 1865. See his file in the Confederate Archives.   [17] Evans, *op. cit.*, I, 628-629.

to the Confederacy. Both came to America with their parents at an early age and were educated in northern states, Pennsylvania and Ohio, respectively. Hagan became connected with the Mobile branch of an uncle's large business house in New Orleans. With other Alabama men he joined Hay's Texas Rangers to help storm Monterey, emerging from the Mexican War as captain of the Third Dragoons as a reward for gallantry. Lane went to Texas in 1836 to volunteer in her war for independence and to face the guns at San Jacinto with his bosom friends, Tom Green and Ben McCulloch, and to share later in numerous Indian engagements, which kept him in fighting trim. Both Hagan and Lane entered the Confederate army with commissions on the strength of fighting experience. The former went out to the field as captain of a Mobile cavalry company, one of the most efficient cavalry troops in the service, to face constant duty throughout the four years of war, and ultimately, in August, 1863, to become a brigade officer under General Joseph Wheeler; the latter entered the war as lieutenant colonel of Greer's Third Texas Cavalry. Lane won his generalship for brilliant action at Farmington and justified it by a desperate charge in April, 1864, when he was coöperating with General Polignac.[18] The name of another Irishman, General Joseph Finnegan, is identified with the defense of the Florida boundaries against Union attacks, especially by Negro soldiers, in the battle of Alcester or Ocean Pond. It was here that the general wrote into history an episode that condemns the soldier in him and exalts the father. His young son, who was on his staff, plunged into the thickest of the fray, but the anxious father, heedless of his own equal danger, called out, "Go to the rear, Finnegan, me B'ye, go to the rear! me B'ye! *Ye know ye are ye mither's darlin'.*"[19]

Instances occur where men highly placed were given the rank of brigadier general as a mark of honor for special service. That may afford an explanation for the appointment of Pierre Soulé to the staff of General Beauregard after his return from his mission to Europe and his elevation to a brigadiership "for special service" after his as-

---

[18] For Lane's record see Johnson, *Texans who Wore the Gray*, 57; for Hagan see Evans, *op. cit.*, VII, 415-416, and Edwin Craighead, *Mobile: Fact and Tradition*, 196. Lane, in the engagement referred to in the text, led a desperate charge, cut off the right wing of the foe, captured many persons, wagons, and twenty pieces of artillery, but was shot from his horse and disabled for months.

[19] Roberts, *Ireland in America*, 143; Nisbet, *Four Years on the Firing Line*, 196.

signment to the defense of Charleston.[20] There may be other instances of this kind which have not been revealed in the research.

The writer has been able to ascertain a certain number of foreign-born who attained the rank of colonel or lieutenant colonel, which ranks will be treated together. In the field and staff of the Sixth Louisiana Infantry appear a surprising number of foreign-born citizens, several Irishmen among them. Their nationality may help to explain the unusual number, six nonnatives out of thirty-six officers in all, for where Irishmen were, there was usually hard fighting and high mortality, even among high-ranking officers. Colonel Henry Strong, leading this regiment after June 4, 1861, in eleven battles, fell at Sharpsburg. Colonel William Monaghan, coming safely through fifteen battles with the same troops, was killed in August, 1864. Joseph Hanlon, a third Irishman of the regiment attaining the position of lieutenant colonel, was captured in October, 1864. The other three foreign-born officers in the regiment were a Frenchman, Louis Lay, who resigned his lieutenant-colonelcy during the first year of the war, a certain Lieutenant Colonel J. G. Campbell of Scotland, who rose from the ranks, and a German who did not rise above a captaincy. Colonel A. R. Blakely, who was scarcely twenty years old when he joined the famous Washington Artillery of New Orleans, served with distinguished gallantry in all the engagements in which he took part, paying the price of war by the loss of his right eye at Second Manassas. He also was an Irishman. Jack Thorington, a lawyer from Montgomery, was another Irishman to attain the rank of colonel, but he resigned on December 1, 1863.[21]

Rather more interesting than any of the other Irishmen of this rank is Colonel James Santiago Reily, who came to the United States about 1840, becoming one of the early settlers in Texas. He early rose to prominence, serving both in the state and national legislature, then being sent to St. Petersburg as consul by President Buchanan. Warm support from such an outstanding Texan as Postmaster Reagan brought a colonel's commission and he was assigned to the Fourth Texas Mounted Volunteers in Sibley's brigade, where he served with

---

[20] *The South in the Building of the Nation*, XII, 411. This may account for the fact that he is not listed with other officers of this rank in the customary lists.
[21] See Record, U. D. C. Memorial Hall, New Orleans; *Confederate Veteran*, XVI, 291, for Blakely. For Thorington see Estes, *List of Field Officers, Regiments and Battalions in the Confederate States Army, 1861-1865*, 124.

distinction and loyalty until he fell in battle near Franklin, Louisiana, in April, 1863.[22]

Colonel George Jackson, entering the United States with his parents at the age of one year, was of English birth. He entered the Confederate service from Maryland in August, 1861, but was not destined for the firing line, as he was quickly made adjutant general and chief of staff of his division. One other colonel was born under the British flag though in the colonies. William G. Robinson was born in Canada, but as a citizen of the United States he secured appointment from North Carolina to the academy at West Point so that he loyally rendered service to his adopted state as commander of the Second Regiment of Cavalry of North Carolina.[23] This probably does not exhaust the list of colonels of British birth in the Confederate army.

In the list of German-born colonels Augustus Reichard would probably be regarded as best known. Before he could march away with his battalion of German troops from New Orleans to Virginia, he had to arrange for the conduct of the office of Prussian consul, which he was filling. He turned it over to his partner, Kruttschnitt, who was bound to the young Confederacy by his marriage to a sister of Secretary Benjamin. According to the view of many, Reichard by his services on the battlefields of Virginia earned a brigadiership which he never received.[24]

In this group of German colonels Leon Toll von Zincken may be regarded as ranking next in importance. Son of a Prussian general and himself once a Prussian officer, he entered the war as a major of the German Battalion of the Twentieth Louisiana. After serving as inspector general on General Breckinridge's staff he was relieved to take command of the Nineteenth and Twentieth Louisiana regiments. He was one of the boldest of officers and was respected for his ability and courage. Several horses were shot from under him at Shiloh and again at Chickamauga so that people began to say, "The bullet has not been moulded for him." The following story is characteristic of his attitude. Ranged in front of his headquarters he kept a long row

[22] For Reagan's letter of Sept. 20, 1861, to Secretary Walker, see Confederate Archives, Reily's File. This is the same person who was sent on a Mexican mission. See above, p. 85.
[23] *Confederate Veteran*, XVI, 133; W. Gordon McCabe (comp.), "Graduates of the United States Military Academy at West Point, N. Y.," *Southern Historical Society Papers*, XXX, 73. *History of the Jews of Louisiana*, 153, is incorrect in claiming a majorality for Kurschiedt.   [24] Kaufmann, *op. cit.*, 575.

of brass cannon. One day a group of men inquired what he expected to do with this array of artillery. "Well, he replied, "if tem dem Yankees come here I make vun hell of a tam fuss!"[25] Record also exists of a Colonel Gustav Hoffman who commanded a German regiment, the Seventh Texas Cavalry, and of a certain nameless German Jew who was presented to the Fifth Texas as colonel but who, after their own crude, jeering fashion, was rejected by the Texans.[26] Colonel James Duff, a Scotchman from Perthshire whom one encounters as commanding the Thirty-third Texas Cavalry on the border, must enter the list here by virtue of his rank. Victor von Scheliha, whom we shall meet more intimately in a later chapter with the engineers, also held rank as a lieutenant colonel.

The young officer from the Swedish army, August Forsberg, will receive special attention in the chapter where special fields of service are discussed, but must be named here with the other officers of his rank for the service he rendered in actual combat. After a year's service on the staff of General Floyd he was made lieutenant colonel first, and then colonel of the Fifty-first Virginia Volunteers. He was severely wounded in the battle of Winchester but lived to serve Lynchburg as city engineer for over twenty years. At least one other Swede, Eric Erson, rose to the rank of lieutenant colonel.[27]

None of this group is more interesting than General A. J. Gonzales, a Cuban by birth who made himself practically an exile by his prominent participation in the uprising in the island against Spanish rule in 1848, and who had engaged in the Lopez filibustering expeditions from outside the borders of his beloved island. He had attended school in New York, where he was a schoolmate of General P. G. T. Beauregard. He became an American citizen by adoption in 1849,

[25] Nancy Telfair, *A History of Columbus, Ga., 1828-1928*, 133. His life was once threatened because a soldier on parole was killed by one of his men. Von Zincken was acquitted in the court-martial, and there was no evidence of prejudice because he was a foreigner.—*Ibid.,* 127.

[26] Kaufmann, *op. cit.*, 568, 572. The unnamed colonel seemed to approve of the tall, sturdy Texans, for he exclaimed with a broad accent, "I tinks I can manage te Texas poys, and I tinks bose togeder we can clean out te Yankees." By jeers and cutting of the tail of his horse, the poor colonel was driven away.—Nicholas A. Davis, *The Campaign from Texas to Maryland,* 18-19.

[27] See *Confederate Veteran,* XVIII, 434, 509, for Forsberg. It is possible that Carl Ludvig Viktor Lybecker belongs here. He is so recorded in the Royal Foreign Office in Stockholm. He was born in 1826, served as Swedish consul in St. Louis, is said to have joined the Confederate army in 1862—first serving as captain of the Flying Artillery Corps, Fourth Division, and attaining the rank of lieutenant colonel on October 31, 1863—retiring on June 6, 1865. He returned to Sweden in 1870. The writer can find no record of him in the American documents.

and in 1856 identity of interests led him to settle in Beaufort, South Carolina, for he married into the Elliot family there. So well known was he that he was indorsed for the Chilean mission in 1857 by the representatives and senators of no less than nine states. The cause of southern self-government made an overwhelming appeal to this Cuban patriot. The official records show that he was perhaps the earliest volunteer, having made the tender of his services on November 30, 1860, to the state of South Carolina, and among the last in service— three weeks after Appomattox. After a brief service as inspector general on Beauregard's staff he was ordered to report as lieutenant colonel of artillery to General Pemberton at Charleston. Two months later he was made colonel of artillery and assigned to duty as chief of artillery in the department of South Carolina, Georgia, and Florida.[28]

France contributed several officers to this grade. Lieutenant Colonel P. F. de Gournay, socially distinguished as the Marquis de Marcheville, was born in Brittany, where he owned extensive lands, but came to this country from Cuba whither he had gone as a young man to manage his father's estates. There he had become identified with the Cuban cause, to which he had rendered distinguished service. His next move brought him to New Orleans where the war found him editor of the *Picayune*. At his own expense, in the magnificent generosity of the day, he equipped a company of artillery, which he served as captain, and went to join the army in Virginia. He served gallantly at Yorktown, constructing and manning the breastworks for the battles around Richmond in 1862. He had reached the rank of major in the Army of Virginia when he was transferred to the Southwest. He was promoted to lieutenant colonel just before the fall of Vicksburg. A severe wound in the breast from a piece of shell at Port Hudson resulted in his being taken prisoner, in which unfortunate condition he remained until the end of the war. He was many times commended for bravery, and proved himself one of the most efficient colonels of artillery in the army. The career of his French compatriot, Colonel Aristide Gerard, resembled De Gournay's, for he also was occupying an editorial position on one of the French papers in New Orleans when the outbreak of war carried him to the field, was brave to the point of rashness, knew much of the science of war, and

[28] U. R. Brooks (ed.), *Stories of the Confederacy*, 290-299. The title of general arose from his association with the Cuban revolt.

was badly wounded at Farmington while with the Thirteenth Louisiana. Upon recovery he was assigned to duty in the Trans-Mississippi department.[29] Closely allied with the French group is the Belgian, Henri Honoré St. Paul, major of the Thirteenth Louisiana, but breveted lieutenant colonel on the field at Seven Pines.

Whether or not it was policy which prompted the appointment of the lone Mexican who appears officially in the ranks of the colonels, it is true that Santos Benavides, who began his service as major of the Thirty-third Texas Cavalry, did attain this relatively high rank and won the commendation of General Bee for his "distinguished services."[30]

The group of perhaps half a dozen Poles who must fit into this part of the picture are as colorful a set of men as ever lifted sword for any country. Colonel Valery Sulakowski has already been identified as the commander of the First Polish Regiment or Fourteenth Louisiana, as it became when it was ready to leave for Richmond, and some hint was given of his power to inspire awe in the most lawless of troops.[31] As an officer on duty he was the incarnation of military law —despotic, cruel, absolutely without mercy. On the other hand no regiment was better looked after for its material needs than his, or obtained more regularly its requisitions. Naturally his soldiers did not love such a martinet, but regarded him as one of the most provident and efficient commanders they ever had. He could shoot down ruthlessly mutineers in his company, but he would treat with tenderness the wife of a sergeant who was killed while helping to restore order. In a placard he could bitterly denounce Duke Alexis of the Romanov house when the Duke appeared in New Orleans on a visit. His impatience of any will but his own virtually ended his military career but not before he had built the best fortifications on the peninsula.[32]

[29] Colonel de Gournay first went to Baltimore after the war, where he taught French and wrote for various publications. After a visit of two years in France, he returned to Baltimore to serve seven years as vice consul for France.—*Confederate Veteran*, XII, 405. For Gerard see John McGrath, "In a Louisiana Regiment," *Southern Historical Society Papers*, XXXI, 119. Colonel A. Rochereau, commanding the French Legion, Colonel A. Ferrier, commanding the regiment of French Volunteers, and lower ranking officers commanding the various detachments of the New Orleans Foreign Brigade are not enumerated, as they were not officers in the regular Confederate service.—New Orleans *Bee*, December 5, 1861. Their service was in an emergency and for a brief period only.

[30] *O. W. R.*, Ser. 1, XXVI, Pt. 1, 284.   [31] See above, Chap. IV.

[32] See Napier Bartlett, "Memorable Deaths" and "Louisiana Troops in the West," in *Military Record of Louisiana*, 43-47.

Sulakowski's pride offended in some way, on February 15, 1862, he tendered his resignation which was accepted, and he returned to his home in New Orleans. Two months later General Magruder urged him to reënter the service of the Confederate army and to take command of the engineer department, but he replied proudly that "under no circumstances" would he reënter the service. Arrest by General Butler's orders brought forth a vigorous protest, dated June 5, 1862, written from the customhouse, where he was evidently in confinement. He denied any connection with or interest in the Confederacy; he even intimated that his hostility would be useful in influencing the Confederates against their government.[33] In view of that vehement letter it is astonishing, to say the least, to find him serving Magruder with the rank and pay of a colonel of cavalry from February 6, 1863, to about January 19, 1864, at Galveston for the district of Texas, and signing himself "Chief Engineer." It appears that he stood in the relation of personal employee to Magruder, a relationship certain to be provocative of friction, for the Confederate government which he refused to recognize would not recognize him. Men whom he attempted to direct as his subordinates were recognized by Richmond as heads of the engineer bureau. Therefore when he found his orders disregarded, on August 27, 1863, he resigned a second time from an impossible situation, though his resignation seems not to have been accepted at once. His personality prevented his advancement so that he left the service without having achieved results worthy of his ability.[34]

Colonel Arthur Grabowski was a Polish count who came to America because he disliked army life and then spent fifty years here in military service. Born in Russia, the son of the well-known Count Frederick Grabowski, he was educated in the Russian military academy in St. Petersburg and in the Royal College of Agriculture. Deciding that a pioneer life in America was preferable to the army, he came to the States at the age of twenty. A brief period of teaching at Roanoke College was followed by experience at the Pennsylvania Military College. In 1861 he went to South Carolina to enlist as a private in the First South Carolina Regiment, participated in the first

[33] For his resignation see letter to General Magruder, August 27, 1863, in his file, Confederate Archives, War Department. Sulakowski's entire file is valuable and highly interesting.

[34] His services as engineer will be dealt with in Chap. VIII.

engagement of the war, the bombardment of Fort Sumter, and fought throughout the struggle. Ability brought rapid advancement to the rank of colonel and during the last few months of the fighting he was with Lee as officer in charge of supplies.[35]

Colonel Hypolite Oladowski was cut from the same block as Sulakowski—perhaps it would be better to say that they had been forged on the same Prussian anvil. He was the same efficient, irascible type of Prussian officer. He had been in the ordnance department in the old army and was serving as ordnance sergeant at the Baton Rouge Arsenal at the time the war broke out. He was not a man of education or position, but we shall hear of him again in connection with special fields of service. Colonel Frank Schaller, who commanded some Mississippi troops, seems to have been one of the few foreigners in the service whose heart was not burning over his wrongs or lack of recognition, though some of his fellows felt that his reward was not in proportion to his merits. By birth a Pole but by adoption a Georgian, and an adept in martial exercises, he was at heart a classical and scientific scholar. He finished his brief career after the war teaching school at Athens, Georgia. One of his comrades declared, "I cannot recall that he ever murmured," and summed him up as a "bold spirit in a loyal breast." One acquaintance declared him in "a large degree, the equal of General Whiting in the range and profundity of his gifts and Acquirements."[36]

A Polish gentleman educated to military life in his homeland, Colonel Ignatius Szymanski had long been known in New Orleans as the wealthy owner of a cotton press, fast horses, and a fast yacht, a genial, cultivated, and liberal sportsman. He became a rebel, so to speak, as a matter of general principle. He was reared as a rebel and poured out satire on those who were ashamed of the title and insisted on being called Confederates. After a brief period of service as adjutant and inspector general, he was made agent of exchange of prisoners for the Trans-Mississippi department, an admirable choice. Over six feet in height, with abundant energy and nervous strength,

[35] His record after the war shows a man tied to a certain career despite himself. He became commandant at Worcester, then went to Pennsylvania State College, and to Maryland Agricultural College. President Cleveland made him superintendent of the Haskell Military Institute, a government school for Indians. He closed his career as president of Defiance College.—*Confederate Veteran*, XXXVIII, 153, 166.

[36] "A Plea for General W. H. C. Whiting," *Southern Historical Society Papers*, XXIV, 277.

he possessed courtesy, tact, knowledge of the world, and social qualities which fitted him eminently for the semi-diplomatic post of exchange of prisoners. He handled his task thoroughly, systematically,
and well. His was the faithfully kept word of a gentleman, and
Union officers with whom he dealt felt that he used his influence to
prevent the ill-treatment of Union prisoners. In a special trip up the
Red River to Shreveport in order to make arrangements with General Kirby Smith for an interview with United States commissioners
of exchange, he was the perfect host, preventing unpleasant topics of
conversation, unfailing in courtesy to his two particular guests, two
Federal officers, thoughtful in catering for the favored few at his
table, "the social inspiration" of the mixed circle of Confederates and
Unionists on board his steamer. His special delight was in his really
fine brass band, which he insisted on retaining on his boat as a means
of promoting diplomatic courtesies, for some of its members were
equally skillful with stringed instruments and could furnish dance
music in the cabin. The approach of the boat was eagerly watched
for, welcomed with ecstatic waving of handkerchiefs, while free-will
offerings of butter, milk, and vegetables were hastily dispatched to
the boat. No man was so popular as "old Sky," as he was lovingly
and appropriately called, for he counted seventy years or more.[37]

An unusual family was the De Coppens who came to Louisiana in
1853 from St. Pierre, Martinique, whither Baron August de Coppens
betook himself from Belgium. Two of his sons became successively
lieutenant colonel of the famous Zouave Battalion, which the elder
had recruited. Georges Auguste Gaston de Coppens enlisted in March,
1861, and fell at Sharpsburg, never attaining the full colonelcy
promised him by General Lee just before that battle. The brother,
Marie Alfred, was appointed captain as early as May, 1861, and succeeded to the lieutenant-colonelcy on the death of his brother but was
retired in the fall of 1864 on account of wounds. It is interesting that
he promptly made his training acquired in the American war count
for another country; he went through the Franco-Prussian War on
the side of France, but ultimately returned to America, only to be
drowned near Galveston.[38]

[37] See the very sympathetic picture of him drawn by one of the Federal officers.—J. M.
Bundy, "The Last Chapter in the History of the War," *The Galaxy*, VIII, 115-117.
[38] In all, four members of the De Coppens family served in the same battalion. The
baron served as assistant quartermaster of the battalion organized by his sons, until cap-

A few more lieutenant colonels and the catalog is complete. The Scotchman, George H. Morton, had sailed from Liverpool and landed in New York in 1852. After a sojourn of two years in the North, he moved to Nashville where he engaged in the mercantile business. Enlisting when the war came, he was elected orderly sergeant of Company A of the First Tennessee Cavalry. Within two months he was serving as third lieutenant and was elected captain in the reorganization of the battalion which placed his company in the Second Tennessee Cavalry in May, 1862. A few weeks more and he was elected major of the Second Tennessee. As major he displayed his talents as leader and disciplinarian and rose within a year to the next rank, that of lieutenant colonel, which post he held until the surrender. So rigid a disciplinarian was he that American-bred lads were inclined to complain but soon came to admire him, especially when he led his battalion gallantly at several engagements. He led it against Sherman's army near Cherokee, Alabama, in October, 1863, with as much courage and pluck as if he had met only his equal in numbers, and won the approval of his superiors at Iuka. A severe wound in March, 1864, disabled him for several months, but he was back in Forrest's expedition by September, 1864, and by his prompt and daring generalship saved a large portion of his regiment from capture. Service to the surrender was his fine record.[39]

A. D. Gwynne, who enlisted at Memphis and rose from second lieutenant to lieutenant colonel at the early age of twenty-three; Michael Nolan, a gallant officer who fell at Gettysburg; James Nelligan, who was court-martialed for leaving his regiment at Gettysburg and Fredericksburg but "whitewashed," as some officer scathingly entered on the record; Michael A. Grogan, a machinist who rose from first lieutenant to the head of a Louisiana regiment; Joseph Hanlon, a reporter from New Orleans who was captured October 19, 1864; and Joseph McGraw, originally a teamster of exceptional ability to command men, who reported back in thirty days after losing

tured on the Buckwater, October, 1864, was released on condition of leaving the country, visited a sister in Paris, but returned to New Orleans after the war. Leon, the youngest son, enlisted at the age of sixteen in this same battalion in 1862, and became second sergeant in Company F before October, 1864. He is the only one who was naturalized. I am indebted for the information about the various members of the De Coppens family to Charles A. Duchamp, grandson of Baron de Coppens.

[39] Richard Hancock, *Hancock's Diary or A History of the Second Tennessee Confederate Cavalry*, 581-583.

his left hand, one of the most respected officers in the artillery corps—
all rose to be lieutenant colonels and all were sons of Ireland.[40] If
the basis of the census had been adopted and the first generation born
in America counted as foreign, Lieutenant Colonel Theodore O'Hara,
who won more glory as author of a famous war song, "Bivouac of the
Dead," than as commander of troops in the field, would enter this
story. B. F. Eschelmann of the New Orleans Washington Artillery,
John P. Emerich of the Eighth Alabama Regiment of Infantry, and
B. W. Froebel, chief of artillery of Hood's division, who was formerly an officer of the Electorate of Hesse, were Germans who
enjoyed the title of lieutenant colonel.

No attempt will be made to enumerate all the names of foreign-
born who attained the rank of major, though a few will be singled
out for comment. It is interesting that most of the chief nations are
represented, although the writer cannot assert that such careful distribution was a matter of shrewd policy to please the various nationality groups in the population. As a matter of course, attention had
to be focused on previous training, and the foreigner who had grown
to man's estate somewhere in Europe was likely to have been subjected to military training. Major William S. Haven, who served at
the head of the Forty-first and later of the Twentieth Arkansas under
General Price; Michael Lynch, a born soldier and efficient officer of
the Twenty-first Georgia; James F. Robinson, who entered the
service as captain and rose to be a major by the close of the first year
of war; and John King, a major at twenty-nine, were Irishmen.
Donald Malcolm McDonald, who came of Scotch Highland blood,
must however be classified as English by virtue of being born in
Davenport, England. In his veins flowed the fighting blood of
Marshal McDonald of Napoleon's army. He enlisted in 1861 from
Missouri as a private in the Confederate service, and fought as a
private soldier in every engagement of any importance west of the
Mississippi save one, despite the fact that he had been promoted to

[40] Gwynne had been in many battles, was badly wounded at Atlanta and captured,
remaining a prisoner on Johnson's Island for three months till exchanged in February,
1865.—Mathes, *The Old Guard in Gray*, 117-118. General Wright said that up to 1863
he had done more important special service than any officer in the brigade.—*Ibid.*, 119.
For Nolan, Grogan, and Hanlon see Record, Field and Staff, Alabama Military Archives;
Record, U. D. C. Memorial Hall, New Orleans; Record of the Officers of the Sixth Louisiana, U. D. C. Memorial Hall, New Orleans (copy in Confederate Archives, War Department); for McGraw see Jennings C. Wise, "The Boy Gunners of Lee," *Southern Historical Society Papers*, XLII, 166-167.

General S. D. Jockman's staff with the rank of major.[41] Robert G. Lowe, who started his war record in the Shreveport Grays but who served in northern Louisiana as major until the surrender, and John Cunningham of the Georgia Reserves were Scotchmen. M. K. Simons and Alexander M. Dechman came from Nova Scotia to Texas. Francis Miller, German despite his Anglicized name, who had served three years under the United States flag in the Seminole War and probably joined the Confederate forces because he had settled in Virginia, led his regiment, the Forty-fifth Virginia, during Early's retreat from the valley. Louis M. Ströbel, who commanded Company F of Terry's Rangers and was elected adjutant in March, 1864, and Gustav Schleicher of Darmstadt, who had been sent to congress from Texas, were representatives of the German element. The last-named was a decided Unionist but felt unable to escape service in the field for his state. His service was chiefly in directing the foundations of fortifications.[42] G. A. Peple, a Rhinelander, was a major in the service of an engineer corps. An unusually interesting officer of this rank was Jacob Wälder of San Antonio. Education in Germany, to which he returned for more than two years to complete his formal training, active service throughout the Mexican War, and several terms in the lower house of the Texas legislature brought him prominently before the people of his section of the state. After assisting Colonel Wilcox to raise a regiment of infantry, he was commissioned a major in the army.[43]

The story of German officers would lose a great deal of flavor if

[41] For Haven and McDonald see the *Confederate Veteran*, XIX, 539, and XI, 288. For Lynch see Nisbet, *Four Years on the Firing Line*, 43; and for Robinson, Descriptive Roll of Officers, Confederate Archives, War Department.

[42] For Lowe see *Confederate Veteran*, XIV, 85. Cunningham is recorded in Biographical Questionnaire, Cornelia Cunningham (granddaughter of the man mentioned in the text), Georgia Archives; Simons appears in Descriptive List of Officers of the Army of the West, Confederate Archives, War Department; Dechman, in Yeary, *op. cit.*, 181. Miller's record is in the *Confederate Veteran*, VI, 108; Louis Ströbel appears in *True Issue*, October 4, 1864, La Grange, Fayette County, Texas; and Ströbel and Schleicher in Kaufmann, *op. cit.*, 570. Joseph Magoffin, though born in Chihuahua, Mexico, was probably the son of American citizens and hence is regarded as native-born. See William E. Mickle (ed.), *Well-known Confederate Veterans and Their War Records*, I, 62. He entered the army in 1861 and was made a major in 1864 in the command of Generals Sibley and James P. Major.

[43] For Peple, see Schuricht, *History of the German Element in Virginia*, II, 85; for Wälder, *Biographical Encyclopedia of Texas*, 116. Several of his letters in reference to assisting Colonel Wilcox in raising a regiment are preserved in the Texas Archives. General Hebert had led Wälder to expect appointment as lieutenant colonel. See Wälder to Col. J. G. Dashiell, March 6, 1862, Papers, Adjutant General's Office, Archives, Texas State Library.

Major Adolph Proskauer had not played his rôle. It will be recalled that he was the person who wrested his majorate from an unwilling colonel and a reluctant Board of Examiners. He put his good brains and steady nerves to effective use on the battlefield. His perfect coolness and apparent indifference to flying bullets, evinced by his frequently smoking a cigar calmly in the thickest of the fight, were constantly commented on. At Gettysburg he issued his orders and animated his men between puffs of his cigar until a bullet through his cheek disabled him and he became a prisoner of war. No longer fit for active service, he became a major of the Invalid Corps at Mobile until January, 1865, when he applied for leave of absence in order to return to Germany for a visit in quest of the sea air and change of scene recommended by his physician. Undoubtedly he would have risen to higher rank if he had not been disabled.[44]

A second striking personality in this rank was Major Gustav Adolf Schwarzmann from Stuttgart. He had already had experience in the Seminole War, where he rose to a lieutenantship in the Fourth Artillery. After his brief service in the post-office department, he secured a commission as major and adjutant general on the staff of General Albert Pike, an old acquaintance. He served with that officer in the Indian Territory for less than a year. General Pike's resignation in 1862 brought misfortune to his subordinate, whom he had sent to Richmond with orders for action contingent upon the acceptance or rejection of his superior's resignation. Long delay terminated in Schwarzmann's commission being vacated in June, 1863, and in severance of his relations with the army.[45]

Foreign-born captains who had embraced American citizenship and who became accordingly Confederate citizens when their respective states seceded were fairly numerous. In view of the constant allusions by southern writers to the large numbers of Germans in the northern army, officers as well as privates, it is interesting that German citizens should have contributed the largest number of captains of any foreign group to the Confederate army, so far as the writer's researches have been able to reveal them. It has been possible to

[44] Park, *op. cit.*, 10; *idem*, "War Diary of Captain Robert Emory Park," *Southern Historical Society Papers*, XXVI, 13. For Proskauer's application for leave to visit Europe, see his letter to the secretary of war, dated February 8, 1865, Confederate Archives, War Department.

[45] Schwarzmann appears in Schuricht, *op. cit.*, II, 84, but the best data was found in his file in the Confederate Archives. It is possible that he should be classified with the colonels, but major is the highest rank in the official records.

collect the names of forty-nine Germans who led companies, of thirty-five Irishmen, thirteen Frenchmen, eight Mexicans, seventeen Britishers, and of a couple of Swedes. The captain of Company C in the Twelfth Alabama was Fred C. Fischer, who had enlisted as a corporal, the type of excellent scholar and officer which the Fatherland can produce. He renounced his American allegiance when a considerable fortune beckoned him back to Hamburg after the war.[46] Captain Franz Melchers was one of the Germans distinguished in civil life before he entered the army. He was editor of the Charleston *Deutsche Zeitung* for thirty-seven years, except for the four war years. He entered the service on April 21, 1862, as first lieutenant of Company B, German Artillery, South Carolina, and rose to a captaincy.[47] In painful contrast with this high type of German stands the picture drawn by the Englishman, R. H. Williams, of the senior captain in the Third Texas Cavalry, Kaupmann, "a heavy, besotted-looking lager-beer Dutchman, a stone-mason by trade, who had got himself elected, no one knew how, and was rarely quite sober."[48] Of the better type again was Emil Oscar Zadek, president of the *Gesangverein Frohsinn* of Mobile in the peaceful days before and after the war.[49] Captain Blayney Townley Walshe is so typical of the Irish officer at his best that his record may well be included. At the call to arms, though he had been in New Orleans but seven years, he enlisted with the Washington Artillery but was soon elected second lieutenant of Company A, Irish Brigade, and later promoted to a captaincy. He shared in all the battles of his regiment from First Manassas to Gaines's Mill. When rendered unfit for duty from a wound received in the last-named battle, he was appointed chief of the passport office in Richmond. As related in an earlier chapter, he became provost of

[46] He is spoken of in the records in terms of real affection and respect.

[47] Some German writers give Melchers the rank of colonel, but the writer can find no confirmation in the official records of rank above that of captain.

[48] Williams, *With the Border Ruffians*, 283. Williams tells an ugly story of how greedy and even dishonest Kaupmann was. Soldiers were to be allowed to select garments for their use from some supplies from a United States brig which had been swept ashore. Williams found sixteen garments with Kaupmann's name affixed, and then he claimed a coat from Williams because, "Gif you vill looke inside de slief, you vill see my name." Williams threw it at him in disgust.—*Ibid.*, 284.

One is arrested by the old-fashioned divisions into which the state was divided. In the private library of Mrs. Pfeuffer is a commission to Captain John Heilmann as captain of "Beat" number 3, Comal County, State Troops, issued by Governor Lubbock on February 12, 1862.

[49] Craighead, *op. cit.*, 302-305.

three parishes in Louisiana. In February, 1865, a subdistrict was created, the Lake Shore, and though he had only two companies of cavalry he broke up the trade between that area and New Orleans. He tried to form an independent cavalry command like Mosby's to operate within the enemy's lines, but Lee disapproved of independent commands, and so the papers were never issued.[50]

Of course the idiosyncrasies of foreign-born officers furnished precious material for amusement to the American soldiers. Lieutenant Jules l'Etondal of the Gardes Lafayette of Mobile, walking with his umbrella raised to protect his very corpulent body against the broiling sun while under heavy fire, provided a household story for generations. And Americans enjoyed marveling at Major Proskauer's strange taste for fried mushrooms. There is enduring human interest in the story of Captain S. Isodore Guillet, who was shot on the very same horse on which three of his brothers had been killed, and which he willed before dying to his nephew.[51] The half-breed Mexican, Vidal, who had command of thirty Mexican Rangers, was clearly a rascal and yielded the army stories of his villainy. But Captain Bustilla and Captain Rafalo Aldrate, heading companies of Mexicans from Texas, seem to have been of a different type.[52]

The experience which Captain T. George Raven had to offer as a graduate of the military college at Addiscombe, England, was not overlooked; neither could the executive experience of a Canadian, John Orr, who had handled large numbers of coolies on the British government sugar farms at Demerara, South America, long escape notice, before his colonel made him adjutant with the rank of captain of the Sixth Louisiana. Every southern boy knows the name of the Irishman, Captain Dick Dowling, who with 42 men checked the advance of 16,000 Unionists and took 400 prisoners at Sabine Pass.[53]

A peculiar interest attaches to two young captains, Confederate by adoption and not by birth—a younger half brother of General Cleburne, who had followed Patrick to America, and the eldest son of the

[50] Confederate Veteran, VI, 576.

[51] "Diary of Robert E. Park, Macon, Georgia," Southern Historical Society Papers, I, 383, 385. For the Guillet story see Telfair, op. cit., 137.

[52] See Muster Roll, Archives Division, Texas State Library, for Vidal. It is dated March 5, 1861. It must be pointed out that there are a few American names on the roll of Aldrate's company from Refugio County: John Casaday, Edward Hicky, Michael Gallaher, etc.

[53] Confederate Veteran, XVII, 318; ibid., XXIV, 368; Maguire, The Irish in America, 580-581.

Irish patriot, John Mitchel. Christopher Cleburne, a youth not yet out of his teens, came to his brother at Missionary Ridge. The general, according to the story, told him, "I can give you a position on my staff, but my advice is that you enlist as a private, and if worthy of it you will win promotion. If not worthy, I do not want you around my quarters." This advice was acted upon, and he became a member of Polk's brigade and served with it in the ranks until General John Morgan offered him a captain's commission. Leading his company, he fell mortally wounded at Dublin, Virginia. John C. Mitchel, Jr., who had shared his father's fortunes from standing by his side in the dock when he was tried for treason against England, through exile in Australia, to his refuge in America, espoused with him the Confederate cause. As soon as the permanent government of the Confederacy was erected at Richmond, he and James, the next younger brother, offered their services. The youngest, William, hastened with the father from Paris in 1862 to proffer service. The young boy enlisted in the First Virginia Brigade but the father was obliged to volunteer in the ambulance corps, as defective eyesight brought rejection as a regular soldier. John, the eldest, promptly received an appointment as lieutenant from the secretary of war and was ordered to a battalion of the South Carolina Artillery stationed at Fort Moultrie. He shared in the famous attack on Fort Sumter, and his company was sent with the Palmetto Guards to garrison the fortress. He shared fully in all the dangers and hardships of the siege of Charleston so that at Colonel Elliott's promotion in April, 1863, it was natural to place him as captain in command of the mass of ruins which still waved a flag as a fortress. On July 20, 1864, while making an observation from the rampart of the fort, he was mortally wounded. He saw the shell coming, but refused to go to the bombproof as he felt he must set his men an example of courage. He died after three hours of agony, saying, "I die willingly for South Carolina, but oh! that it had been for Ireland!"[54]

In the group of lieutenants every nationality under the sun seems to have been represented with an interesting distribution. The author

[54] For Cleburne see Buck, *op. cit.*, 201. For Mitchel see Claudine Rhett, "Sketch of John C. Mitchel of Ireland, killed while in Command of Fort Sumter," *Southern Historical Society Papers*, X, 268-272; Yates Snowden, *History of South Carolina*, II, 786. Mitchel had returned in 1862. The youngest brother was killed at Gettysburg, and James, the second, served as adjutant of General Gordon's Georgia Brigade, losing his right arm in one of the battles near Richmond.—Rhett, *op. cit.*, 269-270.

proposes to give some statistics—not because they are complete or authoritative in the face of the incomplete rolls preserved, but because they are highly suggestive. Ireland heads the list with 63 out of a total of 179 lieutenants identified. Germany ranks second with 59. France, England, and Scotland have a sprinkling. It is perhaps surprising to find Spain, Greece, Hungary, Mexico, and Denmark represented.[55] One notes, in studying the records, that frequently there has been some sort of military experience or some family prominence. Victor D. Fuchs, an Alsatian who had come to Memphis with his family in 1856, had belonged to the old Washington Rifles for four years prior to the war and was promptly elected second lieutenant when his company enlisted in the Fifteenth Tennessee at the outbreak of war. Richard Agar, previously an officer in the British army, suitably entered the First Louisiana Artillery as lieutenant. James Barron entered as lieutenant in Captain Walsh's company of Missouri Light Infantry on the strength of a previous lieutenantship in the artillery of the Missouri State Guards.[56] Lieutenant E. C. McCarthy was the son of the editor of the Limerick and Claire *Examiner,* who had to flee from Ireland with the failure of the contemplated rebellion of 1848 and who had been on intimate terms with General Meagher and with John Mitchel. He was promoted to a lieutenantship very shortly after enlisting in Company A, Thirtieth Louisiana Volunteers. John A. Henneman was a Bavarian who, though unnaturalized, left his jeweler's task to enter the Holcombe Legion as second lieutenant of Company E and who, when wounded so severely that he resigned his commission, entered the cavalry and served to the end of the war.[57] Many were men of ability who commanded the respect of their communities and of their companies in the army.

Promotions occurred occasionally from the ranks. John Finnely of Ireland, to cite a single instance, rose from the ranks of Company

[55] For those who are interested in statistics the table is appended:

Germany	59	Canada	3	Wales	1	Hungary	1
Ireland	63	Scotland	3	Spain	1		
France	8	Mexico	5	Greece	1		
England	4	W. I.	2	Denmark	1		

[56] Fuchs's record appears in Mathes, *The Old Guard in Gray;* for military record of Agar see Bartlett, "Louisiana Troops in the West," *Military Record of Louisiana,* 8; for Barron and the similar cases of John Kenney and Richard C. Walsh, see Descriptive Roll of Officers, Wade's battery, First Division, Confederate Archives, War Department.

[57] See Buehring Jones, *The Sunny Land,* 262, for McCarthy; for Henneman see J. B. O. Landrum, *History of Spartanburg County,* 601-604.

H, Fourteenth Louisiana, to be adjutant of the regiment before he met his fate on the battlefield.[58] A person with knowledge of the manual of arms, whatever his nationality or whatever the company, was valuable. Richard Schevenell, a talented and intrepid Frenchman who had served in the war with Mexico, was chosen first lieutenant of the Mitchell Thunderbolts, a home guard company at Athens, Georgia. He acted as drillmaster and put his group of portly, wealthy gentlemen through hard drills before their elderly joints and muscles were unlimbered. It probably outraged his sense of military propriety to have one of his soldiers hand his gun in the midst of a drill to his trusty slave near by, leisurely raise his umbrella, and stand in rank until disposed again to take over his gun and resume practice. In the regular companies one encounters foreigners as drillmasters, often without assigned rank—Cockins, for instance, the Englishman who drilled the Edisto Rifles in bayonet practice, and a Frenchman who was drilling the Liberty Voltigeurs in Texas in December, 1861 —apparently reserves. William Myer, despite his German-sounding name, informed the adjutant general of Texas that he had been an adjutant in a regular battalion in France, "before I comme to this country in 1850. I would have offered my self for Regular Service, but for Age my held an I could no stand a Campagne but I can learne soldiers."[59]

When one comes to the noncommissioned officers, the numbers are vastly increased. Without attempting to give figures for the entire group, the relation between nationality groups may well be indicated. As usual the Irish far outnumbered the others; next came the Germans, a close second, and then, though only a little less than one third as numerous as the Germans and just one fourth as many as the Irish, came the English; then trailing them, though insignificant in numbers, were the French and Scotch. Interesting are the scattered Italians, Austrians, and Hungarians in this group, while one corporal recorded himself as from the Isle of France, West Africa, and two as from India. One strange name, Mcbroons, certainly suggests a type

[58] Record, U. D. C. Memorial Hall. It is discouraging to find an officer enter on the sheet the statement, "So many non-commissioned officers impossible to state dates of appointment or when reduced," and so the entire record is left blank. This is the case for Company H, Tenth Louisiana.—*Ibid*.

[59] Augustus L. Hull, *Annals of Athens, Georgia*, 270-272; Buck, *op. cit.*, 25; Philip F. Brown, *Reminiscences of the War of 1861-1865*, 42-43. The case of Myer is encountered in a letter from Wm. Myer to the adjutant general from Liberty, dated December 4, 1881, Adjutant General's Correspondence, Archives, Texas State Library.

of name with which the recording official was not familiar and hence a wild effort at interpreting on paper the sounds which met his ear. Almost all the European countries are at least represented in the group.

The men in this class are drawn from the same humble ranks from which we shall see the enlisted men come. They yielded to the same temptation to desert, when the miseries of war appeared no longer endurable, to which the men under them yielded. These low-ranking officers were, as was true of their American fellow officers, good and bad. Professor C. H. Bergmann, schoolmaster of the German school at Charleston, served in the lowly post of an orderly sergeant in Bachman's company during the war; L. L. Ducet, an Englishman-born enlisting from New Orleans, attracted such attention by his gallantry on the field that he was promoted by President Davis himself. So bold was one German corporal that he was the only person besides the captain who cut his way out from a bad situation at Chickamauga. On the other hand Charles O'Connell, an Irish corporal, appeared in only three battles, acted so cowardly at Port Republic while color-bearer that he was deprived of the colors, deserted in September, 1862, and went to Europe.[60] Among the officers of this group desertions are fairly well distributed, embracing English, Germans, and Irish in proportion to their numbers. Some among each of the chief nationalities represented consented to take the oath to the United States. Some conducted themselves so badly as to be reduced to the ranks, and a very few were dropped from the rolls.

The proportion sustained by the foreign-born to the native-born in the allotment of officers can be quickly and easily stated. In the entire Ninth Alabama Regiment, there were only six foreign-born officers and they were in Company B, largely an Irish company. In Company G, First Louisiana, only three of the fourteen officers were foreign-born; in Company C, Second Louisiana, all but three of the twelve officers; in companies C and D, Sixth Louisiana, two of the thirteen; in Company G of the same regiment, almost a German company, three of the four corporals were Germans, the fourth being also a foreigner, an Englishman; and in Company H, a mixed company

[60] Rosengarten, *The German Soldier in the Wars of the United States*, 185-186, records the interesting details about Bergmann. Ducet's record appears on the Record Roll of Company H, Seventh Louisiana, and O'Connell's cowardice is recorded on the Record of Company B, Eighth Louisiana, U. D. C. Memorial Hall.

of privates, one sergeant and one corporal were non-American; companies F and I of the Seventh Louisiana, almost wholly Irish companies, were permitted eight and five foreigners respectively in their full complement of officers. The largest proportions found were in Company E, Ninth Louisiana, the Milliken Bend Guards; and Company G, Fifth Louisiana, Swamp Rangers, where about half of the privates had been born outside America. All the corporals and three of the sergeants were non-native. If this is the proportion in largely foreign companies, one would expect to find none in largely native companies. Yet, strangely enough, a number of the Mississippi and North Carolina companies with relatively few foreign-born in the ranks have one or two foreign sergeants or corporals.[61] One even finds occasionally an Englishman, a Scotchman, or even an Irishman holding office in a purely American company.[62] There are, however,

[61] For accuracy of the record a small table is appended, based on the Descriptive Lists, Confederate Archives, War Department:

Company D, Mississippi State Cavalry, the second sergeant was an Englishman.

Company G, Sixty-first Mississippi Regiment, Lamar Rifles, the fourth sergeant was a German.

Company A, Seventeenth Mississippi Regiment, Buena Vista Rifles, the fourth and fifth sergeants were Irishmen.

Company D, Seventeenth Mississippi Regiment, the fifth sergeant was a German, the third corporal an Irishman.

Company B, Eighteenth Mississippi Regiment, Benton Rifles, the second sergeant was a Welshman, the third corporal an Irishman.

Company D, Eighteenth Mississippi Regiment, Hanover Rifles, the first sergeant was a German, the third corporal an Irishman.

Company E, Eighteenth Mississippi Regiment, Humphrey's Brigade, the third sergeant was an Irishman.

Company K, Twenty-first Mississippi Regiment, Hurricane Rifles, the third sergeant was a German.

Company C, Eighteenth North Carolina Regiment, Columbus Guards, the second sergeant was a Frenchman.

Company D, Seventh North Carolina Regiment, the third sergeant, the first, second, and fourth corporals were Englishmen, the third, Irish.

Company F, Seventh North Carolina Regiment, the fourth sergeant was a Scotchman.

Company F, Eighth North Carolina Regiment, the third sergeant and first corporal were Irish.

Company I, Thirty-seventh North Carolina Regiment, the fifth sergeant was an Englishman.

The statistics here and in the text are gathered from various rolls.

[62] Instances are:

Company A, First Louisiana Regiment, Thomas W. Rollins, Scotch, corporal.

Company F, First Louisiana Regiment, James Spenceley, Englishman, fourth corporal.

Company K, First Louisiana Regiment, ———— Pohlman, German, third corporal.

Company K, Seventeenth North Carolina Regiment, Daniel O'Bryan, Irishman, corporal.

Company H, Forty-third North Carolina Regiment, John Niven, Scotchman, fourth corporal.

Company C, Fifty-sixth North Carolina Regiment, Anthony B. Pierce, Irish, first corporal.

Company C, Sixty-first North Carolina Regiment, John Bolt, Englishman, second corporal.—Record, U. D. C. Memorial Hall; and Original Descriptive and Muster Roll, Confederate Archives.

a few complete regiments, notably in North Carolina and Alabama, where not one officer other than American appears on the records.[63]

The reader would not readily forgive the writer for closing this chapter without some mention of General Gaspard Tochman. If President Davis or Secretary of War Walker were alive today, he would undoubtedly object strenuously to the bestowal on Tochman of the title of general and insist that the only rank applicable was that of colonel. The writer cuts the Gordian knot by calling Tochman by the title which history has bestowed upon him, but denying him a place with the roll of Confederate officers as he never really served the southern republic. No more dramatic figure appeared on the Confederate stage than this fiery Pole, who so long and persistently sought to wrest his "rights" from the Confederacy.

The unsuccessful revolt of Poland against Russia in 1830 had forced Tochman to flee to France and then to the United States where he became naturalized in 1841 and practiced law. His previous residence in Virginia, though in 1861 he was living in Washington, and his natural inclinations would lead him to espouse the cause of a people "fighting against oppression." His explanation of his position in the conflict embraces his fear of amalgamation of the races, his objection to violation of the constitution by the United States, and his obligation under his oath of naturalization to adhere to his state![64] On May 11, 1861, when war was a certainty, he offered his services to the new government at Montgomery to raise ten or twenty companies to be composed of persons of foreign birth, enlisting for the war, to constitute a Polish brigade. In little more than a week he received his authorization to raise ten companies or, if practicable, twenty companies to be organized into a brigade. Such officers of the army as were necessary to enlist the men were to be detailed to such points as Tochman might indicate.[65]

Tochman later held that his authority had been enlarged by the

---

[63] The Fourth Alabama Regiment is an example.

[64] In view of his attitude it is interesting to learn that he offered to go to Paris as consul of the United States "to aid, through the influences known to you, the newly appointed Minister of the United States in preventing, if possible, the recognition, by France, of the independence of the Confederate States." But he made the offer expecting Lincoln to adopt the policy defined in Article V of the Constitution. He withdrew his offer on May 5, 1861. See letter to Seward of that date.—"Dr. Tochman's Letter to the Polish Democratic Societies," *Southern Literary Messenger*, XXXIV-XXXV (May, 1862), 326.

[65] The reply from the war department is dated May 20, 1861.—*Case of General Toch-*

secretary of war in verbal communication with Vice-President Stephens and by implication through a communication of his own to Secretary L. P. Walker, in which he asked removal of the restriction confining him to enlist only persons of foreign birth. Relying on this understanding, which was, at best, rather dubious, he issued from his headquarters at 57 St. Charles Street in New Orleans a proclamation to his "Fellow-Countrymen of the Old World," defining his principles in the issue and calling on them to join him in defense of the Confederate States.[66] By June 20, in less than six weeks, he had raised 1,415 foreigners, exclusive of 285 natives, whom he had organized into 20 companies and was drilling at Camp Anite 50 miles north of New Orleans under 4 officers who had had a military education and had served in European armies.[67]

When Tochman was denied the rank of brigadier general, he suspended his efforts to raise troops and withdrew from the service. A most unpleasant bickering arose between him and the government authorities. The president in a letter of October 17 states that the proposition which he had accepted was for Tochman to raise a regiment *in the North* and that the executive had directed the revision of the letter of acceptance to that effect. Furthermore the question of rank became a matter of contention. Tochman insisted that he had received positive assurance from the secretary of war that he should command the troops which he might raise. A congressional investigating committee felt that it was clear that the president had not authorized higher rank than colonel. Secretary Walker seems to have been at fault here in failing to transmit the president's decision and in thus misleading Tochman.[68]

Tochman's claims seem grandiose. "I had on my list over one

man, *Report of the Committee on Military Affairs on the Memorial of Major Gaspar Tochman,* House of Representatives of the Confederate States of America, April 23, 1863, 1.

[66] This proclamation was published in the New Orleans papers and widely in other southern papers.—New Orleans *Daily True Delta,* of June 3, 1861; *Whig* and *Despatch* of Richmond, dated May 24. Appealing to the principles of self-government, constitutional liberty, and state sovereignty, it recalled the names of LaFayette, Kosciusko, Pulaski, and DeKalb. For the wording see *Report of the Committee on Claims,* House of Representatives, January 15, 1864, 13-14.

[67] Three of these officers were: Colonel Sulakowski, who has already entered these pages; Colonel F. Schaller; and Zeubelon York. The fourth the writer has been unable to identify.

[68] *Ibid.,* 3-4; *Report of the Committee on Military Affairs,* April 23, 1863, Exhibit No. 26, pp. 5, 7-8.

hundred foreign officers who had agreed to come from the North to cooperate with me. With them, under the protection of the Polish Brigade I raised in Louisiana, I could have raised in Missouri alone a large army of Germans. The thirty or forty thousand Germans of Missouri who are now fighting against you would be under my command on your side. You would have had no reason to complain against the indifference of foreigners. They wanted a leader of their own; but not a Prince, whose family's antecedents are not endeared to the progressive liberal part of the European people, and might *probably* have contributed to causing this change in disposition of the Emperor of the French towards the Confederate States which we now witness." He thought it would have checked the enlistment of foreigners in the Federal army by the power of "mere influence" and would have proved the best propaganda for recognition abroad.[69] It is, however, highly probable that he could have raised the full compliment of two thousand troops.

From two quarters Tochman was made to feel the results of his espousal of the cause of the Confederacy. About the middle of December he received a communication from the Polish Democratic societies in France and England, which had been passed on August 26, inquiring into his motives and policy in deviating from the constitution which he had "sworn to support," and censuring him for raising a brigade of troops for the seceded states. His reply from Nashville, concealing his trouble with the authorities, followed the traditional argument that he was a citizen of Virginia and, in consequence of her action in joining the Confederacy, a citizen of the new Confederation. He felt that he had not departed from the principles of the Poles.[70] The second repercussion, from United States authorities, was far more serious for it brought about the imprisonment of his wife in the upper part of her own house in Washington under close surveillance for a fortnight. The Federal authorities ransacked the dwelling and seized her correspondence. After repeated remonstrances she was released.[71]

[69] *Report of the Committee on Claims*, January 15, 1864, Exhibit No. 8, p. 37. The allusion to a "Prince" may have reference to the Bourbon princes who had joined the northern army.

[70] "Dr. Tochman's Letter to the Polish Democratic Societies," *Southern Literary Messenger*, XXXIV-XXXV, 321.

[71] Some of the northern papers tried to make it appear that Madame Tochman was loyal and had no sympathy with her husband's southern sentiments and had no desire to

Tochman then sought monetary reparation from the Richmond government for the sacrifices and losses he had sustained in property, reputation, abandonment of his northern legal clientele, and separation for two and a half years from his family. He claimed that he was entitled under an agreement, which had the nature of a contract, to the pay of a brigadier general for three years, the period for which troops were raised, or his expenses, which he estimated at $5,925 in gold, besides a loan of $1,600 in Confederate currency which he had incurred for his support.[72] By September, 1863, he was pressing on Richmond the blow to Poland's material interests caused by his absence and neglect of the interests of the Polish-Slavonian Literary Society which he had founded in the North.[73] The refusal of a commission had not lessened his identification with the southern cause. It had, "necessarily, deprived the Confederate States of my military experience and services, and myself of the privilege of serving them by the side of those foreigners and natives who had enlisted, and intended to enlist under my command."[74] He represented that Poland had need of his services in the political crisis which had developed there in 1863 and that the payment of his claim might enable him to render her some signal service. He kept urging the president not to refer his claim to the Court of Claims, a body which had not yet been created. He conscientiously points out that the sum of $1,105.33 was deductible as he had been paid in October, 1861, a

see the cause triumph.—*National Republican* (Washington), September 25, 1861. General Scott had before her arrest given her a pass to Richmond to see her husband but then withdrew it.—Day, *Down South*, II, 268-271.

[72] He pointed out as the practice of other governments that military men who undertook to raise troops for their own commands received commissions in rank corresponding to the number of troops raised, with the emoluments attached to their commissions instead of expenses.—*Report of the Committee on Military Affairs on General Tochman's Claims*, 3-4. He claimed that the loss of the fees in a single case involving the heirs of General Kosciusko for the recovery of land in Ohio amounted to several thousand dollars. But he made no claim for compensation for all his losses. He considered them as "losses resulting from the ordinary course of the war, such as you, and other loyal citizens, have suffered, and may suffer, by its incidents."—*Ibid.*, Tochman's Letter to President Davis, September 9, 1862, *Report of Committee on Foreign Affairs*, 3.

[73] See his communications to the secretary of war, of March 2 and 9, 1863; to President Davis of September 19, 1863; to Secretary Benjamin of November 6, 1863; to H. S. Foote, a member of Congress and chairman of the Committee on Foreign Affairs, of December 5, 1863. He was amazed that the executive could have authorized so derogatory a construction of his sacrifices as "the attempt of treating me as a mere recruiting agent."— Letter of March 9, *ibid.*, 1.

[74] Letter of November 6, 1863. He felt that he must elucidate and defend the principles which had induced him to join the Confederacy, presumably by printing pamphlets, and that that undertaking can eventually "but benefit the cause of the Confederacy, and may probably lead to happy consequences."—*Ibid.*, 10-11.

colonel's salary for three months and thirteen days and some small expenses.[75]

The secretary of war, when the case was referred to him by the president, decided that his department had no power to pay for services where no commission had been issued. Tochman then carried the matter to the Committee on Foreign Affairs of the house and finally, on February 20, 1863, filed a memorial with the Committee on Military Affairs of the same body. On January 13, 1864, he had sent papers directly to the senate and the house. In May following he brought his case before the Committee on Claims of a new congress, but on May 18 he learned the discouraging news that congress had agreed to adjourn the last of that month. Finally, at long last, the Committee on Claims recommended unanimously that "Whereas, this Congress highly appreciates said Major Gaspard Tochman's devotion to the cause of freedom and his active and useful exertions in behalf of the cause of the Confederate States of America," the sum still due him be paid. But the committee could not get action that session and so the persistence of General Tochman was doomed to ultimate failure, as action was impossible after that date in the dying Confederacy.[76]

[75] Letter of September 19, 1863, *ibid.*, 3, 4.
[76] *Ibid.; Report of the Committee on Claims*, House of Representatives, 1-2. The date of the recommendation of the committee does not appear on the report.

VI

KNIGHTS-ERRANT AND SOLDIERS OF FORTUNE

IN EUROPEAN armies at the time of the American Civil War many officers were obliged to quit their profession, usually on account of financial extravagance. To these soldiers of fortune the American conflict was a perfect godsend. According to one Austrian visitor, they all espoused the northern cause, not because it was dearest, but because it was nearest. Very few foreign officers even visited the southern states, according to this same observer. He records Colonel Fremantle as the only other tourist whom he had noted during his visit of nearly a year's length. The accuracy of these observations will be tested in this and a later chapter.[1]

Knights-errant who came to offer their swords to the cause were most warmly welcomed at the beginning of the war, as each volunteer might be interpreted as indicating the crystallizing of sentiment in his country in favor of the Confederacy. Estvàn, for instance, an officer in the Austrian army, states that he was most enthusiastically welcomed by Major Ripley and his officers as he arrived in Charleston just prior to the fall of Fort Sumter, as he was "almost the only European officer serving under their flag."[2] To each new arrival, whether in camp or in Richmond drawing rooms, was accorded that gracious hospitality for which the South was justly famous.[3]

This natural eagerness for tangible evidence of favorable sentiment abroad toward the new state was undoubtedly stimulated by the fanfare given each new knight-errant who appeared on the northern side. The Comte de Paris and the Bourbon princes joined the Union forces late in 1861. Reports of their coming were well authenticated on October 2, 1861. Knowledge of a commission granted to Major Bausenwein, late aide-de-camp to Garibaldi, was instantly current in the South.[4] The persistent rumors of the acceptance by Garibaldi

---

[1] Ross, *A Visit to the Cities and Camps of the Confederate States*, 219-220. See Chap. XI.
[2] Estvàn, *War Pictures*, I, 15.
[3] Von Borcke, *Memoirs*, II, 17-19; French, *Two Wars*, 146.
[4] "Lincoln, according to telegraphic report, has accepted the tender of the military services of the Count de Paris and the Duc de Chartres. They will probably enter Gen.

himself of a command in the Union army occasioned much heart-burning in Confederate breasts. Well might the South be anxious and envious, for Garibaldi had about him on his farm on the rocky island of Caprera off the Sardinian coast a changing group of old comrades, utterly devoted to their leader and impatient for new adventures, who would readily have followed him to do battle in America.[5] These rumors persisted until late in the second year of the war. Reports of other distinguished Europeans hastening to draw a lance for the northern side could not but awaken longings on the part of the Confederate for similar knight-errantry for their side. Their longings were to be realized for, if fewer in number, those who came lent brilliant luster to the Confederate cause and won fame for themselves.

Despite the open rejoicing over new adherents to the cause, the warmth of southern hospitality, and warm personal gratitude and affection for individual foreigners, in general there was a disinclination in the Confederacy to give high rank to distinguished foreigners, or to give commissions at all to undistinguished aliens. So far as the government was concerned, its action was circumscribed during the early period of the war by the fact that all officers, except the general and staff officers, were elected by the men. Later, however, even when more of the officers were appointive, no undue partiality by the authorities toward foreigners is discernible.

Promotion was accorded charily to so general a favorite as Heros von Borcke, the Prussian knight-errant, even when urged by another favorite, General Stuart. The latter had tried repeatedly to have the stranger promoted to a brigadier-generalship, in consideration of his services and ability to handle large bodies of troops. These recommendations had been approved by General Lee and desired by the officers and men of the cavalry corps, but were rejected by the Richmond officials. The highest rank which he attained, as we shall see, was that of colonel. Slowness of recognition undoubtedly had much to do with Estván's disgruntled attitude toward the Confederacy and

---

McClellan's staff.   Major Bausenwein, late aide-de-camp to Garibaldi, has today been commissioned into the military service of the United States."—*Daily True Delta*, October 2, 1861.

[5] Secretary Seward did offer Garibaldi a commission as major general in the Union army.   See the article by H. N. Gay, "Lincoln's Offer of a Command to Garibaldi," *Century Magazine*, LXXV, 63-74.   It is probably not amiss to remind the reader that Garibaldi had lived in the United States for parts of four years, 1850-1854, though he never became a United States citizen.

Colonel Heros von Borcke, chief of staff to General Stuart. By courtesy of the Confederate Museum, Richmond, Va.

ultimate departure in the midst of the war.[6] Just as great parsimony was manifested in regard to posts in the low ranks. The Scotchman, Watson, who served with intelligence and ability in the Baton Rouge Rifles, relates his experience when the onerous and not too desirable post of orderly sergeant fell vacant and he, a third sergeant, was selected for the position. In the course of his examination before a board of officers, in which he was sustaining himself well, it was revealed that he was not a citizen. This was considered by the examiners an obstacle, but after a lengthy consultation it was decided that he might be allowed to pass, as he was being considered for a noncommissioned office; but he was given clearly to understand that he need expect no higher rank and could not hold a commission unless he became a citizen. He was advised to get his preliminary papers at once. Like a true Scotchman, the episode only strengthened him in his determination never to forswear his British citizenship.[7]

One grand exception to the general rule of reserving the highest rank to citizens[8] was made in favor of Prince de Polignac, scion of blood royal, though even he did not vault at once into the exalted rank of major general. Camille Armand Jules Marie, Prince de Polignac, was the son of that Prince de Polignac who had served as president of the Council of Ministers of King Charles X of France. The son had been born at Millemont (Seine-et-Oise) on February 16, 1832, so that he was still a very young man, only twenty-nine years old, when he placed his sword at the service of the Confederacy. He enjoyed not only the prestige of distinguished position, but also military experience, for he had changed from his original regiment to the Fourth Hussars in order to participate in the Crimean War from the beginning of hostilities. He conducted himself with sufficient valor to win a lieutenantship in the Fourth Regiment of Chasseurs and to be awarded the Crimean medal. His adventurous spirit could not brook the inactive life of a provincial garrison, and so he secured his discharge early in 1859, and entered upon a study of plant life in Central America.[9] When war was declared between the northern and southern sections of the United States, it was quite in character for

---

[6] See what Von Borcke himself has to say on the subject.—*Op. cit.*, II, 306.
[7] Watson, *Life in the Confederate Army*, 140.
[8] Patrick Cleburne, the only other foreign-born person who attained this high rank in the Confederate service, was, it will be recalled, a naturalized citizen.
[9] *Confederate Veteran*, XXII, 389.

him to offer his sword to that side which personified for him the righteous cause, especially when it coincided with his instinct to defend the weak. His offer was accepted, no doubt with much secret satisfaction, and he was accorded on July 16, 1861, the relatively high rank of lieutenant colonel of infantry, and made chief of staff to General Beauregard.

We may perhaps be permitted a picture of him as he appeared about that general's camp. He was the typical Gaul, tall and thin, grave of face, looking fully his years by virtue of a Napoleonic beard, with possibly a hint of the medieval knight of romance in his mount. He was often pelted, as he rode past, by the rough humor of the soldiers with one of their favorite jibes, "Come out 'er them boots! We see yer mustache!" Yet with the soldier was combined the simple gentleman and courtier, as the following story illustrates. On one occasion, when a Richmond belle was congratulating him on his promotion to a brigadiership, which came by January, 1863, she corrected herself to address him as "Count." As simply as a child he replied, "No, Madame: God made me that; the other I made myself!"[10] He seems to have been very democratic in his relations with common soldiers, for Mercer Otey of the signal corps records that he felt it quite a feather in his cap to be permitted occasionally to enter into conversation with a "live" prince.[11]

His promotion in rank seems to have been well earned. When General Beauregard set to work at Corinth to reorganize his army, he was ably seconded by his chief of staff. The active part taken by Polignac on the day of the battle of Corinth and the bravery there displayed was thought by some to have merited special notice in Beauregard's report—which was not accorded.[12] In any case promotion was promptly forthcoming, for by January, 1863, he was serving as brigadier general with the command of General Dick Taylor who was operating in Louisiana under General E. Kirby Smith.

Let General Richard Taylor tell how the French nobleman won over a command of belligerently provincial soldiers. "I assigned him

---

[10] Thomas Cooper de Leon, *Belles, Beaux, and Brains of the 60's*, 332, tells this delightful story.

[11] W. N. Mercer Otey, "Operations of the Signal Corps," *Confederate Veteran*, VIII, 129.

[12] " . . . why it was not done, can only be attributed to the aversion to render justice to a foreigner, generally attributed to the Southerners, who are jealous of any one else sharing their own glory."—Estvàn, *op. cit.*, II, 100.

to the command of a Texas brigade of about seven hundred men, who had been recently dismounted and were accordingly in an ill humor, who swore that a 'dam frog-eating Frenchman' whose very name they could not pronounce, and whose orders were Greek to them, 'should never command them,' and mutiny was threatened. I went to their camp, assembled the officers, and pointed out the consequences of disobedience, for which I should hold them accountable; but promised that if they remained dissatisfied with their new commander after an action with the enemy, I would then remove him."[13] It was uphill work at first, notwithstanding General Polignac's patience and good temper. The adjustment called for was as great, as General Taylor suggests, as if a crude Texas colonel, drawn from some cattle ranch, were to be sent to command a brigade of the Imperial Guard.[14]

In the first week of 1864 the United States sent a gunboat expedition up the Ouachita River. The expedition was defeated and the boats driven off. Polignac, by his judgment and coolness under fire, gained the confidence and respect of his men, as he soon gained their affection by his care and attention. They got on famously once he had proved his leadership, and he made capital soldiers out of that brigade, which ever after swore by him. It probably only endeared him to his rough troops that on occasion he could swear "like a trooper." When excited, he was addicted to a multitude of imprecations and, though they were not the expressions an American cowboy used, their meaning was perfectly intelligible to the latter.[15]

General Polignac displayed great valor and spirit at the battle of Mansfield during the famous Red River campaign against General Banks, where he won a complete victory, and secured the rank of major general to date from the day of that victory, April 8, 1864.[16]

[13] Taylor, *Destruction and Reconstruction*, 153. The Richmond government may have transferred Polignac from the East in expectation that he would receive a brigade of Louisiana Creoles.

[14] *Ibid.*, 132.   [15] Duke, *Reminiscences*, 132-133.

[16] *Confederate Veteran*, XXII, 389. It is of passing interest to know that his daughter, Agnes de Polignac, the Marquise de Courtivron, consented to become a member of the New Orleans chapter of the Daughters of the Confederacy. In 1918 the Marquise came to America with her husband, a liaison officer of the French High Commission, and while in America visited the battlefield of Mansfield, where occurred her father's most signal victory. On her return home she was instrumental in organizing the Paris chapter of the United Daughters of the Confederacy. This chapter took as one of its objectives the erection of a monument to General Polignac and on April 8, 1925, on the sixty-first anniversary of the battle, it was unveiled by the general's son, Prince Victor Mansfield Polignac, in the presence of his mother, the widow of the general. The prince himself lived until 1913.—Thomas, *Arkansas in War and Reconstruction*, 261, n.; *Confederate Veteran*, XXIX, 352, XXVI, 270, XXII, 221.

As stated before, he was the only person owing allegiance to a foreign flag who attained this high rank. At the very close of the war, as has been related, he rendered service of an entirely different nature in the diplomatic field.[17]

The strangeness of his foreign name to their untutored ears led the western soldiers to make a rude jest which brought its well-deserved punishment. Distorting his name into the designation of a certain animal of odoriferous ignominy, they would hold their noses when he appeared. When his curiosity was sufficiently piqued, he sought enlightenment on the reasons for their peculiar conduct. He thereupon proceeded to give them a sharp lesson, for he led them off on a long, hard ride through woods where presumably their quest might bring them in contact with the scents of the animal which they so studiously avoided.[18] And yet these were the men he could set wild with amusement and enthusiasm by placing his hand on his heart and exclaiming with *empressement*, "Soldiers, behold your Polignac!" They beheld him and followed him with ardor and devotion.[19]

While the prince spoke English fluently, and in his calm moments with absolute correctness, American camp slang baffled him. It is not surprising that he was puzzled when a handsome Creole lad came to his headquarters one morning while he was stationed in Virginia and, after the customary salute, said, "Colonel, I have been off on a two-week's furlough and am just back. I belong to Colonel Censer's 'lay-out,' but don't know where it is. Will you please tell me where it is?"

"Colonel Censer's what?" shouted Polignac, his eyes bulging with amazement.

"To Colonel Censer's 'lay-out,' " repeated the boy. "You know it, it belongs to your 'shebang.' "

"Well, d—n my eyes to ze deep blue h—l," groaned Polignac. "I have been militaire all my life. I was educated for ze army. I have heard of ze compagnie, ze battalion, ze regiment, ze brigade, ze division, and ze army corps, but—, —! 'my soul to ze—ef evair I hear of ze 'lay-out' or ze 'shebang' before."[20]

Probably the most picturesque figure among the foreigners who

[17] See above, Chap. III.
[18] The story was told the writer by an old soldier as one current in Polignac's camp. See also the version by B. Giraud Wright, *A Southern Girl in '61*, 93.
[19] Caroline E. Merrick, *Old Times in Dixie Land, A Southern Matron's Recollections*, 74.
[20] Duke, *op. cit.*, 132-133.

came to break a lance in behalf of the South was the tall Pomeranian officer, Heros von Borcke, who possessed many of the same qualities which made his superior officer, General J. E. B. Stuart, so romantic a soldier, and which probably made the two so companionable. Descendant of a noble house which had furnished famous captains to all the line of Hohenzollern kings, he was born with the lust of battle in his veins. The year 1861 found him serving on the staff of the prince of Prussia, but he secured leave of absence, ran the blockade in May, 1862, and became chief of staff to General Stuart. He brought to the aid of the Confederate cause a splendid equipment, physical and mental. He was not only a superb tactician and organizer, but was very well educated and well read in the literature and art of Europe. With his high attainments he had the simplicity and gentleness of the most cultured German gentleman.

When he appeared among the Confederates he was a giant in stature, six feet four inches in height, as tall as Prince Polignac but more muscular and with the stretch and chest of a prize fighter. He was a virile-looking blonde, with great golden curling mustaches and wide-open blue eyes in which lurked the expression of a singularly modest boy. If he had hailed from one of the Scandinavian countries, he would have been called a Viking. His appearance in the dress of Stuart's cavalry must have been striking in the extreme. We owe to his fellow countryman, Scheibert, a description of his appearance when the latter first met him. "As the time drew near when I must leave the headquarters [Lee's], there came riding up to headquarters one day a tall, stately major, in a feathered hat, tall boots, and great gauntlets to whom I was presented without understanding his name."[21] It was said that he rode the biggest horse and wielded the heaviest sabre in the army,[22] which he swung as easily as if it were a thing of straw, making his appearance in skirmish or battle a living terror to the enemy. From the first, winning high place in the esteem of his fellow officers and superiors, Von Borcke, whom the troopers

[21] *Sieben Monate in den Rebellen-Staaten*, 20.
[22] Many tales were told of that sword, which had an unusually long blade made to order. It was longer than the regulations prescribed and so an officer reported Von Borcke to King William IV, who ordered the colonel never to use it again in Prussia. The latter laid it aside for use in fighting for some other oppressed nation. On the occasion of his visit to the South in 1886 his sword was returned to him. He then presented it to the state of Virginia to be preserved as a relic.—Schuricht, *History of the German Element in Virginia*, II, 83. Polignac also wore a sword that rivaled Colonel Skinner's famed blade, and used it most effectively in personal combat.

styled "Major Bandbox," gained brilliant renown in the saddle and equal popularity in Richmond society.

He was, of course, welcomed in the highest social circles of the South. "To dance with him in the swift-circling, never-reversing German fashion was a breathless experience," writes Mrs. Harrison, "and his method of avoiding obstacles was simply to lift his partner off her feet, without altering his step, and deposit her in safety further on." His difficulties with the English idiom were a source of great entertainment. Waxing enthusiastic over a Confederate belle, he declared, "Ach, she was most beautiful in von home-spun dress and von self-made hat."[23]

The South will never weary of repeating the tales of his prowess, of his scouts for General Stuart, of his boyish pranks when his chief, with a few congenial spirits in his command, rode all night for a frolic. Once he captured the officers of a cavalry regiment of the Union army and their orderlies singlehanded and without a shot when he was out scouting alone, a favorite sport with him. Stuart admired and loved him and remarked of him, "A splendid, proud fellow!" He was designated by the same epithets by every cavalryman, all of whom knew him and loved to boast of his deeds.[24] Probably no better indication of Stuart's opinion of him is to be found than the remark that he made to Scheibert when Von Borcke introduced his fellow countryman to the general. Stuart, after bidding Scheibert especially welcome as a Prussian, said, pointing to Von Borcke, "If you have more men like him over there, send them all over here."[25]

After more than two years of brilliant service with General Stuart, he was severely wounded in the throat on June 19, 1863, in the bloody strife at Middleburg as the Army of Virginia was advancing in the Gettysburg campaign. Scheibert tells in detail the story of how a small group placed him carefully in Stuart's own ambulance, sent back by the general for that purpose, and of how, as the little cavalcade proceeded along the rocky mountain, Von Borcke shuddered at each jolt. Just as they found themselves caught between the two armies and the Confederates retreating, they fortunately discovered an inn, on the estrade of which they deposited him in the care of the

[23] *Recollections Grave and Gay*, 130, 135.
[24] Scheibert, *Sieben Monate in den Rebellen-Staaten*, 23.
[25] *Ibid.*, 20.

innkeeper and made off despite his pleas and demands to be taken along.

It reveals much of Von Borcke's character that he could laugh at such a time. A Negro who had been left to tend the horses while the group carried the wounded officer to the inn had slipped off the halter to let the horses graze, and when Scheibert, hearing the Yankees coming, came dashing up to make good his escape, the Negro failed to understand the need for haste. Scheibert's English failed to meet the occasion, and so, with no time for a long parley, he talked German, but made his meaning intelligible to the Negro by blows of the sword on the head until he got the slave mounted on the white mule, Kitty, and then by further blows got him off into the forest at a gallop. Von Borcke, lying on the piazza, wounded and deserted, still had to laugh over the ludicrous scene.

When within a half-hour the fight was ended and the combatants again with the command, Stuart inquired with black looks about his absent friend. When he learned that Von Borcke was apparently in the hands of the foe, he was inconsolable until convinced that everything possible had been done for him. "I must cut him out; he may still be unobserved," he declared, a view shared by all the other cavalrymen. Scheibert remained in the neighborhood some time to learn what could be done in Von Borcke's interest. As he set off in sorrow over the latter's fate, he met General Longstreet, who gave his word to rescue the Prussian the next morning if he were still in the besieged house and had not been carried off. "It would be a shame for the army to leave so brave an officer in the foe's hands so long as it is possible to save him."[26] A brigadier who rode beside Longstreet rejoiced when he was given the agreeable commission to free this general favorite. The rescue was effected and the wounded hero was sent to Richmond. The northern papers rejoiced prematurely over the death and burial of "Stuart's right arm," for they knew that a prominent Confederate had fallen and even thought for a time that it might be Stuart himself.

Von Borcke had already had the gratification of knowing how sincerely the Confederacy would mourn his loss when a rumor of his death at Chancellorsville spread and was accepted as true throughout the South. Besides many letters of condolence sent to Stuart, a

[26] *Ibid.*, 80-82. The accounts of Scheibert and Von Borcke do not agree at all points.

dispatch was sent Lee by Governor Letcher, requesting that the body be forwarded so that Virginia might justly have the privilege of interring it with all the honors of war. To this demand, General Lee laconically replied, "Can't spare it! It's in pursuit of Stoneman." Von Borcke, during his convalescence, received from General Stuart the following touching letter: "My dear Von, my camp seems dull and deserted to me since you left. On the battlefield, I do not know how to do without you and I feel as if my right arm had been taken from me."[27]

The wound proved to be from a heavy Minié ball, which had to remain in his lung as the surgeons dared not operate. He lived the next months under great suffering with constant attacks of strangling at the least exertion. He was tenderly nursed back to life by the family of Professor Thomas R. Price of South Carolina, which was then residing in Richmond.[28]

Stuart on his deathbed expressed a desire for Von Borcke's promotion to his command, but the Richmond authorities did not see fit to comply with this request, possibly because of his physical inability to take the field, but also perhaps because he was a foreigner. Congress did, however, take the unusual step of honoring him by a special vote of thanks, phrased in the very words with which Lafayette had been similarly honored.[29] And finally, at the end of 1864, he was promoted to a colonelcy by President Davis and intrusted with a mission to England, as is related elsewhere.[30] Undoubtedly his services and experiences in the war in America enhanced the value of his services to his native land when he hastened home from England to

---

[27] *Memoirs*, II, 257-258, 306.

[28] He was warned that if the cyst, which had formed about it, moved, the ball would drop into his windpipe and strangle him. Nevertheless he went gallantly into society. Consternation seized the young women if they dropped a thimble or handkerchief. Mrs. Harrison tells how once in her home, in leaning over the back of a sofa to pick up a thimble he brought on a frightful fit of coughing which her mother dealt with skillfully while the young women were reduced to tears. She also contrasts the picture of the emaciated Von Borcke with that of his early vigorous appearance.—*Op. cit.*, 130-131.

[29] "Whereas, Major Heros von Borcke, of Prussia, having left his own country to assist in securing the independence of ours, and by his personal gallantry in the field having won the admiration of his comrades as well as that of his commanding general, Resolved . . . That the thanks of Congress are due, and the same are hereby tendered to Major von Borcke, for his self-sacrificing devotion to our Confederacy, and for his distinguished services in support of its cause."—*Statutes of the Confederacy*, First Congress, Fourth Session, Joint Resolution, No. 4, Jan. 30, 1864. Von Borcke quotes the resolution in his *Memoirs*, II, 306-307.

[30] Heros von Borcke und Justus Scheibert, *Die grosse Reiterschlacht bei Brandy Station*, Anhang, 177. See above, Chap. III, for his special mission.

participate in the Austro-Prussian War in 1866. After Sadowa he retired to his farm, living the life of a plain, hard-working farmer, which was broken in 1884 by a visit to the southern states, which was, like LaFayette's, almost a triumphal procession.[31]

Besides Heros von Borcke there was a considerable group of foreigners of various nationalities who attained the rank of colonel. Probably the most distinguished next to Von Borcke was Colonel George Gordon of the British army, who had involved himself in some trouble in England and hence came to cast in his lot with the South. He was a big, soldierly-looking man with red whiskers, and with such beautiful manners that he was received as a constant visitor in many of the most refined southern homes. Despite his constant support of the corps which maintained a notorious gambling "club" near the Spotswood Hotel in Richmond, he was recognized as a real fighter. General Stuart, who seemed to have the ability to recognize an able warrior when he saw one, placed Gordon on staff duty and seems never to have felt that it was an error. The Englishman later served on General A. P. Hill's staff and then as second in command of a North Carolina regiment, and was finally badly wounded in the assault by Trimble following the Pickett charge at Gettysburg.[32]

Certainly no stranger character appears in the pages of Confederate history than Colonel Bela Estvàn, a Hungarian who had seen much service on the fields of Italy and Hungary. He had served in the Austrian army under Radetzky in Italy and had been present at the defense of Sebastopol in the Crimean War, but had then come to America, for which he seemed to entertain a real affection and for the misfortunes of which he grieved when secession threatened to disrupt the republic.[33] His prominence in the Virginia militia and the fact that he had been a colonel in that body at the time of the John Brown raid, in addition to his European experience, may explain his early

[31] Schuricht, *op. cit.*, II, 82, 83; Von Borcke, *Memoirs*, II, 298-299. In the 1886 edition he has a chapter on his American visit.

[32] De Leon, *Belles, Beaux, and Brains of the 60's*, 335; Ross, *A Visit to the Cities and Camps of the Confederate States*, 232; *Confederate Veteran*, XXV, 201, XXXVIII, 263. Ross tells how Gordon took part in the grand assault with Pickett's charge which miscarried. His men were very reluctant to go.—*Op. cit.*, 64-65; *Confederate Veteran*, XXXVIII, 263.

[33] His long residence in the South was the main inducement to his taking service for the Confederacy. "To America, my second home, whose image I cling to with fond attachment, I cannot look back without sorrow for her misfortunes."—*Op. cit.*, Introduction, iv. See also for his earlier record, Pivány, *Hungarians in the American Civil War*, 10.

prominence in the war. Almost immediately after South Carolina had seceded from the Union he received a commission from two of the most influential southern leaders with directions to proceed at once from Richmond to South Carolina to superintend the arrangements for the bombardment of Fort Sumter. This commission was followed by an order to start for General Bragg's headquarters in Florida to make a report on the state of affairs there, as Bragg had been given orders to take Fort Pickens. Thereupon he was sent to Raleigh to work out plans with Governor Clark to defend the North Carolina coast. He saw eighteen months' service as a colonel of cavalry with the Confederate forces. He was first attached to the cavalry under General Polk and was then sent to the Wise Legion. He was in the peninsular campaign against McClellan in 1862; he served in Stuart's cavalry raid around McDowell, and at Seven Pines his regiment was attached to Longstreet's division. Stricken by yellow fever in the swampy rice fields of Savannah in the middle of the year 1862, he, according to his own story, applied for a pass to the North, and was allowed by the Federal government to go to New York. There he quickly recovered his health, and was able to proceed to England where he devoted himself to a book relating his Confederate war experiences.[34]

The account of "Count" Estvàn given by Schuricht presents a very different story, the perfect accuracy of which the reader is forced to question. There seems to be much bitter animus back of it as the following excerpt indicates. "He [the so-called Count] lived there [in Richmond] upon the earnings of his two ladies, his wife and his sister-in-law, who gave lessons. . . . He himself was a very good-looking jovial man and knew how to play the part of an upright Austrian country nobleman to perfection. When the Civil War commenced, he pretended to have recruited in North Carolina a regiment of Lancers and was authorized to draw from the Ordnance Department the necessary equipage." He was reported to have taken it all to North Carolina and to have sold it there. Claiming to have deserted, he went to Washington in the full uniform of a Confederate

[34]Estvàn, *op. cit.*, I, 417-418, II, 128, 239 ff. The entire book is, of course, the story of his experience in the American war. Naturally, press comments in the Confederate papers after his departure for the North were caustic. "In these war times, they [deserters] are plentiful under the uniform of military officers. Estvàn, the soi-disant count, who ran to the North after playing out his calls here, was one of a particular class."—*Daily Richmond Examiner*, February 5, 1864.

colonel, where he was received with great distinction, even by President Lincoln. After he had completed his book in England, he revisited Vienna, where, according to some reports, he was arrested and prosecuted as a criminal. Schuricht says the Germans were eager to disclaim him.[35]

A perusal of his book leaves no doubt that though his strictures on the Confederate authorities may not have been uninfluenced by personal feelings, at heart he was a Unionist; he therefore did the natural thing when he resigned his commission and should, doubtless, never have taken service under that banner. That he played the rôle of deserter or that he failed to discharge his duty while wearing the gray is not indicated by the evidence.

Casual references occur to several other men who held rank as colonels, sometimes by name, sometimes without label. In the Confederate records there is note of a Reverend James Sinclair who had held a colonel's commission in the Confederate army, but who in October, 1863, wanted to return to England. Although Secretary Benjamin ruled that he was, alien citizenship notwithstanding, liable to conscription under the rules then in effect, he suggested that on the grounds of expediency, Sinclair should be excused. Colonel Henderson of the English army served for a period in the gray uniform; Lord Talbot had a son who continued in the service until the close of the war, receiving the rank of colonel. Lieutenant Colonel von Scheliha, a Prussian, served as chief of staff to General Buckner and acted also later as chief engineer of the department of the Gulf. The book which he published in London in 1868, *A Treatise on Coast Defense*, he dedicated to Prince Adelbert of Prussia.[36] There is also reference to a Colonel Este, a Prussian, in General Wise's brigade.[37]

One knight-errant who got himself into serious danger of the hangman's noose instead of honorable death on the field of battle from too candid expression of his opinion was Colonel Adolphus H. Adler, a Hungarian who had recently served on Garibaldi's staff. He

[35] Schuricht, *op. cit.*, II, 88-89.

[36] For Sinclair see Bonham, *British Consuls in the Confederacy*, "Columbia University Studies," XLIII, 246; for Lord Talbot, Jacob R. Freese, *Secrets of the Late Rebellion*, 83; for Von Scheliha, Ross, *op. cit.*, 148.

References may often be found to some vague French or German colonel or major of whom account can scarcely be taken, as they are not named. Bartlett, for instance, speaks of a "French colonel who had accompanied us as a volunteer" and of one or two Prussian officials.—"A Soldier's Story of the War," *Military Record of Louisiana*, 34-35.

[37] Catherine C. Hopley, *Life in the South; from the Commencement of the War*, II, 85.

was assigned to the post of engineer in chief to General Wise's brigade and rendered some real service in the line of his engineering duty, but insisted on airing unfavorable opinions of his superior's military talents, declaring him "no soljare, no soljare." He was thrown into Libby Prison under suspicion of northern sympathies. When informed that he would be hung, he tried to cut his throat and lived in constant dread of an ignominious end until he effected his escape north after ten months' imprisonment.[38]

The list of majors owning foreign allegiance is not imposing, and it is not always possible to determine whether or not they had become naturalized. A Major Ford is referred to as an experienced English officer. Major Nocquet, who had served several years in Algiers as engineer officer in the French army, took service with the Confederate army in September, 1861, as chief engineer to Major Gilmer of Bragg's army. He was appointed major of the engineer corps in October, 1862, and won high praise from his superiors. Singing the "Marseillaise" as his comrades gathered about the blazing camp fire at night to fight over again their famous battles, he appeared a zealous and devoted follower of the Stars and Bars; yet in the fall of 1864 he deserted to the foe, as we shall see in due course of time.[39] Major Scheibert served for so short a time and in such individual relationship that he is reserved for special treatment in a class by himself.

Holding the relatively unimportant office of captain were a more numerous and interesting group of foreigners. Denied to the plodding foreigner who had been settled in their midst and who entered the war under compulsion of one sort or another, the title of captain was bestowed readily on knights-errant who slipped through the blockade to join the southern armies for a season. Many officers of foreign armies on leave of absence were found fighting on both sides in America, and often distinguished themselves with brilliant gallantry.

None can exceed in sheer interest the clever, handsome, venturesome English lad, Frank Warrington Dawson who, in his ardor to share the fortunes of the Confederacy, slipped aboard the *Nashville* on New Year's Day, 1862, at Southampton, reported to the officer of

---

[38] William C. Harris, *Prison Life in the Tobacco Warehouse at Richmond*, 87.
[39] *Confederate Veteran*, XXIX, 21; Day, *Down South*, II, 298; J. P. Austin, *The Blue and the Gray*, 50.

the deck that he had been ordered by the captain to report for duty and was duly mustered into service by signing the articles. Captain R. B. Pegram had demurred during his first interview with Dawson at enlisting a mere lad, especially of another nation, but there seemed nothing else for him to do but to accept him when he found him aboard, as the ship was sailing precarious seas and there was no place for other than members of the crew. Dawson ultimately won a new country as well as fame, for he remained after the war to become an American citizen of the restored Union. Upon landing, as he feared that there would be little activity in the naval branch of the service, he went to the navy department alone, in order to avoid the possible objections of Captain Pegram, who had come to recognize his worth and who had treated the lad with marked kindness. He thought of joining as a private the Purcell Battery, commanded by William Pegram, a nephew of Captain Robert Pegram, though the latter insisted on his waiting for something better; but with youthful impatience he went out to the battery and reported for duty a few days before the opening of the Seven Days' Battles. His appointment as a commissioned officer was not long delayed, as with such powerful influence as that of Captain Pegram he was listed as lieutenant under an act of congress, authorizing the appointment of forty lieutenants of artillery for duty as ordnance officers. At Richmond he asked Colonel Gorgas, chief of ordnance of the army, to assign him to Longstreet's corps and mentioned that he did not want duty in the rear. To oblige him, Colonel Gorgas in his letter to Longstreet asked that the lad be given any "particularly hazardous service" in his line of duty.[40]

He had therewith won the first gilt bar on the red collar of his gray jacket. The second step upward came with his appointment as chief of ordnance. His fellow countryman, Ross, found him in 1863 acting in that capacity in Bragg's army near Chattanooga, when Colonel Manning was wounded, a highly responsible post to entrust to a captain, when it is usually given to a lieutenant colonel. The end of the war came while he was awaiting promotion for gallantry on the field. Cool, brave, and reliable, he was still a fresh-faced stripling.[41]

[40] Harrison, *op. cit.*, 179; Dawson, *Reminiscences*, 54, 56; De Leon, *Belles, Beaux, and Brains of the 60's*, 333-334. Dawson's entire book presents a full account of his war experience. See also *Confederate Veteran*, XXV, 201.

[41] Ross, *op. cit.*, 151. After the war Dawson worked as a journalist on several southern papers, became editor of the Charleston *Courier*, and finally met a tragic end in May,

Neither alien citizenship nor lack of technical knowledge had been allowed to stand in the way of Dawson's promotion to a captaincy. He had been recommended strongly for promotion, but an examination was necessary. Dawson boldly confronted Secretary of War Seddon to tell him that he had been too long in the field to know as much as a youngster who had just been graduated from college, and that if promotion depended on a knowledge of conic sections and calculus, he would probably remain a lieutenant. After listening patiently to the outburst, Seddon replied that an examination was inevitable but endorsed on Dawson's papers for the benefit of the board that it would "make due allowance for any deficiency in theoretical knowledge which may have been caused by the engrossing nature of his duties in the field."[42]

Captain Byrne, who was on Cleburne's staff, and who, despite losing a leg at Manassas, insisted on fighting through the war; Captain Edgar J. Franklin, serving on General Drayton's staff under General Magruder in the Trans-Mississippi Department, and participating in the brilliant engagement at Galveston on January 1, 1862; and Captain Edward Lees Coffey, an Irishman who had served in India, were all natives of the British Isles and subjects of Queen Victoria.[43]

Captain John Cussons, aide to General Law, was a tall, long-haired, wild-looking Englishman who had already indulged his love of adventure in digging for gold in California. The men used to call him "General Law's wild man." He was the sort of person who would pass along the point of a Federal picket or skirmish line for half a mile or more, a target for Unionists all the way, and never seem to pay any attention to them. He was taken captive at the battle of Gettysburg and carried off to Johnson's Island. He either scratched under or climbed over the prison wall and escaped back to Dixie. He happened on the house of a charming widow, which was located a few miles north of Richmond, a beautiful place called

1889, in a private quarrel protecting a woman.—De Leon, *Belles, Beaux, and Brains of the 60's*, 334. In his editorials he rendered much service to his adopted city and state. His campaign against duelling brought him prominently before the country so that Pope Leo conferred on him the Order of St. Gregory the Great.—*The South in the Building of the Nation*, XI, 271.   [42] Dawson, *op. cit.*, 112.

[43] Ross, *op. cit.*, 129-130; Dawson, *op. cit.*, 131; *Confederate Veteran*, XXV, 201; Harrison, *op. cit.*, 158. Coffey was appointed as drillmaster with the rank of first lieutenant. See his file, Confederate Archives.

Glenallen. He immediately claimed exemption from the Confederate service, as a British subject, married the charming widow, and, in the words of the storybooks, "lived happily," if not ever after, until her death in 1900.[44]

Captain Prendergast was another Englishman, an ex-member of the British army who served in the Tenth Tennessee. He was wounded in 1863 at Chickamauga and again in September, 1864, on his way to Mississippi. Unlike most Britishers, he was vocal about his privations and held that General Hood's army had met sufferings almost beyond endurance.[45]

The career of Justus Scheibert in the Confederate army must be treated as a thing apart because of its brevity and the peculiar nature of the service. He was primarily a visitor but, as a military man, he could not resist the temptation to enlist when the conflict pressed close. A major in the Prussian engineer army corps, he was sent by the royal Prussian war minister to the United States in the winter of 1863 to observe military tactics in the War of Secession.[46] He left Berlin for London in February, 1863, to get letters of introduction from Mason to influential Confederates and advice as to how to pass the blockade. He was given Charleston as his objective, a decision agreeable to him as he wished to observe the siege of that place. By the middle of the month he sailed from Liverpool to Charleston, via New York and Nassau. Arrived at Charleston on March 15, he offered Beauregard his services as a volunteer. The latter graciously put Scheibert on his staff and charged his adjutant with securing the necessary equipment for him.[47] Although he had intended to join the Army of the Tennessee, as it was the general belief that the decisive conflict would occur there, he decided first to visit the Army of Virginia, then in camp near Fredericksburg. It thus happened, by an accident, that he was an eyewitness and participant in several important engagements in the East, including the all-important Gettys-

---

[44] William C. Oates, *The War between the Union and the Confederacy and its Lost Opportunities*, 176-178. Cussons' indifference to a superior officer led to a challenge between him and Colonel Connelly, in which Major Belo met Cussons while the colonel met Captain Terrell. Before serious damage could be done, the colonel unconditionally withdrew the challenge.—*Ibid.* Cussons' File does not show claim of exemption, but leave as a paroled prisoner.—Confederate Archives, War Department.

[45] Cumming, *A Journal of Hospital Life*, 103; Bonham, *op. cit.*, 129-130.

[46] Scheibert was born in Stettin, May 16, 1831, so that he was at the time of his visit not quite thirty years old.—Von Borcke und Scheibert, *op. cit.*, Anhang, 178.

[47] Scheibert, *Sieben Monate in den Rebellen-Staaten*, 10-11.

burg campaign. Here he was first received at Lee's headquarters and then invited by General Stuart, with whom he was brought into contact through his fellow countryman, Heros von Borcke, to Stuart's headquarters at Culpeper. Because he was a fellow officer and a friend of Von Borcke, he was allowed to accompany the expedition of General Stuart to Kelly's Ford and to the battle of Chancellorsville. He threw discretion to the winds and impetuously volunteered for actual combat as a captain of cavalry, with scarcely time, before the cavalry was off, to sew on the insignia of his rank, necessary to save him from the fate of a spy if he were caught.[48] Their task was to watch the passage of the foe at Kelly's Ford, to harass it continually, and to push it toward General Lee, meanwhile keeping that officer, who was marching against Hooker, informed of the enemy's movements.

Again by a mere throw of the dice, he was assured participation in the Gettysburg campaign. A serious fever prevented him from carrying out his intention to visit Vicksburg in order to study, as an engineer, the methods of defense until Grant had that city entirely surrounded and entry was impossible. He thus escaped capture by the Federals and gained participation in the greatest battle of the war, for at this moment came an invitation from General Stuart to join him, as an important expedition, apparently toward the north, was in prospect. Rapid recovery of his health in the salubrious air of the Virginia foothills where Stuart had pitched his camp made possible his presence at the cavalry engagement of Brandy Station on June 9 and the opportunity of being an eyewitness, from the vantage point of a very tall tree overlooking the entire battlefield, of the three days' battle of Gettysburg. So good was the view that General Lee twice came to the foot of the tree to question him about movements of the enemy.[49]

The writer has said that Scheibert belonged in a class of his own. Not quite! One must take note also of a handsome and plucky young Englishman, Lord Edward St. Maur of the family of the Duke of Somerset, who evidently came as a visitor, but was unable to resist

[48] As a matter of fact the staff did ride off before he was ready so that he could only follow the tracks, lost on the pavement of Culpeper, and did not catch up with the general until noon.—*Ibid.*, 25.

[49] *Ibid.*, 63, 65; Von Borcke und Scheibert, *op. cit.*, Vorwort, v-vi; J. Scheibert, "Letter from Maj. Scheibert of the Prussian Royal Engineers," *Southern Historical Society Papers*, V, 90. One of the best accounts of Gettysburg is from his pen.

the temptation to fight. He came to Richmond with the Marquis of Hartington in the spring of 1862 and seems to have borne himself well in the Seven Days' Battles around Richmond and under hot fire with Longstreet at the battle of Frayser's Farm. It would appear that these were his only battles here, for he soon crossed into the Union lines by flag of truce and returned to England to the regret of Richmond society.[50]

Service on the staff of some general was, of course, one convenient way to honor the chivalrous stranger within the gates—a method which involved necessarily neither high rank nor the emoluments which went with that rank. Enough instances occur where foreign citizenship is indicated to justify the writer in making the above statement. This practice resulted in a very cosmopolitan air at some army headquarters.

Foreigners seem to have been particularly favored as aides-de-camp. Perhaps they were among the most useful and hardest-worked officers of the army; there were among them English, French, and German dignitaries who had crossed the ocean to study an American war. Marcus Baum, a German Jew who enlisted early although exempt from military duty as a foreigner, affords such an instance. General Joseph B. Kershaw, to whom he was acting as special aide and whom he rescued from danger at the price of his own life, said of him, "No braver man, no one truer to the cause, no soldier more loyal to his chief ever breathed than Marcus Baum of Camden, South Carolina."[51] Baron von Massow is another unquestionable instance of a foreign subject serving in this capacity. He was a Prussian cavalry officer who came to Richmond in 1861 to enter the Confederate army from eager desire for actual war. Not successful in securing a commission, he joined Mosby's independent troop and acted as one of his aides.[52] Several other instances of foreigners serving as aides are Baron Barke, a Prussian officer who served as aide-de-camp to General Stuart; a Scotchman whose name cannot be recovered, who was aide

[50] *Confederate Veteran*, XXV, 201; Harrison, *op. cit.*, 131-132. He met the sad fate of being mauled and eaten by a tiger while game hunting in India.

[51] Baum's white horse covered with foam and blood returned riderless from the field, but his rider's body was never recovered because of the great confusion.—*Confederate Veteran*, XXII, 170. If knights-errant be confined to non-residents, Baum does not, of course, belong here.

[52] John W. Munson, *Reminiscences of a Mosby Guerilla*, 154. Schuricht records his subsequent career.—*Op. cit.*, II, 87.

to General Martin in command of North Carolina troops; and Major Atkins of the British army, who will soon be referred to as an aide to General Wheat.[53]

Foreigners certainly served on the staff of practically every general in the Confederate service, but whether they had become naturalized or were still aliens is exceedingly difficult to determine. The following general statement, however, is certainly admissible. There was scarcely a general who did not have several foreign-born assistants, naturalized citizens or aliens, on his staff in one of the many capacities available—as adjutant, as inspector general, as ordnance officer, as provost marshal, as scout, or even as chief of staff. It might be recalled in this connection that at least two Germans were selected as chiefs of staff—Heros von Borcke by General Stuart and Colonel von Scheliha by General Buckner—while one English subject, Colonel Grenfell, acted for a time as General Morgan's chief of staff.

The statement has been frequently made that large numbers of English officers obtained leave of absence in order to secure active experience in the American war—indeed the number has been placed at thousands. As to the actual numbers it is difficult to secure statistics. But sufficient evidence exists to prove definitely that some absences from the British service were used in that way. Allusion has already been made to the arrival at Wilmington on the *Stag* of several English officers and of their pure motives in coming to enlist under the standard of the "peerless Lee." Even here no intimation is given of the numbers who arrived on that particular ship.[54] Hobart Pasha comments on the presence of several Englishmen among the officers composing General Lee's staff who had come out to see active service, which they had, unquestionably, he adds, "found to their heart's content." They seemed to him the sort of men who would do credit to their country.[55]

The story told by a northerner about an officer of the Horse Guards is worth quoting in this connection. "After leaving [New York for Nassau] I hobnobbed a good deal with an Englishman, an ex-officer in the Horse-Guards, who had given up his commission for

[53] It seems clear from the context that the first two were still subjects of other countries. Barke is referred to as "a Prussian officer who had recently joined the Confederate army," and Estvàn again tells of the Scotchman in terms which suggest that he was an alien.—*Op. cit.*, II, 136, 224-225.   [54] See above, Chap. II.
[55] Hobart Pasha (Augustus C. Hobart-Hampden), *Sketches from My Life,* 162.

a time to enter the service of the Confederacy, whither he was now bound. A nice, plucky fellow he was, of gigantic, athletic build. He served the war out like a man, as I afterwards heard, and then returned to England, having gained no distinction for his trouble, but perfectly satisfied with his adventures nevertheless. I was told that he never complained of the hardships and privation of campaigning, but only grumbled at the difficulty of procuring mounts suitable to his unusual weight."[56]

Henry Weymss Fielden, second son of Sir William Henry Fielden of Fenniscowles Hall, Lancashire, who after seven years' service as a commissioned officer in China and India resigned in order to gain active service in the Confederacy, gave efficient service in the siege of Charleston. He was accorded successively the post of assistant adjutant general on the staffs of Generals Beauregard, Sam Jones, and Hardee with the rank of captain, serving from 1862 to 1864, and lived to review the book of his American comrade, Captain John Johnson, *The Defense of Charleston*, published in 1890. Captain Fielden took home with him as his wife a daughter of South Carolina.[57] Major Hodges, on the staff of General Beauregard, was the son of an English lord and did faithful service till the close of the war.[58] Captain Charles Murray, later Lord Dunmore, a descendant of Virginia's last royal governor, served on the staff of General Lee after three years' equally thrilling service in blockade-running.[59] Sidney Herbert Heth was inspector general on the staff of General Haney Heth and always, according to Captain McCabe, wore his Crimean medals when in action. Captain Stephen Winthrop of the Twenty-second Regiment Foot landed at Charleston on January, 1863, and went straight to Petersburg, where Lee put him on Longstreet's staff. Just a year later he was granted a three months' leave of absence to visit England. Though he had been educated at Sandhurst and had served years in the British army, he retired temporarily in May, 1862, probably with the thought of a new experience in

[56] "Experiences of a Northern Man in the Confederate Army," *Southern Historical Society Papers*, IX, 373.

[57] *Confederate Veteran*, XXV, 201. Ross met Captain Fielden and drove with him to Governor Bull's home.—Ross, *op. cit.*, 112; *Confederate Veteran*, XXXIII, 329. Fielden was strongly recommended for major, but it was not granted.

[58] Freese, *op. cit.*, 84.

[59] *Confederate Veteran*, XXV, 201. For his service as a blockade-runner see below, Chap. IX.

America.[60] Burnes was a young ensign from the British navy who had secured leave of absence. He had succeeded in running the blockade into Charleston a few months before Chickamauga, and for his zeal was appointed to General Bragg's staff with a captain's commission. He was that type of cocky young officer who irritated the American officers, for one of them writes of him: "He was chockful of conceit and had a lordly contempt for anything not English. . . . He was an enthusiastic advocate of Southern rights and bitterly denounced the United States government for presuming to resist the efforts of the Southerners to establish a government of their own according to their own ideas." But even this advocacy did not prevent the writer of the above description from remarking caustically that the stranger was aching to have his name "emblazoned alongside Lafayette's in American history."[61]

Knights-errant there were, of course, from other lands than England. Service on General Lee's staff was, naturally, particularly desired. One takes with a grain of salt the beautifully vague statement that a French count, left nameless, served for a while in some position on General Lee's staff. But a bit from one of General Lee's letters to his wife cannot be questioned and adds, perhaps unconsciously, a touch of humor. "The cars have arrived and brought me a young French officer, full of vivacity, and ardent for service with me. I think the appearance of things will cool him. If they do not, the night will, for he brought no blankets."[62]

While it is not the purpose of the writer to attempt to establish the names or numbers of aliens who held the lowest commissioned and noncommissioned positions in the Confederate army, it may be permissible to cite a few cases which have turned up in the course of the research, because they are intrinsically interesting and because they are probably typical of many. William Henry Baron von Eberstein enlisted in the Washington Grays, Seventh North Carolina Volunteers, on April 22, 1861. He was appointed fifth sergeant and was advanced to orderly sergeant of the company, then known as Company K, Tenth North Carolina State Troops. Transferred later to another regiment, he was promoted to the post of sergeant major of

[60] *Confederate Veteran*, XXV, 201, for Heth; for Winthrop see letters in his file, Confederate Archives, War Department.   [61] Hyde, *A Captive of War*, 39-41.
[62] *Confederate Veteran*, XXVIII, 417; Robert E. Lee, *Recollections and Letters of General Robert E. Lee*, 93.

the regiment. While acting as adjutant, he was wounded at Charleston, at Petersburg, and at Drewry's Bluff and was recommended for further promotion by General Beauregard. General Clingman thought him worthy of a general's bars. The youth who ran away from school in England to fight for his mother's country and her grave in South Carolina, as he wrote his father, was entrusted with the regimental colors during the battle of the Wilderness and paid a fearful price for his devotion, as he lost an eye and the hearing of one ear. One Lieutenant Seymour, adjutant in one of the regiments of "galvanized Yankees," proves to have been an old Crimean soldier.[63]

Knights-errant there were in the ranks, too—by no means a negligible number. One reads of a young lord from England, who ran the blockade via Nassau into Wilmington, so full of life and so eager for the fray that he insisted on going ashore in the yawl which had come out to meet his boat and pulling an oar all the three miles to land. One encounters M. Claude Pardigon, a French knight-errant who is rescued from oblivion by the tale that he had challenged the captain of a vessel to mortal combat because he had furnished no toothbrush for guests, even though he thought he had fully discharged his duty by virtue of a comb and brush chained to the boat! M. Bonnegros, son of the French consul at Baton Rouge, was so fired by devotion to the land in which he was residing that he took up arms and fought until captured on the battlefield.[64]

More striking, if possible, is the history of Bennett G. Burleigh, the son of a master mechanic of Glasgow who was welcomed by imprisonment in Castle Thunder after running the blockade from New York into Richmond. He had brought with him the model or drawing of a submarine battery, an invention of his father's which he wished to submit to the Confederate authorities. He was finally, after repeated requests for release, taken before Captain John Brooke, inventor of the Brooke cannon, who recommended his discharge. Joining John Y. Beall and other Confederate refugees in Canada, he participated in the attack on Johnson's Island in September, 1864, to liberate three thousand southern prisoners of war confined there. The young Scotch knight-errant was arrested in Canada, was surrendered

[63] Emily Mason, "Memories of a Hospital Matron," *Atlantic Monthly*, XC, 318; *Confederate Reveille*, 69.

[64] French, *Two Wars*, 145; Ellen Wise Mayo, "A War Time Aurora Borealis," *Cosmopolitan*, XXI, 137.

by the Canadian authorities to the United States, was twice sentenced to death, but finally escaped from prison to England where he served as war correspondent of the *London Telegraph* for many years, participating in British wars in India, Egypt, and South Africa.[65]

With this group belongs a young German, Benno Albrecht Hollenberg, who had come from Osnabrück, Germany, to visit a brother at Huntsville, Alabama. Here he deepened the friendship formed at a German university with two young Americans who had studied abroad, and with warmhearted impulsiveness embraced the Confederate cause on the assumption that, "as this is my friends' fight, it must be a right fight," straightway enlisting in Company F, Fourth Alabama Volunteers. Samuel P. Mendez is a particularly interesting native of Kingston, Jamaica, son of a Jamaican planter and surgeon in the service of the British army. On his mother's side he was said to be a lineal descendant of Ferdinand and Isabella. In school in Baltimore when the war broke out, he warmly espoused the southern cause and enlisted as a private in Lee's army. Wounded and captured at Gettysburg, he spent five months in prison on David's Island, New York, when a parole sent him South to spend the rest of the war in a Confederate hospital and in the first-aid corps.[66] Even these instances hardly prepare the reader for the remarkable statement of a saddler soldier from Jamaica, who with his three brothers had been urged by their father to embrace the southern cause as a righteous one, that eight hundred men had come over from Jamaica, or for the further statement that there were thousands of British subjects in the southern army fighting for the freedom of the South.[67]

And now we come to the real soldiers of fortune, men who are drawn to a new field of action as naturally as the bar to the magnet. For purposes of unity the soldiers of fortune, naturalized citizen and alien alike, are treated together. It is fairly certain, for instance, that Henningsen, if he had been a naturalized citizen of France instead of the Confederacy, would have hastened to America when his old nostrils scented the fray. It was a mere circumstance that he

[65] *The South in the Building of the Nation*, XI, 143, 144; W. W. Baker, *Memoirs of Service with John Yates Beall*, 49.

[66] *Confederate Veteran*, XXII, 469. Hollenberg served faithfully till captured and sent to the Federal prison in a Nashville penitentiary. After the war he studied medicine and settled down to practise in Memphis, but crowned his career by a record as a nerve specialist in New York City.—*Ibid.* For Mendez see *ibid.*, XXXIV, 144.

[67] Wm. W. Malet, *An Errand to the South in the Summer of 1862*, 278.

happened to be fighting for his adopted country. The same statement applies to Colonel Buchel of Texas.

Men of all sorts they were, high and low, good and bad, but similar in one thing—their love of a fight. Obviously we cannot aspire to having culled from among the million soldiers on the southern side all these interesting characters, and we would not burden these pages with each one's record if we could. But a few typical characters may well be permitted their moment upon the stage. First, then, comes Karl Friedrich Henningsen, London-born of German parentage, who had fought seven years in Spain in the Carlist armies, whence he carried away the decoration of the orders of St. Ferdinand and Isabella; had fought against the Circassians with the Russian army; had been a revolutionist in Hungary in 1849, accompanying Kossuth to America; and a leader in the filibustering expedition to Nicaragua in 1859, before he became in 1861 military adviser to Governor Wise in Virginia. Though his title in the Confederate army was colonel, he is usually referred to by the higher title which he claimed in the filibustering fights. At the outbreak of the war a naturalized citizen of Georgia, he accepted the post of second in command in Wise's legion. With a superior German education, speaking eight languages fluently, he was a highly gifted man and amiable companion. He had invented improvements for firearms and had earned a reputation as a military authority by a number of histories of the wars in which he had participated. His history of the Spanish war was of sufficient merit to win the favorable opinion of Wellington and Marshal Soult. The type of fighter he was is sufficiently attested by the fact that in Nicaragua he cut his way to the coast through an overwhelming force of the enemy. When associated with Wise and his brigade, in which he must have felt at home for there were congregated in it many old Nicaraguan filibusters, he was a tall gaunt man with sandy hair and florid complexion, wearing a slouched hat and monkey jacket and walking with a staff. Henningsen had no opportunity to display his genius in behalf of the southern cause, as General Wise was no favorite of the president or of his secretary of war, who feared the ex-governor's influence on the people. And so the Wise legion was ordered off to untenable positions, requisitions were not supplied, and General Wise was placed in the difficult position of supplying his needs from his own resources. It seems strange that Henningsen's very marked abilities and wide experience were ignored when important posts were to be filled and the fact can only be explained by the supposition that he was looked upon as an alien, despite his naturalization and marriage to a niece of Senator Berrien of Georgia.[68] When Wise and Henningsen were sent to Roanoke Island, away from the real theatre of war as they felt, Henningsen took charge of the artillery, Colonel Estvàn of the cavalry, and General Wise set about reorganizing the infantry. After the defeat of Jackson at Cheat Mountain in 1861, there was a general reorganization. Wise and Henningsen were ordered to Richmond to defend themselves against the charges brought against them for their failure to hold Roanoke. During their absence General Floyd was appointed to the chief command of the brigade. For some reason Henningsen was not employed after the operations in the vicinity of the Virginia coast and did not, of course, attain a rank higher than that of colonel. Perhaps he cannot be better summed up than in the words of Parker, "He was the most perfect Major Dalgetty I ever met."[69]

Colonel George St. Leger Grenfel had had as wide a career as Henningsen. An English officer of the British army, he found the adventure his soul craved. He had seen service in the armies of half a dozen nations, had fought in all quarters of the globe, and bore the scars of fifteen wounds carved into his flesh by bullet and blade. He was a splendid horseman, an expert swordsman, an excellent marksman, and a man wholly devoid of fear. Descendant of a family of wealth and distinction, he seemed to break with all their traditions, running away as a mere lad because his father denied his consent for him to join the army.[70] From a private in a regiment of French

[68] The writer has encountered no evidence of personal hostility to Henningsen at Richmond, but he doubtless suffered from his association with General Wise.

[69] Wm. H. Parker, *Recollections of a Naval Officer*, 244. For other accounts of Henningsen see Estvàn, *op. cit.*, I, 196, II, 107-108, 302-304; Schuricht, *op. cit.*, II, 87-88; and Barton H. Wise, *The Life of Henry A. Wise of Virginia*, 286. There is also a brief account in the *Confederate Veteran*, XXIV, 445. The most telling evidence that he felt the neglect he received from the War Office is the following: A friend said, "Tell me, General, what post are you going to fill during the present campaign?" "I am going," the brave veteran dryly but good-naturedly rejoined, "to apply for a Chaplaincy," an ironical way of pointing to the generalship bestowed on Bishop Polk.—Day, *op. cit.*, I, 103-104.

[70] The story goes that his elder brother had served with Wellington in Spain and had been court-martialed because his servant took a kid from a Spanish peasant for his master's mess. The father's mortification lay at the base of his refusal to allow his younger son to enter the army.—Duke, *op. cit.*, 151.

cavalry troops in Algeria, he won his way to a lieutenancy, and attracted the attention of the French commander in chief, Marshal McMahon, by the excellent discipline of his troops. He became a follower of Abd-El-Kadir, and then turned private again in the Turkish army. A few years more and he was on his own account exterminating the Riff pirates who infested the Mediterranean coast of Morocco. Then followed a period of service in South America with Garibaldi. After these many years of soldiering with barbarians he came home to serve England in her army and to learn civilized warfare, entering the British service as a commissioned officer, through the help of friends. He fought in India during the greater part of the Sepoy Rebellion and then in the Crimean War. When England was enjoying a respite from warfare, his restless spirit drove him to seek it elsewhere. It was thus that he was with Garibaldi in South America, and it was thus that he entered the American scene. When the American Civil War began, he found it impossible to deny himself such an opportunity for adventure and secured leave of absence. Other than as a field for exciting adventure, he seemed to care little for the cause and accepted no pay for his services.[71] Remittances came regularly from England, and enabled him to keep splendid horses and two enormous dogs. He came in the spring of 1862, armed with letters of introduction to Lee, and when he explained the kind of service to which he had been most accustomed and which he desired, the general very naturally sent him to General Morgan with the request that he be given every opportunity to gratify his extraordinary appetite. Morgan immediately put him on his staff where he became assistant adjutant general and soon chief of staff. When he joined Morgan he was nearly sixty years old, but showed no sign of age or diminution of physical powers; rather, he seemed to be in the prime of manhood. A fellow officer compared him to the Templar in *Ivanhoe*, and has left this description of his appearance. "He was tall, erect, and of thoroughly military bearing. His frame was spare but sinewy, and athletic, and he preserved the activity of youth. His bold, aquiline features were scorched by the Eastern sun to a swarthy hue, and his face, while handsome, wore always a defiant and sometimes fierce

[71] This is a moot point. Basil Duke says that Grenfel was devoted to the southern side.—*Ibid.*, 152. The writer is inclined to the other view after a study of his character and actions. See also *Confederate Veteran*, XXIII, 439.

expression."[72] He was also represented as a very reticent man. He proved a most efficient officer and his long experience in a somewhat similar service—he always compared the Confederate cavalry raids to the expeditions by Abd-El-Kadir into French territory—was naturally of benefit to Morgan's chief of staff. In Morgan's first fight at Cynthiana, Colonel Grenfel led a furious charge, routing the foe and completing the victory. This is the charge in which eleven bullets pierced his horse, clothing, and himself, but he was not seriously hurt. Morgan more than once bore tribute to his ability.[73]

In 1863 he resigned his position as adjutant general of Morgan's command to accept that of inspector of cavalry for the Army of the Tennessee. But rigid British discipline did not work with the wild western cavalrymen of the South so that, according to Ross, Grenfel looked back with regret to his stirring days with General Morgan. Hence, in disgust he resigned and, after a short period with the Army of Virginia, departed for Canada, expecting to return to England.[74] Then through meeting some old friends he became involved in the plan to liberate five thousand prisoners of war from Camp Douglas near Chicago at the time of the Democratic convention in August, 1864.[75] Although once again by his resignation a British officer, he must perforce volunteer for such a hazardous venture, but the Federal authorities seem to have learned of the plans of the conspirators and doubled the guards about the city and the prison so that the plotters had to abandon their plan. Strangely enough, Grenfel was one of two who lingered too long, so that he and Colonel Vincent Marmaduke of Missouri alone were tried by court-martial and condemned to death. President Lincoln commuted the death sentence to life

[72] Duke, op. cit., 152. Ross also says, "Few young men of twenty are as active and full of life as Colonel Grenfel."—Op. cit., 312.

[73] Concerning one skirmish, Morgan wrote, "To my personal staff I am deeply indebted. Col. St. Leger Grenfel, acting adjutant general ably supported me."—How It Was, 200.

[74] During his short period of service with the Army of Virginia he was employed by General Stuart as an inspector. A story is told of his conduct at the battle near Jack's Shop, which explains his abrupt departure for Canada. The fighting was close and hot and Grenfel became somehow demoralized. When he saw one of the Confederate regiments recoil from a charge directed by the Unionist General Kilpatrick, Grenfel concluded that the day was lost. He took to the bushes, according to the story, swam a river, and reported at Orange Court House that Stuart, his staff, and whole command had been captured. His mortification was so great, when he learned his mistake, that he did not again appear in the Confederate camp.—McClellan, The Life and Campaigns of Major-General J. E. B. Stuart, n., 375-376.

[75] For an account of this undertaking see, Duke, op. cit., 154; O. W. R., Ser. 1, XLV, Pt. 1, 1077-1082.

imprisonment. Although Marmaduke was pardoned after the close of the war, Grenfel was sent to Dry Tortugas, a barren isle south of Florida which was being used as a Federal military post.

At this desolate prison, he was goaded to desperation by cruel treatment, wearing a ball and chain, shut up in a dungeon for ten months with every orifice closed except one, denied speech, light, books, or papers. He was gagged twice, tied up by the thumbs twice for having written a friend of some punishment inflicted on one of his fellow prisoners.[76] During an epidemic of yellow fever, with which he had had large experience in his varied career, in September, 1867, he nursed the stricken for twenty-one days and nights without cessation. Quite desperate at last, the intrepid old soldier determined to turn to the ocean for a refuge or a grave to end it all. Accordingly, one dark night with two companions in misery he stole out from the prison to the beach, embarked in a frail craft and put to sea. A storm ended his stormy career, for he was never heard of more.[77]

With these soldiers of fortune must be classed Augustus Buchel of Indiana, Texas. By accident of birth a German, a Rhinelander, he was educated at the military academy of Mayence, to which was added French training at the École Militaire of Paris. In recognition of his talents and capabilities for war, he was selected by Ali Pasha to accompany him to Turkey, where he was given the important post of military instructor of the Turkish army, carrying with it the rank and pay of colonel, though as a Christian he could not expect promotion. When the Carlist war broke out in Spain, he hastened to enter the army of Queen Marie Christine. For meritorious conduct he won the honor of the Cross of the Order of Golden Crosses. In 1845 he betook himself to the new Lone Star Republic. Naturally when General Taylor called for volunteers for the Mexican War in May, 1846, he raised a company of which he was elected captain. He was soon promoted to the rank of major on General Taylor's staff. He was commended for his bravery at the battle of Buena Vista, and might have

---

[76] This statement depends on a letter written by him to H. L. Stone, whom he had befriended in the army and with whom he had become friendly. The letter is dated January 15, 1868, and shows a spirit becoming broken at last.—Henry L. Stone, *Morgan's Men, A Narrative of Personal Experience,* 28-29.

[77] For fuller accounts of Grenfel see Duke, *op. cit.,* 150-154; *Confederate Veteran,* XXIII, 439, XXXVI, 446, XIV, 61; Ross, *op. cit.,* 311-312; Stone, *Morgan's Men,* 26-31; and François Joinville, *The Army of the Potomac,* Appendix, Note G, "The Partisan Jackson," 111.

been made a foreign minister if President Taylor had lived. The Crimean War was a battle cry to him; he formed a company and led it to the scene of action. At the outbreak of the American war, he took office as a lieutenant colonel of Luckett's regiment, but soon became colonel of the First Regiment of Texan Cavalry. While leading his forces at the battle of Pleasant Hill, April 9, 1864, he received the fatal wound which terminated his adventurous life four days later. He was described as a quiet, unassuming man, and though apparently a secessionist, not nearly so violent as his superior, Luckett.[78] A citizen of the Confederacy but a soldier of fortune if ever there was one!

Captain Robert Goring Atkins, who found service under the Confederate flag as aide to General Bob Wheat, was a County Cork man, son of an Anglican rector, who had sought adventure in Italy with Garibaldi, and who was attached in 1864 to the staff of General Elzie, commandant of Richmond. After serving from September, 1861, for over two years, he secured a four months' furlough to return home on account of his father's serious illness. A letter, preserved in the Confederate archives, written on black-bordered paper from Ireland to the war department, tells its own story. It carried his resignation as he had to attend to family affairs, but also bore the announcement that it would be delivered by his brother, John Atkins, desirous of drawing a sword for "Secessie."[79]

Allusion has already been made to the presence of aliens among the partisan commands, but the service in these distinctive commands was so attractive to the soldiers of fortune and knights-errant that they merit more than a passing reference. Munson in his *Reminiscences* definitely lists among the followers of Mosby "foreign soldiers of fortune," and a "titled adventurer here and there." Conspicuous among the titled adventurers was the Baron von Massow, noted earlier as aide to General Mosby, a Prussian officer who came on a quest for adventure. He also had a more serious desire to study Mosby's tactics. Reared under a foreign code of conduct, his reaction to Mosby's tactics is worth recording. He was riding by the side of

[78] Johnson, *Texans Who Wore the Gray*, 62-63; Kaufmann, *Die Deutschen im amerikanischen Bürgerkriege*, 567.

[79] The data on Atkins are to be found in his file, Confederate Archives. Unarmed, he took prisoner three Federal officers at the battle of Manassas by commanding them to surrender.—Day, *op. cit.*, II, 298.

Captain William Chapman on a midnight raid into the heart of a cavalry camp near Fairfax Courthouse, which was surrounded by thousands of Union soldiers. In a whisper Chapman explained to the baron what they were doing, and how to do it artistically, incidentally stressing the boldness and danger. The baron proved an apt pupil but after a time whispered very quietly to Chapman, "This is not fighting, this is horse-stealing." He proved with Mosby the mettle which was to bring him after his return to his native land the command of the crack cavalry corps of the imperial German army and to cover his breast with medals. Munson pronounced him one of the handsomest men he had ever seen. It is worth while to see him through the eyes of an eyewitness as he rode into the fight at Dranesville, Virginia. "A long red-lined cape was thrown back from his shoulders exposing his glittering uniform. From his hat waved a big ostrich plume and he dashed into the fray with an old German sabre flashing in the light. I have not the slightest doubt that he was mistaken for Mosby, for he was a very conspicuous figure and drew a perfect rain of bullets and sabre thrusts from the enemy. He saw Captain Reed and charged him. Reed threw up his pistol hand and surrendered to the Baron, who passed him by to charge on the next man. When his back was turned, Reed shot him through the body. I saw the baron lying in the road with his martial cloak around him magnificent in his colors and looking every inch a hero." He pulled through only after a long and painful illness and returned to Germany the following summer to fight as a lieutenant of dragoons in 1866 in the Austro-Prussian War.[80]

Captain H. E. Hoskins, son of an English rector, had served in the Crimean War and had won the Crimean medal as a captain in the English army. He sold his commission in order to join Garibaldi in one of his campaigns and later came to America, his thirst for excitement still unquenched. But here his adventures came to their end for he was mortally wounded in one of the Mosby raids and was buried in a little family churchyard at Greenwich, after lingering two days in the home of an Englishman near by. "Thus died," wrote Mosby himself, "as gallant a gentleman as ever pricked his steed over Palestine plains. He had passed without a scar through the fire of

[80] Munson, *op. cit.*, 87-88.

the Redan and the Malzkoff to fall in a petty skirmish in the American forest."[81]

Richard Carpenter was an Irishman who had served in the British army and navy before he joined the Derhenny Guards in New Orleans; Lanigan came from Ireland to fight in the Orphan Brigade of Kentucky; Lieutenant O'Leary had served as a petty officer in the British navy in the Black Sea and in the Shansen Brigade, when it marched to the relief of Lucknow; Hugh McVey was a veteran of Waterloo, over seventy years old but still ready for battle, who died on the field of Shiloh, serving in Company D, Fourth Kentucky Regiment.[82] The group of English adventurers not mentioned before included Colonel Collis P. Moore, a trained journalist by occupation, a citizen of California by residence, and a soldier of fortune by profession, who commanded a Mississippi regiment; Frederick Crouch, who came over to wear the gray, and stayed on in Baltimore after the war; Edmund Langley Hunt and two brothers, distinguished members of the British army, who ran the blockade to join their brother-in-law, General J. E. Erskine of Louisiana, on the side of the Confederacy; and a certain Montague, who had served in the British Eleventh Hussars in the Crimea.[83]

F. A. Scheidecker was an old Crimean soldier of the French army, whose lust for battle led to his enlistment but whose old wound early forced his discharge. The palm for interest among French privates must be awarded to Monsieur Chillon, a veteran officer of the French army who had had to leave his home because of some political trouble, and who was living in California in 1861. To reach Louisiana he had to pass through New Mexico and Indian Territory on foot, his only companion a faithful donkey to carry his tent and supplies. He was aiming at a Louisiana regiment because he hoped to find in it men who could speak his native tongue; he found a haven in the ranks of the Iberville Grays, a company of Creoles, where he became a sort of attaché. His fellow soldiers made allowance for his years and made of him and his donkey, Jason, general favorites; indeed the Third Louisiana Regiment, in imitation of the well-known practice in

[81] Mosby, *Mosby's War Reminiscences and Stuart's Cavalry Campaigns*, 147-148.
[82] *Confederate Veteran*, XXIII, 439, XXXIV, 26, XXX, 304; Russell, *Pictures of Southern Life*, 136.
[83] *Confederate Veteran*, XIII, 90; H. W. Johnstone, *The Truth of the War Conspiracy of 1861*, 8; Russell, *The Civil War in America*, 86.

the British army, made this donkey a sort of mascot. He had shared his master's tent in the long journey over the plains and hence often intruded into the tent of the lieutenant colonel, whom old Chillon strikingly resembled, to the vast amusement of the "boys."[84]

Julius Herr, though born in Germany, had fought not only with German armies, but also with the army of Great Britain in the Sepoy campaign before he enlisted in Company H, Ninth Kentucky, in May, 1862. He fought many good fights before his final wound at Chickamauga. William Schirmer, who had some of the earmarks of a soldier of fortune, was a six-foot Dane with the build and spirit of a Viking. He had seen service on water and on land as a boy of sixteen during the siege of Sebastopol. Residing in New Orleans in 1861, he naturally joined a Louisiana company in March, 1861, as soon as war was certain, became a favorite, and was advanced to the rank of lieutenant. Careful of his men, but utterly indifferent to danger for himself, he was killed while making a round of sentries at Port Hudson the night before the surrender. F. A. Karl was an old soldier who, after surviving three years in the Russian Royal Artillery and the Hungarian revolt, succumbed to a sunstroke as he stood in the ranks of the Washington Artillery on the suffocatingly hot day of their departure. Strikingly enough, the author of the poem "Farewell to Johnson's Island" was a Hungarian soldier of fortune, Thomas Usher Tidmarsh, who wrote it on the wall of the prison just before leaving on an exchange.[85]

Lord Charles Cavendish, who swaggered in Richmond and imposed on some experienced society people, was a very different type of adventurer. He reported to General Fitzhugh Lee for staff duty as assistant engineer about the middle of May, 1864, representing himself as the cousin of the Duke of Devonshire, and as holding a commission in the Eighteenth Hussars. Unquestionably he was a thorough soldier, but when he disappeared, leaving checks which his noble "relatives" in England did not honor, his dupes began to make inquiries in England. It appeared that his name was Short, and that he had been merely a corporal or sergeant in one of the English

---

[84] Estvàn, op. cit., II, 182; Thompson, History of the First Kentucky Brigade, 649; Watson, Life in the Confederate Army, 264-267.

[85] Thompson, History of the First Kentucky Brigade, 918; Bartlett, "A Soldier's Story of the War," Military Record of Louisiana, 18 n.

cavalry regiments. With complete inconsistency, he had been punctilious in the discharge of his duties at headquarters and had paid his mess bills promptly.[86]

Of a slightly different nature is the story of another Englishman, Lieutenant Ewing, though he, too, was strictly a soldier of fortune. He had been a sergeant in the United States army in the company of General W. H. Jackson in the west when that officer resigned to tender his services to the Confederacy. Later when Jackson, in command of a division of cavalry, was operating in North Mississippi and Ewing's company was stationed near Memphis, the latter deserted his Federal command to enter the Confederate lines. He was rescued from prison in Richmond by his old commander and ordered to report to him for duty on his staff. He served faithfully until the close of the war.[87] Allusions to many soldiers of fortune who are left nameless are scattered through the war literature.

The reader who pictures Henry M. Stanley threading the jungles of Africa in search of Livingstone may be surprised to learn that he has a record as a Confederate soldier—one quite in character with his love of adventure and his history. As a warrior he was strictly a free lance and fought under many flags—that of the United States, the Confederacy, England, and Belgium, and commanded thousands of King M'tesa's followers as allies during the most dangerous portion of his march through Central Africa. The Welsh lad, to become famous as Stanley, the explorer, whose real name was John Rowlands, had come to New Orleans in 1859, enlisted at the age of about sixteen in a Confederate company, the Dixie Grays, recruited in Arkansas, saw much service, and made a record as a hard fighter. Imprisonment after capture at Shiloh ended with his enlistment in the Union artillery and discharge within a month on account of his physical condition. After a short visit home he enlisted again, this time in the Federal navy, serving on the *North Carolina* and *Minnesota* as landsman and ship's writer until February, 1865, when he deserted at Portsmouth, N. H. It is said that he swam under fire some

---

[86] De Leon, *Belles, Beaux, and Brains of the 60's*, 335; Dawson, *op. cit.*, 134-135. Lee recommended him for promotion but there was no vacancy. See Cavendish's file, Confederate Archives, War Department.

[87] *Confederate Veteran*, VI, 525.

five hundred yards to make fast a hawser to a Confederate ship, thus enabling the Federal fleet to tow her off as a prize.[88]

The cosmopolitan air which the presence of these knights-errant and soldiers of fortune cast about the Confederate camps can scarcely be better summed up than with the picture sketched for us by the pen of the reporter Russell. "Into one of these I am escorted, and find myself at a very pleasant mess, of whom the greater number are officers of the Zouave Corps, from New Orleans—one, a Dane, has served at Idstedt, Kiel, Frederickstadt; another foreigner has seen service in South America; another has fought in half the insurrectionary wars in Europe."[89]

[88] *Ibid.*, II, 332. A story was published concerning his Confederate service in the *Missouri Republican*, very much to his discredit. It was said that while acting as paymaster's clerk he absconded with the funds intrusted to him with which to pay the regiment.—*Ibid.*, 16. The writer has not seen this story authenticated elsewhere.

[89] *The Civil War in America*, 110. Europeans were, of course, far from having a monopoly of the profession of soldiers of fortune. The searcher of war records turns up Colonel Bradfute Warwick of the Fourth Texas Infantry, who had won honorable distinction in Italy under Garibaldi (Putnam, *Richmond during the War*, 150-151); young Spenser, son of the American consul at Paris, who served as captain under Garibaldi, though not yet of age (*Mobile Daily Advertiser and Register*, December 21, 1860); Dr. Morton of Buckner's staff, who had been with the Russians at Sebastopol (Ross, *op. cit.*, 148); and Fontaine, who was one of the most cold-blooded of the type the world ever produced (Lamar Fontaine, *My Life and My Lectures*, 69, 127-128). These are a few Americans who loved fighting for the sake of the fight.

VII

SCATTERED THROUGH THE RANKS

CERTAIN STATEMENTS have been accepted without challenge among writers on Confederate history. If there was one thing more than another which the southern veteran believed as gospel truth, it was that he was defeated by the hordes of European mercenaries in the Union army. Let one quotation from the many speak for this point of view. Speaking of General Lee's "honorable" surrender, a writer says, "Not to *Northern* foes [did we surrender]; we have always thought we could have *vanquished* them. But we could not stand before a combined army of German, Irish, Dutch, French, Spanish, Russians, and English!"[1]

The following excerpt undoubtedly reflects the Confederate's usual conception of his own army: "A conspicuous feature of this Southern army is its Americanism. Go from camp to camp, among the infantry, the cavalry, and you are impressed with the fact that these men are, with very few exceptions, Americans. Here and there you will encounter one or two Irishmen. Very, very rarely, you will meet a German, like that superb soldier, Major von Borcke, who so endeared himself to Jeb. Stuart's cavalry. But these exceptions only accentuate the broad fact that the Confederate army is composed exclusively of Americans." The assertion has also been made that the total number of Confederate troops exceeded the foreigners in the United States army by little more than a hundred thousand.[2]

There were hordes of German and Irish-born soldiers in the northern army. No one will challenge the accuracy of that statement. But as to the other claim, the almost complete absence of foreign-born

[1] Southwood, *Beauty and Booty*, 284. Another writer phrases it thus: when the Confederate States' cause "began to wane before the overwhelming legions of foreign mercenaries that flocked over the sea in 1864 to get good rations and $900 bounties . . ."— C. W. Read, "Reminiscences of the Confederate States Navy," *Southern Historical Society Papers*, I, 337. See also Putnam, *Richmond during the War*, 168; *Inaugural Address of Gov. Thomas H. Watts*, December 1, 1863; "War Diary of Captain Robert Emory Park," *Southern Historical Society Papers*, XXVI, 8; *Confederate Veteran*, I, 195, XVIII, 313.

[2] Randolph H. McKim, "Glimpses of the Confederate Army," *American Review of Reviews*, XLIII, 434; *Confederate Veteran*, XXVI, 374; Ross, *A Visit to the Cities and Camps of the Confederate States.*

in the southern army, we shall see. It is true that a very few writers noted the presence of some foreigners in the southern ranks. De Leon observes: "While, as a general thing, the rank and file of the state regulars were composed of the laboring classes, foreigners and the usual useless and floating portion of their populations, officered by gentlemen of better position and education, appointed by the governors, the volunteers had in their ranks men of all conditions, from the humblest laborer to the scholar, the banker, and the priest."[3] Russell in more pointed fashion, when discussing the question of the franchise with a southerner on the train, called attention to the presence of foreign soldiers. The southerner had just expressed vehemently his view that the right to vote should not be given foreigners in the new confederacy. "Are not many of your regiments composed of Germans and Irish—of foreigners, in fact?" "Yes, Sir," admitted his companion. The English writer could not refrain from pointing out in his book the inconsistency which would deprive of the suffrage the very men whom the leaders did "not scruple to employ in fighting their battles."[4] And finally the English combatant, "E.T.C.," testifies that there were not a few from the Emerald Isle in every regiment of the Confederate army.

It is often difficult to distinguish between the naturalized citizen and the alien in the case of officers; with the private in the ranks it is quite hopeless. That there were many aliens among the Confederate soldiers is substantiated in various ways,[5] among others by the discharges on the ground of alien citizenship, almost invariably dated 1862.[6] Therefore in this chapter the subject of discussion is the

[3] *Four Years in Rebel Capitals*, 93.
[4] *The Civil War*, 186. The South attributed her crimes, brutal shootings, etc., to rowdies who rushed in and took control.—*Battle-fields of the South*, I, 162. An English correspondent, probably Russell, also bears witness to the fact that, "whatever may be said of Irish and German mercenaries" in the Union army, "the best classes of Americans have bravely come out for their country. I knew of scarcely a family more than one member of which has not been, or is not in the ranks of the army. The youths maimed and crippled I meet on the highroad certainly do not for the most part belong to the immigrant rabble of which the Northern regiments are said to consist . . ."—George F. P. Henderson, *Stonewall Jackson and the American Civil War*, II, 418.
[5] The chief source is, of course, the various descriptive rolls.
[6] The writer has accumulated a considerable list of such discharges from the rolls in the Confederate Archives, War Department, in Washington, from the rolls in the various state archives, and from the Confederate Discharges in the Georgia Archives. A typical discharge reads as follows: Thomas Comisky, private, Wise's Regiment, Artillery, born in Ireland, thirty-seven years of age, occupation—laborer, enlisted for one year, discharged under the Act (referring to the Act of Confederate Discharges, Georgia, April, 1862).
For the change in attitude on the part of the Confederate government when it began to refuse to honor alien citizenship, see below, Chap. XIII.

foreign-born private, regardless of whether or not he ever embraced American citizenship. In view of the inducements held out by politicians and the natural aptitude of the Irishmen for politics, there is probably little doubt that the great bulk of the Irish and Germans had become citizens in order to exercise the privilege of the franchise.

In addition to the distinctly foreign companies, described in Chapter IV, there were many foreign-born scattered through the service, amounting in many companies to as much as one half of the total number of privates. About half of Company B, Ninth Alabama, were Irish-born; about one half of Company B, Captain James Wright's company, the Waul Legion, were a mixed group of foreigners; about one half of Captain Edward's Texan Company A, Rio Grande Regiment, were foreigners; Company F, First Louisiana, Company D, Seventh Louisiana, and Company B, Fifth Louisiana, had one half born abroad. Company E, Eighth Alabama; Captain Nelis's company of Texas Artillery; Company K, Fifteenth Louisiana, Crescent Blues; Company B, Eighteenth Mississippi; and Company C, Rio Grande Regiment of Texans, had each about one third foreigners. De Saussure's cavalry of South Carolina had about one fifth foreign-born. There might be many more such companies than the large number identified if it were possible to examine the lost records of all the companies in the Confederate States army.[7]

It is true that there are a few companies, relatively few so far as revealed by the rolls which the writer has been able to locate, and even an entire regiment here and there, which contain no foreign-born, officer or private. It is a significant fact, however, that even North Carolina, which boasted of possessing a population almost purely Anglo-Saxon, can produce only two entire regiments which had no foreign-born, officers or privates; namely, the Thirty-fourth and the Forty-fourth Infantry. There were several other regiments which had a perfect native record except for a single alien-born member in some one of its companies. To put it conversely, North Carolina had at least one hundred and sixty-six companies in which all the members were American-born. The original muster and descriptive rolls are complete for this state but the blank space provided to record the nativity is not always filled in.

[7] The writer is convinced that a long list of companies with one sixth to one half foreign-born would appear for most of the states if the records were complete.

Mississippi, on the other hand, which is also regarded as largely Anglo-Saxon, according to the rolls extant, shows only nine companies which are completely filled up by natives, though a few of her rolls are also left blank so far as place of nativity is concerned. In the entire Fifteenth Alabama there were only eight foreign-born. Indeed there were many companies made up wholly of native-born from the rural sections of Alabama.[8] The companies of Arkansas Cavalry also show a very high record of native members: McGehee's regiment apparently had seven such companies; Davis' battalion had five, and Regan's, the Thirtieth Arkansas Regiment of Cavalry, had three. Dobbin's regiment had but three aliens in its complement of six companies. Even in the Twenty-third Arkansas Infantry there is no alien-born indicated in the five companies for which rolls can be found.[9]

The Missouri cavalry also records several solid native companies, but it must be recalled that Missourians volunteered for the Confederacy—were never conscripted—made their way often with great difficulty to a point of enlistment, and must, therefore, have been imbued with a real devotion for the cause, a devotion which was unlikely to occur except where one had been bred in the traditions of slavery and states' rights.[10]

The Orphan Brigade of Kentucky boasted that it had a lower percentage of men of foreign-birth than did any other command in either army, Union or Confederate. If the rôle compiled by Thompson is complete and accurate, it makes good its claim, as it had only about one third of one per cent non-native.[11] But let it be remembered that,

[8] For the completeness of the record an appendix (V) is added to show the exact status of the north Alabama companies. Alabama is selected as a typical state, for there were many foreigners in Mobile, as will be recalled, while in other sections there were very few.

[9] It should be noted that the rolls for Arkansas are very unsatisfactory. The author has been unable to locate any except the few rolls in the Confederate Archives, War Department, at Washington. The writer is inclined to view the Parole Lists of Company E, First Arkansas Cavalry, and of Companies D-L, Tenth Arkansas Cavalry, with suspicion as we know how many cavalrymen rode off home without being paroled. Only 3 are shown as foreign-born.—Confederate Archives, War Department.

[10] See Muster and Descriptive Rolls of Burbridge's Fourth Missouri Cavalry; M. L. Chardy's Battalion of Missouri Cavalry; Ninth Missouri Cavalry; Fifteenth Missouri Cavalry; and the Eighth Missouri Cavalry (Jeffers's Missouri Volunteers). In fifteen companies the writer found only one foreigner, in Company B of M. L. Chardy's Missouri Cavalry. The number of men in each company was remarkably small—7, 11, 28, 29, 33, 38, etc.—Muster and Descriptive Rolls, Confederate Archives, War Department; also Records of Parole at the Surrender, May, 1865.

[11] Confederate Veteran, VII, 341, and for the Record, Thompson, History of the First Kentucky Brigade, 571-924.

if the two separate North Carolina regiments had been combined into a brigade, they would have surpassed this record.

Certainly in some parts of the Confederate army foreigners were scarce. Isaac Hermann, a Frenchman who joined the Washington Rifles of the First Georgia Regiment from Washington County, Georgia, was regarded as a curiosity. He tells an amusing story of how man after man stopped at his tent to take a look at a real live Frenchman. When he learned the cause of such inordinate curiosity, he mounted an old stump and introduced himself to his fellow soldiers as a native Frenchman, "who came to assist you to fight the Yankees."[12]

Despite the fact that there were perhaps two hundred companies examined with "nary" a foreigner in their midst, in the vast majority of them there were scattered a few. Frequently in the memoirs of a Confederate veteran one encounters the statement that there was a "paddy" in almost every company of every regiment in the service, and that statement was certainly correct. Yet a member of the First Alabama Regiment alludes to Mike Brogan as "the only Irishman that ever belonged to our company," as if his company were exceptional. McKim, describing the composition of his mess in the First Maryland Infantry, presents a rare group of men serving as privates, and in the group were to be found a country gentleman of large means, a lawyer, several college-bred men, and one whom he calls Redmond, "a highly educated Irishman."[13] The Orphan Brigade would seem to have had only sixty-three Irishmen all told, and yet one of the most touching stories encountered in this study is of "Little Oirish," an eleven-year-old lad who turned the tide of battle at one point at Shiloh by his courage. When the flag had fallen and an old cannon was lost, apparently beyond hope of recovery, this Irish waif picked up the flag, carried it joltingly to the cannon, crawled up the wheel, and waved frantically with wild yells. He infused fresh courage into the men and the field was won.[14]

[12] Hermann, *Memoirs of a Veteran*, 14-15. He will be discussed later among the buglers in Chap. VIII.

[13] Edward Y. McMorries, *History of the First Regiment, Alabama Volunteer Infantry, C. S. A.*, 111; Randolph H. McKim, *A Soldier's Recollections; leaves from the diary of a Young Confederate*, 51.

[14] The fate of "Little Oirish" should be recorded at least in a note. Lanigan was an Irishman who loved and adopted the lad from the time he appeared at camp. One day the lad was found injured in the head; though he seemed to recover, his happy smile and impish fun were gone. One day after a battle the boy and Lanigan, who had prayed not

The proportion sustained by the foreign-born to the remainder of the company, as revealed by the company rolls, tells much of the story we are seeking. Naturally it varied widely through the different companies, but after eliminating the foreign companies and those in which there was a noticeable foreign proportion, the record runs something like this for several Alabama companies: six in a company of eighty privates—two Germans, one Italian, one Swiss, one Scotch, and one from the West Indies; one in eighty privates; seventeen in one hundred and twenty-six privates; four in one hundred and four privates; and five in one hundred and ninety-seven privates. The proportions run similarly in some Texas companies: three in a total of eighty-eight, including officers; one in a company of eighty-one, including officers; ten in seventy-six privates; and five in a company of one hundred and thirty-two privates. Louisiana foreigners assuredly were not confined to certain foreign companies. It proved impossible to find in the rolls available for this state on which the nativity is entered a single company which did not have at least one foreigner. In the DeSoto Blues there were four in a total of one hundred and thirty-three privates; in the Louisiana Volunteers (Company G, Ninth Louisiana), one Irishman appears among the one hundred and eleven privates; in the Brush Valley Guards (Company H, Ninth Louisiana), two Irishmen served with the one hundred and thirty-six natives; in the Davenport Rebels (Company F, Fifteenth Louisiana), twelve in the small company of seventy-seven—and the names do not suggest foreign connections; in the St. Landry Guards (Company C, Sixth Louisiana), fourteen were foreign-born; and in the Attakapas Guards (Company C, Eighth Louisiana), nine out of one hundred and forty-four had been born abroad.

It is rare in the Mississippi companies not to find at least one Irishman or Canadian, frequently more, ranging from two to twenty-one. Company K, Thirteenth Mississippi, had five Germans in a total of 162 privates; and Company D, Sixteenth Mississippi, had ten alien-born in a small group of twenty-one, one lone German with nine Irishmen. In Company B, Seventeenth Mississippi, the number

---

to be parted from him, were found dead. Even more touching is it to read that after they were buried, to the grief of the entire brigade, Old Frank, a dog with which "Little Oirish" had shared his scanty rations, was found two days later lying dead on the grave of his little master.—*Confederate Veteran*, XXX, 303 ff., 336 ff., 377-379.

Though told in story form, this was based on fact as the writer has been able to ascertain.

of non-natives mounted to seventeen in a total of 149 privates, a mixture of several nationalities. Company D of the same regiment came close to the top in this list with fifteen among 115 men, who came chiefly from the British Isles and from her colonies. The Sam Benton Rifles and the Pettus Rifles, perfectly good Anglo-Saxon titles, had eight alien-born each on their rolls. Company D, with twenty-one foreign-born in a total of 160, and Company E, Eighteenth Mississippi, with nineteen in 139 privates, top the list.[15]

Foreigners were found, as is to be expected, in the other two main branches of the service, the cavalry and artillery. The proportions run very similar to those in the infantry companies: one in seventy-six privates in Company K, Seventh Alabama Cavalry; two in fifty-eight in Lee's battery, Alabama Light Artillery; and three in Company D, in Colonel R. H. Taylor's regiment, consisting of 126 men and officers. There were six in Captain P. William's cavalry company of the Waul Legion in a total company of ninety-six; seven in Company H, Terry's Texas Rangers; and eight in 91 in Captain Harwood's company of cavalry in the Waul Legion—all Texan companies. Among the Mississippi cavalry companies one notes in Company C, Second Battalion, and in Company G, Ninth Mississippi, one Irishman in each group; in Company H, Ham's regiment, eight Irishmen and Germans in a company of 102.[16] One finds them scat-

---

[15] Note the proportions taken at random in the following companies:
Company A, Second Alabama, 6 in 80 privates—2 Germans, 1 Italian, 1 Swiss, 1 Scotch, 1 of the West Indies.
Company C, Eighth Alabama, 17 in 126 privates.
Company B, Tenth Alabama, 2 in 104 privates—2 Englishmen.
Company K, Fifteenth Alabama, 11 in 113 privates.
Company H, Forty-seventh Alabama, 1 in 80 privates.
Captain Donnelly's Company, Rio Grande Regiment, 10 in 76 privates.
Company D, Terry's Texas Rangers, 5 in a company of 132.
Company K, Seventeenth Texas Volunteers Infantry, 5 in 132 privates.
Company F, Ninth Louisiana, DeSoto Blues, 4 in 133 privates.
Company H, Ninth Louisiana, Brush Valley Guards, 2 in 138 privates.
Company F, Fifteenth Louisiana Davenport Rebels, 12 in 77 privates.
Company C, Sixth Louisiana, St. Landry Guards, 14 in a total of 131 privates.
Company C, Ninth Louisiana Attakapas Guards, 9 in 144 privates.
Company K, Thirteenth Mississippi, Pettus Guards, 5 in 162 privates.
Company D, Sixteenth Mississippi, 10 in 21 privates.
Company B, Seventeenth Mississippi, Mississippi Rangers, 17 in 149 privates.
Company D, Seventeenth Mississippi, 15 in 115 privates.
Company F, Seventeenth Mississippi, Sam Benton Rifles, 8 in 146 privates.
Company I, Seventeenth Mississippi, Pettus Rifles, 8 in 149 privates.
Company D, Eighteenth Mississippi, Hamar Rifles, 21 in 160 privates (nativity unknown—16).
Company E, Eighteenth Mississippi, College Rifles, 19 in 139 privates.
[16] The above was compiled from the Record Rolls in the Alabama Military Archives; from the Muster and Descriptive Roll of Horses, Arms, Equipment, etc. for the Twenty-

tered in most commands. The Irishman heard his name at roll call in the Texas cavalry, served in the Kentucky troops, and rode with Mosby's and Forrest's commands.[17] Britishers from England, Scotland, and Canada rode with Scott's Louisiana cavalry, with Morgan, with Mosby, and Forrest, and with the Sixth Texas Cavalry under Captain Ross, and splendid troopers some of them made. J. G. Hawkes, for instance, was an Englishman who arrived in this country, a mere youth, when the war was at its height, enlisted as a private, had a number of horses shot from under him, and was one of the First Louisiana Cavalry Regiment which cut its way through the Federal army rather than surrender.[18] German troopers may be noted especially in the Texas and Mississippi cavalry commands; Frenchmen and even Mexicans are found in companies doing guard duty on the Texan frontier.[19]

It could be taken for granted that there would be Arkansas Irishmen in the battery of artillery organized by General Cleburne. One encounters Irishmen also in the Rockbridge Artillery from Virginia, sometimes, like Tom Martin, soldiering for the pure love of it; in Chew's Light Horse Battery, South Carolina; in Beauregard's division of the Army of the Tennessee; and in the famous Curran Bat-

second Texas Mounted Reserves and the Roll for Colonel R. H. Taylor's Regiment of Cavalry, Confederate Archives, War Department; Muster Roll of Captain P. William's Company; Muster Roll of Terry's Rangers, compiled by John M. Claiborne; Muster Roll of Captain T. M. Harwood's Company, Cavalry, Waul Legion, Texas State Library; Descriptive List of Captain Regan's Company, and of Captain Jennings Crosby's Company, Confederate Archives, War Department. The writer has been unable to locate rolls in any other of the states for cavalry companies which furnish the information as to the country of birth.

[17] Erwin B. Thomas was an Irishman who served in Company A, Third Texas Cavalry; William Ryan was another, who was in Company F, Third Texas Cavalry. See Johnson, Texans Who Wore the Gray, 249, 319. Tom Murphy and Thomas Quirk rode in the Seventh and Second Kentucky Cavalry, John Hughes in Mosby's battalion, and an Irishman, unnamed, in General Forrest's command.—Confederate Veteran, IV, 343, XIII, 174, IV, 346.

[18] For Hawkes see Carter, A Cavalryman's Reminiscences of the Civil War, 120-121. John Miller Menie, born in Scotland, came to North Carolina in the late fifties and joined the cavalry company from that state. See his autobiography, a manuscript in possession of the North Carolina Historical Commission. E. A. McKenney, a Canadian, enlisted as a private in Company C, Sixth Texas Cavalry, at Waco, June, 1861.—Yeary, Reminiscences of the Boys in Gray, 495.

[19] Gustavus A. Madgen of Company D, Fourth Texas Cavalry, John Adams Lorenz of Company D, Fifth Texas Mounted Volunteers, and W. H. Foxel of Company C, Thirty-second Texas Cavalry, are a few illustrations of many.—Ibid., 241, 449, 458. Herman Wohleben was a German enlisted in Miller's battalion, Mississippi Cavalry.—Confederate Veteran, XII, 544. General Basil W. Duke in his Reminiscences tells of a Frenchman who had but recently settled in Paducah, Kentucky, who entered Forrest's command, 288. Felipe Vargas was a Mexican who enlisted at San Antonio in June, 1863, in Company F, Third Texas Regiment.—Yeary, op. cit., 764.

tery of Withers' artillery, which did valiant service in many battles around Vicksburg. The writer duly discharges her duty by recording yet again the fact that it may have been an Irishman, P. O. Donlon, sent from Nashville to Charleston, who fired the first gun at Fort Sumter.[20] English gunnery is famous throughout the world and so it is no surprise to find British and Scotchmen serving the guns for the Confederacy all the way from New Bern in North Carolina to Shea's Coast Artillery in Texas.[21]

Most of the students of Confederate history will identify Bachman's battery as one of the three artillery companies composed of sturdy, determined Germans from Charleston. It may not be as well known that one of the companies in Waul's Texas Legion, Company C, in which there were a number of Germans, was transformed during the fight at Fort Pemberton into an artillery company for the rest of the war. The fact that good soldiering is quite independent of nationality is emphasized again by the record of a certain German, Sergeant Henry Worth, in the Louisiana Horse Artillery connected with Colonel John S. Scott's First Louisiana Cavalry. He was regarded as one of the best artillery men in the service with no superior as a gunner in either army. His comrades claimed that he could kill a man a mile off by sighting the piece with his hand only. His eight years of service in the Prussian army had made him almost perfect in all the details of a soldier.[22]

It may come with a shock to some readers accustomed to think of the Washington Artillery as composed of the elite of Louisiana to be informed that there were many foreigners in the five companies of that famous organization, amounting to 167 in a total of 1,039. It should be noted that foreign-born thus constituted over 16 per cent of

[20] *Confederate Veteran*, II, 6; Edward A. Moore, *The Story of a Cannoneer under Stonewall Jackson*, 259; *Confederate Veteran*, XVII, 242; Yeary, *op. cit.*, 191. For authority that P. O. Donlon was the name of the man who fired the historic shot at Sumter see Yeary, *op. cit.*, 191. For Germans in the Rockbridge Artillery, which was a very cosmopolitan body, see Moore, *op. cit.*, 257.

[21] The Scotchman, Alexander Brown, had arrived in Wilmington, North Carolina, only late in 1860, but the next April he enlisted as a private in the artillery company of Captain James D. Cumming, Battery C, Thirteenth Battalion, and saw much hard service, ultimately rising to a lieutenantship.—Sprunt, "Confederate Heroes," *Chronicles of the Cape Fear River*, 312. Thomas Clark, another Scot, served as private in Company B, Shea's Coast Artillery in Texas and S. L. Makeig, of England, served in the First Texas Heavy Artillery, Company K.—Yeary, *op. cit.*, 137, 459.

[22] *Ibid.*, 453, tells of transforming Company C, Waul's legion, into an artillery company. The story of Sergeant Worth is found in Carter, *op. cit.*, 136.

this presumably native company. In one company the proportion was not large, as the company had no less than 330 members on the roll. The foreigners were of many nationalities and were for the most part used as drivers of the horses for the canons. However in a few instances they rose to commissioned positions.[23] The position of driver was not one without danger, for the horses must often be hitched and unhitched under fire to move the guns to other positions, for, of course, during the artillery fire the horses must be removed out of range of the fire.

Enough has been said in earlier chapters to indicate that many nationalities were represented in the Confederate army. That is stating the situation mildly. There was hardly a country or clime of the earth, even a remote and small portion of the globe, but had its representatives. It would be a work of supererogation to dwell upon the chief European nationalities—the Irishman, who appeared in nearly every company; the German, who in many sections of the army disputed priority in numbers with the Irish; the Briton, who as Englishman, Scot, or Welshman was present in such liberal numbers. From nearly all the provinces of Canada, provincials had made their way to the South before and during the conflict—from Nova Scotia, from Montreal, from New Brunswick. The claim has been made by Canadians that they had 40,000 in the Confederate ranks.[24] In the opinion of the writer that is probably a gross exaggeration, but that there were some thousands she will readily concede.

A remark concerning the Irish should be quoted to be refuted. One writer on the Irish in America says that most of the emigrants from that island flocking to the United States before the Civil War went North to offer to that section their unskilled labor and that Confederate soldiers of Irish origin were almost entirely recruited from the descendants of the colonial Irish who had pushed South from Pennsylvania, while the newer Irish were generally found in the Union ranks.[25] This writer has certainly not studied the record rolls of the Confederate army. The four Scandinavian countries are all represented, though the general statement made by a Norwegian

[23] The Record, Washington Artillery Companies, Louisiana.
[24] D. W. Pipes of New Orleans, a survivor of the Washington Artillery, told the writer that such a claim had been made to him by Canadians.
[25] Roberts, *Ireland in America*, 142.

writer that except for a very few, especially from Texas, they served on the northern side is correct.[26] A Hungarian appears occasionally upon the roll, recorded in one instance as "Hongard," for the enrolling clerk probably had difficulty in interpreting the recruit's faulty English. An Austrian, a Chinaman, a Pole, a Russian, a Greek, a Belgian, and a Hollander attract attention by their infrequency. A Cuban or a Peruvian is less striking than an Egyptian or Syrian.[27] Several of the West Indian islands were represented, besides Cuba, St. Thomas, Jamaica, and Martinique. The insertion on the record of the names of outlying bits of larger geographical divisions sometimes reflect a foreigner's provincial pride, as when he had himself recorded as from Corsica, Sardinia, the Isle of Man, the Madeira Island, and the Ile de France. It is perhaps surprising that the name Germany appears so persistently in the absence of a unified nation, though the names of the sectional units, Saxony, Bavaria, Württemberg, are far from absent from the rolls. The large, beautifully vague designation, Europe and Asia, leaves one wondering if ignorance on the part of the enlisting recruit or of the clerk is to be read between the lines.[28] The distortion which these geographical names suffered at the hands of the scribes, combined with hasty, poor penmanship, sometimes leaves the reader puzzled. Pauland, Wayles, Jermany, Cannady, and Yermany, each appears as the country of birth of some recruits.

One marvels when one recalls a company like Company G of the Sixth Louisiana, where men from no less than seven nationalities were rubbing elbows in the congested quarters of a camp, or a regiment like the First Louisiana, where there were assembled thirty-seven nationalities, that fights were not more frequent than they were. On the whole, outbursts of nationalistic feeling seemed rather to be turned against representatives of another country in the northern army, or indeed against fellow countrymen for the treason of being on the opposing side. Irishmen often expressed contempt for Germans, denouncing the German bounty men of the Union army as "poor crea-

[26] "Bortract fra nagle faa, isarheleshed fra Texas, tjiente de alle i Nordstaterna. Haer aller Floade."—David M. Schoyen, *Den amerikanske Borgerkrigs Historie*, 108. There were only about 150 Swedes in Texas in 1860. The writer does find a few scattered in various companies outside of Texas.   [27] See below, p. 212.
[28] Several interesting entries of men born in Persia and Allahabad, North India, must be rejected, as they proved to be sons of American missionary parents. Albert L. Holladay, born in Persia of Presbyterian missionaries, was living with his parents in Virginia in 1861; and the Reverend J. L. Wilson, though born on the Ganges in India, had lived in America ever since he was a small child.—*Confederate Veteran*, XXVI, 168, XVII, 468.

tures." When in a good mood, they would declare that "Shield's Boys," who were chiefly Irish, were worth fighting. Usually, however, they condemned General Meagher and his Irishmen for fighting the patriots of the South, who were struggling so gallantly for their liberty and their homes, and felt that the traditions of their beloved Ireland should have led all sons of Erin straight to the support of the oppressed. One reads amusing stories like that of a warmhearted Irishman from South Carolina who brought a wounded Irishman from Pennsylvania back from the field but at the same time scolded him every step of the way for fighting on the wrong side.[29] On the other hand, the northern Irishman could not find words harsh enough for John Mitchel and his "ilk." "Their General," referring to Meagher, "is an Irishman thrue to the sod, none of your rinegade spalpeens like John Mitchel—fighting for slave-holders in Ameriky, and against Lords and Dukes in Ould Ireland, and the slave-holders as Father Mahan tould me the worst of the two, more aristocratic, big-feeling, and tyrannical than the English nobility." He added that the "blackguard" could never visit the "ould sod" again unless he landed in the nighttime, and hid himself by day in a bog up to his eyes, and even then the Father said he "believed the blessed memory of St. Patrick would clean him out after the rist of the varmin."[30] The northern Irishman was shocked at sons of Ireland fighting against the flag of liberty. Neither could understand the position of the other.

Much has been written about the Federal soldiers who could not speak English; great bitterness has been expressed by southerners against these foreign mercenaries. But nothing has been said by historians about the Confederate soldiers who knew no English. A nurse tells of her encounter with a Mr. Chillion, an old Frenchman in the Twenty-fourth Alabama Regiment whom she was taken to see because they were fellow citizens of Mobile. The poor old soldier actually cried when he found out who she was, but she could scarcely make him understand her. The same nurse tells of a German in the Twenty-first Alabama, the ranks of which were filled largely with

[29] Nisbet, *Four Years on the Firing Line*, 95; Spencer G. Welch, *A Confederate Surgeon's Letters to His Wife*, 25-26. Thomas Ellis tells a similar story of Irishmen on a hospital boat.—*Leaves from the Diary of an Army Surgeon, or Incidents of field, camp, and hospital life*, 70.
[30] Henry Morford, *Red Tape or Pigeon-Hole Generals as seen from the Ranks during a Campaign in the Army of the Potomac*, 87-88.

Mobile foreigners, who could not understand anything said to him. One can sympathize after all these years with the German who gasped in broken English, "Ach! How hard to die, when I have been in this land only three months."

There is also the mysterious figure of the Syrian or Egyptian—no one knew exactly which—of whom Dr. Daniel tells. He was a small, dark-skinned man, apparently about thirty years of age, with fine white teeth, coal-black hair, scant beard, small mustache, and small, sharp black eyes. The surgeon thought that he came from the near East, though certainty was impossible as he could not speak a word of English. He had the aspect of a hunted animal, watching the door narrowly. As the surgeon approached his bed, his eyes showed concern, though he did not of course answer questions. He seemed to apprehend however that one of the doctor's concerns was with the condition of the tongue, for he kept his out all the time the doctor was in the ward. But when the latter palpated the injured region of his body, suspecting typhoid fever, the patient struck the doctor as hard as he could, resenting the action apparently as an indignity to his person. Probably the war had caught him in New Orleans or Mobile and swept him into its maelstrom.[31] Then we learn of a primitive sort of man from the German forests who lived entirely by himself, even in camp; and constructed a shelter of brush and leaves, like a bear preparing to hibernate. In his ignorance of the use of an axe in felling a tree, he was seen to throw it so that it fell on and killed a horse tied near by. His language was scarcely intelligible.[32] The more intelligent among these non-English-speaking soldiers made their meaning clear even when laconic in their paucity of vocabulary. This is well illustrated by the Frenchman who had arrived in Paducah, Kentucky, just prior to the war and who had joined a cavalry regiment attached to Forrest's command. He was accosted by a former acquaintance as he was riding along the street of the Kentucky town during the war.

"Hello, Charlie," said the friend. "What did you fellows come into Kentucky for this time?"

"More horse," was Charlie's brief but clear-cut answer.[33]

[31] Cumming, A Journal of Hospital Life, 97; Yeary, op. cit., 6-7; Ferdinand E. Daniel, Recollections of a Rebel Surgeon, 134-136.
[32] Moore, op. cit., 258.   [33] Duke, Reminiscences, 288.

In the camp and on the field, it might be accurately stated, there were two official languages in the southern army—English and French. The Southern Guards, Italians and French, many of whom did not understand English, recruited, it will be recalled, in Mobile, were transferred from the Twenty-first Alabama to the First Louisiana, which was composed of French and Italian Creoles, on account of the language used in the drill. Nationality was also an important consideration to the commissary department, it may be stated parenthetically, early in the war before soldiers were glad to eat whatever could be had, for it was necessary as far as possible to provide suitable food supplies. French and Italian methods of preparing food were a factor in keeping the men properly nourished with food they would eat. Irishmen even in a regular company of native Americans would frequently mess by themselves, appointing one of their own number cook, so that their food could be sufficiently flavored with onions and shallots.

It is surely a picturesque glimpse that McGrath gives us of the Thirteenth Louisiana, when he described how, after getting his soldiers aboard the boat to leave camp at Mandeville, he discovered that the patriotic citizens had bestowed too much whiskey on the "boys" as a parting gift. As a means of pacification, he suggested that the men sing songs of their native land and soon "a dozen voices were raised in as many languages, and the singing, interspersed with a few fights, continued until one after another the drunken soldiers fell asleep upon the decks."[34]

Cosmopolitanism and provincialism certainly rubbed elbows in the Confederacy when war brought Creoles and the heterogeneous crowds from Louisiana in contact with the country boys from backwoods Georgia. The latter listened openmouthed as Colonel Polignac drilled his battalion at the new fair grounds in Richmond.

"That-thur furriner he calls out er lot er gibberish, an thumthur Dagoes jes maneuvers-up like Hell-beatin'-tan-bark! Jes like he wuz talkin' sense!" records Colonel Nisbet as the words of one of his

[34] For the interesting comment on the transfer of the Southern Guards to a Louisiana regiment, the writer is indebted to a note appended to p. 32 of a manuscript headed, "Partial List of Mobile Companies," compiled by the United Daughters of the Confederacy, Alabama Archives; for the note on the Irish partiality for onions, see the *Confederate Veteran*, IV, 308; and for McGrath's account of the singing, see "In a Louisiana Regiment," *Southern Historical Society Papers*, XXXI, 108-109.

mountaineers.[35] This story might be recalled when one is told of the northern camps where several of the tongues of Europe were used in drill. As a last touching bit, it might be added that out of the mixture of languages emerged certain hybrids which contributed to the southern vocabulary of the time, such as "sacredam," which first fell from the lips of General Beauregard.

The Confederate soldiers were of all ages and all stations of life. The great majority were, as in every army, young men between twenty and thirty-five, but as the war killed off the men of ideal age for fighting, the age curve began to swing out, for foreigner as for native, at both ends until it extended from the thirteen-year-old French orphan lad, Frank Maurvre, to the seventy-year-old veteran from the battlefield of Waterloo, Hugh McVey. The range of vitality extended from the apparently inexhaustible vigor of the Irishman who jumped and shrieked in the midst of battle like a maniac to John Cahill, of Company D, Fourth Kentucky, who was briefly described as "old and feeble."[36] As has been often stated, mere youth or age was no bar to eligibility, as every male capable of bearing a gun was accepted without question. Such discrepancies in age eligibility brought about enlistments of father and son among the foreign-born, as with the native Americans. Such an instance is afforded by James H. Miller, an Irish pioneer residing in Virginia, who enlisted with his son Patrick in Hupp's battery of artillery at Salem, Virginia. A second son, William Miller, later joined this same company.[37] However from the fact that the ranks were recruited from many foreign laborers, seeking in the southern cities of the United States the work denied them at home, one could correctly infer that most of them were single men.

Likewise every rank of society sent representatives to the army from among the foreign-born, the son of a French marquis, the Irish wharf hand, the son of a wealthy Jamaican planter, and the German pack peddler.[38] George Zimpleman, to cite a single case, affords an

[35] *Op. cit.*, 46.

[36] John Cahill is encountered in Edwin Thompson, *History of the Orphan Brigade*, 647. Hugh McVey, the veteran of Waterloo, was pictured as always ready for battle. He died at Shiloh.—*Ibid.*, 650. Since only Thompson's *History of the First Kentucky Brigade* will be referred to hereafter, citations will have reference to that work.

[37] *Confederate Veteran*, XXVIII, 27.

[38] The marquis referred to is De Gournay de Marcheville, who rose to be a lieutenant colonel.—*Confederate Veteran*, XII, 405. Samuel P. Mendez was the son of the Jamaican planter, who enlisted in Lee's army as a private. He is discussed among the knights-errant. See above, p. 188.

excellent instance of the man of fine background who served in the ranks. On his father's side descended from an influential family of Bavaria, on his mother's from a general, he had become fired with enthusiasm for the new republic of Texas and could not rest until he had fulfilled his dream of settling in the New World. From raising stock on a ranch near Austin, in 1861 he entered the Confederate ranks in defense of his adopted country as a member of Terry's Texas Rangers and became that excellent soldier whom his superior praised highly.[39] We are accustomed to think of many college-bred youths of the old families of the South nobly joining the ranks to set an example of devotion to country—and they were found there to the everlasting credit of the ancien régime—but we are likely to think of the foreigners in the ranks as coming from the poor and illiterate class, the dregs of European society. Such an impression yields a picture far from complete. The friends of Private Thomas J. McElrath, a college-bred youth, used to boast that their Scotchman was the best classical scholar in the Fourth Kentucky Regiment.[40] Most of the knights-errant came of good family, and were highly educated. Furthermore many sons of families which had moved to this country, probably to better their fortunes, received a good education here. The "English Combatant," to whom allusion has been frequently made, had attended some southern college, for he referred to recruits from Kentucky, whom he had known personally "when in college." Another fellow countryman, Samuel Pasco, who had left London in 1834, had graduated from Harvard in 1859, and was teaching in Florida when the war came on so that he served in a company of the Third Florida. One trooper enjoyed the distinction of having been born in an old castle in Westphalia and of having studied, first for the priesthood, and then for the practice of medicine. When the family moved to Louisville, he joined General Bridgemann's cavalry.[41]

In occupation the alien-born ran the gamut of possible activities of the human race, but with this distinction from their native-born comrades in arms—the vast bulk of foreigners were drawn from the humbler ranks of manual labor. The brief record of the occupations of the Emerald Guards of the Eighth Alabama as noted on the

[39] *Confederate Veteran*, XIX, 114. See above, p. 231.
[40] George D. Mosgrove, *Kentucky Cavaliers in Dixie*, 253.
[41] *Battle-fields of the South*, 178; *Confederate Veteran*, XXVI, 214; *ibid.*, XXIV, 328. The trooper, William Häcker, will be encountered again in Chap. VIII.

record roll might almost serve as a cross section of the foreign-born privates of the entire army. There were a few merchants, a few clerks, a number of farmers, a few mechanics, a couple of painters, bakers, ropemakers, tailors, a cabdriver, and a cooper, but the greater number were "labourers," to use the spelling of the day. A few were drawn from the army, men who had drifted into the United States army. The Washington Artillery, when it departed from New Orleans for Virginia, was accompanied by a French colonel and two Prussian officers in the ranks. A Scot, whose father had long held a post in the garrison at Baton Rouge, might be called a soldier by tradition and seemed to have no difficulty in discharging the duties of a second lieutenant in the Baton Rouge Rifles. William Aimison, whose father had been a French soldier under the great Napoleon but had emigrated to Nashville with his young son after the Napoleonic wars were over, gravitated naturally to the Forty-fourth Tennessee Infantry at the first call to arms. Frederick Körper, whose father, despite his Prussian nativity, had also followed Napoleon, dropped his fashionable "barbering" at Memphis to snatch up a revolver for McDonald's cavalry company.[42]

Followers of the art of Aesculapius were found dropping the scalpel to seize the gun. One of the most cosmopolitan members of the Confederate army was a doctor whose genealogy and career are worth tarrying over for a few moments. Henry Joseph Warmuth, the son of a Bavarian father and a Spanish mother, had been born in the city of Mexico, where his father was an importer. At the ripe age of six Henry, together with a younger brother, was sent to New Orleans and then to Paris for his formal education. Study at the Lycée Bonaparte was followed by a literary course at the Gymnasium of Würzburg, and then by a medical course at the University of Würzburg. When the call to arms came in America, he enlisted as a private in Company A, Ninth Georgia Artillery, on February 27, 1862, at Atlanta. Equally varied was the career of a much humbler follower of the medical profession. C. E. M. Pohle had come from Prussia in 1844. A period as an actor in a German theatre in New York, Palm's Opera House, was followed by three years in the United States navy

---

[42] Bartlett, "A Soldier's Story of the War," *Military Record of Louisiana*, 34-36; Watson, *Life in the Confederate Army*, 146; for Aimison see *Confederate Veteran*, XII, 402; for Körper see Thomas Jordan and J. P. Pryor, *The Campaigns of Lt. Gen. N. B. Forrest and of Forrest's Cavalry*, 166-167, note.

band, and later by an appointment as prosector of the anatomical department of the Richmond Medical School for this versatile Teuton. We shall later find him filling the congenial post of drum major in the First Virginia Militia Regiment. Tossing off two German dramas and many German poems good enough to be published should have saved this son of the Fatherland from death in a Confederate soldier's home.[43] A Canadian, George Osborn Elms, although his history for eight years previous to the war showed him engaged in railroad construction as a civil engineer, enlisted as a private in Company A, Twenty-eighth Louisiana, in April, 1862. His natural intelligence and training quickly brought him to an adjutant's position, but it was only after two confinements in northern prisons that he qualified as a lieutenant in the corps of engineers.[44]

Newspaper men, printers, and clerks were represented also, but it was the mercantile class which next to the artisan and labor classes was most heavily drawn upon. It is unnecessary to enumerate the many fields of business represented or to cite many examples. Bookkeepers and clerks were naturally numerous and often valuable in the offices of adjutant generals, even after wounds had rendered them unfit longer for the field. In the home guard units it was those men who had had sufficient energy and acumen to build up successful businesses and who had thus become leaders among their respective nationality groups to whom the government looked for aid when crises threatened certain cities. In Mobile it was Julius Hesse, a fine type of German, and J. Domingo, an Italian leader, who preserved order when the troops evacuated that city.[45]

It would be a work of supererogation to overemphasize the dif-

[43] *Confederate Veteran*, XL, 383; Schuricht, *History of the German Element in Virginia*, II, 39-40.
[44] *Confederate Veteran*, XX, 232. Note also Hugh G. Gwynn, an Irishman, who was a railway engineer.—*Ibid.*, XXXIV, 27, 88. This was later the Twenty-seventh Louisiana.
[45] Patrick Walsh is a good example of the newspaper class. Arriving from Ireland in Charleston in 1852, he was apprenticed at the age of thirteen to the Charleston *Courier* to learn the printing trade. He studied and worked his way up until in January, 1863, he became local editor of the Augusta *Daily Constitutionalist.*—*Ibid.*, VII, 177. For other cases see *ibid.*, VI, 274; X, 421 (Eccles Cuthbert of Ireland); Watson, *Life in the Confederate Army*, 241. Peter Mallow furnishes an example of recruit from the clerical force. He was a young Irishman who was disabled when shot through both hips at Rheatown but two months later he was rendering good service in the adjutant general's office of his regiment, the Fourth Kentucky.—Mosgrove, *op. cit.*, 257. The Muster and Descriptive List of the Mobile Home Guards afforded this helpful information about Julius Hesse. For J. Domingo, see statement of Judge P. Williams to T. Owen in 1911.—Alabama Military Archives.

ferent classes which were represented in the Confederate army. A cross section of the industrial life of the foreigners as presented in the first chapter of this book is a faithful picture of the way they classified themselves on the military rolls. Occasionally the record is enlivened by such unusual entries as artist, for so one Terrenhorie of Italy designated himself; teacher, professor of music—almost invariably a German, this last; peddler, frequently a German Jew; or even shepherd, who usually proved a stray Scotchman or Swiss from the Texan ranches. A few lines of work which had been pursued by the Confederate private have vanished, such as farrier, burrer, and carriage maker.[46]

The reader is probably impatiently demanding the numbers of foreign-born in the Confederate armies—the number of each nationality largely represented and the total. This is probably the most difficult point in the entire study because of the disappearance of many descriptive rolls and carelessness in filling in the blanks of others. A few rough estimates have been made by writers interested in special nationalities and will be here given for what they may be worth. First, let the total enlistments in the southern armies, as computed by so careful an investigator as Livermore, be again recorded as about 1,000,000; of this total it has been claimed that 95 per cent were native-born Americans. We may readily grant that the Irish constituted by far the largest proportion of the foreign element in the armies. In one brigade half of the 10,000 who recruited its ranks were Irishmen, all of whom could have been excused at the time of enlistment as aliens. John Mitchel said in a letter to the Dublin *Nation* that there were 40,000 Irishmen in the southern armies.[47] Schuricht estimated about 1,500 Germans born in the Fatherland in the Louisiana regiments, 1,000 in the Virginia companies, about 80 in a Georgia artillery company, and about 400 in all the German companies of South Carolina—a total of only about 3,000. It is to be noticed that he omits entirely any figures for the Texas troops, for Captain Cornehlson's company in North Carolina, and the large num-

[46] The data relative to the occupations are all gathered from the various descriptive rolls. A burrer seems to have indicated an engraver or maker of metal burrs. A farrier means, of course, a blacksmith.

[47] Thomas L. Livermore gives as total enrollment 1,082,119.—*Numbers and Losses in the Civil War in America, 1861-65*, 63. See also London *Times*, February 7, 1863; Henderson, *op. cit.*, II, 418, n. 2; Roberts, *op. cit.*, 143.

bers in the aggregate scattered through most of the companies which were thought of as native companies.

There are many ways to approach the problem, all of which are unsatisfactory. An effort has been made to ascertain the proportion of the foreign-born in such published lists of soldiers as Miss Yeary's, Sid Johnson's, and Thompson's,[48] but their very mode of procedure prevents reliability and completeness. Questionnaires were sent out to all living veterans on the list of the compiler and additional names solicited. But that method precluded the most humble who were not likely to rise to the distinction of getting on a list. It excluded also those who were resting in nameless graves. Such compilations as that made by Booth of Louisiana soldiers is even less helpful, for he was quite uninterested in the details of nationality, the most important data for this study. The writer is therefore driven back to the descriptive rolls, utterly inadequate though they are in number and often incomplete or quite barren for this investigation.

After repeated endeavors to work out the problem on various mathematical lines the writer has been reluctantly forced to the conclusion that any figures can be little more than a guess and must, therefore, lack all authoritativeness. She has handled descriptive rolls for about 800 companies and has examined the records for about 97,022 soldiers, native and foreign-born. It will be recognized that the available rolls cover only a little less than one eleventh of the men enrolled. To apply the principle of strict proportion and multiply by eleven the number of foreign-born ascertained from the rolls would be simple—and quite erroneous. Access to the enrollment of the companies of Louisiana has been possible to a remarkable degree, though even here 165 rolls, as the reader has been told, are missing. In this state was congregated the largest number of foreigners and hence, obviously, the ratio of foreigners in the companies would be unduly high. Even for the Louisiana companies which are not classified as foreign, there is a strikingly high proportion of foreigners— 49 in a company of 137 men, 22 in 80, 24 in 143, 49 in 127, to cite a few ratios. Likewise the deduction which should be made for wholly native companies presents insuperable problems on any proportional basis. Two hundred and ninety-five such companies have been turned up in the search. To multiply this number in exact proportion to the

[48] Yeary, *op. cit.*; Johnson, *Texans Who Wore the Gray*; Thompson, *op. cit.*

portion of the army for which descriptive rolls do not exist would be absurd, for in the 295 companies located were included the companies of North Carolina, concededly the state with the strongest Anglo-Saxon strain. As the rolls for this state are complete and as the rolls for the rural portions of Alabama, the other section where many companies of pure native stock were discovered, have been available, strong doubt exists if many more rolls, if extant, would have added largely to this number. A third method of approach is to endeavor to strike a general average of foreigners per company. Hence some two hundred companies, drawn from a widely distributed area and representing wide variations in number, were studied and yielded an average of 10 per company—a proportion which the writer is convinced would be too low. However here another problem had to be surmounted as the number in a company varied tremendously from a tiny cavalry group of 35, or even 26, in Texas to the swollen figure of 338 for the Fifth Company of the Washington Artillery of New Orleans. Again the principle of working out an average number for each company was invoked and applied to the 200 companies mentioned above. An average membership of 102 was the result. When an average of 10 per 102 men was calculated for the entire army, the number became so large that figures would inevitably be challenged. Therefore the only course left is to state the bare facts that there were tens of thousands of foreign-born in the ranks, many more tens of thousands in the reserve home guards, and, to express the author's conviction that there must be some truth in the reports that thousands of aliens entered the fight for the Lost Cause. One fact is certain: the last man from the foreign element, as the last man from the native group, was called upon. When a country was fighting with its back to the wall, when authorities were pressing into the ranks every male who could shoulder a gun, when most of the foreign-born were relatively young, single men, the alternative for any able-bodied man was pretty certain to be military service or departure from the country —and ere long no alternative.

The authorities at Richmond were doubtless very much more aware of the importance of the foreigner in filling the places in the ranks than their descendants have been in the long interval since the war. They no doubt watched their thinning ranks with the deepest concern and noted with envy the German recruits who were reported to be entering through the New York port by the thousands, disguised as laborers. It was not enough to try to prevent such Federal recruiting abroad by pressure through Confederate diplomatic agents;[49] anxious citizens were constantly pointing out to the government the desirability of embarking on some method of recruiting abroad for the Confederate armies. A glimpse will now be taken at some of these projects.

One of the earliest proposals came almost immediately after the outbreak of the war. A Mr. Denis Meade wrote Governor Clark of Texas on May 9, 1861, that he was returning to Mexico after fourteen years' residence in Texas in order to recover money due him to meet the dire needs of a large family. He considered himself so well acquainted with Mexico and the authorities there from nineteen years' previous residence that he felt that in an emergency he could raise a few hundred picked men, well armed and mounted, to aid the Confederacy. He would act strictly under private orders so as not to interfere with the neutrality laws, though just how the affair could be handled so as not to violate these laws, he does not divulge.[50]

The next suggestion was more direct and went immediately to the central government. James McConaughey wrote to Secretary of War Seddon from Marshall, Texas, on March 10, 1864. The former after serving in the quartermaster's and in the adjutant general's departments had been obliged in October, 1863, to resign on account of his health. He then conceived a plan which would, as he thought, be mutually beneficial to the Confederacy and to himself, as an ocean trip had been recommended for his health. He therefore modestly proposed that he visit Ireland to recruit an Irish brigade for Con-

[49] The diplomatic officials of the Confederacy stationed abroad were greatly concerned with this subject. James D. Bulloch, charged with securing arms and ammunitions abroad in what was very properly called the secret service, tells how he was warned one day in the very height of the war of the imminent arrival in Liverpool of some recruits for the United States army to be embarked on an American ship, then lying in the river. Though Bulloch, from the nature of his duties, which required secrecy, could do nothing, the matter was brought through other channels to the attention of the British authorities. The vessel was detained a day or two but sufficient evidence of the charge of shipping recruits was not forthcoming.—Bulloch, *The Secret Service of the Confederate States in Europe*, I, 309-310, 313. Secretary Benjamin instructed Mason, the regular Confederate official representative, to inform Earl Russell that there were extensive enlistments in Ireland of recruits for the Federal armies.—Callahan, *Diplomatic History of the Southern Confederacy*, 170, n. 3. This part of Confederate history is not regarded as a legitimate part of this story.

[50] Governor's Letters, March-May, 1861, Edward Clark, Archives, Texas State Library.

federate service during the war; and, equally modestly, he desired a commission to command any such so raised. He wished all field and line officers to be appointive by the president unless some chivalrous Irishman of ability and position should lend his influence in raising the troops, and thus merit a high office of which McConaughey would wish to assure him. The expense of transporting 3,000 men from Belfast to Matamoros, which he estimated at from $200,000 to $250,000, he thought might be met by shipping 5,000 bales of cotton to Liverpool under charge of a special quartermaster agent, sent along with McConaughey, any amount realized from the sale of the cotton above the cost of transportation of the troops to be invested in arms and supplies to equip those troops. Seddon's endorsement on the paper was brief and the only one dictated by common sense: "Impracticable or extremely difficult either to export the cotton or bring in the men. The scheme must be declared as visionary and beyond our ability to comply."[51] McConaughey, however, was not to be deterred by Seddon's mild discouragement in a letter of April 23, for on August 20 he is found again elucidating his idea. He declares now that it was not his idea to raise a brigade in Ireland but merely to "emigrate" men from Ireland to Texas, there to be organized into a brigade. He points out that the mere conversion of the cotton, thousands of bales of which were being destroyed through gross neglect, into needed supplies was a worthy object. In addition he had "reliable evidence from Ireland that the South can get twenty men where the North can get one—inducements being equal." With a wave of the hand he brushed away Seddon's objections to its practicability. If he had the authority, he could soon get all the cotton belonging to the Confederate States into the Trans-Mississippi Department, and the bringing in of the men was "perfectly easy," as Irishmen could emigrate to Matamoros and cross the Rio Grande as easily as the St. Lawrence. He counted on many wealthy and influential friends in Ireland, among whom was a member of the British parliament, to assist him.[52] If Seddon vouchsafed another reply, it has not been preserved.

Late in the same year came a similar proposal, this time from

---

[51] Letters Received by Confederate War Department, Confederate Archives, War Department.
[52] See McConaughey's letter to Seddon, dated Marshall, Texas, August 20, 1864.—*Ibid.*

South Carolina, for a responsible agent to station in every important town in France a French representative to recruit for the Confederacy. The ostensible object would be to secure artisans or laborers to replace the men sent to the field, or, if this plan proved impracticable, to help the Frenchmen to emigrate to Mexico. The proposer suggested as bait an offer of public lands, and a stipulated sum of money, together with free passage, of course, urging the old suggestion of the sale of cotton to raise the bounty money. He selected France as the scene of recruitment because the Frenchman's character accorded with the southerner's in innate chivalry, because the French emperor had manifested more sympathy with the Confederate cause than had any other potentate, and especially because French occupation of Mexico made possible emigration to that country without exciting suspicion. Finally the proposer reveals, without surprise to the reader, his willingness to be the agent to execute the plan, and states as qualifications his study of the law, his French citizenship, and his membership in an influential French family. This letter was sent to H. M. Fuller of Beaufort, a member of the Confederate senate.[53]

Yet once more General Gaspard Tochman and Colonel Sulakowski must tread the stage in the most picturesque and romantic of the gestures made to add recruits from abroad. The Poles had in 1863 revolted yet once more against Russian rule. Failure threw into western Europe—Germany, France, and England—between 12,000 and 15,000 fighting exiles, including statesmen and military leaders, and other thousands into Moldavia and Wallachia. Colonel Sulakowski was the first to sense the possibilities for the Confederacy in the situation of these Polish exiles. As early as June, 1863, he addressed a letter to his chief, General Magruder, for whom he was acting at that time, it will be recalled, as chief engineer. Sulakowski proposed to go to France to induce the Polish exiles there to organize into an association to enter the Confederate service. He flattered himself that his known sympathy with the existing French Empire would prevent any obstacles being placed in his way; but in order not to infringe the neutrality laws he proposed to give out publicly

[53] This letter is dated Blackville, South Carolina, November 19, 1864. The context of the letter makes it clear that the writer was not a citizen of the Confederate States.—Miscellaneous Letters to Officers and Members of Congress, Confederate Archives, War Department.

the project of the exiles as establishing a new home in the state of Nuevo Leone in Mexico. Settlement in a country partly inhabited by Indians and in a constant state of revolt would fully explain the equipment of rifles and ammunition. He proposed thus to bring into the field for the fall campaign about 5,000 of the "best fighting men my country affords." His plan to meet expenses was only a slight variation on the old plans: a subscription among patriotic and discreet citizens for $400,000, to be subscribed in cotton or Confederate bonds, deposited with a mercantile house in Matamoros as security for funds to be raised in France by Slidell or some suitable agent. The subscribers could be reimbursed from a fund raised by allowing citizens to hire these Poles as substitutes at $2,000 to $4,000 apiece. He also proposed to buy arms from Garibaldi's reputed store of 1,000,000 muskets. He naturally proposed assurance from Governor Lubbock that each man after service during the existing war would be given 200 acres of land by the state of Texas. Without mincing words he asked to be put in command of the entire force, with the proper rank.[54] The proposal seems merely to have been buried in the governor's files.

Tochman, ever alert to the actions of his fellow Poles and, be it added, to the interests of Gaspard Tochman, addressed a letter to President Davis from Columbia, South Carolina, on September 20, 1864, in which he expressed his zeal to prevent emigration of these exiles to the United States and their enlistment in the Union army, and his desire, on the contrary, to secure them for the Confederate States service. He believed that his reply to the resolution of censure passed on him by the Polish Democratic societies in France and England in August, 1861, for espousing the Confederate cause had contributed to giving them a "clearer view" of the American situation. Otherwise the Polish delegation then in Richmond would not have been sent. He feared that the Poles might be unable to withstand the misrepresentations of the Federal government and be induced to form a Polish legion for the northern armies. As might be expected, he suggested that his services be employed and requisite means be placed at his disposal to enable him to go to Europe to counteract the Federal emissaries; and he draws his usual grandiose

[54] G. O. Correspondence, Archives, Texas State Library.

vision of a success so great that the Union would not receive thereafter a single recruit from any European country except Russia, should the czar authorize emigration from that country to the United States—not a probability. His plan was to enter his soldiers through Mexico with the aid of the Polish societies in western Europe.

Tochman sought the coöperation of Secretary Benjamin and Representative Miles for his new venture. "Let then," he urged Davis and the Honorable W. P. Miles, member of congress, "the Congress of the Confederate State seize this opportunity, and in consideration of the services of the sons of Poland, rendered to Christianity, civilization, and the first American Revolution, pass an Act, offering in the name of the people of the Confederate States, to the Poles banished from their homes, an asylum, protection, rights, and privileges." In December he professed utter indifference as to the person to command the Polish army, offering to go to Europe, even at his own expense, to forward his plan. Davis held an interview with Miles and General Marshall on the subject shortly before December 4, but the latter concluded that it would be improper to recommend to congress any action while the president was considering executive action.[55] Herewith Gaspard Tochman makes his final exit from the Confederate stage.

Meanwhile a more significant gesture came from the exiles themselves, from the Poles in refuge in Moldavia and Wallachia. A delegation of four had run the blockade into Wilmington and had appeared in Richmond late in August, 1864: Colonel J. Smolinski, Colonel A. Lenkiewicz, Major P. Bninicki, and Chaplain J. Mayewski. In a communication to the "Government and people of the Confederate States," they declared their desire to fight for the southern cause, "as did Pulaski and Kosciusko"; they asked the assignment of territory for a home of refuge, to which they could transplant their own institutions, laws, and customs. On August 31 Secretary Benjamin replied first officially to the overture in a typically warm, friendly letter, assuring them of the president's belief in the disposition of congress to make a grant of public land to those

[55] Tochman's letters of September 20 and November 8, 1864, the draft of the Joint Resolution to be presented to congress, and Tochman's letters to the Honorable W. P. Miles of December 4 and 11 are to be found in the House of Representatives Bills, Resolutions, etc., Confederate Archives, War Department.

who should imperil their lives by battling for the independence of the Confederate States.[56]

An interview with President Davis was arranged for the party on September 1.[57] The government did not feel it expedient fully to comply with the wishes of the delegation. To grant territory for the exclusive use of a colony in such manner as to deprive other citizens of the right of settlement in such territory was felt not to be in accordance with American institutions; grants of land were made only to individuals, not to communities. The president, it was stated, hoped at the close of the war to make grants of land to individuals who might then settle together and thus control the political and municipal legislation of the territory by constituting a majority of the population. The government promised, however, that the Poles could organize into companies and regiments—electing their own officers—and into Polish divisions if numbers justified.[58]

While disappointed in the chief object of their mission, the delegates felt that several thousand of the exiles would be glad to become Confederate citizens, if transportation were provided. While the executives recognized the difficulties in international law of recruiting outside the borders of the Confederacy, they did agree to provide free passage for able-bodied exiles and to welcome them as brothers in arms if they chose to enlist after arrival. Benjamin remitted £50,000 to defray their expenses to Colin J. McRae, treasury agent in England. Violation of international law was to be avoided by conveying the emigrants to Matamoros, a neutral port, the destination to be concealed in order to protect the passengers against Federal cruisers. Each emigrant was to receive on arrival cancellation of the expenses for his passage if he felt moved to enlist. Emigrants were further to be informed by their own delegation that all residents in the confederacy were liable to military service in defense of the country. They were to be received at Matamoros by the regular Confederate agent, Richard Fitzpatrick, who would supply them with passage to Texas, where they would be received by another agent. McRae and his agents were not to attempt to induce any to come, and were to receive none incapable of military service.

[56] Benjamin to the Delegation, August 31, 1864.—N. R., Ser. 2, III, 1196-1197.
[57] See Benjamin's letter to the delegation, August 31, 1864.—Ibid., 1197.
[58] For the statement of the government's policy see ibid., September 5, 1864, 1201-1202.

With the four delegates he was to select the ports from which vessels were to sail, and he was warned that the exiles might have to sail from a Mediterranean, or even a Black Sea port, so widely were they scattered. In addition, McRae was to provide the delegation and some eight or ten others, whom they might associate with them, with necessary sums to enable them to travel to the principal European points where the exiles were congregated. Where the poverty of the exiles made this absolutely necessary, the agents were to advance the cost of transportation to the ports. They were also to take care to insure good faith on the part of the Poles. Benjamin, endeavoring not to be unduly optimistic of results, added, "We scarcely expect more than a few thousand men to be desirous of emigrating without their families. Fourfold this sum or more would be willingly spent if the number could be increased to fifteen or twenty thousand." He assumed that the whole affair could be given the appearance of a private arrangement by the Poles to found a colony in Central America, the able-bodied going in advance to prepare for the reception of the rest. That the action was wholly an executive one is clear from the fact that the money for expenses was taken from the secret service fund.[59] The delegation was provided with transportation to Wilmington, and Collie and Company was requested to provide their passage through the blockade.

Rumors echoed, of course, in the Union as well as in the southern states. One catches the usual exaggeration in the following quotation from a prominent southerner, even after due allowance is made for the clearly revealed personal hostility to President Davis: " . . . it was more than rumored that a *secret compact*, wholly unauthorized by the Confederate Constitution, with certain Polish commissioners, who had been lately on a visit to Richmond, had been effected, by means of which Mr. Davis would soon be supplied with some twenty or thirty thousand [*sic*] additional troops, then refugees from Poland, and sojourning in several European states; which latter force, when it should arrive, not being levied under congressional authority, would be completely at the command of the President for any purpose whatever."[60]

[59] For Benjamin's letter of instructions to McRae, dated September 1, 1864, see *ibid.*, 1197-1200.

[60] Henry S. Foote, *War of the Rebellion; or Scylla and Charybdis*, 375-376. It might be noted that the Pole, Okelomski, mentioned in Chap. I, above, was for some reason in

For a moment in the fall of 1864 the leaden skies of the Confederacy seemed shot with a ray of light. Besides the hope of reenforcements from the Polish exiles, Lieutenant H. R. Hislop McIvor, a knight-errant who had come over from London in September, 1861, and enlisted in a company of the Virginia Partisan Rangers, which called itself suggestively "Scotia," offered big hopes from Scotland. He resigned from the service on August 17, 1864, on account of physical debility and because private business demanded his return to Scotland, but with the fixed intention of reëntering the Confederate army as soon as he had settled his private affairs. What was infinitely more important was that he expected to persuade many hundreds of his countrymen to emigrate as the Poles proposed to do. The government made for him the same arrangements as for the Poles with precisely the same conditions of free passage for him to Europe on "public business," and to America for prospective Scotch volunteers.[61] Evidently this attractive method of recruiting the exhausted armies of the Confederacy "died a-borning." No group of Polish or Scotch exiles fought to save the cause, for, despite the contract, no Polish saviors were delivered.

The relative fighting ability of the various nationalities in the Confederate armies is a delicate question which could easily provoke controversy even at this late date. On the whole the palm would seem to have been awarded by the chief Confederate generals to the Irish. A general, one of the fiercest fighters of the war, gave his opinion in the following terms: "If tomorrow I wanted to win a reputation, I would have Irish soldiers in preference to any other; and I'll tell you why. First, they have more dash, more *élan* than any other troops that I know of; then they are more cheerful and enduring—nothing can depress them. Next, they are more cleanly. The Irishman never failed to wash himself and his clothes. Not only were they cheerful, but they were submissive to discipline when once broken in—and where they had good officers that was easily done; but once they had confidence in their officers their attachment to them was unbounded. And confidence was established the moment

---

New York in May, 1861, and that from that point he, together with fifteen other Poles, offered his services to the Confederacy. See Adjutant and Inspector General Letter Book, 0-7, 1861, Confederate Archives, War Department. It does not appear whether their services were accepted or not.   [61] *N. R.*, Ser. 2, III, 1202, 1203.

they saw their general in the fight with them. . . . I repeat, if I had to take from one to 10,000 men to make a reputation with, I'd take the same men as I had in the war—Irishmen from the city, the levees, the river, the railroads, the canals, or from ditching and fencing on the plantations. They make the finest soldiers that ever shouldered a musket."[62]

Certain racial characteristics undoubtedly contributed to making Irish troops successful soldiers. The chief of these traits is his innate love of a fight, a personal fisticuff encounter with a fellow Irishman or a mortal combat on the field of battle. This trait once manifested itself remarkably on the battlefield in a personal encounter between two Irishmen on the opposing sides. There was an Irishman named Burgoyne in the Ninth Louisiana, a huge muscular fellow, so full of fire and fight that he had never had his fill of noise and scrimmage. If the musketry fire slackened while the artillery was in action, he would have to slip over to the nearest gun to take someone else's place. On one occasion he had come over to the artillery, seized the sponge staff and rammed home the charge, meanwhile giving vent to his enthusiasm in screams and bounds like a catamount. Standing on the other side of the gun was another Irishman, a Federal prisoner who was an even finer physical specimen than Burgoyne. He broke out with the words, "Hey, ye spalpane, say, what are yez doing in the Ribil army?"

Burgoyne's retort came as quick as a flash, "Bedad, ain't an Irishman a freeman? Haven't I as good a right to fight for the Ribs as ye have to fight for the Yanks?" "O, yes!" pursued the Federal Irishman, "I know ye, now you've turned your ougly mug to me. I had the plizure of kicking yez out from behind Mary's wall, that time Sedgewick lammed yer brigade out o' there!"

"Yer a liar," shouted the other, "and I'll just knock yer teeth down yer ougly throat for that same lie," and with that he vaulted lightly over the gun, and in a trice the two men were at it in true Irish fashion with their fists. At that moment a Confederate officer, who was Burgoyne's superior, noticed the Federal soldier's gory fist —two fingers had been shattered in the battle—which he was just about to drive into the other's face, with the result that a truce was

[62] Maguire, *The Irish in America*, 576-577.

called, and the sound Pat said to the other, "You're a trump, Pat; give me your well hand, we'll fight this out some other time. I didn't see ye were hurt."[63]

No better illustration of this thirst for a fight, combined with a strong sense of loyalty to their comrades, could be offered than the conduct of the Second Tennessee which was largely composed of Irishmen, when it was stationed at Columbus on the Mississippi. A report was brought into the camp that the Yankees had been guilty of bayoneting the sick men in Russell's regiment, likewise constituted of Irishmen, during a battle at Belmont across the river. Instantly the regiment was aflame and swore to swim the river, if necessary, to wreak their vengeance on the guilty foe. At the roll call, which followed immediately, seventy-nine of the one hundred and three of the company were present; soon four came hurrying in from the hospital, pining for a share in the fight, and fourteen were recalled from guard duty so that the company was nearly full.[64]

A second excellent trait possessed by Irish soldiers is their devotion to a good leader. Captain St. Clair Morgan had raised a company of Irish in Nashville whose devotion to him was such that he believed any one of them would die for him. One understands that devotion, for his solicitude for his "boys" was equally great. He went from the front to Marietta, Georgia, to get shoes for them and did not cavil on his return to carry them on his arms and about his neck till he looked like one huge bundle of shoes. He would have been willing to look much worse to put shoes on his barefoot boys.[65] A third trait, and its importance is incalculable, is their indifference to danger or discomfort. Many are the tales in both armies of their imperturbability under fire.[66] Lastly, come their usual cheer and

[63] This fine story is told in Stiles, *Four Years under Marse Robert*, 212-214. The writer has quoted the conversation exactly, but slightly condensed the rest of the tale. Another instance of this Irish sense of fair play appears in the case of two members of a Missouri brigade. Blows were falling thick and heavy when one exclaimed, "Shtop a minit, till I fasty up my breeches; they're comin' loose." The other desisted coolly until notified to pitch in again.—R. S. Bevier, *History of the First and Second Missouri Confederate Brigades*, 330.

[64] Stevenson, *Thirteen Months in the Rebel Army*, 68-74.

[65] Morgan, *How It Was*, 51.

[66] The writer has had occasion before to refer to Hugh McVey of Company D, Fourth Kentucky. His end is an admirable example of the very trait last mentioned in the text. At Shiloh he was struck by a ball, but when a lieutenant told him to go back to the surgeon, he said, "No Leftenant, no I'll die on the field!" Not long afterwards he was hit a second time, and again he was urged to retire, but again he plied his rifle and answered as before. A third shot killed him instantly.—Thompson, *op. cit.*, 101. It was also of an Irishman, a "dreadful, dirty, snuffy, spectacled old Irishman," that William Dame

wit, traits which make them good soldiers off the field in a campaign —when whiskey could be kept from them.

While it is believed that the above tribute to the Irish soldiers as a group is not too warm, haste is made to add that just as fine specimens of individual soldiers, if not complete groups, were to be found among the Germans, the English, and the Scotch. In other words, among soldiers, as human beings everywhere, no nation has a monopoly of virtue—or vice. Military discipline can do much, but it cannot completely alter a man's character. A colonel of a Georgia regiment said that he wished he had a thousand men like the Frenchman, Hermann, and he could "walk through Yankeedom."[67] But it was a German whom General Buckner praised as the best nonprofessional soldier he had ever known. It was of another German that an officer declared, when asked who was the best soldier in the Terry Rangers, that the name of George Barnhart Zimpleman always came to his mind. That private was often honored by being selected for desperate attempts. He fought in more than four hundred battles and skirmishes from October, 1861, to May, 1865, received two wounds, one of which maimed him for life, and had more horses killed under him than any other man in the group. It was his own fault that he remained a private to the end. The coolness and courage of two German brothers of Company B under conditions which would have tried the loyalty and devotion of any one became proverbial in the Fourteenth Georgia. The stoicism of a Mexican under the surgeon's knife should be recorded. Dr. Nash was attending him after the battle of Cold Water near Senobia, Mississippi. Five of the seven balls which had entered his left leg had to be extracted. While the surgeon was cutting, the patient was smoking an old cob pipe, furnished him by the lady of the house. No chloroform was used, as there was none to be had. When asked if it hurt, he replied, half in Spanish, "Who cares for that?" It is pleasing to record that he recovered and fought through the war. Furthermore, it was a Mexican, Juan Ivara, who charged a squad of forty Federals, forcing them to retreat.[68] The bulldog tenacity

said, "Old Close was as brave as a lion. He had as soon go in a fight as not; a little sooner."—*From the Rapidan to Richmond and the Spottsylvania Campaign*, 133-134.
[67] Hermann, *op. cit.*, 141.
[68] For the two German brothers see James M. Folsom, *Heroes and Martyrs of Georgia*, 156; for the story about the Mexican, see Bunn, *Reminiscences of the Civil War*, 190; and *O. W. R.*, Ser. I, XXXIV, Pt. I, 648.

of the Englishman is justly famous as well as his inherent honesty even when he seems to be deviating from the path of rectitude. The latter quality wins a grudging respect for the Britisher in the following story. An Englishman who had no relatives in this country applied for leave because of the death of a grandmother, after an order was issued to grant furloughs only when deaths occurred in the family. The leave was approved, but his colonel, unusually kindly—or suspicious—kept pressing him, as he was leaving the tent, about details of his grandmother's death. Finally, the Englishman replied bluntly, "She's been dead forty years, sir. I can't lie about it, but I ought to get a furlough on it," and doggedly returned to his quarters. The sequel to this story is too entertaining to omit. A few days later he was shot in the leg, and shouted happily, "Thirty days and no death in the family!"[69]

In sharp contrast with the Englishman appears another, an incorrigible fellow who had to be frequently punished. The poor fellow was sometimes fastened to a cross, with his face placed directly under the spout of the pump, even when the weather was bitterly cold, and water pumped onto his face until respiration was suspended —a remedy known as the cold-water cure and highly efficacious. At other times he was placed in a barrel shirt—a barrel with holes through which the arms protruded—and compelled to mark time in the snow for hours. Contrasted with Zimpleman, for whom his superiors could not find sufficient praise, was "Old Hines," a German probably, of the second Richmond Howitzers who "never performed any duty in camp or on the field," and who walked calmly back to his mess if placed on guard. He never missed a battle and never did any fighting yet by his coolness he was an inspiration to those who did, for as the bullets flew he plied his needle as he mended his clothes and sang his one song, "Shoo Fly, Don't Bother Me."[70]

Irish companies were by no means all joy for their officers, for their love of a fight often degenerated into a pure quarrelsomeness and "raising Cain." As has been hinted, liquor had a disastrous effect upon them and it was practically impossible to keep it from them.

[69] Theodore Gerrish and John S. Hutchinson, *The Blue and the Gray*, 297.
[70] "A Confederate Veteran," *Southern Historical Society Papers*, XIX, 257-261. Old Hines's only associates were his messmates, two Germans, and so it would appear likely that he also was German, though he seems to have talked not at all.

Such encounters as the following could hardly have been pleasant for the officers in charge and were sadly frequent. A lieutenant, not knowing what to do with an Irishman who, wild with drink, had threatened to kill his captain, threatened to tie him. "Oh yis," sang out the culprit, "yis, yis; ye con tie me and ye con gag me too; I've been in the army before, and if you don't know how, I'll tell ye." The officer had him tied with a stout rope to a post, and then went to headquarters for further instructions. On his return he found the offender fast asleep, but untied, the rope bitten through with his teeth. Bright and early next morning the officer was accosted by a sober but hungry Irishman, "I say, Captain! will you not send somebody up to my quarters to get me some breakfast and a jug of *whiskee?*" The officers must have been terribly put to it to know what to do with a mad mob of lawless Irishmen, when two companies fell out and decided to settle it with their fists. At first a colonel was likely to summon an armed guard to arrest the belligerents, but with sad results, for the whole brigade would be in an uproar and the affair made bad blood between the contesting companies. As the Irish never used deadly weapons, the officers learned to let them settle their little family quarrels in the time-honored Irish way with hard knocks with fist and stick on hard skulls, followed by the resumption of the most pleasant and friendly relations.[71]

The description of one Burke, then in a prison camp, may be regarded as typical of an average Irish soldier. "The former [Burke] is a genuine Celt, full of expletive and nervousness, and is noted, for accepting a challenge to fight at ten paces, with double charged muskets and fixed bayonets, is all impulse, and, like all Irishmen, is ready to fight, if you 'tread on the tail of his coat!' "[72]

At a time when officers were notorious for their swearing, it might appear squeamish to note the oaths of a common soldier or of a group. But the Irish seem to have had a special capacity in that direction. "Irish Emmett in the Rockbridge Artillery was noted in his section of the army for growling out oaths through half-clenched

[71] Richard Irby, *Historical Sketch of the Nottoway Grays, afterwards Company G, Eighteenth Virginia Regiment, Army of Northern Virginia*, 9. For another story of an incorrigible Irishman see George W. Booth, *Personal Reminiscences of a Maryland Soldier in the War between the States*, 21-23. For Irish companies see Hunter, *Johnny Reb and Billy Yank*, 98; McGrath, "In a Louisiana Regiment," *Southern Historical Society Papers*, XXXI, 108, 113-114; Watson, *Life in the Confederate Army*, 311.

[72] Joe Barbière, *Scraps from the Prison Table at Camp Chase and Johnson's Island*, 107.

teeth that chilled the hearer's blood," according to the record, but the curious reader is denied samples.[73]

The statement has been made that it was impossible to keep Irishmen and liquor apart if they were in the same vicinity. This applied when the whiskey was the personal property of an officer and must have been irritating, to say the least. General Bevier tells the tale of a keg of whiskey which had been mysteriously emptied to the surprise and embarrassment of the officer who had offered it to the regimental surgeon. However, a "cut in the side of the tent, a gimlet hole in the keg, a long straw on the ground near the gimlet, and nearly every member of two Irish companies as drunk as Bacchus" solved the mystery.[74]

The Irish were not the only group to give trouble. The Germans in the West were a deeper cause of anxiety. Distrusted from the start, they amply justified that distrust by their mutiny at Fort Jackson. The troops which had been retained for the defense of Louisiana were largely foreign troops; those at Fort Jackson were Germans whose wives had represented to them the uselessness of the struggle because the city had already surrendered. They were also told that Captain Duncan, in charge of the fort, intended to blow it up over their heads rather than surrender. Hence during the night of April 27, 1862, they spiked some of the guns, dismounted others, and loudly demanded surrender, even threatening the lives of their officers. This marked an important turning point in the war, for there can be little doubt that, if Duncan had held the forts a few days longer, General Lovell could have removed a large amount of stores, guns, and other war materials from the forts and from New Orleans. The garrisons from all the batteries, erected for the defense of the passes to the city, were withdrawn by General Lovell to be concentrated at Vicksburg. Some detachments followed the flag, while others, many of them foreigners, dispersed to their homes.[75]

Usually the Mexicans enlisted in the Confederate service proved utterly unreliable. With no particular affection for American institutions, whether Unionist or Confederate, they tended early in the war to slip back across the Rio Grande River to participate in the

[73] Moore, *op. cit.*, 257.   [74] Bevier, *op. cit.*, 313.
[75] *The Journal of Julia Le Grand, New Orleans, 1862-1863*, 42-43; John Paris, "The Soldiers' History of the War," *Our Living and Our Dead*, II, 270.

turmoil which soon beset their own land. The authorities tried to conscript Mexicans under Texan laws, which at the beginning of the war required residents of ten days to submit to military service. But General H. P. Bee found in December, 1863, when state troops tried to enforce a draft, that the effort only produced bad feeling, drove the Mexicans across the Rio Grande, and provoked a protest from their government, which insisted fairly that under the treaty of Guadalupe Hidalgo citizens of Mexico who continued their residence in Texas were not liable to forced military duty. General Bee, accordingly, wisely suspended the Texan law. Let us take evidence from one of their own number. Clemente Bustilla, who was seeking to recruit a company of his fellow countrymen, frankly stated that he could organize a company only if he were furnished arms, rations, and quarters. "I could get a list of names on paper enrolled as a company, but I could not depend on their being ready at any call of the Government, unless I had them then in quarters."[76]

Since many of the substitutes came from the foreign population, and since, also, late in the war many of the foreigners were in the ranks because they had been conscripted, it can hardly cause surprise to learn that desertion was common among the foreign-born soldiers. Through the rolls one encounters frequently the notation that a certain soldier was serving as a substitute; he was almost certain to be a foreigner. The system of allowing substitutes became a vicious system on the part of both parties to the bargain. Certain Confederates speculated freely and profitably in the traffic. First they set about "running a Mick," professional slang for getting an Irishman drunk; then they induced him to enlist for two or three hundred dollars, obtaining, however, five times that sum from some citizen desirous of procuring a substitute; and, after sending him to the camp in the forenoon, brought him back to town towards evening to sell him again to some other native seeking to escape the service.[77] This was a game played also by parties of the second part. These same substitutes were frequently deserters from other commands, especially from

[76] General Bee to General W. R. Boggs, writing from Victoria, Texas, December 4, 1863.—*O. W. R.*, Ser. 1, XXVI, Pt. 2, 479. For Bustilla's opinion see his letter to Wm. Byrd, adjutant general, May 21, 1861.—Adjutant General's Correspondence, Archives, Texas State Library. For an instance of rebellion by a Mexican, Captain A. I. Vidal, see *O. W. R.*, Ser. 1, XXVI, Pt. 1, 447-452.

[77] Junius H. Browne, *Four Years in Secessia; adventures within and beyond the Union Lines*, 288.

the infantry service entering the cavalry, or they accepted substitute service merely in order to pocket the money, desert, and play the game again.[78] The hiring of substitutes was not confined to natives, for the rolls show occasionally that a certain foreign-born citizen, usually a merchant and presumably comfortably off in this world's goods, was "discharged by a substitute." Toward the close of the war the supply of foreigners on hand became scarce, as resident foreigners were conscripted, but occasionally an alien made his way into some southern point and was snapped up. It is interesting to note a Scotchman thus seizing on another Britisher to secure his release from the service. Williams, whom we have already met as a Britisher serving with the "border ruffians," as he terms them, happened to be accosted by an English sailor on the streets of Brownsville, Texas, just when he was yearning to get free of the hateful command of his captain, a villain named Duff, "to serve under whom," he declares, "was a disgrace to a self-respecting man." The sailor had come over in a coaster from New Orleans, had been discharged, was sick of the sea, and was thinking of joining the Confederate service. Here was a gift straight from the gods for Williams, and so one hundred and fifty dollars changed hands and Sailor Osborne became a Confederate soldier while Williams was once more a free man.[79] Sometimes Mexicans were coerced into the army by a method which was conscription, but without even the formality of enlistment.

That the conscription net would drag in the foreign-born citizens, reluctant for one reason or another to enter the service, was a foregone conclusion. Kaufmann offers the broad generalization that most of the Germans from Louisiana served under compulsion. Many in Texas refused to serve until they were conscripted; some, as we shall see in a later chapter, refused to renounce their Union convictions and suffered accordingly. Some of the few Swedes, only some hundred and fifty in all, were drafted. We read of Mrs. Palm, who came over from Sweden in November, 1848, with her nephew, S. M. Swenson, and settled near New Ulm, grieving over the conscription of her sons. We note the independence and pluck of John Palm, who fled to

[78] Captain Robert E. Park made the following entry in his diary on May 22, 1863: "Ed. Mahone, of Auburn, brought in four Irishmen as substitutes. They are frauds and should not be accepted. Some, I feel sure, are deserters from other commands."—"War Diary of Captain Robert Emory Park," Southern Historical Society Papers, XXVI, 10.
[79] Williams, With the Border Ruffians, 307-308.

Mexico to escape the dragnet, for though barely sixteen, he knew that neighbors were saying that he was big enough to carry a gun and go to the front. The record of Company B, Eighth Texas Infantry, which was recruited from near New Braunfels and Victoria, is very illuminating: twenty-five of the one hundred and three Germans were conscripted and most of the rest doubtless volunteered to escape conscription.[80]

While it is not surprising that desertion appeared among the foreign-born soldiers, it is amazing that it appeared in an exaggerated degree among the Irish recruits. This statement seems to be necessary, even when due allowance is made for the fact that the Irish had furnished a larger proportion of the foreign element than any other nationality. In a necessarily limited study of some rolls from North Carolina, Mississippi, Texas, Louisiana, and of one Virginia record— incomplete, the reader must again be reminded—the figures for desertion stand as follows: Irishmen, ninety-eight; Germans, forty-two; English, fourteen; with a small scattering of other nationalities. It is conspicuous that no nationality seemed to escape the disease—Canadian as well as Dane became infected, Scot as well as Norwegian, Swiss as well as Frenchman.[81] Mexicans seem to have been addicted to desertion, which was particularly easy, as most of them were serving on the Texan border and found it temptingly simple to pass over the Rio Grande to fight, if fight they were going to, in their own land. It would almost seem that when a Confederate officer detected a few isolated Mexicans, he was prone to take them for deserters. Williams, for instance, chased four Mexicans whom he encountered twelve miles from San Antonio. "After a deal of prevarication they at last confessed they were deserters from the confederate service,

[80] Kaufmann, *Die Deutschen im amerikanischen Bürgerkriege*, 140. For the treatment of Unionist foreigners see below, Chap. XIV. For the drafting of the Swedes see Anderson, *Hyphenated*, 119, 208-209, 213. The important data showing the conscription and place of recruitment of Company B, Eighth Texas, were obtained from a record of this company owned originally by Mr. Lichtenstein of Corpus Christi, loaned to the Confederate Archives, War Department.

[81] Some Descriptive Lists of Deserters from Companies A, C, and F, Fifty-ninth Virginia, and of the Alexandria Light Artillery have provided unexpected material on this point; also a Descriptive List and Account of Pay, Clothing, etc., Confederate Archives, War Department. A Descriptive Roll in a Company Book, preserved in the Alabama Military Archives, Company C, Forty-fifth Alabama, yielded some data. A mixed group of twenty-three Irish, Germans, Swedes, Poles, and Italians deserted to the foe from the Askew Guards, Company C, Fourteenth Louisiana.—Record, Company C, Fortieth Louisiana Regiment, U. D. C. Memorial Hall.

running for Mexico. Down on their knees they went, and begged and prayed, as only Mexicans can, that I would let them go." Though duty indicated that he should take them to San Antonio, he let them go, as he knew that with the lawlessness characteristic of the border a mob would hang them if he brought them back.[82] At Corinth, Mississippi, 400 Germans from a Louisiana regiment which had been sent out on outpost duty came into the Federal lines in a body with white flags on their guns—probably the Twentieth Regiment as it would be hard to find so many of that nationality assembled in any other regiment from that state. Another group of 150 or more, "almost entirely foreigners of a low class or ignorant conscripts from western Louisiana," were reported as deserting from Port Hudson.

There were desertions to the Confederate side by foreigners, as well as from it. One of the most interesting is the case of a Scotchman named Black. He had relatives in the South and as one means of reaching them deliberately joined the Union army with the intention of deserting. Opportunity afforded itself when he was on picket duty at the Potomac, for under pretense of a bath, he was able to strike out for the Virginia shore. Midway in the stream, he turned to shout, "Goodbye, boys; I'm bound for Dixie!" and in the spirit of the slavocracy shouted in answer to the threats of shooting him, "Shoot, and be d—d, you white-livered nigger-thieves." In a shower of Minié balls he landed on the Confederate side, to which he rendered admirable service.[83]

In nearly every company there were privates to whom attention is attracted because of family connections or of personal idiosyncrasies. To this class belong Edmund Ruffin, an elderly Englishman long resident in America; the Irishman, Campbell by name, who as a rebel deserter in the Union forces shot General Morgan; Charles Anderson, the young English Confederate who died during the war, whose chief claim to fame is that he was the father of the celebrated actress, Mary Anderson; Carlo Patti, brother of the great prima donna, who

[82] Williams, *op. cit.*, 275.

[83] One of the odd coincidences with which the history of this war is filled concerns this Scotchman. One night he was escorting with a mere corporal's guard a full company of Federal prisoners. The captain of the Federals recognized Black's voice and directed a question to Black concerning his identity. The latter admitted it and said, "I hope you're well, captain, you and all the boys. I couldn't stay with you, you see; it wasn't because I feared to fight, but I like to fight in the right cause always." Black was escorting his old Union company.—*Battle-fields of the South*, II, 156.

enlisted in the Second Tennessee; and E. W. Barnwell, the Russian consul at Charleston. He entered service in the ranks—this last a native.[84]

Any company was in a poor condition which did not have some personality who afforded amusement or who provided tales which could go the round of the campfires. The dull German or Irishman was usually made the butt of such stories of new recruits as that which represented him on guard demanding the countersign by declaring stoutly, "Halt, you can't pass here unless you can say 'Natchez!'" The mere calling of the roll of an Irish company was sufficient to attract Anglo-Saxons to hear the O'Parions, O'Flaritys, O'Flannartys, and O'Connells called, though most of the former would admit that these same O'Connells and O'Flaritys could not be surpassed in battle, playing cards in camp, or stealing provisions on the march. The informality of the Irish before the drill had whipped them into some semblance of discipline must have been highly diverting. The reporter Russell retails their conduct as he saw them in May, 1861. An order to fix bayonets elicited a wonderful amount of controversy in the ranks. "Whar are yer Dhrivin' to?" "Sullivan, don't yer hear we're to fix beenits." "Ayse the strap of me baynit, sergent, jewel." "If ye prod me wid that agin, I'll let dayloite into ye." Again, an officer reading the muster roll might call, "Number 23, James Phelan." No reply. Voice from the ranks—"Faith, Phelan's gone; sure he wint at the last dipot."[85]

The conversation of several Irishmen was usually diverting to listeners. One of them in the Thirteenth Louisiana was overheard to lament that he had no "gurl" to weep for his departure. "Be me soul," cried another, "I'm glad I've no wun. If I get kilt me people will never know what became of me, and the only monument I'll get will be an entry on the Company books—Killed in battle, Mike Morissy—and that's not me thrue name at that." The zest with which they could pursue food even in battle became a byword with Colonel von Zincken when he heard one of his desperately wounded Irishmen cry out to his comrades, "Charge them, boys; they have cha-ase (cheese) in their haversacks."

[84] Parker, *Recollections of a Naval Officer*, 217; George F. Robertson, *A Small Boy's Recollections of the Civil War*, 80; Craighead, *Mobile: Fact and Tradition*, 333; Mary Polk Branch, *Memories of a Southern Woman "Within the Lines,"* 27.
[85] Russell, *The Civil War*, 175-176; Watson, *Life in the Confederate Army*, 171; R. M. Collins, *Chapters from the Unwritten History of the War Between the States*, 171.

Of quite a different type was the diversion afforded by "Dummick," a Frenchman in Stuart's Horse Artillery, as famous in the Army of Northern Virginia as the big Grenadier in Napoleon's army. He and Dr. Evans, who was very proficient in artillery tactics though a mere boy, were great chums. Dominick proposed a contest with their respective guns to see who could load and fire in the shortest space of time according to the manual. The doctor's victory only won Dominick's greater admiration. The Frenchman, after fighting through all the bloody battles at Petersburg, disappeared suddenly during the siege of that city. He had been dismounted and deprived of a horse he had used for a long time. Dominick had said to Dr. Evans, who chanced to meet him, "Sammie, dey take my horse, put me down in company Q. Damm, me fight no more." And the man who had fought so bravely and faithfully was seen no more.[86]

If the Irish manifested clannishness by enlisting in companies composed exclusively of men of their race, the Germans manifested it also in camp. Nothing is more characteristic of the Teuton than his instinct to celebrate anniversaries. This urge appeared even in camp. On January 14, 1863, the members of the Houston *Turnverein* who composed three companies of Waul's legion were lying in camp near Grenada, Mississippi, after General van Horn's retreat behind the Tallahachie River. All felt the same impulse to celebrate the anniversary of the *Verein*. Consequently a general meeting was called in a tent, speeches full of vigor and patriotism were delivered, and the event celebrated in typical German fashion, concluding no doubt, though the scribe does not say so, with German songs, merry or solemn, ringing through the camp.[87]

[86] McGrath, "In a Louisiana Regiment," *Southern Historical Society Papers*, XXXI, 115-116; D. H. Hill, "Chickamauga," *Century Magazine*, XXXIII, 960; *Confederate Veteran*, V, 82.
[87] Tiling, *History of the German Element in Texas*, 167.

VIII

SPECIAL FIELDS OF SERVICE ON AND OFF THE FIELD

IN THE DISTINCTIVE divisions of the army, the engineer corps, pioneer corps, ordnance, quartermaster, and commissary departments, the reader looks for foreigners and not in vain. It is natural that the army authorities should find aliens who had served in European armies especially fitted for services which called for specialized training.

While General Gonzales—a Cuban, it will be remembered—rendered sufficiently important service at the bombardment of Fort Sumter to be mentioned along with others of the staff by General Beauregard, and shared in the battle of Honey Hill in December, 1864, it was in organizing the coast defenses that he made his distinctive contribution. As a special aide-de-camp to Governor Pickens, he surveyed and studied the entire coast between Georgetown and Savannah in order to determine the resources and extent of the coast defenses and suitable locations for fortification. He then submitted to the general of the department plans for the efficient use of barbette and siege guns with special reference to the speedy change of batteries and the concentration of fire toward any requisite point. During 1861 he spent two months in Richmond, procuring orders from the war department on the Tredegar works, superintending the manufacture and forwarding the most effective pieces of armament to South Carolina. His work was definitely effective. For nearly four years the Charleston and Savannah Railway, although it crossed many navigable tidewater streams, was held intact despite the fleets of the enemy only a few miles distant. This was achieved by the mounting of heavy siege guns on special artillery wheels, and by moving them from point to point with the aid of hundreds of men and horses. In thus mobilizing heavy guns Gonzales and the South were pioneers. This method of handling heavy artillery was used a generation later in the Boer War and a few years later still by the Japanese in the siege of Port Arthur.[1]

[1] See Brooks, *Stories of the Confederacy*, 292, 293, 294, 296-298. For the battle of Honey Hill see *Charleston Daily Courier*, December 5, 1864.

An Englishman who had gone out as a member of Captain Ketchum's battery of artillery was transferred by early May, 1862, to Mobile to join the engineering department, in which division he had served while in the British army.[2] When General Floyd found himself in a most awkward position near Gauley Bridge in his campaign in West Virginia against Generals Cox and Rosecrans of the northern army in 1861, his infantry on one side of the river, his artillery on the other, he ordered his chief of engineers to build boats—and was told that it was impossible. The latter set off for the camp of Wise and Henningsen for aid. In this emergency General Henningsen sent over his chief engineer, Captain Bolton, also an Englishman, with engineering experience in the British army, who found it possible to construct floats quite capable of taking the troops across the river now badly swollen by heavy rains.[3] Captain T. George Raven, a native of Lancashire, brought to the South Carolina Rangers as independent volunteer the training which England gives the graduates of her military college at Addiscombe. The government discovered by 1863 that it had better use for his technical skill than for his sword and made him military engineer on the staff of General Wayne, placing him in charge of the fortifications at Etowah Bridge. Evidently the promotion was no mistake, for he is honorably mentioned in the adjutant general's report. He did not live long to serve his adopted country, for he contracted pneumonia while on duty at Resaca, Georgia, where he was sent after completing the work at Etowah Bridge, and died at Milledgeville.[4] Enlistment as a private in Company A, Twenty-eighth Louisiana Infantry, later the Twenty-seventh, in which he rose to the rank of a lieutenant and an adjutant within a year, together with two periods of imprisonment in northern prisons, seems to have obscured the qualifications of George Osborn Elms of Canada for construction work, despite the fact that he had been engaged for the eight years just preceding the war in railroad construction work throughout the South. It was only after his exchange in late March,

---

[2] Cummings, A Journal of Hospital Life, 22. This was a Mr. Goden.

[3] Estvàn, War Pictures, I, 209. See O. W. R., Ser. 1, V, 285 ff.; Battles and Leaders of the Civil War, I, 142-143, for details of the campaign. Floyd, it will be recalled, had been defeated at Gauley River.

[4] Raven had been brought to America by commercial pursuits but married in Charleston and remained here. In 1860 he had joined the Washington Artillery of Charleston, serving with that battery until the fall of Sumter, but subsequently joined the South Carolina Rangers as an independent volunteer.—Confederate Veteran, XVII, 318.

1865, that he qualified as first lieutenant of the corps of engineers, to which he had been appointed the November preceding, in which capacity he served to the surrender. With this group of British subjects belongs a well-educated Irish engineer, Brennan by name, who came to America on a pleasure trip in 1851, married here, and then settled in Nashville.[5]

There was a distinguished group of Germans in the engineering corps. Meriting, possibly, first mention was Colonel Victor von Scheliha. The student encounters him first in Kentucky in December, 1861. Between this date and May, 1862, when he became a prisoner of war through the surrender of General Mackall at Island No. 10, he had served as staff engineer to Generals Polk, Zollicoffer, Crittenden, and Mackall. Stationed from January, 1864, to the close of the war at Mobile, he appears in the records as chief engineer in the department of the Gulf and erected a new and extensive line of forts around that important point which proved models of strength and judicious arrangement. It was for service in this same field that Gustav Schleicher won the relatively high rank of major, as he constructed several forts, notably Fort Sabine, though obviously his prominence as a member of the Texas state legislature, first as representative and then as senator, had not been left out of consideration.[6] Ernst Kurth, born in Cologne near Meissen, Germany, but resident in Richmond for many years before the war, had gained considerable prominence by his work for the Society for the Construction of Railways in Virginia and by his plan for the Danville railroad bridge over the James River near Richmond. He served as an engineer in the Army of Northern Virginia. The Prussian, G. A. Peple, with whom the reader will soon have a bowing acquaintance because of meeting him at the Confederate Marine School on the *Patrick Henry*, had visited the technical schools of Geneva and Vevey in pursuit of his mechanical interests, and acted as topographical engineer during the early period of the war. Another German engineer officer, sent from

---

[5] *Ibid.*, XX, 232. Elms was brought by his family from Canada to Lyman, New Hampshire, at the age of six, but he went south in 1852 at the age of twenty-one. For Brennan see *ibid.*, XII, 297.

[6] For Scheliha see *O. W. R.*, Ser. 1, XV, 1015, 1059; XXIII, Pt. 1, 391; XXVI, Pt. 2, 431-432, 501-504; XXXIX, Pt. 2, 706, 772, 782, 841, 859; XLV, Pt. 1, 1230-1231, 1249-1250, and Pt. 2, 707-708, 734-735; Ser. 2, III, 864-865, 874. For Schleicher see Faust, *The German Element in the United States*, I, 499-500; Benjamin, *The Germans in Texas*, 108-109.

Richmond for service in the wretchedly constructed fort at Cobb's Point, two or three miles below Elizabeth City on the Pasquotank River, North Carolina—not of his construction, be it added—remained bravely at his post when the men of the garrison ran away. Record has been preserved of several Germans in the engineer department in Texas: Captain William von Rosenberg, John von Rosenberg, and H. R. von Bieberstein. Undoubtedly the most distinguished engineer who served in Texas was the Pole, Colonel Valery Sulakowski, with whom the reader is well acquainted by this time, who built many fortifications along the Texas and Louisiana coast. General Magruder pronounced him an officer of the highest merit. No one could study his plans for removing the "raft" from the Brazos River and for erecting defenses on the Guadalupe and other Texas rivers without feeling that he had ability to render real service to the cause, if his plans could have been executed. It was a loss to the Confederacy that his personality came into conflict with the Richmond authorities. Magruder was right in trying to find some way of utilizing his badly needed talents for the best interests of the service.[7]

Colonel August Forsberg has been noted as one of the few Swedes to attain high rank in the army. It is rather remarkable that his recognition came in the line of service on the field of battle, for, although a regular army man, his distinctive work for his native country, Sweden, and his initial service for the Confederacy had been as an engineer. At the age of twenty-two he was serving as lieutenant in the engineering corps of the Swedish army when a fellow countryman wrote from America to Stockholm for an assistant on a government building to be erected in Columbia, South Carolina. Forsberg was the man selected to be sent. The Danish consul warned him at the outbreak of the war to leave the northern city, where he had migrated after the completion of his work in Columbia, as he was in danger of arrest because of his well-known southern sympathies. Forsberg heeded the advice, gave up a fine position, and set out for

---

[7] See Schuricht, *History of the German Element in Virginia*, II, 56, 85, for Kurth and Peple; for the German at Cobb's Point see Parker, *Recollections of a Naval Officer*, 238. After the garrison had fled, Parker, as captain of the *Beaufort*, and his crew were ordered to take charge of the fort. The Prussian's name was Heinrich. See Oliver D. Kinsman, "A Loyal Man in Florida, 1858-61," *War Papers*, No. 81, p. 11, for a northerner against a mob. For letters by W. von Rosenberg from Austin, dated January 25, 1864, see G. O. Correspondence, Archives, Texas State Library. For Sulakowski's service see his file, Confederate Archives, War Department.

Colonel August Forsberg. By courtesy of his children

the South in a fishing vessel, reaching Charleston during the bombardment of Fort Sumter in April, 1861. Here he was accorded the post of topographical engineer in the Charleston Harbor defense work. However by June of the first year of the war he was given a regular commission as lieutenant for the field service, and climbed rapidly to marked distinction, reaching the rank, as recorded, of colonel of the Fifty-first Virginia. He had doubly endeared himself to the Confederates by espousing their cause, though not a native, and by deserting the North to do so.[8]

The record of the lone French engineer on the southern side whom the writer has discovered is not so creditable. He was General Bragg's chief of engineers, a little, polite, black-bearded Frenchman known as Major Nocquet. Reading backwards, one can see that his final action toward the Confederacy was foreshadowed one night when Bragg's army was on its way into Kentucky. Around the camp-fire there was an animated discussion as to the future of the new republic. Nocquet insisted, with his characteristic foreign shrug, that democracy had proved a failure and that nothing except a monarchy could heal the American dissensions. Oddly enough, some of the native Americans inclined to his view, but there was found at least one to combat it. He won high praise from his superiors, especially Colonel Gilmer, "as active and earnest in his duties, showing much skill and intelligence in locating works for the defense of our position and in directing their construction. Few men possess greater qualifications for usefulness with an army in the field or more zeal for the cause of southern independence." In 1863 when he was acting as chief engineer to General Buckner, just before the battle of Missionary Ridge, he absconded to the Federal army with one hundred and fifty thousand dollars from the army chest and betrayed to the North valuable information as to Bragg's position and works. Leaving the southern army ostensibly for Tennessee to purchase engineer supplies, he was last seen in citizen clothes and was duly dropped from the rolls.[9]

[8] *Confederate Veteran*, XVIII, 434. His marriage was a war romance, for he met a Mrs. Otey (née Morgan) while he was in the hospital, recovering from a severe wound received at Winchester. Their marriage followed very shortly. He served as city engineer of Lynchburg for twenty-one years after the war.

[9] Austin, *The Blue and the Gray*, 49; Ross, *A Visit to the Cities and Camps of the Confederate States*, 143. Ross states that Nocquet robbed the southern army chest. For his irregular departure see his file in the Confederate Archives, War Department. See also Gilmer's letter of January 21, 1862.—*Ibid.*

le Pioneer Corps was a distinct division of the Civil War armies, ̣h members seem not to have been prevented from fighting wh̲ɪ̲e in that corps. A certain Christian Bosche, a native of Germany, was in command of that group for the First Kentucky Brigade with the rank of captain during 1862-63. Several Irishmen and another Prussian are noted as serving in the Pioneer Corps of the First Brigade, First Division, Army of the Mississippi.[10]

A special field of service, though definitely, of course, an integral part of the army and a highly important part, was that of the sharpshooters. As in all other branches, some foreigners appear in this service, which called for fighters of the heroic type. John M. Ozanne, one of the best shots in his company of sharpshooters and utterly fearless, was a native of France, though brought to America when he was ten years old. Incidentally he rendered a far more significant service to his fellow soldiers, if not to the Confederacy, when he resigned his commission as lieutenant because he could not buy his provisions and clothes with the pay. His action changed the law so that thereafter officers, along with privates, received their supplies. John R. Williams was a Scotchman who lifted himself above the ranks by his keen eye and sure aim. He was put in charge of a brigade of sharpshooters in the Army of Virginia and always took his place at the head of his brigade in their numerous perilous engagements.[11]

Scouting and the secret service were special fields of service often necessarily performed at a great distance from the camp or scene of hostilities. Possibly because of their unassumed accents and alien appearance the foreign-born were especially desirable for this branch of service. In any case one finds here a sprinkling of aliens and foreign-born. Captain Tom Quirk, a "dare-devil, 'Blue Grass' Irishman," was made by General John Morgan captain of about fifty scouts or vedettes to obtain information concerning the enemy. He soon attracted attention by his reckless activity and utter indifference to danger, but lacked the caution which is requisite for a real leader. A blue coat, we are told, was to him a red flag which he had to attack at any

[10] Thompson, *History of the First Kentucky Brigade*, 914; Descriptive List of the Pioneer Corps, First Brigade, First Division, First Corps, Army of the Mississippi, Confederate Archives, War Department. There is a single reference to an Irishman, Daniel McCarty, who was transferred to the sappers and miners.—Thompson, *op. cit.*, 616. It is not felt desirable to give a separate handling to this division of the army in this study.

[11] *Confederate Veteran*, XV, 128; XVII, 566.

cost. He never let anyone get ahead of him in entering a fight and he never knew how to retire. Another interesting Irishman in Morgan's command was John D. McRohan. Despite a crippled foot on which he hobbled through life as a result of rescuing a child from a burning building when he was scarcely more than a child himself, he enlisted for active cavalry service in Company D, Eighth Kentucky Cavalry. He was often detailed on secret service on account of his bravery and discretion. A third Irishman in our tale had grown up in Canada, but, caught in the South by the war, served three years under General Forrest. In 1863, when on recruiting service he was cut off from his company by Sherman's raid up the Yazoo River, he reported to General Wirt Adams and was assigned to the scouts under Captain W. A. Montgomery, with whom he served to the end of the war.[12]

The German lad, Joe Kruse, just over from Europe in 1861, proved himself so active, brave, and sagacious that his officers soon found him invaluable as a lone scout. He was not even required to report regularly to his captain. His name became such a terror to the enemy and such a safeguard to unprotected women and children that the marines of the Union army did not often land when they were told by the Negroes that Joe Kruse was about. The word "surrender" did not exist in his vocabulary, and that kind of dauntless courage enabled him to escape from situations where escape seemed utterly impossible.[13] On many occasions Herman Wohleben, a member of Miller's battalion of Mississippi cavalry, was detailed for the perilous duty of entering the enemy's lines to secure information for the commanding general. Another, "Harvey's Dutch scout," was a character well known to Ross's Texas brigade; he was a Presbyterian preacher and a scout, who captured over one hundred men in the Sherman raid. Dr. William J. Häcker was another German in scout service for Bragg's army. Captain John Karner was a Bavarian who may justly be classed as a scout, though his great feat was crossing

[12] *Ibid.*, XIX, 118; XXVIII, 268. The name of the third Irishman mentioned in the text was George Roder.—Mathes, *The Old Guard in Gray*, 185.

[13] Although he seldom allowed himself to be taken by surprise, he was once surrounded by fifty Federal cavalry while eating his dinner. He walked to the front gate with a pistol in each hand, firing unerringly. He jumped on his horse, cut his bridle reins, and, thrusting his spurs deep in the sides of his horse, broke through the ranks of the enemy and escaped.—T. H. Bowman, *Reminiscences of an Ex-Confederate Soldier or Forty Years on Crutches*, 25-26.

the Mississippi from Texas to carry clothing, mail, and supplies to three companies of Texans in Granbery's brigade, Cleburne's divison.[14]

One of the finest pieces of spy work recorded was performed by an English physician, Dr. William T. Passmore, who had a varied career in the Confederate army. Enlisting in the Lunenburg troops of Virginia from the section where he was living, he saw service under General Loring in the mountainous counties of western Virginia, but his skill as a physician soon led to his being detailed for duty in the medical department. However his biggest contribution, probably, was as a disguised scout. General Lee sent him to spy on General Burnside's army. Recognized by a Union man, he still pressed on. He disguised himself as a ragged, mentally deficient man, selling market produce from an old cart to the Union soldiers. He played so cleverly the rôle of the half-wit frightened by so many soldiers that Burnside wrote him a pass, allowing him to enter the lines daily with supplies. From the general conversation, indulged in freely no doubt before a supposed half-wit, he gathered the needed information; hence in a few days General Lee was ready to fight one of the greatest battles of the war, Fredericksburg. Finally a Welshman, Llewellyn William Lloyd, served in the secret service for a brief period during 1862, visiting Baltimore, Washington, and Philadelphia, and reporting back safely to Lee.[15]

Closely related to the spy is the smuggler, Paul A. Fusz, who, though born in Héricourt, France, had lived in St. Louis since he was a child of six. Little more than a child when the war began, scarcely fifteen, he ran away with two other lads to join the southern army. He was caught while he and a comrade slightly older were smuggling quinine and some valuable papers through the lines. The boys promptly chewed up the papers, for which act the elder of the pair was hanged, but Fusz, on account of his youth, was sent to the prison at Jefferson City. Tradition has it that the pardon of this youthful soldier was Lincoln's last official act.[16]

[14] *Confederate Veteran*, XII, 544; V, 573; XXIV, 328. General Bragg gave Captain Karner a pass to go "anywhere in the Confederacy." After the exploit recounted in the text he returned to Texas and served in the army on Galveston Island eight months.— *Ibid.*, IX, 465.

[15] *Ibid.*, XVII, 236-237; Yeary, *Reminiscences of the Boys in Gray*, 433. Lloyd was also for a time chief of ordnance in the field for Mississippi.

[16] *Confederate Veteran*, XVIII, 244.

The ordnance department is so distinct from the fighting force that it has seemed desirable to separate it for discussion from the regular army, for treatment with the special fields of service. A Captain E. von Buchholz was singled out to take charge of ordnance in Virginia. He was a native of Württemberg, the son of the chief ranger, and had served as cavalry and artillery officer for ten years in the royal army of that German principality before his emigration to America and location in Richmond. Governor Wise, recognizing merit, engaged him to survey the state and to draw a reliable topographical map. As a result of that personal contact with the distinguished Virginian he accompanied Governor Wise to Harper's Ferry as a member of his staff at the time of the John Brown raid. At the outbreak of the war the governor, utilizing Buchholz's military experience, ordered him to organize the artillery of Wise's brigade, but he was soon placed in charge of the ordnance stores of the brigade. Early in 1862 he was transferred to Richmond to take charge of the ordnance department of the state of Virginia with the rank of captain, where he remained for the remainder of the war. Buchholz is also to be noted for having clearly foreseen the coming of war. He had written some instructions for field service, for fortification and coast defense, and was engaged on a work on tactics, though he was dubious about finding a publisher. He was one of the small group of Germans who were early in the field with the tender of their services, which appears in a letter of November 13, 1860, to Governor Wise.[17]

The ordnance officer of both southern armies who deserves by all odds to be remembered was the Pole, Colonel Hypolite Oladowski. Some one facetiously remarked that he had been captured along with the rest of the ordnance at Pensacola by General Bragg. If so, he was a valuable prize, for he had but two gods: General Bragg and ordnance supplies. "What the spending of a dollar is to the miser, the wasting of a cartridge was to Oladowski, and it rent his very soul in agony." This penuriousness in ammunition brought, of course, frequent conflicts with the other officers, even in spite of mutual respect. At Dalton an officer under General Cleburne, when making a requisition for supplies, offered Oladowski some suggestions. The first suggestion rendered the officer guilty of an extravagance, and the

[17] Schuricht, *op. cit.*, II, 86. As there were no funds to complete the survey after the war, Von Buchholz went to California as superintendent of a factory for the manufacture of explosives.

second of a presumption, according to the irate colonel, offenses not to be tolerated, and so the paper was returned with a sharp endorsement. Oladowski ever after referred to the offending officer as "that d—d Frenchman, 'Piree!'" The appellation was probably suggested by the name and the traditional hostility of the Teuton and Gaul, but Pearre happened to be of pure native origin. The belligerent colonel did not, however, allow his personal animosities to interfere with his innate respect for the good of the service, for when a short time later Richmond called for recommendations for advancement in rank, and the divisional ordnance officer asked Oladowski whether he was going to send in Pearre's name, his reply was, "I would be one d—d fool if I did not recommend Piree." Furthermore, this was in the face of personal defeat, for Cleburne had taken up the matter of the suggestions and had sustained the young officer by a counter endorsement, thus winning the case for his subordinate and overruling Oladowski.

Occasionally an under officer could fit out a company with ammunition in spite of Oladowski. This proved to be the case with the young English lad Dawson, who, incidentally, was a second foreigner to act as ordnance officer in Bragg's army, though his was a temporary appointment during the disablement of his superior. Dawson was very anxious to complete the equipment of his corps, but he could not have overcome Oladowski's love of red tape and reluctance to part with any of his stores and would have failed except for the fact that he had prudently brought with him from Virginia a quantity of Enfield rifles. This youth's comment on the old colonel contributes one more bit to the picture. "Oladowski could out-curse any man in the army I ever met, except Jubal Early and M. Gray." It was one of his boasts that he had "evacuate Murphreysboro' with zee whole army and lose only one grindstone." But, alas, after Bragg's disastrous defeat at Missionary Ridge, he could no longer congratulate himself on the loss of "only one grindstone."[18]

It was quite in character that Oladowski should be out of sympathy with innovations in the army, and should scorn the signal corps. He dubbed them the "flip-flops" on account of the movement of the flags when signaling according to the Morse code. Once when observing a dispatch being sent to a station some miles distant on a mountain

---

[18] For details concerning this strange character see Buck, *Cleburne and his Command*, 228-230; Dawson, *Reminiscences of Confederate Service*, 104-105.

top, he burst out, "Ah! watch those flip-flops; they go dis way three times and dat way three times," suiting the action to the word with his handkerchief, "and de lieutenant he say now, darn you, you get on your horse and ride to that man on de mountain and tell him what I say!" Like others, only human, when the war seemed incapable of being longer endured, he had his moments of repining, for he was heard to say, "Vell! Vell! Vell! I wish I was in h—ll ten years before dis war begin."[19]

Other foreigners were, of course, detailed to the ordnance department in various subordinate positions—the Irishman, E. Mahoney, for instance, who was detailed early from the Forty-third Alabama and served in ordnance to the end of the war.

The writer has encountered but one alien-born who seems to have been assigned a position as quartermaster. That was Joseph McMurray, a Jamaican who entered the Confederate service as a private on March 27, 1862, and received his assignment to this department a month later, on April 26, 1862. The men who at one time or another received assignment as assistant quartermaster represented several nationalities—German, Hungarian, Irish, and Norwegian. Captain Fred Wolf was a German who had sacrificed a university education to join the tide of emigration to America and had finally settled in Memphis. The secretary of war made him assistant in this department for a Tennessee regiment with the rank of captain after some months in the Washington Rifles from that city. He was one of several Germans who filled this post. A Hungarian who had enlisted in September, 1861, at Houston, was appointed quartermaster sergeant in the Terry Texas Rangers by Colonel Terry but later discharged. A Norwegian transferred from the Twenty-sixth Texas Cavalry to the office of the quartermaster made good, for he served in this capacity until the end of the war. Italy, France, and one of the West Indian islands also sent natives to the South who filled this post during the war.[20]

[19] The first story of the signal corps is told by Otey, "Organizing a Signal Service," *Confederate Veteran*, VII, 549; the second story, by Dawson, *op. cit.*, 104. Of course Oladowski was the type soldiers love to play tricks on. As a Pole, he was, naturally, a devout Catholic. Pretending that coats were available for the officers and men at a remarkably low price at a certain point, Captain T., a Frenchman, managed to get the colonel to burst in rudely upon a communion service, thus committing a sacrilege. "Mea culpa," groaned the unhappy son of the church as he withdrew.—W. J. Hardee, "The Haversack," *The Land We Love*, VI, 337-338.

[20] McMurray's name and position appear on a Descriptive Roll of Officers, Confederate

Since paymasters were in the quartermasters division in the Confederate army, this is the proper place to include the services of Captain Frank Potts, a North of Ireland man who had established a large commission house in Richmond a few years before the outbreak of the war. Although fitted by physique, age—he was only twenty-six years old—and every impulse for the field, he was not allowed to remain in the Montgomery Guards, Company C of the First Virginia, in which he had enlisted as soon as Virginia seceded. His business experience caused him to be assigned very quickly to the post of assistant quartermaster in Longstreet's command, by which general he was commended for efficiency during the Tennessee campaign. But later he was called on to serve as corps paymaster, a position which he was filling with the rank of captain when the Confederacy received its deathblow.[21]

Napoleon has made the commissary department so famous by his terse if inelegant expression, "An army fights on its stomach," that its importance is established for all time. It is only necessary here to point out that its members did not ordinarily fight to justify its classification here. Herman Kaminski was a German Pole whom the prospect of hard work with but scant opportunity of advancement had driven from his homeland to Charleston seven years before the outbreak of war. Though he enlisted in the Tenth South Carolina Volunteers, his executive ability soon singled him out to become regimental commissary. A Scotchman filled the same post, commis-

---

Archives, War Department. A brief account of Fred Wolf appears in the *Confederate Veteran*, XVI, 355.

Some assistant quartermasters were Samuel Frank, who resided at Holly Springs, Mississippi; John F. Griber, of Louisiana; John C. Caldwell from a Louisiana cavalry regiment—all Germans. Frank M. Harney from Louisiana was an Irish assistant quartermaster. Jack Murphy, Irish, and A. B. Vaccaro, an Italian, Joseph de Meza, presumably a Mexican from the West Indies, Chloris Bohled, a Frenchman, and John Schmidt, an Irishman, served as quartermaster sergeants. M. F. Bollegathey was a Hungarian appointed to the last-named post in the Terry Texas Rangers. Thomas Newman was the lone Norwegian.—Mickle, *Well-Known Confederate Veterans and their War Records*, I, 68.

The above has been gathered from various Records and Descriptive Rolls. The data about the Hungarian were taken from a roll compiled by J. M. Claiborne with historical remarks, apparently for a reunion in Galveston on February 20, 1882. It is preserved in the Archives, Texas State Library.

[21] He has to be listed with the captains, for, although he had been advised that he would soon be promoted to the rank of major, he had not received his commission when the republic fell. For details see *O. W. R.*, Ser. 1, XXXI, Pt. 1, 465; XLII, Pt. 2, 1247; *Palmetto Leaf*, a local sheet, reprinted, October 22, 1928, by D. S. F.; also Frank Potts, *The Death of the Confederacy*, Foreword, iv, a letter by Frank Potts to his brother, the Reverend John Potts.

sary general, for the Sixth Louisiana Regiment with the rank of lieutenant colonel.[22] The executive abilities of Major Purvis, who was removed from the captaincy of the Scotch Guards with which he had rendered distinguished service during the siege of Vicksburg, were fully recognized by the military authorities when he was made manager of subsistence and commissary stores for the subdepartment of Mississippi. Daily, commencing work at midnight, he butchered and scalded a thousand hogs and baked a correspondingly huge number of loaves of bread. Louis Volmer, a German, Captain John Ormsby Treanor, an Irishman, and E. A. McKenney, a Canadian, all served in the commissary department of their respective commands after having seen active combat on the field.[23]

Because the personal or body servants, as they were occasionally termed, were so constantly concerned with securing commissary supplies for their masters' tables, a word about them at this point is in order. General Lee, to begin at the top, had as a personal orderly an Irishman named Bryan, perfectly devoted to the general. In his opinion there was nothing too good for the general's mess. He was an excellent caterer, a good forager, and would undoubtedly have provided a good table if the general had not frowned sternly upon anything remotely approaching lavishness. Toward the close of the war Bryan was so handicapped by the scarcity of all provisions that his skill as a cook was utterly wasted.[24]

As usual Louisiana could provide even the most colorful cooks and attendants. Some of the members of the Washington Artillery took off with them to the field a French cook from Victor's famous restaurant in New Orleans. He was a man of resources; his dishes were superb, the object of envy of all visitors who did not regularly enjoy the luxury of a French cuisine. Edouard soon tired of the monotony of camp life, grew indignant when his utensils were ignominiously thrown into the ditches by the roadside when transportation had to be curtailed, felt that his reputation was at stake, and finally with his pet

[22] Kaminski had worked his way through high school after his arrival in America, and his preparation for his war work as commissary had been a clerkship in Georgetown, S. C.— James C. Hamphill (ed.), *Men of Mark in South Carolina*, I, 200. The Scotch commissary of subsistence was J. G. Campbell, who was promoted from the ranks.—Record of the Officers of the Sixth Louisiana, Confederate Archives, War Department.

[23] Napier Bartlett, "The Twenty-Second Louisiana," *Military Record of Louisiana*, 35; *Confederate Veteran*, XXII, 472, XX, 233; Yeary, *op. cit.*, 495.

[24] Lee, *Recollections and Letters of General Robert E. Lee*, 132.

fox took French leave.[25] The colonel of this artillery regiment added a rare touch to his domestic arrangements by selecting for his major-domo one John Bahr, a plethoric, full-breasted, bow-windowed native of Germany who had volunteered with the command as hospital steward. John looked after the colonel's physical demands well, riding many miles for provender for the mess. If he were unfortunate enough to be espied by the men as he returned from his foraging expeditions, they would demand a toll from his fine supplies and threaten dire vengeance if he reported them to the colonel. The stolid German would reply, "All recht; vait dill dot pay master koms. I get you even on der leetle game of boker." The colonel's French servant, François, who was not without his sense of humor, furnished another touch of color. Once, while unloading the head-quarter's wagon, he found that one leg of the small camp stove was missing. François, with a grim smile and a shrug of the shoulders, replied to the angry colonel's demand to know where it was, "Mus-choo Col-o-nel, I do not know, but I dink it must be left on the battle-field."[26] One wonders sometimes why the southerners ever used aliens as servants instead of the black men we naturally expect. Day tells us, for instance, of an Italian, Lanzaroni by name, encountered at a mountain inn in Virginia, who could not speak English, and who would have been arrested as a suspicious character, except for the interference of his master. The soldiers had been amusing themselves by prodding him with the points of their bayonets. Occasionally a servant fought with his master on the battlefield. In one of the companies of the Lee Battalion was found an officer who had brought along to Virginia as his attendant an Irish boy named Flannagan. During the Seven Days' Battles around Richmond, this child procured a small shotgun and fought like an old soldier.[27]

The post of color-bearer was regarded in the Confederate army, as elsewhere, as one of honor. It is noticeable that, in the little group of soldiers so honored which the writer has collected, the natives of the Emerald Isle stand well to the front. Of Doneley—his first name

[25] William M. Owen, *In Camp and Battle with the Washington Artillery*, 21.

[26] *Ibid.*, 20, 22. One Joe Keno, tired of the hardships of army cook, gained exemption on the ground of French citizenship, and delivered lamb and kid at the kitchen door for the mess—which often proved to be dog.—Hull, *Annals of Athens, Georgia*, 297.

[27] Day, *Down South*, I, 284-285. Fannie A. Beers in *Memories. A Record of Personal Experiences and Adventures During Four Years of War*, 275, tells the story of the Irish boy servant.

has not survived—first color-bearer of Company C, Ninth Alabama, it was said that he was "recklessly brave," a fact which probably explains his falling in the bloody battle of Cold Harbor. Dennis O'Halloran became color sergeant of Company I, Fifth Regiment of the Orphan Brigade, in 1864 after he had displayed his bravery in many battles and had been severely wounded. Of only one Irishman has a record of faithlessness to the colors been encountered. He was entered on the roll of the Eighth Louisiana as acting disgracefully at Port Republic, as has been noted in another connection, running off with the colors, for which he suffered reduction to the ranks. His desertion shortly afterwards probably occasioned no surprise. It is noticeable, however, that it was to a small, wiry son of France that Colonel Hall decided to entrust the colors of the Twenty-sixth Louisiana. In order to make the office significant, he had the regiment drawn up in line, called Sergeant Britsche to him, and asked his promise to carry the colors wherever ordered. Through the dead cold words of a printed page one feels the strength and sincerity of the new color sergeant as he replied in a firm, quiet, meaning tone, "Je le jure, Colonel."[28]

A distinctive part of the army was the regimental bands, although the men of which they were composed held their positions in the fighting ranks. At the beginning of the war, bands were in general conspicuous in the southern army by their absence or inferiority. "The Southerners are said to be extremely fond of music, though they seldom take the trouble to learn to play themselves, and seem not very particular as to whether the instruments they hear are in tune or not."[29] This was the opinion formed by Captain Ross when he made his visit in 1863-64. Many of the regiments had little bands of three or four musicians, who played rather discordantly, and such bandsmen as they had were almost all Germans. Bands were allowed by the regulations and much money was expended in procuring instruments, but the soldiers felt it dishonorable to "exchange a musket for

[28] James E. Saunders, *Early Settlers of Alabama*, Pt. 1, 129; Thompson, *op. cit.*, 773; Record, Confederate Archives, War Department, gives the facts about C. O'Connell, the faithless color-bearer. Hall, *The Story of the Twenty-Sixth Louisiana*, 53-54, tells the story of Britsche.

[29] Ross, *op. cit.*, 40. Wolseley seems to have found bands general in Lee's army, for he remarks, "Almost every regiment had a small band of brass instruments. I cannot say much for the music; but it was at least enlivening, and served to mark the time for the men as they marched."—"A Month's Visit to the Confederate Headquarters," *Blackwood's Edinburgh Magazine*, XCIII, 23.

a horn." They were willing, however, to contribute their money for the purpose. For instance in one regiment not less than twenty-five hundred dollars had been collected to buy instruments but, except for the band leader, a Frenchman, and two German volunteers, there was no one to play them. Some regiments succeeded in getting up bands, which were wretched for the first few months. This was in marked contrast with the condition in the United States army, which, the southerners acknowledged, had splendid bands, for there were Italians, French, and Germans by the tens of thousands to play in them. The Confederates explained their deficiency in this respect by the fact that their chief ruling foreign element was the Irish and, "though they are passionately fond of music, they still cling to the musket, and make music of their own in the hour of battle."[30]

The Irish of the Seventeenth Virginia Regiment tried to get up a band, but the scratching sounds produced by inexperienced musicians were impossible. Then they managed to produce a fifer and a drummer, a tall countryman and his little son, trying to keep up with his tall father and missing every other beat in consequence. The boy was so short that his coattail swept the ground behind, while his drum touched it in front. This spectacle taxed the discipline of the regiment too severely. "Is it music ye would be getting out of the likes of him, wid his blowing one way and looking another?" demanded one of the Irish boys.[31]

There were some few good bands in the Confederate armies from the start. A band from the garrison at Mobile was able to furnish excellent music to a group including the governor of Alabama, General Maury, and Admiral Buchanan, which was sailing down the bay to visit the outer defenses, and provided music for dancing in the saloon.[32] The Louisiana regiments occasionally had good music and the band of the first Virginia Foot was one in a thousand. But one could not fail to note the predominance of German names in its list of members.[33] The Twenty-sixth Louisiana enjoyed a deserved reputation for the quality of its music. Its chief musician, Theodore C. Minvielle, taught and drilled the members with great skill and

[30] *Battle-fields of the South*, II, 101.
[31] Arthur Herbert, *Sketches and Incidents of Movements of the Seventeenth Virginia Regiment*, 3, a paper read before the Robert E. Lee Camp about 1909.
[32] Concerning the Mobile excursion see Ross, *op. cit.*, 242.
[33] Charles T. Löhr in his *War History of the Old First Virginia Infantry Regiment* prints in the back a list of all members, designating the band members and the drummers.

patience so that his music gave much life to the command.[34] The Second Virginia Cavalry had the only complete band from Virginia in the cavalry corps. It had a fine set of instruments captured from a New York regiment near Haymarket. Again one is forced to note many German names in its membership. Later in the war cavalry bands were used as an auxiliary in battle, the scream of shell mingling with the bands at Antietam.[35]

The laborious manner in which a band had to be organized is well exemplified by the experience of E. W. Krause, who enlisted in the summer of sixty-one at Brenham, Texas, as bandmaster in Waul's legion. He had been engaged as music teacher in a "female" college at Waco, Texas, at the outbreak of the war and wanted to share the fortunes of his adopted country. He must first secure instruments, then select sixteen suitable men, a task which would have been uphill work without the full support of the colonel, and then teach them to play. He found the "boys" able to make astonishing progress, due to their determination and to the military discipline. In three weeks he dared to venture out with some easy march music for guard mount and dress parade. From that time the band was kept busy serenading the officers' friends "of the gentler sex."[36] It was not, however, until April 20, 1862, that the Thirty-fourth Arkansas had appointed a head musician.

Another bandmaster merits individual mention, not only for his ability to construct a band out of raw materials, but for his own arresting personality. Carlos Maximilian Cassini—a Frenchman and not a Spaniard, despite a name which lodged him in prison in New Orleans to expiate the crime of a real Spaniard until the error was discovered —was old enough to have served on the United States frigate *Constitution*. When the war descended, he was employed in a tailor shop in Bainbridge, Georgia. Although greatly overage, he was induced by one Lewis, who was trying to recruit a regiment, to enlist by promise of the post of bandmaster, as he was a splendid musician with teaching knowledge of all the usual instruments in a band. A set of battered brass horns, which had been somehow obtained and somehow repaired, was turned over to him. Deep in the forest in a primitive

[34] Hall, *op. cit.*, 30-31.
[35] McClellan, *The Life and Campaigns of Major-General J. E. B. Stuart*, 423; T. Francis Rodenbough, *From Everglade to Cañon with the Second Dragoons*, 251.
[36] This is the story as told by Krause himself.—Yeary, *op. cit.*, 411-412.

booth covered with palmetto leaves while the regiment was camping near Savannah, he taught his raw recruits until they could play fairly well. His figure, when he led the parade, provoked smiles, for he insisted on wearing a black broadcloth Prince Albert and a high black beaver hat. Alas, however, for his hopes and prayers to get "at least one Yankee," for when the regiment reached Virginia, the old man was utterly unable to continue the march, and had to go to the hospital, finally being sent back to Georgia.

The bands were in demand for more than dress parade. During bad weather officers learned to keep up the spirits of the soldiers by ordering music by the band instead of letting the men lie about a smouldering fire, wrapped in their blankets until they were half doped by smoke and vile air, as in the first winter of the war. The more enterprising of the bandsmen also soon knew how to turn their accomplishment to their own practical advantage. When the band was not wanted in camp at night, it could forage a good supper by selecting the most prosperous-looking house near the camp. One of the number would enter first, almost without invitation and, seating himself at the piano, he would soon have the household in the room. An invitation to supper for the entire group invariably followed.[37]

In time, however, the Confederacy possessed a number of creditable bands. The garrison at Fort Pickens near Charleston was reinforced in March, 1862, by two companies of the Washington Light Infantry. They brought with them Müller's band, made up mostly of Germans who were professional musicians, and thus contributed a great deal of pleasure to the fort. Stag dances to the measures of this band became a popular amusement.

The Twenty-ninth South Carolina apparently had an excellent band. On May 1, 1864, when it was camping on the Citadel Green at Charleston on its march to Virginia, many of the officers and men started out when it grew dark to serenade General Samuel Jones, commander in the city. Like a group of college youths, the party then went on a general serenading tour through the city. This was one of the last nights of music and gaiety in Charleston, for it was just before the city was surrendered.[38] General Richard Taylor in his account

[37] W. W. Parker, "How the Southern Soldiers Kept House during the War," *Southern Historical Society Papers*, XXIII, 327. The story of Cassini appears in *Confederate Veteran*, XXXIV, 333.

[38] John G. Pressley, "The Wee Nee Volunteers of Williamsburg District, South Caro-

of a Virginia campaign also describes what must have been a very fine scene, when three thousand men went marching through the valley of Virginia, bands playing at the heads of their regiments, all the men in line without a straggler.

While it is true that a larger number of Germans than of any other nationality appear on the rolls as musicians or as privates "transferred to the regimental band," it is possible to find as musicians Swiss, English, Mexicans, and even a number of Irish, credited though they were with being able to make music only with their muskets. Individual musicians who lent "local color" to their respective regiments were not lacking. As ever, the palm for the most picturesque figure must go to the Louisiana Zouaves. "The elder musician was a most perfect picture of the *Turco*. He had served in Algiers, and after the war in Italy brought a bullet in his leg to New Orleans. He was long past fifty—spare, broad-shouldered and hard as a log of oak. His sharp features were bronzed to the richest mahogany color, and garnished with a mustache and a peak of grizzled hair a cubit and a span—or nearly—in length. And the short grizzled hair had been shaved far back from his prominent temples, giving a sinister and grotesque effect to his naturally hard face. Turc was a favorite with the officers, and his dress was far cleaner than that of the others; a difference that was hardly an improvement."[39]

Drum majors must, of course, head the bands, and they hailed also from many lands—Poland, Scotland, England, to give a few of the variations. One Scotchman in the Baton Rouge Rifle Volunteers had been nearly all his life a soldier by choice, had been in the United States army nine years, knew every tactic and regulation, and had been also a drum major. He was now appointed drum major in a Louisiana regimental band. A certain Prussian, already alluded to, who seems to have been everything from actor in a New York German theatre to musician in the United States navy band, filled the position of drum major in the First Virginia Militia band with particular pleasure and accompanied it to the war.[40] It is probably no

lina, in the First (Hapgood's) Regiment," *Southern Historical Society Papers*, XVI, 128-129, 179.

[39] De Leon, *Four Years in Rebel Capitals*, 72.

[40] The Rolls; Watson, *Life in the Confederate Army*, 152, 192; Schuricht, *op. cit.*, II, 39-40. The Prussian, C. E. M. Pohle, was referred to earlier in this chapter.

stretch of the imagination to picture each of these drum majors six feet tall with a fine physique and a splendid bearing.

Long before there were regimental bands of any kind, creditable or the reverse, there were buglers, fifers, string bands, and drummers who went upon the field. Major W. W. Parker's bugler of the Virginia Light Guard was a highly educated German who had served an apprenticeship in music, so to speak, for seven years, and possessed a good voice, so that with the major's wife's guitar and two good violins the regiment did not lack good music. Jacob Gans, Forrest's favorite bugler, also was a German. One notes that there were hazards to bugle as well as bugler, when one reads that Gans's instrument was disabled by three balls while General Forrest's company was on a ride to Pulaski, Mississippi. The terse statement about Jacob Brown, a German musician in the Orphan Brigade, tells much: "He was almost always on the field as bugler when not fighting in the ranks."[41] In his checkered career in the Confederate army, the Frenchman Hermann was once appointed bugler with the rank of sergeant, and under Jacobi, leader of the Thirty-second Georgia band, he soon learned all the calls. When he was demoted from the post of bugler, he broke the instrument, his own, as an act of defiance. Lameau's company boasted of having the best bugler in the Hampton Legion, an Englishman named King.[42] Francis Crouch, composer of "Mavourneen," was bugler in the Richmond Howitzers. Old Charley Benja of Macon, Alabama, the first and last fifer of the Macon Volunteers, was regarded with such affection by the members of the company that, although he had been left behind on account of age, they sent for him after they reached camp. A group of the company who were across the river, hearing his fifing, raised the shout, "Old Charley has come," and hastened to camp to join the jubilee over his arrival.[43] Any story of the war would be incomplete without a drummer boy and, accordingly, we produce Pat M. Griffin, born in Galway, Ire-

[41] Parker, "How the Southern Soldiers Kept House during the War," *Southern Historical Society Papers*, XXIII, 327. See Thompson, *op. cit.*, 915, for Jacob Brown.

[42] Hermann's career is worth charting briefly. He served one year in Jackson's foot cavalry; he helped to form an artillery company; he served as bugler in the Thirty-second Georgia band; he defied Captain Howell and Colonel Roland and landed in prison; he was discharged finally on account of his health. He was a heated, fiery man, and yet a fine fighter. See his *Memoirs of a Veteran*, 74, 136, 138. For King see Samuel E. Mays, "Sketches from the Journal of a Confederate Soldier," *Tyler's Quarterly Historical and Genealogical Magazine*, V, 47.

[43] *Daily Post* (Montgomery, Alabama), May 24, 1861.

land, and brought to the United States as an infant, who was drummer boy in Captain Randall McGavock's company, Sons of Erin, later Company H of the Tenth Tennessee. He served throughout the war with distinction and was ultimately advanced to a captaincy, when McGavock became colonel of the regiment.[44]

It is of peculiar interest, albeit probably no surprise to some readers, to learn that the author of "Dixie," as we know it, was a German. In 1852 a German musician named Arnold came to America with his three sons, all educated musicians. The youngest son, Hermann, organized and conducted a concert orchestra, toured the South, and married a native of Montgomery, where he settled down to teach music. When the citizens of that city set about making plans for the inauguration of President Davis, Arnold was put in charge of the inaugural music. When he could find no score in his musical library which he thought suitable, his bride suggested that for the parade he play "Dixie," a pretty, catchy air which had been current in the South. He played the air through and then scored the music for the band. On February 18 Arnold's band led the parade and as Davis stepped into his carriage to drive to the capitol the band struck up "Dixie." Its first notes so thrilled the great crowd in the square and avenue that one hundred thousand loyal Confederates broke into the rebel yell. Without act of congress it was accepted as the official song of the Confederate States of America.[45] It was not unnatural that Victor Knaringer, professor of music at Hamner Hall, a seminary for young women at Montgomery, should have dedicated his composition, "A Phantasie," to the president of the infant republic, but it was a tribute to this German composer that President Davis honored with his presence its first rendition at a concert at Hamner Hall on March 22, 1861.[46]

It was another alien who made "The Bonnie Blue Flag" popular in the South. Jacob Tannenbaum—and it is unnecessary to suggest his nationality—was so talented that he was a court musician in Hanover at the age of nineteen and had already composed music. Armed

[44] *Confederate Veteran*, XXIX, 269. Griffin also did effective work when transferred to Hood's scouts and when detailed for special work in derailing trainloads of Federal supplies.
[45] *The Sun* (Baltimore), October 21, 1934, Magazine Section, 6-7; "When the Band First Played Dixie," in *Miss Rutherford's Scrap Book*, VIII, 11-12 (August, 1923). The words were written by one Emmett but it was the tune which caught the heart of the South.
[46] Montgomery *Daily Advertiser*, February 19, March 22, 1861.

with letters of recommendation he visited a sister in Mobile and from there went to Paulding, Mississippi, just in time to be entangled in the war. He organized a brass band for a newly recruited regiment of Confederates at Enterprise, Mississippi, and became a military bandmaster at Corinth. But his colonel, probably feeling that an alien should not sacrifice his artistic talent in another country's quarrel, advised him to resign. He returned to Mobile, accordingly, in time to join Harry McCarthey, the author, in making the first popular song of the Confederacy, "The Bonnie Blue Flag," known to every maiden who could finger the keys of a piano and to every street urchin who could whistle or hum.[47]

The chaplains constitute still another nonfighting group receiving appointment from the military authorities and definitely attached to the army. The regiments composed of Irish or French Catholics had usually a priest as chaplain, often foreign-born. While the number of Protestant chaplains was noticeably smaller, they were by nc means lacking, and among them were to be found a few adopted sons.

In view of the controversy so long waged concerning the place of nativity of the famous Father Abram J. Ryan, the writer hesitates to classify him as foreign-born; on the other hand, in the face of the positive assertion of a relative that he was born at Limerick, Ireland, she fears to exclude him.[48] Therefore he will be included for good measure, and attention drawn to his unique service in giving to the South one of its most cherished poems. There is no dispute, however, over the fact that he became a chaplain in the Army of Northern Virginia and that the death of a brother in one of the early battles of the war inspired an ardent patriotism for the Confederacy. At a later period, during 1862-63, he was in New Orleans, where he visited the sick in the prisons and hospitals. Toward the end of the war, while

[47] Tannenbaum soon went north to enroll with a minstrel troop. He returned to Mobile, however, in 1872 to spend most of his life there.—Craighead, *Mobile: Fact and Tradition*, 275. For McCarthey see Wm. V. Izlar, *A Sketch of the War Record of the Edisto Rifles, 1861-1865*, 24.

[48] The writer will content herself by merely stating the two claims. It is said that his baptismal certificate is lodged in the safe of old St. Mary's Catholic Church in Hagerstown, Maryland, and bears the record of his birth at Hagerstown, February 5, 1838, son of Abram Joseph and Mother Ryan of Limerick, Ireland.—*Washington Post*, January 6, 1928. Kate M. White of Knoxville, Tennessee, a cousin, writes in the *South Atlantic Quarterly*, XVIII, 70, January, 1919, that he was born in Limerick, Ireland, in 1836, the son of John Thady Ryan, and that he came to America with his parents in 1839, landing at Charleston, South Carolina, whence the family went to Norfolk to join relatives. One waits for someone to clear up the riddle, possibly by disclosing two Ryans of exactly the same name.

acting as parish priest in Knoxville, Tennessee, he wrote "The Conquered Banner,"[49] indubitably the most celebrated war poem produced on the southern side.

The Irishmen of the Second Tennessee brought with them to the field Father Daly, whose labors in their behalf seemed unremitting. He celebrated mass in the morning, preached a sermon in the afternoon, and in the evening settled the drunken rows of his troublesome children—entirely too numerous. His influence was described as "vastly important as a governing power, and he wielded it wisely and kindly." It must be noted that Father Bannon served unofficially for a year in General Price's army, in which many of his parishioners had enlisted. On solicitation of the Bishop of Mobile he was regularly appointed a chaplain to date from January 30, 1863. This was before his mission to Ireland.[50] Another alien priest who was in this country at the outbreak of war was the Most Reverend Francis X. le Ray, who had come from his native land, France, to the United States in 1843 and was ordained a missionary priest in 1852. He proved enthusiastic in his allegiance to the South and came forward to offer his services as chaplain. He knelt amid shot and shell on many a battlefield to minister to the dying of his faith in both armies. On more than one occasion, indeed, he was seized by Federal forces as a prisoner of war, but was always released immediately, as soon as his character was recognized.[51] Father D. H. Hubert was a French Jesuit who went to Virginia with the First Louisiana Regiment as chaplain in May, 1861, serving with it until late in 1862 when his health demanded a leave of absence. After another period of service in the field, he requested assignment to hospital work in Richmond, as he was incapacitated for further field duty. It was of him that a historic roll bears the notation by a military officer, "A perfect son, always with his regiment. We cannot express what we thought of him." It is not strange that an officer who wrote of him in the tenor suggested above should beg him to return to his army in March,

---

[49] After the war he edited religious and literary papers in New Orleans and Knoxville and had charge of the church at Mobile. In 1870 he published his poems, many bearing on the war.—Johnson, *Texans Who Wore the Gray*, 388.

[50] Stevenson, *Thirteen Months in the Rebel Army*, 43. For Father Bannon see Dom Germain, *Catholic Military and Naval Chaplains, 1776-1917*, 107-110.

[51] *Biographical and Historical Memoirs of Louisiana*, II, 137-138. He returned to France in the hope of recovering his health in 1877 but died very shortly in his native land.—Dom Germain, *op. cit.*, 123-124.

1865, but the end of the war came too soon to produce any fresh chapters in Father Hubert's career.[52]

The Reverend Hippolite Gache was another priest of French birth who was commissioned Confederate chaplain and went out to the field with the Tenth Louisiana Regiment. He was present at thirty engagements, including Sharpsburg, Second Manassas, Chancellorsville, and Gettysburg. As late as March 28, 1865, he was in the trenches before Petersburg.[53]

The German Catholics also furnished chaplains. The Redemptorists placed one of their number in the service of the Confederacy. Father P. Sheeran, who went out with the Louisiana Tigers in January, 1862, served for at least three years as field chaplain.[54] Scattered through the regiments were undoubtedly many of these spiritual servants of many nationalities whose names are lost. The following incident is a testimony to the devotion of one of them. A soldier was sitting on an old log during one of the Seven Days' Battles around Richmond, awaiting his turn at the hands of a surgeon, when a Catholic priest came up and offered to dress his arm, as he had had a great deal of experience in the Italian army in the war between France and Austria. He ripped back the sleeve and most carefully washed and dressed the wound, telling the soldier that he would not need any attention during the night.[55] Such records make one realize that among the priesthood there were men who might appropriately be termed spiritual knights-errant.

Among Protestant clergymen was the Reverend James Barnett Taylor, born in England, brought to the United States in his infancy, and to Virginia in 1817. The war interrupted the work of the foreign mission board of the Baptist church, with which he was identified, and he became a regular chaplain in the Confederate army, laboring chiefly in hospitals. England furnished another chaplain in the person of a rector of the Anglican Church. That classification seems not inappropriate, for although the Reverend T. D. Ozanne was serving an Episcopal parish on the Gulf coast of Mississippi, and though he

[52] *Ibid.*, 117-122; Historic Roll, First Louisiana Regiment, U. D. C. Memorial Hall.

[53] Dom Germain, *op. cit.*, 117.

[54] John H. Deiler, *Zur Geschichte der deutschen Kirchengemeinde im Staate Louisiana*, 44-45; Dom Germain, *op. cit.*, 132-133. There is doubt about Father Sheeran's first name. I have used P. as the initial as that is clearly the letter I have found on the rolls, but note the comment in Dom Germain.

[55] This story is told by George Clark, *A Glance Backward*, 23-24.

had been living in this country since 1835, he had never been naturalized, and was in 1862 making every effort to return to England.
Meanwhile, obliged to remain in the country, he established himself
at Terry, a point only seventeen miles from Jackson, Mississippi,
where he helped care for the soldiers on the retreat from Shiloh. He
then took upon himself the duty of chaplain in a hospital just established near-by where he served for eighteen months while waiting to
cross the lines. His opinion that a clergyman's usefulness was much
greater in the hospitals than in camp and that it was a governmental
error to appoint chaplains only to troops in actual service is worthy of
note.[56] The Reverend Mr. Patterson presents the arresting fact of
Greek nativity despite his Anglo-Saxon name; he came to this country
when a grown man and proved a very valuable chaplain at Chimborazo Hospital. The study has discovered but one Jewish rabbi who
went to the field as spiritual comforter to Jewish soldiers, Rabbi Jacob
Frankel. The Reverend M. Thomas, rector of the Episcopal church
at Griffin, Georgia, was truly a victim of the war. A Welshman born,
he had been reared in Georgia so that, when the war broke out, he
felt the same obligation to resign his chaplaincy in the United States
navy, and join the Confederate forces as did many of the southern-
born. By April, 1865, he was living on his farm near Macon, Georgia, striving by manual labor to save his family from starvation.[57]

The foreign-born surgeons connected with the southern hospitals
were probably superior to the native-born in general, owing not only
to superior training, but to the fact that they were likely to be men of
years and experience, whereas the need for surgeons was so great that
many native students whose training was far from complete were
rushed into the medical staffs—and committed crimes in the form of
bungling amputations and in causing deaths from blood poison which
could have been avoided. Dr. Henderson belongs to the group of
aliens. He came from England in the fall of 1863, and received on
his arrival a commission in the Confederate army medical corps. He

[56] In August, 1862, he succeeded in getting passage from New Orleans to New York
and so returned to England. His long residence in the South so affected his feelings that
it is amusing to note his confusion of pronouns. One moment he refers to Davis as
"our" executive; the next to the Confederates as "you."—*The South As It Is or Twenty-
One Years' Experience in the Southern States of America*, 257, 273.

[57] "History of Chimborazo Hospital, C. S. A.," *Southern Historical Society Papers*,
XXXVI, 92; Townes R. Leigh, "The Jews in the Confederacy," *Southern Historical Society Papers*, XXXIX, 178; Cumming, *op. cit.*, 174.

became surgeon of a hospital in Mobile, but often went to the front when a battle was reported in progress. At Gamble Hospital, which was located in northern Alabama, was stationed another Englishman, Dr. Wildman; at Gilmer Hospital, Chattanooga, still another, Dr. Cannon, had charge of a ward. One inclines to the view that some of these British surgeons, like Dr. Henderson, in coming to this country were actuated by the opportunity to study war surgery at first hand. Dr. William T. Passmore, on the contrary, had come from England to Baltimore as a child and had graduated in medicine from an institution of that city.[58] Dr. Henry J. Warmuth, whom we have encountered as a private in Company A, Ninth Georgia Artillery, despite foreign birth and European education received his actual medical degree at Rush Medical College, Chicago, in 1862. His training was too greatly needed to be wasted by allowing him to remain a private in the infantry and he was, therefore, promptly made assistant surgeon and in March, 1863, full surgeon to his old command. After Chickamauga he was sent to the rear as hospital surgeon at Marietta, Rome, and Covington, Georgia. In the fall of 1864 he returned to Johnston's army as surgeon of the Seventeenth and Eighteenth Texas regiments then consolidated; and after the battle of Franklin he was left by General Forrest in charge of the hospitals between Smyrna and Murfreesboro, Tennessee. His career as an army surgeon was abruptly terminated in December, 1864, by his capture at Murfreesboro.[59] Dr. Hermann Bauer, born in Germany, was an example of a man who was trained in medicine in the South, graduating from South Carolina Medical College in 1861. He served throughout the war with the Second Alabama Regiment. Dr. Schulz is another German chirurgeon of the Confederate armies whose name has come down to us.[60] One finds a group of Irish surgeons: one, Dr. P. J. McCormick, who had had his medical education in this country, as surgeon of the Forty-sixth Mississippi; another, Dr. George H. Doran, a young man who served with the Rio Grande Regiment of

[58] Miss Cumming has much to say of these English doctors.—*Ibid.*, 136, 137. Dr. Cannon was both a doctor and a clergyman in the Episcopal church. For Dr. Passmore, see *Confederate Veteran*, XVII, 236-237. [59] *Ibid.*, XL, 383.

[60] Dr. Hermann Bauer worked his way up in America, where he arrived in 1847 at the age of seventeen, from typesetter, through tutor and professor of French and Hebrew at Wofford College, to surgeon.—"Necrology," *South Carolina Historical and Genealogical Magazine*, II, 166. Kaufmann, *Die Deutschen im amerikanischen Bürgerkriege*, 571, mentions Dr. Schulz.

Texas. One learns of an Irish surgeon of the old school who did not believe in babying the soldiers. When a recruit who had got a bullet in his heel at Vicksburg was asked at the hospital whether he desired an anesthetic, this stern old Irish surgeon replied for him, "No, this ain't no baby you're dealing with, that's nothing but a splinter, you nigger hold that foot." Almost before the soldier who had thus been endowed with Spartan courage knew what they were about, the surgeon had cut out the bullet.[61] Particular interest attaches today, because of his famous son, to Dr. Simon Baruch, descendant of a family distinguished in medicine and the law for generations, who had left Poland in 1853 for America and settled in South Carolina. Fresh from medical college, he doctored and fought for four years with Lee's ragged followers.[62]

In this group of well-trained Europeans must also be mentioned Dr. William Häcker, whose thrilling war experiences in General Bragg's command place him rather with the fighting unit than with the medical corps. The combination puts him in a class apart but his medical service deserves recognition in its due place. Destined by his father for the priesthood, it will be recalled, he was saved from it by a wise uncle, himself a priest, who persuaded the father to allow his son to pursue his own predilections. He brought to the Confederate surgical service the excellent training afforded by Bonn University, experience in the practice of his profession in Paris, and almost a decade of practice in Louisville, Kentucky, where his skill was so recognized that he had been made demonstrator of anatomy at the medical college in that city. After about nine months' service in Bridgeman's cavalry battalion of General Bragg's command, in which he fought in many skirmishes, he was made surgeon of General Raines's brigade. During the march through Kentucky with General Bragg, he was cut off from his command by undertaking a visit to his wife, who was with her people at Bridgeport, and had many breathtaking escapes from the Federals before he succeeded in returning to his battalion. Later when, his ability in scout work having been

[61] Dr. McCormick came from Ireland as a youth, received a good classical education, taught school, and then graduated in medicine in 1857.—*Confederate Veteran*, XIII, 156. Dr. Doran appears on a Muster Roll, Texas State Library, Division of Archives. The Irish surgeon last mentioned appears in W. B. Crumpton, *A Book of Memories, 1842-1920*, 76.

[62] *New York Times*, June 4, 1921. Bernard Baruch, his son, was reared on the traditions of the Lost Cause.

demonstrated, he was detached and placed in the secret service for a period, he was taken prisoner and carried to Camp Chase. With seven comrades he made a daring escape during a violent storm and reached the Confederate army in Nashville. He shared in Morgan's raid through Kentucky, Ohio, and Indiana, was captured, but again made a thrilling escape from the train while on his way to Cincinnati. Then followed his longest period of army service in the line of his regular profession, for he had charge of the hospital at Bean's Station in Tennessee for more than a year from August, 1863, to 1864. As the army had run short of medical supplies, Dr. Häcker was selected to go to Cincinnati to purchase them. Success in the venture was so widely chronicled in southern papers that the Federal government offered a reward for him, whereupon he assumed another name, Dr. Thomas White. Capture for a third time on December 11, 1864, resulted from participation in another scouting expedition into Eastern Kentucky. This time he was court-martialed and exiled north of Mason and Dixon's line for a term of three years. Again his profession came to his rescue, for as Dr. White he practiced medicine in Jasper County, Illinois, till President Johnson's amnesty proclamation allowed him to resume his own name.[63]

By all odds the most interesting assistant surgeon encountered was an Italian, one Dr. Coutre, who turned out to be a Federal spy. A prisoner was brought into General Ashby's command while it was in the valley of Virginia, in February, 1862—a small man of slight, sinewy figure, grey eyes, light hair, dark-brown mustache and Vandyke beard. His manner and voice, as well as his entire appearance, proved him to be a foreigner, though his English was so correct that but for his gutturals he might have passed for an Englishman. He represented himself as a surgeon by profession and the son of General Coutre of the Italian army. In a spirit of adventure, he explained, he had secured a commission as assistant surgeon in the United States army but, as his sympathies were completely with the South, he had revealed his sentiments by imprudent talk and had been ordered under arrest for a court-martial. He had succeeded in making his escape and now sought an appointment as surgeon in the Confederate army. General Jackson, however, felt considerable doubt about the

---

[63] *Confederate Veteran*, XXIV, 328-329. He was one of the first advocates of the germ theory and became one of the leading bacteriologists of the country.

authenticity of his story and referred the case to Richmond, meanwhile confining him to the camp. The war department prudently declined his services, ordered him away from the army, and forbade his presence within less than twenty miles of any Confederate outpost. Coutre wept but went to Woodstock in the Valley, where he secured board with a German family and began the practice of his profession. His accomplishments were many—he spoke German, French, Italian, and Spanish as well as English, and proved his skill as a swordsman against two of Ashby's best men at the same time. Within a few months, through the intervention of a member of congress from that district, he received, to his extravagant joy, a commission as assistant surgeon in the army in the Valley. As he was one of the surgeons left behind on the other side of the Potomac to aid the Confederate wounded after the battle of Sharpsburg, and apparently could not refrain from airing his feelings toward the Union army, he was arrested and sent to Point Lookout despite his protests of immunity as a surgeon. He bribed the guards, got help from Washington friends, and soon turned up again with his old companions of the Seventh Virginia Cavalry. He then went to Richmond to press his exchange so that he might get back into the service. Finally a lieutenant became suspicious because of his abundance of gold and some remarks dropped in his sleep, and the truth was ferreted out—he was a Union spy. He seems to have escaped the fate reserved for spies.[64]

In addition to the surgeons and assistant surgeons, of whose technical training proof is not always forthcoming, there was naturally a large group of disabled soldiers, detailed for various purposes to the hospitals, as nurses, stewards, clerks, and to care for hospital stores. It is conspicuous that frequently the men in these positions who were praised most highly were foreigners. The methodical training so characteristic of the German appears in the young Teuton who was assigned to the nurse, Mrs. Fannie A. Beers, whom we shall meet again, to keep the linen room in order. He was well educated and had taught music before entering the service. His position was no sinecure as he had to keep a full account of all stores in the department, and had full charge of the laundry and the laundresses, whom he was always having to placate. For this reason the surgeons rechris-

[64] For details on this interesting character see David Humphreys, *Heroes and Spies of the Civil War*, 26-28, 50-54, 146 ff.; *Richmond Enquirer*, April 19, 1864; *Richmond Dispatch*, April 19, 1864.

tened him "General Blandner." He was methodical and his books excellently kept. Likewise a Scotchman who could have made large sums of money as hospital steward was praised for his perfect honesty.[65]

The ambulance drivers were drawn from just the ranks one would expect from knowledge of the class which discharged the duties of teamster before the war: Germans in Lee's and Longstreet's armies, with perhaps an occasional Frenchman; Germans and Mexicans in Ross's and Sibley's brigades in the department of the Trans-Mississippi. It is perhaps natural that it was a German who had charge of all the ambulances of Bate's division in the Army of the Tennessee, on whom was bestowed the praise of "acquitting himself with the highest credit under perilous and trying circumstances." In sharp contrast to this German was a disgruntled Frenchman, acting as an ambulance driver, who revealed a foreigner's indifference to a cause in which his heart was not engaged. Mrs. Pryor tells of his pouring forth a torrent of abuse of the Confederacy in his broken English. A woman in the small party he was transporting suggested that she might be able to arrange a transfer to some other post which he might find more congenial. "Nevare! nevare!" cried the man, "I transfare to my own koontree! I make what you call 'desairt.' Mon Dieu! dey now tell me I fight for neeger! Frenchman nevare fight for neeger."[66]

It seems surprising that the overburdened authorities at Richmond had time to give thought to an ordnance laboratory. Yet the unavoidable variation in the ammunition made at the different arsenals indicated early in the conflict that there must be a general supervision of all the laboratories, and that some one must be vested with power to inspect and supervise their materials and operations. For this purpose a laboratory of the Nitre Bureau was decreed and a chemist of distinction who had for some years been professor at the University of Alabama was placed in charge of this delicate and important task. The comment passed upon the choice by a leading official is illuminating: "I attribute much of the improvement in our

[65] Miss Cumming speaks of two Irishmen who had been detailed as nurse and dining room steward to the hospital at Chattanooga. See *op. cit.*, entry of May 31, 1863, 70. For "General Blandner," see Beers, *op. cit.*, 75, and for the honest Scotchman, Cumming, *op. cit.*, 151-152.

[66] Ross, *op. cit.*, 28; Rose, *op. cit.*, 18. Mathes, *op. cit.*, 227, quotes the high praise bestowed on Fred Wolf of Bate's division. See also S. A. Pryor, *Reminiscences of Peace and War*, 281.

ammunition to this happy selection. A more earnest and capable officer I cannot imagine."[67] The officer chosen was John William Mallet, of English ancestry but Irish birth, whose selection was amply justified by his training as well as experience. Young Mallet might almost be called a civil engineer by inheritance, for his father was a distinguished member of that fraternity, a member of the Institution of Civil Engineers, and a fellow of the Royal Society. After graduating at the University of Dublin, and obtaining his doctorate at the University of Göttingen in 1855, the son came directly to the United States and began work as chemist for the geological survey of Alabama. For the next five years he held the chair of chemistry at the University of Alabama and then filled a similar position in the medical college in Mobile. He accomplished the first important work in physical chemistry performed in this country, the determination of the atomic weight of lithium. This work firmly established his reputation as a chemist of the first rank; when the government authorities were casting about for the man to direct the manufacture of explosives, they transferred him to the artillery arm from General Rhodes's staff, where he was serving as aide-de-camp, for he had enlisted in the army in November, 1861, as a first lieutenant.[68]

The erection of a central ordnance laboratory for the production of standard ammunition, including that for field artillery, was determined upon in September, 1862. A tract of land consisting of about 145 acres, located near the city of Macon, Georgia, was immediately purchased, a branch of the Macon and Western Railroad run out to it, and the plant begun by Dr. Mallet, now Colonel Mallet, for the service he was asked to render was held worthy of the rank of a lieutenant-colonelcy on the field. The three main buildings, connected with each other, had a frontage of about 1,200 feet, the middle building being the longest, fully 600 feet. In addition to the main structure there were over 40 other buildings. The bricks for these were molded in a great brickyard near Macon, conducted by ordnance officers. From England came a large assortment of specialized machinery, in which were included several large steam engines, much of

[67] Opinion of General Josiah Gorgas, quoted in "Notes on the Ordnance Department of the Confederate Government," *Southern Historical Society Papers*, XII, 87, an unfinished paper, highly valuable, which was found among General Gorgas' papers and published.
[68] J. C. Wise, *The Long Arm of Lee; or, the History of the Artillery of the Army of Northern Virginia*, I, 45; *The South in the Building of the Nation*, XII, 154.

which had arrived in Bermuda before the blockade completely disrupted trade with England.[69]

The scientific research work soon began to show results. Nitric acid could be made from saltpeter which, together with mercury and copper, was necessary for the manufacture of percussion caps and friction primers. Mercury was to be had from Mexico, but no adequate supply was available after the fall of Vicksburg. The ordnance chemists discovered, however, a mixture of chlorate of potash and sulphide of antimony which they could use instead of fulminate of mercury. The requisite supply of copper was secured by collecting all the turpentine and apple brandy stills in the country, cutting them up, and rolling them into strips! Generals Gorgas and Rains, Colonel Mallet, and Colonel St. John, superintendent of the Mining Bureau, who by providing the metal for the projectiles was first aid to the ordnance department, all together achieved a really remarkable result. After the autumn of 1862, when the powder mills were completed, no requisition of an army in the field was ever dishonored![70] For military protection two companies of infantry and a section of guns were kept at the Macon plants ready for action at all times; they were called out three times to repel attacks. The forces were really efficient as they included among their number some detailed soldiers.[71] In a closely related department, the Mining Bureau, O. Julius Heinrich, a Saxon by birth, put his training in architecture and mining at the Dresden Academy to work for the Confederacy.[72]

It is certainly an interesting circumstance that the laboratory for supplying the Confederate army with medicines and for testing the drugs brought in from abroad by blockade-runners should have been conducted by a non-American. Dr. Charles Theodore Mohr, a native

[69] Wise, The Long Arm of Lee, I, 46.

[70] Wise makes this broad claim.—Ibid., 45. Colonel Rains invented the method of steaming the mixed materials for gunpowder just before incorporation in the cylinder mills, thus largely increasing the capacity of the plants and greatly improving the quality of the powder. That constitutes his claim to a share in the above glory.—Ibid., 46-47.

[71] Ibid., 58. After the war Dr. Mallet went back to the classroom as professor of chemistry in the medical department of the University of Louisiana. In 1868 he went to the University of Virginia. In 1880 he was chosen by the National Board of Health to report upon the proper methods for the analysis of drinking water. He was thereby introduced to a new field of usefulness, for he established himself as an expert on sanitary water supply. His advice was sought far and wide on this subject, and he was frequently called in as an expert witness in legal cases involving chemical questions. He was called to several institutions of higher learning, serving last at the University of Virginia as head of the school of chemistry from 1885 to his retirement in 1911. He died one year later.—Ibid., 45, n.   [72] Schuricht, op. cit., II, 32-33.

of Württemberg, on the eve of the war was conducting a drug and chemical business located at the corner of Dauphin and Frank streets in Mobile. A rich background of education and experience lay behind him: education in natural science at Stuttgart; travel to the headwaters of Dutch Guiana as botanist of an exploring expedition; a period of service in a chemical factory in Moravia; experience in a chemical factory in Cincinnati, when the revolution of 1848 drove him from Europe; study of plant life on the Pacific coast when he was swept there by the gold craze; and, finally, arrival again empty-handed in the States. While there is no way to evaluate the worth of such a laboratory, it must have been very great to a country practically deprived of reliable drugs and medicines.[73]

A last field of special service connected with the army was the prison camps. And here, because our study is confined to the foreign-born, we have to do, except for guards and wardens, who were largely Irish,[74] with a single person. It is not regarded as necessary in this study to narrate the trial of Captain Wirz, to weigh the evidence of guilt, or to pass judgment on him. No name connected with the entire war has been so execrated by northerners and none probably more unjustly. In a sense, he was made the scapegoat of the Confederacy, certainly not with the consent of its leaders—rather, in spite of them. Henry Wirz was a Swiss,[75] not a German as has carelessly been asserted because his native speech in Zurich stamped him with a German accent. It was his misfortune that he did not stay in the North where he spent the first years after his arrival in America instead of moving to Louisiana where he was practicing medicine on a very slight professional foundation, it must be admitted. Here the war caught him. He became a violent partisan of the southern cause and first appears on the Confederate scene as a clerk in Libby Prison at Richmond. Here began his acquaintance with John H. Winder, through whom came many of his appointments—perhaps, indeed, a misfortune. As a deputy provost marshal, he was sent throughout the

---

[73] Craighead, *op. cit.*, 223-229. Dr. Mohr did valuable work for Alabama after the war, from 1865 to 1900, in a study of her mosses, ferns, forests, grasses, and geological resources. He did it so well that there has been no need to do it again.

[74] Hyde mentions Noles, an Englishman in Andersonville who attended to the daily counting, as a "big-hearted fellow, though a great stutterer, a Confederate by force of circumstances, and always dressed in black velvet."—*A Captive of War*, 130.

[75] To call him a Swiss mercenary is, of course, absurd and merely reflects the prejudices of the time.

South on an inspection tour of the prisons in 1862-63. The following summer he was deputed by President Davis to be the bearer of secret dispatches to the commissioners Mason and Slidell and to the Confederate financial agents in Europe, as has been related. Soon after his return in January, 1864, he came to Andersonville with the aid of his patron or evil genius, Winder. However, in the light of his experience, his appointment to the superintendency of Andersonville Prison would seem to have been a very appropriate one. This appropriateness is more marked when the fact is added that he was barred from active service by a severe wound received in battle, his right arm being shattered by a ball. It might be noted incidentally that he was thus physically unable to ill-treat prisoners as some have charged. It should be noted to his credit that the government thought him worthy of promotion to a captaincy for bravery on the battlefield and of a majorate a few months before the close of the war. He had had a good education and spoke several languages fluently, but he was a man of impulsive, some say rough, manner. This apparent roughness of manner sometimes arises in foreigners from difficulties of language, and is a manner which can be easily distorted into offensiveness, though none was intended. The most bitter tales have been printed of his cruel treatment of prisoners. It is possible that, harassed and worried by the necessity of receiving thousands of prisoners in excess of those that he could decently care for, unable to get requisite supplies of any sort, he was less considerate at times than was desirable. But, on the other hand, everyone knows the wild exaggerations bred by war, the tales repeated by eyewitnesses—later proved untrue—which the relater sincerely believes to be true. It is also possible, as Hohenwart says, that Wirz may have exceeded his instructions with the zeal of the Teuton to fulfill the letter of the law.[76]

But charges of brutality do not square with what quite reputable Confederate officers tell. He asked General Imboden to get more shelter put up; he wanted to establish a tannery and shoemaker's shop, as the prisoners could then make shoes from the skins of the thousands of animals which were killed there. The testimony of General Richard Taylor cannot be swept away as whitewashing, as he so clearly had no interest to subserve except that of justice. Let his testi-

[76] "Der Commandant war ein Schweizer, der womöglich seine Instruktionen noch überschritt."—Hohenwart, *Land und Leute in den Vereinigten Staaten*, 76.

mony be heard in his own words, "In this journey through Georgia, at Andersonville, I passed in sight of a large stockade inclosing prisoners of war. The train stopped for a few moments, and there entered the carriage, to speak to me, a man who said his name was *Wirtz*, and that he was in charge of the prisoners near-by. He complained of the inadequacy of his guard and of the want of supplies, as the adjacent region was sterile and thinly populated. He also said that the prisoners were suffering from cold, were destitute of blankets, and that he had no wagons to supply fuel. He showed me duplicates of requisitions and appeals for relief that he had made to different authorities, and these I indorsed in the strongest terms possible, hoping to accomplish some good. I know nothing of this Wirtz, whom I then saw for the first and only time, but he appeared to be earnest in his desire to mitigate the condition of his prisoners."[77] His loyalty to President Davis is a matter of record from the testimony of his attorney as published by the latter on April 4, 1867; namely, that when he was told the night before his execution that his sentence would be commuted if he would implicate President Davis in the atrocities at Andersonville, he replied, "If I knew anything of him [President Davis], I would not become a traitor against him or anybody else to save my life."[78] The bald facts are that he, a Swiss by birth, was tried, condemned and executed, in November, 1865, after the conclusion of the war; that no other keeper of a military prison so suffered; and that the sole execution because of the war was a foreignborn. The verdict of history is that he doubtless did the best he could with what the Confederacy could provide him, but that the inflamed war feeling demanded a sacrifice.[79]

As in every recent war, soldiers were detailed for all sorts of duties—special fields of service—from that of expert accountant to blacksmith, from headquarters postmaster to tailor, from manager of a shoe factory to butcher. Frequently details were disabled men no

[77] Taylor, *Destruction and Reconstruction*, 216.

[78] *Confederate Veteran*, VIII, 364, 365. Louis Schade, who acted as his attorney, had promised to publish these facts as soon as the time should be propitious.

[79] Reams have, of course, been written on this subject. The reader is referred to the official record of his trial; the statement of Louis Schade, referred to above, the many articles in the *Confederate Veteran*, XIV, 446-452, XVI, 199, 253-254, XVII, 270, XXXV, 173; Spencer, *A Narrative of Andersonville*, 55-56; and W. B. Hesseltine, *Civil War Prisons*, 237-247. A very harsh view by a prisoner is presented in Hyde, *A Captive of War*, 187-188, but this view should be compared with that of another Union prisoner, Jacob Kautzler, printed in the *Confederate Veteran*, XVI, 253-254.

longer available for the field, but frequently, for a task requiring special skill, only the able-bodied soldier could be used. Certain tasks would brook no delay, even if they took men from the ranks for their performance. Among the details for nearly every class of service, that calling for expert ability as well as that of a menial character, foreigners are found. A blacksmith's job could call for courage—and it was displayed by Patrick O'Connor, one of the many Irishmen of that name in the army. He was known often to go on the battlefield while the battle was raging, knock off the shoes from the feet of the slain horses, and carry them off to the forge. He thus managed to keep a supply of horseshoes on hand. A Prussian, John A. Lindbauer, was detailed after six months in the field to take charge of a large government shoe factory at Cahaba, Alabama.[80]

Few soldiers had a more varied career than Llewellyn William Lloyd, a true Welshman from Beumaris, in northern Wales. Enlistment in a cavalry company in January, 1861, in Mississippi, turned into service in the infantry under Beauregard, as the government was not then prepared to accept the former type of service. Appointment as chief of ordnance in the field for Mississippi by Governor Pettus was followed by a visit to Washington, Baltimore, and Philadelphia in the secret service under Lee's orders, as has been related. He also mounted guns at Charleston, Fort Moultrie, Richmond, and other points. He is classified here, however, by virtue of the fact that he was detailed to take charge of the East Tennessee and Virginia and also of the East Tennessee and Georgia railroads. During the siege of Knoxville he succeeded in removing all the railroad machinery to Athens, thus preserving for the Confederacy invaluable means of transportation for the soldiers.[81]

To no one in the Confederacy fell a more romantic career than to a Canadian of Welsh descent. The name of George A. Ellsworth conjures up to the reader familiar with this phase of war history the story of the wizard telegraph operator who had an entire Union army baffled and bewildered. He put his training under the great Morse in the national capital to good use for the Confederacy. He was called

---

[80] The story of the blacksmith is told in W. S. White, *Contributions to a History of the Richmond Howitzer Battalion*, 212. For Lindbauer see Mathes, *op. cit.*, 143. Mrs. Pickett speaks of a daring, fearless Italian, Jacaheri, in her husband's employ as headquarters postmaster.—*Pickett and his Men*, 12.

[81] Yeary, *op. cit.*, 443.

from Houston, Texas, where he had been an operator since 1861, to serve under General Morgan, who had known him in Kentucky, so that his soldier life began in Chattanooga. He made two thrilling escapes to Canada from captivity, which he promptly followed by a return to the South, the second time on a blockade-runner. The exploits which made the land ring with his name were connected with sending misleading messages in the Morse code for Morgan and with tapping the wires with field instruments to learn orders and locations of Union officers. He would frequently attach his wire to the main telegraph line at some convenient spot where there was little fear of interruption, and take off the messages. When fuller information was requisite or when Morgan desired to send off misleading messages, Ellsworth would enter some telegraph office and hold the station operator prisoner until he had performed his task so that no alarm was possible. Then to cap the climax, Ellsworth would calmly take the operator's seat and carry on a brisk conversation with other operators who chanced to be on duty at points in which he was interested. His remarkable success, even after his tricks were known, is difficult to explain. A part of the explanation lies in the fact that he knew personally many of his brother operators, in Kentucky and Tennessee, and was perfectly familiar with the habits of the guild. Even where he was suspected, he could throw the men off the scent by a careless, gay answer. He would sometimes force the poor captive at the point of the gun to tick off a dictated message. Such messages thoroughly confounded the Union commanders and sent them galloping madly in all directions—except the right one—to find Morgan. All this, of course, delighted the southern soldiers and made "Lightning Ellsworth," as he was not inappropriately called, very popular.[82] His was a career of great hazard, valuable service, and thrilling interest.

[82] *Confederate Veteran*, VIII, 35; Duke, *Reminiscences*, 126-128. David Flannery, a Limerick man the reader need not be told, also served as superintendent of telegraphs from Memphis to New Orleans for most of the war. See Mathes, *op. cit.*, 250.

IX

FOREIGNERS AS AIDS ON THE SEA

THE LAWS OF neutrality as slowly established by international law dictated the policy of the chief European governments toward the two belligerents in the American struggle. Great Britain through a proclamation by the queen forbade British subjects to enlist in the army or navy; recruiting of soldiers or sailors within British dominions was forbidden; and the fitting out of vessels within territory subject to her jurisdiction was of course likewise prohibited, as were efforts to break a lawful blockade or to carry contraband articles in British vessels. Any subject who violated these commands, based on statutes passed in the reign of George III, did so at his own peril and should not expect to receive protection from his country. France and Spain issued similar decrees, especially forbidding acts of privateering in their ports. Some veiled efforts at recruiting for the Confederate army were made abroad, but it was particularly in connection with the Confederate navy that friction developed between the new nation and foreign governments.

The Confederacy in her brief history advanced just one naval officer to the high rank of admiral and he was a native son—Admiral Raphael Semmes; but the person who ranks next to him in importance in the Confederate navy was born a citizen of Great Britain. John Newland Maffitt was born at sea as his parents were en route from Dublin to New York, which they reached in February, 1819. The lad was reared by an uncle in North Carolina, was sent to school in the North, and was awarded a midshipman's post in the United States navy from North Carolina. He did not, however, receive a lieutenant's commission in the navy until 1843, some time after completion of his training. When his state withdrew from the Union—he had by this time become a citizen of Georgia—he followed the example of most of his fellow southerners in the service and resigned. Within a few days he was appointed a first lieutenant in the prospective Confederate navy and two years later, April 29, 1863, was made commander. His promotion to commander in the Provisional navy came for gallant conduct in running the steam sloop *Florida,* fully armed for a cruise and flying the English flag, in and out of the port of Mobile under the very nose of the Union commander, Prebble, who was in charge of the blockading fleet.[1] He rendered other significant service.

Several of the other commanders of vessels in the Confederate fleet had been born in lands over which the stars and stripes did not float. Washington Gwathmey, originally a British subject, had, like Maffitt, served as lieutenant in the United States navy. With appointment to the navy from Virginia he followed his state and took service under the Confederacy. He was made first lieutenant on October 23, 1862, to rank from October 2, and was commissioned a first lieutenant in the Provisional navy a little more than a year later. He had command of the Confederate steamers *St. Philip, Jackson,* and *Carondolet* on the New Orleans station during 1861-62. He was on Jackson Station and Richmond Station during 1862, and on Wilmington Station in 1864. In the meantime he had seen army duty commanding Fort Caswell in North Carolina during a period in 1862-63. John F. Ramsay was a second Englishman-born but differed from Gwathmey in entering the Confederate service still a British subject on June 9, 1863. He had been formerly in the East India service, and was given rank in the Confederate service upon the recommendation of General Maury. He was made lieutenant for the war in January, 1864, to date from his entry into the service, and promoted to first lieutenant in the Provisional navy in June, 1864, to rank from the preceding January 6. After serving on the *Rappahannock* in European waters, he was in command of the steamer *Laurel* during 1864, and was again abroad in the closing months of the war. A lone Prussian, Philip F. Appel, who rose from master's mate in July, 1861, to the command of the steamship *Bayou City* during 1861-62, and who resigned in November, 1862, appears in the register of officers.[2]

Jack Lawson, coming to America from England in 1825 at the age of seventeen as engineer of the first railroad locomotive run on a

---

[1] For details as to J. N. Maffitt, see James Sprunt, "John N. Maffitt," *Southern Historical Society Papers,* XXIV, Ser. 1, 162 ff.; *Register of Officers of the Confederate States Navy, 1861-65,* 126; *American Annual Cyclopaedia,* 1862, 600; *Dictionary of American Biography,* XII, 195-196; Emma M. Maffitt, *The Life and Services of John Newland Maffitt;* Wm. M. Robinson, Jr., *The Confederate Privateers,* 59.

[2] The dates of appointment of these officers are to be found in *Register of Officers of the Confederate States Navy,* 78, 159, 4.

short line between Baltimore and Susquehanna, had already had a long record as engineer, captain, and owner of a steamboat on the Tennessee and Mississippi rivers before the war came to have need of his services. He attracted much attention at the outbreak of war by hoisting on his boat, the *Cherokee*, a pure white flag, bearing the picture of a hog, by which he meant to suggest the slogan, "Root hog or die." Upon her return to New Orleans at the declaration of secession by Louisiana, the *Cherokee* stayed South till sold to the Confederate government, when she was converted into a gunboat and made a part of the mosquito fleet of Memphis. Lawson was soon made executive officer of the gunboat *General Polk* and shared in the battle at Belmont. After the *General Polk* was burned he was placed in charge of the transport steamer *Chasm* which he commanded up to May, 1863. When the siege of Vicksburg made it evident that the Red River region must be the great source of supply, Lawson was ordered there and showed considerable resourcefulness in getting stores hauled to Vicksburg by wagon, when his boat was cut off by the Federal gunboats. His resourcefulness again came to the fore when he raised one of the boats which had been sunk in the Yazoo River to recover the machinery, which he transported through the country on ox wagons to Selma, Alabama, a truly perilous undertaking. He was thereafter with the army until the surrender.[3]

Command of a torpedo ram, which attempted to explode a torpedo against the new ironsides, at that time the most formidable fighting craft of its kind, is not exactly the same type of command, but is placed here in order to group commanders of vessels together. The effort against the Federal ironsides in Charleston harbor was set for the night of August 20, 1863, and Captain James Carlin, a plucky Englishman, was in charge with a guard of eleven men under Lieutenant Eldred Fickling of the regulars from Fort Sumter. Carlin gave to General Beauregard a very modest report of a perilous undertaking and revealed in the face of defeat the usual English coolness, which alone saved the band from capture. He had just lowered the torpedo and ranged alongside the *Leviathan*, which was protected by five monitors in the immediate vicinity, when he was hailed by the ironsides. He promptly represented his little craft as

[3] *Confederate Veteran*, V, 3.

the United States steamer *Live Yankee* from Port Royal. When his order to put the helm "hard a-starboard" was not properly obeyed, he had to face the problem of escape instead of success in his daring scheme. He answered another hail from the enemy evasively, thus assuring himself that the Federals would withhold fire, and he made full steam for Charleston, leaving the Federals to fire too late.[4]

The list of alien-born who as lieutenants may be considered second in command is short. One encounters George W. Harrison, born in the West Indies, who resigned his commission in the United States navy to accept appointment as first lieutenant in the new navy in May, 1861; Charles H. Hasker, born in London, who served the Confederate navy as boatswain on the *Merrimac* and later as first lieutenant; and John Low, a Liverpool man resident in Savannah, Georgia, who shortly after the outbreak of war went to England to join Bulloch for special service, and whom Bulloch promptly sent to the *Finegal* as second officer in order to utilize his previous experience in the British mercantile marine.[5]

Among the list of physicians for the southern privateers were two aliens. One was Dr. Barrett, a warmhearted Irishman who volunteered for the *Florida* while it was in harbor at Cardenas, Cuba. He gave up an excellent situation in the government hospital in Havana to demonstrate his devotion to the South, which residence in Georgia had inculcated. The other was Dr. David Herbert Llewellyn, not Welsh, as his name would indicate, but English, who was appointed assistant surgeon on August 25, 1862. He served on the *Alabama* and was drowned in the important naval engagement between the *Alabama* and the U.S.S. *Kearsarge* off Cherbourg on June 19, 1864.[6]

Some aliens found their way into minor posts on board the pri-

[4] Snowden, *History of South Carolina*, II, 784.

[5] These lieutenants are recorded in the *Register of Officers in the Confederate States Navy*, 82, 84, 117. Hasker was boatswain in the United States navy and became boatswain in the C. S. navy on June 11, 1861, attaining the rank of first lieutenant of the Provisional Navy only in June, 1864, to date from January 6, 1864. He was also captured September 7, 1863, and taken to Fort Warren (*Confederate Veteran*, XXVI, 459), paroled and exchanged in the fall of 1864.

Low went first to Virginia in a cavalry corps from Georgia, but was properly placed in the navy, for Bulloch praised him "as an able seaman, a reliable and useful officer in every situation." He was also sent with the *Florida* to J. N. Maffitt at Nassau. The *Register* gives his place of birth as Georgia. The writer is inclined to think this an error, but see Bulloch, *The Secret Service of the Confederate States in Europe*, I, 113, 159-160.

[6] Maffitt, *op. cit.*, 250-251; *Register of Officers of the Confederate States Navy*, 116.

vateers. When the British lad whom we have already met in the ordnance department, Francis Dawson, first entered the American story, it was as a member of the crew on the *Nashville*. When the lad won Captain Pegram's consent to ship as a sailor before the mast on the *Nashville*, which was lying in the harbor at Southampton— the captain feeling certain that he would not accept so lowly a post— his romantic and fantastic preparations included the purchase of a bowie knife, a sea-chest, and a sailor's outfit, even to the cloth cap and long black ribbon. Captain Pegram failed purposely to notify him of the date of sailing, but the determined warrior betook himself to Southampton and presented himself to the officer of the deck on New Year's Day, 1862. Captain Pegram then ignored him until satisfied of the sincerity of his purpose, whereupon he secured from the secretary of the navy authorization to appoint him master's mate.[7] There were several other aliens who were appointed to the same post on the various cruisers: an Englishman on the *Alabama*, who participated in the fight with the *Kearsarge*; two Germans on the *Alabama*, one a member of a noble family, who likewise shared in that famous fight; a Frenchman, who served the brief span from September 16 to November 5, 1863, on the *Florida*; and another Englishman, appointed from South Carolina, who served on the Confederate Launch Number 1 on New Orleans Station during 1861-62 and on several other stations. Since the two Germans, born in Prussia and Hanover, enlisted from Cape Town, Africa, one suspects that they were smitten with the same romantic conception of adventure which drove Dawson to America.[8]

Several engineers were drawn from foreign parts: the Canadian, James H. Hood, on the *Nashville*, the only foreign-born of twenty-

[7] Dawson, *Reminiscences of Confederate Service*, 4-10, 33.

[8] The list of these master's mates follows:

George T. Fullam, acting master's mate, July 29, 1862, on the *Alabama*, 1862-64, appointed from England.

Max von Meulnier, Prussian, appointed from Cape Town, Africa, master's mate on the *Alabama*.

Julius Schröder, born in Hanover, appointed from Cape Town, Africa, on the *Alabama*. T. G. Eyre, born in (left blank). Appointed from France, acting master's mate, September 16, 1863, resigned November 5, 1863, served on the *Florida*. The writer infers from the name and place of enlistment that he was French.

Richard S. James, born in England. Appointed from South Carolina, acting master's mate, October 10, 1861. Served on C. S. Launch, Number 1, New Orleans Station, 1861-62, on Jackson Station, 1862. His name was on a list of paroled prisoners who wished to be exchanged. Received on Steamer *Louis D'Or* near Baton Rouge, Louisiana, October 9, 1862; on Charleston Station, 1862-63.—*Register of Officers of the Confederate States Navy*, 57, 66, 99, 133, 174.

three officers on that vessel; the Irishman on the *Virginia*, who had held a similar post in the United States navy and had come to serve at Gosport Navy Yard, on the Savannah and Richmond stations, and finally in the James River Squadron; on the *Florida*, a second assistant engineer who later served on the *Tennessee* in the Mobile Squadron; on the *Shenandoah*, during 1864-65, the second assistant engineer, who was a Scotchman-born; and on the *Alabama*, an Englishman who served up to the time of the famous battle with the *Kearsarge* off the French coast.[9]

An Englishman served as ship's carpenter during an early period of the war on the *Florida*, another Englishman as sailmaker on the *Alabama* and later on the *Shenandoah*, while an Irish-born carpenter and a paymaster of the same nativity transferred their allegiance from the Federal to the Confederate navy, filling the same posts respectively. The official record reveals only one alien-born, an Englishman, serving as boatswain, and only one foreigner officially recorded as acting gunner, serving on the *Georgia* and *Albemarle*, respectively, during 1864.[10] However in an account of the battle of Roanoke Island, a naval officer of the *Beaufort* relates how his men worked their gun coolly and deliberately, as the gun captain was an Englishman from a British man-of-war trained on the gunnery ship *Excellent*, as was also his gunner's mate, both of whom held the Crimean medal.[11]

The naval authorities were obliged to depend upon foreigners for

[9] James H. Hood, Canadian, was chief engineer on the C. S. cruiser *Nashville*, 1861-62. Michael Quinn, Irishman, was chief engineer on October 23, 1862, to rank from October 2, 1862, served on the *Virginia*, 1864.

John Hayes, Englishman, rose to second assistant engineer in the Provisional Navy, June 2, 1864. He served on the C. S. S. *Florida*, 1862-63; on the C. S. S. *Tennessee*, 1864, was captured August 5, 1864, paroled, November 13, 1864, and took the oath to the United States on January 25, 1865.

John Hutchinson was the Scotchman who was made second assistant engineer, October 19, 1864, and served on the *Shenandoah*, during 1864-65.

William Robertson was appointed from England, third assistant engineer to the *Alabama* and was drowned in the *Kearsarge-Alabama* battle, June 19, 1864.

Richard Finn, born in Ireland, is recorded as appointed second assistant engineer from Texas, July 3, 1863, and granted a two months' leave of absence on July 4, 1863, from which he does not seem to have returned by 1864.—*Register of Officers of the Confederate States Navy*, 91, 158, 84, 96, 166, 60. See also Wm. C. Whittle, *Cruises of the Confederate States Steamers "Shenandoah" and "Nashville,"* 24.

[10] *Register of Officers of the Confederate States Navy*, 2, 45, 59, 189. There is a record of one Hugh Lindsay, born in Ireland, who became carpenter on August 14, 1861 (ex-United States navy carpenter), and who resigned June 22, 1863. It does not appear on what ship or ships he served.—*Ibid.*, 114.

[11] Parker, *Recollections of a Naval Officer*, 231. These men are not to be found in the *Register*.

manning their cruisers. It was found impossible to ship crews at home, as there was a great scarcity of sailors in the South, and landsmen naturally preferred the army. Since open enlistment in foreign ports was of course not permissible, the question of securing a crew to man the Confederate ships remained a serious problem. To smuggle a ship out of one port of the European continent and her equipment out of another, and to engage men for a voyage in one direction and for one announced purpose and then to assure their being willing to go in another direction and for quite a different purpose was no slight undertaking, as Bulloch pointed out to the secretary of the navy.[12] Though there was a goodly sprinkling of other nationalities, especially from the seafaring nations, the majority of the crew secured were usually Britishers. It may well be that the readiness with which British seamen had served on American boats before the war had established a tradition of American service and that they questioned little whether it was with North or South. Sir William Russell tells of finding a number of British seamen on a steam ferry plying between Baltimore and Norfolk, who had been attracted to the American service from the West Indies where they heard how "Uncle Sam treated his fellows." When Russell exclaimed at five men out of seven being British subjects, the reply was, "Oh! aye that is—we onct was—most of us now are 'Mericans, I think. There's plenty more of us aboard the ship."[13] There is no doubt that numbers on the Confederate privateers came from the Royal Naval Reserve.

Bulloch, who had been sent to England for the special duty of creating a navy, was active in securing crews for the various privateers as they became ready to go to sea. Bulloch's opinion on the ease or difficulty of securing crews is entitled to the highest consideration. "No very great difficulty was experienced in getting crews for the *Alabama* and *Florida*, and I think that any vessel fitted out to cruise against commerce, thereby holding out to the men not only the captivating excitement of adventure but the positive expectation of prize money, might almost at any time pick up a goodly number of passable seamen. But the iron-clads are too evidently for other purposes to deceive any mere adventurers. Their grim aspect and formidable

[12] Bulloch to Mallory, March 17, 1864, dated Liverpool.—*N. R.*, Ser. 2, II, 607.
[13] *My Diary North and South*, 82. Nineteen recruits came from the Royal Naval Reserves.—Frederick M. Edge, *England's Danger and her Safety*, 22-23.

equipment clearly show that they are solely intended for the real danger and shock of battle, and I do not think reliable crews could be obtained from among the floating population of European seaports."[14] His idea for manning war vessels was to collect a crew at home to put aboard as soon as the ironclad had destroyed the blockading fleet and entered the home port, since the men at the guns must be actuated by pure patriotism. The evidence of the commander of the *Shenandoah* corroborates this view, for he declared that he had "myriads" of applications to enlist for that vessel, as its privateering character was naturally suspected, but he refused all applications in order not to violate the queen's proclamation of neutrality. Even with the utmost care to keep men not belonging to the ship from getting on board, he found forty-two stowaways aboard when finally at sea.[15] Though this zeal would seem to indicate ease in filling up the crews of privateers, ardor was by no means always so great,[16] and the equally serious question of quality of the crew remained to harass the officers later, as we shall see. The representatives of the Federal government were vigilant and protested constantly to the British government against enlistments of crews for the Confederate cruisers. Efforts to fill up the crews of Confederate ships and corresponding vigilance on the part of Union officials were not confined to England but appeared in France, Belgium, and several other continental countries.[17]

The chief source of recruitment seems to have been the crews on the prizes captured by the Confederate privateers. This was true from the very beginning of the war. The steamer *Winslow*, a small side-wheel boat taken over from the United States navy by the Confederates, was very active in cruising outside of Cape Hatteras as a privateer. Many of the men on the vessels captured by her, generally foreigners, entered the southern service. When the *Beaufort*

[14] *N. R.*, Ser. 2, II, 455. The letter is dated July 9, 1863.

[15] Wm. C. Whittle, "The Cruise of the Shenandoah," *Southern Historical Society Papers*, XXXV, 249-250.

[16] S. Barron, who assisted Bulloch, wrote Secretary Mallory from Paris on November 10, 1863: "The *Florida*, Commander Barney, is now in Brest undergoing repairs. She has only 27 men on board and there seems much difficulty in getting a crew for her."—*N. R.*, Ser. 2, II, 519.

[17] The United States consul at Antwerp wrote on April 10, 1864, to Captain Winslow, in command of the *Kearsarge:* "I take the liberty of informing you that an agent of the *Rappahannock* has engaged about twenty-five seamen at our port during this day, and I am informed that they will leave here this evening for Calais."—*N. R.*, Ser. 1, III, 13. See also *ibid.*, I, 23.

was being fitted out with a crew, it was made up principally of men who had been in the prizes captured by the *Winslow*. On the *Beaufort* there was but one American, a green hand who shipped as a coal heaver. Otherwise the crew was composed of Englishmen, two of whom were splendid men from ships-of-war, of Danes, and of Swedes. The captain declared that he had never sailed with a better crew. He marveled at their eagerness to go into battle, considering the fact that they knew nothing of the cause of the war. He found difficulty only in shipping a cook and steward and finally had to take as cabin boy a youth of fourteen who before long deserted the ship.[18]

The way in which seamen shifted allegiance is well told by Midshipman Morgan, who said: "We had treated these unfortunates kindly; they received the same rations our own men did, and one-half of them were released from their irons and allowed to roam about the deck in the daytime. They must have become attached to us, for first one man and then another asked to be permitted to talk to our first lieutenant, and when this was granted, would request to be allowed to ship aboard. To our surprise the second and third mates and the twenty-seven seamen joined us and afterwards proved to be among the very best men we had."[19] Indeed the ease with which the privateers were generally able to secure volunteers from captured vessels was a striking peculiarity of the Civil War. There seemed to be no very great attachment to any particular flag. In truth, the crew of a prize vessel often appeared to take pleasure in knocking down bulkheads on their own vessels in order to insure a good draught for the flames and in collecting combustible materials to burn the prize. The presence of many foreigners in the American merchant marine is doubtless the explanation of such lack of loyalty, along with the desire to escape close confinement or irons.[20]

The methods pursued by southern officers in securing a crew often followed the time-honored way. Individuals were wooed. For instance a British sailor who had just returned to Liverpool was invited to dine with an old friend who had left the service for trade. He found four men with his friend at the hotel. The talk soon turned to the Confederacy, in the course of which great contempt was ex-

---

[18] Parker, *Recollections of a Naval Officer*, 211, 220.

[19] James M. Morgan, *Recollections of a Rebel Reefer*, 122-123.

[20] Bulloch refuses to explain why the captured crews expressed so little veneration for the flag, but states it as a fact.—*Op. cit.*, II, 147, 148; Grimball, "Career of the Shenandoah," *Southern Historical Society Papers*, XXV, 120.

pressed for the North, and the presence of a Confederate vessel lying at Birkenhead adroitly referred to with the assurance that the prize money would be enormous. Her crew was to be picked men, all old men-of-war tars, while her speed would enable her to give the "tow rope" to anything in the Yankee navy. The bait worked in this instance. The youth, although he held British papers, reasoned that the "service promised plenty of adventure," he liked the cause, and was not "indifferent to the prospect of prize money."[21]

Preparations were carefully made to secure recruits for the *Alabama*. The true nature of the venture was cautiously concealed from a crew which had signed ostensibly for a simple merchantman's cruise to Nassau. Captain Bulloch instructed several of his officers to circulate freely among the men as they were sailing away on the *Bahama* to induce them to continue on the *Alabama* after they had reached Terceira, a Portuguese island in the Azores. Two sets of articles had been prepared, one for men shipping for a limited time, the other for those willing to sign for the duration of the war. When the two ships met at Terceira, Captain Semmes ran up the Confederate flag to the accompaniment of "Dixie" and addressed the crew exactly as if he were commanding an English man-of-war, appealing to them as Englishmen. He spoke of the glory won by British seamen, their hatred of oppression, told of the horrors of the war as waged by the North against the Confederacy, and indicated the great career before recruits. "Now, my lads," said he, "there is the ship" (pointing to the *Alabama*), "she is as fine a vessel as ever floated; there is a chance which seldom offers itself to a British seaman—that is, to make a little money. There are only six ships that I am afraid of in the United States Navy. We are going to burn, sink, and destroy the commerce of the United States. Your prize-money will be divided proportionately, according to each man's rank, something similar to the English navy."[22] A great many of the crew

[21] Phil D. Haywood, *The Cruise of the Alabama*, 9 ff.

[22] We do not lack for reports of the history of the *Alabama*. In addition to Semmes's own account, we have that of his paymaster, Yonge, who was one of those officers who had instructions to circulate among the men.—Montague Bernard, *A Historical Account of the Neutrality of Great Britain during the American Civil War*, 348-349; *Narrative of the Cruise of the Alabama*, by one of the crew who attempts to quote a part of Semmes's speech, 4-5; that of Haywood, *op. cit.*, who became often disgruntled; and G. T. Fullam, *The Cruise of the "Alabama"* from her Departure from Liverpool until her Arrival at the Cape of Good Hope.

This critical feeling of Haywood's colored his story when he wrote it. He criticizes Admiral Semmes in the following terms: "Here was Captain Semmes, who had commanded

signed, some eighty in fact, but some hesitated as they feared that the service would be long and monotonous, as the vessel was bound to steer clear of ports; besides none of them cared to undervalue the courage and worth of the American navy and knew that as long as "England was doing a large trade with American ports, she was not likely to quarrel, no matter if a Yankee cruiser hung the whole of us." Some of them feared to take action under another flag, as they were naval reserve men, but Captain Semmes reassured them by promising to put them in English ports every three months where they could get their books signed.[23] Ultimately, through the efforts of the fourth lieutenant, most of the men did sign up. Forty-eight men, however, most of them firemen, resisted all arguments, and left an hour later on the *Bahama* which had brought Captain Semmes to the Portuguese harbor. The crew was composed almost exclusively of British subjects or of men on a lawful voyage entitled to British protection. As on other privateers, volunteers were accepted from captured vessels so that before long the *Alabama* had a full complement. The basis of division of the prize money on a privateer was one half to the owners of the vessel, one half to the officers and crew, unless some other written agreement had been made.[24]

It did not prove so easy to get a crew for the *Shenandoah*, even though in picking out the crews for the two vessels, the *Laurel* and *Sea King*, which were to carry the men to the place of rendezvous with the *Shenandoah*, particular efforts had been made to secure adventurous spirits and to avoid married men. Out of the fifty-five men present only twenty-three, about 25 per cent of the requisite quota, proved willing to embark on such a privateering enterprise. The force was too weak to weigh anchor, and the undertaking would have failed except for the spirit of the young Confederate officers, who threw off their jackets and with cheers raised the anchor. As usual it completed its crew from the prizes and, in this case, from

an American man-o'-war, addressing his crew as Englishmen, and urging them to do their best to injure and disgrace his own countrymen. No English officer would do that, I think, under any circumstances."—*Ibid.*, 32-33.

Yonge, the paymaster, was dismissed from the ship at Jamaica. He afterwards went to England and furnished evidence to the American legation concerning the violation of neutrality.—Bernard, *op. cit.*, 349.

[23] Haywood, *op. cit.*, 25-26; *Narrative of the Cruise of the Alabama*, 5.

[24] This division of the spoils had been fixed by law.—*Statutes of the Provisional Congress*, Vol. II, Chap. III (1861), Sec. 5.

a large number of stowaways who slipped aboard at Melbourne to appear on deck later and enlist in the crew.[25] The vessel enlisted fourteen men from the prize *Abigail* on January 10, 1864, eight from twenty-four whalers which were captured in the Caroline Isles, so that ultimately there were no British in the crew when it dropped anchor in Liverpool, November 6, 1865, seven months after the war was over. It might be more accurate to state that when the crew was mustered for examination at Liverpool by the British authorities everyone swore he was a southerner.[26]

The *Georgia* would probably have met insuperable difficulties in securing a crew except for the activity of a Liverpool firm, which equipped her and shipped a crew of forty-eight British subjects for her, ostensibly for Shanghai. Again, when that same vessel was at Cherbourg with much discontent and many desertions disrupting the crew, the same firm again came to her rescue, enlisting in Liverpool some twenty seamen and sending them to Brest. The *Japan*, also built in England, was manned by Englishmen, conveyed on board surreptitiously.[27]

The care with which the attitude of important men, such as the chief engineer, in a crew on a privateer was ascertained may well be noted. Bulloch's methods with the men in running the blockade to bring in the *Finegal* in November, 1861, are typical. The vessel was cleared for Nassau, but Bulloch intended to sail directly from Bermuda to Savannah, Georgia. Until after the ship had left St. George's harbor, Bermuda, not a word was said to the crew or even to the captain about running the blockade but, during the passage from England, Bulloch had kept an eye on the men, and his second in command had been much with them so that the two officers felt certain the crew suspected the mission of the boat. Bulloch was especially anxious about the engineer and so had often dropped into the

---

[25] S. A. Ashe, "The Shenandoah," *Southern Historical Society Papers*, XXXII, 321; Grimball, "Career of the Shenandoah," *Southern Historical Society Papers*, XXV, 118. They secured about 42 men at Melbourne from the stowaways, almost all of whom claimed to be Americans. They proved to be good, faithful men.—Whittle, "The Cruise of the Shenandoah," *Southern Historical Society Papers*, XXXV, 250-251. They added 8 men from 4 captured whalers.—*Ibid.*, 252.

[26] This is the Confederate vessel which, it will be recalled, sailed the north Pacific for months after the war was over in utter ignorance that hostilities had ceased, and never entered Liverpool to surrender to the British government until November, 1865.— Charles Lining, "The Cruise of the Confederate Steamship 'Shenandoah,'" *Tennessee Historical Magazine*, VIII, No. 2, 111.

[27] Richard Cobden, *Speech of Mr. Cobden on the Foreign Enlistment Act*, 23-24.

engine room. This man, McNair, was a silent, steady, reliable Scot, "immovable and impassive as the Grampian Hills when it was proper to stand fast, prompt, quick and energetic when it was necessary to act," according to Bulloch himself. He had cause to feel sure of McNair and made good use of him later, for he proved of great service in fitting out the *Alabama* and had charge of her engines until she was turned over at Terceira to Captain Semmes and his regular staff of officers. Shortly after the *Finegal* left Bermuda, Bulloch called the crew aft and told them of his intention to run the blockade, offering to put into Nassau if any refused to continue with the ship. Not a man backed out, though he made it clear that he would fight any United States ship trying to stop him. He equipped the men with rifles and revolvers, and set a few old ship-of-war men among them to drilling the rest. It was revealed that the engineer had been expecting the information, for he had put aside a few tons of the best and cleanest coal for the final dash into harbor, assuring Bulloch he hoped to drive the ship at the rate of eleven knots an hour for a brief spurt. As is well known, he made good and the *Finegal* entered Savannah safely.[28]

The most conspicuous failure in securing reliable men was that of the *Alabama*. The men were a "scratch crew," in the parlance of the time, such as could be had at any time in Liverpool through shipping agents. With some fine, adventurous seamen there were also about fifty sailors picked up from the streets of Liverpool, who looked from the start as if they would call for some strict warship discipline. The major part of the crew were obviously seamen, stout, hardy fellows, and the rest dockside loafers and turnpike sailors. "Any one familiar with roads leading out of Brighton and Margate," reports Haywood, who was one of the crew, "will recognize these last [the loafers and turnpike sailors]. They are picturesquely nautical in their talk. . . . I need not say that they are always thirsty and penniless. These are the characters that figure in the 'cruelty log' in merchant ships. They article as ordinary seamen, and have most likely never stepped a spar, and their officers soon find this out, and to correct their deficiencies beat them blind and silly.

"The real seamen were nearly all 'run sailors,' as most of the 'Dicky Sands' (a cant name amongst shipping men for 'Liverpud-

[28] Bulloch, *op. cit.*, I, 118-122; Bradlee, *Blockade Running*, 53-54.

lians') are; that is, they ship from port to port, and a more reckless and desperate set do not exist."[29]

British captains, according to Haywood, would not ship these "run men" for long voyages if they could possibly avoid it, but they made up what efficiency there was in the *Alabama* crew. They were mostly English, with a few Irish, Danes, and one Russian or Finn, whose real name, Jackalanwiski, was promptly converted by his fellows to "Jack-O-Lantern." It is interesting at this point to contrast the personnel of the crew with that of the *Kearsarge*, the United States vessel which met the *Alabama* in deadly combat; among the 140 men composing the crew on the United States vessel there were only 11 foreigners.[30]

It is worth while to see through the eyes of one living through the experience what life was among the heterogeneous dregs of Europe on a southern privateer. The bad traits of many soon began to come to the surface. "The bullies commenced to haze the quieter men, and tried to impose on all but the captain of our mess. A Scotchman named M'Gregor put a stop to it in our watch by seizing one or two ruffians, throwing them up till their heels struck the carlings, and then dashing them down on the deck, banging the life right out of them for the time. Indeed, the law between decks was that of the strongest, and God help the weak ones; they would have been as well off in a pirate ship, as no reporting was allowed." Old M'Gregor merits an individual description as one type, albeit an extreme one, of sailor serving the sacred cause of the Confederacy. He was a rigid Calvinist so that the mess watch echoed with clashes of opinion on fate, free will, and foreknowledge, but for all that he impressed Haywood as the worst man he ever knew, "a cool remorseless, determined villain" who once told Haywood with his hard, incisive speech "that he would cut the throat of his father if enough money was forthcoming." His very appearance must have struck chills of terror. "He had a hard, colorless face, and light gray eyes that seemed covered with a film like a snake's; when excited they glittered under his shaggy brows with a sinister, venomous light."

[29] This encouraging picture of the crew of the *Alabama* was drawn by Haywood, *op. cit.*, 33-34.

[30] *Ibid.*, 30; Frederick M. Edge, *An Englishman's View of the Battle between the Alabama and the Kearsarge*, 34. Hereafter cited as *The Alabama and the Kearsarge*.

It is no surprise to learn that he had been a "slaver," mutineer, and pirate in the Windward Isles.[31]

It was regarded by Union officials as illuminating concerning the character of the officers on the *Alabama* that George T. Fullam, an Englishman, after pledging his honor to return to the *Kearsarge* if allowed to bring off prisoners from the *Alabama* which was sinking, steered directly for the Confederate steamer, the *Deerhound*, and cast his boat adrift.[32]

Before we come to the natural consequence of shipping such a crew on the *Alabama*, it might be well to sum up the character of the crew on several of the other Confederate privateers. Dawson found but eight seamen on the *Nashville*, representing almost as many different nations—an Irishman, a Belgian, a Swede, a fat Cockney Englishman, a Frenchman, a Spaniard, and a Scotchman. He found them to be "mean, treacherous, and obscene" and wished to say no more about them than was absolutely necessary. But he speaks well of one Lussen as a "thoroughly instructed sea-faring man, a very intelligent man," whom he welcomed as a roommate and acceptable companion. This man described himself as an officer in the navy of one of the South American republics, expecting to receive an appointment in the Confederate service. The captain of the *Beaufort*, on the other hand, never sailed with a better crew—composed of Englishmen, Danes, and Swedes, but recruited, it will be remembered, from Union ships taken prize by the *Winslow*; and the crew of the *Shenandoah*, stowaways, or men picked up from any old whaler, behaved well.[33] Indeed the crew of the *Beaufort* had the utmost contempt for their cook, a delicate-looking Spaniard who had been captured as part of a prize and shipped with the *Beaufort*, for protesting just before the battle at Elizabeth City that he didn't want to fight. Falling on his knees before the captain of the vessel, he kept repeating, "Captain, me no wanter fight." Placed in the magazine by direction of the captain, he was hauled before that harassed officer in the thick of the fight by two men who had caught him flee-

[31] Haywood, *op. cit.*, 38-40. There is no reason to feel that the description is over-colored by any special antagonism on the part of the writer.

[32] Edge, *The Alabama and the Kearsarge*, 13. It is noticeable that Edge, an English writer, comments on the crew of the *Alabama* as *almost exclusively English*—with, in addition, one Irishman, one Portuguese, two Welshmen, one Scotch, and one German.—*Ibid.*, 38-41.

[33] Dawson, *op. cit.*, 10-11, 22-23; Parker, *Recollections of a Naval Officer*, 220; Whittle, "Cruise of the Shenandoah," *Southern Historical Society Papers*, XXXV, 247 ff.

ing. Returned to the magazine he fled a second time and beat the entire crew to Norfolk.[34] One can only say of the sailors, as of the soldiers, that there were all kinds on all the boats, good and bad, and nationality had little to do with their characters and abilities.[35]

The difficulties of desertion and mutiny which beset the path of the *Alabama* might have been anticipated. Four of the crew, three of whom were Englishmen, deserted at Jamaica. The fireman was taken back to the boat, but one man was able to prove that he was a naval coast volunteer of Her Majesty's Ship *Majestic*, and was released.[36] Finally, when the vessel reached Martinique on November 18, 1862, insubordination reached the point of mutiny, led by one George Forrest, an American-Irishman who possessed the qualities of leadership. Forrest had been brought to the *Alabama* from the prize brig *Dunkirk*, had been recognized by Captain Semmes as a deserter from the *Sumter*, been tried by court-martial, and condemned to loss of pay and of shore liberty. Forrest only laughed at the punishment but conceived a murderous hatred of the captain, which culminated in the effort at mutiny. Again he was court-martialed but, instead of being shot, the usual penalty for mutiny, he was dismissed in disgrace. As he left the ship, he freely stated his opinion of the officers and crew. Discipline undoubtedly suffered from this leniency, for the type of men aboard probably interpreted it as indicating that the officers did not dare punish and that the gravest offenses would meet only with irons or with being sent ashore. The mutiny had not been a success but insubordination never ceased while the vessel was afloat.[37] Certainly Captain Semmes, able to keep such

[34] Parker, *Recollections of a Naval Officer*, 238.

[35] The commander of the *Arkansas* called a tall athletic young Irishman "one of my best men."—George W. Gift, "The Story of the Arkansas," *Southern Historical Society Papers*, XII, 115.

[36] Haywood, *op. cit.*, 73; *Narrative of the Cruise of the Alabama* (by one of the crew), 8. If Mason wrote this last sketch, there were but three who deserted. Desertions occurred on other ships, such as the *Shenandoah*, from among men who had been on captured ships. Attempts to bring them back were obstructed by United States consuls.—Grimball, "Career of the Shenandoah," *Southern Historical Society Papers*, XXV, 128.

[37] This was the opinion of Haywood, *op. cit.*, 49, 54, 60. See also Fullam, *op. cit.*, 12. Desertion of a different character occurred when men who had served on the Confederate cruisers gave testimony of one kind and another against these vessels. Such an instance is illustrated in the following story. One Jones, ex-boatswain of the *Oreto*, probably at the instigation of the United States consul, made declaration that the *Oreto* was a Confederate gunboat. Captain Hickley of the American *Greyhound* seized her and put the case in the court of admiralty. A southern woman concludes the story with a burst of intense feeling, "The Yankees rejoiced, and the excellent rascal Jones, a low, dirty, Liverpool dock-rat, went to Washington, and as the hero of a great event was made an acting lieutenant in the Federal Navy."—Maffitt, *op. cit.*, 239.

a crew in working order, was no ordinary man; only a man of exceptional courage, determination, and seamanship could have accomplished it.

Desertions to the foe occurred, of course, from the navy, as well as from the army. Let a single case suffice. Some time after Fort Pulaski, which was located at the mouth of the Savannah River, had been taken by the Union forces, a small picket boat in charge of a Confederate midshipman, and rowed by four sailors, two of whom were Irishmen, set out in the direction of the fort to reconnoiter. The two Irishmen had been conscripted into the Confederate navy and were then serving on board the *Atlantic*, a blockade-runner which had been converted into an ironclad. The boat was on her way back when the officer, taking off his jacket, tossed it to the bowman to stow under the bow, with a caution about the revolvers in it. Quick as a flash Pat had the pistols out of the coat, handed one to his fellow Irishman, and pointed the other at the midshipman with the peremptory order to steer straight for Fort Pulaski. At the fort Pat communicated important information about the *Atlantic*, for which the Federals were on the lookout, and which they accordingly captured.[38]

Occasionally alien residents became involved in maritime enterprises which led to diplomatic negotiations. A British subject was convicted of a plot to seize a vessel in San Francsisco harbor and to take it out as a Confederate privateer. He was saved from the results of his folly only by direct intercession of Cobden Bright of England.

The second case concerned a British subject, Vernon G. Locke, who, under the assumed name of Parker, had been put in command of the privateer *Retribution* by the man named as her commander at the time the letter of marque was issued. Locke proceeded to issue commissions to British subjects in New Brunswick, on British soil, though he had no authority to do so and was not even himself in the Confederate service. It would appear next that a certain Braine, who was thought by Secretary Benjamin not to be a Confederate citizen, got possession of the vessel and went to the British colonies where, for the ostensible object of securing fuel to continue his voyage, he sold portions of the cargo at different points on the coast entirely against the rules of legitimate warfare. In his capacity of privateer he seized the United States vessel *Chesapeake*, where-

---

[38] Maguire, *The Irish in America*, 571.

upon the Washington authorities demanded of England that the parties engaged in the capture be surrendered under the Ashburton Treaty for trial by the courts of the United States on charges of murder and piracy, but this was refused by the New Brunswick authorities. The simple facts of the case are probably that some aliens, sympathizing with the South, erroneously believed themselves authorized to act as belligerents under Parker's letter of marque and so were guilty of violating England's neutrality proclamation. Benjamin very properly disavowed all responsibility.

A third highly irregular performance involved five Irishmen residing in Matamoros. A Marylander named Hogg who had gone South at the outbreak of hostilities, and who was on the Mexican border in November, 1863, devised a plan to capture several Union merchant vessels. He secured from General Bee, commanding at Brownsville, a paper sanctioning his project and from the Brownsville collector of customs a blank form for a ship's register into which could be inserted the description of any prize vessel he might capture. Hogg then secured the coöperation of five Irishmen residing in Matamoros just beyond the Mexican border. In November the little party of six took passage in the United States schooner *Joseph L. Gerrity*, which was laden with cotton and bound for New York, rose against the Yankee captain the second night out, set him and his crew ashore in a small boat on the Yucatan Peninsula, and, by virtue of the blank register, passed the prize off as the Confederate blockade-runner *Eureka*, and sold the cargo. To escape the charge of piracy lodged by the owner of the vessel, Hogg, with one of the Irishmen, escaped to Nassau, only to learn that three of his men had been arrested in Liverpool on this charge by the efforts of the United States consular service. Benjamin intervened in behalf of the three Irishmen at the request of Hogg, though disclaiming sanction of such irregular warfare by noncitizens who were not in the Confederate service. The British court held piracy a nonextraditable offense, and discharged the prisoners after the Confederate government had spent £458 for counsel in their defense.

The last case involved John Y. Beall, as ill-starred in this venture as he was to be in his proposed rescue of Confederate prisoners from Johnson's Island,[39] and a comrade, an invalided army officer. The

[39] See above, pp. 187-188.

two men received on March 5, 1863, commissions as acting masters in the naval service with the right to enlist men not subject to conscription and to draw equipment for them. Though they were therefore part of the naval establishment, they embarked on a private venture. In other words, they must find their own boats and pay themselves out of their future prizes. The first two recruits were young Scotchmen, Bennett G. Burleigh and John Maxwell. When the expedition had enrolled ten men, it set out from Richmond about April 1, 1863. Beall was left without aid by the restoration of his comrade to active duty and appointed one Edward McGuire and the two Scots as acting masters. By September, when the force had attained a total of eighteen and possessed two boats, Beall began to function as a marine coast guard by capturing eight vessels in all—fishing scows, sloops and schooners, of which the *Alliance* was the most important. Later the little band—now reduced to fifteen—was captured and threatened with the extreme penalty meted out to piracy, but a threat of reprisals by the Confederacy brought the amenities of war and the prisoners, including the two Scots, were in due course exchanged.[40] One of these Scotchmen was the same Burleigh who was associated with Beall in the Great Lakes unhappy venture.

There appears to be a dearth of information as to the crews on the few Confederate men-of-war. The impression made on one observer by the men of several vessels is worth repeating, even though we are left in ignorance as to the vessels in question. "This was the first time I had seen any specimen of our infant navy, and must confess the splendid appearance, quickness, cleanliness, neatness, and obedience of the seamen were in favourable contrast with the sleepy, lackadaisical dandyism of the officers—many of whom were mere lads. The men were truly magnificent specimens of bone and muscle —mostly foreign-born, from the merchant navy; and, dressed as they all were in the neat blue uniforms captured at Norfolk, reminded me much of what I had seen of the British navy in American waters —bronzed and rosy fellows, active as cats, and fit to fight a brigade at any odds." A goodly number of men were transferred from the army to the navy, beginning in February, 1862—Irishmen, English,

<hr />

[40] For the first case, see Brougham Villiers and W. H. Chesson, *Anglo-American Relations*, 161. For the second case see Benjamin's letter to the Honorable J. P. Holcombe, dated April 20, 1864, which sets forth the entire case.—*N. R.*, Ser. 2, III, 1095-1097; the third case is described in Robinson, *op. cit.*, 206-209; and the last in *ibid.*, 222-227. Burleigh is spelled variously in the different sources.

and even a Russian. A stray Austrian, resident in Mobile at the opening of the war, enlisted as early as 1861 in the embryo navy.[41]

The number of foreigners enlisted on the Confederate cruisers can be computed with some slight approximation to accuracy, but no figures are possible for the ironclads or gunboats serving in American waters. Exact figures are possible for the *Shenandoah*, the *Florida*, and the *Alabama*, and indicate 167 foreigners scattered among the crews.[42] Based on the ratios which prevailed on the three vessels above-named, or about two thirds of the crew, allowing perhaps 100 for half a dozen minor boats, of which the *Arkansas* is the chief, we reach possibly 400 as the number of foreigners in the naval service, but beyond that we cannot go. An approximation is possible for the *Tallahassee* with its crew of 110, the *Georgia* with its crew of fifty, and the *Nashville* with its crew of forty. Estimates for the proportions of foreign-born in the crew of 300 on the *Merrimac* and for the rams and for the fifty-odd armed vessels constituting the river defenses would be mere guesses. That there were foreign-born on these vessels in fair proportions is reasonably certain.

Probably nothing attempted by the Confederate government was more ambitious or showed more pathetically the lack of solid foundation than the Confederate Naval School—note the careful omission of the more pretentious title of academy. It enters our story because one of the teachers was born abroad. To chronicle anew the history of this unique and fascinating institution is no part of this story. It will be sufficient to recall that the establishment of a naval school for the proper training of young officers for the navy had been Secretary Mallory's thought from his very entrance into office; but,

---

[41] *Battle-fields of the South*, I, 301. The transfers appear on the various Descriptive Lists and Accounts of Pay and Clothing; in Thompson, *History of the First Kentucky Brigade*, 686, 720, 732. The record of the Austrian recruit is in a report to the U. D. C. at Mobile, December 6, 1909, a manuscript preserved in the Alabama Archives. The *Daily Richmond Examiner* for November 1, 1861, reports the offer of a resigned British naval officer, Captain S. J. Short, to join the C. S. navy, but he does not appear on any official list.

[42] By calculation from figures given in various writings on privateers, the writer has attained the following on foreigners, officers and crew:

SHIPS	FOREIGNERS
Shenandoah	58
Florida	49
Alabama	60
Tallahassee (total, 110)	74
Georgia (total, 50)	34
Nashville (total, 40)	26
Minor vessels, *Arkansas*, etc.	100-150

although such a school was amply authorized under the statutes approved on March 16, 1861, steps to form an academy did not prove feasible until 1863. The number of acting midshipmen had been limited by act of congress in 1862 to 106 and that of passed midshipmen to 20. Mallory laid the cornerstone of the school, figuratively speaking, by an order on March 23, 1863, for examination by a board of officers of the acting midshipmen at the several stations in various subjects, such as seamanship, gunnery, mathematics, navigation, English, French, drawing, and drafting. Several captains were designated as examiners; Lieutenant William H. Parker was named commandant of the embryonic school and directed to draw up regulations: and the steamship *Patrick Henry* of the James River squadron indicated as the school ship, on which quarters were fitted up for the midshipmen. In the fall of 1863 the navy department selected an academic staff of 10 instructors assisted by 2 surgeons, a paymaster, gunner, boatswain, engineer, and sailmaker. Strangely enough, the staff remained almost unchanged except for the commandant from the day it opened with 50 acting midshipmen in the fall of 1863, offering instruction in 6 departments, until the fall of the Confederacy. It was closely modeled on Annapolis. The ship was usually stationed near Drewry's Bluff in the heart of hostilities so that the lads became versed in the practice as well as theory of warfare, being frequently called to seize cutlass and carbine or to take their places in trenches facing an actual foe. Their final duty proved to be to guard the train on which the government archives and the bullion of the treasury were being conveyed from Richmond.[43]

The one foreigner identified with the naval school was George A. Peple, born at Henry-Chapelle in the Rhine province of Prussia and educated for a teacher. After graduation a predilection for the mechanic arts led him to visit the polytechnic schools of Geneva and Vevey in Switzerland. Emigration to America changed his homeland but not his profession at first, for he was for years engaged in educational work. In 1859 he went to Richmond and during the early period of the war acted as topographical engineer, then as commissary sergeant at Buchanan. Finally he was appointed professor

---

[43] For a fuller account see John T. Scharf, *History of the Confederate States Navy, from its Organization to the Surrender of its Last Vessel*, 773-781; Hanna, *op. cit.*, 5-6, 31-35, 61-63.

of history and modern languages at the Confederate Marine School on board the school ship stationed in the harbor at Rocketts, Virginia. In this position he ranked as acting master or major of the army. Toward the close of the war he also edited for some time the *Richmond Anzeiger,* which the government had purchased. He was long a leading spirit among the Germans in America.[44]

Romance tends to cling around the Lost Cause, but certainly no aspect of the history of the Confederacy is more truly romantic than the story of the blockade-runners. The names of the fortunate vessels which were able to elude the Federal chasers successfully for a number of runs became familiar to and beloved by the Confederate civilians in the chief ports of entry. An interesting set of names they were with all sorts of connotations. One can fairly picture by the name bestowed on a given vessel the sort of commander who ruled her destiny, ranging from the quiet captain of the *Lillian* to the swashbuckling commander of the *Let Her Rip;* from the cautious type of business man who ran the *Chicora* to the fierce captain of the *Vulture* or *Falcon;* from the sentimental, fatherly type who ran the *Dream* to the staid states'-rights patriot who christened his ship *Virginia.* Sometimes a vessel seemed to personify its name, for the *Siren* was indeed an enchantress; the Yankees were never able to touch her.[45]

During the first two years of the war the blockade-runners were almost exclusively officered by English and Scotch but, during the last two years when the danger was very much increased, the additional incentive of patriotism was required to induce men to venture loss of fortune in the service and to run the danger of imprisonment. Nearly all the officers during the last two years were Confederates.[46]

Many of the captains during the early period were drawn from the very cream of the English navy, officers of prolonged naval experience who, tired of the inertia of life on half pay, were drawn to volunteer in the Confederate service by the lure of the rich profits,

[44] Schuricht, *History of the German Element in Virginia,* II, 85. Schuricht must be in error as to the birthplace.

[45] Without any special effort the author has collected the following list of blockade-runners: *Lillian, Little Hattie, Florie, Agnes E. Fry, Chicora, Let Her Rip, Let Her Be, Condor, Falcon, Flamingo, Ptarmigan, Vulture, Owl, Bat, Fox, Venus, Dream, Story, Estelle, Atlanta, Rob Roy, Virginia, Charlotte, Banshee, Night Hawk,* the *Siren,* the *Don.* Bradlee gives a list of all the blockade-runners into Charleston.—*Op. cit.,* 96-98.

[46] This is the statement of Sprunt, *Chronicles of the Cape Fear River,* 394. He lived in Wilmington, served on several of the runners, and was in a position to know.

of experience in their profession, and of adventure, which was a battle cry to those old sea dogs. The sympathies of so many of the English were with the Confederacy that probably other naval officers would have gone in for blockade-running if the United States had not threatened to send all British naval officers taken on a blockade-runner to England in irons.[47] As evidence that interest was confined largely to Britishers, one might note the efforts of the French partner in the Charleston firm of Fraser, Trenholm, and Company, who was eager to have a French vessel in the blockade-running trade. A steamer was set aside for the purpose. To make her legally French, a French captain and crew were obligatory, but although high wages were offered, no men could be found.[48]

The English officers in this service usually operated under an assumed name. For instance, Captain Roberts, who commanded one of the first little twin-screw steamers, called the *Don*, was in reality a titled officer in the English navy, the Honorable Augustus Charles Hobart Hampden, son of the Earl of Buckinghamshire. He was post captain in the Royal Navy, and for a time commander of Queen Victoria's yacht, *Victoria and Albert*. He had seen service in the war against Emperor Nicholas in 1854 under the British admiral, Sir Charles Napier, and after the order, "Lads, sharpen your cutlasses," had boarded the Russian warships before Kronstadt, helped storm the seven forts which guarded the entrance to the harbor, and sailed up the Neva to St. Petersburg. With the coming of the American war he obtained leave of absence to try his skill at this new game of blockade-running. He was very proud of his craft, in which he made six trips between Nassau and Wilmington. He returned to England with a snug fortune. The *Don* was captured on her very first trip after the command had been renounced by "Captain Roberts," and the chief officer was assumed by his captors to be Roberts. He did not reveal his identity and the northern newspapers upon the arrival of the prize at Philadelphia were full of the capture of the "notorious Captain Roberts." Their chagrin, when they learned the mistake, equalled their former elation. Dramatic to the end, unable to endure the dull routine of service ashore, Hobart accepted

<hr />

[47] Thomas Taylor, *Running the Blockade*, 87; John Bassett, "Running the Blockade from Confederate Ports," *Historical Papers*, "Trinity College Historical Society," Ser. 2, p. 63; Bradlee, *op. cit.*, 42-43.
[48] Rhodes, *History of the United States*, V, 397-398; Bradlee, *op. cit.*, 61.

the command of the entire Turkish navy at the outbreak of the Turkish-Russian War. He died, in accordance with his character, Hobart Pasha, admiral of the Turkish navy.[49]

The *Condor,* one of a fleet of fast three-funnel boats, was commanded by Admiral Hewitt of the British navy, who won the Victoria Cross in the Crimea and who was knighted by Queen Victoria for his distinguished services as ambassador to King John of Abyssinia. When this steamer was stranded near Fort Fisher, off the North Carolina coast, the celebrated spy, Rose Greenhow, was on board and entreated Hewitt to send her ashore through the breakers. He assented reluctantly and only after several refusals, a consent which brought, by drowning, the tragic end to her colorful life.[50]

Murray-Aynsley of the Royal Navy, known among blockade-runners as Captain Murray, was perhaps the most successful of the British naval blockade-runners and was a great favorite with the prominent people of Wilmington, especially with Colonel Lamb of Fort Fisher. In the *Venus* he had many hairbreadth escapes, the best known of which was the running into port in broad daylight in full view of the northern fleet. Colonel Lamb loved to describe the scene—the *Venus* closely chased by several blockaders, fired upon by other Union vessels, steaming straight ahead with old Murray on the bridge, his coat sleeves hitched up almost to his armpits—always a sign of intense excitement with him—but otherwise as cool as a cucumber.[51] This sight was, as Lamb declared, one never to be forgotten. He served for three years, commanding the *Nashville,* the *Hansa,* and other blockade-runners, ever ready to aid a blockade-runner in distress.

Another notable British officer in this group was the gallant Burgoyne, who later went down in the ironclad *Captain* in the Bay of Biscay as he was commanding it on its unfortunate voyage in September, 1870. The type of fearless spirit he was is indicated by the fact that he too was a wearer of the Victoria Cross. Captain Lionel Campbell Goldsmith, an Englishman of Jewish descent, served also

---

[49] Hobart made one trip with the *Falcon.* His book, *Sketches from My Life,* has been criticized as fantastic, but the chapters on his blockade-running experiences do not seem exaggerated. See also Bassett, *op. cit.,* 63-64; Taylor, *Running the Blockade,* 90-91; Sprunt, "Tales of the Cape Fear Blockade," *North Carolina Booklet,* I, No. 10, 69-70.

[50] *Ibid.,* 98; Joseph Hergesheimer, *Swords and Roses,* 185.

[51] Taylor, *Running the Blockade,* 92; Sprunt, *Chronicles of the Cape Fear River,* 432-433.

for a time as captain of the famous *Venus*. Eventually, after a terrific experience on another vessel with yellow fever, which killed off a considerable number of his crew in a half hour, he gave up the game of blockade-running, then fast drawing to its close. The *Siren* was also commanded by an Englishman, "who dreaded the coast as the devil does holy water," and was actuated apparently only by the desire to run off again when he touched soundings, instead of by the determination to run the blockade.[52] Tom Taylor, who lived a thrilling life for several years as supercargo on the *Banshee* and *Night Hawk*, was assistant to a firm of Liverpool merchants, trading chiefly with India and the United States in 1861. Early the next year one of the partners in his house informed him of the purchase of a steamer by him and a few friends, in order to have a fling at blockade-running and offered Taylor a chance to go as supercargo. He jumped at the chance—a stroke of luck for a youth of twenty-one. He served in various capacities on the *Banshee* and on the *Night Hawk*, and became endeared to the children of the South as the Santa Claus of the war.

All of these British visitors, serving the Confederacy by bringing in the sinews of war as truly as if they had served on her ironclads or privateers, trod Confederate soil every time they came over. A favorite spot visited by them was a humble cottage, in reality a pilot's house converted by a woman's magic into a home, nestling among the sand dunes and straggling pines and blackjack north of Fort Fisher. It adds to the romance to know that the spirit which presided over the hearth there was a Rhode Island maid, married to a Virginia youth. She insisted on staying near-by to help the post hospital and to set meals for soldiers and sailors and indeed for anyone who was lending a hand to the cause.[53]

Equally helpful but not so familiar were a group of lesser figures. The captain of the *Lillian*, which finally fell a prey to a Federal chaser, reported himself to the examining officer as Daniel Martin, a native of Liverpool, who once had to spend three weeks in Wilmington repairing the boiler which had been injured in the chase

[52] Hergesheimer, *Swords and Roses*, 185; Bradlee, *op. cit.*, 142, 145; *Confederate Veteran*, XXV, 201; Taylor, *Running the Blockade*, 91.

[53] Sprunt, *Tales and Traditions of the Lower Cape Fear*, 100-101; Taylor, *Running the Blockade*, 59-60.

in running in.[54] Quite at the other end of the Confederate States a Scotchman was pursuing the same business. William Watson had lived in the southern states for about eight years before the war and had enlisted from Baton Rouge, as we have seen, in the Confederate army, but had secured his discharge as an alien. He regarded the prospects of continuing in his old prewar business as impossible and so invested in a small vessel to engage in the highly speculative business of blockade-running. Though he was by profession an engineer, he had served as a seaman, had a fair nautical education, and was therefore a tolerable navigator. Accordingly he sailed out of New Orleans one dark night on the *Rob Roy* under the very walls of the forts and became ultimately a blockade-runner between Galveston, Havana, Belize, and Matamoros. Captain Carlin, who made twenty-three voyages without having a gun fired across his bows but had to burn his vessel on the twenty-fourth, was an Englishman who had been in the United States Coast Survey for years.

Patrick Pepper was a County Clare man who found his sale of dry goods at the *Golden Sheep* in Mobile terminated by the blockade and accordingly added the importation of munitions to dry goods, as far more profitable. He went as supercargo on his own ship, the *Cuba*, making a great success of his voyages to Havana. At last the vigilance of the Federals was rewarded and the *Cuba* was overhauled just off Mobile bar. The supercargo had disappeared but he emerged from the hatch, shouting that he had set the boat afire, which was full of powder from stem to stern. His blockade-running days were over, for the ship went up with a bang, and he was lodged in Fort Warren, whence he departed for Mexico until the war was over. One recalls him for his proud reply to the Federal officer's inquiry as to his nationality. "I am an Irishman by birth and a Confederate by choice."[55]

In a slightly different category belong Henry Sulter and John Stump because both were Germans long resident in America and were in all likelihood Confederate citizens. The former had run away from Hinterbruck to go to sea and had visited most of the

---

[54] Morgan, *Recollections of a Rebel Reefer*, 195-196.

[55] Watson, *Adventures of a Blockade Runner*, 8; Wm. C. Dundas, "Blockade-Running during the Civil War," *The Bellman*, XXVI, 607. For Patrick Pepper, see Craighead, *op. cit.*, 356-357.

corners of the world. The gold fever had carried him to California; finally he had settled down in Savannah. His long seafaring experience made him more valuable to his adopted country as a pilot taking vessels through the blockade than as a soldier; therefore he was allowed to leave the German Volunteers of Savannah with which he had enlisted. He became captain and owner, among other vessels, of the *Lida* and the *Mary Baker*. Less fortunate than some of the British whose fortunes we have been following, he was captured no less than four times during the war and emerged at the end penniless. John Stump, on the other hand, had no record of experience on the sea, though he had been in the Mexican War, but embarked upon the business of running several ships between Richmond and New York, all of which were eventually captured.[56]

It is worth while to note a few of the foreigners serving in various minor capacities on the boats. Captain Wylie, a Scot who came over with the *Advance*, which the governor of North Carolina wisely bought in England to run the blockade into Wilmington with supplies for the soldiers and people of that state, stayed to become her sailing master. One of the engineers on the *Advance* was James Maglenn, an Irishman, who was chief engineer on her last trip and was carried with her into New Bern. This resourceful Irishman made his escape from there, however, to Baltimore, where some friends aided him in his further flight to Canada.[57] The writer has also encountered one instance of a Frenchman serving as chief engineer. James Sprunt was a native of Glasgow—and he never foreswore his British citizenship though he lived in America long after the war— who came to North Carolina at the age of six. Too young to enlist in the war and unable to enter the naval service, though he had already been studying navigation, he accepted an appointment as purser on the *Advance* and sailed to Bermuda. He made one successful voyage on the *North Heath*, and four on the *Lillian* under Captain John N. Maffitt. With all on board that vessel he was taken

[56] *Confederate Veteran*, XVIII, 245, XIV, 320.
[57] Sprunt, *Chronicles of the Cape Fear River*, 379-380, 391. Maglenn assured his escape by his quick wits on the train to Canada. An officer and guard entered to take a straw vote in the impending presidential election. Many reported they had voted for McClellan, and he noted that the officer's eyes brightened when anyone said Lincoln. Therefore when the officer eyed him sharply, he replied loudly, "I cast my vote for Lincoln."

prisoner in August, 1864, and held for eight months. His last war record was as purser of the *Susan Beirne*, another blockade-runner.[58]

With the exception of one or two Danes, the crews of the runners were either Britishers or southerners. It is a question whether the citizens of any other European country had the combination of business enterprise, capital to invest, seafaring experience, and adventurous spirit to carry out blockade-running on a large scale. Not only were capable, daring leaders requisite, but for the crew a large number of men who would trust their leaders and each other. In the crew must be found cool, daring spirits to steer the vessel safely through what often seemed certain capture and to crowd an engine to its last inch of speed. In other words, the members of the crew must also be adventurers, attracted to the service by enormous bounties and wages paid in gold or silver.

The crew of the *Rob Roy* as described by its owner was a heterogeneous set, embracing, besides its Scotch owner, a native of Cork as captain, and as cook a burly Englishman with a broken nose who delighted in the sobriquet of "Cheshire Bob." For one voyage from Havana to Galveston, Watson seems to have acquired a worthless set for his crew; on arrival at port some of the firemen and trimmers tried to slip to a boat which was lying alongside. They had some difficulty in explaining their motives for deserting. They did not want to be captured, shipwrecked, worked to death, starved, or otherwise abused, as they had been on the vessel they were forsaking. Upon Watson's demanding of the engineer what they meant, the latter said that some of the crew had been picked up about the grogshops of Havana and a more "worthless, despicable set he had never seen"; that they had been recently imported by the loafers and sea lawyers who infest seaports and had come to Havana to prey on the blockade-runners; that they had intended merely to get their advance pay and desert, but that the strict laws of Havana had prevented that manoeuvre. Watson remarked dryly that the provost

---

[58] Sprunt was educated at the Grove Academy of Kenansville and at Mr. Jewett's school, but when ready to enter the University of North Carolina, it proved impossible to send him. He was always studious and read widely so that his writings and collections on the history of the Cape Fear region are valuable.—J. G. de Roulhac Hamilton, "James Sprunt," in *Literary and Historical Activities in North Carolina*, I, 92. He found pleasure in the fact that he once took the regular pilot's place in bringing in the *Don*.

guard would promptly conscript them into the army, an "excellent place for straightening up such fellows."[59]

Fortunately sometimes for the blockade-runners, quick wits were scattered among the crew as well as among the officers. The *Night Hawk* owed her escape from destruction on her very first run to one of her Irish firemen. The vessel had grounded on the bar at Wilmington and was boarded by men from the United States launches. The captors had put the crew into the boats and had just applied the torch to the ship, when the Irishman sang out, "Begorra, we shall all be in the air in a minute, the ship is full of gunpowder!" Off rushed the northern sailors to their boats in a panic, rowing off as fast as they could, but leaving behind them in their haste seven captives and the burning vessel to be ultimately salvaged.[60]

Blockade-running became ultimately an extra-hazardous occupation. The northern consuls and officials bought photographs of blockade-runners at Nassau and Havana, together with whatever information was available concerning them. This material was preserved in Ludlow Street Jail in New York with the result that, if a native southerner tried to pose as an Englishman, he was often identified and sent off—not to England—but to Fort Lafayette or Fort Warren. A certain Charleston mariner on board a British vessel with a crew on his way to take charge of a new ship at Bermuda was surprised to have a Federal officer produce his own photograph with his history written on the back and tell him exactly where he was bound for, even identifying the members of his crew.[61]

The value to owners of cargoes borne by these blockade-runners was very great. During the four years of the war about 66 vessels left England and New York to run the blockade into Wilmington; of this number more than 40 were destroyed by their own crews or captured, but most of them, before coming to this sad end, succeeded in making several runs and thus abundantly repaid their owners for the investment. The *Advance* ran the blockade seven or eight times. The regularity of her trips was remarkable under the conditions. It was common to hear on the streets of Wilmington the remark, "The *Advance* will be in tomorrow." And she was. The

---

[59] Watson, *Adventures of a Blockade Runner*, 37, 39, 73, 301-302.

[60] Taylor, *Running the Blockade*, 121-122.

[61] Told by Captain Usina after the war to a Confederate veterans' association. See Sprunt, *Chronicles of the Cape Fear River*, 390-391.

profit on 1,000 bales of cotton and on the goods carried in exchange would net $250,000 on a transaction covering only two weeks.

The cargo carried by the *Venus*, to take a concrete instance, could generally be computed at $250,000 and consisted of blankets, shoes, manfactures of all sorts, and mysterious cases labeled "hardware." Badeau states that in little more than a year before the capture of Fort Fisher, which defended Wilmington, the ventures of British capitalists and speculators entering that port alone had amounted to $66,000,000 in gold, and that $65,000,000 worth of cotton reckoned in gold had been exported in payment for the goods brought in. Cotton, purchasable in the Confederate States for three cents a pound, was sold in England at the equivalent of forty cents to a dollar a pound, and the profits on some kinds of goods introduced into the Confederacy were as great. It is no exaggeration to say that this trade during the war period, if the initial cost of the ships be included, approached close to $150,000,000 in standard gold currency.[62]

The fever of speculation infected everyone, of course, foreigner as well as native, who had money to invest. According to a clergyman who wrote the governor of New York in October, 1861, a British consul at New Orleans was interested in a blockade-runner then being loaded at Montreal, where the deputy consul general was supposed to be helping him. The German Jews of Richmond were supposed to be extensively involved in the traffic with Baltimore and northern cities.[63]

If a run was profitable to the owners of the cargo, it was also profitable to the officers and crews on the boats. Captains received as high as $5,000 for the round trip, one half in advance—a rule which applied also to the crew; the chief officer, $1,250; the second and third mates, $750; the chief engineer, $2,500; the members of the crew and firemen, about $250; and the pilot, $3,500. Pilots had to be especially well paid after it became known that the United States dealt severely with them. They were not exchanged.[64]

Officials had to be propitiated, as on their favor depended in great measure the possibility of a quick turnover, and so the narrow, trim

---

[62] The calculations are from *ibid.*, 372-373. His statement of the number of vessels in the trade appears in "Tales of the Cape Fear Blockade," *North Carolina Booklet*, I, No. 10, 74.

[63] *O. W. R.*, Ser. 2, II, 123; Putnam, *Richmond during the War*, 203.

[64] Bradlee, *op. cit.*, 143-144.

vessels became the scenes of prodigal hospitality. In the words of Taylor: "There never was too much to eat and drink there [Wilmington], and the commonest luxuries were almost things of the past; so when it became known that there was practically open house on board the *Banshee* friends flocked to her. She soon attained great popularity, and it was really a sight when our luncheon bell rang to see guests, invited and uninvited, turn up from all quarters. We made them all welcome, and when our little cabin was filled, we generally had an overflow meeting on deck.

"What a pleasure it was to see them eat and drink! Men who had been accustomed to live on corn-bread and bacon, and to drink nothing but water, appreciated our delicacies, our bottled beer, good brandy, and, on great occasions, our champagne warmed their hearts toward us. The chief steward used to look at me appealingly, as a hint that our stores would never last out; in fact we were often on very short commons before we got back to Nassau. But we had our reward. If any special favor were asked it was always granted, if possible, to the *Banshee*."[65]

Hobart's picture of the feast prepared in celebration of a successful entry includes the beverage prepared for the toast. "The drink we mixed in two horse buckets cleaned up for the occasion; a dozen or so of claret, a couple of bottles of brandy, and half a dozen of soda water, the whole cooled with two or three lumps of ice (of which article, as if in mockery, the Southerners had heaps)."[66]

One instance of the way in which blockade-runners were hindered may be in point. William Watson found his vessel, the *Rob Roy*, seized by the government to do duty at Fort Velasco at the mouth of the Brazos River, as the authorities had been warned that a large Union force was meditating a descent on the coast to offset the failure at Sabine Pass. In the recovery of his vessel, luck played a large rôle, for Watson happened to encounter at Magruder's headquarters an officer with whom he had been left wounded on the battlefield of Corinth. In a word, army officers were reluctant to lend aid to

[65] Taylor, *Running the Blockade*, 64-65.
[66] Hobart, *Sketches from My Life*, 16. In another place he speaks of "visits from thirsty and hungry Southerners of all ranks and denominations, many of whom had not tasted alcohol in any form for months, to whom whatever they liked to eat or drink was freely given."—*Ibid.*, 102.

blockade-runners, as they were likely to suspect them of being Yankee spies.[67]

For blockade-running foreign subjects had certain assets. While a Confederate citizen had to expect, if caught trying to break the blockade, imprisonment for the duration of the war, an alien was usually early in the war released and dismissed to his own country. They were much more likely to have had sea experience than the numerous inland-born natives. When the war broke out and ports were blockaded, every old barge or river flatboat was picked up and made seaworthy to run the blockade. Foreign-born were usually prime movers in this enterprise.[68] They seem to have rendered valuable service as pilots in bringing the blockade-running boats into port. One of the most interesting of these pilots was an Englishman near the Brazos River in Texas who did not hesitate to take vessels drawing as much as six feet over the bar. When he appeared aboard in a sou'wester, his "weather-beaten face ribbed like the sea sand, a grizzled beard curled round his mouth in round tufts exactly like barnacles," he might well have been the old man of the sea in person. His salutation inspired confidence, "My name is Lyon, I am Lyon by name and lion by nature; the British Lion they call me here, so now the British lion has got you in charge, and you are out of all danger."[69]

The foreign blockade-runners proved also the one means of communication with the outside world. A newspaper correspondent of the London *Times* intrusted to Hobart some of his articles for the *Thunderer*. Taylor was regularly the bearer of dispatches from the Confederate agent at Nassau to Richmond, and to facilitate his journeys within the Confederacy held a pass, which could, however, jeopardize his status as a neutral if his journeyings took him into debatable territory; and Watson, when there was no longer safe conveyance between Texas and the rest of the world via Brownsville, was charged by General Magruder with important messages to be delivered to the Confederate consul at Havana or mailed to him at Tampico or Vera Cruz.[70]

---

[67] Watson, *Adventures of a Blockade-Runner*, 54-59, 62-63.
[68] See the record of one Dave McLusky, a Scotchman, who had settled on the Trinity River in Teras.—*Ibid.*, 89-91.   [69] *Ibid.*, 45-46.
[70] Hobart, *op. cit.*, 177-178; Taylor, *Running the Blockade*, 133-135; Watson, *Adventures of a Blockade Runner*, 105-136.

This organized attack by neutrals against the Federal blockade opened a new era in the history of blockade. The United States had to contend with something new—with neutral merchants forming public companies with the express object of breaking the blockade, and establishing regular bases almost in the enemy's waters. When the United States government, driven to extremes to throttle this trade, tried to blockade neutral ports where her enemy was operating, England objected with the result that the United States had to yield to international law. Thomas E. Taylor, mere youth though he was, was the chief organizer of a great and systematic attack on the blockade of the southern ports, such as had not been witnessed before.

No wonder that the toast among blockade-runners ran in this wise: to "the Confederates that produce the cotton; the Yankees that maintain the blockade and keep up the price of cotton; the Britishers that buy the cotton and pay the high price for it." To this might well have been added "and to the foreigners of every nation who man the boats." With a rousing cheer the toast concluded, "Here is to all three [four], and a long continuance of the war, and success to blockade-runners."[71]

[71] *Ibid.*, 305.

X

FOREIGNERS IN THE CIVILIAN POPULATION DURING THE WAR

To say that there was a tremendous division of sentiment in the nation as a whole over the question of secession is a truism. Inability to see eye to eye on the most burning question of 1861 up to the actual outbreak of war was manifest in many parts of the South and even in many families, as is well known. That same division of opinion extended, as we have seen, to the foreign population with the cleavage most marked in the German element. In general, however, once war was certain, sentiment crystalized strongly among the native whites in support of a new Confederacy and in strong opposition to coercion by an oppressive North. The foreign elements reacted in much the same way. A striking illustration is afforded by one Captain Henry Hunsicker, a native of Germany, who was so eager to go to the front that he turned over the post office at Shreveport to the first person he could seize and dashed off to join the Shreveport Rebels.[1]

The Germans, as has already been asserted, were almost everywhere opposed in principle to slavery, and were inclined to take their oath of allegiance to the government of the United States seriously. Left to themselves they would almost unanimously have preferred to remain neutral. But no such position is allowed by a dominant majority in any war. Pressure was brought to bear in its many diabolical guises by vigilance committees; public opinion and vigorous propaganda induced many to enlist, and the reluctant were shortly subjected to the conscript laws. It was only a very small minority, and that in localities where they could be protected by an overwhelming majority in the local population, which could resist such pressure.

At first there was complaint of the failure at New Braunfels, Texas, to respond promptly to the call for volunteers. It will be recalled that Comal County had been one of the few German communities in Texas which supported secession in the referendum vote on the action of the convention. While not for slavery, the natural con-

[1] O'Pry, *Chronicles of Shreveport*, 169.

servatism of an upper bourgeois class feeling inclined them to avoid a break with their American-born neighbors, and to prefer to see their state secede with her sister states of the South. Yet a T. J. Thomas complained to the governor on April 20, 1861, of his fellow towns-men at New Braunfels: "They have not done much as yet. They are hard to move. There are few Americans here and we feel our re-sponsibility. I would earnestly urge upon your Excellency to arm our men here who may not be able to arm themselves. This is the only excuse they have offered and should they not respond nothing short of a force Draft upon them will stir and start them."[2] In a similar strain wrote Dr. Felix Bracht to Governor Clark a few days later. Dr. Bracht had secured a commission from Colonel van Dorn to raise a company of infantry in Morris County but, as a nonmilitary man, he had had it transferred to a Gustavus Hoffman, while he sought a surgeon's appointment. "Our people are rather slow to move and there will be some delay, but finally there will be as full and a good company mustered in Comal County."[3] But by the fol-lowing September he is sharper against his fellow New Braunfelsers. "Our people won't move, and although a somewhat better feeling prevails, among the young men, that ought to come forward now is the greatest reluctance firmly grown against any service whatever. Older persons even such as used to be not over patriotic before, are quite enraged and would like to see the laggards drafted. I know you feel great reluctance to that yourself, and therefore I beg you to permit Mr. Hoffman to make this last trial."[4]

It is noticeable, however, that the German press had become cir-cumspect. The conservative position of the *Neu Braunfelser Zeitung* under the leadership of Lindheimer from the moment the results of the 1860 election were known has been noted. The order for martial law, proclaimed by General Robert Bechem, printed, naturally, for the German section of Texas in both German and English,[5] dated

[2] Governor's Letters, March-May, 1861, Governor Edward Clark, Archives, Texas State Library. Governor Houston, it will be recalled, had been removed by this time and the lieutenant governor, Edward Clark, had succeeded him.

[3] *Ibid.*, Bracht to Governor Clark, April 26, 1861.

[4] Governor's Letters, June-December, 1861, Archives, Texas State Library. That the good doctor had either secured his medical training with too little attention to English or had forgotten what he had learned will be the reader's first reaction, but one must recall that he came from Germany in 1849.—Viktor Bracht, *Texas in 1848*, Preface, xi-xii.

[5] The writer has seen a copy of this proclamation in the Pfeuffer Library in New Braunfels.

June 14, 1862, cowed some of the German citizens. Some of the hardier souls left for Mexico or for the North; some evaded actual service by securing exemptions or were detailed as teamsters, while some evaded the conscript officers by hiding in ravines and thickets.

It is not necessary to rest upon the general statements regarding the way in which the Germans sought to evade service. One does not dig very deep into the records concerning them without uncovering some instances—cases with which one can very readily sympathize. Before the war descended the more farsighted who were able to get away took steps for their departure. Viktor Bracht, born at Düsseldorf, brother of the Dr. Felix Bracht already encountered, was a wholesale grocer in San Antonio, who had taken his family to New York in 1860. After a six months' visit he wisely sailed, with his stock of merchandise, not for Texas, but for Mexico, where he remained in business until 1866. Another case in point is August Santleben. His father had come to Texas from Hanover in 1845 and had settled on a farm near Castroville. By July, 1850, the father had taken out his American citizenship papers. Although he had voted against secession, he submitted to the will of the majority. Partly with a view to providing employment for his son and possibly with a view to keeping him out of the army, he engaged in freighting cotton from Columbia to Eagle Pass by ox team. In September, 1862, the son, then nearly seventeen years old, under age and "without political prejudices," which probably meant that he was not for the Confederacy, went to Mexico where he would surely escape the service.[6] The story of how the government dealt with these recalcitrants belongs to a later chapter. It could not criticize a man who, like Henry August Miller, after several years' residence in Fredericksburg, Virginia, found himself rejected by the army because of low stature. A wise man, knowing from experiences in Europe the conditions of a country under war, he returned to the Harz Mountains until the war was over.[7]

Meanwhile the German women on the Texas farms and in the villages suffered just as did the other women in the Confederacy and were driven to the same expedients. They took cornhusks from their

[6] H. Castro to Governor Clark, San Antonio, Texas, June 15, 1861, Governor's Letters, June-December, 1861, Archives, Texas State Library.

[7] Personal testimony of his granddaughter, Marian Reed.

bedticks to weave hats, they used nuts and sumac berries for dyes. But they enjoyed some advantages over their American neighbors, for, because of their European connections, they were able to bring in calico from France through Mexico, so that the little German girls strutted about in "imported" dresses to the envy of little native-born lasses who had to don dull homespun.[8]

The attitude of the Mexicans scattered through the civilian population varied with the individual—some were coöperative, others distinctly troublesome. One of the most curious letters encountered in this study came from the pen of a Mexican residing in San Antonio, written shortly after the opening of the war, in which he cordially placed his services at the disposition of the governor and tendered much gratuitous advice as to how resources might be procured. "The eminent services I rendered Texas since twenty years are well-known to Your Excellency. My doctrine being that is nothing done, long as it remains some things to be done. I take this opportunity to tender my concurs to the state in any way you think proper. My long and practical experience in financial affairs may yet be useful to the country if properly applied by Your Excellency."

In the same letter he offers the services of his nephew, Lorenzo Castro, "the most intelligent young man of the state, so judged by public opinion at large." He also "tender his service to you. He has already been employed to procure the sensus in Several countys. Also has act as commissioner for claims embracing Indians depredations. And is at this moment county commissioner of Bexar. He has never received any compensation for his labors. But will serve the County without any regard for remuneration so long as the State needed credit and help from his Citizens."[9] In an additional letter two months later he urges "Thresory Bonds as the most simple way to obtain the desired effect" of a currency to meet current expenses.[10] At the close of his second letter of August 22 he renews the offer of his nephew's and his own services and of those of his grandson, Angelo Causui. It does not appear that the state of Texas availed itself of the generous offers of the Castro family but the desire of

[8] The writer is indebted for these bits to Mrs. D. Crockett Riley of Fredericksburg who was herself one of these favored Germans girls and remembered the war deprivations vividly.

[9] H. Castro to Governor Clark, San Antonio, June 15, 1861, Governor's Letters, June-December, 1861, Archives, Texas State Library.

[10] August 22, 1861, from Austin.—*Ibid.*

these Mexicans, whether aliens or adopted citizens, to serve the country seems clear.

On the other hand, acting impetuously or obstructively, a group of Mexicans did cause the state authorities annoyance. In Zapata County, bordering on the Rio Grande, a band of thirty or forty Mexicans shortly before April 12, 1861, organized and armed themselves to go to the county seat to prevent the officers from taking the oath to the Confederate government required by the Texas convention. They threatened the collector of customs, the assessor, and collector of taxes, and the few who had taken the oath. The action seems, so far as it is possible from the meager records to judge, to have been an impetuous gesture of loyalty to the United States.[11] In general, however, the Confederate and Texan authorities were not troubled with a positive attitude toward the Federal government on the part of Mexican residents, but rather with a negative attitude toward the Confederacy. They refused to enroll in either state or Confederate forces, retired across the river, and sometimes raided ranches on the Texas side. They were accused of being sympathetic with the United States, but it is hard to determine whether their actual sympathy extended further than to a desire to stay out of the Confederate army and a readiness to join lawless Mexicans in plundering their neighbors. When conscripted, they made unreliable soldiers in general, as has been already stated, and gave much trouble by desertion.[12] Everywhere in the portions of Texas where they constituted a considerable element in the population, they had to be reckoned with by the civil and military authorities. The army found difficulty, because of the barrier of language, in buying soldiers' provisions from them. One soldier relates how the commissary sergeant became so worried in dealing with the Mexican owners of cattle that to escape a harassing situation with which he did not know how to deal he feigned illness. The relator of the tale was then designated to provide the beef for the day's rations. He called upon each of the Mexican companies having beeves for sale and secured the needed meat rations by the simple

[11] Related in a letter by Henry Redmond to Colonel John S. Ford, from Carizo (county estate?), Zapata County, April 12, 1861.—Governor's Letters, March-May, 1861, Governor Edward Clark, Archives, Texas State Library. It is not clear that a letter of B. F. Neal to Governor Clark, dated Corpus Christi, April 21, 1861, refers to the same episode.—Ibid.

[12] See the comment of an officer in O. W. R., Ser. 1, IV, 131-132, 137.

device of pointing out the beeves desired and then having them roped and butchered.[13]

Meanwhile Mexicans were to be encountered on the ranches during the war years much as they had been before. A war so remote was scarcely noticed or realized by the *vaqueros*, the local name for helpers or hands on the ranches, who usually understood little or no English, or by the few Mexican women who did the cooking and housekeeping on some ranches and were as unreliable as the men. The wife of a Confederate surgeon tells how her Mexican servant went off, leaving her alone with a day-old baby.[14]

Complaints arose from civilians that the vote of the Mexicans was abused—probably by no means a new complaint. In the gubernatorial election of August, 1861, in Texas it was charged that every Mexican was provided with a Lubbock ticket and that Mexicans not over sixteen years of age were allowed to vote. Occasionally they were involved in illicit transactions such as negotiating for the sale of counterfeit Confederate money.[15]

As was to be expected, the large owners of property, slaves, and plantations among the foreigners in the South were both sympathetic and helpful to the cause. Mr. Thornton, an Englishman possessing a very handsome estate a mile from Centreville, Virginia, had fled on the approach of the Union forces before the first battle of Manassas. As he was returning later to ascertain the fate of his buildings and stock, he noted large columns of troops on a detour to flank Sudley Ford. Penetrating the woods by cowpaths known to him but not to the enemy, he was able to evade them though almost surrounded and to furnish General Evans with valuable information.[16] Another gentleman of the same nativity, in charge of or owning an estate near Suffolk, Virginia, with a permit to pass the Union lines at will and to purchase supplies for his estate, abused this favor to an alien in order to procure large supplies of sugar, coffee, clothes, bacon, shoes,

[13] H. A. Graves, *Andrew Jackson Potter, The Fighting Parson of the Texan Frontier,* 137.

[14] For allusions to Mexicans in Texas during the war period, see North, *Five Years in Texas,* 177-178, and especially Williams, *With the Border Ruffians,* 316, 317, 318. The experience of the surgeon's wife is told in a letter to her mother, unsigned, undated.—Confederate Museum at Richmond, S 788.

[15] For the complaint about the Mexican vote in the election see Walter Oakes to Governor Clark, August 27, 1861, Governor's Letters, June-December, 1861, Archives, Texas State Library. For the charge of Mexican complicity in counterfeit money see letter from J. A. Quintero to Secretary Benjamin, *O. W. R.,* Ser. 2, V, 842.

[16] *Battle-fields of the South,* I, 55-56.

medicine, surgical instruments, and tools from Norfolk for the Confederate troops. The only trouble the pleasant arrangement cost the Confederate general was the necessity of placing a permanent and trustworthy guard to insure safe landing of the boats.[17] Always the foreign-born planter found it prudent not to oppose the views of his neighbors. It is interesting to note a Scotchman of good education in Mississippi who, after many years of industry, had acquired an estate of four hundred acres of land but who owned only two Negroes. Even though he professed to be a strong secessionist,[18] he had the grace to be very angry over the denial of her salary to a teacher on the grounds that the treasury was empty, for he attributed this action instead to the fact of her being from the North.

When the tables were turned and the Union recovered control, the alien, however zealously he strove to maintain a neutral position, often found himself caught between the two millstones. Such a record has come down in the case of Mr. U., a Scotchman of good reputation and social standing who had been for many years a citizen of New Orleans. Refusal to participate in the secession movement, retirement from business, and seclusion did not save him when General Butler descended upon New Orleans. Shortly after the order to deliver up all arms by a certain date had gone into effect his house was searched, and U. lodged in jail when an old fowling piece, which had evidently been "planted" under some lumber in his rear courtyard for the sake of the reward, was found. Release came only with the payment of a very large ransom.[19]

In some parts of the country, especially in remote Texas, the planters and ranchers went about their affairs much as if there were no war. Some settlers, like two Scotchmen by the name of Cockburn, kept on about their ranches, planting, tending cattle, and fighting Indians, killing the marauders or being scalped, just as in the days before the war.[20] A certain Britisher sold out his interest in a ranch and came to Brownsville to seek passage to England on a blockade-

<hr/>

[17] French, Two Wars, 155.

[18] "Sometimes I thought that he really was what he professed to be, at other times, I doubted it, thinking that, perhaps, he only advocated those sentiments to keep in the good graces of his more affluent neighbors. . . ." This was the opinion of the victim, as voiced in her account of her experiences.—E. C. Kent, Four Years in Secessia, 5-6.

[19] Watson, Life in the Confederate Army, 435-436.

[20] Williams, op. cit., 397, tells of how these two brothers were attacked by Comanches in April, 1865. The two men fought desperately for their lives and property, but both men and the entire family of the married brother were killed.

runner from the mouth of the Rio Grande. After years of living in Canada and Texas, he had turned his face homewards, probably only hastened in that determination by the conditions into which war had thrown the country. He died in Brownsville before he was able to set sail.[21]

Some of the group of English and Irish who had settled in Peters' Colony, Texas, were too old for military service by the time the war came. They continued to live on their ranches during the war years, but rendered service vicariously by paying their taxes in kind. A Spaniard who owned a fine piece of property in Eastern Texas probably reflects the feeling of many foreigners who became victims of a war which they neither understood nor were truly interested in, but which they saw threatening their possessions. A Unionist who was seeking to escape north through the eastern part of Texas, because it was inhabited chiefly by Spaniards and Mexicans, accepting the hospitality of this Spaniard, described him as seemingly "very much depressed by the sad condition the secessionists had brought the country to."[22]

The number of professional men of foreign birth who pursued their various callings, often under difficulties, during the war years was not negligible. German pastors and Irish priests, and even French-born priests in Louisiana, are to be expected, but hardly an Irish Methodist clergyman or an English cleric ministering to a Presbyterian congregation. The greatest anomaly was the beloved rector of fashionable St. Paul's in Richmond, where President Davis, General Lee, and many notables worshiped, the Reverend Mr. Minnigerode, a German who conducted the Episcopalian services with a strong Teutonic accent and prayed fervently for the success of the southern arms. With a career as varied in America as it had been in Europe, where political activity in the revolt of 1830 had driven him into prison and then into voluntary exile, he moved from a position of eminence as teacher and orator in Philadelphia to the chair of classics in the College of William and Mary in Virginia. Thenceforth he adopted the cause of the southern slaveholders, joined the church which seemed the bulwark of slavocracy, and in 1848 left his chair

[21] *Ibid.,* 301 ff.
[22] Jackson, *Sixty Years in Texas,* 66-71, 75-76, 84, 91-92; Alfred E. Mathews, *Interesting Narrative; Being a Journal of the Flight of Alfred E. Mathews,* 17. Nacogdoches was still chiefly inhabited by Spaniards and Mexicans.

for the pulpit, thus estranging himself somewhat from his German brethren. He was called the father-confessor of the secession and remained loyal to the leaders in their misfortune, visiting Jefferson Davis repeatedly during his imprisonment at Fortress Monroe to carry to him spiritual consolation. He was a brilliantly gifted man and was held the best pulpit orator in the South.[23]

The Reverend T. D. Ozanne—whom we have seen serving as chaplain in a Mississippi hospital—returned to England late in 1862 after many futile efforts for more than a year to find a more salubrious climate, a complete convert to the southern point of view. We shall meet him yet again when we attempt to evaluate the influence of resident aliens on European opinion, as he presented a defense of the southerner's rights and a warning against northern bigotry.[24] In the Government Street Presbyterian Church in Mobile the Reverend William Thomas Hamilton, born in Sheffield, England, had served for more than twenty-six years up to the opening year of the war.[25] Dr. Smyth, another Presbyterian clergyman and non-American, was long a resident of Charleston and became such a partisan of secession that he wrote a bitter article for the issue of the *Southern Presbyterian Review* for April, 1863.[26] After the importing business, with which the young German clerk, Conrad, repeatedly mentioned in these pages, was connected, was moved to Wilmington when Charleston was virtually closed by the capture of Morris Island, he found living accommodations in the home of an unmarried Methodist minister, an Irishman. The pastor reserved two rooms for his own use, and turned the rest of the house over to Conrad and six other guests in return for his board. Conrad remarks that the clergyman was too

[23] See Schuricht, *History of the German Element in Virginia*, II, 42-43; Kaufmann, *Die Deutschen im amerikanischen Bürgerkriege*, 569; Frederick Kapp, *Aus und über Amerika. Thatsachen und Erlebnisse*, II, 374. Kapp's comment gives an insight into the type of man he was: "Er ist ein fein gebildeter Mann, in der deutschen Politik linkser als der radikalste Fortschrittsmann, aber in amerikanischen Dingen weniger für das Zuckerbrot als für die Peitsche."—*Ibid.*

[24] His view was that by a violent disruption of the ties that bind master and servant, abolition of slavery would, in attempting to benefit the slave, destroy both.—*The South as It Is*, 161 ff. He affords a sharp contrast with the Reverend J. R. Balme, another Englishman, who settled in the South after becoming naturalized. Instead of accepting the southern view on slavery, he lifted his voice against it with the result that he narrowly escaped lynching, and was obliged to leave the country. He returned to England before the war. See extract from *Morning Journal*, Appendix, in Balme, *Synopsis of the American War*.

[25] Craighead, *Mobile: Fact and Tradition*, 247.

[26] Note also the comment about it in an article, Wm. C. Dundas, "Enmities and Barbarities of the Rebellion," *Danville Quarterly Review*, IV, 568-569.

generous, a liberality which he explains as probably actuated by a desire to win them to his church—a vain hope. The reader takes some satisfaction, in the interest of justice, in the reflection that the clergyman must have fared well, as the guests had access through their blockade-running ships to all the delicacies which entered that port.[27]

A number of German pastors serving charges throughout the South come to view. A church in the Tennessee synod of the German Lutheran faith, St. John's near Wytheville, Virginia, was open throughout the war, under the care of the Reverend J. A. Brown until 1862, then of the Reverend E. H. McDonald, and finally of the Reverend W. D. Rödel. Despite his German name the last-mentioned had to conduct services in English. While Scheibert was visiting in Charleston he met a German preacher from Berlin whose name is not mentioned, to whom he acknowledged his indebtedness for an insight into many peculiar customs and institutions of the South, especially the slavery question.[28] The pastor of the Clio Street church in New Orleans during the war period was a Herr Pastor Pressler, who seems to have definitely advanced the interests of his congregation by establishing a parochial school and by so increasing the membership that in 1864, during one of the blackest years of the war, it was decided to build a larger church as soon as possible. Presumably the German churches continued to be served by German clergymen. With this group belongs James K. Gutheim, who came from Prussia in 1845 and served in a synagogue in New Orleans through the war.[29]

There may have been a small group of Scandinavian pastors scattered through the South, but the writer has been able to uncover but one. Inasmuch as the Norwegian settlement at Prairieville, Texas, erected a church as early as 1854 and called a Lutheran minister from Norway, A. E. Fredericksen by name, who arrived the next year, it is possible that he was still serving the parish throughout the war period.[30] The Swedes located near Austin bewailed the fact that they had no pastor.

[27] Conrad, *Schatten und Lichtblicke*, 90.
[28] Schuricht, *op. cit.*, II, 46; Scheibert, *Sieben Monate in den Rebellen-Staaten*, 11-12. It is probable that the clergyman was the Reverend Louis Müller, pastor of St. Matthew's Lutheran Church, 1848-1898.
[29] Deiler, *Zur Geschichte der deutschen Kirchengemeinde im Staate Louisiana*, 26. Pressler had this charge from 1859 to 1869. Gutheim is mentioned in Isaac Markens, *Hebrews in America*, 29.
[30] Blegen, *Norwegian Migration to America, 1825-1860*, 188. The presence of S. B. Newman, a Swedish Methodist minister who landed in Mobile in 1842 is no evidence

The first Catholic bishop of Natchitoches, consecrated at New Orleans in December, 1853, who served there until his death in 1875, had been born in Brittany, France—the Reverend Augustus Nary Martin. Father Mullen and Father O'Riley were Irishmen, as their names indicate. A French priest saved the Catholic church at Alexandria, Louisiana, for Father J. G. Belliel stood at the front door to threaten death to any Union soldier who attempted to apply the torch to the "house of God." His courage under fire, so to speak, may be attributed to the fact that he had been trained in the French army and attained the rank of lieutenant of cavalry before studying for the priesthood. Versatile to the end, it might be added, he was serving as professor of French at the Louisiana State Seminary at the time of his death in 1867. Out on the Texas plains another French missionary priest, the Reverend P. F. Parisot, an Oblate Father, was serving in the eastern part of the state, and was often called upon to shrive a dying soldier, Union or Confederate.[31]

In the neighborhood of Knoxville, Tennessee, a couple of Confederate soldiers stumbled on a French home where the family, great "Rebs," delighted to do all they could for these Confederate soldiers. The head of the family proved to be a clergyman, of what denomination does not appear, but obviously Protestant as other families in the neighborhood collected for his sermon, which was given in French as "some of them did not understand English." True to the tradition of French cookery, the clergyman treated the soldiers to a "splendid dinner" and served each of them a glass of homemade wine.[32]

---

that he remained there until 1865.—*Year Book of the Swedish-American Society of America,* 1908, 120-121.

[31] *Biographical and Historical Memoirs of Louisiana,* II, 140; Mary Gay, *Life in Dixie during the War,* 66; *Confederate Veteran,* II, 334; G. P. Whittington, "Rapides Parish, Louisiana—a History," *Louisiana Historical Quarterly,* XVIII, 39; P. F. Parisot, *Reminiscences of a Texas Missionary,* 105. Another very interesting Catholic priest who was serving on the Texas border in 1857 on the eve of the war cannot be included in the absence of proof that he was still there during any part of the war period, but the wide sweep of his territory is so illuminating concerning the time as to merit a place at least in the notes. Reference is made to L'Abbé E. Domenech, whose charge was the German Catholics scattered in the towns, colonies, and villages of northwest Texas, and the Irish soldiers among the United States troops who were stationed in the frontier army posts. It included the wide sweep from Castroville, thirty miles west of San Antonio, to Fredericksburg and New Braunfels.—Emmanuel H. Domenech, *Journal d'un Missionaire au Texas et au Mexique.* A translation exists called *Missionary Adventures in Texas and Mexico,* 42.

[32] For a Catholic service an altar would have to be erected, which could, of course, be done in a private home; but the absence of reference to it and the emphasis on the sermon makes the inference that it was a Protestant service seem a just one.—Richard Hancock, *Hancock's Diary, or a History of the Second Tennessee Confederate Cavalry,* 39 n. The

Surprisingly enough, the research has turned up very little about the professional group practicing medicine. The name of one lone German has been encountered, a Dr. Wilhelm Grebe, a Richmond surgeon who, according to a notation on a record roll, was detailed as a practicing doctor from Company A, Nineteenth Virginia Militia, for the months of July and August, 1864. Yet obviously the civilian population required the care of attending physicians, and it is entirely unlikely that there were not at least a few foreigners among them. Fremantle encountered an Irish physician at Jackson, Mississippi.

Whatever the southerners of the ante-bellum days may have thought of the superiority of Anglo-Saxon blood in general, they certainly must have had a very great respect for the educational training of Europe, or they would never have intrusted the education of their children in so great a degree as they did to Germans and French. If these foreign teachers had been restricted to French men and women to impart the proper French accent and to teach dancing, their selection would have been explicable, but we find in addition a goodly sprinkling of teachers of many nationalities throughout the educational system of the South, from tutors of children in the home, too young to be sent away to school, to the incumbents of university chairs.

In the list of such teachers probably the most distinguished who served during any portion of the war was the Swedish-German, Maximilian Schele de Ver, who after 1844 was professor of modern languages at the University of Virginia. A colleague at this institution was Professor George Frederick Holmes, who filled the chair of history and literature from 1857 to his death in 1897. Holmes had been born in British Guiana, educated in England, and had built a reputation as an educator at various southern colleges. At the University of Alabama a Frenchman, a M. Andre Deloffre, was a professor in the department of modern languages during all the war years until the university buildings were burned during General J. T. Croxton's raid on Tuscaloosa on April 4, 1865. Madame Deloffre saved their home by placing a French flag on the front door. But her husband was unable to save the university buildings, not even the library, although he, as librarian, led the commanding officer of the Union forces to

clergyman was probably M. Esperendieu. See Samuel C. Williams, "John Mitchel, The Irish Patriot, Resident of Tennessee," *East Tennessee Historical Society Publications*, 1938, No. 10, 56.

that building and unlocked the doors to display the valuable collection of books. "It is a great pity," was the reply of the northern officer, "but my orders are imperative."[33]

Scattered through the smaller colleges and seminaries were a number of persons of greater or less obscurity, some of whose names have not been lost. Professor David Duncan, an Irish graduate of the Scottish university at Glasgow, was filling the chair of ancient languages at Wofford College in 1861; James Kennedy Patterson, who had been born in Scotland, dropped from the professorship of Latin and Greek in Stewart College, Tennessee, to the principalship of the Transylvania High School, where he served throughout the war and helped to keep education going. Another Irishman who had received his formal training at Trinity College, Dublin, was William Irwin, principal of the St. John's Military Academy at Spartanburg during the war.[34] Barhamville Institute, on the outskirts of Columbia, South Carolina, was conducted by Madame Sophie Sosnowski, of Polish ancestry though born in Baden, the daughter of the court physician. She had arrived in America with her husband, an ex-officer of the army, in 1838 and settled somewhere in the North, but after his death a very few years later had moved to Columbia, South Carolina, where she had established with her two daughters a school for girls. She had the daughters of some of the best families of the South in her school and her responsibility in protecting her young charges when Sherman swept through Columbia was no light one. She tried to return to their homes those whose parents were residing in the

[33] The writer hyphenates De Ver because he was born in Sweden, but had been reared in Germany. After his first arrival in America he edited for a time the *Alte und Neue Welt* in Philadelphia, and then went to Charlottesville in 1844, as stated in the text.— Eickhoff, *In der neuen Heimath*, 204. For Holmes see *The South in the Building of the Nation*, XI, 505. He had served as president of the University of Mississippi for a single session, 1848-49.

After the war M. Deloffre returned to France, where years later Major Caleb Huse, purchasing agent for the war department, met him on the streets of Paris. He lived there in reduced circumstances to a very great age. For the completeness of the record it should be added that M. Deloffre came to the university in 1853, serving as tutor that year and as instructor in 1854.—*Historical Catalogue of the Officers and Alumni of the University of Alabama, 1821-1870.* The writer owes the intimate details to Miss Alice Wyman, present librarian at that institution.

[34] For Duncan see J. B. O. Landrum, *History of Spartanburg County*, 469-470. Just prior to teaching at Wofford College, he had been at Randolph-Macon College. Patterson seems to have been a schoolman of considerable ability, for after the war he was sent by Kentucky to the International Geographical Congress in Paris and to the British Association in Bristol, England, and in 1890 represented his state at the British Association which met at Leeds, England.—*The South in the Building of the Nation*, XII, 253. Irwin is mentioned in *Carolina Spartan*, January 19, 1860, December 11, 1862, and December 10, 1863.

upper part of South Carolina, but the rest she dispatched to North Carolina. It is interesting, although entirely natural, to know that General Tochman visited Madame Sosnowski at Columbia during the war.[35] At this institution was located Captain Strawinski, an exile of the Polish Revolution of 1830. The singing master at the school was an Italian, Torriani. His family was overheard, during the soul-rending days at Columbia when Sherman's army was destroying that city, praising in French "la sublime civilisation américaine." In the same city there lived also a German music teacher, who evidently had no connection with Barhamville, but gave private lessons. One also comes across an Englishwoman seeking a passport at Richmond in order to go to Warrenton, Virginia, where she was to teach music, and the ubiquitous German, a Mr. Brinkeman, at Greenville, Tennessee, who combined the functions of music teacher, orchestra director, and vinedresser, and was, in addition, a veteran of the battle of Waterloo.[36] Aldehoff's Seminary, located at Lookout Mountain, was conducted by a German, who was a most enthusiastic pro-southerner, owing his attitude partly perhaps to his wife, who was a descendant of Governor Sevier. Poor Professor Kliffmiller upon his return to Eufaula, Alabama, from New York, on August 23, 1861, where he had gone to place his wife and her sister on a vessel bound for Germany—probably to escape the war—became an object of solicitude to the Vigilance Committee. That body on examination, however, found him "true and loyal," and worthy of double praise in that, "foreigner as he was," he did not remain outside the lines but returned and "stood by us like the true man he is." He was returning to his position and probably to his salary at George H. Brown's Female School.[37]

Prominent among the instructors from Paris who established

[35] Sophie Sosnowski, "Burning of Columbia," *Georgia Historical Quarterly*, VIII, 200; Brooks, *Stories of the Confederacy*, 22. For Tochman's visit see *Report, House of Representatives Committee on Foreign Affairs*, C. S. A. Congress, 11.

[36] Sosnowski, *op. cit.*, 199-200, 209-210, mentions Strawinski and Torriani. Conrad, *op. cit.*, 111, tells of the German music teacher. At her request in order to afford her protection, because he was Hanoverian consul, he betook himself, with a tin box, in which he had placed valuable private and official papers, $600 in a leather belt about his body, and the Hanoverian flag, to her home. For the English lady see Hopley, *Life in the South*, II, 84; and for the German vinedresser, Robertson, *A Small Boy's Recollections of the Civil War*, 77.

[37] Morgan, *How It Was*, 24, speaks of Aldehoff's Seminary. Kliffmiller's case is described in "Reminiscences of Green Beauchamp," the Scrapbook of Barbour County Chapter, U. D. C., 1910, Alabama Military Archives, W. 80, Index.

schools in this country were M. and Mme Dieudonne de Felhorn, who opened a most unusual school at Mobile, bringing with them the teachers and paraphernalia for instruction exclusively in French. They also made an innovation in the school calendar by conducting classes the year round, holding the winter session in Mobile, the summer session on Spring Hill outside the city. The purpose was to "finish" young southern women according to the most approved Parisian manner. Since social intercourse was held more valuable than book learning, no textbooks were used, but young "ladies" must learn to observe and think and express themselves elegantly.[38]

At a boy's academy in Clinton, Louisiana, was an excellent teacher from Poland, De Brinsky by name. He was a very small man, not as large as some of his pupils, but able to command them by his personality. The record of a private school at Greenville, Tennessee, run by a "most excellent Irish lady, Miss Charlotte Wolfendon," has escaped oblivion.[39] Mr. Schardt, a German whom we have encountered in connection with the communistic community of Claiborne Parish, Louisiana, and who married the elder daughter of the founder of the community, was a music teacher and piano tuner who traveled about Louisiana in the vicinity of Bastrop.[40]

Nashville Female Academy, chartered as early as 1817, was under the direction of Dr. C. D. Elliott for the two decades preceding the war. In 1860 it boasted no less than seventeen music teachers, thirteen of whom had been drawn directly from the musical centers of Europe to give instruction to its 425 students of music. Elliott wrote Count Cavour and other prominent persons abroad for his teachers. At that time Nashville was surpassed as a music center only by New York, Boston, and New Orleans. Presumably some of these foreign musicians were still connected with the school during the one war year that it was still functioning. Data are not available but it is

[38] Craighead, op. cit., 166-167, describes this school at length: "The class wandered out in the open, or under the skies and the teacher read aloud or talked, and encouraged the pupils to give their impressions. Each teacher had a band of such followers. . . . The Felhorn girls may not have been profoundly learned, but they made an impression wherever they were, and in after life were quite successful as wives and mothers."

[39] The Clinton school rests on the oral testimony of D. W. Pipes of New Orleans, who attended his school in 1861-62 before he enlisted in the Washington Artillery.—Robertson, op. cit., 71, speaks of Miss Wolfendon.

[40] Schardt never became a member of the community. During the fifties he had conducted a German school in New Orleans and directed several German choral societies in New Orleans. As a forty-eighter he had many enemies so that he moved his family eventually to Hot Springs, Arkansas.—John H. Deiler, Eine vergessene deutsche Colonie, 3, 10.

likely that foreign-born teachers were to be found in the thirty-five colleges and 274 academies in Tennessee which claimed some 15,790 pupils at the outbreak of the war. All surely did not close their doors instantly in April, 1861.[41]

A very distinctive contribution to the cause of education was made by "Professor" J. J. Ayres, a Frenchman who was a member of the faculty in the Female Seminary at Edgeworth, North Carolina. In order to get some school textbooks stereotyped, the publishing firm of Sterling and Campbell of Greensboro, North Carolina, sent him to Liverpool, England, where he succeeded in getting some stereotypes made, and in bringing them back on Governor Vance's famous blockade-runner, the *Advance*, on its first successful run home. Cotton was sent by the firm to pay for the work. When General Stoneman circled the town of Greensboro in 1865 at the very end of the war, Campbell had the stereotypes buried in the basement of the office, as he feared the fall of Greensboro, though he did not anticipate the collapse of the Confederacy. It is surprising to learn that there was a great demand for books until the occupation of Greensboro by United States troops after Johnston's surrender.[42]

Private tutors, living on the plantations as members of the family, are harder to locate, though we know that they existed. The Swiss gentleman, Mr. Weidemeyer, who lived for many years, including at least the first war years, as tutor in the Dulany connection about Upperville, Virginia, may be taken as illustrative of a group—the size of which cannot be estimated. The tutor was passed from one family to another as his young charges outgrew him.[43] A particularly interesting illustration is Sarah L. Jones, an English teacher who was engaged by Governor John Milton of Florida as tutor to his children, and who found herself, when she went North in 1862, regarded as a rebel.[44]

[41] H. M. Doak, "The Development of Education in Tennessee," *American Historical Magazine*, VIII, 76-77; Libbie L. Morrow, "The Nashville Female Academy," *Nashville Banner*, June 22, 1907. Among the private papers of the Elliott family, preserved in the Tennessee Historical Society at Nashville, is a manuscript history of the institution by Elisabeth Elliott.

[42] James W. Albright, "Books Made in Dixie," *Southern Historical Society Papers*, XLI, 60.

[43] He was so serving June 15, 1862.—Marietta Andrews, *Scraps of Paper*, 19-20. The above is taken from the journal of her aunt, Mrs. Henry Grafton Dulany, of Oakley, Virginia.

[44] Sarah L. Jones, "Life in the South from the Commencement of the War," *Florida Historical Society Quarterly*, II, No. 2, 41.

The French and Italians served as instructors of swordsmanship. A southern mother writes that her son was being instructed by a drill master in military science during the day, and drilling with the States' Rights Guards at night. His parents were willing to "give him to our country," and were sparing no trouble or expense to fit him for a soldier's duty, but were clearly thinking of an officer's commission, for his teacher, a Frenchman, felt that in two more weeks he would be ready for a captain's duties.[45]

The practice of the profession of music in almost any form was left to foreigners, even though, for the sake of having a regimental band, a native son in the army might consent to learn to play an instrument. In the orchestra pit of the theatres, for instance, one saw Germans chiefly. The implication in the following excerpt is sufficiently clear: "The theatres were a great temptation [to the soldiers], and as convalescents were permitted to attend them with properly signed 'passes,' these places were nightly crowded with military audiences, scores having arms in slings or bandaged heads. Such pieces, such music, such yelling and laughter were never heard before; the poor Germans in the orchestra were tired to death with repeats of 'Dixie,' 'My Maryland,' and the 'Marseillaise'—tunes which the audience accompanied with vocal efforts of their own, or embellished with a running accompaniment of stamps and howling."[46] It was a French musician, designated as "seedy," and "of course, a political refugee," who played the steam calliope on a steamboat plying the Alabama River at the opening of the war. He composed a hymn to the South for General van Dorn.[47]

Likewise the more outstanding of the artists proved to have been born outside the boundaries of the Confederacy. L. M. D. Guillaume, a French student, worked carefully and industriously at his studio in Richmond, though during the late, lean war years he could scarcely have had many commissions. While touched with the mannerisms of the French school, his canvases had distinct merit and have delighted thousands of southern people.[48] The question of which artist designed

[45] Merrick, *Old Times in Dixie Land*, 30. The writer dismissed the Frenchman's name by saying, "whose name I cannot spell." [46] *Battle-fields of the South*, II, 30.
[47] De Leon, *Four Years in Rebel Capitals*, 44. The writer has been unable to identify this hymn.
[48] *Ibid.*, 300-301. It is clear that he painted many portraits of prominent southerners during the fifties, and that he lived on in Richmond into the war period. Oddly enough, one of the most celebrated of the artists of Confederate subjects, E. B. D. Julio, who

the Confederate flag has been a matter of much controversy and is even now in doubt. It is proper, however, that the claims of Nicola Marschall to that honor be here set forth. This musician-painter of Prussia first came to America as a youth, in the gold-fever days, but returned to Europe for further training in Munich and Italy in 1857-59. The war caught him teaching art and violin at the Marion Female Seminary in Alabama. After serving for a time in the Confederate army as a private at Forts Morgan and Gaines, he employed a substitute for something over a year at the instance of a friend. He enlisted again when a new call for volunteers came and served to the end in the second Alabama Regiment of Engineers under Colonel Lockett. The story of the designing of the flag upon which his fellow citizens of Marion insist is that Mrs. Lockett, the wife of a wealthy Marion planter, after a contest inaugurated by congress had failed to bring satisfactory results, selecting him undoubtely because he had already made portraits of many Alabama planters, asked him to design a flag, not too unlike the United States flag but distinguishable at a distance. Of the three designs he drafted, dashed off, according to tradition, in twenty minutes, the first was adopted. The flag, two red stripes and one white, with a blue field upon which was arranged a circle of seven white stars in the upper left corner, was first flung to the breeze on March 4, 1861, at Montgomery. The honor of having conceived the design for the stars and bars is also claimed for Major Orren Randolph Smith of Louisburg, North Carolina. Probably the conclusion reached by Peter Brannon in a paper read before the Daughters of the Confederacy at Marion is the only just and reasonable one: the design was probably drawn by Marschall, but this cannot be proved. No such doubt attaches to his designs for a Confederate uniform, which Mrs. Lockett returned to ask him to draft. Recalling the dress of the Austrian sharpshooters, gray with green trimmings, which he had seen when passing through Verona, he made several rough sketches in color to denote the different branches of the service.[49]

The attorneys discovered, who pursued their profession in a more

---

painted the famous "Last Meeting of Lee and Jackson" did not move to New Orleans till the late sixties, and did his work still later.

[49] Based upon the manuscript of Brannon's address at Marion, Alabama, preserved in the Alabama Military Archives, W, Index. The best collection of material on this subject is in the North Carolina Collection at the University of North Carolina.

or less active way during the war, are not numerous, though undoubtedly there were others of whom no mention is made here. Michael Hahn, who was to be inaugurated as governor of Louisiana in March, 1864, under Lincoln's famous 10 per cent plan, was a Bavarian who was graduated from the law department of the University of Louisiana and continued to act as notary under the Confederacy, though he was allowed to omit the oath of allegiance to that government, strangely enough in view of the fact that he was an openly avowed Union and anti-slavery man.[50] There is also record of an Englishman, J. A. Brear, who practiced law in Newton, Alabama, and of the Irishman, Michael Ryan, who became one of the leading lawyers of Alexandria, Louisiana, noted earlier. We note that the blockade-runner Watson, when arrested in New Orleans under Butler's regime for treasonable language and hauled to the custom-house, sent a note to an English lawyer, who was, he understood, solicitor for the British consul, and who generally attended to cases of British subjects.[51] A man of the distinction of Christian Roselius was allowed to continue quietly about his practice, undisturbed by the government although known to be a Union man. It might be noted, however, that he refused to accept the post of chief justice of the supreme bench under the United States government when that authority resumed control of New Orleans because he would be subject to military interference.[52]

Business was profoundly altered by the war. There were still some big businesses being conducted, some by native firms, like the large importing house of Bee in Charleston, some by foreigners who were counting on a rich harvest. A "pompous Englishman" named Payne, who had amassed a fortune at New Orleans, and who apparently was held there as late as 1863 by his interests, made himself a nuisance at the little Calvary Church by his criticism of the volunteer singers.[53] It is pleasing to read of the liberality and loyalty of

[50] In a proclamation of December 8, 1863, Lincoln declared that he would recognize as the true government of any of the seceded states, except Virginia, the organization set up by loyal citizens, provided that they constituted one tenth of the voting population of the state in 1860. See Ficklen, *History of Reconstruction in Louisiana through 1868*, 57 n.; *Dictionary of American Biography*, VIII, 87-88.
[51] W. R. and M. B. Houghton, *Two Boys in the Civil War and After*, 6; Whittington, *op. cit.*, 548; Watson, *Life in the Confederate Army*, 409.
[52] Rightor, *Standard History of New Orleans*, 400-401.
[53] *Journal of Julia LeGrand*, 125. The pettiness of human nature continued in wartime. "Mr. Payne has since had almost a contention with a Mrs. Hedges, a Scotch lady, who has taken Rosa's place; she sings songs and ballads sweetly and with much taste,

some adopted sons. A German Jew of Bavaria, Simon Gumbel, a man of means in Louisiana, placed at the disposal of the government a steamboat which he owned and others in which he had an interest, which were used to great advantage as transports. Mark Downey, an Irishman, furnished provisions and equipment to various bodies of troops. This was in addition to his duties in the civilian guards, for, though too old for the field, he promptly enrolled in the reserves and was ready to turn out for the defense of Richmond at any time.[54] A second prominent business man in Richmond was Emil O. Nolting, a Prussian of distinguished lineage, probably best known to history as the consul for Belgium during the war, but doing a large exporting business in tobacco in Richmond and Baltimore until 1865. Robert Mure was a prominent Scotch merchant of Charleston, cousin of the British consul at New Orleans.[55] Messrs. Depasseur conducted a French house in New Orleans of such importance that banks secured their Paris credits through it and it became involved in the difficulties between Count Mejan and General Butler.[56] A Mr. Burnside continued to live in his magnificent establishment in New Orleans, a brownstone mansion surrounded by extensive grounds with exquisite rare plants and flowers, and prevented its preëmption by General Butler for military headquarters by the presentation of British citizenship papers. His business does not appear if indeed he had any.[57] The firm with which William Watson was connected at Baton Rouge must have had a business of considerable size as, in addition to engineering, it carried on a sawmill, a wood factory, and a coal and steamboat business. In northern Alabama, even during the darkest days of the war, the Irishman named Jere Boyle still carried on extensive construction works on the railroads and in the coal mines, and suffered severe personal losses at the hands of General Wilson's northern army. In Austin, Svante Palm and S. M. Swenson conducted a large store until the latter was obliged to flee to Mexico.[58]

but does not sing church music correctly, they say, Mr. Payne says so. He doesn't look as though he had an ear."

[54] *History of the Jews of Louisiana*, 97. For a note on Mark Downey see *Virginia Magazine of History*, II, 435-436, 336.

[55] *Ibid.*, I, 343-344; Harriette K. Leiding, *Charleston, Historic and Romantic*, 228.

[56] Letter of Sulakowski to Governor Clark, Archives, Texas State Library, Texas Archives. For the involvement of this house and Butler, see *American Annual Cyclopaedia*, 1862, 650.

[57] Southwood, *Beauty and Booty*, 64-65.

[58] Watson, *Life in the Confederate Army*, 60. For Boyle the writer is indebted to a

Some aliens cloaked questionable activities under the guise of business pursuits and occasionally involved themselves in difficulties with the Federal authorities. It appears that an individual by the name of Charles Heidsieck, the head of a great French house which dealt in champagne, had come to the southern states to collect from delinquent creditors and had made his residence for some time in Mobile. Entering his name as bartender on some steamboats which General Butler was permitting to convey provisions to New Orleans, he carried between New Orleans and Mobile a large quantity of letters with treasonable information. On the conviction that there could be no channel except the employees of the boat, as no passengers were allowed, and having his suspicion deepened by the discovery that Heidsieck had been aboard in disguise and that he spent all the time between trips in New Orleans, Butler arrested him as a spy. In his pungent style he declared, "I arrest him as a spy—I confined him as a spy—I should have tried him as a spy, and hanged him as a spy if I had not been interfered with at Washington." He was caught red-handed, for he had in his possession at the time of his arrest a canvas wrapper about the size of a peck measure, covering letters from the French, Swiss, Spanish, Prussian, and Belgian consuls, together with a large number of letters to private persons, mostly rebels or "intermeddling foreigners," which contained contraband intelligence. A number of French residents in New Orleans petitioned Butler to release Heidsieck, allowing him to find safety in Europe for the period of the war, a concession which that stern general made "as an act of clemency." When the French consul promptly betook himself in behalf of the accused to Washington, the alleged spy, however, refused parole, and insisted that all suspicion as to his neutrality should be allayed because he was acting in coöperation with Count Mejan, the French consul stationed in the Louisiana metropolis. But General Butler promptly swept aside Count Mejan as a shield by recalling that the latter's "propriety of conduct and neutrality has, by subsequent revelations, been shown to be worse than doubtful." The chief charge against the consul was that he had allowed his office to be the repository of about a half million dollars in specie, which had been loaned by a bank of New Orleans to the Confederate govern-

manuscript in the Alabama Military Archives.—Mary Duffee, "Sketches of Jones Valley," No. 10, 6-7.

ment to purchase army clothing, and had consented to accept a commission for his services. For this violation of neutrality, Count Mejan was, as is well known, recalled by his government. Disposition of the case of Heidsieck was taken out of Butler's hands by the government at Washington.[59]

In the cotton trade there was some connivance of foreigners with northerners. A shrewd trader in New York would purchase several bales of cotton at perhaps eight cents per pound from a person whose home and cotton were within the Confederate lines. There next stepped into the game an alien, pleading exemption from the restrictions of trade which must hamper the noncombatants of belligerents, or deceiving an unsuspecting Union general by offering evidence of ownership of the cotton through forged and fraudulent bills of sale. One particular instance of this sort of connivance reveals a Frenchman agreeing to land cotton in New Orleans as his property in return for $20,000. When that sum had changed hands, the northern dealer got his cotton.[60] One naturalized Irishman found no reason to quarrel with his luck when he discovered that he could convert the misfortune of the death of a mule into an asset by allowing the use of its carcass to convey $10,000 worth of quinine and morphine. He even helped in the ruse to get it through the Union lines.[61]

Naturally aid in the perfecting of munitions was eagerly welcomed from native or foreigner and determined the business activities of some of the latter. An Englisman, John Hardcastle, paid a heavy price for having consented to carry out some inventions and improvements in armaments for the Confederate government. He was arrested by the Union government on the lower Potomac on his way homeward through the northern states.[62] An Irishman who had pronounced aptitude for mechanical engineering and had graduated with distinction from Trinity College had settled down in Nashville to the manufacture of locomotives. During the war his skill was utilized by the government. The Military Board of the state of Tennessee

[59] Parton, *General Butler in New Orleans*, 96-97.
[60] George H. Gordon, *A War Diary of Events in the War of the Great Rebellion, 1863-1865*, 312.
[61] G. A. Hanson, *Minor Incidents of the Late War*, 16-17.
[62] Lawrence, *Border and Bastille*, 206-208. This Britisher showed the doggedness and courage for which his nation is famous. A fellow prisoner said of him, "There was nothing remarkable about the little, round, ruddy man, except a joviality which never seemed to droop in the heavy prison air; when I wrote that an honest laugh was never heard here, I ought to have made that one exception."—*Ibid.*, 206-207.

engaged Thomas M. Brennan's services for the manufacture of cannon, shot, and shell and his product ranked with the output from the few reliable factories. When his works were seized in 1862 by the Union forces, he moved to Elyton, Alabama, to continue making munitions.[63] The searcher turns up a Welshman by the name of Walter S. Withers, who had wandered to Atlanta by 1853. In 1862, with a partner, he started a foundry to make buttons, spurs, and such small objects for the central government. To be near the raw materials, he sold the Atlanta business and moved to Bartow County, Georgia, but still continued to make government supplies.[64] Another British subject, an Englishman this time, made sabres for the Confederacy in a stone mill on the Chickamauga Creek in Georgia which were known as the "Joe Brown pikes," evidently in derision of their inferiority. General James Green Martin, in command of all state forces of North Carolina, hired two Frenchmen to make swords and bayonets. In the museum at Fredericksburg in the Texan hills stands a tiny brass salute gun, twelve to fifteen inches in length, made by Father Terillion and Engelbert Krauskopf, the latter having been brought to Texas by Müsebach, the founder of Fredericksburg, as his gunsmith. This gun was used by the Confederate forces during the war.[65]

It is very noticeable that the manufacture of swords seems to have been largely in the hands of Germans. Louis Fröhlich, after an unsuccessful venture with Bela Estvàn, the Austrian officer in Confederate service, embarked on the making of swords alone at Kenansville, North Carolina, and maintained a small plant, employing fifteen to twenty hands until it was burned by the Federals in 1864. The largest sword factory in the Confederacy, that of Louis Haiman and Brother, located at Columbus, Georgia, was conducted by two Prussians, who happened to be tinners by trade. The factory which they opened in 1861 covered a city square the next year. The output was 100 swords a week, to which they later added revolvers, leather equipment, and cooking utensils until they were operating a plant which was employing over 500 men. Clanton's regiment was armed

[63] *Confederate Veteran*, XII, 297.
[64] *Pioneer Citizens' History of Atlanta, 1832-1902*, 352.
[65] See *Confederate Veteran*, I, 48, for sabre maker on the Chickamauga Creek; the note on General Martin was found in a typed manuscript in the North Carolina Historical Commission; the salute gun in Fredericksburg was duly labeled with the information recorded in the text.

entirely with Haiman sabres. The plant continued to operate until April, 1865, when it was burned by the Federals.[66]

Another business enterprise which, with munitions, was felt to occupy a privileged position was that of manufacture of cloth—cotton or woolen—and clothing. William Jordan, Sr., who came to Fredericksburg, Texas, in 1854, made the first Confederate suits used in that state. Few letters which have been unearthed in this search can exceed in curious expression and revelation of alien attitude that addressed to the governor of Texas by a Charles J. Mathis from Frelsburg in Colorado County, dated November 22, 1862. Though a poor school teacher—a fact which he stresses strongly—he was undertaking to open a cotton and wool factory, "fortified" apparently by the credit of his friends. Colonel Delany had granted him exemption for some men, but he was now pleading to be allowed exemption for five more. As might be expected from that part of Texas, Colorado and Austin counties, the names of the five men are suspiciously German. As he makes out a good case for himself, he should be allowed to continue his plea in his own words.

"Majesty! It is very hard for me to demand so many men from you now, but having been found myself unfit to perform military service, I began to think how I could assist the government in another way. As a Frenchman I have seen many things in my own country as well as in Ohio; I began to build a cotton and wool factory with about $2,500 worth, my whole property, that is now swallowed up. I am just building on credit. The spinning frame is my own invention and merits therefore the right of invention—If your Majesty will please to assist me and with the help of my friends, my factory will soon be increased so that there can be made from 100 to 3 or 400 yards a day of good cloth. Believe me, Dear Majesty, as soon as I do not need a man, I will release him that he may join the army." He then adds a bit of flattery to strengthen his cause. "But Mr. Greedens, our Tax collector for the war assured me that your Majesty is not such a man [as to let his whole property be swallowed up] and that if you are well informed of the state of affairs you will not hesitate a moment to assist me in your manner."

There is another thing which he felt moved to tell his "Majesty." "There is a man here, called M. Malsch, this man, although a good

[66] R. D. Steuart, "Confederate Swords," *Confederate Veteran,* XXXIV, 12-13.

man and dealer for his pocket is a major, and I believe, an enrolling officer for the militia he does his very best to my workmen believe that they will be drafted anyhow, if they work for me or not and so it is, that the completing of my factory goes on only slowly. Mr. M. Malsch of Frelsburg is a new storekeeper and thinks probably that his business will not go on so lugratively if my when mine will go once."

It seems a pity that we are left uninformed as to whether the governor was as pleased as the petitioner thought he would be to see factories established in Texas.[67]

It was to the petty merchants and small traders that war wrought the greatest changes. The testimony from all the larger cities, except New Orleans, which remained strikingly cosmopolitan,[68] that Jewish merchants had largely acquired possession of the stores is too overwhelming to deny. Some few Jews went North to find refuge there while the war lasted,[69] but others came in to take the chances of rich profits in a fluctuating and rising market. A sharp criticism made of General Winder's administration as provost marshal in Richmond was that he only caused annoyance to honest men and soldiers, while permitting the city to be overrun by rogues, speculators, spies, foreigners, and blockade-runners.[70] "In every city and village of the Confederacy," declared Mr. Foote of Mississippi to the lower house of congress, "it might be safely estimated that at least nine-tenths of those engaged in trade were foreign Jews, spirited here by extraordinary and mysterious means. In this city one had only to explore the streets to convince him that four out of five of the tradesmen in

[67] Governor's Letters, Archives, Texas State Library.

[68] Note the impression made on a northern spy who went into this city in 1862. "Sit down in a stall, over your tiny cup of excellent coffee, and you are hobnobbing with the antipodes—your next neighbor may be from Greenland's icy mountains or India's coral strand. Get up to resume your promenade, and you will hear a dozen languages in as many steps; while every nation, and tribe, and people—French, English, Irish, German, Spanish, Creole, Chinese, African, Quadroon, Mulatto, American—jostles you in good-humored confusion."—Richardson, The Secret Service, 48. Many types began to flock in from the North after capture by the Union forces.—W. C. Corsan, Two Months in the Confederate States; including a Visit to New Orleans under the domination of General Butler, 9-10.

[69] Putnam, Richmond during the War, 272, charges that some pretended to be going to Europe, rather than to the northern states to prevent the confiscation of property left behind, as they would then be alien friends, not alien enemies. It is interesting, on the other hand, to find a German, Lewis Long, going to Reading, Pennsylvania, after his family. A letter from the mayor of Fayetteville, North Carolina, recommends him to the favor of all southern citizens to facilitate his passage.—Letter File, Military Board, North Carolina Historical Commission.   [70] Shotwell Papers, I, 383.

our principle thoroughfares were Jews." He permitted himself to indulge in a malicious thrust at Secretary Benjamin, whose presence in the cabinet was bitterly resented by many southerners who could not rise above their prejudices. Rumor had given some explanation of this mystery, he declared, and held that it was by official permission that this swarm of Jews from all parts of the world had come to this country and were permitted in many cases to conduct illicit traffic without official examination into the transactions. At the proper time he would expose what he held to be an outrage.[71]

All sorts of northern or European goods quickly became very scarce and expensive, indeed scarcely procurable, because of the blockade, and traffic in them seemed to be confined to Jewish merchants. They seemed to have some secret system of communication by which the merchandise found its way across the lines by hidden, intricate channels, to be stored in undiscoverable recesses in the southern cities.

Even before the war descended, many of the Jews with their native shrewdness quietly laid in immense stocks of merchandise and wares which they were able to retail at enormous advances in prices for cash within the next year or two. Gentiles complained that these merchants seldom had much of value to sell for Confederate script, such "goots" not being obtainable in the Confederate States, but the exhibition of a gold piece often produced the desired article. A certain store in that part of Richmond known as Rocketts, kept by a German Jew by the name of Heisenberger, became famous among the soldiers as "Noah's Ark"; it seemed capable of producing anything from a needle to firearms. Anything not to be had in the fashionable precincts was almost always forthcoming here. It was a general resort for the soldiers in town on leave, for they were always charged with errands for their comrades. They connived to torment the owner by stealing and met his threats to "tole General Lee" with laughs. Loudly he lamented, "I fills mine ouse mit goots, and ven a veek hab gone away, dey am all gone, and I hab not ask much monish ash pwhat I gib for dem."[72]

---

[71] "Proceedings of the First Confederate Congress," 3 Sess., *Southern Historical Society Papers*, XLVII, 121-122.

[72] Gerrish and Hutchinson, *The Blue and the Gray*, 330-331. One can quite understand the mystification of one Jew who had been lodged in Castle Thunder for receiving treasury notes for some garments. No sooner was he inside the prison than a young man employed there entered the citizen's room to ask if anyone had greenbacks to sell. The Hebrew held that "it vast a tam pretty pishness to put a shentlemans in such a tam hole

A British merchant noticed the large number of Semitic faces in a Charleston hotel. "Fully one-half the large number of guests in the House seemed as if they had just stepped out of Houndsditch, and reminded me of what a friend in Mobile said, that, 'I should meet more Jews in Charleston than I could see in Jerusalem.' They all seemed absorbed in the study of the auctioneer's pamphlets, and the long advertisements of sales which half-filled the papers. I found these sales were all of goods which had run the blockade, and the quantity seemed very large, and very varied."[73] He soon saw the large store opposite crammed with these same men while a large stock of foreign goods was auctioned off.

On the eve of the expected evacuation of Richmond in 1862, when the presence of large packing cases on the pavements was correctly interpreted by these shrewd businessmen, a hectic excitement seized the little Jewish and German merchants, who were feverishly converting their goods into cash at ruinous rates of discount, sometimes gladly paying $400 in paper for $100 in cash, or exchanging merchandise for tobacco to be stored away in cellars until the entrance of McClellan's soldiers should afford an opportunity for a lucrative sale.[74] The story of how a German Jewish lad of sixteen in Richmond exchanging his real name of Solomon Guthman for the American one of James Wilson had made enough money in two months by smuggling goods from Nashville to Atlanta to plan to return to Germany is quite credible.[75]

Of course the Jews did not have a monopoly of all business during the war. One reads of a small grocery store, the Light House, a little way down the Alabama River from Montgomery, conducted by a "Dutchman"; of an Englishman who at the close of the war had had to leave a watch repair and jewelry shop in Montgomery to retreat to his little farm six miles away;[76] of another English watchmaker at Columbus, Georgia; of a Frenchman, M. Pierre Abadie,

---

as dat for doing vat de tam Rebels vash doing demselves."—Browne, *Four Years in Secessia*, 305-306.

[73] Corsan, *op. cit.*, 126.   [74] *Battle-fields of the South*, I, 316-317.

[75] John Fitch, "Police Record of the Spies, Smugglers, and Rebel Emissaries," in *Annals of the Army of the Cumberland* (Appendix), 490-491. The lad was caught by the Federal officers.

[76] This Englishman's wife was French. When the French officer Hermann stopped at their cottage one night, they sang French songs, but when they reached the "Marseillaise," and other patriotic airs, she was quite overcome.—Hermann, *Memoirs of a Veteran*, 180.

who conducted a small furniture store at 130 Dauphin Street, New Orleans; and of an Irish-Scotch hotelkeeper at Newnan, Georgia, who impartially bestowed upon two of his daughters the names of Caledonia and Hibernia. Pizzini became famous in Richmond as a restaurateur who was able to keep up a wonderful table all through the war when the rest of Richmond was starving.[77] There still lingered in the war-torn Virginia valley an English clerk at a Staunton hotel to understand British prejudices and to give Wolseley and his two companions a room to themselves with three beds; and there were still German cobblers in the Confederacy when leather was so scarce that one of their number was glad to repair a pair of shoes for the scraps of leather left over from the piece provided by the patron.[78] When trade descended to the level of peddling, it was pretty likely to be conducted by an Irishman or a German Jew. Probably the supreme illustration of determination to sell was exemplified on the sandy waste between San Antonio and Brownsville far from human habitation, where a German Jew had pitched his tent near a muddy hole to sell hard crackers, cheese, and "rifle whisky" to the passing troops, demanding Uncle Sam's currency, but accepting, under compulsion, Confederate paper.[79]

Probably no group under the Confederate jurisdiction was more important than the mechanics and munition workers, and in large number they were foreign-born. Very early in the rebellion an extensive plant for the manufacture of field artillery was established in New Orleans, which made excellent batteries. The factory was conducted by the aid of northern and foreign mechanics. The government searched out trained mechanics in the towns and among the troops and detailed the latter to work in the ordnance establishments. A German only arriving in Knoxville in 1860, who had learned the gunsmith's trade in his fatherland, became an active member of the ordnance department.[80] Occasionally a petition would be presented

[77] Telfair, *A History of Columbus, Ga.*, 136; Southwood, *op. cit.*, 191; Cumming, *A Journal of Hospital Life*, 110; Dame, *From the Rapidan to Richmond*, 32.

[78] "A Month's Visit to the Confederate Headquarters," *Blackwood's Edinburgh Magazine*, XCIII, 15; Hopley, *op. cit.*, II, 77.

[79] Williams, *With the Border Ruffians*, 278, tells this story of German-Jewish enterprise in Texas. Orville J. Victor (ed.), *Incidents and Anecdotes of the War*, 283, tells of two Irish peddlers who came alongside a Union vessel at New Orleans to sell milk and eggs. They professed great loyalty to the United States.

[80] See Stevenson, *Thirteen Months in the Rebel Army*, 82, for the plant in New Orleans; for the German from Knoxville see *Confederate Veteran*, XX, 59. The primitive type of ordnance factory is well set forth in the account of H. O. Nelson, the German alluded

in favor of exempting a foreigner because he was "familiar with the process of making shot,—able to inspect munitions."[81] In general it may be stated that the most important and valuable workmen in the Confederate armories, arsenals, and ordnance foundries were German, and this is exactly where this foreign element in the civilian population was to be found. Even the men who were out of sympathy with the Confederacy were obliged to work at that employment.[82]

The lack of skilled labor was a source of difficulty to the war and navy departments and great efforts were made to supply the deficiency by importing artisans from abroad. The secretary of the navy wrote Bulloch urgently on April 11, 1863, pressing him to send over mechanics and a superintendent to direct the manufacture of Bessemer steel. Bulloch found it difficult to find men of character and skill willing to take the risk of capture in running the blockade and to endure the hardships after arrival. Only large monetary inducements would prevail with them. He found it impossible to induce anyone capable of producing Bessemer steel to go, and doubted the practicability of undertaking the making of that article in the Confederacy. However he engaged a certain Thomas Ludlam who had been foreman of a large iron works to organize a party of skilled mechanics to go out under his charge in a vessel to be provided by Bulloch. He declared him capable of taking charge of a foundry for any kind of work, of selecting the site, of superintending erection of buildings and machinery, and of making the ordinary tools required. He was dispatched in due course with his party of about ten men, but

---

to above. A shipyard to afford repairs to the infant navy was located at San Jacinto, Texas, at the junction of the San Jacinto River and Buffalo Bayou where both join Galveston Bay. An old abandoned sawmill was converted into an armory, where flintlock guns were changed for percussion caps, and where bowie knives were fashioned. A razor-like edge was put to every weapon that left the armory, with a cowhorn for a handle, and copper guard made from the boiler tubes within the mill. A rawhide scabbard hid the vicious instrument.

[81] Frequently on the army rolls occurs the notation that a man has been detailed as a machinist. See also Wise, *The Long Arm of Lee*, I, 58. William Latham, an Englishman, was detailed as a finisher of cannon from Company B, Fourth Kentucky.—Thompson, *History of the First Kentucky Brigade*, 668. The petition referred to in the text was found in behalf of Henry Augustus Gunther, a native of Prussia, but now a citizen of North Carolina, sent up from Wilmington.—Letter File, Military Board, November 17, 1861—September, 1862, North Carolina Historical Commission. A list of names taken from a time book of machinists rifling a smoothbore gun for South Carolina is very suggestive: Duc, Mustard, Sigwald, Petsch, Duncan, etc. Of course, the name is not proof of foreign nativity.—*Charleston, South Carolina, The Centennial of Incorporation*, 235.

[82] Marks, *The Peninsular Campaign in Virginia*, 380-381, emphasizes the loyalty of the German workmen and their wives to the United States government.

they had to be separated at Bermuda, as all could not be accommodated on the same blockade-runner. The greater part of the group did enter the country to discharge their engagements but, because of insurmountable local difficulties, it proved impossible to construct new works or to enlarge those already existing. In addition, another difficulty arose with these Britishers. The agreement with them called for their pay in gold, which had so soared in price as to make their pay enormous; fulfillment of the contract would, moreover, have brought utter demoralization among the native operatives. An offer to pay half the wages in gold to their families in England, if they would take the remainder in Confederate money, proved unacceptable. The intermediation of the British consul proved unavailing to modify the contract, and so there remained nothing to be done except to return them on the next steamer, paying their passage back to England. This experience cost the government only 2,000 pounds in gold or around $40,000.[83]

It is superfluous to draw attention to the fact that the war years cut off completely the normal immigration from Europe to the South, relatively slight at best compared with that of the North. Such evidence as one encounters of unskilled labor performed by whites during the critical war years is corroborative of the fact that it was undoubtedly performed by the foreign-born already resident in the South, continuing to carry on labor in accustomed lines. The instances which appear are, of course, of Irishmen.[84]

It is hardly surprising that an economy which had depended for its labor on illiterate slaves had found it necessary to import its horticulturists. And so one notes without surprise that the horticulturist who had had charge of Capitol Square prior to the war was

[83] See Bulloch's account of the episode.—*The Secret Service of the Confederate States in Europe*, II, 231-232, and also Gorgas, "Notes on the Ordnance Department of the Confederate Government," *Southern Historical Society Papers*, XII, 84. Note how far short of the cost Mallory's calculations came.—*N. R.*, Ser. 2, II, 623. The Railroad Convention, meeting April, 1863, adopted a resolution calling on the government to import 500 artisans, machinists, and miners to supply the shops of the government and the railroads.—*O. W. R.*, Ser. 4, II, 510. See also Bradlee, *Blockade Running*, 239.

[84] *Daily Richmond Examiner*, March 12, 1864. It is odd that space could be found for details like the following so late in the war. Two Irish blacksmiths won the attention of the Richmond public by staging a fight and so gaining space in the paper for themselves and for several other Irish witnesses in the police court trial which followed. Some Irish fishermen off Old Point Comfort likewise appeared in a Norfolk paper by their gruesome haul of human arms and legs instead of the fish for which their seines were intended. The strange haul was undoubtedly the result of amputations at the fortress located at that point. See also *Battle-fields of the South*, II, 226 n.

E. G. Eggeling, a native-born German who was during the period of the Confederacy transferred to the presidential mansion as steward. Charles Page in his capacity of war correspondent encountered this same state gardener in Richmond, as the triumphant Union army entered the capital. After ingratiating himself with a bouquet of choice blooms from the conservatory, he sought to enlist the good services of the northerner in procuring a pass to the North. One would infer that he was no longer enamored with his post.[85]

Scattered along the southern lines of railroad was a sprinkling of foreign-born workers, Irishmen and Englishmen, in various capacities. Judging however from one list of officers and employees on the Alabama and Florida Railroad, one could not assert that foreign-born constituted even a majority of the personnel. This list had been com-piled to provide the government with an authentic list of men exempt as indispensable for the 119 miles of railroad. Only 14 of the 119 necessary to run the road showed the place of birth as outside the United States.[86] Sometimes these railroad mechanics proved of the highest service to the government. William Rushton was one. He had been brought from Philadelphia, to which point he had emi-grated from Ireland when a child, to Atlanta by the Georgia Rail-road as master machinist in 1847. During the war he invented and constructed a cannon which did effective service, and often contributed helpful ideas for the fortifications in and around Atlanta.[87] When Governor Brown wanted guns in 1861 he turned to an Irishman, Anthony Murphy, who was connected with the Western and Atlantic Railroad, to assemble the men to make them. It was this same man who prevented the success of the daring attempt of some Unionists in the secret service to cut the Confederate line of communication be-tween Big Shanty and Chattanooga. The Unionists, posing as southern refugees, aroused his suspicion, and by chasing their engine with a handcar he ruined their plan.[88] But in general most of the railroad

[85] Schuricht, *op. cit.*, II, 50; Charles A. Page, *Letters of a War Correspondent*, 329.

[86] Irishmen can be located connected with the Atlanta and West Point Railroad Com-pany as engineers and with the Western and Atlantic Railroad. An Englishman was master of machinery at the Atlanta Rolling Mills.—*Pioneer Citizens' History of Atlanta*, 305, 319, 374, 382, 387. The list of employees on the Alabama and Florida Railroad is preserved in the Alabama Military Archives. A similar list of 186 employees on the Mont-gomery and West Point Railroad for September 1, 1864, was useless for our purpose as it did not give the place of nativity.

[87] *Pioneer Citizens' History of Atlanta*, 321-322.

[88] "Helped Capture Engine 'General,'" *Southern Historical Society Papers*, XXXVII, 264-265; *Pioneer Citizens' History of Atlanta*, 303 ff.

mechanics had been northern men and most of the few foreigners among them left the Confederacy to escape the hardships of war. The railroads were hard put to it to maintain service, and one of their serious difficulties arose from the scarcity of mechanics.[89]

In time of war the distressed families of poor soldiers have a special claim upon more fortunate members of society. The stringency of the blockade increased the suffering greatly in this war, and only the generous gifts of the planters and wealthy townsmen prevented actual starvation. Naturally this suffering appeared most acute in the large cities. Foreign-born were both recipients and donors in this charity. Goods and supplies were brought in by railroad and shipped down the rivers at special prices to enable the cities to care for their poor. Public soup houses were opened in the city buildings. In two cities this charity assumed the form of what was called the Free Market—in New Orleans and in Mobile. For eight and one-half months this market was open in the Crescent City twice a week. The number of families receiving help on each occasion rose from 723 on the day it was opened to 2,000 on the day when Commodore Farragut entered the city and the storehouse was closed. Probably the average number of families thus receiving help can be estimated at 1,875.[90] Naturally many of the poverty-stricken were the helpless families of the foreign-born, some of them deprived of their breadwinner, but foreigners were also donors and generous donors. A committee had already collected considerable sums, which had been contributed by the patriotic spirit of the Germans in New Orleans for the support of the families of the soldiers of their nationality in the field before the Free Market was instituted. On September 26 the committee was again in a position to turn over to the Free Market Committee $300 for the same purpose. The Swiss Guard, a small group of young men, gave $21 on April 9, 1861, to the Free Market.[91] Altogether millions were subscribed by private persons to relieve suffering in that city.

[89] For the condition of the railroads and dearth of mechanics see the letter of Quartermaster F. W. Sims to Brigadier General Lawton, dated February 10, 1865.—O. W. R., Ser. 4, III, 1091-1092. Sims was, naturally, serving as superintendent of railroad transportation.

[90] Rightor, Standard History of New Orleans, 154; Kendall, History of New Orleans, I, 242. General Butler claimed that he distributed food to 10,490 families, little more than 1,000 being natives.—O. W. R., Ser. 3, II, 724.

[91] Louisiana Staatszeitung, October 1, 1861 (New Orleans); Southwood, op. cit., 80.

The Free Market in Mobile had so similar a history that it is unnecessary to give the details. There remains only to add that a Dane, Lewis Peter Waganer, after being discharged from Company A, Fifteenth Cavalry, as over age, was appointed contractor of the Free Market, in which post he gave fine service.[92] Finally it was to the German and Irish inhabitants of Richmond that Estvàn appealed in behalf of some Union prisoners of war whose deplorable condition excited his sympathy; in a few hours that appeal had won a response. Money, bottles of wine, and parcels of lint, prepared by German women, made their way to the hospitals; and the Irish also brought what linen they could spare to the surgeons for the use of the wounded prisoners.[93]

However if the German and Irish women could respond generously to the call of the suffering, they could also be quite unreasonable on other occasions and play something of the rôle of the fishwives of France. The city council of New Orleans, to relieve the scarcity of small change, authorized the issuance of checks, as specie payments had been suspended by the Confederate government. Business houses began to issue notes and certificates, which acquired the telling if inelegant name of "shin-plasters." Butchers and barkeepers were among the most prolific creators of this kind of money; even streetcar tickets were current instead of five-cent pieces. The inevitable quickly happened: as the value of the medium declined, the cost of food and clothing rose. Finally the market people, largely Germans, Gascons, and French, refused to accept the "shin-plasters" until the city authorities intervened and forced their acceptance.[94]

In Richmond the story is one of violence rather than of mere unreasonableness. On a certain spring day in 1862 a mixed crowd of Germans, Irishmen, and free Negroes—men, women, and children—armed with pistols, knives, hammers, hatchets, and axes, and every other kind of weapon for defense or offense in breaking into stores, gathered in the lower city in an ugly mob. They quickly broke into stores and could soon be seen emerging laden with booty. Women who were bowed almost double under heavy sides of sole leather or who dragged after them heavy cavalry boots, meanwhile brandishing

---

[92] This detail is contained in a report to the U. D. C. in Mobile, made December 6, 1909.
[93] Estvàn, *War Pictures*, I, 292-293.   [94] Kendall, *op. cit.*, I, 241-242.

huge knives, swore that they were dying of starvation, though they bore the appearance of being well nourished. It is difficult to imagine just how cavalry boots or sides of leather were designed to assuage hunger, so that, as always, history had to record the Richmond mob spirit as descending to mere theft and arson. Nerves were frayed and patience exhausted by the deprivation and hardships of a war which seemed to be dragging on without sight of the end and which concerned this class of humble foreigners little except to impose even greater hardships.[95]

The isolation which the blockade forced upon the South was difficult for the native-born, but it was especially distressing to the foreign-born, who was often cut off from his nearest and dearest. The English youth, Williams, living on a ranch in Texas, by the merest accident received some mail from his family. Asking for mail for a friend at the post office in Matamoros, he found letters from his mother, addressed in care of the South Western Express Company, which had existence only in the imagination of an English newspaper man, who had advised anxious Britishers to address relatives or friends in the South through that medium.[96] Exiles rejoiced over finding English newspapers at Wilmington little more than a month old.[97] Presumably a woman living on Sullivan's Island on the South Carolina coast would be pretty well isolated at all times but, with the restrictions of travel imposed by war, she would find her life resembling that on St. Helena. One understands then with what eagerness an "Elsässerin" living there welcomed her guest, Conrad, when he was ordered to Sullivan's Island for the sea air to expedite his recovery from typhoid—at last she had some one with whom she could converse in her beloved mother tongue![98]

One element in the population of the cities was quite temporary, but not to be disregarded on that account—the group of men connected with the blockade-running business. Oddly enough this foreign element was not confined to the ports, as might possibly have been expected, but extended to inland cities. For instance Augusta, a thriving little city of fifteen thousand inhabitants on the Savannah River, became the distributing center for the interior of most of the

[95] Putnam, op. cit., 208-209.
[96] Williams, With the Border Ruffians, 309.
[97] Ross, A Visit to the Cities and Camps of the Confederate States, 183.
[98] Conrad, op. cit., 45.

goods which ran the blockade into Charleston and Wilmington. Here they were sold at auction.[99] Captain Ross encountered several English friends in that city engaged in the business. Everyone seemed absorbed in trade, and the shops were filled with supplies and customers.

Our study has already brought us into contact with the young Englishman, Thomas E. Taylor. He was scarcely twenty-one when he landed in the Confederacy to represent a firm engaged in blockade-running. It is impossible to prove that Taylor's agents were British, but the names and logic suggest that they probably were, as the firm would naturally want young active men whom they knew and could trust, and men who could be depended upon to remain at their posts instead of Americans who were certain to be snapped up for the army. Accordingly it is reasonable to suppose that each British house engaged in the business had a little group of resident agents to handle the incoming and outgoing cargo of the ships, thus swelling the population of the ports.[100] An exception to the general rule of sale to the highest bidder by auction was the firm of Bee, Jerny, and Company, an old Charleston business house which was so fine that it did not auction off its goods but offered them in stores at a fixed price with a set profit. It also erected branches in Columbia and Richmond in order to bring needed supplies to the residents of those inland points. This arrangement explains the constant traveling in which their young secretary-treasurer, our friend Conrad, was engaged. When Charleston was seriously threatened he was moved to Wilmington; when that point became uncertain, Conrad, forced to act on his own initiative, decided on Columbia, South Carolina, as offering the greatest safety. Accordingly he was transferred to that city in the spring of 1864, but had to make regular trips to Wilmington when their ships came in. We have followed so long the fortunes of this enterprising, faithful young German that the reader will hardly be willing to let him pass from the scene of Confederate history without a final sentence to indicate his fate. He lived and suffered through

[99] *Ibid.*, 75, 76, 95.

[100] Sprunt, *Chronicles of the Cape Fear River*, 410-411, gives a picture of Thomas Taylor. Taylor himself speaks of Tom Power and Arthur Doering as loyal lieutenants at Wilmington, when Taylor was promoted to conducting the vessel through the blockade.— *Running the Blockade*, 64. Ross found his blockade-running friends, last seen in Augusta, Georgia, in Wilmington, when he reached that point, living in a fine large house, to which they invited him.—*Op. cit.*, 130, 182.

the burning of Columbia by Sherman, was able to locate his employer, Mr. Bee, at Spartanburg, departed for the North and for Europe on March 20, 1865, and was robbed on his way to the Potomac. Because of some southern letters intrusted to him, he was imprisoned by the Federal agents, but released with a lecture on neutral obligations. He rendered a last service to his employer by sailing to Liverpool rather than directly to Germany in order to stop payment on the checks of the Bee company.[101]

Occasionally an English or German agent for the purchase of cotton to run the blockade might have been encountered in Mobile or even in Texas,[102] but the place where their presence was felt was the East. Wilmington was, until its capture by the Federals at the close of the war, the most important port of entry. There were often during the early years a dozen blockade-running steamers lying at the wharves, loading cotton and unloading all manner of stores. There were many Englishmen in the town, representing shipowners and manufacturers. Some of them were worthy and acceptable temporary residents, but some quite the reverse. But all lived well. The Britishers and other foreigners gave a cosmopolitan air to the streets. They generally cultivated a social life of their own, rather convivial and expensive, in which foreign liquors brought in by the blockade-runners played an important rôle.

Fortunately a picture of Wilmington as it was during the war has been preserved. "At every turn you met up with young Englishmen dressed like grooms and jockeys, or with a peculiar, coachman-like look, seeming, in a foreign land away from their mothers, to indulge their fancy for the *outre* and extravagant in dress to the utmost. These youngsters had money, made money, lived like fighting cocks, and astonished the natives by their pranks, and the way they flung the Confederate 'stuff' about. Of course, they were

---

[101] Conrad, *op. cit.*, 110 ff., 140-141.

[102] An illustration of the foreign agent in Texas, as well as of the hazards of the business, is given by Watson. An English agent had sold a large amount of goods in Texas and had bought cotton with the proceeds. He then proceeded to convey the cotton across the plains, but an official of the cotton bureau took possession of the Englishman's cotton, as it was handy, giving in exchange a Confederate receipt. The official easily got a permit to take government cotton out of the country and crossed it by ferry to Matamoros. But here the owner suddenly appeared with his bill of sale. Mexican authorities would recognize no ownership other than that shown by the bill of sale and the Confederate official was without jurisdiction on Mexican soil, so that the Englishman in the end got his cotton.— *The Adventures of a Blockade Runner*, 28-30.

deeply interested in the Confederate cause, and at the same time wanted cotton.

"They occupied a large, flaring yellow house at the upper end of Market Street. There these youngsters kept open house, and spent their pass and the Company's money, while it lasted. There they fought cocks on Sundays, until the neighbors remonstrated and threatened prosecution. A stranger passing the house at night, and seeing it illuminated with every gas jet (the expense, no doubt, charged to the ship), and hearing the sound of music, would ask if a ball was going on. Oh, no! it was only these young English Sybarites enjoying the luxury of a band of negro minstrels after dinner. They entertained any and everybody.

"But, alas, there came a day when these Masters Primrose, with brandy flushed faces, faded away, and were scattered like their namesakes before a chilling north east wind, and Wilmington knew them no more."[103]

[103] This description appeared in a magazine article soon after the war, which magazine is not stated.—Andrew J. Howell, *The Book of Wilmington*, 120-121, 131.

XI

FOREIGN VISITORS TO THE CONFEDERACY*

CAPTAIN ROSS OF THE Austrian Hussars, who was traveling through the Confederacy from May, 1863, to April, 1864, remarks on the paucity of visitors in that land. He expressed surprise that so few foreign officers visited the southern states, especially at so interesting a period. He states that except Colonel Fremantle and a young English officer of engineers, no other "tourist," so far as he was aware, visited the country during his sojourn there.[1] We shall, however, have occasion as we move on through the pages of this chapter to note the visitors with whom Ross himself came into contact in the course of his travels. In addition to the visitors whom we can identify there were probably many others who because of their obscurity never entered the records. Probably many Englishmen or other Europeans who found themselves in New York heard such conflicting accounts that they decided to visit the southern states in order to secure first-hand evidence. Like an unidentified visitor they probably slipped secretly across the lines when the passport forbade entry into any insurrectionary state. This particular individual managed to cross the Confederate line into Kentucky, passed through Tennessee, Alabama, Georgia, and North Carolina, visited Charleston and Richmond, a number of camps and plantations, talked with people of all classes, and succeeded in getting back to New York, all within the short space of a month, from mid-September to mid-October, 1861.[2]

Britishers were distinctly out of favor with the Washington government by 1862 for they were all regarded as rebel sympathizers. That they could desire to visit the southern republic merely for pleas-

* Some of these visits, especially those of the military men and of the newspaper reporters, have been alluded to earlier, but it seems desirable to set them clearly before the reader as events in themselves which had a certain influence on the fortunes of the new republic.

[1] *Visit to the Cities and Camps of the Confederate States*, 219-220. Ross refers to Fremantle merely as Colonel F., but initial and date leave no doubt as to whom he means.

[2] The visitor carefully conceals his identity in the article published in *Blackwood's Edinburgh Magazine*. The writer is stated to be an officer of the British army on a short leave of absence. He writes, "We found ourselves at New York, with a few weeks' holiday in hand."—"A Month with the Rebels," *Blackwood's*, XC, 755-767.

ure or with a disinterested desire for firsthand information was, at least, a matter of question in the minds of Union officials. Each Englishman was held a possible suspect in smuggling through the lines arms, quinine, tea, or sugar, or a possible sharer in some political conspiracy in aid of the "rebels," as one visitor rather bitterly remarks.[3] Hence passes to visit the South were not to be had for the asking.

The first visit by an alien of sufficient importance to enter the records is that of Colonel Charles A. de Arnaud, a Russian, which occurred almost before hostilities were begun. He was making an extensive visit to the South and was in the newborn Confederacy when Beauregard's guns roared against Fort Sumter and precipitated the war. Upon his return to Washington he reported to Baron Stoekl, the Russian minister to the United States, who strongly advised him to go west to make his observations in that section of the Confederacy, as the baron was convinced that the west would be the important theatre of war. He went, accordingly, to Louisville and, after another extensive tour through the South, reported to General Ransom his opinion that there would be a general war of extensive proportions, not merely a repression of local insurrections. At General Ransom's urgent insistence he went to St. Louis to set forth the general situation to General Frémont. Then began De Arnaud's active military service, which aligned him with the Union forces and places his further visits to the South in the category of spying expeditions, thus removing him from the scope of this study.[4]

A group of military visitors was to be expected by both North and South. Wherever war is being waged, the men whose business war is are going to go to watch the war machines in action. The most distinguished of this group was Colonel Garnet Wolseley, later Lord Wolseley, who ran the blockade of the Potomac with Frank Lawley, reporter of the London *Telegraph*. After four arduous campaigns in the Crimea, India, and China, Wolseley was enjoying eighteen

---

[3] The writer of these sharp words was Wolseley.—"A Month's Visit to the Confederate Headquarters," *Blackwood's*, XCIII, 2. A third visitor, an anonymous Englishman, gives his impressions in "Some Account of Both Sides of the American War," *Blackwood's*, XC, 768-779.

[4] De Arnaud was appointed aide on the staff of General Frémont and was requested to make a reconnaissance into Kentucky and Western Tennessee in order to correct the maps of that area. This hazardous journey he made from August 12 to September 5, 1861. This was followed by a tour of observation along the banks of the Tennessee River, from October 9 to November 14, 1861, covering a period of five weeks. He received his discharge from Frémont and sailed for Europe, February 7, 1862.—*Reminiscences of the Union and its Ally, Russia*, 3-4, 10-11, 17, 19-20.

months' well-earned leave, writing his first book and hunting in Ireland, when he was suddenly ordered to Canada as assistant quartermaster general in December, 1861. The incident of the *Trent*, the forcible seizure and removal from a British mail vessel of the two Confederate commissioners, Mason and Slidell, who were on their way to Great Britain and France, had led the British government to decide as a precautionary measure to organize the Canadian militia. A visit to the Confederacy, about which he could get no reliable information while the Civil War was in progress, was a natural desire; he secured a two months' leave the latter part of August, 1862, from the general officer commanding in Canada, without, of course, betraying his plans. This was more than a difficult, really a hazardous, adventure, for, if he escaped seizure as a spy, he was undertaking an enterprise highly reprobated by the officers of the British government, and one which entailed risking his commission. He determined upon a visit to army headquarters as a species of humorous revenge. "I knew from personal experience how much all loafers are hated at the Headquarters of every army in the field. But I felt a sort of justification in presuming to inflict myself upon the staff of the Confederate army, should I succeed in joining it, because I had myself so often been similarly bored by the presence of traveling gentlemen at the Headquarters of armies with which I happened to be serving in the field."[5] He visited the scene of the Seven Days' Battles around Richmond and made his way to Lee's headquarters near Winchester. It was on this visit that he met Generals Lee and Jackson, for both of whom he expressed unbounded admiration in his article on the American war which was published anonymously in *Blackwood's* in January, 1863. He was in the Confederate States from September 11 to October 21, 1862.[6]

There entered also for longer or shorter periods other observers from the various European armies. Next to Wolseley the most distinguished from the British army was Lieutenant Colonel Arthur Fremantle of the Coldstream Guards, then a young man of only twenty-eight, who was using a furlough for a hasty tour through the Confederacy to take a look at the army and to become acquainted

[5] Wolseley, *Story of a Soldier's Life*, II, 120.
[6] When in Winchester he is said to have been frequently at the home of Mrs. Hugh (Fitzhugh?) Lee and to have corresponded with her up to the last years of her life. He never lost his interest in the South or in the friends he made there.—*Confederate Veteran*, XXV, 200-201.

with the officers. In order to avoid breaking the rules of the block-ade, he entered Texas by way of Mexico, crossing the Rio Grande at Matamoros and consuming eleven days of his three months' leave by a three-hundred-and-thirty-mile trip through Texas. Crossing the Mississippi at Natchez, he visited Jackson, the Mississippi capital, Mobile, and Chattanooga, accompanied General Polk to Shelbyville, and was for a few weeks the guest of that general at Beechwood, the Tennessee home of Mrs. Andrew Erwin, which was serving as headquarters for a number of officers of the Army of the Tennessee.[7] Returning to Chattanooga, he traveled east to Charleston and Rich-mond, accompanied the army to Gettysburg as Longstreet's guest, and retreated with the army to Hagerstown. Fremantle was received by most of the chief generals of the Confederate army: Lee, Jackson, Johnston, Longstreet, Bee, and Magruder. His open frank manner seemed to win the hearts of the southern women,[8] while his appre-ciation of the camp cuisine delighted the officers at the front. Cap-tain Otey has left a description which bears repetition. "Our gumbo fillet was quite *au fait*, and he could hardly credit our chef's remark that it was made from the tender twigs of the young sassafras bush that grows so lavishly in the South, with the photograph of a chicken that had done service in the days gone by. Our champagne was quite delectable on a hot and dusty march to wash down the dust that gathered in our gullets. It was made in an old molasses barrel and contained about three parts water to one part of corn and mo-lasses sufficient to sweeten, when after a few days of fermentation it could be drawn and served minus the effervescence."[9] Immediately after his return with Lee's army from the Pennsylvania campaign he made his way north, crossing the Union lines without difficulty by a perfectly frank avowal of his status as a British officer and by

[7] This intimate detail comes from *ibid.*, VII, 324. At Beechwood he met a number of the prominent women of that region—Mrs. Erwin herself, the Misses Hardee, Mrs. Greene, and Miss Rowe Webster. Both his father and grandfather had been associated with the Coldstream Guards as adjutants and he had held the same office.—Noll (ed.), *Doctor Quintard, Chaplain C. S. A. and Second Bishop of Tennessee,* 77.

[8] Mrs. Harrison gives her impression as follows: "No one ever heard Colonel Fremantle spoken of by his Southern comrades save in terms of enthusiastic praise."—*Recollections Grave and Gay,* 133.

[9] Otey, "Operations of the Signal Corps," *Confederate Veteran,* VIII, 129. After Fre-mantle's return to England he published a book, *Three Months in the Southern States,* which was very acceptable to the Confederates due to its presentation of the southern side. "By the next season we were all eagerly reading this *brochure* reprinted in Mobile for circulation in the army," says Mrs. Harrison.—*Op. cit.*

a full statement of places he had visited in the South. He denied having in any way entered the Confederate service and gave his word that he did not have in his possession any letters, public or private, from any person in the South.[10]

Lieutenant Colonel Fletcher of the Scots Fusilier Guards was indubitably a more impartial observer than some other British officers who visited the Confederate States for he set out with the distinct purpose of seeing both sides. The kindness of General McClellan permitted him to reside at the headquarters of the Army of the Potomac during the campaign of the peninsula, including the siege of Yorktown, the Seven Days' Battles, and the retreat to the James River. Only a short time later, through the courtesy of the authorities of both combatants, he was enabled to enter and traverse the Confederate States. This, incidentally, fixes the date of his visit as in the late summer of 1862.[11]

Captain Fitzgerald Ross, a cavalry officer of the Austrian Hussars, had the benefit of a very much longer period of study of the Confederacy and of its leaders. He entered "Secessia" by way of the underground railroad from Baltimore to the Virginia shore in May, 1863, and did not leave it until April, 1864. After a short stay at Nassau and Havana he concluded his American tour with a visit to the northern states and to Canada. During his stay of nearly a year in the South he visited all the principal cities and armies and witnessed many interesting events, including the battle of Gettysburg, the bombardment of Charleston, and the battle of Chickamauga. He was fortunate enough, with the help of obliging military officers, to reach Lee at Chambersburg on the eve of the great battle. After some weeks with the western army he returned to the east, visiting Augusta, Charleston, and Wilmington. Christmas he had the pleasure of spending with General Stuart, with whom there followed the opportunity of inspecting troops near Fredericksburg. Late in January he made a trip to Mobile, inspecting the defenses and sharing in the social life, even to the degree of serving as groomsman at

[10] Scheibert states that he had entrusted with Fremantle "news" to his bride and parents in Germany.—*Sieben Monate in den Rebellen-Staaten*, 96. Pollard gives the story of Fremantle's crossing the Union lines, in *The Second Year of the War*, Appendix, "The Battle of Gettysburg and the Campaign in Pennsylvania," 367-370. Through the sub-title, "Diary of an English Officer in the Confederate Army," and the content, it is simple to identify the writer as Fremantle.

[11] Henry C. Fletcher, *History of the American War*, I, Preface, v.

the wedding of his friend Von Scheliha, whom he had met at Ringgold and whose relatives he knew in Europe. He made his return pleasantly by steamer up the Alabama River to Montgomery, by rail across to Charleston and ran the blockade out of Wilmington to Nassau. There is hardly a Confederate of prominence in civil or military life who does not figure in the pages of the book which records his Confederate experiences. Ross appeared in America in the full uniform of the Hungarian Hussars and was with difficulty dissuaded from donning it for his sojourns with the army, but friends tried to paint to him the invariable custom of the Confederate privates of never allowing the slightest peculiarity of costume to pass without a constant flood of jokes, bound to become boresome to the victim.[12]

A host of lesser military men found their way south of Mason and Dixon's line. The number of young officers who, sent to Canada from Great Britain when war with the United States over the *Trent* affair seemed probable, took advantage of their relative nearness to use their leaves for a visit to the front cannot be estimated. But Wolseley gives a clear-cut picture of the interest felt by them in the American war. "It is not easy to describe the breathless interest and excitement with which from month to month, almost from day to day, we English soldiers read and studied every report that could be obtained of the war as it proceeded."[13] Among the young officers who succeeded in viewing the war at first hand were Lord Dunmore, of the Scots Fusilier Guards, who had gone to Richmond and Charleston incognito under his family name of Murray; Captain Phillips of the Grenadier Guards, who had been present with Pelham at one of the artillery engagements and had been given a red and blue striped necktie to wear around his hat as a talisman; Colonel Bramston, also of the Grenadier Guards; Captain Bushby; and an officer of engineers who crossed the lines on foot, visited the Army of Virginia, and even reached Charleston.[14] To this group may

---

[12] His story appeared first in the pages of *Blackwood's* as "A Visit to the Cities and Camps of the Confederate States," XCVI, XCVII, 1864-1865. It was later published in book form. See Pollard, *op. cit.*, 340.

[13] Wolseley, "An English View of the Civil War," *North American Review*, CXLIX, 725.

[14] Morgan, *Recollections of a Rebel Reefer*, 104; Philip Mercer, *The Life of the Gallant Pelham*, 136. Phillips requested the gift of the necktie to be preserved as a memento of his experience.—Ross, *op. cit.*, 220. The officer last mentioned in the text came in with

belong an English captain who visited General Jackson at Moss Neck, and who found him drying out his guest's great overcoat when the visitor went to the headquarters tent to bid his host good-bye; and some British officers who appeared at Memphis and wished to visit the encampment in that vicinity.[15]

A group of three French visitors to the camp of the First Maryland Regiment while it was in camp at Swift Run Gap in May, 1862, excited some suspicion, though they might well have been army officers, as they claimed. Indeed one specifically identified himself as De Beaumont of the Chasseurs d'Afrique. Foreign vessels in the harbors brought visitors from among the officers aboard to the port before which they were lying, notably to New Orleans, where the hostilities of the Union men-of-war drew both French and English vessels for the protection of their respective subjects. Record exists of the visit to Norfolk of two officers of the Brazilian navy, whose ship lay at Fortress Monroe. Imagination must cover many unrecorded visits.[16] A German baron who came over from Washington to learn Mosby's tactics and the secret of his success learned them only too well when some of the general's scouts in Fairfax County took him for an imposter and "went through him," the Mosby men's term for robbing him of all he had. When he reported the outrage at Mosby's headquarters, displaying his papers, he was informed that that was "part of our tactics." His sojourn was brief.[17]

Colonel le Mat was a visitor who came for quite a different purpose—to teach, in one sense, rather than to learn. He was the inventor of the "grapeshot revolver," the cylinder of which, filled with

---

only a small kit, and cannot be the unidentified person first mentioned in this chapter, as the dates do not accord. Colonel Bramston is mentioned by Von Borcke, as is Bushby.

[15] Elihu S. Riley, *Stonewall Jackson*, 49; Markinfield Addey, "Stonewall Jackson," *The Life and Military Career of Thomas Jonathan Jackson*, Addenda, 229. This Englishman had brought a box from Nassau to General Jackson and had received an invitation to visit him in his camp. General Thompson had taken charge of the English visitors to Memphis, had boasted loudly of his state troops as by far the best in point of instruction and discipline in the West, and then drilled them all night in order to show them off to his visitors next morning. But one old ex-sheriff, who could never acquire the least smattering of drill, proved to be Thompson's Waterloo.—Duke, *Reminiscences*, 82-83.

[16] McKim, *A Soldier's Recollections*, 87. One of the amusing stories of the early days of Union control in New Orleans relates how two French officers noted that the streetcar on which they were riding was frequently hailed by women, but boarded by none. When they learned that it was because their uniforms were being mistaken for Federal uniforms, they left the car in order not to deprive the ladies of their ride!—Southwood, *op. cit.*, 298. See also Ellis, *Leaves from the Diary of an Army Surgeon*, 30-31, for the Brazilian visitors.

[17] J. Marshall Crawford, *Mosby and his Men*, 190-191.

bullets, revolved around a section of the gun barrel, the barrel itself being loaded with buckshot. Le Mat's English vocabulary was limited, and his sole subject of conversation his invention, which he was trying to sell to the Confederate authorities, so that men whom he insisted on posing in order to illustrate his invention were inclined to fight shy of the imaginative Gaul.[18]

As always happens in time of war, there also came to the scene of conflict a group of distinguished civilians. One of the earliest was also one of the most distinguished. On August 16, 1861, Prince Napoleon arrived in Charleston to be the guest of General Beauregard for two days. It will be recalled that this son of Jerome Bonaparte bore the pompous name of Prince Napoleon Joseph Charles Paul Bonaparte, but acquired the nickname of Plon-Plon, a corruption of Plomb-plomb, bestowed upon him because of supposed cowardice in the Crimean War. He had been made a prince in 1852 and was destined to become the head of the Bonapartist party upon the death of the prince imperial in 1879.[19]

The visit to Richmond of Count Mercier, the French minister to the United States, was certain to attract attention, even if he had not expressed to the friends of the fearless Unionist sympathizer, John Minor Botts, great anxiety to converse with him on the subject of the war, as he placed great reliance on his views. This was not, of course, allowed him, as Botts was at that time reposing in prison for too frank an expression of his views. It is, however, asserted that a copy of the letter which Botts had prepared in October, 1861, for the French consul in Richmond, setting forth the history of the secession question, was placed in Count Mercier's hands during his visit.[20]

Lord Edward St. Maur came to America with the Marquis of Hartington, whom we shall encounter in another group directly, and

[18] Morgan, *Recollections of a Rebel Reefer*, 94.
[19] Bartlett, "A Soldier's Story of the War," *Military Record of Louisiana*, 51 n., August 16. Space is not taken here to record the visit of Dr. Rudolph Mathews Schleiden, minister for Bremen, 1861-64, who made a flying visit to Richmond on April 25-27. He went for the express purpose of mediating a truce but without official authority from Lincoln and therefore hardly classifies as a visitor in the sense used in this chapter; furthermore, the war was scarcely yet on, for Virginia was ratifying the provisional constitution of the Confederate States on the very day of his arrival. See Ralph H. Lutz, "Rudolf Schleiden and the Visit to Richmond, April 25, 1861," *Reports of the American Historical Association*, 1915, 209-216.
[20] John M. Botts, *The Great Rebellion*, xv.

was in Richmond for a brief period in 1862. He fought in the battles of the Seven Days around Richmond and distinguished himself for gallantry on the field at Frayser's Farm. It was what he told Wolseley, with whom he spent a few days in Canada before sailing for England, that fixed the former in his determination to visit the Army of Virginia. Lord St. Maur was preëminently a visitor, rather than a knight-errant, though noted, of course, with the latter.

A special magnet drew Lord Talbot to the Confederacy when in January, 1863, he ran the blockade into Charleston from Nassau. He had a son who was a colonel in the service and who continued in the army until the close of the war. In November of the same year Lords Harvey and Kartwright were in Richmond, having also entered via Nassau.[21]

Other English gentlemen of rank, including Colonel Leslie, chairman of the Commons Committee on Military Affairs, were soon to appear. Leslie spent a week in General Jackson's command and departed, enthusiastic about that soldier, as most visitors were.[22]

Besides these visitors who can be identified by name, the researcher finds many allusions to others, mentioned casually or by the first letter of the surname in accordance with the prejudices of the time, which seem to have regarded the bold printing of names as indelicate. The Englishwoman who had come over as a sort of assistant housekeeper with an English mistress to their South Carolina plantation tells in her memoirs of the war of the arrival from England of her mistress's brother, who came to break to her the news of her mother's death. This brother, Mr. "M," a rector of the Church of England, had great difficulty in getting through the United States.

[21] *Confederate Veteran*, XXV, 201; Freese, *Secrets of the Late Rebellion*, 84. The facts concerning the presence of distinguished visitors are so striking that it would not have seemed necessary to spread rumors of other persons being present, but Dame Rumor was busy from an early to a late period. To give just two illustrations: The *Huntsville (Ala.) Advocate* (not extant) on April 24, 1861, printed the statement that Baron Rothschild was in New Orleans then and had agreed to take the entire loan of $5,000,000 which had been advertised.—Reprinted by Montgomery *Daily Post*, May 2, 1861. And the *New York Times* on January 24, 1864, published a translation of a private letter from a Frenchman in Richmond, formerly an officer in the Confederate service, reporting the arrival at Richmond from Nassau of an agent of the French emperor, named Martigny, with whom President Davis had held conferences. It was reprinted by the *Daily Richmond Examiner*, February 3, 1864. It is probably needless to say that the writer has found no corroboration of these canards.

[22] He is quoted as saying: "He is a revelation to me; Jackson is the best informed soldier I have met in America and as perfect a gentleman as I have ever known."—Riley, *op. cit.*, 182. The Baltimore *Sun*, September 12, 1911, retells the story in the article, "Stonewall Jackson."

It is interesting to note that the amenities of the profession were extended to this visitor by a fellow clergyman even in wartime. The Presbyterian minister of the town near which the English woman was living, Conwayboro', extended an invitation for the stranger to preach at his church, which he felt that he could not well refuse, even though he was not of the same denomination. The congregation, we are assured, seemed very much pleased with the English minister's sermon. Late in the war, in August, 1864, after the death of her employer, Captain "W," who had entered the Confederate service and had died ultimately of disease contracted from hardship, another brother of her mistress, Clement E—, ran the blockade from Bermuda to escort his sister home to England. The stringency of the authorities at Washington at this date, late in the war, may be noted, for they refused him a passport. This British subject resided at Conwayboro' about three weeks, the length of time required to settle Mrs. "W's" affairs and to make the necessary preparations for leaving the country.[23] The memoirs and diaries of the war frequently speak of an Englishman or stranger encountered on the train or at some friend's home, or as running the blockade.[24]

Legislators seem to feel a special call to visit the scene of action during a war and doubtless it is highly desirable that some of the members of a body which is to pass the statutes regulating the attitude of a neutral nation should have primary evidence as to actual conditions. In any case some of the men who were sitting in the British parliament penetrated the lines of the Confederacy. Among the earliest of these visitors were Sir James Ferguson and the Honorable Mr. Burke, who witnessed a review of the Stonewall Brigade by Generals Johnson, Beauregard, and Smith sometime before October, 1861. It would appear that some in the South looked upon the visit as official, but Sir James stated to a Mrs. Hopley, an Englishwoman, that it was an unofficial visit, that his stay would be but

[23] Elizabeth Collins, *Memories of the Southern States*, 19, 99. She alludes always to her master as Captain W., and to her mistress as Mrs. W. He was evidently Lieutenant Governor Plowden C. J. Weston, elected December 16, 1862, with Governor Borham. The clergyman brother, the Rev. W. W. Malet, made several trips into nearby states, embodying his observations in *An Errand to the South in the Summer of 1862.*

[24] John Lewis Peyton, on his way from Richmond to Charleston, affords an illustration. "I could not restrain a burst of laughter at the remark of an Englishman, a fellow-traveler en route to run the blockade from Georgia, who in gazing at one of the stations at the confusion worst confounded, said it seemed to him 'as if hell had broken loose.' "—Peyton, *The American Crisis*, I, 176.

a short one, and that England would remain entirely neutral.[25] Mr. Burke, however, had proceeded farther South.[26] The Marquis of Hartington, son of the Duke of Devonshire and member of parliament from North Lancashire, and Colonel William Leslie, member from Monaham, were apparently next on the scene and seem to have entered by crossing the Upper Potomac sometime early in February, 1863.[27] George Thompson, whose special interest in parliament was forwarding the cause of the laboring class, was visiting the Confederacy in December, 1864. Last to arrive, the Honorable Peter Connolly, an Irish member from Donegal, was present to see the death throes of the Confederacy. At the request of General Lee he was allowed a room in the cottage of a Mrs. Pryor near Petersburg and messed with the general on his scanty fare. He ran the blockade on the *Owl*, expecting to land at Wilmington but, when the stars and stripes were detected flying above Fort Fisher, which had been captured only a few days before, the *Owl* turned tail and landed Connolly and two other passengers a short distance below the fort, from which point they readily made their way to Raleigh. But the full sets of horse equipment, including saddle, bridle, and stirrups, which the warm-hearted Irishman was bringing as gifts for General Lee and each member of his staff were never delivered. Governor Vance of North Carolina turned the visitor over to General C. M. Wilcox, who took him to Richmond and to army headquarters near Petersburg and escorted him along his own skirmish line. The Irishman became so enthusiastic on witnessing a slight skirmish that he offered his services for the approaching campaign to General Wilcox, who thereupon tendered him a place on his staff as volunteer aide. He left for Richmond on a Saturday evening to get his luggage, expecting to report early Monday morning, but on Sunday morning the lines were broken and the army was retiring toward Appomattox.

[25] It is possible to fix the approximate date of this visit from letters written by a young soldier. See Philip Slaughter, *A Sketch of the Life of Randolph Fairfax*, 18; Hopley, *Life in the South*, II, 71.

[26] Sir William Henry Gregory, M. P. for Galway, had recently visited the United States, North and South, but the writer has no evidence that it was after the war commenced. In fact it was probably before the outbreak of hostilities, for, back in London, as early as May, 1861, he was urging recognition.—"The Civil War in America," *The British Quarterly Review*, XXXIV, 204.

[27] The date is fixed by a statement in Lawrence, *Border and Bastille*, 67, where the author states that these two men had been forwarded across the river shortly before his arrival.

Connolly's next appearance was in New York ten days after the surrender, where he arrived after much difficulty, naturally, in reaching the railroad from Richmond. The impulsive Irishman there encountered General Wilcox, urged the paroled Confederate to return with him to Ireland, and tried to press his purse upon him.[28]

The correspondents of the great British newspapers formed a group quite distinct, yet they were brought into frequent contact with the other visitors. The earliest and probably most prominent of the group was Sir William Howard Russell, who represented the London *Times* and who has left us so many invaluable writings on the war. Russell was then about forty years old and at the height of his powers, with a rich background of experience as war correspondent in Denmark, the Crimea, and in India during the mutiny in 1858. He came from New York to Washington, entered Virginia at Norfolk about the middle of April before the fall of Sumter had drawn military lines, and spent the next two months in the Confederacy. He then returned to the North, as he foresaw that constant reports to his paper would be impossible from Richmond. His reports to the *Times*, especially his account of the first battle of Manassas, in which he bantered the Federals unmercifully, gave great offense to the North and brought down upon his head a torrent of newspaper condemnation and a flood of anonymous letters which threatened tar and feathering and even assassination. Finally when Secretary Stanton, a bit spitefully it must be confessed, refused to allow him to accompany General McClellan to the peninsula, he felt that his opportunity for usefulness to his paper in America was barred and accordingly set sail for his native country in the closing days of December, 1861. This virtual expulsion of Sir William may have been a mistake, as his letters would doubtless have painted to Europe the magnificent sacrifices, the enormous preparations for war made by the North, and might thus have brought an earlier modification of the views of the *Times*. One needs to recall the frenzied passion of wartime to realize why his criticisms, frankly expressed

[28] C. M. Wilcox, "Defense of Batteries Gregg and Whitworth, and the Evacuation of Petersburg," *Southern Historical Society Papers,* IV, 21-22, n. General Lee's request to Mrs. Pryor is characteristically courteous, as always: "General Lee has been honored by a visit from the Hon. Thomas Connolly, Irish M. P. from Donegal. He ventures to request you will have the kindness to give Mr. Connolly a room in your cottage, if this can be done without inconvenience to yourself."—Pryor, *Reminiscences of Peace and War,* 330.

of the Confederates also, failed to make his writings appeal to the Unionists as the impartial statements of a neutral.[29]

Francis C. Lawley, who slipped across the Potomac with Colonel Wolseley in mid-September, 1862, was the representative of the London *Telegraph*, became subsequently the editor of that paper, and ultimately was sent to parliament. Son of Lord Wenlock, he had been private secretary to Gladstone and was already well known in London society. He soon won a place in Richmond society by his personal charm, for he was spoken of as "one of the handsomest and most agreeable men ever known." Even Wolseley said of him that he never knew anyone with a "more charming voice or a more seductive manner." His resemblance to the best pictures of George Washington was remarked on wherever he went in America, and that likeness recommended him particularly to southerners. When one adds to handsome appearance and a pleasing voice the quality of being a companion who leaves no dull moments, one understands why Richmond society promptly took him to its heart.[30] The third outstanding newspaper correspondent, who with Lawley followed the stirring events of the war until the beginning of 1864, was Frank Vizetelly, correspondent, but, more particularly, artist for the *Illustrated London News*. He was equally clever with pen and brush, a rollicking fellow, full of fun, and incomparable as an aid to the young girls of Richmond and their soldier "boys" when they endeavored by tableaux and private theatricals to forget the war. He had followed all the recent campaigns—had been at Sebastopol, in China, with Garibaldi in Italy. But he was a reckless sort of person, capable of neglect in the matter of debts.[31]

Less prominent than any one of these three and without contact with them, of course, because of an earlier entry was S. Phillips Day, reporter for the London *Herald*, who traveled through a considerable portion of the southern states, especially in the area of the battle-

[29] The full record of his observations is to be had in *My Diary North and South*.
[30] See De Leon, *Belles, Beaux, and Brains of the 60's*, 334. For Wolseley's opinion of him see his *Story of a Soldier's Life*, II, 128.
[31] De Leon tells a story of a dinner given by Vizetelly, Lord Cavendish, and Colonel Gordon, lasting from two o'clock to midnight, which was never paid for—by them. He died while on service for England in Egypt and a tablet to his memory was placed in St. Paul's crypt.—*Belles, Beaux, and Brains of the 60's*, 334, 335. See also *Confederate Veteran*, XXXII, 285. For an excerpt from the *Illustrated London News* for April 2, 1864, which records his departure from Lee's camp for England after nearly two years in America, see XLIV, 314.

fields of the East in the summer of 1861. When he reached Washington, the provost marshal called upon him to recall the pass which he had been granted only a few days earlier by General Scott to visit the Union camps on the Virginia side of the Potomac. Day attributed the "undignified and scurvy treatment" accorded him to a statement published in the *New York Herald*, accusing him of secessionist proclivities of too strong a character for him to be allowed full liberties. He considered such treatment as a personal insult and so "derogatory to the important journal and the English interests" which he represented that he decided to stay no longer in a country "where the liberty of the press is virtually ignored, and free thought and free opinion, and the publication of facts, are regarded as hostile to the interests of a nation which has vaunted so long and so loudly of its free institutions!" Percy Greg, who after the war contributed a number of articles on the war to the London *Standard* and other periodicals, was in the Confederacy during a part of the war and constitutes one of the line of British visitors.[32]

The only instance encountered of a correspondent acting as a spy was an Englishman detected by General Baker only after he had imposed upon Secretary Seward and had received letters enabling him to visit the outposts whenever he wished. He boldly crossed the Federal lines, entered General Jackson's camp, and boasted of his deceptions until his secret meetings with well-known secessionists in Washington aroused General Baker's suspicions and lodged him in Old Capitol Prison.[33]

Through the correspondence conducted by the British consul at Charleston, Robert Bunch, one catches a fleeting glimpse of one Gabriel Cueto, who had come to America as correspondent of a Scotch newspaper but had somehow landed in the military prison at Salisbury, where he was languishing in November, 1862. Though debarred from writing he had managed to smuggle a letter to Bunch, in which he protested against being held without charges being brought against him. Bunch's demand for an investigation finally

[32] Day published his experiences and views of the war in *Down South*. The bitter outburst quoted in the text against the United States occurs on 293-294. For Greg see *Manchester Guardian*, December 30, 1889; W. E. A. A., "Percy Greg," *The Academy*, XXXVII, 45.

[33] LaFayette C. Baker, *Spies, Traitors, and Conspirators of the Late Civil War*, 209-215. Baker was chief of the Federal secret service during the war.

produced the report from the war department that Cueto had no passport, as he had deliberately decided not to get one in Washington, seeking to avoid the difficulties which had beset the path of William Howard Russell after his mission became known. When arrested, Cueto had used incendiary language, a fact which had caused his detention. The authorities offered to deliver him to the consul on the condition that he leave the Confederacy.[34]

The degree to which the newspaper reporters and visiting military men were thrown together and "chummed" together would strike the most careless reader. Scheibert and Von Borcke, as fellow countrymen, struck up a friendship as soon as the former appeared at General Stuart's headquarters shortly before the battle of Middleburg. Scheibert was with Von Borcke shortly after the latter was wounded, it will be recalled. On the way to Gettysburg, to cite other instances, we find Colonel Ross and Reporter Lawley occupying an ambulance together in General Longstreet's train, while Colonel Fremantle was a guest in the same corps. Scheibert and Ross were naturally drawn to each other as fellow cavalry officers and formed a friendship which was cemented in Richmond and Charleston. On the actual battlefield of Gettysburg, Scheibert, Lawley, and Fremantle watched the progress of the conflict from the same oak tree, as has been related.[35]

In Richmond the group of congenial aliens foregathered, Fremantle, who had been obliged to depart for England, being replaced by a young French consul who joined the quartet. They jestingly called themselves the Congress, as four great powers were represented.

[34] Bonham, *British Consuls in the Confederacy*, in "Columbia University Studies," XLIII, 104-105. George Alfred Lawrence cannot enter this story, for, though he came from England equipped with letters of introduction from Dudley Mann and Slidell to most of the influential persons of the Confederacy, he heeded Colonel Mann's advice to enter through the northern states rather than to run the blockade. He might better have followed his own instinct, for he was arrested by the United States and so failed in his enterprise. See his own account in *Border and Bastille*.

[35] It is almost amusing to get these contacts reported first by one and then another of these visitors, alluding to the others. See Ross, *op. cit.*, 46-47; Scheibert, *op. cit.*, 79, 88; Pollard, *op. cit.*, 347. Scheibert's description of how he located a good vantage point at Gettysburg is interesting: "Ich hatte an diesem Tage die ganze Front abgeritten und gesehen, dass man von keinem Punkte des Thales aus auch nur einen einigermassen günstigen Blick auf das Vorterrain hatte, bis ich auf dem Berge, auf welchem General Lee zu halten pflegte, eine Eiche und oben in der Eiche den Oberst Fremantle erblickte, dem ich mich zugesellte. Von hier aus lag das Schlachtfeld wie ein Panorama vor uns. Ich bin deshalb des 2. und 3. Juli keinen Schritt breit von dem Baume gewichen, von dem aus ich oft rapportiren musste, was ich sah.—*Op. cit.*, 87-88. See also above, p. 182.

Scheibert and Ross had adjoining rooms at the Ballard House and arranged to go together to Charleston where great events were daily awaited.

In Charleston Scheibert and Ross were associated with Vizetelly, whom Ross recognized from having seen his photograph, and all had become acquainted with the French, Spanish, and English consuls with whom they had a very pleasant relationship. On the night the bombardment began the other two aliens gravitated breathlessly to Scheibert's room.[36]

When Captain Ross moved on to the army in the west about the middle of September with Vizetelly, he encountered Colonel von Scheliha on General Buckner's staff, and Captain Dawson, now in Longstreet's quartermasters department. Then Lawley appears on the scene of interest. Here again there was much merrymaking at Chattanooga with Vizetelly the leader in the frolicking. It was no uncommon thing, according to Dawson, to see half a dozen officers late at night dancing to the music of "The Perfect Cure," one of the favorite songs of the day in the London music halls, which was introduced in the west by Vizetelly.[37]

Back in Richmond by early December, the two reporters and Ross found another attractive companion in Von Borcke, who was slowly recovering from his wound. As an old habitué of the Confederate capital, he introduced the newcomers to the Oriental Saloon, where a capital supper was to be had even thus late when the chef was likely to be handicapped in his art by the absence of ingredients. The trio who had wandered about the battlefields together so long spent the Christmas of 1863 in camp with General Stuart, but the note of separation was sounded in the farewell dinner given to Lawley at the Oriental on January 14, as he was leaving almost at once for Europe. Ross however was to make his last trip in January and February, this time to Mobile, as the reader is aware, and alone, for Vizetelly left him at Wilmington to sail for home in early April, 1864. In the Gulf city Ross was received as an old friend by Von Scheliha, now chief engineer of the department of the Gulf. When the accommodations at the hotel proved unsatisfactory, the engineer insisted on sharing his quarters with him and placed a horse at his

[36] Ross, *op. cit.*; Scheibert, *op. cit.*, 113, 116.
[37] Dawson, *Reminiscences of Confederate Service*, 102.

disposal so that they had many rides together.[38] The Austrian also finally left by running the blockade from Wilmington.

On the boat on which he sailed for Europe from Nova Scotia Scheibert found as fellow travelers the Prince de Joinville, whom he condescendingly describes as a "harmless, agreeable young man," and Major Anderson of the British embassy at Washington, whose opinions confirmed Scheibert in his own views as to Confederate fortunes. One more contact, and the circle is finished. Von Borcke, when in Richmond for Pelham's funeral in March, 1863, encountered Lawley, who presented him to Prince Polignac. Englishman, Austrian, Frenchman, German—all must cross each other's path within the confines of the Confederacy.[39]

That business men would be drawn to a nation at war and in need of all sorts of supplies was as inevitable as that military men would be drawn there, though the magnet was quite a different one. The two months' visit of Lord John Brewerton to the South during October and November, 1863, evidently was made to measure the cotton resources of the South. His lordship had just reached New York, ready to return to England from a trip to Washington, when a cablegram sent him back to Lord Lyons and then to Richmond in an effort to secure an interview with President Davis. A certain Colonel Ralph Abercrombie[40] accompanied him to arrange and make the trip overland to Richmond with the eminent nobleman in disguise as a farmer. President Davis, when Lord Brewerton's presence in the city was made known to him, insisted on the distinguished Englishman's becoming his guest at the executive mansion. For a day or two the two men were in consultation alone, and then came a procession of cabinet members, army officers, and other prominent men. A reception was given soon after in his honor at the president's home, one of the most brilliant given there during the war, with the grounds illuminated festively with fireworks, military bands in attendance, and many of the chief notables in civil and military life

[38] Ross, *op. cit.*, 204, 229, 240-241.

[39] Scheibert, *op. cit.*, 126; Von Borcke, *Memoirs of the Confederate War for Independence*, II, 191.

[40] Colonel Abercrombie was appointed by President Davis to conduct foreigners between Washington and Richmond. He was outstanding among such guides in his boldness and courage and was adept in disguises. His assistants were so reliable and his plans so well conceived that only once was he arrested and then he succeeded in making his escape. His route was the same both ways, with the same guides and the same stopping places.— Freese, *op. cit.*, 65-66, 87-91.

present. It had been arranged that the women, from the president's wife down, should be attired in calico as a compliment to the cotton manufacturing interests of England, though, if the truth were told, there were few silk or satin gowns left to wear. Within about two weeks after the grand ball the visiting nobleman started through the Confederate States on an inspection tour, being especially interested in the places where vast quantities of cotton were stored. The trip swept from Wilmington to Mobile and consumed about two months. It was reported that upon the visitor's return to Richmond he expressed his complete belief in the final success of the Confederate cause, assuring President Davis that he and his associates would furnish whatever money, arms, and provisions were required by the Confederacy in exchange for cotton, and that the South would continue to receive the support of all the upper classes in England. After a final week of consultation in Richmond, Colonel Abercrombie escorted the nobleman, again in disguise, back to the British embassy in Washington. It was said that he attended a grand reception at the White House, and was regarded as a firm friend of the Union.[41]

On one of his trips Abercrombie took a Charles R. Dangerfield, a large manufacturer or agent of British manufacturers of arms, successfully through the lines. The object of the visit was to negotiate contracts at Richmond in exchange for cotton, contracts which were consummated and signed after a trip to all the larger cities and storage places in order to satisfy him of the availability of the cotton. Still a third British manufacturer who can be identified is a Francis Miller, who, like the two just noted, was conducted through the lines by the same expert guide. After the usual tour through the Confederacy, he made contracts to furnish arms, accouterments, saddles, and clothing which were to be paid for in cotton.[42]

There was a mysterious visitor at Mobile in 1862, a Mr. Cassell, whose task was to collect the gold in payment of interest on the Alabama state bonds held in England. Shortly before the middle of July he apeared in Mobile, a man of travel and culture, about twenty-five years of age, displaying British citizenship papers together with all the papers necessary to secure immunity from arrest and

[41] *Ibid.*, 76-83.
[42] *Ibid.*, 87, 88. These stories have to rest on the statement of Dr. Freese, as the writer has found no corroborative testimony. His accounts are very circumstantial.

winning the courtesy of being entertained by the midshipmen's mess on board the gunboat *Morgan* which had escaped up the river after the fall of the forts of Mobile Bay. One day in July he was on board the *Crescent* as she was sailing down the river for the bay with the British flag flying from her flagstaff. She pulled up alongside the British corvet *Rinaldo* as the British consul, who was also aboard, wished to communicate with the captain of the *Rinaldo*. Both the consul and Cassell boarded the *Rinaldo* while some small boxes, evidently containing gold, were hurriedly passed through a porthole of that vessel. Cassell seemed to be in charge of the *Rinaldo* and remained aboard after the consul returned to the *Crescent*.[43]

Another British merchant, Corsan, who spent two months in the Confederacy, October and November, 1862, does not seem to have received the kindly ministrations of Colonel Abercrombie and experienced considerable difficulty in being able to leave. Evidently he was not negotiating public contracts with the government. In retaliation for the Federal order which forbade the flag of truce boat to carry any passenger except consuls to or from City Point, Secretary Randolph issued a peremptory order that no person could leave the Confederacy. First Corsan had to break down the Confederate order by his persistence, prolonged through ten or twelve days, and do it unaided—for the British consul could lend him no aid—and then he found himself, despite his British passport, position, and Confederate pass, curtly refused, on the ground of his being an Englishman, by the Federal official of the flag of truce boat which once or twice a week came from Fortress Monroe to City Point for the exchange of paroled prisoners. And so back to Richmond he had to go. He finally made his escape via the Shenandoah Valley by running the lines somewhere on the Upper Potomac; after an interesting week of travel he entered Maryland and was finally free to return to his native land.[44]

A man of the prominence of Baron Émile Erlanger in the business and social world could not send agents for a visit to the Con-

[43] This story is told by a midshipman who was detailed to the *Crescent* on special mission in citizen's clothes and told to observe and report all he saw. Cassell came up to speak to him, evidently recognizing a former host, and frankly stated the mission of the *Crescent*.—Peter Brannon, "Through the Years, The Gunboat Morgan," Montgomery *Advertiser*, September 29, 1935. The story was originally told by Thomas G. Garrett, the midshipman, in the *Advertiser* in 1909.
[44] Corsan, *Two Months in the Confederate States*, 246-248, 254, 255.

federacy without attracting attention. As is well known, this wealthy German had banking houses at Frankfort, Paris, and Amsterdam, and it was to him that Colonel J. G. Gibbs turned when he was sent to Europe in December, 1862, to dispose of fifteen million dollars worth of Confederate cotton loan bonds after he had failed to place them in England. After some weeks of negotiation the French banking house of Erlanger et Compagnie proved willing to float a loan, but the Jewish financier ridiculed the idea of such a small issue when a much larger figure could easily be negotiated, for cotton was then bringing sixty to eighty cents a pound in Liverpool whereas the bonds called for redemption in cotton at only ten cents a pound. Erlanger finally took up the entire issue at about eighty cents on the dollar.

M. Émile Erlanger, a member of the firm, under the impetus of such a market, decided to send his agents directly to the new state. At Washington they secured a pass to Richmond without difficulty, for they were not recognized as representatives of the famous banking house, and soon appeared on the streets of Richmond. In contact with President Davis and Secretary Memminger they urged a much larger issue of the cotton bonds. But Davis, relying on his secretary's judgment, proved indifferent. Fortune, smiling upon the author in respect to the identity of the Polish delegates who came to negotiate for a homeland in return for military service, denied her favor in regard to the names of these financial agents. Hence the contract was drawn up for the small sum stipulated and signed secretly by the secretary and the three visiting Frenchmen on January 28, 1863. The banker, accustomed to speculation, advertised the bonds at a minimum bid of ninety cents, which was far too high. The actual value of the loan netted to the government was only $6,250,000. There are still people who feel that, if a foreigner's advice had been heeded, the Confederacy would have had a permanent history.[45]

It seems desirable, though perhaps not strictly logical, to classify Charles Frédéric Girard with the visitors. Although he had come to America from Switzerland with the scientist Agassiz in 1847, had served with him three years at Harvard, had then become identified with the Smithsonian Institution during the decade before the war,

[45] See "If We Had the Money," *Southern Historical Society Papers*, XXXV, 201-203. For a fuller account of the affair see Schwab, *The Confederate States of America*, 30-36. Richardson, *The Secret Service*, 361-362, proves that there were three agents sent by the Erlanger Company.

and had even become naturalized, his service to the Confederacy was to all intents that of a foreigner. Caught in France when the war broke out, where he had gone in 1860, he accepted a commission from the Confederate government to supply its army with drugs and surgical instruments. Despite great difficulty in securing entrance, he ran the blockade into Charleston on the *Junon* on the night of July 8, 1863. From General Beauregard he secured a pass to Richmond, where he sought out General Cooper, an acquaintance from Washington days. That acquaintance opened all doors so that he met the Confederate statesmen and visited the patent office and the Tredegar works. During the summer he visited Virginia and the Carolinas and embodied his observations in a book which he gave to the French reading public, emphasizing by its very title the fact that it represented the view of an outsider, *Les Etats Confédérés d'Amérique Visité en 1863.*[46]

There appears as the agent of Messrs. Huller and Company, large French contractors, a M. Luel who was in Richmond in the summer of 1861 to superintend the purchase of tobacco for the French empire, thus giving great impetus to this branch of trade, and giving rise to the hope that the blockade would be short-lived. While the newspaper reporter Day was being conducted over some of the huge warehouses, nine hundred hogshead of tobacco were pointed out as belonging to the French government. A Mexican, José Oliver, was in Richmond in 1862 to negotiate with the government for the sale of saltpeter.[47]

It is sufficient here merely to recall the visit of the Polish delegation which was sent to Richmond in September, 1864, by their fellow exiles in Moldavia and Wallachia.[48]

Visitors were received with true southern hospitality by everyone, civilian or officer on the field. One marvels at the readiness with which the stranger could secure access to the highest officials, and how heads of government departments, burdened with the cares of state, could find time to accord a friendly hearing to each curious or sympathetic stranger. Of course they were eager to win friends

---

[46] Preface, vi, 10, 33-34, 68, 81, 85. For Girard's career in America see *Dictionary of American Biography*, VII, 319.

[47] Day, *op. cit.*, I, 82. Four hundred hogsheads were of an old, and 500 of a new purchase; Secretary Benjamin was unable to close a contract with Oliver.—*O. W. R.*, Ser. 1, VI, 864, 48.   [48] See above, Chap. VII.

for the "Cause," but even knights-errant, expecting commissions and claiming time, must have become burdensome. One may regard the procession as beginning with Sir William Russell. He was received by President Davis, Secretary of War Walker, Attorney General Benjamin,[49] General Beauregard, General Whiting (major then), and Senator Wigfall and was invited by Mrs. Davis to an "At-Home" in the temporary White House in Montgomery.[50] Each visitor required the ministrations of a long line of officials. Perhaps one could not do better than to note the many persons involved in the reception accorded to Captain Ross of the Austrian Hussars in Richmond on June 18, 1863. He delivered his introductions, chiefly in the form of photographs, as letters had been considered too compromising, secured an interview with Secretary of War Seddon, who wrote a pass for him to the army; he met the chief of the Signal Corps, the under-secretary of war, and Burton Harrison, private secretary to President Davis, who furnished him with letters of introduction to their friends in the army. He had a long and "most interesting" conversation with Benjamin, by this time secretary of state, and escorted by the president's secretary saw President Davis, who was very courteous and "conversed some time" with him. Major Morris was "particularly obliging" and made all arrangements for his journey to overtake Lee. Major Carrington telegraphed to Staunton in order to assure him a place on the stage and provided him with a letter to the quartermaster there, and went down to the station to see him off at six o'clock in the morning, securing for him a seat in the ladies' car, and particularly charging the conductor with taking proper care of him. "Everybody seems to take pleasure in doing all they possibly can to oblige a stranger," is Ross's very natural conclusion. "It is enough to know that you are a foreigner, and all will do their utmost to assist you."[51] Passes seem to have been freely issued to the strangers, knights-errant, or mere visitors, and letters of introduction to the various military generals and commanding officers were forthcoming. Of course everyone wanted to meet

[49] It will be recalled that this versatile statesman started as attorney general.
[50] Russell, "Recollections of the Civil War," *North American Review*, CLXVI, 372-373.
[51] Ross, *op. cit.*, 23. For the full story see 15-23. Scheibert, while showing appreciation of the burdens of the secretary of war, was, naturally, impatient of delay for himself. "Am folgenden Tage begab ich mich zu dem unter der Arbeitslast fast erdrückten Kriegsminister Herrn James A. Seddon, bei dem ich bei seiner vielen Beschäftigung leider nie vor 11 Uhr Abends ein Audienz erhielt."—*Op. cit.*, 15.

General Lee, and the present-day reader feels that Richmond might have been a little more considerate of his time and strength. Ross found that his anxiety about transportation to the front was needless, as a government wagon was placed entirely at his disposal for reaching Lee's headquarters. When a bit of pressure was necessary to get hotel accommodations, it was forthcoming, and a Colonel Allen, acting commandant at Chambersburg, secured admission to the inn for Captain Ross. When the strangers needed a mount to ride with the army, it was promptly provided.[52]

The generals extended a kindly and cordial reception, accompanied usually by entertainment. Frequently high ranking officers accompanied the visitor on the tour of inspection. Captain Lee, the general's brother, showed Wolseley round the works at Drury's Bluff, pointing out all new improvements in guns, carriages, and projectiles. General R. E. Lee kept him a long time in his tent, conversing on a variety of topics. He regretted that he "couldn't put him up," but placed horses or a two-horse wagon, as he preferred, at his disposal.[53] When Ross visited the army in the west, he rode with General Breckinridge and General Custis Lee, and dined with General Gracie. General Beauregard personally escorted the relatively insignificant reporter, Day, over the battlefield of Manassas.[54]

General Stuart, with his tremendous energy and exuberance of spirits, probably thoroughly enjoyed guests. Certainly he was not required to invite Lawley, Vizetelly, and Ross to spend Christmas at his headquarters near Orange Court House in 1863. When the two last-named put in their appearance—Lawley was prevented from accepting—they were warmly welcomed, and Vizetelly, who was a great favorite of the general, contributed some of his best stories to the Christmas cheer. Stuart, the perfect host, gave up his tent and blankets to Ross when they retired. Of course Stuart rode with his friends on a tour of inspection. Christmas morning the two guests rode over to pay their respects to General Lee. He pressed them to remain to share his Christmas fare, but they felt under obligation to return to General Stuart's table. Unfortunately just as they had started back, a messenger came galloping up to advise them to accept

[52] Ross, op. cit., 25, 38, 49.
[53] "A Month's Visit to the Confederate Headquarters," Blackwood's, XCIII, 12, 21. Captain Lee extended the same personal attention to Ross when he visited Drury's Bluff.— Ross, op. cit., 19-20.   [54] Day, op. cit., II, 72.

an invitation to dinner, if it were extended, as the turkey, ducks, and other delicacies expected had not arrived. Nevertheless General Stuart managed to serve his guests a fairly good dinner.[55]

Probably no more thoughtful act of hospitality could be found in the annals of war than that extended to Scheibert, and it must be credited to that perfect gentleman, Robert E. Lee. Although Lee was lying ill in a farmer's house close to his headquarters near the Rappahannock, he sent to Scheibert in response to his letter of introduction a warm invitation to regard the general's tent as his and expressed the hope that Scheibert would remain at headquarters long enough to view the army and for Lee to meet him.[56] To Captain Ross, when he was presented to the general near Chambersburg shortly before the battle of Gettysburg, Lee extended an invitation to share his dinner. Ross's comment is sufficiently illuminating: "It was a frugal meal, and simply served."[57]

Sometimes the courtesy to the stranger was well and promptly repaid. This proved the case when Hobart Pasha, the blockade-runner, was utilizing a few days' stay in port for a visit to Richmond. It was owing to the presence in the party of General Custis Lee, a son of the commander in chief, that Hobart and his friends were able to get through the lines of the southern army, which they had been skirting. The staff, when the party reached headquarters, gave them a hearty welcome, in return for which the blockade-runner offered such delicacies as cases of sardines, bologna, sausages, and condiments for a feast.[58]

Kindness and friendliness were poured out also by the civilians on the knights-errant and visitors in overflowing measure. They were indeed accepted into the inner circles of society.[59] An invitation to Ashley Hall, some five or six miles from Charleston, the home of Colonel Bull, descendant of the last royal governor of South Carolina, afforded the group of aliens—Ross, Scheibert, and Vizetelly— an opportunity to see a southern plantation under delightful conditions. The reader, too, can almost forget the war as he spends the

---

[55] Ross, op. cit., 204-206, 207-208.
[56] Scheibert, op. cit., 17.   [57] Ross, op. cit., 43.
[58] Hobart Pasha, Sketches from My Life, 161-163. Hobart makes the error of thinking General Custis Lee is a nephew of R. E. Lee.
[59] Ross, op. cit., 242, 251. At Mobile, Ross had to burst into eulogies of the "gentler sex." "The reports I had heard of the charms of the fair sex at Mobile I found to be not at all exaggerated."—Ibid., 240.

day with them, "roaming over cotton-fields and rice plantations, through woods, and park-like meadows, studded with the most magnificent live oaks," wanders through an artistic garden with winding walks, small lakes, and all sorts of flowers and trees, and finally enters a comfortable though simple house in the English style.[60] Captain Pegram took the lad Dawson with him, when they landed from the *Nashville*, to his home in Sussex county, Virginia, for a visit. There Dawson met a Nat Raines, a wealthy planter, who was so captivated by the youth that he made him one of his family. It was to this home that Dawson repaired when he was given a furlough to recover his health. Equally fortunate in Richmond, Dawson found a second home with Mr. and Mrs. John H. Tyler, parents of one of the ordnance sergeants in his regiment, where long after the war a chair was still kept for him at the table as regularly as if he had been a son.[61] The southern people seemed to feel that any foreigner taking up arms in their behalf must not be allowed to feel the absence of parents and relatives. The Frenchman Hermann bears testimony that his friends all over the county, when he returned to Georgia, took pride in performing the duty of relatives; the Scotchman Watson tells how the people of Baton Rouge had a packet of blankets, clothing, shirts, shoes, stockings, and many little gifts sent him, accompanied by affecting letters from mothers, thanking him for his care over their boys. He was deeply moved and inspired for the cause by this thoughtfulness.[62]

Nothing could exceed the tender care lavished upon the knights-errant wounded in the defense of the beloved southland. While Dawson lay wounded in Richmond, the fact was noted in the Richmond *Dispatch*. His old friends in the navy—and he remarks that navy officers are more clannish and stick together more closely than army officers—came at once to visit him. First came his "dear friend," Captain R. B. Pegram, who chided Dawson for resigning from the navy without informing him of his intention. Commodore Hollins, Commodore Forrest, and Captain Arthur Sinclair were all "exceedingly attentive."[63]

[60] *Ibid.*, 112-113. See also Scheibert's description of that excursion, *op. cit.*, 114-116. The description in the text is a composite formed from the impressions of the two visitors.
[61] Dawson, *Reminiscences of Confederate Service*, 34-35, 100, 119.
[62] For an instance of Secretary Benjamin's kindness to a stranger see Hermann, *Memoirs of a Veteran*, 70-71; Watson, *Life in the Confederate Army*, 247, 249.
[63] Dawson, *op. cit.*, 51.

The romantic figure of the Prussian Von Borcke was known the length and breadth of the land, and so his serious wound, causing his life to hang by a thread for months, was a source of grief everywhere. He was taken by Dr. Eliason in General Longstreet's private ambulance[64] to the doctor's home near the Blue Ridge, where he was nursed by the women of the family with the loving care which would have been bestowed on a son of the house. Here he lay for months until he could be moved to Dundee, where it was thought the mountain air would hasten his recovery. In Richmond kindnesses were heaped upon him and his friends suffered with him when the slightest exertion brought on a paroxysm of strangling.

The devotion of General Stuart to his chief lieutenant, Von Borcke, was a feeling far deeper than gratitude to the man who comes to aid in a desperate venture. There sprang up between the two men a Phythias and Damon friendship, one of the beautiful by-products of the field and tent. This chapter can close in no more fitting way than with the scene between this dying native-born son of Virginia and the beloved alien within her boundaries. Von Borcke, still an invalid, had come to bid his chief the last farewell and was sobbing as frankly as a child. To his foreign friend, for whom he had sent, Stuart addressed these words—they were his last conscious words: "My dear Von, I am sinking fast now, but before I die I want you to know that I never loved a man as much as yourself. I pray your life may be long and happy; look after my family after I'm gone, and be the same true friend to my wife and children that you have been to me." The scene offers a beautiful companion picture to the visit paid not a great while before by Stuart to the grievously wounded Prussian when no hopes were entertained for his recovery.[65]

[64] Captain Scheibert, at the first news of Von Borcke's being wounded, hastened from the distant army headquarters, bringing Longstreet's private ambulance, and with it many kind messages from that officer.—Von Borcke, *Memoirs*, II, 297-298.

[65] *Ibid.*, 313-314.

XII

FOREIGN WOMEN FURTHER THE CAUSE

A DISCUSSION OF THE women of the Confederacy who chanced to be born under an alien flag as distinct from the rest of the civilian population would have little meaning except as they furthered the interests of the new republic. Hence this brief chapter is devoted to a presentation of their special activities in connection with the war or with the individual state.

Except the German and Irish women who occasionally even ventured to aid northern soldiers,[1] the foreign-born women were as fanatically devoted to the Confederate cause as the women who were bound to the South by generations of American blood. They were as enthusiastic as the American-born in their support of the government at Richmond, as bitter in their denunciation of the foreign "vandal," and as eager to assist the brave "boys in gray." The desire to be of service sometimes took strange forms. An Englishwoman heard the report of the illness of a soldier and offered a grave in her family plot. One very touching story of loyalty comes from the northern-born but southern-wed Flora Adams Darling, wife of General Darling, who had been killed in battle. By special arrangement of generals on both sides, Mrs. Darling was returning to her New England home and had reached Mobile. The evening before her departure from that city General Garner called with several of her Louisiana friends to bid her good-bye. There was also in the group an Italian woman, a guest at the Battle House, whose husband had been killed in the patriot army under Garibaldi. An enthusiastic supporter of the Confederacy, she sang the war songs of her adopted country with ardor and supported the cause of freedom zealously from an Italian point of view. As the group was about to separate,

[1] A northern officer tells how in Richmond, when a train of injured Union soldiers was waiting to be taken to the hospital, now and then a German woman thrust out her hands and gave a little cake to some soldier who aroused her special pity. When commanded by the guards to stand back and give nothing, she answered, "Ich verstehe kein Englisch." Later the same author relates how these German women would pass along the line of northern soldiers with baskets and slip a cake to the soldiers when they could, despite positive orders against such charities.—Marks, *The Peninsular Campaign*, 379-380, 397.

someone proposed that they sing the "Marseillaise," each in his or her own tongue—and "there, in Italian, French, and English, the battle-cry was taken up, with an ardor that must have reached Heaven, for it came from the hearts of men and women who knew the import of the soul-stirring words that have led so many on to 'victory or death.' In memory I can see that lady at the piano, with almost inspired look, as she sounded the key-note of liberty, and sang the noble words of that grand old hymn that fires the souls of patriots with a fixed resolution, regardless of consequences."[2]

In the long list of persons sent abroad by the government on one mission and another, it is interesting and surprising to find the names of two women. Mary S. Hill, whom we shall meet again in hospital work, was an Irishwoman who had been brought to America in early life and had grown up in New Orleans. When her brother enlisted, she took up the cause with her whole heart. President Davis sent her, because of her mental alertness and loyalty, to Europe on a diplomatic mission, the nature of which seems to have been successfully concealed even from the prying search of the modern historical scholar. The second such emissary was a Mrs. Grinnell who had come to New York only a few years prior to the war and was accepted as the daughter of an English baron. She was sent by the surgeon general to buy bandages which, a fellow countryman rather spitefully remarked, "nobody else but Mrs. Grinnell could get."[3]

As soon as the war was really under way, and the southern women began to assume for themselves a share in its activities, the Irish and German women came forward with their contribution. Their work was most apparent in communities where there was a recognized German community, such as Richmond or Wilmington or German Texas. A record has been left in Wilmington to the effect that "the German women of the city entered into the work, zealously giving their means as well as their time to the call of their President." It might be inter-

[2] "I shall never hear any music this side of the Eternal City like the last strains that fell on my ears in the land of memories; nor have I ever been guilty of attempting to sing since that memorable night, for I would not willingly dispel the impression of the heart-thrilling words. . . ." Darling, *Mrs. Darling's Letters of Memories of the Civil War*, 151.

[3] See *Confederate Veteran*, X, 124, for Miss Hill. Sprunt, in *Chronicles of the Cape Fear River*, 455, speaks very disparagingly of Mrs. Grinnell. "She was an English woman of that class and with those manners which any man, if he has traveled much, has often seen. She gave herself out as a daughter of an English baronet, and had first come to New York several years prior to the war."

esting to find here the names of some of the more prominent German officers repeated in the activities of their wives, but the scribe merely states that "were it not open to a charge of invidiousness, a few women might be singled out as especially helpful and interested in serving the country of their adoption."[4] Such helpfulness was not limited of course to group action where a number of Germans or Irish could gather to make clothing for the soldiers, to scrape lint, or to make bandages, but included numerous instances of the bringing in of linen and delicacies, which they could ill afford to spare, for the soldiers. Mrs. Burton Harrison has left a pretty picture of two rosy Irish sisters employed in the hospital with which she was associated who brought in linen sheets and pillowcases spun by their mother in the old country and given them for their "hope chests" in the new world. "On 'seein' the Yankees don't seem of a mind to spare us husbands anyhow, we'd be proud for you to use 'em, miss, in your beyoutiful room that's like a palace beside the rest."[5]

Oddly enough, the number of good women who went to the hospitals to nurse the wounded and ill soldiers was not as numerous as one would naturally expect, for a great deal of that labor of love was left to men. According to Kate Cumming, one of the devoted band who did render valiant service in this field, it was not regarded as ladylike to nurse soldiers in the hospitals. Again and again in her diary she strikes out at this attitude and criticizes the native southern women almost bitterly for their failure to come forward when there was so much work crying out to be done and too few hands to do it. "I know that the women of the South will think I have said too much against them: but let them remember that I, too, am a woman, and that every slur cast on them falls on me also. Will the neglect of the suffering, which I have but too faintly sketched, not serve to make them resolve in future to do better?" Or again, hear her impassioned plea: "Lest this outburst may leave a wrong impression, the writer hastens to reiterate that there were some women of the South whose names were enshrined in the hearts of the soldiers and officers for their selfless, untiring work as nurses."[6]

[4] *Ibid.*, 251. The German women of New Braunfels formed societies to make uniforms for the soldiers. See the master's thesis by Ada Hall, "The Texas Germans in State and National Politics, 1850-1865."
[5] Harrison, *Recollections Grave and Gay*, 184.
[6] Cumming, *A Journal of Hospital Life*, Introduction, 7.

Miss Cumming was herself a Scotchwoman living in Mobile at the outbreak of the war, who, although brought to America as a child, never fails to let the reader feel her nativity. She served as a nurse from April, 1862, to the surrender. She had a brother in the Alabama Artillery in the Army of the Tennessee, and a father still living in Mobile. Her diary leaves no doubt that she rendered splendid service helping to save many a life and soothing the dying hours of many a soldier. When milk was needed, she went out to the citizens and begged it; once, when in utter despair, she went to Dr. Young, the medical purveyor, and begged so persuasively for some wine that she did not come away empty-handed. Out of her own purse, assisted by the charity of the authorities at the hospital, she bought a little milk every day for the worst cases at the hospital at Chattanooga. When she visited the sick men on one occasion and found four who had eaten nothing for some time because they could not eat beef, bread, and coffee, their only supplies—a fact which only strengthened her conviction that many a man died for want of proper nourishment— she did not give up in despair, but wrote to her friends in Mobile for supplies. One needs no imagination to know that her letters were strong enough to bring a response. When a poor Catholic soldier could not die in peace without the last sacraments of the church, she set off posthaste to the home of a priest. Although his housekeeper sought to discourage her by stating that he was out and would have to have a meal and some rest before he could go out again, she insisted on waiting for him and was able to persuade him to come at once to the dying man.

Her foreign birth was an asset at times, as when one of the physicians took her while she was stationed at Gilmer Hospital in Georgia to visit a Scotchman who welcomed a fellow countryman with special pleasure.[7] Her stricture on her sex is especially interesting in view of the eulogies so unceasingly poured out on the women of the South: "I feel confident that very much of this failure is to be attributed to us. I have said many a time that, if we did not succeed, the women of the South would be responsible. This conclusion was forced upon me by what I could not but see without wilful blindness. Not for one moment would I say that there are no women in the South who have

[7] *Ibid.*, 46, 49, 53. The entire book rewards a perusal. For her visit to the Scotchman, see 103.

nobly done their duty, although there was an adverse current, strong enough to carry all with it."

Or one might well read these excerpts: "I have no patience with the women whom I hear telling what wonders they would do if they were only men, when I see so much of their own legitimate work left undone. Ladies can be of service in the hospitals, and of great service. I have heard more than one surgeon say, if he could get the right kind, he would have them in almost every department. I could name many things they could do, without ever once going into a ward."[8]

In all justice to the women it should be added that not all the physicians of the South welcomed women as nurses. In some hospitals, however, they were glad to have their services. Mary Hill, the Irishwoman mentioned above in connection with a diplomatic mission, rendered her finest service in the hospitals. During the Seven Days' Battles around Richmond she was in charge of the Louisiana hospital as matron. It was during this time that she won the name of the "Florence Nightingale of the Army of Northern Virginia."[9]

Because human nature is so rich that it cannot be confined to one field in its services, we encounter Miss Hill in still another capacity. During the time that General Butler held control of New Orleans, she suffered arrest and imprisonment in the Julia Street prison for women because she had been guilty of carrying letters through the military lines investing that city. The British consul interceded in her behalf so that ultimately she was released on the ground of her British citizenship. It is true that she often served as the bearer of messages from wives, sisters, and mothers in New Orleans to soldiers at the front and brought back the replies.[10]

From being the bearer of personal letters it is but a step to being the bearer of information to the military authorities. Among the many women who served the Confederate army in this way there was a Cuban, a Lola Sanchez. Her family, a feeble old father, an invalid wife, and three attractive daughters, lived on the east bank of St. John's River opposite Palatka, Florida. One brother was in the Confederate army, and the three daughters sympathized warmly with the South, conveying information whenever possible. The father had already been arrested and imprisoned at St. Augustine as a spy at the

[8] *Ibid.*, Introduction, 7.
[9] *Confederate Veteran*, X, 124.
[10] *Ibid.*

time of Lola's bold venture. Their place was often surrounded by northern soldiers, both whites and blacks, and the house searched for concealed spies, because information still percolated to the Confederates. But a bevy of attractive girls was likely to bring soldiers to the house for other reasons than to ferret out hidden spies. One evening while Lola was preparing refreshments for a group of Union officers, flitting back and forth from one room to another, she overheard enough to surmise that plans were afoot for two raids on the Confederates the next day—one a gunboat raid up the river against the Confederate camp, the other a foraging expedition south from St. Augustine. She promptly arranged with her sisters for one to entertain the men while the other continued the preparations for the supper. Meanwhile she sped on her mission of warning the Confederates, which involved a journey through a dense forest growth of water oak and pine, through a tangle of scrub vines, which wound itself about her neck with snaky folds, through palmetto and wild jasmine, and across a stream. The message delivered, she made the return journey safely, accomplishing the entire trip in an hour and a half without her absence having been noted by the Union officers. On the morrow occurred a capture by the Confederates instead of by the Yankees.[11] In the records of the Old Capitol Prison at Washington there is note of a French woman charged with having sold dispatches to the Confederate authorities,[12] who was brought in when the famous spy, Belle Boyd, was there.

A picturesque figure, the vivandière, has been known at least since the Thirty Years' War, and has appeared in the European armies frequently since. It is certainly a matter of interest, though scarcely of importance, that there was at least one such person in the southern army, attached to the Washington Artillery of New Orleans. With that military unit went a certain German, John Bahr, as steward, and his wife, Mistress John, whom Colonel Slocomb uniformed as a vivandière. She proved able to bear the fatigue of the campaigns as well as any of the men and made herself indispensable in many ways. The little woman proved as true as steel, and her motherly hand bathed many a soldier's wounds, made many a nourishing broth, or prepared for him a cup of creole coffee which he could drink. Soldiers, ever

[11] *Ibid.*, XVII, 409.
[12] Boyd, *Belle Boyd in Camp and Prison*, 245.

alert for sobriquets, named the good couple, not from disrespect but from a homely affection, "he bear and the she bear."[13] Very similar probably were the two "cantoneers," Mary Ann Perkins and Madame Boivert, who were entered on the roll of the Gardes Lafayette from Mobile. There were several other women of foreign birth who followed the army, though none who enjoyed so picturesque a costume or name as the "she bear" of the Washington Artillery. Mrs. Lucinda Horne accompanied Company K, Fourteenth South Carolina Volunteers, recruited from the German settlement of Edgefield County. To tend to her son and husband she traveled with this company of men through the war and evidently endeared herself to the members of that company, for she was later made an honorary member. There is also record of a Betsy Sullivan, Irish-born wife of a soldier, who went with a Tennessee regiment to cook, wash, and look after the needs of the men.[14] Mary Hill in her varied war record even accompanied the army to the field on several occasions in order to be near her brother. Such was her personality and character that, instead of breeding familiarity, she was treated with reverence by all the soldiers with whom she came in contact.[15]

The nearest approach to "soldiering" in an organized way on the part of any foreign woman in the Confederacy is found in Texas. The women at Castroville, which must have included some German women in that partly Teutonic settlement, organized and drilled with guns and pistols in order to defend their families against Indians while their menfolk were away with the army.

Among the extraordinary and dramatic characters associated with this war—and it is not likely that anyone who has pursued this story so far will deny the presence in the Confederate army of a number of romantic personalities—none was stranger than Mrs. Velazquez, the one foreign woman soldier to fight on the field of battle disclosed by the existing records. Madame Loreta Janeta Velazquez claimed descent from an ancient Castilian family of that name, one of whose sons, it is claimed, was in charge of the expedition which discovered Mexico. Born and reared in Havana, she began her career in the unconventional manner which was to characterize her: she was mar-

[13] Owen, *In Camp and Battle with the Washington Artillery*, 21.
[14] Chapman, *History of Edgefield County*, 483, 489-491. It is possible that Mrs. Horne was a descendant of Germans rather than German-born.
[15] *Confederate Veteran*, X, 124.

ried secretly in 1856 to a young American officer of the United States army. Upon the secession of his state, his wife persuaded him, though with considerable difficulty, to forsake the government which he had served so long and to throw in his fortunes with the Confederate forces. Then a yearning for a distinguished and active career seized her; "wild about war," she decided to raise a sword against the North with or without the consent of her husband.

In spite of her husband's remonstrances and the ugly picture he drew for her of the objectionable sides of a soldier's life, she carried out her plan after he had rejoined his regiment. Her first problem was, of course, a uniform and one which would prove an adequate disguise. In this she manifested considerable ingenuity. As soon as she reached New Orleans, she went to an old French army tailor in Barancas Street, whom she knew to be very skilful, and who, as she phrased it, "knew how to mind his own business by not bothering himself too much about other people's affairs." She had him make for her half a dozen fine wire net shields, which completely disguised her figure. Once assured of complete disguise in her uniform, she raised a regiment of recruits and spent her spare time in a conscientious study of the army regulations. When her quota was filled, she entrained at New Orleans and was met at Pensacola by her amazed husband to whom she had telegraphed her intention of proceeding to that place. Proud of her cleverness in carrying out her intentions, and acknowledging the futility of further argument, he took command of her men and began their military training. As he was explaining to one of the sergeants the use of the carbine, the weapon exploded in his hands and instantly killed him. Left utterly alone by the accident, Madame Velazquez, instead of being diverted from her original plan, now devoted her entire mind to a military career.[16]

She found herself under some disadvantages in not having a regular commission and in not being attached to some regular command. That fact exposed her to some slights which she would not otherwise have met and prevented officers from appointing her to commands which she might otherwise have achieved, as she was always ready to perform faithfully any task assigned her. On the other hand, as she

[16] This may have been the very woman of whom Colonel Fremantle speaks, a woman who was pointed out to him as having fought at Perryville and Murfreesboro in a Louisiana regiment. He was told, furthermore, that she was not the only woman in the ranks, but the writer has no evidence that the women referred to were foreigners.

herself admits, her independent position enabled her to a great extent to choose her own position in battle, and thus gave her probably greater opportunity to distinguish herself than would otherwise have been hers. As the routine of camp made her restless, she went within the United States lines in order to get reliable information of the movements of the enemy. Craving excitement and wishing to render service to the Confederate States in such signal manner that the authorities could no longer ignore her, she turned spy. She did ultimately attain the rank of lieutenant, being known as Lieutenant Harry T. Buford. Toward the close of the war she sampled life as a blockade-runner. But she found time during her exploits as spy and officer and during a highly adventurous life to be married three times and to become the mother of four children.[17]

[17] The above account of Madame Velazquez is drawn from C. J. Worthington (ed.), *The Woman in Battle*. Liberal excerpts from this book, written by Madame Velazquez herself, may be found also in Menie M. Dowie (ed.), "Madame Loreta Janeta Velazquez," *Women Adventurers*. Ross alludes to Madame Velazquez in his book.

XIII

THE ATTITUDE OF THE CONFEDERACY
TOWARD FOREIGNERS

THE QUESTIONS of domicile and liability to military service on the part of resident aliens have not always been adjudicated in the same way through the centuries of history. They have not been viewed alike even by the commentators on international law and their learned opinions have been, in turn, frequently susceptible of differing constructions. The opinion of modern writers is that citizens or subjects of one country resident in another can never be compelled to take up arms in behalf of the country in which they are resident. At the time of the Civil War this was an open question. It would perhaps be a fair presentation of the international law on the subject in 1861 to say that a resident alien should contribute to the preservation of order, and in return for shelter and protection should do his bit for defense against foreign invasion. He should not be required to serve in the regular army because such obligation might prevent his leaving the country at will, and might force him to place his life in jeopardy for objects in which he had no personal concern, or might by virtue of his bearing arms against the state of his allegiance even lay him open to the charge of treason. Obviously every resident must obey the law of the land, national and state. If any material change was to be made in his legal situation, he had a right to expect a reasonable time for withdrawal from the country. From any illegal exercise of force he had a right to be immune, and, if that right were violated, the country of which he was a subject could intervene in his behalf. Citizen and alien must be treated with equal justice.[1] In the Confederacy as in the United States the problem was complicated by the fact that some states which were eager for immigrants had allowed the right of the franchise to residents before they had acquired citizenship.

The question of legislation regulating citizenship and naturalization

[1] John B. Moore, *Digest of International Law*, IV, 52, 54-55; Bernard, *A Historical Account of the Neutrality of Great Britain during the American Civil War*, 443.

was a matter which necessarily engaged early the attention of the authorities in the Confederate States. Inasmuch as secession restored sovereign power to each state until it entered a new union, some of the states legislated on this question before the Confederacy was even formed. On February 7, 1861, for instance, the Louisiana convention passed a law conferring the right of citizenship on all persons resident in Louisiana at the date of the adoption of the secession ordinance. South Carolina bestowed citizenship on anyone who within the next year moved to that state to reside permanently.[2] The Confederate government took thought promptly on this important question. As early as February 16, 1861, the Committee on the Judiciary reported a bill which prescribed uniform rules of naturalization. The bill was read twice, and ordered placed on the calendar of the secret session.[3] The constitution of the Confederate States, when it was drafted, conferred on congress power to establish a uniform law of naturalization for aliens.[4] It was almost a year, however, before any bill on the subject was again introduced, and then on January 29, 1862, a bill was offered to repeal so much of the laws of the United States adopted by the congress of the Confederate States as authorized the naturalization of aliens. Although this strange bill was passed, it was vetoed by President Davis on several grounds: first, that it did manifest injustice to such aliens as were already domiciled in the Confederate States and had already begun proceedings for naturalization; and, second, that the several states had surrendered the power formally exercised by some of them—permitting aliens to vote until naturalized as citizens of the Confederate States with the clear expectation that congress would exercise the power granted to it; and finally, that the general policy indicated by the bill was not in accordance with the civilization of the age, and hence productive of evil effects on the foreigners in the new state.[5] His veto was sustained.

The next attempt at legislation on the subject shows clearly the prejudice against foreigners which existed in the minds of at least

[2] *American Annual Cyclopaedia*, 1861, 430. The Louisiana convention had adopted the secession ordinance on January 26, 1861. For South Carolina see *Ex Parte Henry Spinchen*, Vol. I, Chaps. 12, 14.

[3] *Journal of the Congress of the Confederate States of America*, I, 56.

[4] Art, I, sec. 8, par. 4.

[5] *Journal of the Provisional Congress of the Confederate States of America*, I, 720. For the veto message, dated February 4, 1862, see *ibid.*, 758-759.

some of the legislators. On February 5, 1863, Mr. Miles offered a resolution that the committee on foreign affairs be instructed to inquire into the expediency of regulating by law the subject of naturalization with a view to such discrimination against aliens as might best tend to promote the "stability and purity of our political and social institutions."[6] And finally on May 3 of the next year yet one more resolution sought to restrict citizenship by providing against future possession of the rights of citizenship by persons of foreign birth unless they had had "active participancy in our present struggle for independence."[7] Therefore the only action taken on the question during the life of the Confederacy was an act signed by the president in August, 1861, which conferred upon every noncitizen in the military service protection during the war and the rights of a citizen, together with the right to become naturalized and entitled to all the rights of citizenship upon taking an oath to support the Constitution and to renounce his former allegiance and indicating of which one of the Confederate States he intended to become a citizen.[8]

The act of banishment of August 8, 1861, ordering every male citizen of a hostile nation over fourteen years of age to leave the Confederacy and the arrest of all Union men who did not tender their allegiance or leave the Confederate States within forty days affected very seriously the German colonists in Texas who adhered to their antislavery convictions. A confiscation act followed very promptly, under which all the property of Union men who did not proclaim their allegiance or who had left the country should be confiscated.[9] This proclamation against alien enemies occasioned at first considerable uneasiness among a number of British subjects who misunderstood its purport. The office of the British consul at Richmond was besieged for days afterwards by persons seeking advice. Frightened Irishmen arrived in scores under the impression that they were "alien enemies" until their fears were dissipated. While all persons who had a domicile or who were carrying on business within the state with which the Confederacy was at war, no matter whether they were citizens or not, were classified by the law as alien enemies, relatively

---

[6] *Ibid.*, VI, 71-72.
[7] *Ibid.*, VII, 17. [8] *Ibid.*, I, 384, 621.
[9] Act of Banishment is given in *American Annual Cyclopaedia*, 1861, 147; Confiscation or Sequestration Act, signed August 31, in Herbert H. Bancroft, *History of the Pacific States of North America*, XI, 458; *Journal of the Congress of the Confederate States of America*, I, 457, and *Statutes at Large*, Provisional Congress, 3 Sess., Chap. XIX, Sec. 2.

few foreigners were affected. In fact a clerk in the war department records on October 1 that only a few hundred alien enemies departed from the country.[10]

Legislation prescribing the rules for military service became of the highest importance to foreigners. On April 9, 1862, the Confederate congress completed the first draft law, which authorized the president to place in the armies for three years all white men between eighteen and thirty-five years of age who were residents of the Confederate States and who were not legally exempted by force of municipal law or international law.[11] Substitutes were allowed under this law. Only a few months later, September 27, 1862, a second more stringent law was enacted. The conscription net now took in all white male residents between thirty-five and forty-five years of age not legally exempted.[12]

The effect of the conscription laws on the foreigners was unfortunate. Not fully understanding how the laws would be administered, many hundreds who had been resident in the South only a few months when the war broke out but who had volunteered and served for one year regarded them as oppressive and even despotic. To put such men on an equality with those born on the soil who had not as yet served at all seemed like the absolutism many had experienced in Europe. There was, accordingly, much murmuring, and many, rather than serve indefinitely in the army to win citizenship, abandoned the cause and sought protection from the consuls of the country of their nativity.[13]

The first legislative act by any of the states looking directly to-

[10] Day, *Down South*, I, 261-262. Jones, in *A Rebel War Clerk's Diary*, I, 73, 82, says that the order for aliens to leave caused little excitement except among the Jews, but Day seems explicit. Representative Sparrow on March 1, 1862, presented a memorial from J. J. Amonett, an Italian, in reference to the Sequestration Act, which was referred to the judiciary committee.—"Proceedings of the First Confederate Congress," Sess., *Southern Historical Society Papers*, XLIV, 72.

[11] *Public Laws of the Confederate States of America*, 1 Cong., 1 Sess., Chap. 31. There was a clause in that law, struck out on April 19, 1862, which is illuminating as to the attitude toward foreigners: "That all persons who shall claim to be exempted from said military service on the ground that they are foreigners, and who shall have exercised the right of suffrage, shall be notified by the officer before whom such claim shall be entered to leave the Confederate States, and if within 30 days after such person or persons shall claim and establish such exemption he or they shall be found within the jurisdiction of the Confederate States, he or they shall be . . . and shall be imprisoned and otherwise dealt with as such."—*Journal of the Senate of the Confederate States of America*, II, 204. President Davis signed the law on April 16.

[12] *Public Laws of the Confederate States of America*, 1 Cong., 2 Sess., Chap. 15.

[13] *Battle-fields of the South*, I, 313.

ward coercion of the alien was passed in Virginia during the same year. To foreign-born citizens who had not declared their intent to be naturalized it prohibited the issue of licenses to sell any kind of merchandise. The motive actuating its passage was clearly to prevent avoidance of the draft by claim of foreign citizenship by depriving many of their means of livelihood.[14]

Five days after the first conscription act passed congress, an act defined the terms of exemption but did not touch the question of the foreigner. Already in December, 1863, no person liable for military service was permitted to furnish a substitute; and a few days later it was enacted that no person liable to service should be exempted by virtue of having furnished a substitute. Finally, on February 17, 1864, congress reached out for all white male residents between seventeen and fifty years of age. Those between forty-five and fifty and between seventeen and eighteen were to form a reserve corps which would not serve outside the state of residence. Lines were also drawn somewhat more sharply regarding exemption. Very different was the legislation for service in the navy where the numbers needed were comparatively few. On June 14, 1864, an amendment to the act establishing the volunteer navy still made enlistment a privilege for resident foreigners and Marylanders.[15]

From the beginning of the enforcement of the conscript laws, there was necessity for executive interpretation of the meaning of "resident." Consuls began to protest to state and Confederate authorities, who naturally turned to the war department for authoritative interpretation. One of the very early replies in May, 1862, from Attorney General Watts at the request of the war department held that congress must have intended domiciled foreigners, at least, to be included; that is, those who had acquired habitation with no intention of removal. Such persons, having acquired a *nati* character in the Confederacy, had a right to expect its protection, but such protection carried with it the correlative duty of defending the country. Any foreigner who had not chosen to leave before the actual beginning of hostilities might be presumed to consider the Confederacy his

---

[14] *American Annual Cyclopaedia*, 1862, 798-799; *Session Laws of Virginia*, 1861-62, Chap. 3; *Journal of the Senate of the Confederate States of America*, II, 204.
[15] *American Annual Cyclopaedia*, 1864, 31; *Public Laws of the Confederate States of America*, 1 Cong., 4 Sess., Chap. 65. For provisions for the navy see *ibid.*, 2 Cong., 1 Sess., Chap. 49. The president's proclamation, offering letters of marque to those desiring to aid the Confederacy by service in private vessels, was open to all nationalities, of course.

domicile; he might yet leave with permission; but when a reasonable interval after the opening of hostilities had elapsed, the right to change domicile was subordinate to public safety.[16] One conscript officer held that purchase of real estate was tantamount to establishment of domicile; but the superintendent of conscripts then issued instructions denying the conclusiveness of such evidence as ownership of real property, marriage in the country, exercise of the privilege of the franchise, or even the declaration of intention to acquire citizenship. The evidence must "satisfy the mind fairly and reasonably that the party has not only changed his domicile in point of fact, but that he so intended." Assistant Secretary of War Campbell gives such a fair opinion concerning one element in the foreign population that it is worth quoting: "As a general thing the French population of this country retain the domicile of their nativity and rarely mingle in the public concerns of the country of their residence. They generally retain a purpose to return to the land of their birth, and are seldom willing to forego their relations with the Empire, which is an object both of affection and pride. It would be an act of injustice to coerce men of this description to fight our battles."[17] The secretary of war interpreted the act to mean to include among the conscripts all who had acquired a domicile in the Confederate States. The whole issue then turned on the definition of domicile. Since the question of domicile was a question of law, the head of the war department ruled that the issue should in each case be determined by the facts and by the opinion or oath of the person concerned. The law was to be so construed as not to impose forced military service upon mere sojourners or temporary residents, but only on such as had rendered themselves liable under the law of nations to be considered citizens *de facto* by having established themselves as permanent residents without intention of returning to their native land. Mere length of residence was not proof of intention to remain unless accompanied by abnegation of allegiance elsewhere.[18]

At first the department was lenient as to proof. The oath of the

[16] For Attorney General Watts's full view see Bonham, *British Consuls in the Confederacy,* in "Columbia University Studies," XLIII, 92-93.

[17] *Ibid.,* 93; *O. W. R.,* Ser. 4, II, 366.

[18] The phraseology in the text is suggested by Benjamin's statement of the interpretation. As secretary of state he had to set forth the view repeatedly in dealing with foreign countries and with their protests.—Bonham, *op. cit.,* 237-239; Richardson, *Messages and Papers,* II, 576 ff.

party supported by the oath of one credible witness was deemed sufficient.[19] It allowed the discharge early in the war at the end of their term of enlistment of all undomiciled foreigners. Several hundred aliens were thus discharged, but the same interpretation served as a shelter to a large number who had previously been regarded as permanent residents.

Of course army officers became involved in the complexities of this law in the course of the administration of their duties. General Orders Number 82, issuing from the adjutant general's office at Richmond, dated November 3, 1862,[20] set forth the interpretation as given above, but General Magruder declared one Britisher, resident at Houston, liable for service because he had in 1854 declared his intention to be naturalized. The consul at Galveston promptly carried an appeal to the secretary of state.[21] General Whiting followed his own judgment when he ordered all conscripts and all foreigners sent to camp for examination in order that all who were liable might be enrolled, although the assistant secretary of war, to whom the case came finally, declared his method irregular.[22]

The ultimate authority before which the alien could bring his case was naturally the courts. And cases soon came before the tribunals. The decisions generally held that persons not domiciled—not having permanent residence—in the Confederate States were exempt from service in the regular armies. Some of the judges, however, went much further in the demand for military service from domiciled aliens. Judge Hull of the Georgia Supreme Court, for instance, in his charge to the grand jury at Atlanta in the spring of 1862, recommended the prosecution of all foreign-born citizens who had exercised the rights of citizenship and then claimed exemption from military service on the ground of foreign allegiance. He intimated that if such cases were brought before him the offenders would receive penitentiary sentences, as such an act constituted a misdemeanor. At Richmond in 1863 Judge Meredith decided in a habeas corpus case that every foreigner, as well as every citizen of Maryland, had acquired domicile by enlistment in the army, no matter for how short a period,

[19] *O. W. R.*, Ser. 4, II, 70. See order of Secretary Randolph to Major G. W. Swanson, dated August 26, 1862. [20] *O. W. R.*, Ser. 4, II, 164.
[21] Bonham, *op. cit.*, 184. No further attention seems to have been given it by the state department and no further move made by Consul Lynn.
[22] Bonham, *op. cit.*, 108-109.

and was therefore liable to conscription. Judge Jones at Mobile held that in return for protection aliens owed a temporary and qualified allegiance. And in a very lengthy opinion, analyzing exhaustively the differences between domicile, residence, and itineracy, Judge Magrath of South Carolina ruled that aliens were liable for service in military organizations confined to the district of their residence, subject, however, to a call for defense in any part of the state.[23]

Some of the consuls attempted to insist that no alien was subject to enlistment by ex-post facto legislation, which altered an alien's status by a law not in existence at the time he took up residence, unless an opportunity were afforded him to leave. Many Confederate authorities, on the other hand, felt that ample warning had been given between the commencement of the war and the passage of the first conscription law—a period of a whole year.

As a matter of fact the number of exemptions allowed by Confederate authorities on the ground of foreign citizenship, according to the report compiled at the very close of the war by General Preston, head of the Conscription Bureau, is astonishingly small. The largest number, only 167, is strangely enough recorded for North Carolina and Alabama, states which, it will be remembered, prided themselves on the small percentage of foreign-born; and the lowest number, zero, for no less than three states—South Carolina, East Louisiana, and East Tennessee. The total for the eight states for which a record is noted was only 373.[24] The record obviously shows the situation at a given moment, February 20, 1865, or just prior to this date, and offers no statistics for the Trans-Mississippi Department or for parts of Louisiana and Tennessee or for the entire period of the war. A special record for Galveston has features of striking interest. In July, 1862, it was noted that 298 aliens had claimed exemption and had

[23] See *American Annual Cyclopaedia*, 1862, 494, for Hull's opinion; Frank Moore (ed.), *The Rebellion Record*, VI, 49, for Judge Meredith's; *Savannah Republican*, July 9, 1863, and Bonham, *op. cit.*, 223, for Judge Jones's view. For Magrath's full opinion see *Ex Parte Henry Spinchen*, a pamphlet. Jones, in *A Rebel War Clerk's Diary*, I, 270, declares that the secretary of war and the president agreed with the court decisions, but frequently gave consideration to the question of expediency in their decisions on cases.

[24] *O. W. R.*, Ser. 4, III, 1103. The record was compiled in February, 1865. The table in condensed form stands as follows:

Virginia	25	Mississippi	1
North Carolina	167	Florida	1
South Carolina	0	East Tennessee	0 (or 3?)
Georgia	12	East Louisiana	0
Alabama	167	Total	373

applied to their respective consuls for protection papers, an action which the Galveston natives stigmatized as "shirking."[25] For Galveston, 298, and only 373 for the entire country! Obviously the record is woefully inaccurate.

There were many Confederates who would have pressed the law much further in order to enforce service from aliens. There was much discontent throughout the war because aliens were not conscripted. It was felt that people who had lived in America for some time, who had voted, had held property, or had declared their intention to be naturalized were under moral obligation to assist in the defense of their homes. Men were cognizant that in some towns practically all business was done by aliens, who charged extortionate prices and contributed their share toward depreciating the currency. It exasperated them and filled them with a sense of injustice to see a man, after serving a short enlistment, demand and receive exemption as a foreigner. All he had a right to expect was a reasonable length of time to settle his affairs and leave the country. They saw no reason why foreigners should be exempt when old men and mere lads were shouldering muskets, especially when they recalled that many foreigners had been rabid secessionists before April, 1861. Leading newspapers such as the *Charleston Daily Courier*, the *Daily Richmond Enquirer*, and the *Daily Richmond Examiner* crusaded for conscription of aliens.[26]

Many extreme measures were introduced into congress and received serious debate. On August 28, 1862, "whereas, many persons because of foreign birth have sought the protection of consuls to secure exemption from military service, and are therefore accumulating property to the demoralization of adopted citizens," a resolution was offered and agreed to for the Judiciary Committee to inquire whether such exemption can legally be extended by foreign consuls whereby the person or property of any inhabitant of the Confederate States shall be relieved from that tribute "now exacted of all citizens in their persons and property."[27] On January 17 following a bill was introduced in the house providing for the enrollment of persons of

[25] Lubbock, *Six Decades in Texas*, 387 n.

[26] See *Charleston Daily Courier* of March 2, April 10, and July 8, 1863; *Daily Richmond Enquirer* of April 7, October 6, July 27, and August 27, 1863; *Daily Richmond Examiner* of March 22, 1864.

[27] *Journal of the House of Representatives of the Confederate States of America*, V, 322.

foreign birth in the army, but on March 30 the Committee on Military Affairs asked discharge from its further consideration and secured its reference to the Committee on the Judiciary.[28] On February 5 a member secured passage by the house of a resolution for that same committee to inquire into the expediency of a recommendation by congress to the several states to prohibit by law unnaturalized foreigners from holding real estate; but the committee, in asking discharge from its further consideration on April 13, succeeded in having it laid on the table.[29] A bold bill to conscript alien residents was placed on the calendar of the senate on April 4, 1863, considered on April 13, 14, 21, and 23, but failed on April 24. A somewhat similar bill in the house about the same time, providing for placing in the military service citizens of Maryland and foreigners resident within the limits of the Confederacy with an amendment for exemptions by the president, passed the house.[30] Deep and bitter feeling against foreigners and especially against Jews became manifest in the debate over this house bill. Mr. Baldwin of Virginia thought it time to protest against Richmond's being made a city of refuge for foreign adventurers. The bill should be extended in its range of operation to all the numerous foreigners who were there from all parts of the world claiming protection for their persons and property, getting the benefit of every blow struck for independence, and sheltering themselves from military service under consular protection. The Confederacy had no official notification of such governments as Great Britain and France. He would have the plough of conscription run over the foreign consuls themselves. It was time that foreign nations should discover that recognition was a game at which two could play and that the Confederacy owed those countries no comity whatever.

Mr. Hilton of Florida was prepared to take action against the Jews. They had swarmed to the South, he asserted, as the locusts of Egypt. They ate up the substance of the country, they exhausted its supplies, they monopolized its trade. They should be dragged into military service. The high prices under which the country suffered were not the result of competition among consumers but of competi-

[28] "Proceedings of the First Confederate Congress," 3 Sess., *Southern Historical Society Papers*, XLVII, 144; *Journal of the House of Representatives*, VI, 256.
[29] *Ibid.*, 70, 335.
[30] *Journal of the Senate of the Confederate States of America*, III, 236, 283, 291, 321, 324, 334, 340; *Journal of the House of Representatives of the Confederate States of America*, VI, 8, 442-443.

tion among buyers for the purpose of extortion. The latter flocked as vultures to every point of gain. The speaker mentioned the instance of a small vessel which got through the blockade on the Florida coast. The government had decided to appropriate the cargo when at least one hundred aliens flocked there, led even to this remote point by the scent of gain, and had to be driven back actually at the point of the bayonet.[31]

By December feeling on this subject had become so thoroughly aroused that it was possible for Mr. Brown of Mississippi to offer in the senate a resolution authorizing the president to command by proclamation all male foreigners to make their choice within sixty days: to take up arms or to leave the country. He was tired, he declared, of feeding drones. So long as the country was blessed with abundance and these people were of no disadvantage, he was willing to tolerate their presence. But now that they were eating out the land's substance and by their speculation depreciating the currency, they were of no earthly use; on the contrary, their presence was a great disadvantage. He knew of no international law which forbade saying to them: "The time has come when we can entertain you no longer." It might be safely assumed that nineteen twentieths of those people were engaged in traffic. They were the men who ran the blockade, and any man who secretly brought in goods from the Yankees, knowing that he was violating the law, was not to be trusted for fear of his communicating with the enemy. He would rather have a regiment of Yankees turned loose on Richmond than longer tolerate the presence of such people. In the midst of plenty the wives and children of their soldiers were starving, and their "limbs exposed to the blasts of winter. Will Congress arouse itself from its lethargy and apply a remedy?"[32]

Early in January, 1864, members were no longer debating a presidential proclamation for aliens to choose between army service or departure but a bill to require all white male residents between the ages of eighteen and forty-five to enter the army after February 1, without regard to claim of "alienage," but granting the president power of exemptions "upon consideration of equity and justice or of public necessity." George Vest, member for Missouri, would allow

[31] "Proceedings of the First Confederate Congress," *Southern Historical Society Papers*, XLVII, 121, 122-123.

[32] *Journal of the Senate of the Confederate States of America*, III, 455. For the résumé of Brown's speech see *American Annual Cyclopaedia*, 1864, 206-207.

exemptions to aliens upon payment of two thousand dollars in coin or its equivalent in foreign exchange.[33]

A few voices were lifted in opposition to such extreme measures. Mr. Miles thought that it would only make enemies for the Confederacy and produce unwilling soldiers. It would also embroil her in difficulties with foreign nations. If such a law passed, England, France, and other powers would probably retaliate by expelling all the Confederate citizens from their dominions. De Jarnete of Virginia held that the government had no right to conscribe citizens who acknowledged their allegiance to a foreign country. The power was a dangerous one, such as had never been claimed by any nation in the world.[34] Undoubtedly the faint hope of foreign intervention alone held congress to a liberal policy toward aliens.

Finally on February 17, 1864, the long-debated bill became law. As has been indicated, white male residents between the ages of seventeen and fifty must enter the military service of the Confederate States for the war; those between eighteen and forty-five must remain in the service, but the problem of conscription of aliens was not specifically dealt with as such.[35]

We have to do, however, not only with Confederate statutes, but with state militia laws, some of them antedating the existence of the central government, others passed when the exigencies of war dictated desperate measures to meet desperate situations. Under the militia law of South Carolina, dating back to 1839, free white aliens or transients between eighteen and forty-five resident for six months in the state were liable for patrol or militia duty within a restricted area. The convention which adopted the ordinance of secession in Georgia passed an ordinance declaring that each alien then within the state with bona fide intention of making it his permanent abode should be regarded as a citizen unless within three months he made declaration before a court of record that he did not wish to be so considered. Aliens, therefore, who failed to make such a declaration were conscripted for the army; all claims for exemption brought subsequently

[33] *Journal of the House of Representatives*, VI, 585, 590. Mr. Moore of Kentucky charged that there were many who had taken out naturalization papers in the United States and had then come to the Confederacy and taken out foreign exemption papers.— *Daily Richmond Examiner*, January 11, 1864.

[34] *Ibid.*, January 6, 8, 1864. The *Daily Richmond Whig* of July 11, 1863, feared foreign war if aliens should be conscribed.

[35] *Public Laws of the Confederate States of America*, 1 Cong., 4 Sess., Chap. 65.

were denied.[36] Tennessee in October, 1861, enacted a law constituting the white male population of the state between eighteen and forty-five a Reserve Military Corps, subject to duty upon the call of the governor, and all the able-bodied white male population between forty-five and fifty-five into a Military Corps for defense to be called into actual service only after all the Reserve Corps had been called out into actual service.[37] In Louisiana aliens within the usual prescribed age limits of eighteen to forty-five with the usual exemptions were after sixty days' residence liable to militia service for five years. In accordance with this statutory provision the governor issued a proclamation just prior to October 1, 1861, warning aliens that they must hold themselves ready to defend their hearths and to join a home guard company or lose the right to seek reparation for any loss incurred in the event of the enemy's reaching New Orleans.[38] One other state had a regulation for militia service. Every white male, resident in Texas one month and in his militia district ten days, was required to serve; in case of threatened invasion, even this slight residence requirement was waived.[39]

With these exceptions the drastic steps taken by the various states later in the war in establishing their own militia seem to have marked efforts to meet emergencies and crises in the struggle. In May, 1862, when the Federal forces were perilously near the city of Richmond, the long roll was beaten, and every man and boy able to carry a gun was, without respect to age, marched off to Capitol Square where they were formed into companies and sent to the fortifications.[40] At the November session of the Louisiana legislature, 1860-61, the militia was declared composed of "all free white males capable of bearing arms, residing in the state, 18 to 45 years of age, not exempt under

[36] Session Laws of South Carolina, 1839, Chap. 13, Sec. 1; American Annual Cyclopaedia, 1863, 449; for Georgia, Confederate Records of Georgia, I, 457. When Consul Fullarton asked permission for two drafted Britishers to quit Georgia with leave to remain in the state thirty days to arrange their affairs, he was referred to this law.—Governor's Letter Books, 1861-65, 546-547, Georgia Archives.

[37] Session Laws of Tennessee, October, 1861-1862, Chap. 26, Sec. 1.

[38] Revised Statutes of Louisiana, 1856, Art. 60, Sec. 1, pp. 75, 78. For the governor's proclamation see Louisiana Staatszeitung, October 1, 1861. The above explicit statement in the text is given in a report of Albin Rochereau, Chef de Bataille, to the Légion Française, in an undated pamphlet in the Howard Memorial Library at New Orleans. Rochereau explains to the members of the Legion that the consul had no right or means to save his compatriots from the action of the law.

[39] A Digest of the General Statute Law of the State of Texas (1859), Art. 1426.

[40] Kent, Four Years in Secessia, 19-20, describes the scene in Richmond when the men were called out.

this law." As danger approached New Orleans, every individual who had resided in the state sixty days was ordered enrolled in the militia, which could be called on to fight, not only within the city, but also at any other point within the territory of the state where the governor and state authorities decided to send it. Even more drastic, at least in wording, was the definition of the militia as formulated at the legislative session of December, 1862, to January, 1863, held at Opelousas. The militia was to be composed of all the free white males capable of bearing arms between the ages of seventeen and fifty, whether citizens of the state or residents thereof, "temporarily or permanently, unless specially exempted."[41] The South Carolina legislature passed an act on September 30, 1863, authorizing the governor "for the purpose of suppressing insurrection and repelling raids" to enroll all white males between eighteen and forty-five, including, among other groups enumerated, "resident aliens." This action came at a critical moment: Charleston was being bombarded, the reverses of Gettysburg and Vicksburg were recent, money was low, and the state desperate.[42] North Carolina in July, 1863, ordered the enrolling in the militia of all white male residents between eighteen and fifty, "including foreigners not naturalized" who had been residents in the state thirty days, as a guard for home defense against invasion and for the suppression of insurrections. Mississippi legislated in December, 1863, that aliens, eighteen to forty-five years of age, who had not volunteered by March 1, 1864, should be forced to leave. When she found herself facing Sherman's raid in August, 1864, she directed the governor to call upon every able-bodied man in the state to "meet the present emergency."[43] In characteristically picturesque language Governor Brown, attempting to stem the tide of invasion into Georgia in the fall of 1864 by the armies of our "barbaric foes," ordered a "levy en masse of the whole free white male population residing or domiciled in this state between sixteen and fifty-five years of age," except those manifestly unable to bear arms

[41] *Session Laws of Louisiana*, December, 1862- January, 1863, No. 42.
[42] *South Carolina Statutes at Large*, XIII, 148-149. The measure was less drastic than that recommended by the governor in his message, for he urged the inclusion of all between sixteen and sixty.
[43] *Session Laws of North Carolina*, Called Session, 1863, Chap. 10; *Session Laws of Mississippi*, November, 1863, 133, Called Session, August, 1864, Chap. 61. Gov. Pettus issued a proclamation on December 8, 1863, for the execution of the act.—Executive Letter Book, 430-431, Mississippi Archives.

or exempted, which meant only the clergy. Legislators and judges, who were exempt by a recent law, were invited—all others were ordered—to report for forty days' service unless the emergency were sooner over. All refusing to report were informed that they would be arrested and carried to the front. On a later occasion, April, 1865, when a military officer ordered the guard, composed of aliens, to the fortifications of Columbus and some of them refused to respond, he appealed to Governor Brown. For the person familiar with the governor's reaction to such situations, his reply would not need to be signed: "Arrest and compel them to go." The mayor of Atlanta, facing an emergency on May 23, 1864, could only "require" all male citizens of the city to report to the marshal of the city, adding lamely that all male citizens unwilling to defend their homes and families "are requested to leave the city at their earliest convenience" as their presence only "tends to the demoralization of others."[44]

One might suppose that Texas, isolated from the major campaigns of the war, would escape emergencies, but not so, for she found that she had an element in her population determined to evade service if it were in any way possible. The legislature had passed a law rendering all able-bodied free white male inhabitants between the ages of eighteen and fifty liable to military duty, with due exemptions, of course.[45] Aliens of conscript age were, furthermore, required by General Orders Number 28, if they held an office or employment connected with the army in Texas, though not in it, to take an oath of allegiance to the Confederacy and to enroll themselves as subject to military duty, or else to furnish substitutes, unless they had been appointed by authorities superior to General Magruder. Failure to comply with the order would entail immediate loss of employment or office.[46]

Obviously these rigorous militia laws worked hardships on the

[44] Governor Brown's executive order is dated Milledgeville, November 19, 1864. For an account of Sherman's march see *American Annual Cyclopaedia*, 1864, 405. The legislative act authorizing the governor's action was passed on November 18.—*Session Laws of Georgia*, 1864, Title VIII, No. 9. For Brown's reply to B. H. Thornton in regard to the alien guard see Governor's Letter Books, 1861-65, 6, Georgia Archives. For the action of the mayor see Reed, *A History of Atlanta, Georgia*, 159.

[45] See *Session Laws of Texas*, November, 1861- January, 1862, Chap. 10, with the alteration of the session of February-March, 1863, Chap. 64.

[46] For General Orders Number 28, February 22, 1863, issued by General Magruder see *O.W.R.*, Ser. 1, XV, 986-988. Article XV deals with the regulations concerning foreigners.—*Ibid.*, 988.

aliens, and many were the protests. James Stewart, for instance, living in Mississippi, complained repeatedly to Governor Pettus. On March 10, 1862, he pointed out that he could not leave the state at once because all his earnings of sixteen years "are now in the hands of the Planters and of course I can't get anything back at the present time." On August 25 he quotes the consul at New Orleans as denying Mississippi's right to force British residents to join the militia. He reiterates that he is preparing to return to Europe as soon as he can put his business in order. By September 6 he promises to leave within sixty to ninety days, as soon as his "family is in better health." But Pettus insisted that resident aliens were liable under the law to repel invasion and suppress insurrection, and that only the legislature could alter the law. James Stewart was, however, discharged on February 4, 1863, by order of General Smedes of the state troops. A. Proniewski was a forlorn, lame foreigner, who could not raise the money to get to Richmond. He sought from the governor a job as cotton buyer, for he had no money to get away from the Confederacy.[47]

The state governors, dealing at close range with the problems of enlistments and untroubled by diplomatic entanglements with foreign powers, were inclined to be drastic as to the obligations of aliens. As early as 1861 Governor Henry Rector of Arkansas suggested that the Germans and Irish should be drafted if they showed a real disinclination to enlist and their reluctance was found not to proceed from the lack of opportunity for promotion. "It is not a wise or just government," in his opinion, "which, in a war like this, taxes native blood and energy alone, leaving the foreign-born at home, reaping the fruits of dear-bought victories."[48] Governor Lubbock of Texas felt that he had the right to prohibit all persons from leaving the state without proper passport, particularly those seeking to go to Mexico or to pass through that neighboring country. He doubtless had in mind the Germans who were thus seeking escape in goodly numbers. In April, 1862, he had made a decision, in supposed compliance with the demands of international law, that British subjects would not be drafted or forced to fight in the militia against the

---

[47] Jas. Stewart to Pettus, March 10, August 25, September 6, 1862; Notation of Pettus on letter of Consul Magee to Pettus, December 4, 1862.—Governor's Correspondence, Mississippi Archives.

[48] *American Annual Cyclopaedia*, 1861, 25.

United States in case of invasion, but within about a year he had shifted his position and stood strongly with the governors of Virginia, Alabama, Louisiana, and Georgia, who insisted on the obligation of aliens to render militia duty to repel invasion and to perform police duty. Arthur T. Lynn, British consul at Galveston, took the governor to task for this change when it was revealed in an order to enroll all British subjects in the Texas state troops. Lynn protested strongly that no such municipal law had existed at the time of establishment of domicile.[49] Governor Shorter of Alabama and Governor Moore of Louisiana insisted that the legislatures should leave no doubt as to the military obligations of aliens. When Governor Smith ordered eight thousand militia in Virginia under arms in 1864 for home defense, he included all foreigners hitherto exempt.[50] Governor Milton proposed to embrace in the state troops of Florida all who had resided in the state as long as five days or those who might be in it one hour for the purpose of speculation, including, of course, aliens. This body was neither to be subject to regular duty in the army nor to be taken away from their ordinary pursuits except to repel invasion or to maintain order.[51]

Governors Smith and Brown agreed that every foreigner should be compelled to perform military duty or leave the country, but only the latter made an issue of it, insisting upon such service as "unquestionably due from all domiciled foreigners by the law of nations."[52] He had insisted upon this view as early as August, 1863, when, after the fall of Vicksburg, he had ordered a draft of eight thousand men for home defense and had arranged for a muster on August 4 in each county which had not already voluntarily raised its quota. This muster was for the entire arms-bearing population: all males from eighteen to forty-five regardless of allegiance or of

[49] Lubbock in a letter of October 15, 1862, to General H. P. Bee declared his intention to prohibit persons from leaving.—Lubbock Papers, Archives, Texas State Library. The best statement of Lubbock's shift in position is found in his *Memoirs*, 387. See also Governor's Letters, Lubbock Papers, 1863, Archives, Texas State Library.

[50] For Governor Shorter's position, see Appleton's *American Annual Cyclopaedia*, 1863, 7; for Governor Moore's see his Message to the Twenty-seventh Legislature of Louisiana, Extra Session, Opelousas, December 15, 1862, *Journal of the House*, 7. For Governor Smith's inclusion of aliens in the call for the militia see Schuricht, *History of the German Element in Virginia*, II, 100. He desired especially to relieve the regulars from guarding prisoners—certainly a very justifiable use of the militia.

[51] *American Annual Cyclopaedia*, 1863, 413.

[52] Governor Brown laid before the Georgia legislature copies of his correspondence with Consul Fullarton.—Governor's Message, November 5, 1863, in *Senate Journal of Georgia*, Annual Session, 1862-63, 29.

previous provision of a substitute. His proclamation stated that "an unnaturalized foreigner living under the protection of our Government and laws . . . is bound to defend his domicile and is liable to be drafted by the State and compelled to do so."[53] He became involved in a very spicy correspondence during July with A. Fullarton, the British consul at Savannah. When Fullarton found it impossible to secure exemption of the British subjects living in Georgia or modification of the order, he felt compelled to "advise those drafted to acquiesce in the military duty until they were required to leave their homes or to meet United States forces, then to throw down their arms, and refuse to render a service directly against the Queen's proclamation of neutrality, trusting to Fullarton's interference in their behalf at Richmond."[54] Logical to the end, Governor Brown, when he found among aliens opposition to defending Atlanta in July, 1864, issued an order on July 28 banishing from the state aliens who refused to do service for the defense of the state. They were allowed the scant margin of ten days for departure, and then were "no more to return, on pain of being dealt with as the laws and usages of nations justify in such cases." Secretary Seddon, refraining from interference in a state executive's quarrel, contented himself with announcing that foreigners leaving under Governor Brown's command should be permitted to sail for any neutral ports, but not for United States ports.[55] President Davis thereupon on September 19 sent a communication to several of the governors suggesting that in any future proclamation aliens employed at labor in occupational trades, at munitions works, or in shoe factories for the Confederate States might not be required to perform military service or be obliged to leave the country. But Governor Brown had long before forestalled that difficulty in one of his replies to Fullarton by declaring that the State would consult her own interests and exempt from military service for local defense any aliens who were more serviceable to the state in civil employ.[56] Governor Smith

[53] Bonham, op. cit., 141-142; Confederate Records of Georgia, II, 464-468. The proclamation is dated July 17, 1863.

[54] For the correspondence between Brown and the consul see Confederate Records of Georgia, III, 372-377, 383-389, 391-394, 403-409; Bonham, op. cit., 142-149; Governor's Letter Books, 1861-65, 529-530, Georgia Archives.

[55] See O. W. R., Ser. 1, LII, Pt. 2, 714, for Brown's order of banishment of aliens; for Seddon's order, see ibid., Ser. 4, III, 604. Seddon's order is dated August 23, 1864.

[56] President Davis' communication is found in "Journal of the Executive of Virginia," Chap. 8, CCIII, 400, Confederate Archives, War Department. It took the form of a

merely stated in his inaugural address his view that aliens should perform military duty or leave, but did not press the matter.[57]

The Confederate army is far from the only one in history in which the companies were filled up by coercion, but it certainly is a flagrant example. Our frank reporter of the London *Times* gives a statement of the situation in New Orleans on his arrival there in late May, 1861. Englishmen will be surprised, he thinks, "to hear that within a few days British subjects living in New Orleans have been seized, knocked down, carried off from their labor at the wharf and the workshop, and forced by violence to serve in the 'volunteer' ranks. These cases are not isolated. They are not in two's or three's, but in tens and twenties; they have not occurred stealthily or in byways; they have taken place in the open day, and in the streets of New Orleans. These men have been dragged along like felons, protesting in vain that they were British subjects."[58] Fortunately their friends did not forget the British consul, who after some strong representations to the authorities secured their release. Governor Thomas O. Moore discharged the men and condemned the practice, even disbanding a company to show his disapprobation. Some thirty-five British enlistments had been discharged by the time of Russell's arrival, but the consul's office was still thronged with women who implored him for the release of their husbands. The consul said that about sixty cases of impressment of British subjects had claimed his attention.[59]

---

circular letter to Governors Bonham of South Carolina, Vance of North Carolina, Watts of Alabama, Brown of Georgia, Smith of Virginia, and Milton of Florida. It is printed in *O. W. R.*, Ser. 4, III, 670-671.

Brown's statement to Fullarton that the state would consult its own interests in exemptions is found in *Confederate Records of Georgia*, III, 406-407.

Possibly one of the strangest uses ever made of the pardon power was by Governor Smith to help fill the thinning ranks of the Confederate army. He was doubtless, like Brown, consulting the interests of Virginia when he pardoned several foreign criminals for grand larceny in order that they might return to the field. One was a German, two were Irish.—"Journal of the Executive of Virginia," Chap. 8, CCIII, 157, Confederate Archives, War Department. Even at that he was more moderate than the mayor of New Orleans when the latter let Coppens go into the jails to recruit for the Zouaves.

[57] For Governor Smith's view in his inaugural see *Virginia Documents*, 1863-1864, No. 18, p. 10. It would appear that North Carolina did not approve of expulsion. Governor Vance wrote President Davis on October 12, 1864, "No laws have been passed in this State oppressive of this class of persons [foreigners] and no edict of expulsion has been or will be adopted."—*O. W. R.*, Ser. 4, III, 724.

[58] *Pictures of Southern Life*, 63. His report of abuses was first printed in the London *Times*, June 13, 1861, but was widely copied; The *Daily Picayune*, July 6; Washington *Daily National Intelligencer*, July 17.

[59] Cases of assault were complained of by the consuls. Moore told of a British subject

Naturally the Louisiana military authorities tried to present as good a case as they could. Colonel Manning, the governor's aide, pointed out that the Carroll Guards, the worst offenders in the use of force to secure recruits, was only an embryo company, without commissions or official standing, and asked correction of misrepresentations. Consul Mure suggested the issuance of a gubernatorial proclamation that no companies formed by impressment of foreigners would be received into service. The aide further pointed out that British subjects had in many cases taken advantage of the opportunity to gain bounty money, a liberal supply of clothing, and good food, which had been held out as inducements by some companies, and had then sent their wives to the consulate, as the time for departure of the companies drew near, to report a tale of impressment. If British subjects volunteered, "whether for bread or bullets," they must not expect the protection of their government. The governor did, however, on second thought issue the proclamation as requested by the British consul in New Orleans. Probably some of the cases arose from the employment by company officers of "runners" who received a commission for each recruit and who were consequently none too careful of their methods.[60] The vast majority of the people of New Orleans condemned the procedure as sharply as did the London *Times* and members of parliament.[61]

There were other cases of coercion of foreign subjects, especially from the border states. During Price's raid into Missouri in September, 1864, some Union men, including several foreign-born, were taken captive at Potosi. They were marched off for General Shelby to look over. The seven Irishmen were turned over to an Irish captain, but no doubt received the same treatment as the twelve native Missourians; namely, enforced mustering into the Confederate service. Several other forced recruits, soon added to their number, proved

---

in Mississippi who had lost one eye by assault and was confined in a bitterly cold prison in Jackson because he had resisted conscription.—Bonham, *op. cit.*, 87.

[60] *Ibid.*, 175-177. Russell was sharply criticized for his statements.—*My Diary North and South*, 553. For unfavorable reactions to Mure see *O. W. R.*, Ser. 2, II, 591.

[61] The London *Times* thought it clear that every strong fellow in New Orleans not obtrusively attached to British allegiance was liable to a most unpleasant degree of persuasion to join some volunteer corps. He might be safe enough from the well-organized corps, but he was liable to be pounced upon by some fellow under no control, roughly used, dragged to some drill house or yard, with some rough fellows to keep watch, and, unless he had a friend to run to the British consul, be marched off to the seat of war.— August 13, 1861. See also Russell's statement to parliament on the subject on June 9, 1864.—Hansard's *Parliamentary Debates*, CLXXV, Third Ser., 1452.

to be foreign-born—two Englishmen, an Irishman, and a Frenchman.[62] It went ill with men who were not able to show foreign citizenship papers, some being clapped into prison for refusing as foreigners to take the oath of allegiance.[63] The arrest of one Peter McSheeley, an employee at the Charleston arsenal, in July, 1863, for refusing to join the Arsenal Guards seems more justifiable, for by that date the policy of enforcing obligation to render home defense had become clearly crystalized. Three more cases were soon added to McSheeley's dossier for General Cooper to pass upon. When they refused to join the Arsenal Guards, they encountered the same penalty meted out to McSheeley.[64]

The coercion of public opinion was a powerful weapon. Many British subjects tried to depart from the country at once, after the outbreak of hostilities, but could not get passes through the lines, although undoubtedly many slipped through informally. Others prudently went about their business until conscripted, resolving then to try to take refuge behind the queen's proclamation of neutrality. This proclamation warned subjects against taking up arms for either belligerent. Consuls kept it posted conspicuously in the consulates and endeavored with a fair degree of conscientiousness to see that its provisions were observed.[65]

Germans were in a worse state, especially in and around Richmond. Many, naturally, tried to leave; straightway arose cries of disloyalty, even of treason. The foreign-born in general and the men who kept away from the enlistment booths in particular were objects of suspicion and all possible influence was brought to force or shame them into the military service. The noncitizens, who had a legal right to claim exemption in Richmond, could receive little protection from their home country. There was no strong united Germany in existence then to offer protection; indeed there was only one German consul in Richmond at that time, a representative of the free city of Bremen. To this consul, Edward W. de Voss, the alarmed and suspected Germans hastened for protection. The usual procedure to

---

[62] Donald Palmer, *Four Weeks in the Rebel Army*, 18, 19. The two Englishmen were brothers, named George. The Frenchman was named Zeno Tibault.

[63] On the boat on which he was traveling from his parish in Mississippi to New Orleans, in hope of passage home to England, the Reverend Mr. Ozanne saw several passengers very roughly handled, some being at once sent to prison for refusing to take the oath.— *The South as It Is*, 281.

[64] Bonham, *op. cit.*, 124.   [65] *Ibid.*, 79.

secure foreign papers was for the alien to take an oath that he was a citizen of the designated country, and to pay a fee of a dollar, whereupon he received a certificate from his consul. Usually the oath included affirmation that he had never taken an oath of allegiance to the United States, to the Confederate States, or to any other foreign nation. For some time these certificates were respected by the Confederate authorities but they did not increase good will on the part of the natives toward the foreigners.[66] Many of all nationalities had resided so long in the South that few of their neighbors remembered their foreign nativity; indeed one investigation revealed that two Irishmen had come from Ireland so long before that they had forgotten their native county. Some had taken out naturalization papers for business reasons, yet considered themselves British subjects in feeling. This situation was certain to create complications and ill will on both sides.

As soldiers became more precious, the foreign papers were challenged and subjected to closer scrutiny. The merchant Corsan, for instance, tells how on one train, just as it was ready to start, a guard with fixed bayonet was posted at the door of each car, while an officer demanded papers of each passenger. Corsan's British passport produced no effect. He was asked to prove that he was the person named in the passport; failing that, he would be held as a conscript. Fortunately for him, he was able to satisfy the conscript judge, before whom he was marched, by his personal cards, letters, and papers of his identity.[67] Even Conrad, the agent for the well-known house of Bee, who by his constant trips in and out of Wilmington must have been well known to many of the authorities, had difficulty in escaping the militia patrol at Wilmington, for his consulship was acknowledged only for South Carolina. He therefore judged it prudent to remain hidden all day on one occasion when he was in Wilmington, and only in the evening went to his train with his travel pass.[68]

For a man once in the army, the authorities did not smooth the path for discharge, as is well illustrated by the difficulties experienced by William Watson when his term of enlistment had expired. The

---

[66] Schuricht, *op. cit.*, II, 91.

[67] Corsan, *Two Months in the Confederate States*, 81-86. The conscript judge was ensconced in a wooden hut, which had once been a grocery store.

[68] Conrad, *Schatten und Lichtblicke*, 103. The *Daily Richmond Examiner* of February 17, 1864, tells of a German boy, aged 17, who stole $1,600 from his employer in order to get back to Germany to escape the conscript officer.

Scotchman applied for discharge on the ground of being a neutral foreigner. His colonel did not seem inclined to grant a discharge under the clause in the Conscript Act providing for discharge of aliens at the expiration of their original term of enlistment, evidently fearing to set a precedent and reluctant to act without specific instructions.[69] He held that Watson could not claim exemption as a neutral foreigner as he had already violated neutrality by participation in several battles. Watson countered by stating that he had not seen the queen's proclamation until after he had already enlisted. In order to regularize his position in the army after his term had expired, as he was no longer an orderly or sergeant and had no right to rations, he was placed technically under arrest—a simple suspension from duties. Since the officers did not wish to bring up the question then for fear of thinning the ranks, the colonel suggested a return to duty with a guarantee of discharge in July along with the other exempts. The discharge was accordingly made in July, 1862.

It is amusing that after all his difficulties in getting the discharge Watson should have been virtually driven back to the army. He found his position exceedingly awkward and unpleasant. There was no kind of occupation open in civil life, for practically all business was suspended and every young man of any spirit had enlisted. Those who had held back were now being hunted by the conscript officers and were regarded with open scorn. Idleness was obnoxious to an active young man, and yet he could not get out of the country to seek work elsewhere. It became increasingly apparent to him that under a military despotism the safest and best place was in the army, and so we see the man who was so insistent about a discharge a few months before, setting off to join his friends in the old company, finding a remnant of it under General van Dorn just as a battle was about to begin. He was wounded at once, captured, and paroled. In rejoining the army he knew of course that he was violating neutrality and forfeiting his rights as a British subject, but there seemed nothing else to do.[70]

There were naturally other ways to put the thumbscrews on re-

[69] A remark made by the colonel to Watson is enlightening as to the number of aliens in the regiment. If Watson received a discharge under this clause, the colonel had no doubt but that there would be thirty applications from the different companies of the regiment within a week.—Watson, *Life in the Confederate Army*, 360-361.

[70] *Ibid.*, 361-387, 419-423.

luctant recruits. Consul Magee of Jackson, Mississippi, waxed very indignant when a Britisher was discharged from an instruction camp as an undomiciled foreigner, armed with a document which urged all persons to give no employment of any kind to this class of exempts as they were a nuisance to the government. Indeed this method was no secret. An order that no white man should work on the levee or on a steamboat was published by the authorities in the *Picayune,* the *Daily True Delta,* and all the newspapers of New Orleans.[71] Furthermore, between frequent summonses and reëxaminations, foreigners had no certainty of escaping service, for physical disabilities allowed by one physician might not pass muster with another.[72]

At the outbreak of the war many aliens certainly tried to escape from the discomforts and dangers of a country involved in war. No sooner had war actually begun than the consulates of the various nations became crowded with persons eager to escape. Those were the days to drive consuls distracted with a multitude of demands for passports, for exemptions from military service, for loans of money, and for the forwarding of mail to England. There was comparative freedom of movement within the Confederacy;[73] nonmilitary individuals had little difficulty in securing passports at Richmond, but to get passes through the lines from the military authorities was quite a different matter. Occasional permits were granted; some foreigners left by the flag-of-truce boats; and, undoubtedly, others slipped through the lines informally or ran the blockade. Consuls often had to discourage would-be travelers by telling them of half a score of persons who had been endeavoring for weeks to find a way of getting out. Tales were rife of families which had reached Washington, to have their luggage detained but themselves returned to Richmond; of persons hiring wagons at the rate of one dollar a mile but with the additional proviso of having to refund the value of the horses

[71] Bonham, *op. cit.,* 154; Southwood, *Beauty and Booty,* 196.

[72] The writer found in the private library of Mrs. S. V. Pfeuffer of New Braunfels a paper from an enrolling officer which bore a list of German names, evidently exempts, with the notation at the bottom, "A great many of these men having certificates are able to serve and ought to be reëxamined."

[73] Secretary Benjamin assured Consul Cridland that neutrals were at liberty to travel and transact business without restrictions other than those imposed by the military.—Richardson, *Messages and Papers,* II, 498; Bonham, *op. cit.,* 159. Of course where military lines ran into a southern state, as in Louisiana, there were difficulties. Watson could come and go between Baton Rouge and New Orleans, posing as a foreigner and a neutral, and transacting business for planters who did not deem it quite safe to venture within General Butler's reach.—*Life in the Confederate Army,* 433.

if they were impressed; of a French professor starting for Paris afoot via the Tennessee Mountains; and of persons arrested as spies in both Washington and Richmond.[74] The road between Richmond and the Potomac was crowded with wagons of refugees, Germans and Irish, going to Washington to take the oath of allegiance and to seek better fortunes.[75]

At the other end of the Confederacy similar scenes were taking place. One reads of a party gradually being gathered to depart from San Antonio for Laredo and then through Mexico to Matamoros to board a boat for Europe: a Scotchman, two Irishmen, a Swede, three or four Englishmen, and also some Texans. Others escaped via New Orleans after it had passed into Union hands.[76]

The Seven Days' Battles around Richmond during the midmonths of 1862 brought the war close to many people and, together with the conscript laws of that year, encouraged a fresh exodus. In December, 1862, the rumor that Charleston was to be reduced brought the British man-of-war *Cadmus* to that port to carry off any British subjects who wished to leave. Some took advantage of the opportunity.[77] Human nature being what it is, numbers of passports were "informal" and many foreigners were arrested in transit and brought to Richmond on the charge of evading the laws. An observer declared that it was remarkable how many were desirous of getting away. At the collapse of the Confederacy the office of the provost marshal in Richmond was thronged from morning till night, chiefly by people pleading for passes to Baltimore. Numerous British workmen in the different government workshops were anxious to leave but were denied passports.[78] The total estimated to have left the Confederate States up to December, 1864, is 36,462, most of whom

[74] Hopley, *Life in the South*, I, 370-371.

[75] Harrison, *Recollections Grave and Gay*, 106. An English mechanic working for the government sent his frail wife with her baby north.—Hopley, *op. cit.*, II, 365.

[76] Frances H. Fearn, *Diary of a Refugee*, 49. A very humble Irishwoman and her husband went from New Orleans to Havana.—Watson, *Adventures of a Blockade Runner*, 245. See Anderson, *Hyphenated*, for Swenson's escape.

[77] The reaction of the *Daily Richmond Examiner* of December 29, 1863, to the conscript law is interesting. "If the objects of the law are to drive such persons [foreigners] from the Confederacy, and not to put them in the service, then no better plan could have been adopted. Its effect, we fear, will be to paralyze business, close many business places, and drive enterprising capital from the community, without benefitting the country and filling up the army to the extent it was anticipated." For the *Cadmus* see Bonham, *op. cit.*, 118. Ellis comments on the departure of a small steamer from Richmond.—*Leaves from the Diary of an Army Surgeon*, 184.

[78] The *Daily Richmond Examiner* printed on January 14, 1864, the statement of the arrest of foreigners. For the British workmen in the shops see Bonham, *op. cit.*, 91.

were undoubtedly foreigners, as combatants were not allowed to leave.[79]

The efforts made by the home countries to come to the aid of their subjects caught by the war within the boundaries of the Confederate States must, at least, be touched upon. If a Britisher, notwithstanding the queen's proclamation of neutrality, entered the military service of the Confederacy, he violated the enlistment act and rendered himself liable to punishment and could consequently make no claim to the protection of his country. However the British government would not admit that the action of sailors enlisted in the service of a power recognized by Great Britain as a belligerent constituted piracy under international law. She would not admit as recognized by international law the interpretation of the law by the United States which visited privateering with the death penalty.

When the complaints from British subjects began to descend on the consuls, they naturally turned for instructions to the only diplomatic representative of their government on this side of the water, Lord Lyons at Washington. Lyons issued a circular of instructions to the consuls on November 12, 1861, which became in general the guide to conduct for those officials. While Great Britain could allow her subjects voluntarily domiciled in a foreign country to bear the obligations incident to such domicile, including service in the militia or local police for maintenance of order, or, even to a limited extent, service for defense of the country against foreign invasion, she could not countenance her subjects being embodied and compelled to serve in regiments, though nominally militia, where they would be really exposed to the ordinary accidents and chances of war and liable to be treated as rebels and traitors in a civil war. Many questions were involved in which they, as aliens, could not, simply by reason of their domicile, be supposed to take an interest and as to which they might be incompetent to form an opinion, yet in the determination of which they were precluded from freedom of choice and action. No state could justly pass laws to compel aliens resident within its territories to serve against their will in armies ranged against each other in civil war. A fortiori, in the absence of any such law it could not enforce the service.[80]

---

[79] American Annual Cyclopaedia, 1864, 31.

[80] Bonham, op. cit., 113-114. Lyons stated also in the circular that there was no hope of securing in practice any legal decision of a competent court favorable to the exemption

As the states began to amend their militia laws to embrace aliens temporarily resident, the British foreign office, in reply to a request by Lord Lyons for instructions, took note of what was in effect *ex post facto* legislation. In a circular dated October 11, 1862, it declared that no alien could be forced to render service if there were no law to that effect in existence when he took up his residence in a given state unless he were given the option of withdrawing.[81]

There next arose the problem of the property of neutrals under the sequestration act. Lord Russell of the British foreign office held the confiscation of property of neutrals contrary to international law and issued explicit instructions to one of the British consuls to remonstrate strongly on the injustice and hardship of confiscating such property. Copies of this communication were sent to the other consuls.[82] In August, 1862, an official decision went from London to Acting Consul Magee at Mobile as to the advice to be given British subjects whose property was destroyed in the Confederacy to prevent its falling into the hands of United States officials. It was the opinion of England that foreign owners of cotton in the southern states had no ground of complaint against a *de facto* government if cotton were destroyed with the sanction of that government to prevent its falling into the hands of the opposing forces. That was a liability to which foreigners were exposed in a state which was carrying on war. It was suggested that evidence of ownership of destroyed property be preserved, as appeal could later be made for equitable adjustment in the event that the Confederate States survived.[83]

In July, 1864, arose the question of the status of British subjects residing in Memphis, Tennessee, then under martial law. Lord Lyons was instructed by the home government to inform such residents that Great Britain could not interfere with the operation of that law in a foreign state, and that, if British subjects wished to enjoy British protection, they must discontinue their residence in places under such military control.[84]

The attitude of Great Britain as to domicile became definite as

---

as a matter of right. For the full text of the dispatch see *Sessional Papers*, 1864, LXII, 414, cited in North America, No.13.   [81] *Ibid.*, 415.

[82] See *ibid.*, 1862, LXII, 116-117, for Russell's letter to Consul Cridland. For the sequestration act, see above, p. 385.

[83] Bonham, *op. cit.*, 197-198. See also *New York Times*, August 27, 1862; Richmond *Record*, July 10, 1863.   [84] Bernard, *op. cit.*, 456.

the war progressed, for she refused to intervene for subjects who had been long resident in any of the southern states. Joseph Hansard, for instance, who had been a resident of Georgia for twenty-five years, was informed, when he applied to Lord Russell for protection on the eve of return from England to the Confederate States, that he must return to that state, if he chose to do so, at his own risk. In the case of another British citizen taken on a blockade-runner and condemned by court-martial to two years' imprisonment by the United States, Britain declined to interfere as he had been a resident in the South for many years and in addition had taken an active part for the Confederates. It would thus appear that Great Britain in judging the question of domicile definitely considered length of residence and attitude toward the *de facto* government. She was even more generous in her interpretation of Confederate claims than the Confederate secretary of war.[85]

Far less has entered the records concerning the attitude of France and her efforts in behalf of her subjects than concerning the British attitude. Count Mercier denied that French citizens had lost their rights to protection by exercising the privilege of the franchise; in other words, his position would seem to have been that a foreigner was immune from military duty until he had actually become naturalized. M. Drouyn de l'Huys, who held the portfolio of foreign affairs under Napoleon III, complained to Slidell in an interview that frequent and grave complaints had been made of the forced service of French subjects in the southern armies; that such a policy would produce a bad feeling between the two countries; and that he hoped for its discontinuance. Slidell replied that he had reason to believe that, when the facts were ascertained, it would be found that all demands of French natives claiming exemption from military service had been impartially examined. He made the usual claim that French subjects should expect to defend their own property if they chose not to avail themselves of the option of leaving.[86]

Both the British and French governments gave to their subjects the protection afforded by the presence of vessels in the ports of a country which was the scene of war. French and British ships lay

---

[85] The second case cited in the text was that of a Mr. Gray.—*Ibid.*, 455-456.
[86] For the correspondence between De l'Huys and Benjamin see Richardson, *Messages and Papers*, II, 684-685.

in Mobile Bay and one French frigate came up the river. Both countries had ships of war stationed near New Orleans. The commandant of the French sloop, Captain de Clouet, addressed a note to Commodore Farragut of the United States fleet in protest against the threat of bombarding New Orleans in forty-eight hours. Sent by his government to protect the lives and property of thirty thousand French subjects in New Orleans, he protested against the short delay, considering it ridiculous, and demanded sixty days as the time to be allowed for the evacution of the city. He concluded with very strong language, indeed, a threat, "If it is your resolution to bombard the city, do it; but I wish to state that you will have to account for the barbarous act to the power which I represent. In any event, I demand sixty days for the evacuation."[87]

The presence of these boats in the harbor afforded an opportunity for the exchange of social courtesies between the officers aboard and the citizens of the port city and must have provided a pleasing diversion for people cut off from the outside world by the blockade. Mrs. Southwood describes such a social occasion aboard the British man-of-war *Rinaldo*, lying off New Orleans. "The midshipmen were returning some of the many courtesies they had received from the civilian population by a tea aboard the vessel. The band played the southern airs, the vessel, gaily lighted, with the flags floating in the breeze, presented a beautiful spectacle in the moonlight to the crowd gathered on the levee to enjoy it until dispersed by Butler's myrmidons."[88]

On the whole it must be admitted that under the circumstances the Confederate authorities afforded the best protection possible to their alien population. When Galveston was taken by the United States forces in October, 1862, communication with the city by the Confederates in the interior would necessarily be cut off. The Confederate military authorities invited the citizens without regard to nationality—and foreigners at that time constituted a majority of the population of that port—to remove to the interior, offering free transportation to all, and warning them when all communication must cease. Consul Lynn wished to know if he were to be prohibited from obtaining provisions from the state for the aliens remaining at the port. Despite the expiration of the time limit allowed, General

[87] Lossing, *Pictorial History of the Civil War*, II, 344.
[88] *Beauty and Booty*, 118-119.

Magruder patiently renewed his offer of transportation to the interior and stated that he was trying to arrange with Federal officers for supplies to enter the city by steamer under a flag of truce.[89]   In March, 1863, Beauregard advised ordering all foreign civilians to depart from Charleston. On the following February 17, when the Federal bombardment seemed about to begin, he issued a warning of the expected attack to all residents of Charleston and Savannah and ordered all noncombatants to retire. In July the mayor of Charleston issued a similar proclamation, followed in August by one from the governor of South Carolina.[90] Due care of the civilian population had surely been taken.

Probably, however, the most burdensome task imposed upon Confederate authorities by the foreign-born was the constant flood of official inquiries from European countries concerning subjects in the Confederate army. The Army Intelligence Office, created primarily to supply information concerning native soldiers to their anxious relatives, became an angel of mercy to some foreign families abroad. The overburdened president became the recipient of official requests from foreign countries for information concerning individuals. He referred all inquiries to the Intelligence Office. Foreign civilians resident in the Confederacy must, however, take advantage of such means of communication, surreptitious for the most part, as were available. Occasionally the only sure means of communication was a personal messenger. The most expensive "letter" which the writer has encountered was the clergyman who was sent by anxious relatives in England to convey to Mrs. W. in South Carolina the sad news of the death of her mother.[91]

The story of the consular service in the Confederacy, a volume in itself, is not regarded as a part of this story, yet it cannot be altogether ignored. The consuls constituted a small group, about twenty-five in number, foreign-born with one or two exceptions, exerting an influence out of all proportion to their number. Most of the British consuls, at least, had been in office for some time, and were, as a natural consequence, in more or less veiled sympathy with the seces-

[89] *O. W. R.*, Ser. 1, XV, 911.
[90] Bonham, *op. cit.*, 128; *O. W. R.*, XIV, 781; *Charleston Mercury*, July 10, 1863; *Charleston Daily Courier*, August 17, 1863.
[91] W. A. Crocker, "The Army Intelligence Office," *Confederate Veteran*, VIII, 119. For the case of Mrs. "W," see above, p. 356.

sion. They were drawn in one direction by their sympathies and in another by their superior officers, Lord Russell and Lyons, the latter of whom, at least, inclined to sympathize with the North. C. C. Cridland, British representative at Norfolk when the war began and later at Richmond, had strong sympathy for the South and did some practical work in its behalf. There was one American-born in the group. E. W. Barnwell, acting-consul at Charleston for Russia at the opening of the war, was a South Carolinian, member of a famous family, but his exequatur was revoked when he entered the military service. M. Théron, who was acting at Galveston for France and Spain, was suspected of attempting to alienate Texas from the Confederacy and so was dismissed by Benjamin in the fall of 1862.[92]

The duties of these commercial representatives, in the absence of regular ambassadors, assumed a diplomatic character. Throughout their stay their chief task was the protecting of foreign subjects from impressment into the army. They made numerous remonstrances to the governors, to army officers, and to the departments at Richmond, to which uniformly courteous replies were made by the urbane Benjamin, followed often by investigations and, where justifiable under the Confederate interpretation of the law, by discharges. While the British consuls seem to have been most active, protests are to be found from Count Mejan against imposition of active service on French subjects.[93] William Mure, British consul at New Orleans, seems to have been alert to the needs of his fellow countrymen, especially those in poverty and sickness, some of whom he cared for at his own expense, a practice which Russell said was common with the consuls in spite of their poor pay.[94] The consulates, as ever in time of war, became places of refuge. At first the consuls sought to transmit letters

[92] This detail concerning the individual consuls is found in Bonham, op. cit., 15, 16-17; for Théron see Pickett Papers. The granting of Raven's exequatur is noted in Journal of the Congress of the Confederate States, V, 422 ff. See also North American Review, CXXIX, 349-350. The list given by Bonham is for only the British consuls.

[93] O.W.R., Ser. 1, XV, 776. For an interesting example of a protest to a state, see statement of January 9, 1863 from George Moore to the governor of Virginia, protesting against the impressment of John Gallaher and John Berry.—"Journal of the Executive of Virginia," Chap. 8, CCII, 317, Confederate Archives, War Department. This is one of only two protests made to the state of Virginia which the writer has encountered.

[94] Mure's activity was favorably noted in the London Times, in Russell's article of August 3, 1861; New York Times, October 12. He befriended a sailor formerly of the Royal Navy, who had been wounded in the Crimean War, and later was blockaded on a merchantman in Mobile. Consul Magee sent him to New Orleans, where Mure sent him at his own expense to a hospital for an old wound, which had broken out afresh.—London Times, June 19, 1861; Bonham, op. cit., 178-179.

to Europe for anxious exiles in the South. Cridland, and Bunch in slightly less degree, were the chief offenders in this respect. The former forwarded them sometimes by private messenger. In October, 1861, he sent by a personal agent to the consul general in New York a large bag of dispatches which was seized in Baltimore and duly forwarded to Fort McHenry. Seward dispatched only the few official letters for the foreign office, retaining the rest as improperly forwarded by a consul. In the dispute between Lyons and Seward the latter had rather the better of the argument. Meanwhile Lyons arranged for the transmitting of official correspondence by men-of-war, and consuls, British and others, were warned against inclusion of private correspondence. That became the procedure thenceforth. Bunch had learned his lesson so well that in 1862 he declined to forward the letters of an Englishwoman and discouraged her attempts to smuggle them through the blockade.[95]

The Richmond authorities experienced constant friction with the consuls. The latter manifested indifference toward securing exequaturs by submitting the proper credentials, a disregard of the state department which was little short of insulting. On June 5, 1863, Secretary Benjamin wrote Moore at Richmond that the president refused to recognize him as consul as he had neglected to submit his credentials. The secretary of state inclosed a copy of the letters patent revoking his exequatur and also published a statement in the local press. In a letter to J. M. Mason in England Benjamin said that the consuls would be respected in the future so long as they confined themselves to the sphere of their duties and did not evade or defy the Confederate States government. This was followed immediately by an order restricting all communication of consuls to neutral vessels arriving from neutral ports in order to prevent communication between foreign agents in the Confederacy and those in the United States. A few days later the government felt it necessary to refuse to allow Cridland to serve at Mobile and to request him to leave Alabama. When he went from Richmond to Mobile, he had declared the change of residence the act of an individual, but straightway on arrival he presented to Admiral Buchanan a document from Minister Lyons, creating him consul at Mobile. No government could countenance such action and

[95] *Ibid.*, 45, 78-79; Hopley, *op. cit.*, II, 129, 222.

so on June 8, 1863, Cridland was told to take up his residence elsewhere than in Alabama.[96]

Events were now rapidly moving to a head. The sentiment of the South, a feeling which came to the surface in congress and in the press, was averse to letting the consuls continue their function, partly owing to their zeal in protecting fellow countrymen from army service. The statesmen had not wished to try to force recognition of the Confederacy from foreign governments by demanding new exequaturs. Furthermore the direction of consuls resident in the territory of one belligerent by a minister accredited to the other was, inevitably, as Lord Lyons said, provocative of friction and suspicion. It was suspected that Lord Russell intended to withdraw all consuls from the South to replace them by commercial agents, a policy which would have given British subjects protection without the necessity of consular dependence on Washington.[97] The London *Index* warned the British public that the persons and property of British subjects were dependent on Confederate forbearance and urged Great Britain by prompt recognition of the Confederacy to prevent the revoking of the exequaturs which would leave "tens of thousands of British subjects and millions of British property without consular protection."[98] Consul Fullarton added the straw which broke the camel's back of Benjamin's patience by advising aliens to throw down their arms and refuse to fight in the face of the enemy. Benjamin, acting on his own authority in the absence of the president, summoned the cabinet for an emergency session on October 7, 1863. The cabinet decided to dismiss the consuls. The dismissal was couched in Benjamin's most dignified style: "This assumption of jurisdiction by foreign officials within the territory of the Confederacy, and this encroachment on its sovereignty, cannot be tolerated for a moment; and the President has had no hesitation in directing that all consuls and consular agents of the British Government be notified that they can no longer be permitted to exercise their functions, or even to reside within the limits of the Confederacy."[99] And then to assuage any fears on the part of

[96] Bonham, *op. cit.*, 86 ff., 158 ff.; Richardson, *Messages and Papers*, II, 498-505. Benjamin wrote Mason an account.—Pickett Papers, Benjamin to Mason, No. 25, June 11, 1863.

[97] This policy commended itself to the *Daily Richmond Enquirer.*

[98] See issues of March 12, April 23, 1863.

[99] *American Annual Cyclopaedia*, 1863, 213. The optimism displayed by some of the

Emperor Napoleon as to the care of French subjects, Benjamin instructed Slidell to explain the situation promptly to the French secretary of foreign affairs.[100]

It seems the very irony of fate that it required the interposition of the secretary of war of a country which was to be so grossly outraged by consuls to save two consuls from service in the second class militia of Virginia during the crucial days of the Seven Days' Battles. On June 19 a request for exemption from service in the second class militia from D. von Groning, vice-consul of Italy and E. O. Nolting, vice-consul of Belgium, was forwarded to the governor of Virginia by Secretary of War Randolph. The state executive granted the request only on June 27 when Randolph asked for their discharge on the ground of "courtesy for the Governments represented by these gentlemen."[101]

---

papers is amusing. The *Daily Richmond Enquirer* of October 15, 1863, thought, "We may now expect, ere long, to see a British minister at Richmond, and British consuls asking *exequaturs* from Mr. Benjamin; for England never neglects her subjects, nor leaves them without the shadow of her wing and the guardianship of her flag. The sooner the better; we do not want to hurt either her or her subjects."

[100] *American Annual Cyclopaedia*, 1863, 213; Pickett Papers, Benjamin to Slidell, No. 25, October 8, 1863.

[101] "Journal of the Executive of Virginia," Chap. 8, CCII, 161, 167, Confederate Archives. On June 19 the governor refused the request of the Italian consul and stated that when the application of the Belgian consul came up it would be considered. An additional reason for granting it on June 27 was stated to be that given by Secretary Randolph in his letter—a very poor reason.

XIV

THE PERSECUTION OF THE GERMANS

SOMETHING HAS been said of the disinclination to allow promotion in rank to aliens in the Confederate army and of the prejudice against them on the part of members of congress and of the press. But it is necessary to grasp fully the depth and intensity of that feeling to be able to understand the events to be narrated in this chapter.

This feeling antedated the war and found expression against all, including those from the North, who had not been born and bred in the faith of their peculiar institutions of the South. This sentiment was voiced to Olmsted by a South Carolinian: "The intelligent mercantile class, who come among us from the North, and settle, are generally valuable acquisitions to society, and every way qualified to sustain 'our institutions'; but the mechanics, most of them, are pests to society, dangerous among the slave population, and ever ready to form combinations against the interest of the slaveholder, against the laws of the country, and against the peace of the Commonwealth."[1]

Proslavery men looked on Germans everywhere with hidden or open suspicion because of their well-known opposition to slavery. Their usual success in agricultural, industrial, and commercial pursuits may have awakened envy in the breasts of their less industrious neighbors in certain backward or undeveloped sections; and their love of the Fatherland, manifested by great public festivals commemorating events in the history of Germany, was misinterpreted as lack of affection for the adopted country. The transplanted Germans recognized the situation and resented secretly the political and social neglect which was their portion in the South in even greater measure than in the North.

It was, however, in the newer West, where life was harder and the prejudice which arises from ignorance more difficult to endure, that the most bitter and unintelligent denunciations were given expression. Some of those statements shock us today by the degree of

[1] *Seaboard Slave States*, II, 149-150.

ignorance they reveal and by the utter, unreasoning race hatred be-trayed. At Manchac Spring in Texas Olmsted found some travelers who thought the "Dutch" of the South different from those of the North. In the South they did not appear to have any regular busi-ness. They were thieves and loafers and nothing better than a "set of regular dam'd agrarians." All joined in these denunciations, which appeared to afford them relief, though founded, so far as Olmsted could see, on mere prejudice. His host intimated that he refused them, as outlaws and barbarians, fire and water whenever he had opportunity. "Agrarianism" was certainly a strange charge, as Olm-sted comments, for that new southwestern country to lodge against them but meant probably a predilection for free labor and aboli-tionism.[2]

In Texas amusing ideas came to the fore. Bilious diseases played havoc with the inhabitants in Liberty County, even Americans having to acknowledge a great deal of chills and fever, but they declared that the Germans were served about right, if they so suffered, "for living without bacon, and eating trash, such as 'fresh fish and *ripe cucumbers!*'"[3]

The Texan slaveholders, who had the least acquaintance with the Germans but knew of their sympathy with the slaves, already too near the border for the peace of mind of the owners, disliked having the Teutons settle near their plantations. Actual collisions were rare, as it was only where the population met in equal proportions, as in San Antonio, that there was opportunity for ideas to clash, and there the German shopkeeper or mechanic carefully avoided open expres-sion of views likely to be unacceptable to his American fellowtowns-men. The charge of inciting slaves to escape was repeatedly and vaguely made against the Germans, but Olmsted did not find a single well-defined case to substantiate the charge. He did, however, while he was in the state, encounter a case in which a German was brutally treated due to such a suspicion, which later failed to be substantiated in a slaveholders' court.[4]

An expression of the distaste felt toward the Germans was re-vealed to a northerner in Texas in the midst of the Civil War. He was riding one day into the country with a "genuine" Texan, as he

[2] *A Journey Through Texas*, 132.
[3] *Ibid.*, 374.
[4] *Ibid.*, 328-329.

terms him, who, when they approached a heavy German settlement, called attention to the fine farms and substantial improvements. The Texan burst out, "See the Germans squatted everywhere on the best lands in our State, I'll tell you what I would do if in my power. I would compel them to leave the rich land and go to the sand-hills and sand prairies. I don't think they have any business on these lands, and right under the noses of the better class of citizens."[5] Even De Bow could print such a prejudiced statement as the following: "The exceptions [to acceptance of slavery] which embrace recent importations in Virginia, and in some of the Southern cities, from the free States of the North, and some of the crazy, socialistic Germans in Texas, are too unimportant to affect the truth of the proposition"—that a class conscientiously objecting to the ownership of slave property did not exist in the South.[6]

The prejudice against the foreigner came sharply to the fore, as always, during the war. The feeling of distrust and distaste was sometimes, as was natural, mutual. The clearest expression of this mutual dislike as reflected in the army comes from Captain Francis Dawson. He did not like Longstreet's staff, declaring the general himself reserved and other officers overbearing. Except Colonel Manning, he had not a friend on the staff. "The staff had no 'use' for me, which perhaps was not surprising, as I was a stranger and foreigner, and I was on no better terms with them in 1864 than I had been in 1862."[7] On his way to join Longstreet he and a Captain Taylor, a naval officer with whom he had become acquainted, were held up by the Home Guards, quite naturally, as they refused to show their papers. "I suspect the nautical bearing of Captain Taylor which his uniform did not disguise, and my own fresh color and English accent, had more to do with our trouble than the fact that we were dismounted and alone. I really had some little difficulty in making myself understood at Stevensburg."[8] On one occasion Dawson even came to blows over this question of the foreigner. Major Walton, whom the Englishman heartily disliked, remarked in a con-

[5] North, *Five Years in Texas*, 193.
[6] "The Non-Slaveholders of the South," *De Bow's Review*, XXX (O. S.), 69, an open letter to N. R. Gourdin of Charleston.
[7] Dawson, *Reminiscences of Confederate Service*, 128.
[8] *Ibid.*, 61. That the privates should be conscious of a foreigner is perhaps not strange. Dawson heard a man say as he fell at the battle of Mechanicsville, "That Britisher has gone up at last."—*Ibid.*, 49.

versation that when the Confederate States had their independence, they did not intend to have any "d——d foreigners" in the country. Dawson asked what he expected would become of men like himself who had renounced their own country to aid the Confederacy. A flippant answer brought forth first a warm reply, then a blow, and then a challenge, but the matter was settled by an apology from Walton, which was certainly due.[9]

The constant use of the words "hireling" and "mercenary" as applied to the Irish and, especially, to the Germans in the northern armies was a further reflection of race prejudice entertained in the Confederacy. It was often, of course, utterly unjust, for it took no account of the hundreds of thousands of naturalized citizens of those nationalities long settled in the United States. The utterly callous attitude of a certain fighter on the southern side is not to be understood as typical, even of the Confederate frontiersmen, but is presented as reflecting how far prejudice could sway one man or a very small group of men. After Fontaine, the callous Confederate soldier in question, and one Cozzens, a scout, had captured a group of Federal soldiers, Fontaine declared, "We were sorry that they were Americans, as it necessitated our return sooner than we anticipated, for we did not kill real American soldiers in cold blood, as we did the hirelings of foreign countries. Had they been foreigners, we would not have taken them prisoners, only shot them as we rode up." Again he says, "We killed them in scores, as we could not take care of prisoners, for we frequently had as many as two to one in our front. . . . They were only foreign hirelings, and were here to kill us merely for the greenbacks and gold they received. Therefore, we had no scruples of conscience in disposing of them to the best advantage. Suffice to say I did my level best, and sent as many out of our way as my physical endurance permitted."[10]

This general prejudice made itself heard even against those in the highest positions. Toward Secretary of State Benjamin, it was mixed with and outweighed by particular prejudice against his race, as we have seen.[11] It could even appear against the beloved and highly respected Cleburne. In the discussion which followed his

[9] *Ibid.*, 102-103.
[10] Fontaine, *My Life and My Lectures*, 137, 155.
[11] "Proceedings of the First Confederate Congress," 3 Sess., *Southern Historical Society Papers*, XLVII, 121-122. See above, pp. 335-336.

proposal to arm the Negroes, one officer declared, "I believe Cleburne, though a skilled army officer, and true to the Southern cause, is opposed to slavery, and has not a proper conception of the negro, he being foreign born and reared."[12]

The feeling naturally existed among the civilian population and appeared on the slightest pretext, intensified by the suspicion which war breeds. In Richmond there burst out in September, 1863, a clamor against Irishwomen for buying up a load of muskmelons in the Second Market with intent to retail them. Three women were fined five dollars apiece and the melons ordered confiscated. "It is well," declared the *Daily Richmond Examiner,* that "the attention of the efficient clerk of the Second Market has been called to these creatures. They swarm through the markets every morning, and buy up the major part of the fruit brought in by the country people and take it to their houses to retail. As they understand the world, a jug of whiskey, and a half dozen melons, and a dozen hard boiled eggs, constitute a respectable store."[13] Probably the writer of this tirade had little appreciation of how desperately hard it was for the poverty-stricken foreigner to pick up a living in the capital in those lean war days.

Above all, citizens were rabid against having foreigners in office. There appeared in the Mobile *Advertiser and Register* in the midst of the war a letter signed by an "Alabama Woman" declaiming against "extortioners and speculators and declaring that none but native Southerners must fill office."[14] It is amusing to see some aliens entering heartily into the prejudices against other foreigners. "E.T.C.," an Englishman, declared that after the war there would be thousands of "Jews and Dutch" willing to swear that their sympathies had always been with the South, but he thought that "our people understand *that* question as well as Government, and will take more than usual care to protect themselves against the hordes which have been the chief movers and instigators of all the 'isms, usurpation and despotism, of the North."[15]

Nowhere was the outburst more vehement or unjust than in

[12] Nisbet, *Four Years on the Firing Line,* 265. See above, pp. 39-40.

[13] Moore (ed.), *Rebellion Record,* VII, 54.

[14] August 30, 1863; or Cumming, *A Journal of Hospital Life,* 87. No copy of this issue is recorded as extant in the *Union Catalogue of American Newspapers.*

[15] *Battle-fields of the South,* II, 49-50.

Texas. Letters of Americans printed in the Texas newspapers were showing deep animosity. The San Antonio *Ledger* in its issue of April 29, 1861, printed an article sharply critical of the attitude of the Germans toward the war and grossly unjust. The editor of the Houston *Tri-Weekly Telegraph* came to their defense. He said that unjust charges were being made against them, pointed out that the largest company which went from Houston, one hundred and thirty strong, was composed entirely of Germans, while most of the other companies that went from Houston were composed in part of Germans; that they had faced fire; and that, if they had not volunteered in proportion to their numbers in the population, it was because they did not have means and hence hesitated to leave their families. The southern-born would not give money to help poor soldiers; yet they were loudest in their "curses of the German."[16] Now and then a native realized that it was unreasonable to expect the uneducated foreigner to understand the intricacies of the involved constitutional quarrel of states' rights or to demand that he should be vitally concerned about it.[17] And one cannot forget the kindnesses poured out on individual foreign soldiers who had, as it has been beautifully phrased, consecrated "a sentiment into a sacrifice."

If the Confederate cherished deep feeling against the alien because he was unwilling to take up arms in behalf of the "sacred cause," or even against those who did, it can be readily inferred that he would have scant patience with the disloyalty and "treason" of the foreign-born citizen. Hence the reader may be well prepared for harsh measures against the Germans in Virginia and for the brutal scenes in Texas. Several respectable German citizens who had opposed secession, as H. L. Wiegand, for example, were imprisoned in Castle Thunder where they lay for months awaiting trial. The situation of foreign-born citizens in other cities and towns, but especially of those isolated in the country, was difficult. Bands of masked and armed men harassed these unfortunates, suspect by virtue of their very birth. A German couple, to cite a single instance, located near

[16] April 4, 1862. No copy of the *Ledger* for the date indicated is extant.
[17] See Eliza F. Andrews, *The War-Time Journal of a Georgia Girl*, 36. One cannot but feel, however, when the Louisiana planters near Baton Rouge were urging William Watson, the Scotch engineer, upon his second return from the war, that he might be satisfied with fighting now and could be of more service if he would give them the benefit of his engineering skill, that they were thinking of their lands and of their machinery at least as much as of him.—Watson, *Life in the Confederate Army*, 423-424.

Trevillian, Louisa County, Virginia, had opened a store and become prosperous by their industry. After the beginning of the war a group of spiteful neighbors accused them of two sins: of being secretly abolitionists, and of selling merchandise to Negroes, an illegal act. A band of masked men visited them by night and ordered them to leave within three days. When they returned to burn the house, the wife by sheer grit fought them off by threatening to shoot the first assailant, but the couple was obliged to seek refuge with countrymen in Richmond.[18]

An Englishman, an "involuntary sojourner in Richmond for five weeks" in 1862, as he phrased it, gives a sad picture of the treatment accorded to the Germans. "Natives and foreigners—of the latter class, Germans particularly—have suffered long confinement here; and some have gone hence, seated on their coffins, to the fair grounds outside of the city, where a rope and cross beams stand always."[19]

The presence of large groups of Germans in Texas, settled in communities almost wholly German, was certain to produce problems. Their antislavery sentiments and pro-Union loyalty have been stressed. Furthermore the fact that Texas marked the frontier of civilization with her many refugees from the law should be clearly kept in mind. To the fact that so many of the white natives in that section were desperadoes, criminals, gamblers, and smugglers is to be attributed, in part, at least, the ugly scenes to be depicted. Life was cheap on the frontier.[20]

An effort has been made to draw a rather sharp line of distinction between the attitude of the Germans of the lower Brazos, Colorado, and Guadalupe regions and that of their fellow countrymen settled in the upper courses of the Colorado, Guadalupe, and San Antonio rivers, dependent on the political philosophy in Germany at the time of their emigration. The Germans had migrated from the Fatherland to the former region at a time of strong provincial loyalty

[18] Harshness against the alien-born was not confined to Texas and Virginia, though nowhere else was there such brutality. A butcher with a stall in the First Market was imprisoned for months in Castle Thunder. Schuricht, *History of the German Element in Virginia*, II, 96-98.

[19] "Richmond and Washington during the War," *The Cornhill Magazine*, VII, 100.

[20] One finds a casual reference to the hanging of a Frenchman, Antoine Zimmerman, at Fort Clark on June 9, 1861, by the men of his post. There is simply the record without explanation of his offense. Perhaps he, too, objected to serving for a country of which he may not have been a citizen.—Governor's Letters, June-December, 1861, Archives, Texas State Library.

on the part of the individual citizen for his particular provincial state. Coming to Texas with these ideas, they readily adapted themselves in the lower plantation counties to the provincial conceptions of their plantation neighbors, embraced the principles of the Democratic party, and, if not defending slavery as an institution, at least regarded it as a matter for disposition by the states and not by the Federal government. To this extent they and their children were states' rights men.

In the other area, where the German element was far more numerous, the great bulk of the immigrants had left Germany at a different period in her development, at a time when the tide of nationalist feeling was running strong. Some of them before their exile had been zealous revolutionists in 1848 and took an enforced departure for new lands and scenes. Confronted in little more than a decade in the new environment by the profoundly fundamental issues of secession and war, while the oath of allegiance to the United States was still a comparatively recent act, these Germans probably sympathized with the Union cause.[21]

It is difficult to draw such a sharp line between the political views of Germans entering Texas in 1848 and those entering a decade earlier; it is, however, probably a correct statement to say that the great bulk of the Germans in Texas were not in sympathy with slavery and would almost unanimously have preferred to remain neutral in the war if they had been allowed to escape the pressure of Vigilance committees and of the conscript laws.

Many who had the means and acted promptly enough found an asylum in Mexico. Even there they did not escape pursuit. The Confederate agent, J. A. Quintero, stationed at Monterey, faithfully reported the actions of exiles. He wrote Colonel (later General) McCulloch on January 27, 1862, as follows: "This man Kimmey, Joseph Ulrich, [a partner of one Mr. Jones of San Antonio] and G. Theisen, are our avowed enemies, and like other Germans who have left Texas, have not spared any means to poison the minds of the Mexicans against us. They are constantly taunting and deriding the military weakness of the South and circulating rumors calculated

[21] This view is advanced in Robert P. Felgar's manuscript, "Texas in the War for Southern Independence," 16-17.

to do us harm."[22] Others who felt deeply on the subject departed for New Orleans or the North directly and entered the Union army. General Butler organized the First Texas United States Cavalry from fugitives to New Orleans—almost entirely German Texans. They were abandoning their families to greater misery than they probably realized, for under the sequestration act there was scant hope for anything but the greatest want, deprivation, and ill-treatment at the hands of the Confederate or Texan authorities. Others, unwilling to serve the Confederacy but also unwilling or unable to leave the state, remained at home but managed to evade the conscript officers by temporarily living in ravines or thickets.

Many Germans could not bring themselves to take the oath to the Confederate States but did not want to take the risk of secret flight or of refuge in the brush; hence they remained quietly on their farms in the hope that the war would soon be over. They met the worst sort of fate. They had to take first of all the brunt of the Indian attacks, which burst out as soon as the Union troops withdrew and before the Confederacy was ready to take over the defense of the border. The men on the border fled to the nearest city settlements, Fredericksburg, Kerrville, and Björne, the German settlements which had pushed fartherest west.[23]

Distrust of the Germans was voiced by the Americans from the very beginning of the war. Dr. Bracht retails to Governor Clark under date of May 18, 1861, a report of the departure of two noted abolitionists, both Germans, for Washington on a suspicious errand. "The two traitors are watched and will not be permitted to return to their homes nor families in San Antonio which still live there." He adds unctiously, "It shows that some souls are past redemption."[24]

A small incident preliminary to the persecution of the Germans should not be omitted. Franz van Stucken had recruited in the Fredericksburg region a company of Home Guards among whom were undoubtedly some Unionists who joined in order to remain near

[22] Governor's Letters, March-May, 1861, Governor Edward Clark, Archives, Texas State Library.

[23] Kaufmann, *Die Deutschen im amerikanischen Bürgerkriege*, 154-158. On March 22, 1862, some Americans complained that there were 96 Germans not in the army—vs. 7 natives in Kerrville.

[24] Governor's Letters, March-May, 1861, Governor Edward Clark, Archives, Texas State Library.

their families. Stucken's company was to go to San Antonio at General Bee's order, as exaggerated tales of the activity of Unionists were afloat. Lieutenant August Simering of this company, a Unionist at heart, was intrusted with the escort of several cannon drawn by oxen. He tarried at Fredericksburg, sending the cannon ahead with the command to wait for him at a certain point. He then missed the escort and cannon and came on without them to San Antonio. Although the men soon came in with the cannon, the rumor found credit that Unionists among the escort had taken the cannon away, and thus the distrust against Germans in the Confederate service increased.[25]

Already in the spring of 1862 the papers were writing of the strange fruit which the trees in Texas bore. The San Antonio *Herald* of July 19, 1862, reported of the Unionist Germans, "Their bones are bleaching on the soil of every county from Red River to Rio Grande and in the counties of Wide and Denton [German counties] their bodies are suspended by scores from the 'Black Jacks.'" The persecution of the Germans had begun, especially at the hands of the Vigilance Committee, members of the secret order of the Knights of the Golden Circle with headquarters in San Antonio. Its precept was to convert Union men to the true faith by way of a halter.

The most decisive, and incidentally unfortunate, step taken by the German citizens to maintain themselves in a neutral position during the war was the organization in June, 1862, of the Union Loyal League. Eighteen men only participated in the first meeting, but they were drawn from a rather far-flung area; they might be regarded as representing the Germans of Gillespie, Kerr, and Kendall counties, and some communities of Medina, Comal, and Bexar counties. The chief objects of the organization were to protect its members and their families from disturbance by the Indians and to protect members from coercion into bearing arms against the United States. The original membership did good work, as some five hundred men turned out for a meeting on Bear Creek, in Gillespie County, on July 4, 1862, and took an oath not to enter the Confederate service. Among the questions here discussed was a more effective organization of three military companies from Gillespie,

---

[25] Edward Schmidt, *Fest-Schrift zur Fünfzigjährigen Erinnerungs-Feier an das Gefecht am Nueces,* 8.

Kendall, and Kerr counties. After electing the company officers, they selected Fritz Tegener as major to command the battalion of the three companies. An advisory board with Edward Degener as one of its members was also constituted. After a session of the advisory board with the officers of the three military units, the companies dispersed to await such orders as might be dictated by future developments.[26]

A little later in the same month General Bee, in command of the Rio Grande military district, was given information as to the activities of Unionists, especially of the Germans, and named as provost marshal of the disaffected counties, Captain James Duff, a despicable character, according to one of his own officers. There had spread, probably as an echo of the meeting on Bear Creek, a rumor that five hundred Germans had hidden in the mountains near Fredericksburg and were oppressing the secession planters. Bee placed four companies of mounted troops from San Antonio at Duff's disposal under command of Captain John Donelson. The former was instructed to proclaim martial law in Gillespie, Kerr, and Kendall counties, to exact an oath of allegiance to the state and Confederate governments from citizens on pain of being treated as traitors, and to send out scouting parties to break up encampments and to send into the settlements the families of disloyal Germans.[27]

Shortly after the middle of July, Major Tegener heard of the murder of a man named Steward, whom the Unionists shot as a betrayer of the decisions in their meetings. Whether the Union League should be held responsible for this murder cannot now be determined, but the circumstance that at one of their meetings lots were drawn to see who should perform the deed lays responsibility in some measure on the League. At least it provided a welcome pretext for the southern commander to send Captain Duff and to introduce a rule of terror among the inhabitants of the mountainous region in the vicinity of Fredericksburg. The "bushwackers" must be driven out from the mountains.[28]

Captain Duff issued the proclamation at Fredericksburg, warning bushwackers to come into the camp within three days to take the

---

[26] John W. Sansom, *Battle of the Nueces River*, 2-3. Tegener lived in Austin.

[27] *O. W. R.*, Ser. 1, LIII, 454-455, Bee to Captain S. B. Davis, Assistant Adjutant General of First Texas District, October 21, 1862. For Williams' opinion of Duff see his *With the Border Ruffians*, 236. [28] Schmidt, *op. cit.*, 9.

oath of allegiance, an interval far too short, as the summons could not, in the absence of modern swift means of communication and under war conditions, be spread throughout the extended district in that time. At the expiration of the brief period Duff sent out patrols to harry the neighborhood and throughout the summer continued the hunt of human beings. Two parties of twenty-five each were dispatched with wagons to bring in from the farms the wives and children of those who had taken to the mountains. In four days one party returned with ten Germans who were promptly lynched, the other with four or five men and eight women with their little children. These women and children were sent to Fredericksburg, and the men to the guard tent. Lieutenant Williams, an English resident who had volunteered for frontier service and who had been assigned to Duff's group, was deeply touched by the sight of "these poor folks stripped of their property, such as it was, earned by hard toil and exposure on a dangerous frontier; and I could not but contrast their treatment with that of well-known Abolitionists in San Antonio, who, because they were wealthy, and made friends of the mammon of unrighteousness, were not only unmolested but specially favored in all sorts of ways."[29] One small patrol was sent to Fredericksburg to enforce on the inhabitants the oath of allegiance. Most of them submitted, though some "took to the mountains rather than perjure themselves."[30] Patrols which did not bring in prisoners committed much destruction. Williams on his way to the Nueces River came on one such scene of desolation, the fields as well as the house ruined, all the furniture broken, the cattle driven away, and the population vanished. Some of the farmers who were thus punished had rendered fine service in the Indian wars before 1861.[31] The number thus misused surely mounted to several hundred.

Shortly after the middle of July, Major Tegener heard of General Bee's proclamation of martial law, and of the harsh actions of Duff. He at once called a meeting of the advisory board of the Union League. The board made the important decision to disband the three companies recently organized as concrete assurance to the

[29] Williams, *op. cit.*, 237. He says that a German tavern keeper in Fredericksburg had informed against them to Duff (he calls him Dunn) to pay off old spites. Williams seems to have preferred to disguise slightly the names of the officers he was criticizing.
[30] *Ibid.*, 232, 235.
[31] *Ibid.*, 238; Kaufmann, *op. cit.*, 159-160.

army officers of the Confederacy that no armed opposition to the government was in contemplation. It also decided to invite and to advise all Unionists unwilling to submit to the Confederate authorities to meet with Major Tegener on August 1 at a point on the headwaters of Turtle Creek in Kerr County in order to proceed with him to Mexico.[32]

Tegener, as planned, left the rendezvous on Turtle Creek the afternoon of August 1 with his little band of sixty-one, joined on August 8 by four Americans, also on their way to Mexico. Sansom, who had business in Mexico, served as guide. He was an experienced trapper who knew the way through the desert to the Rio Grande. It is clear that the group were overconfident in thinking that they had eluded the Confederate forces and that under the proclamation they had sufficient time to leave Texas, for they made no effort to waylay their pursuers as they might easily have done in one of the narrow defiles of the river. Furthermore they made no effort to hurry their flight. Tegener pitched camp on the morning of August 9 on the west bank of the Nueces River about twenty miles from Fort Clark, still a day's march from the Mexican border. Here in their overconfidence they were recklessly careless. They did not select a location for their camp which would give them protection and defense in case of an attack; they did not even place a strong guard around the camp for the night. Tegener refused to heed the warnings of danger from Sansom, who sensed the presence of their pursuers. Meantime a man named Burgemann, who had wormed his way into their confidence and had attended the League meetings, proved a spy in the service of the Confederates and had betrayed the place of rendezvous and the route to be followed to Mexico. Armed with this information Lieutenant C. D. McRae, sent by Captain Duff with ninety-four mounted men, a force nearly twice the size of Tegener's, started in pursuit. On the afternoon of August 9 the advance guard discovered the German camp, and McRae secreted his men in a ravine about three miles distant and planned an attack early the next morning.[33]

[32] Sansom, op. cit., 4.
[33] There is no dearth of primary information on this battle. The official report of McRae was written eight days after the battle and is found in O. W. R., Ser. 1, IX, 614-616, McRae to Gray, August 10, 1862. See also the report of General Bee to Captain S. B. Davis, October 21, 1862.—Ibid., LIII, 454-455. The accounts left by Williams,

Shortly before daybreak the Confederates approached the camp and captured one of the other party. Though his life was offered him if he would lead them to the camp of his companions, he refused to betray them and was hanged. About an hour before daybreak firing began, earlier than planned, owing to an unexpected encounter of two German guards with the Confederates. In a few minutes the firing ceased. At break of day McRae and his men charged the camp and broke the line of the Union group. Unfortunately, when they discovered the presence of their enemies, Tegener would not listen to the sound advice of the guide Sansom, to flee to a neighboring hill which was easier to defend, but accepted battle where they were on the Nueces River. After a desperate struggle the fugitives scattered, leaving nineteen of their number killed and nine wounded, and having in their turn killed two Confederates and wounded nineteen. The wounded, left in the hands of the attackers, were murdered in a barbarous manner a few hours later by the victors. Some dying men were dragged to trees and hung; one was thrown or fell on the camp fire when shot down, though just before he expired he was pulled from the fire by Williams, more humane than his comrades in arms. In justice to McRae it should be stated that he was badly wounded during the battle and, according to Williams, knew nothing of the cold-blooded murder. In his official version, written on August 18, eight days after the event, McRae says of the murdered, "They offered the most determined resistance and fought with desperation, asking no quarter whatever; hence I have no prisoners to report." This official statement would seem to argue that

---

op. cit., 242-251, and by John W. Sansom, the guide, op. cit., 57-61, were not published until forty years after the event. Kaufmann, op. cit., 157-162, and Schmidt, op. cit., based their accounts largely on the versions of Sansom and Williams. Don H. Biggers, German Pioneers in Texas, 57-61, gives a brief account.

In addition to the above the writer has used secondary accounts of Lossing, Pictorial History of the Civil War, II, 537; Felgar, op. cit.; and the printed address of James P. Newcomb, given at Comfort on the Twenty-fifth anniversary of the event. The writer is indebted to A. Brinkman for the use of one of these rare pamphlets. Newcomb cites the testimony of Jacob Kuchler, given in 1887. The latter was a commissioner in the Texas Land Office, who sent Newcomb an account of the battle for use in his address.

Though there is considerable discrepancy among the several accounts, there is general agreement in the essentials. Sansom, Williams, and Kuchler are in agreement in saying that the nine wounded Germans were basely murdered by a detachment of McRae's men under Lieutenant Lucke.

North, op. cit., 192-193, tells an astonishing tale which came to his ears of a serious fight about that time northwest of Austin between the state militia and 200 to 300 Indians who had come down from the mountains to steal horses and cattle. But when the war was over, he learned the truth. It was the garbled account of this fight.

all the German prisoners, wounded though they were, fought until life was extinct, a fact which does not strike the impartial reader as plausible. It is more probable that McRae wrote those words with the expectation of shielding his subordinate officer, Lucke. Likewise the praise of his men seems tinged with partisanship, hardly justified by the circumstances: "My officers and men behaved with the greatest coolness and gallantry, seeming to vie with each other in deeds of daring chivalry."[34]

The survivors fled toward the Rio Grande. Of the thirty-seven who escaped, six were later killed by Confederate troops on October 18, 1862, while crossing the Rio Grande River into Mexico; several almost starved in the desert; and eleven, including the guide Sansom, succeeded in escaping to Mexico. Most of the latter became members of the First United States Texas Cavalry and rendered almost three years of service on the Union side. Of the other twenty, some spent the remaining years of the war in Mexico, others in California, and some returned to their homes, secreting themselves from capture by the Confederates by various devices.[35]

The massacre on the Nueces River did not end German disloyalty to the Confederacy. However difficult it became to escape from Texas, many Germans still succeeded in the effort. Sansom alone escorted groups of forty-eight, thirty-six, and nine over the Mexican border. All found their way to the Union army. Their disappearance and that of many others was doubtless noticed by their American neighbors.[36]

The massacre did not prevent the Germans in Austin County from holding secret meetings and from trying to evade the conscript law. At the very end of November, 1862, A. J. Bell, the enrolling officer of Austin County, reported to the superintendent of conscripts in Austin that from 400 to 500 persons were attending secret meetings. At one public meeting they had determined to send a petition to the governor asking that their families be provided for and themselves armed and clothed as a condition antecedent to submission to the conscript laws and to entering military service. Bell considered this, quite naturally, as evidence of a "spirit of insubordination" and suggested that a company of mounted and well-armed men be sent

[34] O. W. R., Ser. 1, IX, 615-616.
[35] Sansom, op. cit., 11, 13-14.   [36] Kaufmann, op. cit., 161-162.

him, as the militia could not be relied on because of their sympathy with the conscript dodgers.[37]

In early December General Magruder was endeavoring to meet this problem in the well-known way of generals when they feel it necessary to avoid strict military discipline. He directed the superintendent of conscripts at Austin to cause all persons of foreign birth manifesting opposition to be sent first of all from the state to regiments in other departments. He urged caution and quiet action in order to obviate, as far as possible, all distinction between loyal and disloyal citizens of alien blood.[38]

Less than five weeks later, on January 3, 1863, the same enrolling officer wrote that the Germans of Austin and adjoining counties were in a state of open rebellion, had openly resisted a recent draft, and had beaten a draft officer with sticks and iron bars. Only eight days later about six hundred people gathered from five counties—Austin, Washington, Fayette, Lavaca, and Colorado—at Shelby Prairie in the upper part of Austin County where a number of speeches, chiefly by Germans, advocated refusal to enter either the Confederate or state service and even open resistance to the government. A resolution was adopted to appoint one man in each beat to organize the men immediately into companies of infantry and cavalry. Drilling had already begun and picket guards were kept mounted and armed to communicate information to the officers. Great excitement was evinced by the farmers near Cat Spring as they felt themselves and their property in danger. The officer thought it possible to enforce the law by prompt action without much bloodshed, but if allowed to continue the situation would call for greater sacrifice of life and property. At least one full regiment of well-armed cavalry should, in his opinion, be dispatched to that section.[39]

General W. G. Webb of the state troops, writing from La Grange on January 4, 1863, reported in Austin County and in Fayette County a number of meetings of Germans, including some Americans, which had been going on secretly for months, to resist the draft. According to his information, partly from loyal Germans, the seeds of disaffection had been sown by native Americans. The disloyal foreigners

[37] *O. W. R.*, Ser. 1, XV, 887. He says that he had it on reliable authority that they were considering resistance to the contemplated draft.—*Ibid.*

[38] *Ibid.*, 890.

[39] *Ibid.*, 925-926. Alarms were also coming in to a Colonel Green.—*Ibid.*, 921.

threatened with destruction every German who would not join them. He had been informed that a German blacksmith in Fayetteville was secretly making spearheads and that the disloyal had been providing themselves with ammunition. The disaffected had served as a deterrent to volunteering, for the loyal were determined to make an issue with the disloyal by compelling them to meet the draft. Webb had had great difficulty in restraining the hotheaded Confederates that he might gain time to ferret out the treasonable plans and thus avoid precipitating civil war. He thought that the greatest disaffection in that part of the state lay about New Ulm and Industry in Austin County and about Round Top and Fayetteville in Fayette County. He wanted a regiment of cavalry sent under pretense of forming an encampment to overawe the disaffected.[40]

About this time at La Grange General Webb was visited by a committee of Germans professing to represent one hundred and twenty of their countrymen of Biegel Settlement, in Fayette County, who presented him with a written statement of their grievances and their unwillingness to defend the state unless they had guarantees that their families should be protected in their absence. They expressly declined to take the oath to the Confederate States because they knew of no law requiring state troops to take that oath. The spirited nature of their protest cannot but command respect. After presenting the destitute condition of their families it concludes: "For these reasons we sympathize with all the unfortunate who have to provide for their own maintenance, and hope that our authorities will look upon us as men and not as chattels. With what spirit and what courage can we so situated fight, and that, moreover, for principles so far removed from us?" They insisted that there was a higher duty than defending their country, that of maintaining their families.[41]

A similar report of open opposition to conscription at Fredericksburg went to Governor Lubbock at about the same time from Lieutenant Colonel H. L. Webb. His description of a meeting in that German town on January 3, 1863, gains by being presented in his own words: "Many inflammatory speeches were made, advising resistance to the draft, the moderates, or conservative portion of the

---

[40] *Ibid.*, 926-928.

[41] The Declaration of Citizens in Biegel Settlement to General Webb.—*Ibid.*, 928-929, 945. It was evidently written in German, for James Paul, private secretary, certified to a translated copy.

persons composing the meeting, were not allowed to speak. . . . About one-third of the persons present were Americans. I am of opinion that there is serious danger, that they will give us much trouble, and from all I could learn, they are determined to keep up their organizations, set at defiance the Laws of the State, and if practicable join any Yankee force that may land on our soil." Evidently a man of action, feeling that there was serious danger, he reported that he was leaving that very morning for Galveston to lay the situation before General Magruder.[42]

Magruder acted promptly, ready for fresh victories after his recent recapture of Galveston. He sent Lieutenant Colonel Hardeman to Alleyton to dispatch several companies of the Arizona brigade with a piece of artillery against the disloyal Germans in La Grange. Magruder on January 8 declared martial law in Colorado, Fayette, and Austin counties and had the ringleaders arrested while the governor himself proceeded to the scene of rebellion. He held a conference at La Grange with the members of the committee from Biegel Settlement, to whom he gave a "very plain, positive talk."[43] His efforts and the activities of the military brought about an enrollment of the drafted men, though some of the disloyal threatened to "hoist the white flag and go over to the enemy" at the first good opportunity.[44]

Lieutenant Colonel H. L. Webb wrote from Alleyton in Colorado County, on January 21, 1863, that the Germans and others had quietly submitted to the draft and had gone to the different rendezvous to be enrolled as soldiers, and also that those who were not drafted professed loyalty with a promise of cheerful submission to the laws of the Confederacy and of the state of Texas.[45] Lieutenant Colonel Hardeman was able to report from Columbus, Colorado County, on January 26, that the Germans in that section were quiet, that almost all had consented to enter the militia, but that he would pursue some of the insurrectionary leaders still at large in the country, and not in the service. General Magruder soon assured Governor Lubbock that "order and a better state of feeling" prevailed in the

[42] Lubbock Papers, 1863, Governor's Letters, Archives, Texas State Library.
[43] *O. W. R.*, Ser. 1, XV, 936, 945. For General Orders No. 39, ordering martial law, see *ibid.*, 955.
[44] *Ibid.*, 945. Webb was trying to secure from someone on oath the statement that desertion was under contemplation. Webb reiterates that the movement was not confined to Germans.—*Ibid.*, 945-946.   [45] *Ibid.*, 955-956.

disaffected counties, and that he had ordered the ringleaders under arrest to be turned over to the civil authorities since their offenses had been committed previous to the declaration of martial law.[46] The display of military force, together with the support of the civil authorities, subdued the disaffected Germans and Americans for a period at least.

There was clearly some abuse of civilians, especially of the women, during the searches and arrests, beginning about January 10 at La Grange and Belleville and continuing into February, which provoked resentment and ill will on the part of the German population. When the report of the character of Colonel Hardeman's command is noted, the reader can scarcely feel surprise at the fact that these humble aliens were not treated with consideration. Colonel Webb reports them as "the most disorderly, outrageous set of men I ever knew," guilty of all kinds of excesses, over whom their officers had no control.[47] This officer's report concerning his official inquiry at New Ulm, after the women of Austin had filed a petition of protest, is probably a fair presentation of the case.

The women declared that the injuries which they had received during the raids had been inflicted by several civilians whom a lieutenant asked to lead him and his detachment by night to the houses of the disaffected Germans. As those men were enemies of the Germans they probably led him to the homes of innocent persons. Dividing his command into two squads in order to make all the arrests at about the same time, he led one group himself and sent the other under a subordinate officer. Webb frankly criticized the lieutenant, named Stone, as unable to enforce discipline and unfit for command, expressed his conviction that "the soldiers behaved badly by pushing the women away from their husbands" and inflicting some bruises, but insisted that the women investigated agreed that the serious injuries were inflicted by the civilian guides. Webb sought to restore better feeling by assuring the Germans that guilty persons should be arrested and punished.[48]

There was some slight complaint of undue leniency toward foreign suspects arrested by civilians. Lieutenant Colonel H. L. Webb, for

[46] *Ibid.*, 960, 974-975. [47] *Ibid.*, 942, 955.
[48] The report is dated February 11, 1863.—*Ibid.*, 981-982. The whitewashing report of Lieutenant W. J. Wheeler, dated February 23, 1863, is obviously biased and hence unreliable. —*Ibid.*, 989.

instance, complained on February 11 that prisoners he had sent from Columbus to the provost marshals of Fayette and Austin counties with directions for their delivery to civil authorities in accordance with General Magruder's order had been immediately discharged and permitted to return to their homes, instead of being held for prosecution by the district attorney.[49]

Far different was the usual tale of proscription and murder. The Latin settlement on the Guadelupe River was devastated. Williams, though a part of Duff's command, which was entrusted with the bloody work, was utterly out of sympathy with the persecution and viewed it with the coldly critical eyes of an Englishman demanding orderly procedure of law even in war time. At Fredericksburg a group of unfortunates, "whose only offense was that they secretly sympathized with the North," were placed under the charge of the guard, and were reported the next morning as having escaped. Instead they had been quietly spirited away and hanged at some little distance from the camp. He also tells the pathetic tale of a man who had been brought in by a patrol one morning under accusation of northern sympathy. He was freed the same night as nothing could be proved against him. His happy release with a pass from Duff was turned into mockery the next morning when his body was found dangling in the woods near by, the throat slit from ear to ear. What makes the record blacker is the fact that many were fathers of large families of dependents, while others were graybeards, of no value to the Confederate army. Williams condemns the hangings as without "shadow of an excuse," with "no possible palliation for these diabolical midnight assassinations."[50]

Equally pathetic is the picture drawn by North of another victim, a white-haired Teuton, fourscore years of age. Because he was suspected of Union proclivities, the Vigilance Committee went to his house and told his aged wife that her husband was needed as an important witness. They placed the man in the saddle, ordered him to ride in front, and, as he was riding out of the gate of his own yard, shot him in the back. The poor old wife went insane with grief and shock.[51]

[49] This was at least the report brought back by the escort concerning the men taken to La Grange, Fayette County.—*Ibid.*, 978-979.

[50] Williams, *op. cit.*, 258-259.   [51] *Op. cit.*, 192.

The opposition of the Germans to conscription continued to the end of the war—as did the lynchings. Even as late as April, 1865, ten Germans who had been kept in prison at Fredericksburg under suspicion of disloyalty were hanged. Williams was ordered out with a detachment to move against them but, as he had been out of sympathy with the persecution of the Germans from the beginning, he sent the first lieutenant with twenty men. In the clash with the military the Germans were badly defeated and several made prisoners. They were placed in the lockup of the little town of Fredericksburg, a flimsy wooden building over which only a weak guard was posted. A mob appeared that night, easily overpowered the guard, burst into the place, taking out the ten prisoners, and hanged them on the live oaks outside the town. Williams strongly suspected that the hanging was with the connivance of the officer in command.[52]

Acting under the orders of their superior officers and in regular line of military duty, the Confederate force may be held as justified for pursuing and attacking the German band of fugitives on their flight to Mexico on the ground of treason, for they were attempting to escape to Mexico there to join the forces of the enemy, but certainly no defense can be offered for the base killing of wounded prisoners. For that the only proper word is murder. McRae probably would not have sanctioned that action if he had not been wounded and had been in personal command. But his statement in his official report that the Germans asked no quarter, and hence he had no prisoners to report, does him no credit. He is too palpably shielding a subordinate. The incident on the Nueces River is one of which no Confederate officer could be proud.

Some Germans have taken the position that Tegener and his little band should have been permitted to depart peaceably to Mexico. They had understood, according to Sansom, that men whose consciences would not permit them to take the oath to the Confederacy had the privilege of withdrawing from the country.[53] The fact that they were assembled in a small band and that they carried arms only for their protection against Indians did not justify the Confederate

[52] Williams, *op. cit.*, 407-408. Mrs. Crockett Riley insisted, to make the story of cold-blooded lynching worse, that they were not all hung at the same time. One was hanged one night, and four killed a week later; one shot, and three hanged to trees still later.   [53] Sansom, *op. cit.*, 11, 13-14.

attack upon them. In point of view of the accepted rules of war that position is hardly tenable, as the government must apply its conscript laws uniformly to all citizens. It was exasperating and irritating to have some citizens refuse to help fight for the cause, and—worse—secretly hope for the success of the foe. In all justice it must be admitted that the southern efforts to stamp out disloyalty were a justifiable action of governmental authority, and no more drastic than those authorized by the Union in dealing with the copperheads of the North. Nothing, however, can be said in extenuation of the hangings of the disloyal. Those peaceful farmers and graybeards were not taken with arms in their hands; there was no hostile force in the vicinity to which they could lend aid or comfort; there was no pretense that the act was one of retaliation. Martial law was in force at the very moment of the hangings so that no plea for the need of summary justice can be entertained. Swift justice could have been executed on any real offender by legal process of drumhead court-martial. Much of the violence was incident to a time of war, incident to life on the border, incident to personal animosities and revenge, and to the zeal of fanatically patriotic men. But families endured physical suffering from being deprived of their breadwinners; innocent men were killed; families suffered the anguish of seeing bands of ruffians drag husbands and fathers out of their homes and hang them to trees. For these acts there were no extenuating circumstances.

XV

THE SERVICE OF THE FOREIGNERS TO THE CONFEDERACY

AN ATTEMPT AT an evaluation of the service of the aliens and foreign-born citizens to the Confederacy is as indispensable as it is difficult. Without attempting a meticulous analysis of the abilities and war record of each of the officers, which would be quite beyond the ability and training of the lay writer and burdensome to the lay reader, it may be rewarding to weigh the contributions of the civilians and to glance at the more obvious military achievements of a few of the foreign-born who rose high enough in the service to affect the outcome of battles and campaigns.

The foreigners furnished some leaders for the civilian posts, though not in proportion to their numbers, as was natural in view of the humble station of most of them and of the prejudice against them. To civil office they furnished a Benjamin and a Memminger, whose merits and contributions have been duly set forth. The value of the services of a diplomatic character rendered by the men sent on missions abroad, measured in the perspective of time, show little to justify the expenditure of money by the government and of effort on the part of the men sent. The number thus singled out for special missions would be surprising if we were not aware that the government was obviously capitalizing the foreigner's knowledge of his country or his mastery of a foreign tongue. From first to last Richmond sent at least eighteen emissaries of foreign birth abroad, each to the land of his nativity or to some point where previous experience was to be used in the interest of the adopted country. Lieutenant Capston, Captain Lalor, and Father Bannon were all expected to understand Irish psychology—and proved that they did. Bishop Lynch was not a native of Italy but knew Rome from his student days and, what was more important, had a personal acquaintance with some of the prelates about the pope.

Confederate diplomatic ventures in the border states of northern Mexico were eminently successful. The scholar could scarcely escape a study of John Quintero's correspondence with the state department and the comments passed upon him by his colleagues without the conviction that here was a clever and resourceful diplomat, able to grapple with many delicate and difficult problems. As a matter of fact his record shows more tangible results than do those of Mason or Slidell. It was he who through Governor Vidaurri opened up the channels of trade in the northern border states of Mexico for the group of Confederate purchasing agents and contractors who swarmed over the border. It is difficult to estimate the volume of trade which flowed over the Mexican border, including, of course, European goods, but the revenues to Mexico from tariff duties had been estimated at $125,000 to $150,000 a month.[1] This Mexican trade was especially important as it was kept open, to a greater or less degree, during the entire war. To Quintero in chief measure must fall credit for this success, as he secured and retained the good will of Vidaurri for the Confederacy and, more than any military leader, though he had the support and aid of the commanders in the Trans-Mississippi Department, he possessed the tact to untangle the difficulties as they arose to threaten friendly relations and the strength to curb border incursions. He proved shrewd and successful in his dealings with all the Mexican authorities, one after the other—Governor Vidaurri, President Juárez, and, lastly, the French Imperialists.[2]

Perhaps it is worth while, in order to show how inadequate is the judgment of the moment, to measure the Confederate agents by comparing their achievements in the light of historic perspective with the effect they seemed to produce at the time. Measured in that way, the missions of Rost and Quintero, of Father Bannon and Bishop Lynch compare well with those of Mason and Slidell; those of Hotze and Capston in their spheres seem to have been as successful as the efforts of Bulloch in an entirely different realm. Praise in unstinted measure was poured out by President Davis himself on Father Bannon and Bishop Lynch. "Mr. Quintero's services are highly appreciated by the Department," wrote Benjamin of the Mexican diplomat,

---

[1] This is the estimate of Frank L. Owsley, *King Cotton Diplomacy*, 128, 144.

[2] For a full account of Quintero's mission see *ibid.*, 119-145. For his own account of his mission as well as the political, economic, and military situation of Mexico see Quintero to State Department, August 19 and 22, 1861, Pickett Papers. The latter comprises the notes on the existing conditions in Mexico. The writer regards it as no part of her task to discuss in detail his mission—in other words to re-do the task already admirably performed by Owsley.

"and he has frequently received the commendation of the Government for his zeal and for the address with which he has managed to maintain cordial relations with all the functionaries on the Mexican border."[3] Yet in truth meagerness of results was in general the lot of the foreign-born, equally with the native-born, emissary in the diplomatic field. Not one won recognition for his country.

The foreign-born civilians of humble station were an asset to the state despite the cry of "useless consumers." Some of them became manufacturers of arms, especially swords, and of minor army equipment. It will not be forgotten that it was a Britisher who provided the first Confederate uniforms in Texas. They furnished the labor in the few factories of the land—munition plants, clothing plants, salt and nitre plants; they constituted in large degree the shopkeepers; a very few worked on the railroads. In other words they were the producers of most of the necessary commodities except food and were the distributors also of food. In a surreptitious way along the boundary lines or near "debatable ground" they aided in getting commodities through the lines for Confederates, official and lay. Aliens sometimes abused favors extended to them as neutrals to traffic for the benefit of the Confederate armies or for neighbors who would be suspected if they tried to pass the Union lines.[4] Some of the many tales of civilians carrying word to some Confederate officer of Federal military movements concerned foreign residents. Several have entered this account and do not require repetition.[5]

Some of the alien-born, even while sometimes acknowledging allegiance to another country, spent generously to equip troops. It is perhaps not surprising to read of the generosity of the South Carolinian, Plowden Weston, later elected lieutenant governor of his state, who furnished a suit of clothes to each man in the company which he raised and ordered the requisite number of rifles for them from England.[6] But more surprising was the gift of an Irishman who had for forty years been a citizen of Kentucky. Immediately

[3] See also Richardson, *Messages and Papers*, II, 77.
[4] See above, pp. 316-317, for an Englishman living near Suffolk; for the service rendered by the Scotchman Watson to his neighbors near Baton Rouge see his *Life in the Confederate Army*, 433. See above, Chap. 13, n. 73.
[5] The reader is reminded of the service of Lola Sanchez in this connection. See above, pp. 378-379. For the work of the English planter, Thornton, who reported the presence of Union forces to Colonel Evans, see above, p. 316.
[6] Collins, *Memories of the Southern States*, 11, 12, 13, 40.

after the outbreak of war he left New Orleans, where he regularly spent the winter season, for his adopted state in order to equip a regiment for the war at an estimated cost of ten thousand dollars. Sulakowski, De Gournay, and Debray each equipped a company.[7]

By their presence at their homes the aliens were able to protect not only their own property, but that of their neighbors. A Patrick Lynch, whose place of origin scarcely needs to be designated as County Meath, Ireland, saved many homes during Sherman's pillage of Atlanta by using his slaves to put out the flames. Not the least of the services of the European Brigade in New Orleans was the protection of property when the Federal boats brought the Unionists to that city. A cry rose from the desperate citizens to burn the city, but the determination of the brigade prevented any move toward its execution.[8]

Like natives, foreigners, exempt or beyond military age, rendered service in the Home Guards for local defense, to preserve order, to guard property, commissary stores, and ordnance, to stand guard at camps of correction, to do provost duty in general, and to guard prisoners. The service of the factory workers, organized into such military units, is obvious. But reference here is to individuals, like one Lionel Simpson, a Scot, living in Texas as a rich slaveowner in 1861, who helped guard prisoners taken by Bourland's men near Gainesville.[9] Such instances could be multiplied everywhere throughout the South.

More tangible and to the anxious Confederates more significant was the service rendered by the foreigners to the military arm of the state. Consideration of the military records of the two major generals, General Patrick Cleburne and Prince Polignac, is clearly indicated. At the opening of the western campaign of 1862 Cleburne's brigade, with one other, was detached and united with General Kirby Smith's column, which from Knoxville was to penetrate Kentucky through Cumberland Gap and form a junction with the main army under General Bragg, which was entering Kentucky by a different route. Kirby Smith's forces encountered opposition at Richmond,

[7] See Montgomery *Daily Mail*, April 27, 1861, for Lynch; for De Gournay, see *Confederate Veteran*, XII, 405.

[8] Lynch also secured with Father Thomas O'Riely's aid a command from the Union authorities for a guard to be stationed around the churches.—*Pioneer Citizens' History of Atlanta*, 317-318. For the scene in New Orleans see *The Bummer Boy*, 15-16.

[9] Jackson, *Sixty Years in Texas*, 65.

Kentucky, in September. Cleburne directed the first day's fighting. In his very first handling of an independent command he was the chief instrument in winning a victory which, in regard to the number of prisoners captured, the amount of stores taken, and the complete destruction of the opposing forces, was one of the most complete of the entire war.[10] We find him again displaying some of his finest abilities at Ringgold Gap on November 27, 1863, on Bragg's retreat after Chickamauga. He put his men in line of battle with sixty pieces of artillery masked just inside the Gap. His plan, he told another officer, was to "salivate" the Union forces when they came up. As the Federals came forward with a rush and whoop, flushed with their recent victory, they confidently expected to carry everything before them. Not a Confederate gun was allowed to be fired until the Unionists were within fifty yards of the southern lines. Then they were given the full blast from the guns, and for six hours this division alone, except for a few cavalrymen, held at bay a large force of Grant's army. Cleburne thus by his heroic defense saved Bragg's army from annihilation and checked any further operation in that quarter for several months. By the time a spring campaign could open, General Johnston, who succeeded Bragg, had his army in very good shape for defensive operations.[11] The value placed upon Cleburne's services at this point was sufficiently attested by a unanimous resolution of thanks tendered him and his command by the Confederate congress a few months later for their gallant defense of Ringgold Gap.[12]

Cleburne served again as a division commander under General J. E. Johnston during the latter's celebrated campaign in north Georgia during the spring of 1864 and distinguished himself in a number of its battles, especially at New Hope Church, by repulsing the enemy with signal firmness and with heavy losses to their charging columns. The retreat from Kennesaw Mountain, which followed shortly, is regarded by some authorities as "the brightest jewel in Cleburne's coronet," for there is no better illustration of his firmness, courage, and force than the manner in which he covered the

[10] Maguire, *The Irish in America*, Appendix, 643.
[11] Austin, *The Blue and the Gray*, 116, 117, 122. To Cleburne's credit it should be stated that he made this splendid defense in obedience to Bragg's order and contrary to his own judgment.
[12] *Daily Richmond Examiner*, February 4, 1864.

retreat of Johnston's army from that point.[13] He commanded an army corps at the battle of Jonesboro, Georgia, and again protected the retreat of Hood's defeated army from that field. In order to secure the safe withdrawal of the remainder of the army from Atlanta it was of the utmost necessity for this Confederate corps to hold its position through the day. The odds were terrific and the battle of the type that tries men's souls, but Cleburne held the position, and the remainder of the army was enabled to retire in safety from Atlanta. He was also in command of a corps at the battle of Franklin, where he fell in storming the second line of the Federal works.[14]

His loss was felt by some leaders as irreparable, for the verdict of military authorities seems to be that as a division commander he had no superior. His officers and men alike had implicit confidence in him, and therefore his orders were obeyed promptly and unquestioningly, a factor which was one of the elements in his success. That success was so uniform that as the war dragged on friend and foe learned to look for the position in battle of his distinctive blue and white battle flag.[15] "Cleburne is here!" meant to the Confederates that all was well. "Where he was, no masses of the enemy could break his lines, no matter how impetuous their attack or fearful the odds. When he led a column, its onslaught was irresistible and never failed to carry the opposing lines—save at one point only, and there is the grave of the Stonewall of the Western Army, and his devoted division."[16]

Cleburne's resourcefulness was truly remarkable. Nowhere was this trait more strikingly illustrated than on the march from Kentucky

[13] Bunn, *Reminiscences of the Civil War*, bound with Nash, *op. cit.*; Bartlett, *op. cit.*, 204-205.
[14] Gordon, "General P. R. Cleburne," *Southern Historical Society Papers*, XVIII, 265-269; Hardee, "Biographical Sketch of Major-General P. R. Cleburne," in Maguire, *The Irish in America*, Appendix, 650.
[15] Buck, *Cleburne and his Command*, 201. It naturally bore a shamrock. As an outward manifestation of the devotion he inspired, the story of his sword should not be omitted. In the spring of 1863 his original regiment, the Fifteenth Arkansas, presented him with a sword, towards the purchase of which every officer and every man had contributed. When it arrived, having run the blockade, it proved a Damascus blade in a plain polished steel scabbard; on the hilt was the device of a shamrock, the belt rings and bands of solid gold, and on the scabbard a gold plate, surmounted by the harp of Erin, bearing the inscription, "To Major-General P. R. Cleburne, from his old Regiment, Fifteenth Arkansas." So highly did he prize this token that he never wore it in battle, but always sent it to the rear for safety, as he did before embarking on his last campaign.—*Ibid.*, 104-105.
[16] Nisbet, *op. cit.*, 259; "A Sketch of Major-General P. R. Cleburne," *The Land We Love*, II, 460.

in 1862. The road which had been selected for the passage of ordnance and supply trains crossed a very difficult hill, at which the trains came to a dead halt. With the enemy pressing the rear and the trains immovable, the order for their destruction to prevent capture by the enemy had already been issued, when Cleburne, off duty because of a wound, came upon the scene. He promptly asked for and obtained unlimited authority. Instantly stationing guards in the road to arrest every straggler and passing officer, he had soon collected a large force with which he organized fatigue parties literally to lift the trains over the impassable hill. The train which he thus saved contained munitions and subsistence of the utmost value to the Confederacy. It is not certain that without these supplies the army could have made its subsequent long march through the wasted and sterile country which it faced.[17]

The qualities which made him great on the battlefield were combined with others equally important for the general off the field. Among the first and most important was the power of firm, wise discipline. While he was still only the colonel of the Fifteenth Arkansas, General Hardee, his superior officer, recognized his sleepless vigilance. It has been said that such a division of men as Cleburne commanded would have made the reputation of any general. This may—perhaps should—be granted, but it must also be admitted that it was a master hand that disciplined and welded them into the fine fighting force they became. There was no officer in the Confederate army who labored so indefatigably for the benefit and improvement of the troops under his command. His command was perhaps the best drilled in the Army of the Tennessee. When his troops were not positively in motion, he required his subordinate officers to keep up a constant course of drill, discipline, and study. He himself, while the army lay at Corinth, Wartrace, Chickamauga, and Dalton, held daily recitations, which each brigadier and field officer in his division was required to attend. Near Dalton he had a schoolhouse built for this express purpose. In the spring of 1863 a copy of a little work on rifle shooting which had been issued as a textbook for the English army fell into his hands. The British imprint was sufficient to enlist the interest and in-

[17] Hardee, "Biographical Sketch of Major-General P. R. Cleburne," in Maguire (ed.), *The Irish in America*, Appendix, 644.

dorsement of a former corporal of that army, and the next step was to give his division the benefit of its teachings. A line officer from each regiment constituted a central group which were to learn the system so thoroughly that they could impart it to the regimental officers and through them to the men. Major Bonham of the staff was to instruct them in the exact working of every part of the rifle and then in marksmanship. Before long the men, bored by the technical details and regarding the system as purely theoretical, lured Major Bonham into telling stories, a practice of which he was very fond, with the result that the daily session was converted into a period of games and general diversion until they were caught red-handed in their sins by their commander. And then the stern north-Ireland schoolmaster appeared in the person of Cleburne, probing in ten minutes the depths of their ignorance and enforcing every morning the study of theory and every afternoon rifle practice until "practise had made perfect." His pains bore fruit, for he organized from among these students of the rifle his famous Whitworth Sharpshooters for the campaign of 1864, men who were taught to judge distance by the eye, as no range finders were yet in use, over ground of varied topographical features. He armed them with special costly guns from England. These men became so proficient that, if one of the enemy's batteries proved especially annoying, the Whitworths, put to work on it, rarely failed to silence or to reduce its fire. At Resaca they repeatedly silenced batteries at eight hundred yards' range and almost annihilated a skirmish line of Federal Kentuckians.[18]

In general, Cleburne's discipline was firm, severe but humane. Punishment followed swiftly and surely any infringement of military rules, but never punishment which humiliated or disgraced the offender, such as "gagging" or "bucking" or "barrel-shirts." It was his conviction that such treatment of soldiers lessened or destroyed the self-respect without which no man could be a good soldier. He punished by extra guard duty, the cleaning of accoutrements, or the loss

[18] The Whitworth Sharpshooters was an élite corps, and, while the service was dangerous, it was exciting and carried immunity from camp drudgery and guard duty. Hence a place in it was eagerly sought. It reported directly to and received orders directly from division headquarters, near which it always camped. The company was rated as equal to a light battery. During the Georgia campaign the casualties amounted to 60 per cent of its members, but vacancies were quickly filled, as each brigade had a waiting list of good men, anxious for transference to this distinguished service.—Buck, *op. cit.*, 224-225. See also *Annals of the Army of Tennessee and Early Western History*, 244-246.

of privileges, such as leave from camp. For grave offenses the culprit went before a court-martial.[19]

Though trained abroad, Cleburne adapted himself to the peculiar conditions of a volunteer army, and thus could meet the crisis when the terms of the three-year men expired. The greater part of his division were Arkansans and Texans, many of whom had not heard from their homes and families for three years. A man of warm sympathies, he felt keenly the sacrifice he was asking of his men and, laying aside the formal manner of the commander, he appealed to them as one man to another, to set above every earthly consideration the consummation of Confederate independence. His eloquence and sincerity inspired them so that he won the early and unanimous reënlistment of his division—a great moral gain over conscription and an inspiration to other portions of the army.[20] Congress later passed its Conscription Act to retain the three-year men in service, but the moral effect of voluntary enlistment was of critical importance.

One of Cleburne's greatest services was the organizing of the secret order of the Comrades of the Southern Cross, which, though partly philanthropic, was also a device to promote zeal for the service. Soldiers obligated themselves to stand by each other, never to desert comrades in distress or to desert their country so long as she maintained an organized opposition. Cleburne attributed the valor of his troops mainly to the effect of this order and held that, if it had existed through all the southern armies, nothing could have checked "exalted oneness of action among the oath-bound members of this order."[21] It is not without significance in the history of the Confederacy that in the record of this lawyer, who at the modest age of thirty-seven was known to Richmond as Major General Cleburne but to his idolizing command as "Old Pat," two nations share.

The services of the knight-errant, Prince Polignac, were also sig-

[19] Buck, *op. cit.*, 103-104. Gagging was the suggestive name applied to fastening a bayonet in the mouth by tying it with a string which passed behind the neck. Bucking was the name applied to tying a soldier's hands together at the wrists and slipping them down over his knees where they were forcibly held in place by running a stick under the knees and over the arms. Bucking from sunrise to sunset, practiced by one general of the Confederate army to break up straggling, was not exactly a pleasant experience; and it was not efficacious in that instance.

[20] Hardee, "Biographical Sketch of Major-General P. R. Cleburne," in Maguire, *The Irish in America*, Appendix, 647; Hardee, "Biographical Sketch of Major-General P. R. Cleburne," *Southern Historical Society Papers*, XXXI, 157.

[21] "A Sketch of Major-General P. R. Cleburne," *The Land We Love*, II, 462.

nificant, even though one cannot escape the feeling that his high rank was partly the result of gratitude to an alien and a tribute to exalted social rank though also undoubtedly partly the fruit of hard work. At Corinth he ably seconded General Beauregard's efforts to reorganize the Army of the West. The active part which he played at the battle has already been commented on.[22] His distinctive contributions to the Confederate cause, however, came later and west of the Mississippi. It was no small achievement and a tribute to his powers of adjustment that this polished Frenchman of court circles could win the confidence of his rough Texans. On March 1 and 2, 1864, his share in repulsing the enemy's gunboats on the Ouachita River gained the thanks of General Taylor in a special order. At the battle of Mansfield and at Pleasant Hill in the Red River campaign he greatly distinguished himself by his gallantry and skill in the performance of his duties. General Mouton, who had been ordered by General Taylor to open the attack on the left, charged magnificently. When the former, together with five of his regimental commanders, fell at Mansfield, the division, according to General Taylor, never halted nor fell into confusion, but under the gallant Polignac pressed stubbornly on. The prince drove the enemy's forces in wild confusion until after sunset, though they had double his numbers and were superior in every respect. Though the Confederates were hopelessly defeated the next day and retreated to the nearest river, the Unionists were in full retreat by the following morning, and Banks had abandoned all thought of further advance, a signal victory for Polignac.[23]

Even more remarkable, in the opinion of the writer, was the ability and method of an alien in rallying native troops to the support of their own country. After Louisiana became isolated and food increasingly difficult to get, his half-starving division showed signs of insubordination. The prince collected his men and addressed them. "I wish I could tell you," he said frankly, "that matters are likely to improve, but on the contrary I fear harder times are in store for us. It is for you to decide whether the cause for which we are fighting is worth the sacrifice we are called upon to make."[24] Thenceforth there was no more murmuring among his troops.

[22] See above, p. 168.
[23] Evans, *Confederate Military History*, X, 314-315; Thomas, *Arkansas in War and Reconstruction*, 261. For the congratulatory order see O. W. R., Ser. 1, XXXIV, Pt. 1, 158; for Taylor's report, *ibid.*, 560-572.
[24] Cecil Battine, *The Crisis of the Confederacy*, 358.

So much has been said of Von Borcke that it seems almost supererogation to add a specific evaluation of his services. As must be abundantly evident to the reader, he was a bold, dashing fighter who helped General Stuart win many a cavalry charge and who must have been responsible for the death of many Federals. He was clearly an excellent scout, for his superior was fond of sending him off on ticklish expeditions to locate Yankee troops. No better estimate of the value of his services can be given than to recall that it was Stuart's desire that the Prussian should succeed him in the command of the cavalry troops.[25]

The services of the Marquis de Gournay, known on the military records simply as Colonel Paul Francis de Gournay, laid obligation on the Confederacy in several ways. First he equipped at his own expense an artillery company, which he as captain led to the field in Virginia. Gallant service at Yorktown, where he constructed and manned the breastworks during the Seven Days' Battles of June, 1862, was followed by distinguished service in the southwest at the four months' siege of Port Hudson. Here he was severely wounded and taken prisoner. He was confined at Johnson's Island till the close of the war. The official appraisal of his merits was that he was "one of the most efficient colonels of artillery in the army." His courage is sufficiently attested by the fact that he was many times commended for bravery.[26]

General Bee's comment on Colonel Buchel who fell at Pleasant Hill was, "a brilliant soldier of Prussia and an irreparable loss to our cause and his adopted country." Commanding the rear regiment in the move on the enemy's line, he drew back in time to avoid the fire of the ambuscade, pass to the left, dismount his men, attack the Federals in their ambuscade, and drive them back to their lines. This gallant and soldierly act, displaying the discipline and hold he had on his men, cost him his life, for he fell mortally wounded.[27]

The contribution of John A. Wagener demands individual recognition as an example of service to a state. Colonel of the First Artillery Regiment of South Carolina, he was ordered in September, 1861,

[25] Von Borcke's own feeling about his scout work on one occasion reflects the mixed feeling of gratification and danger. "Much as I appreciated the honor thus paid me, I did not feel greatly obliged to him [Stuart] on this particular occasion, as I rode forward into the darkness, feeling that I should run a narrow chance of being shot by our men on my return, if indeed, I escaped the bullets of the Yankees."—*Op. cit.*, I, 218.
[26] *Confederate Veteran*, XII, 405.   [27] *O. W. R.*, Ser. 1, XXXIV, Pt. 1, 608.

to Port Royal to strengthen its defenses in order to protect the sea island section of the South Carolina coast. He planned Fort Walker on Hilton Head, which he built with the aid of his German soldiers. His victory at the battle of Hilton Head displays the intrepidity of the South Carolina militia as well as of their commander. Both North and South devined the strategic advantage of Port Royal. The North wanted to take it to shut off the blockade-runners who had safe passage between Hilton Head and Pinckney Island to the harbor of Savannah. The South had to oppose a Union fleet of 75 ships supported by a land force of 10,000 men under General Sherman with two small forts, Fort Walker and Fort Beauregard. The entrance to the harbor was wide and deep so that only the heaviest cannon had the range to reach the ships of the enemy. In addition the defenders were sadly wanting in heavy armament and in proper ammunition. At Fort Walker were stationed companies A and B of Wagener's German artillery with two other companies. When the northern fleet moved to the attack on November 7, the little band of brave troops fought with coolness and courage, the handful holding out for four hours against a powerful fleet. The state legislature felt that Wagener's service there was worthy of a special resolution of thanks to the "brave commander" and to his troops for "their gallant efforts to protect the State from invasion."[28]

Obviously the European military training, the experience with actual warfare, and the higher morale that comes from recent contact with a battlefield on the part of the European-born in the southern army were of the greatest possible benefit to the Confederates. These assets were valuable when they appeared in the ranks, for one such soldier gave steadiness to many about him, but they were invaluable in an officer. Officers who had been on the field of battle could set to the raw recruits who were taking their baptism of fire an example of meeting the flying bullets without flinching. Above everything else the army needed officers to drill and discipline and whip the volunteer army into shape. Standards of military honor, such as proper consideration for the enemy, appeared in many instances first in the foreign officers, as is demonstrated in this work. They helped to teach the masses of volunteers the necessity of obedience and coöperation.

[28] Ratterman, General Johann Andreas Wagener, 18-20; Wagener, "John Andreas Wagener," 56-64; Charleston Deutsche Zeitung, November 3, 1906.

Their soldierly bearing, their words of encouragement spoken at the crucial moment, and their habitual self-discipline created confidence.

An admirable example of what the trained person could achieve was afforded to the Wise Legion with the arrival of General Henningsen, although he won no glory from his share in the Confederate war. A fellow officer, who might easily have manifested jealousy of him, pays him high tribute; Estvàn characterized Henningsen as a man who spoke little but acted quickly and with decision. In a few days, according to Estvàn's judgment, it was manifest that an able soldier had taken the command. The legion underwent a complete reorganization; with the few means at the Englishman's disposal, he effected wonders. Both officers and men placed the fullest confidence in him.[29] With long experience in peculiar military conditions he foresaw the situation likely to arise at Roanoke Island after capture by the Union navy of Hatteras and Ocracoke inlets in 1861, and at a council of war at General Wise's headquarters pointed out the probable consequences to its officers of the neglect of the legion at Richmond in disasters which they could not avoid.[30] Of course any foreign-born officer had to have sufficient power of adjustment to adapt himself to American men and ways, or he would come to grief as did Colonel St. Leger Grenfel, who, for all his thirty years in the British service, became so distasteful to General Morgan's men that that officer was obliged to remove Grenfel from his position as adjutant.[31]

European training and an impersonal attitude toward the foe enabled Estvàn to render humane help to the wounded prisoners. In the first bitterness of war feeling some southerners resented his desire to help "Yankees" and thought it traitorous, but an officer like General Jackson, to whom he appealed for support, warmly approved his humanitarian efforts and ordered him to "shoot any ruffians who may dare to interfere with you in your work of humanity."[32] Estvàn's European experience stood him in good stead here and it was in alleviating the suffering of the Confederates and Union

[29] Estvàn, *War Pictures*, I, 204-205.
[30] He pointed out how Wise's legion was wanting in nearly everything it needed. He was, therefore, of the opinion that, before undertaking the task committed to it, the officers should carefully consider the serious consequence that might result to the legion, through which it might incur the displeasure of the government.—*Ibid.*, II, 111-113.
[31] See above, p. 192. Grenfel was apparently allowed to resign.
[32] Estvàn, *op. cit.*, I, 176. Jackson's words are rather striking. "You are right, as a European officer you must know what a new army most stands in need of. Act, therefore, according to your own judgment."

wounded prisoners of war that he probably rendered his best service to the Confederates. From the center of the battlefield of First Manassas he sent men out with stretchers, bandages, and refreshments to succor the wounded. By evening he had three hospitals in operation: one for the slightly wounded, one for amputations and other serious cases, and one for those wounded beyond all hope.[33] But it should also be remembered to Estvàn's credit that he did his best to rally the fleeing troops at Newbern against Burnside's attack in March, 1862, and so far succeeded that the Confederates sank one of the enemy's gunboats and blew up the forts to prevent their falling into the hands of the foe. With the help of another officer he was able to keep up so strong a fire that, as the enemy fell back, the Confederates were able to save their valuable baggage.[34] Here is a striking illustration of the steadiness of a European officer rallying the raw North Carolina troops.

One field to which the European-born seem to have contributed in striking measure and out of all proportion to their numbers was that of defensive works calling for highly trained engineering skill. It has already been noted that General Gonzales rendered a richer service as engineer than as staff officer on the field. Von Scheliha and Schleicher, Forsberg, Sulakowski, and George Raven, representing German, Swede, Pole, and Englishman respectively, should be recalled as one sweeps in review the defenses of the Virginia coast, of Mobile, Louisiana, and Texas. An important engineering service was even rendered by the Prussian visitor, Scheibert, which has been reserved for presentation here to emphasize the foreign contribution in the technical field. Scheibert was, it will be recalled, connected with Lee's army as a volunteer soldier for only a few weeks. During the retreat from Gettysburg, at the request of General Lee, he rode ahead of the retreating army to the Potomac where the army engineers and pioneers were to replace the bridges which had been destroyed by the Unionists. He helped under the greatest difficulties to direct the building of a pontoon bridge in sixty-eight hours. This bridge greatly facilitated the crossing of the Potomac by Lee's army,

---

[33] *Ibid.*, 177; II, 251-252. He also rendered fine service after the battle of Gaines's Mills. Estvàn draws a very black picture of Confederate indifference to the suffering of Union soldiers. There were probably some such instances as he pictures, but also others of care of the foe. It must also be remembered that he was wholly out of sympathy with the cause. [34] *Ibid.*, 148-149.

as by means of it and the ford, which became passable as the water fell, the entire army made its escape.[35]

The various nationalities brought their characteristic traits as contributions to the Confederate army. The Englishman brought innate honesty and bulldog tenacity, the Scotchman his generally high level of intelligence and stubbornness, the German his patience and persistence. Germans fought well in companies and as individuals. The Frenchman fought with verve, with dash, and could rise to heights of exalted patriotism. His volatile spirits and lightheartedness were often a tonic on the battlefield as well as in the camp. No others were quite so good for siege guns and water batteries. And then there were the Irish. When a general had work to be performed that required soldiers on whom he could rely, he was sure to select an Irish regiment. Let General Dick Taylor pay his tribute to the Irishmen in the southern armies in his own words: "Strange people, these Irish! Fighting every one's battles, and cheerfully taking the hot end of the poker, they are only found wanting when engaged in what they believe to be their national cause." Again, after a hot engagement when his effort to relieve the guards was met by scornful howls of "We are the boys to see it out," he remarks, "As Argyle's to the tartan, my heart has warmed to an Irishman since that night."[36]

The Mexicans who found their way into the southern army were as a group unreliable. The fact is in such contrast with the record of other foreigners that the writer may be pardoned if she labors this point. The testimony from many sources is overwhelming. Perhaps no officer in the Confederate army could speak with more authority than Colonel Augustus Buchel, who as commander on the lower Rio Grande in Texas had several entire companies of Mexicans in his regiment. Already in December, 1861, he was complaining of the escape of some Mexican prisoners with the connivance of the Mexican guard. "I have repeatedly," he writes in December, 1863,

[35] Scheibert, *Sieben Monate in den Rebellen-Staaten*, 95-96. It might be added that Scheibert a few weeks earlier had taken and delivered six prisoners of war to the Confederate authorities. He had gone off in search of fodder for his horse, and, ignorant of the country, had started in the direction of the enemy. Just as he came up to a certain plantation, he encountered six Yankees coming out of the house. Aware that only boldness could save him, he drew his sword and rode up to the astonished Yankees, shouting in broken English, "Surrender, you scoundrels! all my cavalry is right behind me." The Prussian marched the six triumphantly back to Lee.—Von Borcke, *Memoirs*, II, 244-245.
[36] *Destruction and Reconstruction*, 68, 76.

"called attention to the wholly unreliable character of the Mexicans enlisted on this frontier, so far as our cause is concerned. Company C [Captain Parker's], of this regiment is composed entirely of Mexicans. Scarcely a night passes that one or more of them do not desert. This will continue to be the case so long as the civil war continues in Mexico. The company has already been reduced nearly one-half, and in a short time scarcely a corporal's guard will remain. . . . I am thoroughly satisfied that they would desert in a body and cross the river should the enemy attack this post, even if they did no worse. They have no sympathy in our cause, do not understand it, and enlist simply for the subsistence, pay and clothing. They change their allegiance with the utmost facility to whichever party offers the largest inducements." Buchel's suggestion for a remedy was their removal to the interior where the facilities for desertion were not so great. Though greatly in need of more troops he declared that he would "much prefer to be without them," so detrimental were they to the service.[37] In view of the almost universal testimony against the type of Mexican who entered the Confederate service, it is doubtful if their numbers, perhaps a thousand, compensated for the annoyance to their commanders.

Many of the companies and regiments of the Confederate armies won glory for themselves on the field of battle, and it is noticeable that in this number a goodly proportion of the companies of foreign-born must find a place. Cleburne's famous division was made up of, and its honors were shared by, citizens of five states—Arkansas, Texas, Alabama, Mississippi, and Tennessee. There was in it one regiment of Irishmen who illustrated strikingly the characteristics of that race. At the battle of Missionary Ridge, General Cleburne came up on foot just in the rear of the Irish Brigade, saying in a very quiet way, "Boys, take them in." That was quite enough, for the men sailed into the foe, capturing many prisoners, six stands of colors, and many guidons. One soldier captured a whole company that had taken

[37] Buchel to Major S. B. Davis, December 18, 1861.—*O. W. R.*, Ser. 2, II, 1408. Already, by December 5, 1861, he had complained of Captain Parker's company of Mexicans, who, "like all their countrymen, are susceptible to bribes and corruption, and cannot be depended upon." It must be admitted in all honesty that he complained also of Captain Buquor's and Captain Marmion's companies, composed chiefly of foreigners, old soldiers, and deserters from the old Federal army.—*Ibid.*, Ser. 1, IV, 153. See also Williams, *op. cit.*, 348, 350. See above, pp. 126, 128.

shelter behind a big chestnut log.[38] Company H, Fortieth North Carolina, made up principally of Irish, it will be recalled, was always ready, whether for work or fighting, and would go wherever ordered. With this group of Irishmen Lieutenant Joseph Price captured the United States steamer *Water Witch* off Wilmington by boarding it in a night attack—one of the most brilliant of the Confederate exploits on the water.[39] Bob Wheat's wild, thieving Tigers, chiefly Louisiana Irish, were not a crew to be proud of off the field, but on it they could and did fight. At First Manassas the men of this Louisiana battalion were left the sole defenders of the bridge and bore the whole brunt of the enemy's left for the first two hours in the morning. Although few in number, these heroic soldiers sustained every shock with unwavering courage and more than once, dropping their rifles, rushed upon the enemy with long bowie knives. One of their number admitted that he himself was "bate up wid foitin," but when General Beauregard, arriving with reinforcements in the afternoon, told the Wild Cats they had done enough, "Bedad, they wint to the rear and got a few glasses of whiskey, and kem back to 'foit' as fresh as the flowers of May."[40] In the fight at Big Hill seventeen miles from Richmond, Kentucky, Company F of the First Louisiana Cavalry, which the boys called the Irish Brigade, was conspicuous for its gallantry. They formed in an old field to the right of the road, and under a withering fire never flinched but continually advanced until the charge was ordered and the enemy fled.[41] At Port Gibson a handful of brave Irishmen held back a whole regiment of Federals.[42] Everyone knows of Richard W. Dowling, the modest Irish youth of only nineteen years, and his Davis Guards, the little company of forty-three Irishmen at Sabine Pass, who on September 8, 1863, could hold at bay a United States fleet with ten or fifteen thousand men preparing to land for a raid through Texas. With six small cannon and some small arms, two score men killed a large number of the enemy, sank one of the enemy's boats, disabled and captured two other gunboats, drove away the rest, and took a large

[38] Collins, *Chapters from the Unwritten History of the War Between the States*, 180.
[39] Sprunt, "Confederate Heroes," *Chronicles of the Cape Fear River*, 321.
[40] De Leon, *Belles, Beaux, and Brains of the 60's*, 329; "A Month With the Rebels," *Blackwood's*, XC, 766.
[41] Carter, *A Cavalryman's Reminiscences of the Civil War*, 36.
[42] Henry H. Baker, *A Reminiscent Story of the Great Civil War*, 50.

number of prisoners without the loss of a man. A little band of Irish saved all Texas from invasion by the Union army and greatly heightened the morale of the people of that state. Dowling and his brave Irishmen enjoy the proud distinction of being the only command during the entire period of the war whose full muster roll appears in the report of a battle. President Davis said of this exploit, "The success of this company of forty-four men is without parallel in ancient or modern war," and presented each soldier with a little silver medal, the only honor of the kind bestowed by the Confederates during the war.[43] At Fredericksburg it was a Georgia regiment, mostly Irish, which defended Mary's Hill against Meagher's charge. Truly it was, as the southern colonel said before the fight, "Greek versus Greek today."

Bachman's German battery of South Carolina, already mentioned for state service, served through the trying years in Virginia, complimented for gallantry at every turn, and enjoyed a distinguished name for unbounded courage. Among the most trying experiences of the company was their service in the Seven Days' Battles around Richmond; at Sharpsburg, when half of the battery was advanced within close range of the lines of the Federal infantry in an effort to break them with canister; and at Gettysburg, when with Gardner's South Carolina battery it accompanied the infantry of Hood's division in the charge up Round Top Hill, and when the next day it repulsed the charge of the Federal cavalry under General Farnsworth. It saved the army transportation at Gettysburg and was among the last to cross the bridge over the Cape Fear River on the final retreat.[44] General Taylor said of the Germans who fought at Mansfield and in other places in Louisiana, "None of my regiments did better than General Buchel's regiment of Texas Germans, raised around New Braunfels."[45]

[43] In a fight of an hour and a half they killed 50 men, captured 150 men, and 18 cannon.—*Confederate Veteran*, IV, 336-337; North, *op. cit.*, 113. For President Davis' comment on the exploit see Bowman, *Reminiscences of an Ex-Confederate Soldier*, 39. The medal was made of a thin plate of silver with the initials "D. G." (Davis Guards) and a Maltese Cross crudely engraved on one side with the place and date of achievement on the other.—Lossing, *Pictorial History of the Civil War*, III, 221-222.

[44] Brooks (ed.), "Bachman's Battery," *Stories of the Confederacy*, 283; *idem.*, "Hampton and Butler," *Southern Historical Society Papers*, XXIII, 35-36.

[45] Taylor asserts that these Germans had been in Texas some years and had caught the spirit, and that they were fighting for their adopted country.—Nisbet, *op. cit.*, 95. In view of the known attitude of the Texan Germans, it is hard to think their heart was in the fight. It is more likely that they fought well, under the German instinct of duly discharging their duty.

The group of mixed foreigners, misnamed the Polish Regiment, wild and lawless as they were, proved splendid fighting material on many a hard-fought field, and no men knew better how to die gallantly. One striking illustration is afforded at Frayser's Farm, where it lost thirty-three men out of a company of forty-two. The loss was so great in killed and wounded that the regiment was totally ruined for months, and there was not left after the battle a decent company.[46] It was finally consolidated with the Twentieth Louisiana, also reduced to one half or less.

The splendor of Pelham's Frenchmen from Mobile at his batteries is undimmed by time. Most glorious is their record at Fredericksburg, when, at an order from General Stuart, Pelham moved his advanced gun and his Napoleon detachment down the embankment close to the compact lines of Federal soldiers, who had just crossed the Rappahannock and were forming line of battle under cover of the river bank. When the blue line charged, the bayonets glistening in the sunshine and the cannon thundering from across the river, the Napoleon detachment roared its defiance. Pelham soon drew upon himself the fire of half a dozen batteries. Yet his lone gun never ceased to roar and never failed to do slaughter. His was the only Confederate gun in action, and it was not retired until the last round of ammunition had been exhausted. In the half lull between discharges there floated from the Napoleon detachment the strains of the "Marseillaise" while the singers themselves were making history. They delayed the great battle one hour, during which the Confederates were able to make preparations of great consequence.[47]

Space may be vouchsafed to record a few instances of special daring by the humble foreigner who never emerged into the limelight of fame. No nationality had a monopoly of heroism; it was displayed in the ranks by men of every nationality. At the first battle of Manassas, Joe Angell, English by birth, without knowledge of what war was like, still acted with gallant and heroic conduct. When his colonel fell, the soldier stayed with him against his superior's protest and in utter disregard of his own danger. When he found it impossible alone to remove his colonel from the field, he started for aid

---

[46] Bartlett, "Louisiana Troops in the West," *Military Record of Louisiana*, 43-44.
[47] *Confederate Veteran*, VI, 363; French, *Two Wars*, 150.

only to find himself caught in a terrific cross fire from which he could escape only by throwing himself flat on his face. In this position he was stunned by a cannon ball and left for dead by the Federals but, when quiet came once more, he rose and found a comrade to help him carry the colonel from the field.[48]

A second story concerns an Irishman in Scott's regiment of Louisiana cavalry. When the colors of an East Tennessee regiment were captured, a Federal soldier cried out mistakenly that they had "old Scott's colors." But a gallant son of the Emerald Isle, who by valor at Murfreesboro had won the right to bear the colors, whirled his horse around and, waving the flag above his head, cried at the top of his voice, "It's a d—— lie, Scott's colors will never go down." The action was, of course, an invitation to all the Federals near by, an invitation which was promptly accepted. Unfortunately, in the wild retreat the point of the color staff broke against a tree and the flag fell to the ground. In a flash the color-bearer leaped from his horse, tied the banner around his body, and insolently replied to the demand of some Federals to surrender it by vaulting into his saddle and saying, "Now, darn ye, when ye git it, ye'll git me." His colors fell only at Chickamauga a few months later when the bearer fell.[49] At the battle of Shiloh, Frederick Körper, German-born as his name indicates, showed notable courage in the capture of a United States colonel within the enemy's lines.[50]

One encounters records like the following: "We do not know where George Pietz came from or where was his home, (except that he was born in Germany) but we know that he was a good Confederate soldier," and the record substantiates that fact, for even after his fourth wound, so terrible that it was felt necessary to discharge him, he rejoined his company to receive his last wound.[51] Private Lawrence Lutz, a Hanoverian, enlisted in Louisiana on April 16, 1861, was sent to Corinth, took part in Shiloh, shared in a flank movement at Chattanooga, followed Bragg through Kentucky and back to Murfreesboro, and was crippled for life at Chickamauga.[52] Of Captain Werner, a German of Savannah, it was said, "None had

[48] Confederate Veteran, XVIII, 133.   [49] Carter, op. cit., 62.
[50] Jordon and Pryor, The Campaigns of Lt. Gen. N. B. Forrest and of Forrest's Cavalry, 166-167, n.
[51] Carter, op. cit., 112. We do know that he was a member of Co. E, First Louisiana Regiment.
[52] Confederate Veteran's Association, Fulton County, Georgia, 39.

taken up arms in her defense sooner, none suffered privation and imprisonment for her more patiently, and none died more gallantly than Claus Werner."[53] No less than three of the Emerald Guards (Company I, Eighth Alabama) won a place on the roll of honor, while thirty-five of the one hundred and four members were killed.[54] The record of B. Vaccaro, who was born in Italy, reads as follows: he was at Shiloh, Perryville, Murfreesboro, where he was wounded, at Chickamauga, and Missionary Ridge, shared in the Atlanta campaign, was severely wounded at Peachtree Creek, served at Franklin, was captured before Nashville with most of his command, and imprisoned at Camp Chase until the end of the war.[55] L. A. Pires was a Portuguese who served the first year of the war in the Missouri State Guards, was with Lucas' battery, then with General Laws, and after the siege of Vicksburg with the Third Missouri Battery. He was captured at the surrender of Vicksburg, paroled, exchanged, and then sent to Bragg's army at Chattanooga, being under fire in nine battles.[56]

These soldiers endured one thing beyond the suffering of the native Americans—the loneliness of exile. Miss Cumming tells of an Englishman from Yorkshire in Company E, Seventh Arkansas Regiment, who was grieved that he could not even let his people know where he was dying and was cheered when told that his nurse knew a way of getting letters through the blockade. Unfortunately he died before she was able to get the exact address of his family.[57]

Until the harsh conscript laws forbade their employment, the substitutes in the Confederate service were necessarily drawn from among the aliens in the South. These substitutes, instead of making indifferent soldiers, sometimes proved excellent material. Bartholomew Fohrer furnishes a case in point. Replacing the scion of a wealthy family, who must have been at best a delicate soldier, the fiery Gaul was an asset to the Forty-first Tennessee. Thirteen years a soldier in his native France, he had acquired so soldierly a bearing and his burnished gun was so like polished silver that he arrested the trained eye of General Pemberton in a review of the army at

[53] Charles H. Olmsted, "Reminiscences of Service in Charleston Harbor in 1863," *Southern Historical Society Papers,* XI, 123.
[54] Record of Co. I, Eighth Alabama Infantry Regt., Alabama Military Archives.
[55] Mathes, *The Old Guard in Gray,* 209-210.
[56] Yeary, *Reminiscences of the Boys in Gray,* 611-612.
[57] *A Journal of Hospital Life,* 69-70.

Vicksburg. He made one of the best soldiers in the Confederate armies, for the more furious the battle, the more was he in his true element. His enthusiasm rose in direct ratio to the danger, his eyes flashing and his fine face aglow as if the victory were already won when the issue seemed most doubtful. At the battle of Jonesboro as his company was advancing to the wild roar of musketry, Fohrer hailed the right guide of the regiment, "Heigh, Sumner, by Jesus, how you like it?"[58]

Indeed the foreign soldiers, whether aliens seeking the thrills of adventure by participation in the quarrels of another country, or adopted sons coerced unwillingly into the army, rendered much fine military service in the ranks. As is attested by the *Rebellion Records*, they turned the tide of battle at certain points. Thousands are lying in nameless graves; thousands are merely names in compilations of Confederate soldiers;[59] and other thousands are forgotten under the effacing hand of time. But all together they helped to fill up the ranks of the southern armies, suffered through the "hell" which is another name for a battlefield, toiled through the misery of the long hard marches under a grueling sun or over the frozen, icy roads of mountains, or pulled their leaden feet through the Virginia mire in the spring rains. They endured the miseries of camp diseases, camp filth, camp pests; they knew the pangs of hunger and tried to stay them by chewing grains of corn or eating the wild berries gathered from bushes beside the road. They pined in the northern prisons; they languished in the southern hospitals; they were wounded and maimed and paid the supreme price on hundreds of battlefields. The record of their service is on every historic roll. One marvels that it was possible for men to pass through so many hailstorms of bullets and live. But why repaint for the thousandth time the picture of the sufferings of the Confederate soldier? Suffice it to say that foreign-born soldiers shared in them all. It is no uncommon record to count entered on these rolls after a soldier's name eighteen and twenty battles in which he had participated. The longest record the writer has ever seen is of over four hundred engagements—this the record of a foreign-born soldier.[60]

---

[58] *Confederate Veteran*, XVIII, 78.
[59] Even in the *Rules of the German Friendly Society*, 36, of Charleston, the writer encountered the names of several members who had fallen in the war.
[60] The writer is inclined to think that the recorder who gave this figure on the record

Foreigners, besides serving as cannon fodder on the field of battle, also rendered many indirect services to the armies. It must not be forgotten that the brawn of "Pat" and "Fritz" was of great service in digging trenches as they plied their picks with the steady, even strokes of a machine as compared with the uneven, spasmodic blows of the native clerks or bookkeepers at their side. The practiced eye and ax of the Canadians were highly useful in the felling of tall trees to serve as bridges across narrow streams. That same strength was taken advantage of in hospitals when someone had to pinion down the poor victims while a surgeon burned out proud flesh from the wounds or when strong arms were needed to carry the helpless soldiers from operating table to hospital bed in the ward.[61]

For scouts and spies a foreign accent and foreign passport were often very helpful assets. The Frenchman, Hermann, playing the rôle of an alien eager to return to France, a rôle made plausible by his broken English, secured valuable information, though the war ended before he was able to fulfill his real mission of getting a message through to General Forrest.[62]

Some of these foreign-born soldiers did well other things outside the strict line of duty and made distinct contributions to the morale by elevating the tone of the life about camp or hospital. As will be recalled, McElrath's comrades loved to boast of their Scotchman as the best classical scholar in the Fourth Kentucky Regiment. His fellows loved to gather around the bivouac to hear him read some passage from the classics or to hear his eloquent recital of legends. Even in prison, after he was interned at Rock Island, having been captured at Mt. Sterling with his comrades on Morgan's last raid, he thus enlivened many weary hours for his fellow prisoners.[63]

---

roll possibly added an extra cipher. Of course, a soldier who led such a charmed life as to survive all his skirmishes through the entire 4 years of war could conceivably have shared in 400 engagements, at an average of 8 a month. The total number of engagements recorded for the war on all fronts is 2,200, 140 of which only were important battles.—James K. Hosmer, *The Appeal to Arms*, 5.

[61] Alexander Hunter, describing a detail to erect breastworks, declared that one brawny Irishman seemed never to know the meaning of fatigue.—*Johnny Reb and Billy Yank*, 47. The Irish and Germans were not, of course, the only ones to be set at digging trenches and mines. For a Frenchman of Savannah, killed while digging a mine at Petersburg, see *Confederate Veteran*, XXXIV, 61; for the Canadian alluded to in the text see Watson, *Life in the Confederate Army*, 328-330; for hospital service see Collins, *Chapters from the Unwritten History of the War Between the States*, 233.

[62] Hermann, *Memories of a Veteran*, 205, 206-213.

[63] Mosgrove, *Kentucky Cavaliers in Dixie*, 253.

The methodical, scholarly instinct of the German appeared even in the ranks. When Colonel James J. Morehead undertook to prepare a sketch of his regiment, the Fifty-third North Carolina, it was not to one of the 99 per cent of Anglo-Saxons he turned for data but to a German private for a copy of the diary which he had kept from the organization of his company to the date of his capture, May 5, 1864.[64]

When the Frenchman was laid low by bullets or disease, his innate instinct for graciousness smoothed the day for the nurses in the hospital. The comment of a nurse after a drink intended for a treat had been brusquely rejected by a sick captain from Alabama is illuminating: "If you had made it for some Frenchmen who are in the house, they would have taken it for politeness' sake, whether they liked it or not."[65]

The irrepressible humor of the Irishman, his readiness to share his few grains of corn with a comrade in arms, or to supply his strength to help a staggering weaker brother on the march are traits which were noted and valued by the southern officer. The numerous tales of the idiosyncrasies of the Irish were a never-ending source of amusement.

If no nationality had a monopoly on courage and the qualities which go to make a good soldier, no country could be stigmatized as having a monopoly on the vices which curse an army. Probably no crime known to military law is so utterly demoralizing and destructive of the morale of an army as desertion. Noted on the descriptive rolls after countless numbers of names appears the bald statement, "deserted" or "not seen," after a given date. Irish, who have been so lauded for their bravery in the midst of soul-shaking carnage, left by the score, by the hundreds; Germans absconded with appalling frequency; Mexicans simply could not be held in the lines if they decided to leave; even the bulldog tenacity of the "steady" Englishman was not proof against the insidious temptation to escape the horrors of the service. The writer, in fact, cannot recall one single nationality for which she could not cite an instance of desertion. The weakness of the alien, with probably more justification, merely matched that of his native comrades, for it is well known that the

[64] Sprunt, "Confederate Heroes," *Chronicles of the Cape Fear River*, 291.
[65] Cumming, *A Journal of Hospital Life*, 35.

mountains of western North Carolina, to recall a single neighborhood, were full of deserters—native Americans.

The value to the Confederate cause of the service of foreigners
on the sea is incalculable. Note has already been taken of the fact
that the person ranking second in importance in the infant Confederate
navy was an adopted son, Commander John Maffitt,[66] and that several of the other commanders of vessels in the fleet had been born
abroad. Among the men designated as officers on the *Register*, ranging from lieutenant to carpenter, from ship's physician to boatswain,
from gunner to gunner's mate, one counts twenty-four men in the
Confederate naval service who began life as the subjects of foreign
governments. Adding to them the short list of five commanders of
vessels we attain a total of twenty-nine foreign-born officers out of
a complete total of about eighteen hundred officers. It is worth
noting that twenty-six of the entire group were born under the British
flag, including one Canadian and one from the West Indies. Only
one was a Frenchman, and two were Germans. Far different is the
record for the crews, as we have seen.

The men of the cruisers were foreign, the majority British, but
with representatives of most of the sea-faring countries. Praise could
not always be bestowed upon the quality of the crews with enlistment
often actuated by greed. This resulted sometimes in undependable
crews, notably that which shipped on the *Alabama*, as has been pointed
out. On many of the cruisers, however, especially those recruited
from the crews aboard the Union ships captured as prizes, the men
behaved well. In any case, good or bad or mixed, these crews of
foreigners rendered valiant service for the Confederate cause, as they
were an indispensable element in the operation of the cruisers.

It is unnecessary to measure what each Confederate cruiser contributed to the devastation of United States commerce, but it is proper
to record yet again that the *Shenandoah* alone captured four steamers,
seventy-eight ships, four brigs, eighty-two barks, sixty-eight schooners
—in all 278 vessels of nearly 1,000,000 tons burden. The effective-
ness of these cruisers may best be evaluated in terms of the damage
estimated by the United States government when presenting its case
against the eleven cruisers which figured in the Alabama claims. The
sum total of the claims for ships and cargoes, it is well known, was

[66] For details as to his service, see Chap. IX.

almost $18,000,000, of which all but about $4,000,000 was laid at the doors of the *Alabama* and *Shenandoah*.[67] Stated in military terms the victory of the cruisers caused almost the extinction of American commerce. It drove the merchant flag of the United States from the oceans and almost effaced its carrying trade. It is well also to remember that the British firms which allowed the men serving on the privateers to be paid by drafts on their firms were an aid to the Confederate cause, a fact which Uncle Sam did not forget when the day of reckoning with England came.[68] In any ledger casting up the credit and debit pages for the foreigners in the Confederacy, the share of foreign crews in rolling up this huge total would have to be written large on the credit side.

Quite beyond calculation was the value of the service rendered by the blockade-runners. Without the materials to supply the equipment of war for the soldiers—arms, clothing, munitions, and medicines; without the necessities and some of the luxuries to sustain life for the civilian population and to keep up their morale, the war must have ended much sooner than it did. In trying to evaluate the services rendered by the officers of these ships it may be permissible to recall that during the first half of the war they were almost entirely Englishmen and Scotchmen until, indeed, the risks of capture, owing to the increasing number and vigilance of the blockading fleet, became so great as to offset the lure of colossal gains. Augustus Hampden, Admiral Hewitt, Murray-Aynsley, to call them by their proper English names; Burgoyne and Tom Taylor as well as Daniel Martin, Henry Sulter, and William Watson, to name but three of a large lesser group, gave service as valuable, though of an entirely different nature, as did Gordon and Von Borcke and Polignac. Whatever of glory there was in the enterprise, as in the profits, the crews shared, and on the strictly British vessels they were almost exclusively Britishers. Likewise whatever of praise or blame is bestowed on the blockade-runners for prolonging the war the crews must share.

In the long run it was not valor that counted in the effort to win the war. It was the blow to the Confederate States commissariat, the cutting off of the supplies, the starvation of Lee's army, the closure of the last hope of the Confederacy, which gave the victory

[67] The exact total for ships and cargo was $17,900,633.
[68] Leiding, *Charleston, Historic and Romantic*, 231.

of General Curtis in seizing Fort Fisher its lasting importance. To evaluate the importance of the foreign blockade-runners it is necessary to scrutinize closely their aid in getting in supplies and in getting out cotton with which to purchase them. What the blockade-runners were able to do in providing sinews of war to prolong the struggle was a factor of first importance.

Thousands of bales of cotton were carried on the blockade-runners which would otherwise have been stored uselessly in the warehouses. Hobart Pasha boasted that he alone landed 1,140 bales at the Bermudas from Wilmington on his first trip.[69] But for the food supplies run in by the blockade-runners the South would have been far sooner starved into surrender and, for such luxuries as reached her, she was entirely dependent on this gentry. The port of Wilmington sustained the army commissariat for the last two years of the war. The little *Banshee* brought in on one occasion 600 barrels of pork and 1,500 boxes of meat, enough to feed Lee's army for a month, running in through Admiral Porter's fleet of sixty-four vessels. It had happened that late in December, 1864, the commissary general appealed to Tom Taylor, picturing Lee's army in terrible straits with rations for only thirty days, and undertaking to pay Taylor a profit of 350 per cent on any provisions and meat brought within the next three weeks. Taylor telegraphed to have the *Banshee II*, which was then discharging a cargo in Wilmington, made ready for sea at once. He himself hastened to that port, crossed to Nassau, purchased a cargo of provisions there for about $6,000 and landed it at Wilmington in eighteen days, for which he received $27,000. One British subject with one little steamer prolonged Lee's resistance for a month, and thus directly affected the history of the American war.[70]

The total number of vessels engaged in running the blockade into the Atlantic and Gulf ports has been estimated at about 1,650,[71] each vessel having averaged five successful trips. Some were, of course, captured or wrecked on the shore on the first trip, but others have a record of twenty, thirty, and even sixty trips through the blockade. If we accept the estimate of $250,000 as representing the value of a typical cargo, multiply by five, the average number of runs, and then by 1,650, the number of vessels in the business, we reach the stagger-

[69] *Sketches from My Life*, 170.
[70] Taylor, *Running the Blockade*, 139-140.   [71] Owsley, *op. cit.*, 286.

ing sum of $2,062,500,000 as yielding the value of the goods slipped in and out of ports presumably shut off from the rest of the world by a blockade. Rhodes estimates the amount of cotton shipped to England and the Continent from the Confederacy as 541,000 bales; but Owsley computes also the cotton which entered northern ports and reaches well over 1,000,000 bales, perhaps 1,250,000 bales, as running the blockade after the spring of 1862.[72] And finally some idea of the importance of the blockade-runners to the South may be obtained by noting the amount of war munitions which thus secured entry into the Confederacy, a record which is fairly complete on government account. The army was, contrary to the usual opinion, practically supplied with small arms after 1861 by the importation from abroad. Altogether, according to the reports in the *Official War Records,* there were about 330,000 stand of small arms imported into the Cis-Mississippi region by the central government; if to this is added the importation of arms by the separate states, the importation on private account, and the importation to the Trans-Mississippi Department, the sum total may be placed at 600,000 stand of arms.[73]

As important as the amount of goods introduced was the kind. A study of the bills of lading reveals, as has been stated in detail, that, besides munitions, necessities of all sorts slipped in aboard the blockade-runners—clothing, shoes, food supplies in sufficient measure to stave off starvation, manufactures of all sorts, and no mean supply of luxuries.

The foreigners, for they were the blockade-runners, kept a Federal squadron, consisting of three hundred vessels of all kinds—sailing vessels, monitors, ironclads, and cruisers—busy trying to prevent them from entering Charleston and Wilmington. A triple line of ships with many of the fleetest vessels afloat, anchored in a semicircle at each of these ports, policing the ocean between them and the neutral islands of the Bermudas and the West Indies, could not avail to keep out the blockade-runners—until the port cities themselves fell.[74] These vessels of the Union government were thus diverted from their legitimate business of pursuing and destroying the cruisers which had the free range of the five seas.

[72] Rhodes, *History of the United States,* V, 409; Owsley, *op. cit.,* 289.
[73] *Ibid.,* 289-290.
[74] Tom Taylor personally ran the blockade a greater number of times than anyone else.—Sprunt, *Chronicles of the Cape Fear River,* 388. Note also the comment in the preface to his own book, *Running the Blockade,* vii.

Against all these advantages must be weighed two calamities traceable to the blockade-runners. It is believed that the yellow fever which raged in Wilmington late in 1862 and which cost many lives was introduced from Nassau by a vessel running the blockade. More fundamental and far-reaching in its effects was the depreciation of the Confederate currency caused by the draining away of the gold. There were those Confederates who declared that blockade-running did more harm than good, and that, except for war supplies and absolute necessities, it should cease.

Taylor's opinion of the importance of the blockade-running is interesting and entitled to the consideration due the views of a participant: "Had Charleston and Wilmington been retained and blockade-running encouraged, instead of having obstacles thrown in the way, I am convinced that the condition of affairs would have been altered very materially, and perhaps would have led to the South obtaining what it had shed so much blood to gain, namely, its independence."[75] While the modern scholar would probably not subscribe to the opinion that the South might thus have won her independence, still no careful student will deny that the blockade-runners, largely foreigners, greatly and seriously affected the history and course of the war.

The foreigners who were in the Confederate States during the war, whether participants in the fray or onlookers as alien residents, whether military observers who had come over to learn what was to be learned from studying a military machine in operation or civilians who had come over for business or "pleasure," had something to say about the conditions here. In greater or less degree, according to the importance of his station or the penetration of his comments, each observer influenced public opinion in his homeland. Occasional letters slipped through to some foreign land, but there is, of course, no way to measure the influence of private correspondence. We must, therefore, turn to the printed material which appeared on the news stands in the form of articles from press correspondents and in the form of books.

Let us note first the influence of the regular writers for the press. It is natural to begin with the one first on the scene, who was also by all odds the most influential, Sir William Howard Russell, who

[75] *Ibid.*, 137-138.

wrote for the London *Times*. Probably the best indication that he was fairly impartial in his criticisms of both sides is the fact that he awakened bitter animosity on both sides of Mason and Dixon's line. Probably such a comment as the following which appeared from his pen would not incline a southerner to feel too kindly disposed toward the reporter: "Whether it be in consequence of some secret influence which slavery has upon the minds of men, or that the aggression of the North upon their institutions has been of a nature to excite the deepest animosity and most vindictive hate, certain it is there is a degree of something like ferocity in the Southern mind towards New England which exceeds belief. I am persuaded that these feelings of contempt are extended toward England." His letters were copied by the southern papers, exciting great indignation "by their misrepresentations and actual falsehood." One of his letters from Charleston shortly after the fall of Fort Sumter spoke of the preparations and deeds in what the Confederates thought "the most slighting manner" and dared to intimate "that some persons were Unionists at heart." Their new pride of nationhood was bitterly affronted by the statement, "They entertain very exaggerated ideas of the military strength of their little community, although one may do full justice to its military spirit." Rejoinders appeared in the newspapers voicing indignant denials in the name of South Carolina to such statements.[76] When Russell encountered the British consul Mure from New Orleans in Washington a few weeks after the former's comments on the situation in the Louisiana metropolis had been printed, the consul assured the reporter that he was more detested in New Orleans than he was in New York.[77]

Russell gave equal offense and more to the Union. Even though he was only reflecting southern sentiment, as he read it, the northerner did not enjoy the following picture of himself: "Believe a Southern man as he believes himself, and you must regard New England and the kindred states as the birthplace of impurity of mind among men and of unchastity in women—the home of Free Love, of Fourierism, of Infidelity, of Abolitionism, of false teachings in political economy and in social life, a land saturated with the drippings of rotten philosophy, with the poisonous infection of a fanatic press; without honor

---

[76] Russell, *Pictures of Southern Life*, 8; Leiding, *op. cit.*, 231.
[77] Russell, *My Diary North and South*, 553.

or modesty; whose wisdom is paltry cunning, whose valor and man-hood have been swallowed up in a corrupt, howling demagogy, and in the marts of a dishonest commerce." Opinions expressed as to the strength of the South were bitterly resented by northerners. "The North thinks that it can coerce the South, and I am not prepared to say they are right or wrong; but I am convinced that the South can only be forced back by such a conquest as that which laid Poland prostrate at the feet of Russia. It may be that such a conquest can be made by the North, but success must destroy the Union as it has been constituted in the past."[78] So inflamed became feeling that by December, 1861, as has been stated, the Union authorities virtually expelled this frank reporter.

A second reporter, Samuel Phillips Day, whose book, *Down South*, appeared early in the war, in 1862, was much more violently pro-southern than Russell had ever dreamed of being. That many of his opinions were proved by time fallacious does not alter the fact that Confederate sympathizers in England related and gloated over them. With every variety of phraseology Day sought to show the strength of the new republic in food, in finance, on the field, and in purity of motive. "These instances of Southern production and resources will serve to exhibit the utter impossibility of the blockade necessitating a scarcity of provisions—much less 'a famine in the land,' as some Northern croakers professed at the commencement of the civil war." "These bonds are a legal tender in all branches of trade, and are received as a specie medium by the banking houses of the Southern Confederacy, who put them in circulation at their pleasure. By this means the Government possesses an overflowing Treasury, besides value in its possession to meet every obligation." Of the first battle of Manassas he exults, "Never was a victory so triumphant, never a defeat so disgraceful. The 'Grand Army of the North,' so long in formation and preparation . . . have been defeated and put to ig-nominious flight, and by an antagonist far inferior in numbers and resources—in fact, in everything but valour." "The South cherishes no lawless aims, neither indulges in the ambitious project of annex-ation. Justice and equity form the framework of her policy." He dangled before Britishers the bait of trade with the southerners, wrested from the northerners, and ventured upon the emphatic pre-

[78] *Ibid.*, 23.

diction that "whether the unhappy war that now wages be of short or of long duration, one thing is certain—that neither a reunion of states nor of people can ever be effected. . . . The bitter feeling on either side is as strong as death—the enmity as lasting as eternity."[79]

It was difficult for him to find language strong enough to paint the North as black as he thought it should appear. "During my sojourn in the Federal capital, I saw quite sufficient of the Northern army to enable me to form a pretty correct opinion of its character and efficiency. I must candidly confess that it presents a striking contrast to that of the South, which appears to me immeasurably superior in every respect. The former is principally composed of hirelings, many of them the scum of huge cities, who enter the army in order to live, and not to die glorious deaths on the battlefield." "Disaffection in the North," he told his readers, "is much more rife than is generally supposed, or than the Government would wish to acknowledge. It increases every day, and many who refrain from avowing their predilections, only cherish them the more fervently in their breasts." He seemed to delight in picturing acts of vandalism performed by the northern hordes.[80]

Lawrence, the ill-starred reporter who landed in prison instead of in the Confederacy, sought to give the British public the impression of a deeper sympathy in Maryland for the southern cause than actually existed. "I fancy the world is hardly aware of the hearty sympathy with the South—the intense antipathy to the North—which animates at this moment the vast majority of Marylanders. I have heard more than one assert that of the two alternatives, he would infinitely prefer becoming again a colonial subject of England to remaining a member of the Federal Union."[81]

Corsan, the British merchant who spent two months of the year 1862 in the South, visited it when it was at the climax of its strength, energy, and confidence, and so perhaps it is not strange that his views were strongly colored by his rose-tinted glasses. He was sure that

[79] *Down South*, I, 267, 270, II, 1-2, I, 265-266. He so far forgets his English citizenship that he refers repeatedly to "Our troops."—*Ibid.*, II, 3.
[80] "The foreign merchant will have another decided advantage over his Northern competitor, even should commercial intercourse be renewed, owing to the Southern tariff, which will amount almost to prohibition upon goods manufactured on that side of the Atlantic."— *Ibid.*, I, 273. For the prediction of eternal enmity see *ibid.*, 218-219; for the northern army and disaffection, II, 296, 301-302; for vandalism, II, 15.
[81] *Border and Bastille*, 257-258.

the rebellion would not collapse for want of food, clothing, or arms, as the Confederacy was becoming increasingly independent of outside sources of supply. He saw strength in the defenses of Mobile; saw only hatred of the northern conqueror; and found Butler's methods at New Orleans designed effectually to alienate all latent Union feeling.[82] With all desire to avoid exaggeration of the energy and ingenuity of the southern people it was Corsan's conviction that the North could not subdue the South. "If she had all Europe with her, they could not accomplish it."[83]

The Swiss-born Girard, traveling through the Confederate States in 1863, still found a defiant and confident people, taking its cue from President Davis who expressed himself to the visitor as preferring rule by the king of Dahomey to the Yankee yoke. The visitor was scarcely painting to the French public a faithful picture of the situation when he represented the confidence inspired by President Davis as "without limit"; when he dismissed the violent opposition of the Raleigh *Standard* as disappointment in personal ambitions; when he drew a picture of liberty of speech and of the press as untouched; and when he made light of Lee's retreat after Gettysburg as an effort to avoid a campaign during the summer—only in fact a skillful retreat.[84] He seems to have been readily responsive to the arguments which were poured into his ears: that where there was no sovereignty, there could be no rebellion; that where there existed any cleavage of opinion, as in western Virginia, it had been fomented by the Union; that the southern army consisted, not like the Union forces, of mercenaries, but entirely of native-born, all rushing to the defense of their country; that the northern soldiers, in particular General Butler, had committed acts more odious than those of the barbarians against the Roman empire; and that the single state of Texas could furnish the sinews of war for a large army for the period of the war, even if it persisted for ten years. He called upon France to admit the new state into the family of nations, holding out to her, as the British visitors

[82] *Two Months in the Confederate States*, 32, 38-39, 107-108, 267-268, 298.

[83] *Ibid.*, 295-296, 298. As was inevitable for a merchant, he saw the southern hatred toward the Yankees turning that section to Europe for future trade relations which would amount to the tidy sum of $250,000,000 to $400,000,000 a year.—*Ibid.*, 198-199. He quotes Confederates as saying, "No, no! we will send our cotton, tobacco, naval stores, etc. direct to Europe, and buy all we want from Europe. . . . We never will trade with the North again!"—*Ibid.*, 134.

[84] Girard, *Les Etats Confédérés d'Amérique*, 20-21, 67, 68, 97, 130-131.

had done, the lure of commercial advantages which would fall to the country making the first gesture of recognition.[85]

Some of the civilian residents who were fortunate enough to be able to return to the land of their origin gave their impressions to the public and thus helped mold public opinion. The Reverend T. D. Ozanne, who had resided in the South for twenty-one years prior to the war, attempted to show the British people in 1863 *The South as It Is.* His attitude, as might be expected, was decidedly favorable to the Confederate cause. While not defending slavery as an institution —his British upbringing and calling forbade that—he painted it in the best possible colors, declaring that the education of the youth fostered feelings of gentleness and kindness toward the slaves and that brutal treatment of a Negro by an overseer was "punished with instant dismissal, or even by prosecution in a court of law." Probably his assertion that Negroes were seldom overworked, owing to the difficulty of driving them beyond a certain point, is susceptible of some evidence.[86] But when he came to the political issue of secession, he showed less moderation. He declared that the "Black Republican" party in the North, professedly fighting for the Union, was not fighting against slavery because of the moral and religious evils involved but because of the great political power vested in the southern slaveholder, "that splendid class of men of leisure." He renewed, of course, the economic argument that the North desired to retain a monopoly of southern commerce, and inveighed against the unjust tariff legislation of congress. The emancipationist had had his say for many years; it was now high time for the views of the southern statesmen to be presented on this question "which not only affects his pecuniary interests but also the whole of his social and political existence." Like most of the ardent secessionists, he was certain of success. "The South cannot be subdued; the immense extent of its territory, if nothing else, would prevent it; and even if it could be

[85] "Elle diffère de celle des États-Unis en ce que tous ses soldats sont des citoyens nés et appartenant au sol. . . . ils concourrent tous à la defense de leur sol."—*Ibid.,* 105-106. He tells of Union men falling on women and children like wild beasts, tearing jewels from their fingers, ears, and breasts, tying white prisoners together, one ill with smallpox, in order to spread the disease, and amusing themselves by tearing pickaninnies from their mother's arms to throw them into water.—*Ibid.,* 118-120. Of Butler he declares, "On ne connait encore en Europe qu'une faible partie des actes qui ont signalé l'administration civile et militaire du général Butler. . . . Pour écrire cette histoire d'une manière complète et impartiale, il faudra tenir compte d'éléments que la simple prudence ne nous permet pas même d'effleurer aujourd'hui."—*Ibid.,* 124-125.

[86] Ozanne, *The South as It Is,* 77, 78, 81-82.

overpowered, such would be the state of poverty and ruin to which it would be reduced, that it could not share the burden of debt incurred in conquering it."[87]

Sometimes one is forced to wonder how a visitor could so direct his travels as to be able to write in good faith the following passage, penned by a promoter of Confederate recognition from Lancashire who was visiting the South in March, 1864, and who, by his own confession, had traveled through a great portion of the Confederacy. According to his views, the machinery of the government was working as smoothly as if it had been in existence for fifty years; there was no breath of discontent anywhere and none of the food shortage in Richmond which he had seen reported in the London *Daily News* and *Star*. "This is the first I knew of it. Scarcity, I assure you, there is none. . . . As for the destitution that prevails, I can only say that anybody can live here at half the cost they can in Manchester [England]."[88]

The news which found its way into the English newspapers from irregular correspondents on this side, false though it might be at times, undoubtedly had its effect in deluding readers. It may be the same Manchester correspondent reporting to the London *Index* as above, who wrote so confidently of the outcome: "The forthcoming campaign will, no doubt, be the most active and decisive of any during the war. I know for a certainty the arsenals are well stocked, and you may look to hear good news before mid summer."[89]

If the bits from a layman found ready readers abroad, we may be sure that anything written by a military authority was seized upon with double avidity. Articles of this character seem to have been especially welcomed by *Blackwood's Edinburgh Magazine*. The first article, appearing in the issue of December, 1861, the author of which this writer has been unable to identify, purported to give the findings after a month spent with the rebels. Though generally favorable to the Confederates, and thus probably predisposing the British in their favor, it was fair and made claims with regard to clothing and the commissariat which could at that time be substantiated. "The perfect unanimity throughout the whole South in the belief that their cause is

[87] *Ibid.*, 7, 61, 190.
[88] This was written at Richmond, March 29, 1864, and printed in the London *Index*, May 12. It was also copied in the Montgomery *Daily Advertiser*, in its issue of June 14, 1864. [89] *Ibid.*

just, strikes the stranger as one of the most formidable symptoms which the Union has to fear." Probably no scholar will be disposed to quarrel with that as a fair statement of the situation toward the close of the first year of war. The quotation from the lips of a shoemaker soldier concerning defeat is also typical for that period, "They *can't* do it. If they beat us in the field, we'll take to the woods, and shoot them down like squirrels." The writer defended slavery as an institution "which feeds and clothes the world, which protects the negro against the vicissitudes of old age, sickness, and infancy, and keeps him in the only position where he can be useful to society and harmless to himself."[90]

In the October, 1862, issue, the editor offered the second article, "Ten Days in Richmond." Again after eighteen months of warfare, the British public was assured that "it is useless to argue any longer on the original merits of Secession. Separation is now not a question of right, or even of expediency, but a simple matter of fact. . . . Reconstruction of any Union is out of the question. Indeed, no government is possible in which men from the North and from the South should participate on equal terms. In the South there has arisen a general feeling of personal hatred towards the North. Failing success, the men of the South declare they would consent to be dependent, not to say on France or England, but on Spain or on Timbuctoo, rather than ever again have any dealings with such a Government as that which prevails at Washington."[91] Though there are no clues to the identity of the author, the method of discussion disposes the writer to believe that he was a military officer on leave.

The third article, appearing in January, 1863, is the one written by Wolseley. Although anonymous, it was written with a certain air of authority, which, no doubt, told the British public that a man competent to judge was speaking. Such sentences as the following doubtless swayed some: "But my next impulse was to smile at the utter folly they [Federals] exhibited in rushing into a great war of conquest, with the avowed object of bringing into subjection those every way superior to themselves, in all qualities essential to good generalship and the formation of a soldier-like character."[92] When he dismissed

90 "A Month with the Rebels," *Blackwood's*, XC, 757, 758. For the entire article see 755-767.
91 "Ten Days in Richmond," *Blackwood's*, XCII, 399.
92 "A Month's Visit to the Confederate Headquarters," *Blackwoods*, XCIII, 10.

McClellan as "a Napoleon without glory, and a Fabius without success" and praised Jackson and Lee without stint, few paused to reflect that he had come under the personal influence only of the southern leaders. It has never been forgotten that of them he wrote: "With such a leader [Jackson] men would go anywhere, and face any amount of difficulties; and for myself, I believe that, inspired by the presence of such a man, I should be perfectly insensible to fatigue, and reckon upon success as a moral certainty. Whilst General Lee is regarded in the light of infallible Jove, a man to be reverenced, Jackson is loved and adored with all that childlike and trustful affection which the ancients are said to have lavished upon the particular deity presiding over their affairs."[93] Of the rank and file of Lee's army he said, "I have seen many armies file past in all the pomp of bright clothing and well-polished accoutrements; but I never saw one composed of finer men, or that looked more like *work*, than that portion of General Lee's army which I was fortunate enough to see inspected. If I had at any time entertained misgivings as to the ability of the Southerners to defend their country and liberties against Northern invasion, they were at once and forever dispelled when I examined for myself the material of which the Confederate armies are composed."[94] Who can fail to suspect that his ringing challenge to parliament strengthened many a soldier and romantic youth in his own predilections for the southern cause: "Will parliament consider that the time has come for putting an end to the most inhuman struggle that ever disgraced a great nation, such as the Republic of the United States once was, though now it is merely the military despotism of a portion of the States striving under the dictatorship of an insignificant lawyer to crush out the freedom of the rest."[95]

After another interval there appeared the account by Captain Fitzgerald Ross of the Austrian army, his "Visit to the Cities and Camps of the Confederate States" beginning in *Blackwood's* in the December issue of 1864. His view was wholly favorable to the South but came too late to have much effect upon the opinions of its readers. "Were it not for the friendly neutrality of the British government toward the North," Ross declared, "the Confederates would have had a fleet, and the war in consequence would have been over long ago."

[93] *Ibid.*, 19, 21.   [94] *Ibid.*, 24.   [95] *Ibid.*, 29.

Before the year 1863 had run its course another British officer had told his fellow countrymen his impressions of the southern people and their leaders. At the outbreak of the war Colonel Fremantle was inclined, because of the natural prejudice against slavery, to favor the side of the North. During his three months' contact with the Confederates their gallantry and determination won his respect so that before the end of the third year of the war his book, *Three Months in the Southern States*, took its place with those enumerated above, pouring into the ears of Britishers praise and glorification of the Confederate cause. It was reprinted in New York the next year, where the laudation of the South by a foreign visitor did nothing to forward good feeling between England and the United States. But the edition which was brought out by a German house in Mobile, bound though it was in wallpaper, was loved and lauded by the southern women.[96]

In the course of that same year, 1863, there was published in London one of the most surprising books of the period, Estvàn's *War Pictures from the South*. With every critical comment upon the Confederates the reader has to remind himself that the writer had fought on that side for about two years. It is not sufficient to sweep aside his criticisms, as have many southerners, as the pique of a man dissatisfied with his rewards; it is too clear from the very beginning that his sympathies were rather with the Union. He was in the unfortunate position of a man fighting on the wrong side and unable to keep from betraying where his sympathies lay. The irony of his position is clearly revealed in the fact that he dedicated his first edition to General McClellan, his second to "The Soldiers of Both Armies"! Certainly in 1863 no Confederates could have joined him in the prayer "that the American Republic, once the pride of the world, may arise strong and powerful from this disastrous struggle; that the blood which has been shed in torrents during this war may serve to fertilize the soil of liberty, and that a new Union may arise, greater, stronger, and more free than its predecessors."[97]

There is little reason to feel that Estvàn stemmed among book readers in England the tide which was running for the Confederacy, but he may have strengthened the pro-Union sentiment in Germany by the German edition, *Kriegsbilder*, which came out in Leipsic in 1864.

[96] It was printed in Mobile in 1864 by S. H. Götzel, probably a German.
[97] Estvàn, *op. cit.*, II, 282-283.

The books which foreign participants and residents produced for fifty years after the conclusion of the war had, of course, no effect upon the outcome of the war by influencing public sentiment in the various countries interested in the Confederacy, but they have served the cause of truth in shedding much light upon events and characters in the war. Von Borcke's *Memoirs* has given much additional light on the social as well as military history of the period. Scheibert, in collaboration with Von Borcke, has given an impartial account of the battle of Brandy Station. From Williams we get a more impartial and fuller account of the treatment of the Germans in Texas than is to be had from the purged or whitewashed official reports. Without the memoirs of the Scotch nurse, Kate Cumming, and the account of Mr. and Mrs. W. by the maid, Elizabeth Collins, and bits gleaned from similar accounts, this book could not have been written.

Sometimes the eyes of an observant contemporary sum up a situation more accurately and neatly than reams of statistics. This story will close with the comment of the nurse, Kate Cumming, on a remark which she had heard made that none but native southerners must fill office. "I can tell her that if the native southerners, who, when the war was first inaugurated, used to wear their blue badges, and cry 'secession and war to the knife,' had come forward as I know foreigners have done, we would not now be in need of the late earnest appeal for men, by our beloved President. And I not only think it bad taste, but unfeeling, in any of our people to draw distinctions at the present time, when we all know how nobly foreigners have poured out their blood in our defense."[98]

The record is finished. It will probably give offense. Surprises often do not give joy if they overthrow long-cherished conceptions. The descendants of Englishmen who came over during the colonial period may feel that their fathers and grandfathers are being robbed of the distinction of having fought unaided for the great cause to which they devoted their lives. One need only point to the glowing tributes paid by those same ancestors to the German and French companies, to the Swedish and Polish officers who helped lead the troops. Descendants of foreign-born who shared in that struggle may feel that not sufficient credit is given to their sacrifices and resent the recording of enforced service when so many of their number volun-

[98] *A Journal of Hospital Life,* 87.

teered. There is glory sufficient and more than sufficient for all. The story of the heroism and endurance of 9,000,000 people who could sustain an unequal struggle against 20,000,000 for four long years shines with undimmed luster. At the outbreak of the war all, native and foreign-born, sprang to the defense of their states with inspiring ardor. The full record, which now shows practically the last man in the Confederacy, whether native son or foreigner, pressed into the ranks, only fills the modern reader with respect for the leaders who could demand and secure the last ounce of strength from its entire man power.

APPENDICES

APPENDIX I

DISTRIBUTION OF FOREIGNERS BY CITIES

DISTRIBUTION OF IMMIGRANTS BY CITIES*

	Eng.	Irish	Scot.	Br. Am.	Ger.	Fr.	Others	For. Total	Pct. of For.	Total Pop.
Charleston, S. C.	368	3,263	209	33	1,944	133	361	6,311	15.55	40,578
Memphis, Tenn.	522	4,159	113	140	1,412	120	472	6,938	30.66	22,623
Mobile, Ala.	663	3,307	318	141	1,276	538	818	7,061	24.13	29,258
Montgomery, Ala.	34	200	32	23	208	40	41	578	6.53	8,843
New Orleans, La.	3,045	24,398	736	562	19,752	10,564	5,564	64,621	38.31	168,675
Richmond, Va.	357	2,244	199	74	1,623	144	315	4,956	13.07	37,910
Savannah, Ga.	348	3,145	112	53	771	72	151	4,652	20.86	22,292

FOREIGNERS IN NEW ORLEANS*

BORN IN FOREIGN COUNTRIES

German	19,729	Mexico	261
Br. America	562	Portugal	109
Denmark	227	Poland	119
England	3,042	Spain	1,390
France	10,515	Sweden	140
Ireland	24,385	Switzerland	600
Italy	896	West Indies	1,009 (including few Negroes)

Total born in U. S.   90,669
Total born abroad   64,621

* 1860 Census, *Population Statistics*, 615. The figures for these two tables were compiled apparently at slightly different dates.

[481]

APPENDIX II

FOREIGNERS OR FOREIGN-BORN OFFICERS IN THE CONFEDERATE ARMIES

The author cannot hope that after a lapse of three-quarters of a century the following lists can be entirely correct. She has based the classification of rank on the various descriptive rolls, checked by Estes, *List of Field Officers, Regiments and Battalions in the Confederate States Army, 1861-1865,* by the *Official War Records,* and by various printed records. There will, however, prove to be omissions and inaccuracies, owing to the absence of complete rolls. It would be the work of a lifetime to trace the descendants of all the men involved—and not worth while. It is believed, however, that the lists will be suggestive and with corrections, which it is hoped will be offered by readers of this book, in time may be made correct.

MAJOR GENERALS

Patrick Ronayne Cleburne, Irish
Camille Arnaud Jules Marie, Prince de Polignac, French

BRIGADIER GENERALS

Robert Becham, German. Brigadier general of Texas State Troops
Xavier B. Debray, French. Raised and commanded a Battalion of Texas Cavalry
William M. Browne, English. Aide to President Davis. Although the Senate refused to confirm the appointment, he was paroled as brigadier general
Joseph Finnegan, Irish. Appointed brigadier general April 5, 1862
James Hagan, Irish. Made brigadier general August 15, 1863
Walter Page Lane, Irish. Appointed general February 3, 1865
Collett Leventhorpe, English. Appointed general February 3, 1865; declined appointment March 6, 1865. Commissioned general of North Carolina State Troops
Peter Alexander Selkirk McGlashan, Scotch. Colonel of the Fifty-fifth Georgia Regiment, but commissioned brigadier general too late to serve with this rank

Patrick T. Moore, Irish. Appointed September 13, 1864; paroled in Virginia

Pierre Soulé, French. Appointed brigadier general in recognition of special service

John A. Wagener, German. Appointed brigadier general of South Carolina Militia

COLONELS

Adolphus H. Adler, Hungarian. Engineer in chief of General Wise's legion

Santos Benavides, Mexican. Major of the Thirty-third Texas Cavalry; then colonel of Benavides' cavalry

(?)A. R. Blakely, Irish. Connected with the Washington Artillery, New Orleans

Heros von Borcke, German. Chief of staff in General Stuart's cavalry corps. Given rank as colonel for a special mission to England at the close of the war

Augustus Buchel, German. Colonel of First Texas Cavalry (Buchel's cavalry). Buchel's tombstone records him as a brigadier general in the Confederate army, but the writer can find official records of no higher rank than colonel

James Duff, Scotch. Commander of the Thirty-third Texas Cavalry

(?) Felix Dumonteil, French. Colonel of the Fourteenth Confederate Cavalry

———— Este, German. A colonel of this name is reported in the Wise Legion

Bela Estvàn, Hungarian. Rendered various services, but chiefly with General Wise

Augustus Forsberg, Swedish. Colonel of the Fifty-first Virginia Infantry, though his greatest service was as engineer

Aristides Gerard, French. Colonel of the Thirteenth Louisiana Regiment

A. J. Gonzales, Cuban. Chief of artillery of the Department of South Carolina, Georgia, and Florida after January, 1865. Also chief of ordnance to General Beauregard

George Gordon, English. Colonel under General Stuart and on the staff of Stuart and General A. P. Hill

Arthur Grabowski, Pole. Rose from private in a South Carolina regiment to officer in charge of supplies for General Lee

———— Henderson, English. Reference only

Karl Frederick Henningsen, German. Second in command of the Wise Legion

Gustave Hoffman, German. Colonel of the Seventh Texas Cavalry

George Jackson, English. Adjutant general and chief of staff

(?)———— Lovenskiold, German

William Monaghan, Irish. Colonel of the Sixth Louisiana Regiment

P. B. O'Brien, Irish. Colonel of the Louisiana Irish Militia Regiment. This regiment consisted of only eight companies and seems never to have been transferred to Confederate service.

Hypolite Oladowski, Polish. Chief of ordnance to General Bragg. Rank dates from January 11, 1865

Augustus Reichard, German. Colonel of the Twentieth Louisiana Infantry

James Santiago Reily, Irish. Colonel of the Fourth Texas Mounted Volunteers, Sibley's brigade

William G. Robinson, Canadian. Colonel of the Nineteenth North Carolina Volunteers (Second North Carolina) Cavalry

Frank Schaller, Polish. Colonel of the Twenty-second Mississippi Infantry

Gustav Adolph Schwarzmann, German. Colonel and adjutant general to General Albert Pike (or major—the records conflict)

James Sinclair, English clergyman. Served until October, 1863, when he was released and allowed to return to England

Henry B. Strong, Irish. Colonel of the Sixth Louisiana Infantry

Valery Sulakowski, Polish. Colonel of the Fourteenth Louisiana. Served later in Texas as engineer to General Magruder, a personal relationship

Ignatius Szymanski, Polish. Colonel of the Chalmette Regiment of Louisiana Militia and then agent for exchange of prisoners in Trans-Mississippi Department

———— Talbot (son of Lord Talbot), English. Knight-errant, served throughout the war

Jack Thorington, Irish. Colonel in Hilliard's Alabama Legion

Jacob Waldeck, German. Reference to him as colonel of a German Texas State Regiment (son of Count Waldeck, one of the founders of German Texas)

→ Zeubulon York, Polish. Colonel in the Polish Brigade, Fourteenth Louisiana Infantry

Leon von Zincken, German. Colonel of the Twentieth Louisiana Infantry, and then of the Thirteenth Louisiana Infantry

LIEUTENANT COLONELS

J. G. Campbell, Scotch. Commissary general in the Sixth Louisiana Regiment

Georges Auguste de Coppens, French or Belgian. Lieutenant colonel of the First Louisiana Zouaves

Marie Alfred de Coppens, French or Belgian. Succeeded to the command of the First Louisiana Zouaves on the death of his brother, Georges

Paul F. de Gournay, French. Lieutenant colonel of the Twelfth Battalion, Louisiana Artillery

John P. Emerich, German. Served as second in command of the Eighth Alabama Infantry

Eric Erson, Swedish. Lieutenant colonel of the Fifty-second North Carolina Regiment

B. F. Eschelman, German. Second in command of the Washington Artillery of New Orleans

B. W. Fröbel, German. Chief engineer with the rank of Lieutenant colonel of Hood's division

George St. Leger Grenfel, English. Adjutant general to General Morgan and on the staff of other generals. Inspector of cavalry of the Army of the Tennessee

Michael A. Grogan, Irish. Lieutenant colonel of the Second Louisiana Infantry

Andrew D. Gwynne, Irish. Of the Thirty-eighth Tennessee Infantry

Joseph Hanlon, Irish. Second in the Sixth Louisiana

Louis Lay, French. Lieutenant colonel in the Sixth Louisiana Infantry

(?) Carl Ludvig Viktor Lybecker, Swedish. First, captain in the Flying Artillery Corps of the Fourth Division, lieutenant colonel, October 31, 1863 (on the authority of the Royal Foreign Office of Stockholm)

Joseph McGraw, Irish. In charge of Pegram's Artillery Battalion, Mahon's division

John William Mallet, English. In charge of the laboratory, Nitre Bureau

George H. Morton, Scotch. Of the Second Tennessee Cavalry (later the Twenty-second Tennessee Cavalry)

James Nelligan, Irish. Second in command of the First Louisiana Volunteers

Michael Nolan, Irish. Lieutenant Colonel of the First Louisiana Volunteers

Henri Honoré St. Paul, Belgian. Breveted lieutenant colonel on the field at the Battle of Seven Pines. Usually classified as major

Viktor von Scheliha, German. Chief engineer with this rank in the Department of the Gulf. At one time chief of staff to General Buckner

(?) Thomas M. Wagener, German. First South Carolina artillery

MAJORS

(?) ———— Bruch, German. Galveston Home Defense Guards

John Cunningham, Scotch. Of the First Georgia Reserves (Symons' regiment)

Alexander M. Dechman, Canadian. Of the Second Texas Militia. Dechman is not given in the *List of Field Officers*, but the writer has found him on a descriptive roll

———— Ford, English. In command of the First Virginia Infantry Battalion Local Defense (Armory). This is probably the Major Ford spoken of

Hugh Gwynn, Irish. Major in the Twenty-third Tennessee Infantry

William S. Haven, Irish. Of the Twentieth Arkansas Infantry

———— Hodges, English. On General Beauregard's Staff. Such an officer is spoken of by visitors but cannot be identified in official lists

Nicholas Kabler, German. Historians record him as major of the Forty-second Virginia Regiment, but he cannot be located in the official records

(?) John King, Irish. First (Carter's) Tennessee Cavalry

Michael Looscan, Irish. First Texas Cavalry, First Texas Battalion, Arizona Brigade

Robert G. Lowe, Scotch. With the Shreveport Grays, serving in Louisiana

Michael Lynch, Irish. Of the Twenty-first Georgia Infantry

(?) Donald Malcolm McDonald, Scotch. On General Jackman's Staff

Francis Miller, German. Major of Forty-fifth Virginia Regiment

Raphael Moses, German Jew. Commissary of the Army of Northern Virginia

Otto Nathusius, German. In Waul's Texas Legion

———————— Nocquet, French. Chief Engineer to General Gilmer of Bragg's army

Theodore Oswald, German. Of the Fourth Battalion, Texas Infantry

G. A. Peple, German. Ranked as major by virtue of his position as professor in the Confederate Marine School

Adolph Proskauer, German. Major in the Twelfth Alabama Infantry

James F. Robinson, Irish. Of the Twenty-third Arkansas Infantry (Adams' regiment)

Max Römer, German-Hungarian. Served in Wise's legion on his western campaign. Again, this individual cannot be located in the official reports, but Schuricht lists him

Gustav Schleicher, German. Engineer with the Texas Rangers. The Official War Records do not record him with rank above captain, but the German writers give him this rank

M. K. Simons, Canadian. Apparently with the Second Texas Militia

Louis M. Ströbel, German. Associated as officer with Company F, Terry's Texas Rangers and later with the Texas State Troops. It is impossible to determine whether Schuricht is correct in giving him rank as major. The only muster rolls the writer has found in the Texas Archives do not give him rank above captain, but they are for 1861 and 1862

Jacob Wälder, German. He held a commission as major, evidently
of a regiment which he, together with Colonel Wilcox, raised in
the spring of 1862

Henry Wirz, German. In charge of Andersonville prison

Gerbert Albers, German. Long Prairie German Company, Texas

Rafalo Aldrate, Mexican. Refugio County Home Guards, Precinct
No. 2

Robert Goring Atkins, Irish. Aide to Colonel Bob Wheat, and on the
staff of General Elzie. British knight-errant

F. Baredouin, French. Company C, First Mobile Volunteers, Local
Defense

C. Baumann, German. Home Guards, Co. H, Nineteenth Virginia
Militia

———— Behrman, German. Of the Galveston Rangers

Christoval Benavides, Mexican. In command of a company in Col.
Benavides' cavalry

Refugio Benavides, Mexican. In command of a company in Col.
Benavides' cavalry

———— Biesenbuch, German. Company B, Third Texas

———— Bolton, English. Engineer in the Wise Legion

Christian Bosche, German. Company H, Ninth Kentucky Pioneer
Corps

J. Boses, German. Captain of a German Texas Company

C. P. B. Brannigan, Irish. Company I, Eighth Alabama

H. (?) Brumendstadt, German. Florence Guards, Florence, Louisiana

E. von Buchholz, German. Captain of Ordnance, Wise Legion and
then transferred to Virginia Ordnance Department at Richmond

———— Burns, English. British knight-errant

Clemente Bustilla, Mexican. In command of a Texas Company

———— Buxton, English. In command of the British Foreign
Legion of Richmond, Virginia

———— Byrne, English. A British knight-errant

Patrick Caniff, Irish. Company F, Fifth Missouri

P. F. Carney, Irish. Company H, Eighth Louisiana

Christopher Cleburne, Irish. In Third Brigade, Morgan's cavalry

John Clendinning, (?) Irish. Company B, Twenty-third Arkansas

José María Cobos, Mexican. Headed temporarily a home defense company at Brownsville, Texas

Edward Lees Coffey, Irish. British knight-errant

M. T. Connor, Irish. Company F, Sixth Louisiana Infantry

Christopher Cornehlson, German. Company A, Eighteenth North Carolina

John Cussons, English. Aide-de-camp to General Law, knight-errant

Francis Warrington Dawson, English. Chief of ordnance in Bragg's army (temporarily). Held several posts

Henry Döring, German. Headed a German company from Cherry Springs, Texas

Dick Dowling, Irish. Davis Guards, Texas

James W. Fair, English. Company E, Fifth Missouri

Henry Weymss Feilden, English. Assistant adjutant general on staffs of Generals Beauregard, Sam Jones, and Hardee

E. A. Fernandez, Mexican. Company D, Fifth Florida Cavalry

Sylvester Festorazzi, Italian. Southern Guards, Mobile

Frederic C. Fischer, German. Company C, Twelfth Alabama

Melayé Francis, French. Company I, Tenth Louisiana (from Martinique)

Edgar J. Franklin, English. Served on General Drayton's staff in the Trans-Mississippi Department. Knight-errant

L. D. Fremaux, French. Engineer on General Beauregard's staff

(?) ——————— Fremder, German. Captain of the German Hussars of South Carolina after death of Captain Cordes

(?) Leon J. Fremon, French. Company A, Eighth Louisiana

James Garrity, Irish. (?) Company, Fifth Louisiana

——————— Gonzalez, Spanish. Captain of the Spanish Guards, Home Defense, Mobile

Patrick Henry Gormsley, Irish. A Georgia company

Robert D. Green, British. Montgomery Foreign Guards

Robert Gregg, Scotch. Scotch Guards, Mobile

John F. Griber, German. (?) Company, Sixth Louisiana

S. Isidore Guillet, German. Aide-de-camp to Colonel von Zincken

F. W. Hagemeier, German. Company D, First Virginia

——————— Harsh, German. Company E, Twenty-first Georgia

John Heilman, German. Beat No. 3, Comal County, Texas State Troops

John A. Herbig, German. Sanitary Corps, Richmond, Virginia

Sidney Herbert Heth, English. Inspector General on the staff of General Hany Heth

Georges Heuilly, French. Gardes Lafayette, Company A, Twelfth Alabama

G. Hoffman, German. Captain of a company from Comal County, Texas, in Sibley's brigade

——————— Hunsicker, German. Shreveport Rebels, Louisiana

——————— Kaupman, German. (?) Company, Third Texas Cavalry

John W. Keely, Irish. Company B, Nineteenth Georgia

Richard Keough, Irish. North Carolina Rangers

E. Krauskopf, German. Captain of one of the companies from Fredericksburg, Texas

Joseph Kyrisk, Polish. In command of a Polish company from Panna Maria, Texas

Pierre Leclaire, Canadian. Company I, Tenth Louisiana

Albert Leibrock, German. Captain of Marion Rifles, in a Virginia regiment

Maurice Lichtenstadt, German. Steuben Jägers, Georgia

P. Loughry, Irish. Company I, Eighth Alabama (Emerald Guards)

L. A. Allen McClean, Scotch. Assistant adjutant general

R. McFarland, Irish. Company H, Fourth Alabama

Daniel McNeill, British. Company B, British Guards, Mobile

John D. McRohan, Irish. Company D, Eighth Kentucky

Charles Mallory, Scotch. The Scotch Boys, North Carolina

Charles Maréchal, French. Company H, Twenty-first Alabama, French Guards

A. Melchers, German. Palmetto Schützen, South Carolina

Franz Melchers, German. Company B, German Artillery, South Carolina

John C. Mitchel, Irish. Command in a South Carolina Company at Fort Sumter

J. Moore, Irish. Company C, Seventh Louisiana

A. Moroso, Italian. Company D, First Regiment Home Guards, Virginia

———————— Müller, German. Galveston Island City Schützen, Texas

Charles Murray (later Lord Dunmore), English. On General Lee's staff

———————— O'Brien, Irish. Emmett Guards, Twenty-fourth Alabama

Bernard O'Connell, Irish. Company B, Twenty-fourth Alabama (Emmett Guards)

Steve O'Leary, Irish. Southern Celts, Thirteenth Louisiana

John Orr, Canadian. Adjutant to the Sixth Louisiana

———————— Pattina, Mexican. Captain of a small company of Mexicans

José Marie Penaloza, Mexican. Company C, Eighth Texas, Terry's Texas Rangers

Jacob Phiniza, German. Company ————, Eighth Georgia

Alfred Pico, Italian. Italian Company, Nineteenth Virginia Reserve Troops

———————— Podewill, German. Captain of a company in Waul's legion

Augustus Poitevin, French. Captain of Mobile French Guard Volunteers

Frank Potts, Irish. Paymaster, First Corps, Army of Northern Virginia. Rose from Company C, First Virginia

———————— Prendergast, English. Ex-member of British army, in the Tenth Tennessee

Andrew Quinn, Irish. Company I, Eighth Alabama

Thomas Quirk, Irish. Company of Scouts, Second Kentucky Cavalry

Philip I. Rabinau, German. Company C, Fifth Louisiana

T. George Raven, English. South Carolina Rangers

William Robson, Scotch. Captain of a company in the Third Louisiana Infantry, served chiefly in northern Arkansas

Otto von Roder, German. Company A, Texas (from Victoria County)

———————— Rose, English. Company K, Third Texas

———————— Rosenheim, German. Company F, Third Texas

———————— Sabath, German. Company H, Seventeenth Texas

Joseph Santini, Italian. Garibaldi Legion

Justus Scheibert, German. On General Beauregard's staff, later in Stuart's cavalry for very brief period

E. B. H. Schneider, German. Houston Turnverein Company

Hermann Schuricht, German. Company M, Nineteenth Virginia Militia; earlier, Company D, Fourteenth Virginia Cavalry

T. A. G. Scott, Irish. Missouri Company

———— Sherhagen, German. Company G, Third Texas

C. B. Sigwald, German. Captain of Marion Rifles, South Carolina

Jakob Small, German. German Schützen, South Carolina

Peter Stankiewicz, Polish. Polish Company, from near Panna Maria, Texas

John Steigen, German. Georgia Artillery, German Volunteers

A. Stikes, German. Company C, Twelfth Alabama

———— Strauss, German. Company F, Fifteenth Louisiana

Franz van Stucken, Belgian. Fredericksburg Cavalry, Texas

George Tait, Scotch. Company K, Eighteenth North Carolina

Robert Tait, Scotch. Company B, Eighteenth North Carolina

Thomas F. Tobin, Irish. Tennessee Company

John Ormsley Treanor, Irish

Mark Trumper, English. Company B, Fifth Missouri

———— Tucker, German. Aide-de-camp to General Fitzhugh Lee

Charles de Vaux, French. French Guards No. 1, Mobile. Company H, 21 Alabama

Adrian I. Vidal, Mexican. Captain of a Mounted Company of Six Months Volunteers, Texas

Robert Voigt, German. Waul's legion, Texas

F. W. Wagener, German. South Carolina company (brother of John Wagener)

B. T. Walsh, Irish. Company F, Sixth Louisiana (formerly Company A, Irish Brigade)

William Warmut, German. Fredericksburg Company, Texas

Garvin Watson, Scotch. Scotch Guards, Mobile

C. Werner, German. Company K, German Volunteers, Savannah, Georgia

D. Werner, German. Company A, South Carolina Home Guards

———— Wheeler, British. Company A, British Guards, Mobile

J. T. Whitehead, English. Tennessee Artillery

H. Wickeland, German. Waul's legion, Texas

Franz Wilde, German. Company ———, Nineteenth Georgia

John R. Williams, Scotch. Commanded a company of sharpshooters

Stephen Winthrop, English. On Longstreet's staff

Jacob Wittman, German. German Fusiliers, No. 2, Mobile

Hanke Wohleben, German. South Carolina Company

Fred Wolf, German. Assistant quartermaster, in Alabama regiment

Emil Oscar Zadek, German. Company C, Home Guards, Alabama
    Cavalry

APPENDIX III

Major Atkins, Aide-de-camp to General Wheat, English

Baron Barke, Aide-de-camp to General Stuart, German

Marcus Baum, Aide-de-camp to General Kershaw, German

Heros von Borcke, Chief of Staff for General J. E. B. Stuart, German

Captain Burns, Ensign of the British Navy, on General Bragg's staff, British

Captain ———— Bryne, on General Cleburne's staff, British

John Conelly, on brigade staff duty for the First Kentucky Brigade, Irish

Henry Cordes, aide-de-camp on the staff of General Evans with rank of corporal, German

Francis W. Dawson, chief of ordnance, staff of General Longstreet, English

Alexander M. Dechman, assistant adjutant general on the staff of Nineteenth Texas Cavalry, Canadian

George Osborn Elms, adjutant of the Twenty-eighth Louisiana Infantry for Colonel Allen Thomas, Canadian

Bela Estvàn, on staff of General Joseph Johnston, Hungarian

J. H. Fairley, on General Whiting's staff, Irish

Henry Fielden, assistant adjutant general on staff of General Beauregard, son of an English baronet

August Forsberg, on the staff of General Floyd, Swedish

L. D. Fremaux, engineer on the staff of General Beauregard, French

General Gonzales, inspector general on the staff of General Beauregard, Cuban

George St. Leger Grenfel, adjutant on General Morgan's staff, English

Louis Hanauer, on the staff of General Hardee, German

Sidney Hubert Heth, inspector general on the staff of General Hany Heth, British (had been in the Crimean War)

Major ———— Hodges, on the staff of General Beauregard (son of an English lord), English

Henry Kenna, adjutant in the First Louisiana Regiment, Irish

E. I. Kursheedt, adjutant in the Washington Artillery, German

Michael Looscan, adjutant general, staff of General R. Taylor, and inspector general on the staff of General S. B. Maxey, Hungarian

Carl Ludvig Viktor Lybecker, aide-de-camp to General Marmaduke, Swedish

Baron von Massow, aide-de-camp to General Mosby, German

David Mayer, on the staff of Governor Brown of Georgia, German

Franz Melchers, on the staff of General Wade Hampton, German

Patrick F. Moore, on the volunteer staff of General Beauregard during the Seven Days' Battles, Irish

Charles Murray, on General Lee's staff, English (later Lord Dunmore)

Conrad Nutzel, provost marshal on the staff of General Ben Hill, German

P. K. O'Rourke, adjutant for the First Louisiana Regiment, Irish

Prince Polignac, on the staff of General Beauregard, French

Viktor von Scheliha, chief of staff for General Buckner, German

Gustav Schwarzmann, adjutant general on the staff of General Albert Pike, German

Pierre Soulé, on the staff of General Beauregard, French

——————, an English officer on General Longstreet's staff

Captain Stephen Winthrop, on Longstreet's staff, English

APPENDIX IV

ALABAMA

Mobile

Alabama Light Dragoons, Irish

British Consular Guards, Co. A, English

British Consular Guards, Co. B, British

Co. K, Captain Eugene Brooks's cavalry, mixed

Co. E, Citizens' Guards, Captain John F. Leaven's company, mixed

Coast Guards, mixed. Served on Gulf Coast during first month of war, then to Fort Gaines to finish one year

French Guards, organized late under Captain Maréchal

Co. B, German Fusiliers, German, No. I, Captain J. P. Emrich

Co. I, German Fusiliers, under Captain Jacob Wittman, Co. 2

Captain Gueringer's Company from Beat 1, Co. A, Ninety-fifth Alabama Militia, mixed

Mobile Dragoons, Irish

Mobile French Guards, Captain Poitevin

Spanish Guards, Captain Gonzales, chiefly Spanish

Stuart's Horse Artillery, Pelham's artillery, mixed

Co. F, First Mobile Volunteers, or Mobile County Reserves, British

Co. I, Second Alabama, Scotch Guards (later Co. A, Forty-fifth Alabama), Scotch

Co. I, Eighth Alabama, Emerald Guards, Irish except 10

Co. A, Twelfth Alabama, Gardes Lafayette, French

Co. C, Twelfth Alabama, Independent Rifles, largely German

Co. H, Twenty-first Alabama, the French Guards, French, Captain de Vaux

Co. K, Twenty-first Alabama, mixed, Captain Festerazzi, Southern Guards

Co. B, Twenty-fourth Alabama, Emmett Guards, Irish

Montgomery

    Alabama Rebels (firemen), mixed

    Montgomery Foreign Guards, mixed

    The Irish Volunteers

GEORGIA

Augusta

    Irish Volunteers

Savannah

    Frazier's Battery, largely Irish

    Co. K, German Volunteers, Captain Werner, German

    Steuben Jägers, Captain Lichtenstadt, German

    Irish Jasper Greene, Companies A and B, Irish

    German Volunteers, First Georgia Volunteers (artillery), German

    Co. B, Nineteenth Georgia Infantry, Jackson Guards, Irish

    Co. E, Twenty-first Georgia, German Jägers, Captain Harsh (?)

LOUISIANA

Avegno Zouaves, Thirteenth Louisiana, Governor's Guards, mixed with two Irish companies—Southern Celts, and St. Mary Volunteers

British Fusiliers, Major M. Quayle

Co. D, First Louisiana, Emmett Guards, Irish (about two-thirds Irish)

Co. E, First Louisiana, Montgomery Guards, mostly Irish (three-fourths)

Co. F, First Louisiana, Orleans Light Guards, half foreigners

Co. B, Fifth Louisiana, almost all foreigners

Co. C, Fifth Louisiana, Sarsfield Rangers, almost entirely Irish

Co. G, Fifth Louisiana, Swamp Rangers, three-fourths foreigners

Co. B, Sixth Louisiana, almost all Irish (110 of 140 men) and all foreigners except two

Co. F, Sixth Louisiana, Irish chiefly

Co. G, Sixth Louisiana, German largely, all but two born abroad

Co. H, Sixth Louisiana, many foreigners, less than one-third natives

Co. K, Sixth Louisiana, many foreigners (almost three-fourths at one time)

Co. F } Sixth Louisiana, Irish Brigade
Co. I }

Co. D, Seventh Louisiana, Virginia Guards, half Irish
Co. F, Seventh Louisiana, Irish Volunteers, almost solidly Irish
Co. B, Eighth Louisiana, mixed, two-thirds foreigners
Co. D, Eighth Louisiana, mixed, two-thirds foreigners
Co. E, Ninth Louisiana, four-fifths Irish, the rest foreign-born
Tenth Louisiana Regiment, largely Irish, but all foreign
Six companies, Fourteenth Louisiana, half to three-fourths Irish, chiefly foreigners
Co. B, Fifteenth Louisiana, Jefferson Cadets, two-thirds foreigners
Co. D, Fifteenth Louisiana, St. Ceran Rifles, two-thirds foreigners
Six companies, Twentieth Louisiana, Col. von Zincken, German
Four companies, Twentieth Louisiana, Irish
Donaldsonville, two companies, Irish
First Special Louisiana, Bob Wheat's Tigers, chiefly Irish
Florence Guards, Captain Brummenstadt, German
French Company of St. James Parish, Louisiana
Garibaldi Legion, one company of Italians
Louisiana Zouaves, Major de Coppens, French, Italians, Creoles
Polish Brigade (later Fourteenth and Fifteenth Louisiana), many nationalities
Shreveport Rebels, mixed, but all foreign except five

Defense Guards—European Brigade

Austrian Guards, Captain Cegnavich
British Guards, Captain Shannon
French Brigade, Colonel A. Rochereau, five companies of French
French Guards, Colonel Paul Juge, Jr.
French Veterans or Volunteers, Colonel A. Fournier
Hansa Guards, six companies
Independent French Volunteers, Major E. Brogniet
Italian Guards, Major Della Valle
Orleans Guides, Cavalry
Spanish Legion, Cazadores españoles, Commandant P. Avendano
(In addition Co. F, Tenth Louisiana, was probably a foreign company, as all which were decipherable were recorded as from foreign lands)

MISSOURI

Irish Battery under General Price

Shamrock Guards, Irish under General Price

Two Irish regiments under General Bevier's command (probably some American-born of Irish descent)

NORTH CAROLINA

Co. D, Seventh North Carolina, mixed, one-half foreigners

Co. A, Eighteenth North Carolina, German Volunteers, Captain Cornelhson, German

(?) Scotch company, Eighteenth North Carolina, Scotch

Co. H, Fortieth North Carolina, Irish chiefly

A Wilmington Company, Captain Edward D. Hill, Irish

SOUTH CAROLINA

Charleston Battalion, chiefly Irish, served at Fort Sumter, two companies, artillery

Co. C, Charleston Battalion, Captain Schroder, German (unable to determine whether they were not descendants of Germans)

Emerald Light Infantry, Irish (disbursed before January, 1863)

German Schützen, Captain J. Small, Fourth South Carolina Militia, German

German Hussars, Troop G, Third South Carolina Cavalry, Captain Theodore Cordes

Home Guards, Captain Morosso, aliens

Irish Artillery, two companies, Irish

Marion Rifles (Volunteer Corps of Fire Department), Captain Sigwald, German

Old Irish Volunteers, First South Carolina, Irish

Palmetto Schützen, Captain A. Melchers, German, Fourth Brigade, South Carolina Militia

Wagener's Artillery, three German companies
  Captain Bachman's Battery, all Germans
  Light Battery A, Captain F. W. Wagener
  Light Battery B, Captain F. Melchers

TENNESSEE

Second Tennessee Regiment, almost solidly Irish

Tenth Tennessee Regiment, almost solidly Irish

Company I, Fifteenth Tennessee (ex-Memphis militia company), mixed aliens

Company I, Twenty-first Tennessee (later Co. B, Fifth Confederate Tennessee), Colonel Frazier, Irish almost entirely

Garde Française, of Memphis, French (not certain that it entered service)

One German company from Nashville

One Irish company from Nashville under Captain St. Clair Morgan

TEXAS

Battalion of Bürgerwehr, Home Defense under Oswald and Bruch, German

Bastilla's company, Mexican

Benavides' Regiment of Cavalry, Mexican

Captain Pattina's company, Mexican

Captain Redwood's company, Rio Grande Regiment, mixed, Irish in majority

Co. F, First Texas Heavy Artillery, Davis Guards, Irish

Co. E, First Texas Cavalry, Captain Franz von d. Stucken, mostly German

Co. F, Second Texas, partly German (only forty men)

Third Texas Cavalry, Colonel Buchel, mixed with many Germans and Mexicans

    Seven companies from New Braunfels, German

    Captain Buquor's company, Mexican with some other foreigners

    Captain Marmion's company, Mexican with other foreigners, artillery

    Three companies on the Rio Grande River for four months' service, Mexican

    Company C, Captain F. J. Parker's company, Mexican except three

Co. C, Fourth Texas Cavalry, Tom Greene's brigade, German except two

Co. E, Fifth Texas, Mounted Volunteers, Tom Greene's brigade, German

Co. B, Eighth Texas, mostly German, all but fourteen foreign, Terry's Texas Rangers

Co. C, Eighth Texas Infantry, Captain Penaloza, Mexican (fifty-two men)

Co. F, Eighth Texas Cavalry, Terry's Texas Rangers, Captain Louis Ströbel, German

Galveston Davis Artillery, mostly German

Galveston Rangers, Captain Behrman, German

Home Defense Company at Brownsville, under Captain José Maria Cobos

Home Guard, Brownsville, many Mexicans

Home Guards, Precinct No. 2, Refugio County, Jeff Davis Home Guards, Mexicans probably, under Captain Aldrate

Island City Schützen, Captain Müller, at Galveston

Local Defense, Precinct No. 3, Mason County, solidly German (twenty-six men)

Long Prairie Company, Fayette County, German

Captain James Morgan's Company, Coast Defense, mixed

Twenty-fifth Texas Regiment, many Germans (allowed itself to be captured by General Osterhaus)

Turnverein Artillery Company of Houston, Captain E. B. H. Schneider, stationed on Galveston Island, German

Waul's legion

Co. under Captain Nathusius, German, 129 men from Houston

Co. under Captain Robert Voigt, German, 120 men

Co. under H. Wickeland, German, 92 men

Co. A under Captain Bolling, mixed, chiefly German

Co. under Captain Podewill, German, from Comal County

One Company from Colorado County, German

Three companies from Fredericksburg and vicinity

One under Captain Döring of Cherry Springs, German

One under Captain E. Krauskopf, German

One under Captain William Warmut, German (about 100 men)

One Company from La Grange County, mixed

One Polish Company from near Panna Maria, Texas

One small company from San Patricio, Terry's rangers, Irish

VIRGINIA

Artillery Regiment, under Colonel Rains, partly German, from Richmond

Foreign Legion in Richmond, almost wholly British under Captain
Buxton

German Sanitary Corps, Captain John A. Herbig

Irish Battalion, First Virginia, Irish except Company A which was
German

Co. H, Eleventh Virginia, Lynchburg, many Irish

Co. G, Seventeenth Virginia, Alexandria, Irish

Co. I, Seventeenth Virginia, Alexandria, Irish

Nineteenth Virginia Reserves, Home Defense, mostly foreigners
from workshops

One company of Italians under Captain Alfred Pico

Marion Rifles, German

RECRUITED FROM UNITED STATES PRISONERS

Brooke's Foreign Battalion

Tucker's regiment

APPENDIX V

Co. A, 10 Alabama Infantry

Co. D, 10 Alabama—mostly farmers near Alexandria, Sulphur Springs, Polksville

Co. F, 10 Alabama—mostly farmers near Crosswell

Co. I, 10 Alabama

Co. K, 10 Alabama—mostly farmers, Fort William Rifles near Fayetteville

Co. H, 11 Alabama—mostly farmers around Carrollton

Co. C, 13 Alabama

Co. D, 13 Alabama

Co. G, 13 Alabama—mostly farmers around Greenville

Co. H, 13 Alabama—mostly farmers from Coosa County

Co. D, 15 Alabama, Fort Bowder, from Barton County

Co. E, 15 Alabama, Dale County Beauregards

Co. F, 15 Alabama—nativity not stated for last twenty-two members

Co. H, 15 Alabama—Glennville Guards

Co. L, 15 Alabama—Pike Sharpshooters, of Pike County

Co. A, 18 Alabama—Coffee, Talladego, Jefferson counties, etc.

Co. B or G, 31 Alabama (Descriptive Roll not clear)

Co. A, 31 Alabama

Co. K, 31 Alabama

Co. C, 36 Alabama

Co. A, 41 Alabama

Co. F, 41 Alabama

Co. G, 41 Alabama

Co. B, 43 Alabama

Co. K, 43 Alabama

Co. B, 44 Alabama, farmers from around Scottsville

Co. F, 44 Alabama, chiefly farmers of Randolph County

Co. G, 44 Alabama, chiefly farmers of Randolph County

Co. H, 44 Alabama, chiefly farmers of Randolph County

Co. I, 44 Alabama, chiefly farmers of Randolph County

Co. K, 44 Alabama, chiefly farmers of Randolph County
Co. A, 46 Alabama, largely farmers
Co. F, 47 Alabama, largely farmers
Co. G, 47 Alabama, largely farmers
Co. A, 48 Alabama, largely farmers near Bloutsville
Co. B, 48 Alabama, largely farmers near Gadsden, etc.
Co. C, 48 Alabama
Co. D, 48 Alabama
Co. E, 48 Alabama
Co. F, 48 Alabama
Co. I, 48 Alabama, chiefly farmers
Co. K, 48 Alabama, almost all farmers
Co. A, 59 Alabama
Co. A, 60 Alabama
Co. B, 60 Alabama, farmers
Co. C, 60 Alabama, farmers of Ranch, Oakley, etc.
Co. E, 60 Alabama, many farmers near Carstins Bridge and neighborhood
Co. G, 60 Alabama, almost all farmers near China Grove, etc.
Co. I, 60 Alabama, chiefly farmers near Fort Deposit
Co. C, 4 Alabama, Infantry, Magnolia Cadets

BIBLIOGRAPHY
AND
INDEX

PRIMARY

MANUSCRIPTS

In the Confederate Archives, War Department
Now transferred to the National Archives Building
Lists and Rolls

Descriptive Lists and Muster Rolls of the Various Companies of the Confederate Armies

Variously named, Descriptive List and Muster Roll, Muster and Descriptive Roll, Original Muster and Descriptive Roll, Muster Roll, Historic Roll, or Record

Descriptive List and Accounts of Pay and Clothing

Descriptive List of Deserters from the Alexandria Light Artillery

Descriptive List of Deserters from Companies A, C, F, Fifty-ninth Virginia

Descriptive List of the Mobile Home Guards

Descriptive List of Officers of the Army of the West

Descriptive List of the Pioneer Corps, First Brigade, First Division, First Corps, Army of the Mississippi

Descriptive Roll of Horses, Arms, Equipment for the Twenty-second Texas Cavalry

Discharges—Official of Individual Soldiers

Discharges—of the Mounted Reserves

Record of Company B, Eighth Texas (loaned by Mr. Lichtenstein of Corpus Christi, Texas, to the Texas Archives)

Records of Parole

Individual Files of Confederate Officers and Soldiers

Executive and Legislative Manuscripts

House of Representatives, Bills, Resolutions, etc.

Journal of the Executive of Virginia

Letters Received, by the War Department

Letters and Telegrams Sent, A and C. G. O., Vol. XLIII, August 29-December 31, 1864

Miscellaneous Letters to Officers and Members of Congress

Pickett Papers

    Domestic Letters. Package K, Manuscript Division, Library of Congress, Miscellaneous letters from Hotze, De Leon, Helm, and Avengo to the State Department

    Letters of Richard Fitzpatrick to the Secretary of State

    Letters of J. A. Quintero to Secretary of State, June 1, 1861-December 7, 1864

MANUSCRIPTS IN STATE ARCHIVES

Alabama

    Beat Rolls, Muster and Descriptive Rolls, Alabama Military Archives

    Company Book, of Company C, Forty-fifth Alabama

    Letter by John McArthur to Thos. M. Owen, June 24, 1909

    Letter by John B. Rabby to Thos. M. Owen, September 30, 1910

    Letter from Judge P. Williams to T. Owen, 1911

    List of Employees on the Alabama and Florida Railroad

    Record, Military Roll of the Alabama Companies

    Report to United Daughters of the Confederacy of Mobile on Mobile companies, made December, 1909, a manuscript preserved in the Alabama Military Archives

    Scrap Book of Barbour County Chapter, United Daughters of the Confederacy

Georgia

    Confederate Discharges, Georgia Archives

    Cunningham, Cornelia. Biographical Questionnaire

    Governor's Letter Books, 1861-1865. Georgia Archives

Louisiana

    Record, Military Rolls of the Louisiana Companies. Preserved in the Memorial Hall of the United Daughters of the Confederacy, New Orleans, Louisiana. Here are hundreds of rolls, by far the best rolls for Louisiana companies, though some 165 rolls were never recovered from Mr. Booth after he had compiled his record

Mississippi

    Executive Letter Book. Preserved in the Mississippi Archives

    Governor's Correspondence. Preserved in the Mississippi Archives

North Carolina

    Original Muster and Descriptive Rolls are preserved in the Confederate Archives in Washington and are complete

    Petition for Henry A. Gunther, Letter File, Military Board, November 17, 1861-September, 1862. North Carolina Historical Commission

Texas

Many Muster Rolls and Descriptive Lists and Muster Rolls are to be found in the Texas Archives, Texas State Library, copies of which do not exist in Washington

Adjutant General's Correspondence

Adjutant General's Office, Papers

Descriptive List and Muster Rolls

G. O. Correspondence

Governor's Letters, Edward Clark, March-December, 1861

Governor's Letters, Lubbock Papers

Photostat of the Muster Roll of Van Stucken's Company, preserved in the Fredericksburg Museum, Fredericksburg, Texas

Roll about Terry's Texas Rangers, compiled by J. M. Claiborne with remarks, apparently for a reunion in Galveston on February 20, 1882

Virginia

Unsigned Letter by a Confederate Surgeon's wife to her mother, Confederate Museum, Richmond

In Private Collections

Manuscripts in the S. V. Pfeuffer Collection of Texicana

Bechem's Letter of Refusal of a Generalship

Commission to Captain John Heilman as Captain of Beat No. 3, Comal County, State Troops

Lists of Exempts in Comal District

Manuscript in the private library of Alex Brinkman, Comfort, Texas

Letters between Alex and Charles Brinkman

PRINTED PUBLIC DOCUMENTS

Confederate and Union

Congressional Reports on the Tochman Case

Report of the Committee on Claims, January 15, 1864, House of Representatives, C. S. A. Richmond, 1864

Report of the Committee on Foreign Affairs, House of Representatives, C. S. A. Richmond, 1863(?)

Report of the Committee on Military Affairs on the Memorial of Major Gaspar Tochman, April, 1863, House of Representatives, C. S. A. Richmond, 1863

Hansard, Thomas Curson (ed.). *Parliamentary Debates*. Third Series. London, 1830-1891

Journal of the House of Representatives of the Confederate States of America

Journal of the Senate of the Confederate States of America

These two journals are printed as *Senate Executive Documents,* 58 Congress, 2 Sess., Vol. XXV-XXXI, No. 234. 7 vols. Washington, 1904-1905

Kennedy, J. C. C. (ed.). *The Eighth Census of the United States, Agriculture,* 1860. Washington, 1864

———. *The Eighth Census of the United States. Statistics of the Population of the United States,* 1860. Washington, 1864

Matthews, J. M. (ed.). *Statutes at Large of the Provisional Government of the Confederate States of America from February 8, 1861, to its termination, February 18, 1862.* Richmond, 1864

Moore, John Bassett. *Digest of International Law.* 8 vols. Washington, 1906

Official Record of the Union and Confederate Navies of the War of the Rebellion. 31 vols. Washington, 1894-1927

Parliamentary Papers, 1864. London, 1864

"Proceedings of the First Confederate Congress," *Southern Historical Society Papers,* Vols. XLIV-XLVII. Richmond, 1923-1930

Register of Officers of the Confederate States Navy, 1861-1865. Compiled by the Office of Naval Records and Library. Washington, 1931

Richardson, James D. *Compilations of Messages and Papers of the Confederacy including Diplomatic Correspondence, 1861-65.* 2 vols. Nashville, 1905.

Separate Acts of the Regular Congress of the Confederate States of America to the Fall of the Government

The War of the Rebellion: A Compilation of the Official Records of the Union and Confederate Armies. 130 vols. Washington, 1880-1901.

THE VARIOUS CONFEDERATE STATES

Candler, Allen D. (ed.). *The Confederate Records of the State of Georgia.* Atlanta, 1909-1910

Digest of the General Statute Law of the State of Texas. Austin, 1859

Ex Parte Henry Spinchen. [n. p.], [n. d.]. A decision by Judge Magrath of the Confederate District Court in South Carolina. A pamphlet in the Confederate Archives, War Department

Hilgard, E. W. "Memoranda Concerning the Geological Survey," *Journal of the Senate of the State of Mississippi,* Called Session, 1862. Appendix

"Inaugural Address of Governor Smith," *Virginia Documents,* 1863-1864

"Inaugural Address of Governor Thomas H. Watts," December 1, 1863. Montgomery, 1863. A pamphlet preserved in the Alabama Military Archives

Journal of Public and Secret Proceedings of the Convention of the People of Georgia held in Milledgeville and Savannah in 1861. Milledgeville, Georgia, 1861

Journal of the House of Representatives of Louisiana, Twenty-seventh Legislature, Extra Session, Opelousas, December 15, 1863

Journal of the Senate of Georgia, Annual Session, 1862-1863

Journal of the Senate of the State of Mississippi, Called Session, 1862. Jackson, 1863

Revised Statutes of Louisiana. New Orleans, 1856

Session Laws of Georgia, 1864

Session Laws of Louisiana, December, 1862-January, 1863

Session Laws of Mississippi, November, 1863; Called Session, August, 1864

Session Laws of North Carolina, Called Session, 1863

Session Laws of South Carolina, 1839

Session Laws of Tennessee, October, 1861-1862

Session Laws of Texas, November, 1861-January, 1862; February-March, 1863

Session Laws of Virginia, 1861-1862

South Carolina Statutes at Large, Vol. XIII

Virginia Documents, 1863-1864

NEWSPAPERS

AMERICAN

(Austin) *Evening News.* January, 1895

Baltimore American. 1910

(Baltimore) *Sun, The.* September, 1911; October, 1934

Charleston Daily Courier. 1863-65

(Charleston) *Die Deutsche Zeitung.* November, 1860-February, 1861; November, 1906; Jubilee Edition, November 22, 1913

Charleston Mercury, The. November, 1860-July, 1864

(Galesburg, Ill.) *Hemlandet.* August, 1855-July, 1866. After 1858, Chicago

(Galveston) *Union.* December, 1860-1864, scattered copies

(Houston) *Der Texas Demokrat.* 1861- April, 1863

(Houston) *Tri-Weekly Telegraph.* January, 1861

(La Grange, Texas) *True Issue, The.* October, 1861, October, 1864

Louisiana Staatszeitung (New Orleans). October, 1861-October, 1864

(Louisville) *Evening Post, The.* May, 1900

(Memphis) *Commercial Appeal, The.* March, 1905

Mobile Daily Advertiser and Register, The. November, 1860-April, 1861

Mobile News Item. April, 1910

Montgomery (Alabama) *Daily Advertiser.* December, 1860, April, 1861, June, 1864. Broken files. September 29, 1935

Montgomery *Daily Mail.* April, 1861

(Montgomery) *Daily Post, The.* February, 1861-May, 1861

Neu Braunfelser Zeitung. New Braunfels, Texas. 1860-1865

L'Abeille de la Nouvelle Orleans. November, 1860-1863

New Orleans Commercial Bulletin. February-May, 1863

(New Orleans) *Daily Crescent.* May, 1862

(New Orleans) *Daily Picayune, The.* July, 1861-March, 1862

(New Orleans) *Daily True Delta, The.* March, 1860-October, 1861

(New Orleans) *Tägliche Deutsche Zeitung.* November, 1860-June, 1864

New York Times, The. October, 1861-January, 1864, June, 1921

Richmonder Anzeiger. November, 1860-1864. (In the private possession of Mr. August Dietz, Richmond, Virginia.)

Richmond *Dispatch.* June, 1861-April, 1864

Daily Richmond Enquirer, The. March, 1863-April, 1864

Daily Richmond Examiner. November, 1861-March, 1864

(Richmond) *Record.* July, 1863

Daily Richmond Whig. (The exact title varies during the war.) June, 1861-1864

(San Antonio) *Der Texas Demokrat.* December, 1862-March, 1863

(San Antonio) *Texas Staats Zeitung.* December, 1860-January, 1861

Savannah Republican, The. (Exact title varies through the years of the war.) 1862-July, 1863

(Seguin, Texas) *Seguin Mercury, The.* 1860-61

(Spartanburg, South Carolina) *Carolina Spartan.* January, 1860-1863

(Washington) *Daily National Intelligencer.* July, 1861

(Washington, D. C.) *National Republican.* September, 1861. (Title varies during the war years.)

Washington Post, The. March, 1901, January, 1928

BRITISH

Illustrated London News. April, 1864

(London) *Index, The.* March-April, 1863

(London) *Times, The.* June-August, 1861; August, 1862; February, 1863-January, 1864

Manchester Guardian, The. December, 1889

NON-OFFICIAL COLLECTIONS AND COMPILATIONS

Appleton's *The American Annual Cyclopaedia and Register of Important Events,* for the years 1861-1865. (W. T. Tenney, ed.) New York, 1862-1866

Bartlett, Napier. *Military Record of Louisiana.* New Orleans, 1875. (This consists chiefly of "A Soldier's Story of the War," but also of other papers)

Battles and Leaders of the Civil War; being for the most part contributions by Union and Confederate officers. Based upon "The Century War Series." 4 vols. Eds., Robert Underwood Johnson and Clarence Clough Buel. New York, 1887-1888

Biographical and Historical Memoirs of Louisiana. 2 vols. Chicago, 1892

Biographical Encyclopedia of Texas. New York, 1880

Brooks, U. R. (ed.). *Stories of the Confederacy.* Columbia, South Carolina, 1912. (A compilation of many tales by many authors)

Catholic Encyclopedia, The. 17 vols. New York, 1907-1922

Confederate Veterans' Association of Fulton County, Georgia. (Robert L. Rodgers, comp.). Atlanta, Ga., 1890

Dictionary of American Biography (Allen Johnson and Dumas Malone, eds.). 20 vols. New York, 1928-1937

Estes, Claud. *List of Field Officers, Regiments and Battalions in the Confederate States Army, 1861-1865.* Macon, Georgia, 1912

Evans, Clement A. *Confederate Military History.* 12 vols. Atlanta, 1899

Fitch, John. *Annals of the Army of the Cumberland.* Philadelphia, 1864

Germain, Dom Aidan Henry. *Catholic Military and Naval Chaplains. 1776-1917.* Washington, 1929. (A brief abstract has been printed in *The Catholic Historical Review,* N. S., IX, 171-178)

Hamphill, James C. (ed.). *Men of Mark in South Carolina.* Washington, 1907-1909

Historical Catalog of the Officers and Alumni of the University of Alabama, 1821-1870. Tuscaloosa, 1870

Johnson, Allen, and Malone, Dumas. See *Dictionary of American Biography*

Johnson, R. U., and Buel, C. C. See *Battles and Leaders of the Civil War*

Johnson, Sid. *Texans Who Wore the Gray.* Tyler(?), Texas, 1907. (Although this is Vol. I, there seems to be no record of another volume)

La Bree, Benjamin. *Camp Fires of the Confederacy*. Louisville, 1898. (This collection of short stories and anecdotes contains many accounts signed by noted officers of the southern army)

Mathes, James Harvey. *The Old Guard in Gray*. Memphis, 1897. (The editor and author secured much data orally from participants in the war)

Mickle, William E. (ed.). *Well-Known Confederate Veterans and Their War Records*. New Orleans, 1907

Moore, Frank (ed.). *The Rebellion Record: A Diary of American Events, with Documents, Narratives, Illustrative Incidents, Poetry, etc.* 11 vols. New York, 1861-1868. (Still useful though the collections of official reports have been superseded by the fuller and more accurate publications of the government)

Rodenbough, T. Francis. *From Everglade to Cañon with the Second Dragoons*. New York, 1875. (This work is a compilation in part of excerpts, primary chiefly, but is secondary for the portion which treats of the early history of the second regiment)

Rodgers, Robert L. *History of Confederate Veterans Association, Fulton County, Georgia*. Atlanta, 1890

Miss Rutherford's Scrap Book [later *Historical Notes*]; *valuable information*. 10 numbers annually. Athens, Georgia, 1923—

South in the Building of the Nation, The. 12 vols. Richmond, 1909

Sprunt, James. *Chronicles of the Cape Fear River*. Raleigh, North Carolina, 1914. (Sprunt defies exact classification as he combines personal recollections with copious excerpts from other primary sources and with secondary material)

Thompson, Edwin Porter. *History of the First Kentucky Brigade*. Cincinnati, 1868

——. *History of the Orphan Brigade*. Louisville, 1898. (The two works by Thompson have been compiled from records submitted by the soldiers themselves and so classify as sources for those portions of the books)

Victor, Orville J. (ed.). *Incidents and Anecdotes of the War*. New York, 1862

Yeary, Mamie (ed.). *Reminiscences of the Boys in Gray, 1861-1865*. Dallas, Texas, 1912

MILITARY AUTOBIOGRAPHIES AND REMINISCENCES

Adams, Francis Colburn. *The Story of a Trooper*. New York, 1865

Austin, J. P. *The Blue and the Gray*. Atlanta, 1899

Baker, Henry H. *A Reminiscent Story of the Great Civil War.* New Orleans, 1911

Baker, W. W. *Memoirs of Service with John Yates Beall.* Richmond, 1910

Barbière, Joe. *Scraps from the Prison Table at Camp Chase and Johnson's Island.* Doylestown, Pa., 1868

Baruch, Simon. *Reminiscences of a Confederate Surgeon.* New York(?), 1915

Battle-fields of the South. 2 vols. London, 1863. (This work is signed "By an English Combatant" [T. E. C.], and it appears that he was a lieutenant of artillery on the field staff)

Bevier, R. S. *History of the First and Second Missouri Confederate Brigades.* St. Louis, 1879

Blake, Henry N. *Three Years in the Army of the Potomac.* Boston, 1865

Booth, George Wilson. *Personal Reminiscences of a Maryland Soldier in the War between the States.* Baltimore, 1898

Bowman, T. H. *Reminiscences of an Ex-Confederate Soldier or Forty Years on Crutches.* Austin, 1904

Brown, Philip Francis. *Reminiscences of the War of 1861-1865.* Roanoke, Virginia, 1912

Browne, Junius Henri. *Four Years in Secessia; adventures within and beyond the Union Lines.* Hartford, 1865

Buck, Irving A. *Cleburne and his Command.* New York, 1908

Carter, Howell. *A Cavalryman's Reminiscences of the Civil War.* New Orleans, 1908(?)

Chapman, Robert D. *A Georgia Soldier in the Civil War, 1861-1865.* Houston, [n. d.]

Clark, George. *A Glance Backward; or Some Events in the past History of my Life.* Houston, 1920

Clark, Walter Augustus. *Under the Stars and Bars; or Memoirs of four years service with the Oglethorpes of Augusta, Georgia.* August, 1900

Collins, R. M. *Chapters from the Unwritten History of the War Between the States; or The Incidents in the Life of a Confederate Soldier in camp, on the march, in the great battles, and in prison.* St. Louis, 1893

Crawford, J. Marshall. *Mosby and his Men: A Record of the Adventures of that Renowned Partisan Ranger, John S. Mosby.* New York, 1867

Dame, William Meade. *From the Rapidan to Richmond and the Spott-sylvania Campaign.* Baltimore, 1920

Daniel, Ferdinand Eugene. *Recollections of a Rebel Surgeon.* Austin, Texas, 1899

Davis, Nicholas A. *The Campaign from Texas to Maryland.* Richmond, 1863

Dawson, Francis W. *Reminiscences of Confederate Service.* Charleston, 1882

Duke, Basil W. *Reminiscences of General Basil W. Duke, C. S. A.* Garden City, 1911

Dunlop, William S. *Lee's Sharpshooters or the Forefront of Battle.* Little Rock, 1899

Ellis, Thomas T. *Leaves from the Diary of An Army Surgeon, or Incidents of field, camp, and hospital life.* New York, 1863

Estvàn, Bela. *War Pictures from the South.* 2 vols. London, 1863

Folsom, James Madison. *Heroes and Martyrs of Georgia.* Macon, Ga., 1864

Fontaine, Lamar. *My Life and My Lectures.* New York and Washington, 1908

Fremantle, Colonel Arthur James. *Three Months in the Southern States, April-June, 1863.* Mobile, 1864

French, Samuel Gibbs. *Two Wars: an Autobiography of General Samuel G. French.* Nashville, 1901

Gilmore, Harry. *Four Years in the Saddle.* New York, 1866

Gordon, George H. *A War Diary of Events in the War of the Great Rebellion, 1863-1865.* Boston, 1882

Gordon, John Brown. *Reminiscences of the Civil War.* New York, 1903

Hall, Winchester H. *The Story of the 26th Louisiana Infantry in the Service of the Confederacy.* [n. p.], 1890(?)

Hancock, Richard. *Hancock's Diary: or, a History of the Second Tennessee Confederate Cavalry.* 2 vols. Nashville, 1887

Hanson, G. A. *Minor Incidents of the Late War.* Bartow (Fla.), 1887

Harris, William C. *Prison Life in the Tobacco Warehouse at Richmond.* Philadelphia, 1862

Haywood, Phil D. *The Cruise of the Alabama.* Boston and New York, 1886. (This is the account of one of the crew)

Hepworth, George Hughes. *The Whip, Hoe, and Sword; in the Gulf Department in '63.* Boston, 1864

Hermann, Isaac H. *Memoirs of a Veteran.* Atlanta, 1911

Hood, John Bell. *Advance and Retreat.* New Orleans, 1880

Humphreys, David. *Heroes and Spies of the Civil War.* New York and Washington, 1903

Hunter, Alexander. *Johnny Reb and Billy Yank.* New York and Washington, 1905

Hyde, Solon. *A Captive of War.* New York, 1900

Irby, Richard. *Historical Sketch of the Nottoway Grays, afterwards Company G, Eighteenth Virginia Regiment, Army of Northern Virginia.* Richmond, 1878

Izlar, William Valmore. *A Sketch of the War Record of the Edisto Rifles, 1861-1865.* Columbia, S. C., 1914

Johnson, John. *The Defense of Charleston Harbor.* Charleston, 1890

Joinville, François Ferdinand Philippe Louis Marie d'Orléans, Prince de. *The Army of the Potomac.* New York, 1863

Jones, Buehring. *The Sunny Land.* Baltimore, 1868. (Valuable for the appendices)

Jones, Charles C. *The Siege of Savannah in December, 1864, and the Confederate Operations in Georgia and the Third Military District of South Carolina, during Sherman's March from Atlanta to the Sea.* Albany, 1874

Jones, Charles C., Jr. *Historical Sketch of the Chatham Artillery during the Confederate Struggle for Independence.* Albany, 1867

Kell, John McIntosh. *Recollections of a Naval Life.* Washington, 1900. (Kell was an executive officer on the *Sumter* and on the *Alabama*)

Lee, Robert E. *Recollections and Letters of General Robert E. Lee.* New York, 1924

Löhr, Charles T. *War History of the Old First Virginia Infantry Regiment.* Richmond, 1884

McClendon, W. A. *Recollections of War Times by an Old Veteran.* Montgomery, Alabama, 1909

McKim, Randolph Harrison. *A Soldier's Recollections; leaves from the diary of a Young Confederate.* New York, 1910

McMorries, Edward Young. *History of the First Regiment, Alabama Volunteer Infantry, C. S. A.* Montgomery, 1904

McMurray, William J. *History of the Twentieth Tennessee Regiment Volunteer Infantry, C. S. A.* Nashville, 1904

Marks, James J. *The Peninsular Campaign in Virginia or Incidents and Scenes on the Battlefields and in Richmond.* Philadelphia, 1864

Monteiro, A. *War Reminiscences.* Richmond, 1890. (This was written by the surgeon of Mosby's command)

Moore, Edward A. *The Story of a Cannoneer under Stonewall Jackson.* New York, 1910

Morford, Henry. *Red Tape or Pigeon-Hole Generals as seen from the Ranks during a Campaign in the Army of the Potomac.* New York, 1864

Morgan, James Morris. *Recollections of a Rebel Reefer.* Boston and New York, 1917

Morgan, William H. *Personal Reminiscences of the War of 1861-65.* Lynchburg, 1911

Mosby, J. S. *Mosby's War Reminiscences and Stuart's Cavalry Campaigns.* New York, 1887

Mosby, John S. (Charles Wells Russell, ed.). *The Memoirs of Colonel John S. Mosby.* Boston, 1917

Mosgrove, George Dallas. *Kentucky Cavaliers in Dixie.* Louisville, Kentucky, 1895

Munson, John William. *Reminiscences of a Mosby Guerilla.* New York, 1906

Nisbet, James Cooper. *Four Years on the Firing Line.* Chattanooga, 1914

Noll (ed.). *Doctor Quintard, Chaplain C. S. A. and Second Bishop of Tennessee.* Sewanee, Tennessee, 1905. (The work is edited by the Reverend Arthur Howard Noll, who contributes also an introductory chapter on Dr. Quintard)

Owen, William Miller. *In Camp and Battle with the Washington Artillery.* Boston, 1885

Palmer, Donald. *Four Weeks in the Rebel Army.* New London, Connecticut, 1865

Papers of Randolph Abbott Shotwell. 2 vols. Raleigh, 1929. (J. G. de R. Hamilton, ed.)

Park, Robert Emory. *Sketch of the Twelfth Alabama Infantry of Battle's Brigade, Rode's Division, Early's Corps, of the Army of Northern Virgina.* Richmond, 1906

Parker, William Harwar. *Recollections of a Naval Officer.* New York, 1883

Porter, John W. H. *A Record of Events in Norfolk County, Virginia from April 19th, 1861 to May 10, 1862.* Portsmouth, Virginia, 1892. (Largely a compilation of names)

Rose, Victor M. *Ross' Texas Brigade.* Louisville, 1881

Ross, Fitzgerald. *A Visit to the Cities and Camps of the Confederate States.* Edinburgh and London, 1865. (This first appeared in *Blackwood's Edinburgh Magazine*, Vols. XCVI and XCVII, 1864-1865)

Scheibert, Justus. *Sieben Monate in den Rebellen-Staaten während des nordamerikanischen Krieges 1863.* Stettin, 1868

Semmes, Raphael. *Memoirs of Service Afloat, during the War between the States.* London, 1869

Shotwell Papers. See *Papers of Randolph Abbott Shotwell*

Spencer, Ambrose S. *A Narrative of Andersonville.* New York, 1866

Stevenson, W. G. *Thirteen Months in the Rebel Army.* New York, 1864

Stiles, Robert. *Four Years under Marse Robert.* New York and Washington, 1903

Stone, Henry Lane. *Morgan's Men, A Narrative of Personal Experiences.* Louisville, 1919

Taylor, Richard. *Destruction and Reconstruction.* New York, 1883

Tunnard, William H. *A Southern Record, The History of the Third Regiment Louisiana Infantry.* Baton Rouge, 1866

Von Achten der Letzte. *Amerikanische Kriegsbilder aus der Südarmee des Generals Robert E. Lee.* Wiesbaden, 1771

Von Borcke, Heros. *Memoirs of the Confederate War for Independence.* 2 vols. New York, 1938

————. *Zwei Jahre im Sattel und am Feinde.* Berlin, 1898. (This book appeared first in English and was then put into German)

————, und Scheibert, Justus. *Die grosse Reiterschlacht bei Brandy Station.* Berlin, 1893

Watson, William. *Life in the Confederate Army.* New York, 1888

Welch, Spencer Glasgow. *A Confederate Surgeon's Letters to his Wife.* New York and Washington, 1911

White, William S. "A Diary of the War," *Contributions to a History of the Richmond Howitzer Battalion.* 4 vols. Richmond, 1883

Williams, R. H. *With the Border Ruffians.* New York, 1907

Wise, George. *History of the Seventeenth Virginia Infantry, C. S. A.* Baltimore, 1870

Wise, Jennings C. *The Long Arm of Lee; or, The History of the Artillery of the Army of Northern Virginia.* 2 vols. Lynchburg, 1915. (Largely secondary)

Wolseley, Garnet Joseph. *The Story of a Soldier's Life.* 2 vols. Westminster, 1903

Worsham, John H. *One of Jackson's Foot Cavalry.* New York, 1912

Worthington, C. J. (ed.). *The Woman in Battle.* Hartford, 1876. (The portion which treats of Madame Loretta Velazquez is a record of her life as given by Madame Velazquez herself. Excerpts from the same record appear in Dowie, Ménie M. (ed.). *Women Adventurers.* London, 1893)

REMINISCENCES AND ACCOUNTS OF CIVILIANS

Andrews, Eliza Frances. *The War-Time Journal of a Georgia Girl.* New York, 1908

Andrews, (Mrs.) Marietta (Minnigerode). *Scraps of Paper.* New York, 1929

Baker, La Fayette C. *Spies, Traitors, and Conspirators of the Late Civil War.* Philadelphia, 1894

Balme, Joshua. *Synopsis of the American War.* London, 1865

Beers, Mrs. Fannie A. *Memories. A Record of Personal experiences and adventures during four years of war.* Philadelphia, 1891

Bigelow, John. *Retrospections of an Active Life.* 5 vols. New York, 1909-13

Blackford, (Mrs.) Susan Leigh (Colston). *Memoirs of Life in and out of the army of Virginia during the War between the States.* Lynchburg, 1894-1896

Bokum, Hermann. *Wanderings North and South.* Philadelphia, 1864

Botts, John M. *The Great Rebellion: Its secret history, Rise, Progress and Disastrous Failure.* New York, 1866

Boyd, Belle. *Belle Boyd in Camp and Prison.* New York, 1865

Bracht, Viktor. *Texas in 1848.* San Antonio, Texas, 1931. (Translated from the German by Charles F. Schmidt. The preface gives biographical sketches of Viktor Bracht and Dr. Felix Bracht)

Branch, (Mrs.) Mary Polk. *Memoirs of a Southern Woman "Within the Lines."* Chicago, 1912

Bulloch, James D. *The Secret Service of the Confederate States in Europe.* 2 vols. New York, 1884

Bunn, H. G. *See* Nash, Charles E.

Collins, Elizabeth. *Memories of the Southern States.* Taunton, England, 1865

Conrad, August. *Schatten und Lichtblicke aus dem amerikanischen Leben während des Secessions-Krieges.* Hannover, 1879

Cook, Joel. *The Siege of Richmond.* Philadelphia, 1862. (Cook was a correspondent of the Philadelphia Press)

Corsan, W. C. *Two Months in the Confederate States; including a Visit to New Orleans under the domination of General Butler.* London, 1863

Crumpton, W. B. *A Book of Memories. 1842-1920.* Montgomery, 1921

Cumming, Kate. *A Journal of Hospital Life in the Confederate Army of Tennessee, from the Battle of Shiloh to the end of the War.* Louisville, 1886

Darling, (Mrs.) Flora Adams. *Mrs. Darling's Letters or Memories of the Civil War.* New York, 1883

Dawson, Sarah M. *A Confederate Girl's Diary.* Boston and New York, 1913

Day, Samuel Phillips. *Down South; or An Englishman's Experiences at the Seat of the American War.* 2 vols. London, 1862. (Day was a special correspondent of the London *Morning Herald*)

De Leon, Thomas Cooper. *Belles, Beaux and Brains of the 60's.* New York, 1907

———. *Four Years in Rebel Capitals: An Inside View of Life in the Southern Confederacy, from Birth to Death.* Mobile, 1890

Domenech, Emmanuel Henri. *Journal d'un Missionnaire au Texas et au Mexique.* London, 1858. (A translation of this work exists under the title, *Missionary Adventures in Texas and Mexico.* London, 1858)

Fearn, (Mrs.) Frances H. *Diary of a Refugee.* New York, 1910

→ Foote, Henry Stuart. *War of the Rebellion; or Scylla and Charybdis.* New York, 1866

Freese, Jacob R. *Secrets of the Late Rebellion.* Philadelphia, 1882

Gay, Mary A. H. *Life in Dixie during the War.* Atlanta, Ga., 1901

Girard, Charles Frédéric. *Les Etats Confédérés d'Amérique, Visité en 1863.* Paris, 1864

Harrison, (Mrs.) Constance Cary. *Recollections Grave and Gay.* New York, 1911

Hobart-Hampden, Augustus Charles. *Sketches from My Life.* New York, 1887. (He is better known as Hobart Pasha)

Hohenwart, Ernst H. *Land und Leute in den Vereinigten Staaten.* Leipzig, 1886

Hopley, Catherine C. *Life in the South; from the Commencement of the War.* 2 vols. London, 1863. (This book presents a picture of the Confederacy by a blockaded British subject. The introduction is signed S. L. J. [Sarah L. Jones], a pseudonym)

Houghton, W. R. and M. B. *Two Boys in the Civil War and After.* Montgomery, Alabama, 1912

Jackson, George. *Sixty Years in Texas.* Dallas, 1908

→ Jones, John B. *A Rebel War Clerk's Diary at the Confederate States Capital.* 2 vols. Philadelphia, 1866

Kapp, Frederick. *Aus und Über Amerika. Thatsachen und Erlebnisse.* 2 vols. Berlin, 1876. (The portion which deals with Texas contains primary material)

Kent, (Mrs.) E. C. *Four Years in Secessia.* Buffalo, 1864

Lawrence, George Alfred. *Border and Bastille.* New York, 1863

Le Grand, J. *The Journal of Julia Le Grand. New Orleans, 1862-1863.* Richmond, 1911. (By Julia Ellen [Le Grand] Waitz)

Linn, John Joseph. *Reminiscences of Fifty Years in Texas.* New York, 1883

Logan, Kate Virginia (Cox). *My Confederate Girlhood; the Memoirs of Kate Virginia Cox Logan.* Richmond, 1932

Lubbock, Francis Richard. *Six Decades in Texas or Memoirs.* Austin, 1900

Maffitt, Emma Martin. *The Life and Services of John Newland Maffitt.* New York and Washington, 1906

Malet, William Wyndham. *An Errand to the South in the Summer of 1862.* London, 1863

Maris, Martin. *Souvenirs d'Amérique. Relations d'un Voyage au Texas et en Haiti.* Bruxelles, 1863. (Valuable as presenting aspects of foreign settlement, even though the visit was made considerably before the war)

Merrick, Caroline Elizabeth. *Old Times in Dixie Land, a Southern Matron's Recollections.* New York, 1901

Miller, (Mrs.) Susan Francis. *Sixty Years in the Nueces Valley, 1870-1930.* San Antonio, 1930

Morgan, Julia Estelle (Mrs. Irby). *How It Was; four years among the Rebels.* Nashville, 1892

Nash, Charles E. (ed.). *Biographical Sketches of Gen. Pat Cleburne and Gen. T. C. Hindman.* Little Rock, Ark., 1898. Bound with Nash is Bunn, H. G. *Reminiscences of the Civil War*

North, Thomas. *Five Years in Texas, or What did you Hear during the War.* Cincinnati, 1871

Olmsted, Frederick Law. *The Cotton Kingdom, a Traveller's Observations on Cotton and Slavery in the American Cotton States.* 2 vols. New York, 1861

————. *A Journey in the Seaboard Slave States in the Years 1853-1854 with remarks on their Economy.* 2 vols. New York, 1904

————. *A Journey through Texas; or a Saddle-Trip on the Southwestern Frontier.* New York, 1857

Ozanne, T. D. *The South as it Is or Twenty-One Years' Experience in the Southern States of America.* London, 1863

Page, Charles A. *Letters of a War Correspondent.* Boston, 1899

Parisot, P. F. *The Reminiscences of a Texas Missionary.* San Antonio, 1899

Peyton, John Lewis. *The American Crisis or pages from the Note-book of a state agent during the Civil War.* 2 vols. London, 1867. (This agent was sent by Governor Clark of North Carolina to Europe where he served throughout the war. He sailed from Charleston, October 26, 1861)

Pickett, (Mrs.) La Salle (Corbill). *Pickett and his Men.* Atlanta, 1900

Pryor, Sara Agnes (Mrs. Roger A.). *Reminiscences of Peace and War.* New York, 1904

Putnam, (Mrs.) Sallie A. B. *Richmond during the War; four years of personal observation.* New York, 1867

Richardson, Albert Deane. *The Secret Service, the Field, the Dungeon, and the Escape.* Philadelphia, 1865. (This book is difficult to classify as it overlaps with military memoirs)

Robertson, George F. *A Small Boy's Recollections of the Civil War.* Clover, South Carolina, 1932

Russell, William Howard. *The Civil War in America.* Boston, 1861

———. *My Diary North and South.* Boston, 1862

———. *Pictures of Southern Life, political and military.* New York, 1861

Saxon, Elizabeth (Lyle). *A Southern Woman's War time Reminiscences.* Memphis, 1905

Siringo, Charles A. *A Texas Cow Boy.* Chicago, 1886

Southwood, Marion. *Beauty and Booty.* New York, 1867

Taylor, Thomas. *Running the Blockade.* London, 1896

Watson, William. *The Adventures of a Blockade Runner.* London, 1892

Wright, Louise Wigfall (Mrs. D. Giraud). *A Southern Girl in '61.* New York, 1905

PAMPHLETS

Barbee, David R. *An Excursion in Southern History.* Asheville, 1928. (This was originally published in the *Sunday Citizen*, Richmond, May, 1927)

Boggs, W. R. *Military Reminiscences of Gen. William R. Boggs.* "Trinity College Historical Society," John Lawson Monographs. Vol. III. Durham, North Carolina, 1913

Bummer Boy, A. New York, 1868

Chamberlayne, John Hampden. *Ham Chamberlayne—Virginian: Letters and Papers of an Artillery Officer in the War for Southern Independence, 1861-65.* Richmond, 1932

Cobden, Richard. *Speech of Mr. Cobden on the Foreign Enlistment Act.*
London, 1863. (A speech delivered in parliament on April 24, 1863,
and reprinted as a pamphlet)

Confederate Reveille, The. Raleigh, 1898. (A memorial edition published
by the Pamlico chapter of the Daughters of the Confederacy)

Conseil d'Administration, Légion Française. [n. p.], [n. d.]. (A pamphlet preserved in the Howard Memorial Library, New Orleans)

D. S. F. *Palmetto Leaf.* [n. p.], 1928. Reprinted October 22, 1928

de Arnaud, Charles A. *Reminiscences of the Union and its Ally, Russia.*
Washington, 1890

Edge, Frederick Milnes. *England's Danger and her Safety.* London,
1864. (A letter to Earl Russell, Secretary of State)

Fullam, George T. *The Cruise of the "Alabama" from her Departure
from Liverpool until her Arrival at the Cape of Good Hope.* Liverpool, 1863. (This account was published anonymously "By an Officer on Board," but it has proved possible for him to be identified as
above)

Herbert, Arthur. *Sketches and Incidents of Movements of the Seventeenth Virginia Regiment.* [n. p.], 190- (?). (A paper read before the Robert E. Lee Camp at Alexandria, Virginia, about 1909)

*Inaugural Address of Gov. Thomas H. Watts before the Alabama Legis-
lature December 1, 1863.* Montgomery, 1863

Kinsman, Oliver D. "A Loyal Man in Florida, 1858-1861," *War Papers*, No. 81. Washington, 1910. (Read at a meeting on May 4,
1910)

Mathews, Alfred E. *Interesting Narrative; Being a Journal of the Flight
of Alfred E. Mathews.* [n. p.], 1861. (Account of an escape covering the period from April 20 to May 16, 1861)

Narrative of the Cruise of the Alabama and List of her Officers and Men
(By one of her crew). London, 1864

Newcomb, James P. *Address of Hon. James Newcomb* [n. p.], [n. d.]

Potts, Frank. *The Death of the Confederacy.* Richmond, 1928. Edited
by Douglas S. Freeman

Sansom, John W. *Battle of the Nueces River in Kinney County, Texas,
August 10th, 1862.* San Antonio(?), 1905(?)

Tochman, Gaspard. *Virginia: A Brief Memoir for the information of Europeans desirous of emigrating to the New World.* Richmond, 1868

Whittle, William C. *Cruises of the Confederate States Steamers "Shenandoah" and "Nashville."* Norfolk(?), 1910

ARTICLES IN MAGAZINES AND NEWSPAPERS
(Almost all Primary)

Albright, James W. "Books Made in Dixie," *Southern Historical Society Papers,* XLI, 57-60

Aldis, Owen F. "Napoleon and the Southern Confederacy," *North American Review,* CXXIX, 342-360

Article VIII, *The British Quarterly Review,* XXXIV, 203-213. (In a book review on several writings on the American war occur some comments on Sir William H. Gregory of value to this study)

Ashe, S. A. "The Shenandoah," *Southern Historical Society Papers,* XXXII, 321

Bassett, John. "Running the Blockade from Confederate Ports," *Trinity College Historical Society, Historical Papers,* Ser. 2, pp. 62-68

Biesele, R. L. "The San Saba Colonization Company," *Southwestern Historical Quarterly,* XXXIII, 169-183

Brannon, Peter. "Through the Years, The Gunboat Morgan," Montgomery *Advertiser,* September 29, 1935

Brock, Irving A. "Cleburne and his Division at Missionary Ridge and Ringgold Gap," *Southern Historical Society Papers,* VIII, 464-475

Brooks, U. R. "Hampton and Butler," *Southern Historical Society Papers,* XXIII, 25-37

Bundy, J. M. "The Last Chapter in the History of the War," *The Galaxy,* VIII, 113-121

"Capston's Special Mission," *Southern Historical Society Papers,* XXIV, 202-204

Cobb, Irvin S. "The Lost Irish Tribes in the South," *Tennessee Historical Magazine,* Ser. 2, I, 122

"Confederate Veteran, A," *Southern Historical Society Papers,* XIX, 257-261. (This first appeared in the Richmond *Times*)

Crocker, W. A. "The Army Intelligence Office," *Confederate Veteran,* VIII,119

De Bow, J. D. B. "The Non-Slaveholders of the South," *De Bow's Review,* O. S., XXX, 67-77 (an open letter to N. R. Gourdin of Charleston, written by the editor)

Debray, Xavier B. "A Sketch of Debray's Twenty-Sixth Regiment of Texas Cavalry," *Southern Historical Society Papers,* XII, 547-551; XIII, 153-165

Doak, H. M. "The Development of Education in Tennessee," *American Historical Magazine,* VIII, 76-77

"Downey, Mark, Note on," *Virginia Magazine of History*, II, 336, 435-436

Dundas, William C. "Blockade-Running during the Civil War," *The Bellman*, XXVI, 606-608

"Enmities and Barbarities of the Rebellion," *The Danville Quarterly Review*, IV, 557-611. (Address of the General Assembly of the Presbyterian Church in the Confederate States of America to all the churches of the world as reported by the Reverend J. H. Thornwell)

"Experiences of a Northern Man in the Confederate Army," *Southern Historical Society Papers*, IX, 369-378

Ezekiel, H. T. "Judah P. Benjamin," *Southern Historical Society Papers*, XXV, 297-302

Gay, H. N. "Lincoln's Offer of a Command to Garibaldi," *Century Magazine*, LXXV, 63-74

Gift, George W. "The Story of the Arkansas," *Southern Historical Society Papers*, XII, 115-119

Gordon, G. W. "General P. R. Cleburne," *Southern Historical Society Papers*, XVIII, 261-271

Gorgas, General Josiah. "Notes on the Ordnance Department of the Confederate Government," *Southern Historical Society Papers*, XII, 66-94. (An unfinished paper found among the papers of General Gorgas, chief of ordnance)

Grimball, John. "Career of the Shenandoah," *Southern Historical Society Papers*, XXV, 116-130

Hardee, W. J. "Biographical Sketch of Major-General Patrick R. Cleburne," *Southern Historical Society Papers*, XXXI, 151-163

"The Haversack," *The Land We Love*, VI, 79-86

"Helped Capture Engine 'General,'" *Southern Historical Society Papers*, XXXVII, 264-265. (Copied from Richmond *Times-Dispatch*, December 29, 1909)

Hill, D. H. "Chickamauga," *Century Magazine*, XXXIII, 937-962. (N. S.)

"History of Chimborazo Hospital, C. S. A.," *Southern Historical Society Papers*, XXXVI, 86-94. (Abstract from address by Dr. J. R. Gildersleeve, copied from *News Leader*, January 7, 1909)

"If We Had the Money," *Southern Historical Society Papers*, XXXV, 201-203

Jameson, J. F. (ed.). "The London Expenditures of the Confederate Secret Service," *American Historical Review*, XXXV, 811-824. (With note by Dr. Jameson)

Jones, Sarah L. (pseud.). "Governor Milton and His Family," *The Florida Historical Society Quarterly*, II, No. 2, 42-50. (This is a portion of the work which appeared as a book, *Life in the South from the Commencement of the War*)

Keely, J. W. "Handclasps between the Lines, Diary of Cap. John W. Keely," *Atlanta Constitution Sunday Magazine*, March 15, 22, 29, April 5, 19, 1931

Kinsman, Oliver D. "A Loyal Man in Florida, 1858-61," *War Papers*, No. 81

Leigh, (Mrs.) Townes R. "The Jews in the Confederacy," *Southern Historical Society Papers*, XXXIX, 177-180

Lining, Charles. "The Cruise of the Confederate Steamship 'Shenandoah,'" *Tennessee Historical Magazine*, VIII, No. 2, 102-111

Lutz, Ralph H. "Rudolf Schleiden and the Visit to Richmond, April 25, 1861," *Reports of the American Historical Association*, 1915, 209-216

McCabe, W. Gordon (comp.). "Graduates of the United States Military Academy at West Point, N. Y.," *Southern Historical Society Papers*, XXX, 34-76

McGrath, John. "In a Louisiana Regiment," *Southern Historical Society Papers*, XXXI, 103-119. (Copied from the New Orleans *Picayune*, August 2, 9, September 6, 1903)

McKim, Randolph H. "Glimpses of the Confederate Army," *The American Review of Reviews*, XLIII, 431-437

Mason, Emily. "Memories of a Hospital Matron," *The Atlantic Monthly*, XC, 305-318, 455-485

Mayo, Ellen Wise. "A War Time Aurora Borealis," *The Cosmopolitan*, XXI, 134-141

Mays, Samuel Elias. "Sketches from the Journal of a Confederate Soldier," Tyler's *Quarterly Historical and Genealogical Magazine*, V, 30-54, 95-127

"Month with the Rebels, A," *Blackwood's Edinburgh Magazine*, XC, 755-767

Morrow, Libbie L. "The Nashville Female Academy," *Nashville Banner*, June 22, 1907

"Necrology," *South Carolina Historical and Genealogical Magazine*, II, 166

Olmsted, Charles H. "Reminiscences of Service in Charleston Harbor in 1863," *Southern Historical Society Papers*, XI, 118-125

Otey, W. N. Mercer. "Organizing a Signal Service," *The Confederate Veteran*, VII, 549

————. "Operations of the Signal Corps," *The Confederate Veteran,* VIII, 129

Paris, The Reverend John. "The Soldiers' History of the War," *Our Living and Our Dead,* II, 259-290

Park, R. E. "Diary of Robert E. Park, Macon, Georgia," *Southern Historical Society Papers,* I, 383-385

Parker, W. W. "How the Southern Soldiers kept House during the War," *Southern Historical Society Papers,* XXIII, 318-328

"Plea for General W. H. C. Whiting, A," *Southern Historical Society Papers,* XXIV, 274-277

Polignac, J. C. de. "Polignac's Mission," *Southern Historical Society Papers,* XXXII, 364-371. (Copied from Richmond *Dispatch,* May 20, 1901)

Pressley, John G. "The Wee Nee Volunteers of Williamsburg District, South Carolina, in the First (Hagood's) Regiment," *Southern Historical Society Papers,* XVI, 116-194

Read, Capt. C. W. "Reminiscences of the Confederate States Navy," *Southern Historical Society Papers,* I, 331-362

Regenbrecht, Adalbert. "The German Settlers of Millheim before the Civil War," *Southwestern Historical Quarterly,* XX, 28-34

Rhett, Claudine. "Sketch of John C. Mitchel of Ireland, killed while in Command of Fort Sumter," *Southern Historical Society Papers,* X, 268-272

"Richmond and Washington during the War," *The Cornhill Magazine,* VII, 93-102. (O. S.)

Russell, William Howard. "Recollections of the Civil War," *North American Review,* CLXVI, 234-249, 362-373, 491-502, 618-630, 740-750

Scheibert, J. "Letter from Maj. Scheibert, of the Prussian Royal Engineers," *Southern Historical Society Papers,* V, 90-93

"Sketch of Major-General P. R. Cleburne, A," *The Land We Love,* II, 460-463

"Some Account of Both Sides of the American War," *Blackwood's Edinburgh Magazine,* XC, 678-779

Sosnowski, Madame Sophie. "Burning of Columbia," *The Georgia Historical Quarterly,* VIII, 195-214

"Southern Privateers," *The Merchants' Magazine and Commercial Review,* LIII, 445-457

Sprunt, James. "Running the Blockade," *Southern Historical Society Papers,* XXIV, Ser. 1, 162-165. (Portion on J. N. Maffitt)

Steuart, R. D. "Confederate Swords," *The Confederate Veteran,* XXXIV, 12-14

Stock, Leo Francis. "Catholic Participation in the Diplomacy of the Southern Confederacy," *The Catholic Historical Review,* XVI, 1-18

Stone, Grace. "Tennessee: Social and Economic Laboratory," *Sewanee Review,* XLVI, 36-44

"Ten Days in Richmond," *Blackwood's Edinburgh Magazine,* XCII, 391-402

"Dr. Tochman's Letter to the Polish Democratic Societies," *Southern Literary Messenger,* XXXIV-XXXV, 321-327

Washington, L. Q. "Confederate States State Department," *Southern Historical Society Papers,* XXIX, 341-349

W. E. A. A. "Percy Greg" (Obituary Note), *The Academy,* XXXVII, 45

White, Kate M. "Father Ryan—The Poet Priest of the South," *South Atlantic Quarterly,* XVIII, 69-74

Whittington, G. P. "Rapides Parish, Louisiana—a History," *The Louisiana Historical Quarterly.* (The entire account runs through volumes XVII-XVIII)

Whittle, William C. "The Cruise of the Shenandoah," *Southern Historical Society Papers,* XXXV, 235-258

Wilcox, C. M. "Defense of Batteries Gregg and Whitworth, and the Evacuation of Petersburg," *Southern Historical Society Papers,* IV, 18-33

Williams, Samuel C. "John Mitchel, The Irish Patriot, Resident of Tennessee," *East Tennessee Historical Society Publications,* No. 10, 44-56

Wise, Jenning C. "The Boy Gunners of Lee," *Southern Historical Society Papers,* XLII, 152-173

Wolseley, General Viscount. "An English View of the Civil War," *North American Review,* CXLIX, 713-727

Wolseley, Lord (An English Officer). "A Month's Visit to the Confederate Headquarters," *Blackwood's Edinburgh Magazine,* XCIII, 1-29

SECONDARY

GENERAL AND SPECIAL

Abbott, John S. C. *The History of the Civil War in America.* 2 vols. New York, 1863-1866

Addey, Markinfield. "Stonewall Jackson," *The Life and Military Career of Thomas Jonathan Jackson.* New York, 1863

Anderson, August. *Hyphenated or The Life Story of S. M. Swenson.* Austin, 1916

Anderson, Rasmus Björn. *The First Chapter of Norwegian Immigration (1821-1840), its cause and results.* Madison, Wisconsin, 1895

Bancroft, Herbert H. *History of the Pacific States of North America.* 34 vols. San Francisco, 1883

Battey, George Magruder. *A History of Rome and Floyd County, state of Georgia, United States of America.* Atlanta, Georgia, 1922

Battine, Cecil. *The Crisis of the Confederacy.* London, 1905

Belisle, John G. *History of Sabine Parish.* Many, Louisiana, 1912

Benjamin, Gilbert Giddings. *The Germans in Texas.* Philadelphia, 1909

Bernard, Montague. *A Historical Account of the Neutrality of Great Britain during the American Civil War.* London, 1870

Biesele, R. L. *The History of the German Settlements in Texas. 1831-1861.* Austin, 1930

Biggers, Don Hampton. *German Pioneers in Texas.* Fredericksburg, Texas, 1925

Blegen, T. C. *Norwegian Migration to America, 1825-60.* Northfield, 1931

Bonham, Milledge L. *The British Consuls in the Confederacy.* "Columbia University Studies in History, Economics, and Public Law," Vol. XLIII. New York, 1911

Boyd, Minnie Clare. *Alabama in the Fifties.* New York, 1931

Bradlee, Francis Boardman C. *Blockade Running during the Civil War and the Effect of Land and Water Transportation on the Confederacy.* Salem, 1925

Brougham, Villiers, and Chesson, W. H. *Anglo-American Relations 1861-1865.* London, 1919

Butler, Pierce. *Judah P. Benjamin.* Philadelphia, 1907

Callahan, James M. *The Diplomatic History of the Southern Confederacy.* Baltimore, 1901

Capers, Henry D. *Life and Times of C. G. Memminger.* Richmond, 1893

Chapman, John A. *History of Edgefield County from the Earliest Settlements to 1897.* Newberry, South Carolina, 1897

Charleston, South Carolina, The Centennial of Incorporation. Charleston, 1884

Chesney, Charles C. *Essays in Military Biography.* New York, 1874

Chronicles of Shreveport and Caddo Parish. Shreveport, 1928

Congaware, George J. *The History of the German Friendly Society of Charleston*. Richmond, 1935

Cook, John Eston. *Stonewall Jackson: A Military Biography*. New York, 1866

Craighead, Erwin. *Mobile: Fact and Tradition*. Mobile, 1930

Deiler, John Hanno. *Eine vergessene deutsche Colonie*. New Orleans, 1900

————. *Zur Geschichte der deutschen Kirchengemeinde im Staate Louisiana*. New Orleans, 1894

Dodd, William Edward. *Jefferson Davis*. Philadelphia, 1907

Dorman, Lewy. *Party Politics in Alabama from 1850 through 1860*. Wetumpka, Alabama, 1935

DuBose, John Witherspoon. *General Joseph Wheeler and the Army of Tennessee*. New York, 1912

Dworaczyk, The Reverend Edward. *The First Polish Colonies of America in Texas*. San Antonio, 1936

Eckenrode, Hamilton James. *Jefferson Davis, President of the South*. New York, 1923

Eickhoff, Anton. *In der neuen Heimath*. New York, 1884

Faust, Albert Bernhardt. *The German Element in the United States*. 2 vols. Boston and New York, 1909

Ficklen, John Rose. *History of Reconstruction in Louisiana through 1868*. Baltimore, 1910

Fletcher, Henry Charles. *History of the American War*. 2 vols. London, 1865. (The writer was of the Scots Fusilier Guards and visited both sides during the war, though the book is largely secondary)

Folsom, James Madison. *Heroes and Martyrs of Georgia*. Macon, Georgia, 1864. (Recorded as Vol. I, but no more volumes appeared)

Garrett, William. *Reminiscences of Public Men in Alabama for Thirty Years*. Atlanta, 1872

Gerrish, Theodore, and Hutchinson, John S. *The Blue and the Gray*. Portland, 1883

Graves, H. A. *Andrew Jackson Potter, The Fighting Parson of the Texan Frontier*. Nashville, 1881

Hainan, Miecislaus. *The Poles in the Early History of Texas*. Chicago, 1936

Hamilton, J. G. de Roulhac (ed.). *Literary and Historical Activities in North Carolina*. 1900-1905. Vol. I. Publication of the North Carolina Historical Commission. Raleigh, 1907

Hanna, A. J. *Flight into Oblivion*. Richmond, 1938

Hardee, W. J. *The Irish in America.* New York, 1873

Hardy, John. *Selma: Her Institutions and Her Men.* Selma, 1879

Harris, D. W., and Hulse, B. M. *The History of Claiborne Parish, Louisiana, from its Incorporation in 1825 to the close of the year 1885.* New Orleans, 1886

Henderson, George Francis P. *Stonewall Jackson and the American Civil War.* 2 vols. London, 1898

Henry Rosenburg, 1824-1893. Galveston, 1918. (A volume to commemorate his gifts)

Hergesheimer, Joseph. *Swords and Roses.* New York and London, 1929

Hesseltine, W. B. *Civil War Prisons.* Columbus, Ohio, 1930

History of the Jews of Louisiana. New Orleans, 1903(?)

Hosmer, James Kendall. *The Appeal to Arms.* "American Nation Series," Vol. XX. New York, 1907

Houck, Louis. *A History of Missouri from the Earliest Explorations and Settlements until the Admission of the State into the Union.* 3 vols. Chicago, 1908

Howell, Andrew Jackson. *The Book of Wilmington.* Wilmington(?), 1930(?)

Hudson, Estelle. *Czech Pioneers of the Southwest.* Dallas, 1934

Hull, Augustus L. *Annals of Athens, Georgia.* Athens, Georgia, 1906

Ingraham, Joseph H. *The Sunny South.* Philadelphia, 1860

Jordan, Donaldson, and Pratt, Edwin J. *Europe and the American Civil War.* Boston and New York, 1931

Jordan, Thomas, and Pryor, J. P. *The Campaigns of Lt. Gen. N. B. Forrest and of Forrest's Cavalry.* New Orleans and New York, 1868

Kaufmann, Wilhelm, *Die Deutschen im amerikanischen Bürgerkriege.* München, 1911

Kendall, John Smith. *History of New Orleans.* 3 vols. Chicago and New York, 1922

Knight, Lucian Lamar. *History of Fulton County, Georgia.* Atlanta, 1930

Landrum, J. B. O. *History of Spartanburg County.* Atlanta, 1900

Leiding, Harriette K. *Charleston, Historic and Romantic.* Philadelphia, 1931

Livermore, Thomas Leonard. *Numbers and Losses in the Civil War in America, 1861-65.* Boston, 1900

Lonn, Ella. *Desertion during the Civil War.* New York, 1928

―――. *Salt as a Factor in the Confederacy.* New York, 1933

Lossing, Benson John. *Pictorial History of the Civil War in the United States of America.* 3 vols. Philadelphia, 1866-1868

McClellan, Henry Brainerd. *The Life and Campaigns of Major-General J. E. B. Stuart.* Boston and Richmond, 1885

McKinnon, John L. *History of Walton County, Fla.* Atlanta, 1911

Maguire, John Francis. *The Irish in America.* London, 1868

Maloney, Walter C. *A Sketch of the History of Key West.* Newark, New Jersey, 1876

Markens, Isaac. *Hebrews in America.* [n. p.], [n. d.]

Mercer, Philip. *The Life of the Gallant Pelham.* Macon, Georgia, 1929

Moore, Albert B. *Conscription and Conflict in the Confederacy.* New York, 1924

Norelius, Erik. *De Svenska Luterska Församlingarnas och Svenskarnes historia i Amerika.* Rock Island, 1890

Norlie, Olaf M. *History of the Norwegian People in America.* Minneapolis, 1925

Oates, William Calvin. *The War between the Union and the Confederacy and its Lost Opportunities.* New York, 1905

O'Pry, (Mrs.) Maude Hearn. *Chronicles of Shreveport.* Shreveport, Louisiana, 1928

Owsley, Frank Lawrence. *King Cotton Diplomacy.* Chicago, 1931

Parton, James. *General Butler in New Orleans.* Boston, 1864

Pioneer Citizens' History of Atlanta, 1832-1902. Atlanta, 1902

Piványi, Eugene. *Hungarians in the American Civil War.* Cleveland, 1913

Pollard, Edward A. *Southern History of the War. Second Year of the War.* New York, 1864

Qualey, Carlton C. *Norwegian Settlement in the United States.* Northfield, 1938

Ratterman, H. A. *General Johann Andreas Wagener, Eine biographische Skizze.* Cincinnati, 1877

Reed, Wallace. *A History of Atlanta, Georgia.* Syracuse, New York, 1889

Rhodes, James Ford. *History of the Civil War.* New York, 1917

———. *History of the United States from the Compromise of 1850.* 8 vols. New York, 1893-1919

Rightor, Henry. *Standard History of New Orleans, Louisiana.* Chicago, 1900

Riley, Elihu Samuel. *Stonewall Jackson, a thesaurus of anecdotes and incidents in the life of Lieut. General Thomas Jonathan Jackson.*

Annapolis, 1920. (Gathered orally by the author from Jackson's soldiers)

Rippy, J. Fred. *The United States and Mexico.* New York, 1926

Roberts, Edward F. *Ireland in America.* New York, 1931

Robinson, William Morrison, Jr. *The Confederate Privateers.* New Haven, 1928

Rosenburg, Henry. See *Henry Rosenburg*

Rosengarten, Joseph George. *The German Soldier in the Wars of the United States.* Philadelphia, 1890

Ryle, Walter H. *Missouri, Union or Secession.* Nashville, 1931

Saunders, James Edmonds. *Early Settlers of Alabama,* New Orleans, 1899

Saxon, Lyle. *Fabulous New Orleans.* New York, 1928

Scharf, John Thomas. *History of the Confederate States Navy from its Organization to the Surrender of its last Vessel.* New York, 1887

Schøyen, David M. *Den amerikanske Borgerkrigs Historie.* Chicago, 1876. (Vol. III of *Amerikas Forenede Staters Historie*)

Schuricht, Hermann. *History of the German Element in Virginia.* (Published with the Annual Reports of the Society for the History of the Germans in Maryland.) Vols. XII and XIV. Baltimore, 1898-1900

Schwab, John C. *The Confederate States of America, 1861-1865, A Financial and Industrial History of the South during the Civil War.* New York, 1901

Severin, Ernest. *Svenskarne i Texas i Ord och Bild.* [n. p.], [n. d.]

Shpall, Leo. *The Jews in Louisiana.* New Orleans, 1936

Smith, Edward Conrad. *The Borderland in the Civil War.* New York, 1927

Snowden, Yates. *History of South Carolina.* 5 vols. Chicago and New York, 1920

Sprunt, James. *Tales and Traditions of the Lower Cape Fear.* Wilmington, 1896. (Has more secondary than primary material)

——. "Tales of the Cape Fear Blockade," *North Carolina Booklet.* Vol. I, No. 10. (Contains much primary material)

Steinach, S. Adelrich. *Geschichte und Leben der Schweizer Kolonien in den Vereinigten Staaten von Nord-Amerika.* New York, 1889

Stephenson, George M. "Some Footnotes to the History of Swedish Immigration from about 1861 to about 1865," *Year Book,* Swedish Historical Society of America, 1921-22. Chicago, 1923

Telfair, Nancy. *A History of Columbus, Georgia, 1828-1928.* Columbus, 1929

Thomas, David Y. *Arkansas in War and Reconstruction.* Little Rock, 1926

Thompson, Samuel Bernard. *Confederate Purchasing Operations Abroad.* Chapel Hill, North Carolina, 1935

Tiling, Moritz. *History of the German Element in Texas.* Houston, 1913

Victor, Orville J. *The History, Civil, Political, and Military of the Southern Rebellion.* New York, 1863

Villiers, Brougham, and Chesson, W. H. *Anglo-American Relations.* London, 1919

Wheeler, J. H. *Historical Facts of the State of Texas.* Bryan, Texas, 1914

Wise, Barton H. *The Life of Henry A. Wise of Virginia.* New York, 1899

Wolf, Simon. *The American Jew as Patriot, Soldier, and Citizen.* Philadelphia, 1895

Wooten, Dudley G. (ed.). *A Comprehensive History of Texas, 1685-1897.* Dallas, 1898

Year Book of the Swedish-American Society of America. Chicago, 1908 (Especially valuable for the article, "En börtglomd Svensk-Amerikan")

UNPUBLISHED SECONDARY MANUSCRIPTS

Some of these may appear in print before the publication of this work.

Brannon, Peter. "Confederate Flag." Manuscript in the Alabama Military Archives

Duffee, Mary. "Sketches of Jones Valley." No. 10. Alabama Military Archives

Felgar, Robert P. "Texas in the War for Southern Independence." A doctoral thesis prepared at the University of Texas

Gonzales, Jovita. "Social Life in Cameron, Starr, and Zapeta Counties." A manuscript prepared for the master's degree at the University of Texas and preserved in the library of that institution

Hall, Ada. "The Texas Germans in State and National Politics, 1850-1865." A thesis for the master's degree at the University of Texas, preserved at the University of Texas

Rosenquist, Carl. "The Swedes in Texas." A doctoral thesis prepared at the University of Chicago

Wagener, William Yeaton. "John Andreas Wagener." A manuscript in the possession of the author

SECONDARY PAMPHLETS

Edge, Frederick Milnes. *An Englishman's View of the Battle between the Alabama and the Kearsarge.* London, 1864

Johnstone, H. W. *The Truth of the War Conspiracy of 1861.* Athens, Georgia, 1921

Memphis: Her Great Men. [n.p.], [n.d.]

Schmidt, Edward. *Fest-Schrift zur Fünfzigjährigen Erinnerungs-Feier an das Gefecht am Nueces, 10. August, 1862.* San Antonio, 1912

Slaughter, Philip. *A Sketch of the Life of Randolph Fairfax.* Baltimore, 1878. Earlier edition, Richmond, 1864. (Fairfax was a private in the Rockbridge Artillery attached to the Stonewall Brigade)

INDEX

of war, 63-64; secretary of state, 64; won Davis to emancipation plan, 65; instructions to Lieut. Capston, 75; praises Father Bannon, 79 n.; explains Avegno's silence, 83; concerned about recruiting abroad by United States, 221 n.; aid of, sought by Gen. Tochman, 225; reply of to Polish delegation, 225; thrust at by Mr. Foote, 336; praises Quintero for work in Mexico, 440-441; mentioned, 70, 77 and n., 369, 439

Bennett, Thomas, foster father of Memminger, 65

Bergmann, Prof. C. H., orderly sergeant, 158

Bevier, Gen., of Missouri, two Irish regiments in command of, 123

Bieberstein, H. R. von. See Von Bieberstein, H. R.

Black, Scotchman, story of desertion to join Confederates, 238 and n.

Blackwood's Edinburgh Magazine, articles in, on Confederacy, 473-475

Bladen Light Infantry, a company in North Carolina, 133

Blakely, Col. Andrew R., clerk in treasury department, 89; record of, 141

Blockade-runners, captains of, British at first, 299; extra hazardous occupation, 306; pay to officers on, 307; hospitality of, 307-308; advantages of foreigners as, 309; as mail carriers, 309; present new feature in war to United States, 310; service of, 464-466

Bnincki, Maj. P. See Polish delegation

Boerne, Texas, German colony founded by *Adelsverein*, 15; mentioned, 16

Bohemians, bound for Texas, 18; settlement of at Alleyton, 20

Bohlae, Fritz-in-the-hole, cobbler in Montgomery, 6

Bohled, Chloris, French quartermaster sergeant, 252 n.

Boivert, Mme., cantoneer of Mobile, 380

Bokum, Hermann, forsook Tennessee to become Union chaplain, 60

Bollegathey, M. F., Hungarian quartermaster sergeant, 252 n.

Bolling, Capt. E. G., in command of mixed group, 128

Bolton, Capt., builder of floats, 242

Bonnegros, M., son of French consul at Baton Rouge, in the ranks, 187

"Bonnie Blue Flag, The." See Tannenbaum

Borcke, Heros von. See Von Borcke

Bosche, Capt. Christian, German commander of Pioneer Corps, 246

Boses, Capt. J., of a Comal County company, 125 n.

Botts, John Minor, desire of Mercier to converse with, 355

Boyd, Belle, famous spy, 379

Boyle, Jere, Irish railroad construction man, 25 and n., 330

Bracht, Dr. Felix, mentioned, 47 n.; chairman of Comal County mass meeting, 48-49; defeated for secession convention, 50; complained of indifference at New Braunfels, 312 and n.; distrust of Germans, 425

Bracht, Victor, brother of Felix, goes to Mexico, 313

Bragg, Gen., Dr. Häcker in the command of, 267; mentioned, 245, 249, 250, 442

Braine, and the privateer *Retribution*, 294-295

Bramston, Col., of Grenadier Guards, visit of, 353

Bratton, James, transferred from Texas to civil service, 89

Braunfels, Prince Carl. See Solms-Braunfels

Bravery, of all nationalities, 231-232

Brazos River, German settlement on, 17

Brear, J. A., English lawyer in Newton, Ala., 329

Breckinridge, Gen., shows Col. Ross about, 370

Brennan, Thomas M., Irish engineer, settled in Nashville, 243; made munitions for Tennessee, 332-333

Brewerton, Lord John, visit of, 364-365

Bright, Cobden, saves British subject, 294

Brinkeman, teacher at Greenville, Tenn., 324

Brinkman, Alex, in Confederate army, 61

Brinkman, Charles, in United States cavalry, 61

British attitude toward subjects in Confederacy, 408-410

British consul, dismissal of, 415-416

British defenders of slavery, 36

British Guard, at New Orleans, in conflict with Butler, 115-116

British Guards, Company A, British Consular Guards, of Mobile, 99

British knights-errant, large numbers claimed, 188

INDEX

545